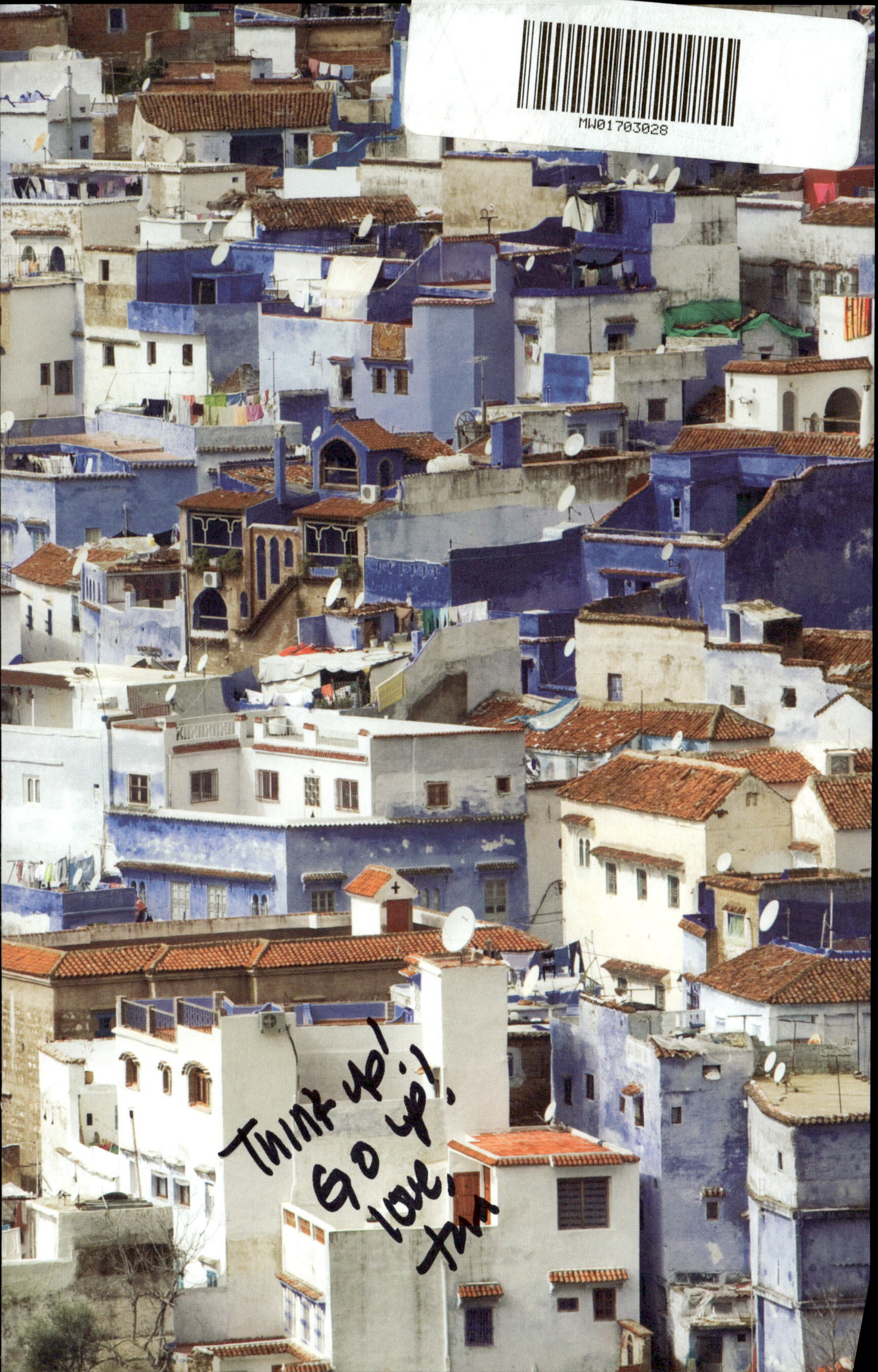

Think up!
Go up!
love,

This is a work of memoir. Some names and identifying details have been changed to protect the privacy of individuals.

Published by The Love Offensive Press
Providence, Rhode Island
www.theloveoffensive.com

Design by Risa Kent
Edited by Jennifer Liese

ISBN: 979-8-9937527-3-0 (Hardcover)
ISBN: 979-8-9937527-2-3 (eBook)
ISBN: 979-8-9937527-1-6 (Audiobook)

First Edition — Limited Gold Foil Printing, 2026

Printed in China

10 9 8 7 6 5 4 3 2 1

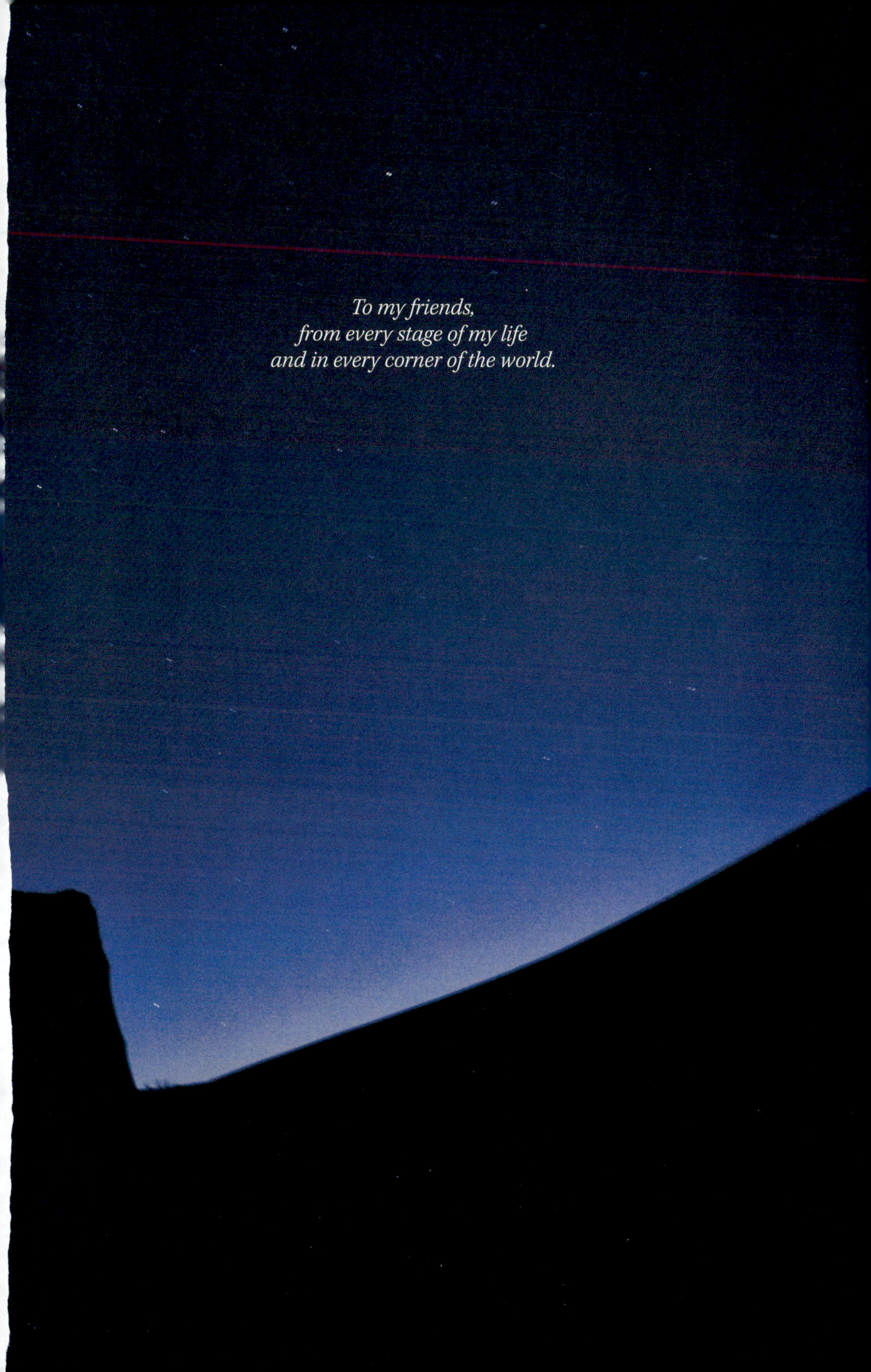

To my friends,
from every stage of my life
and in every corner of the world.

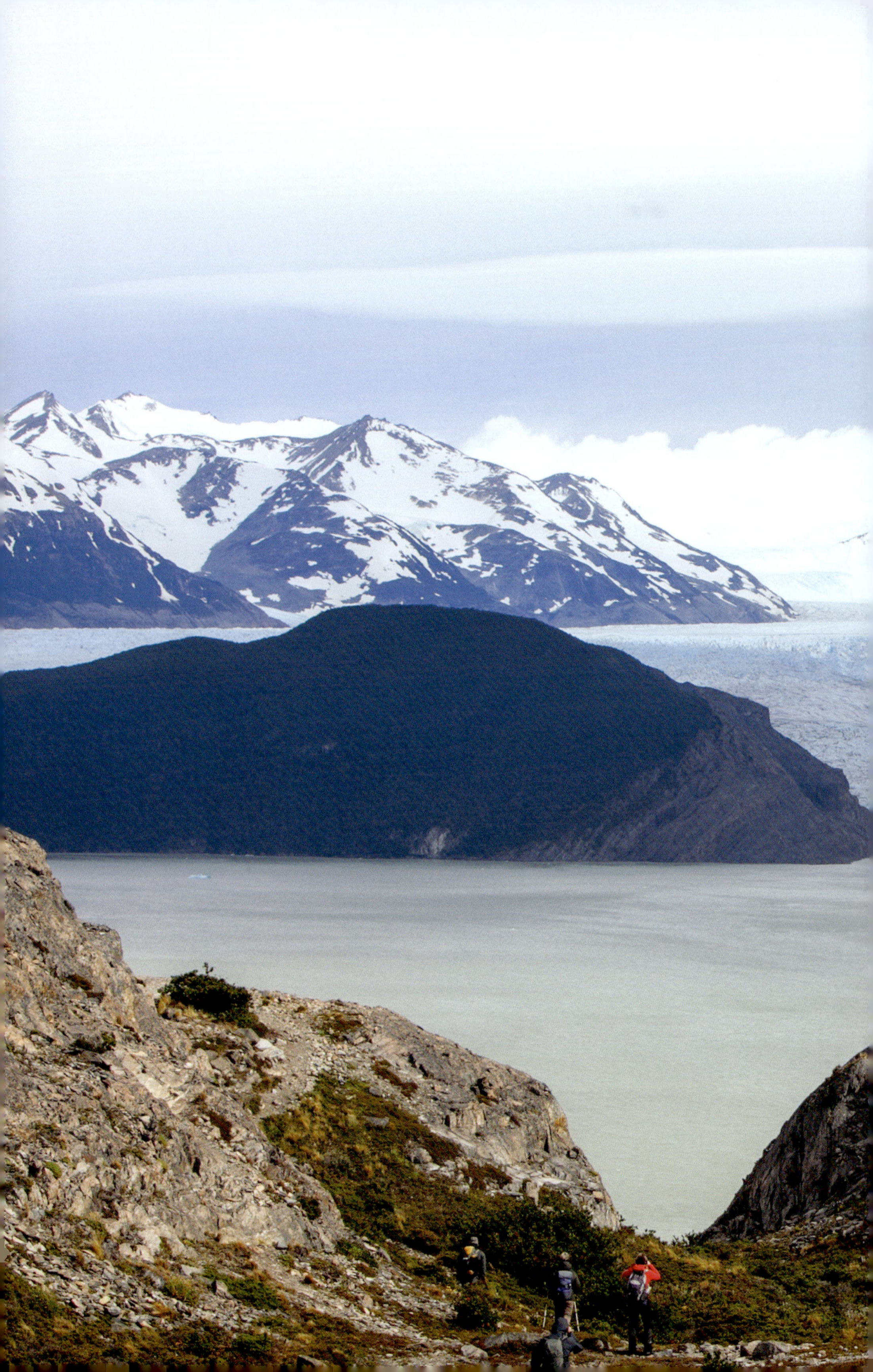

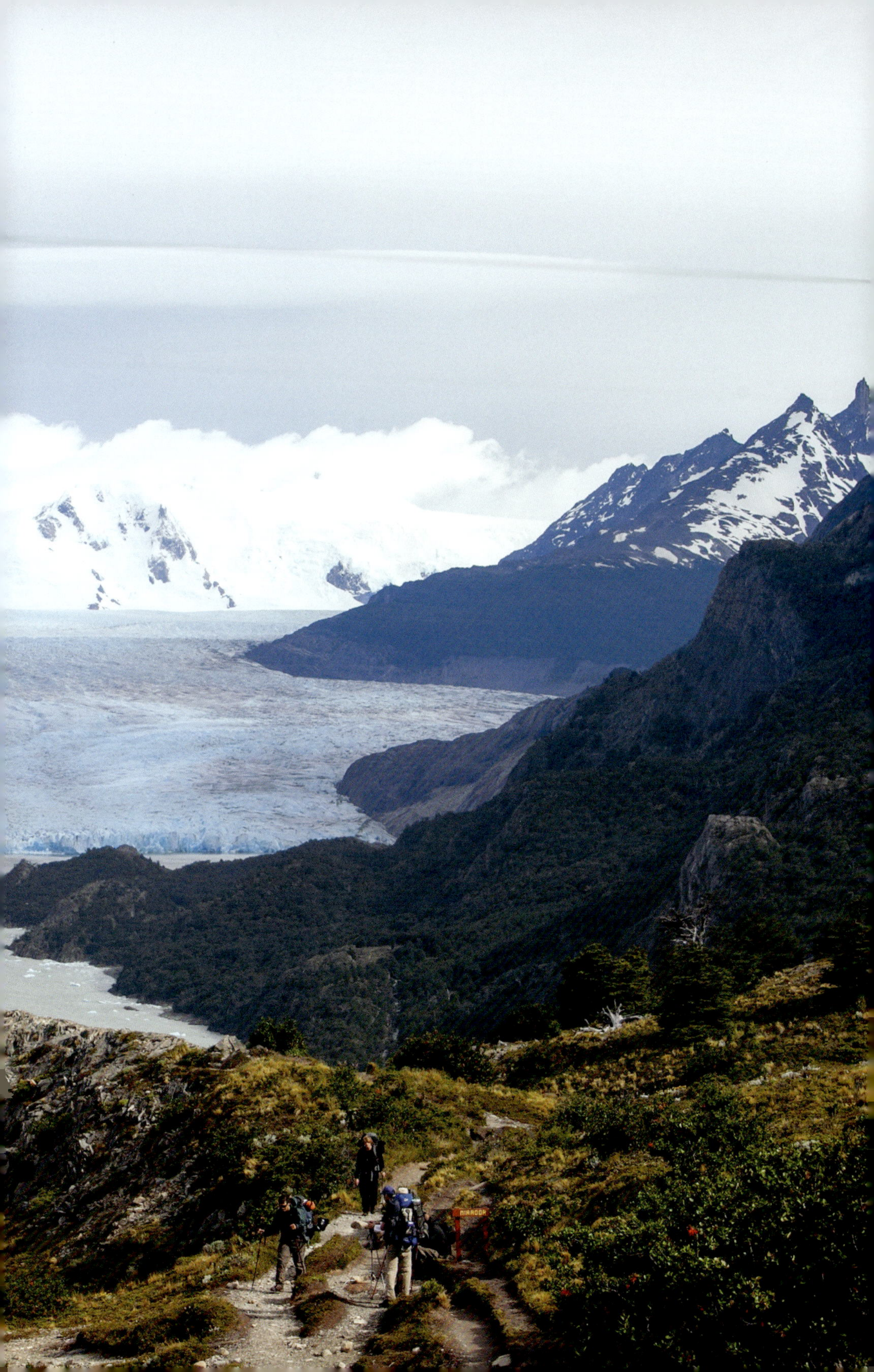
MIRADOR

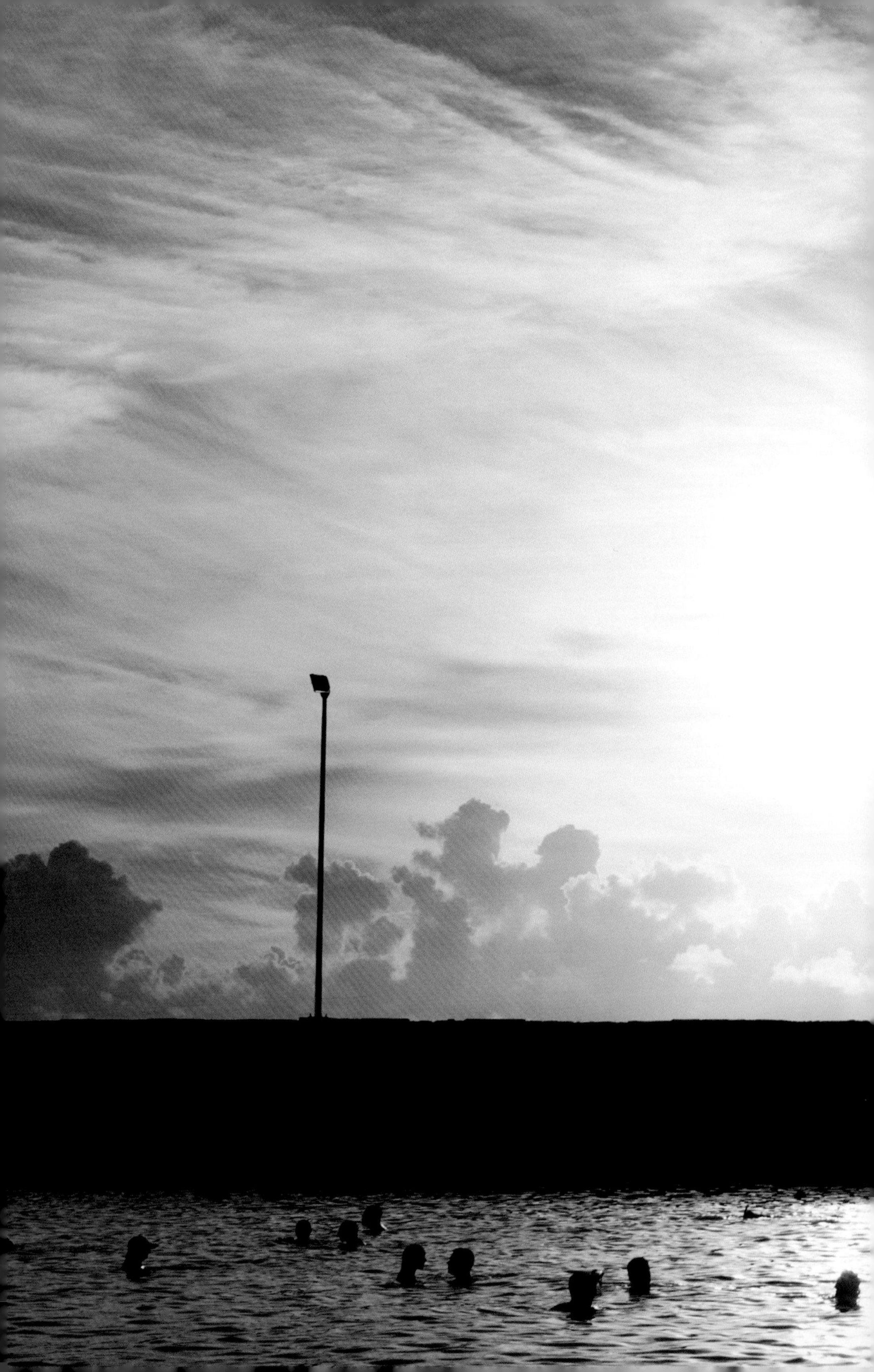

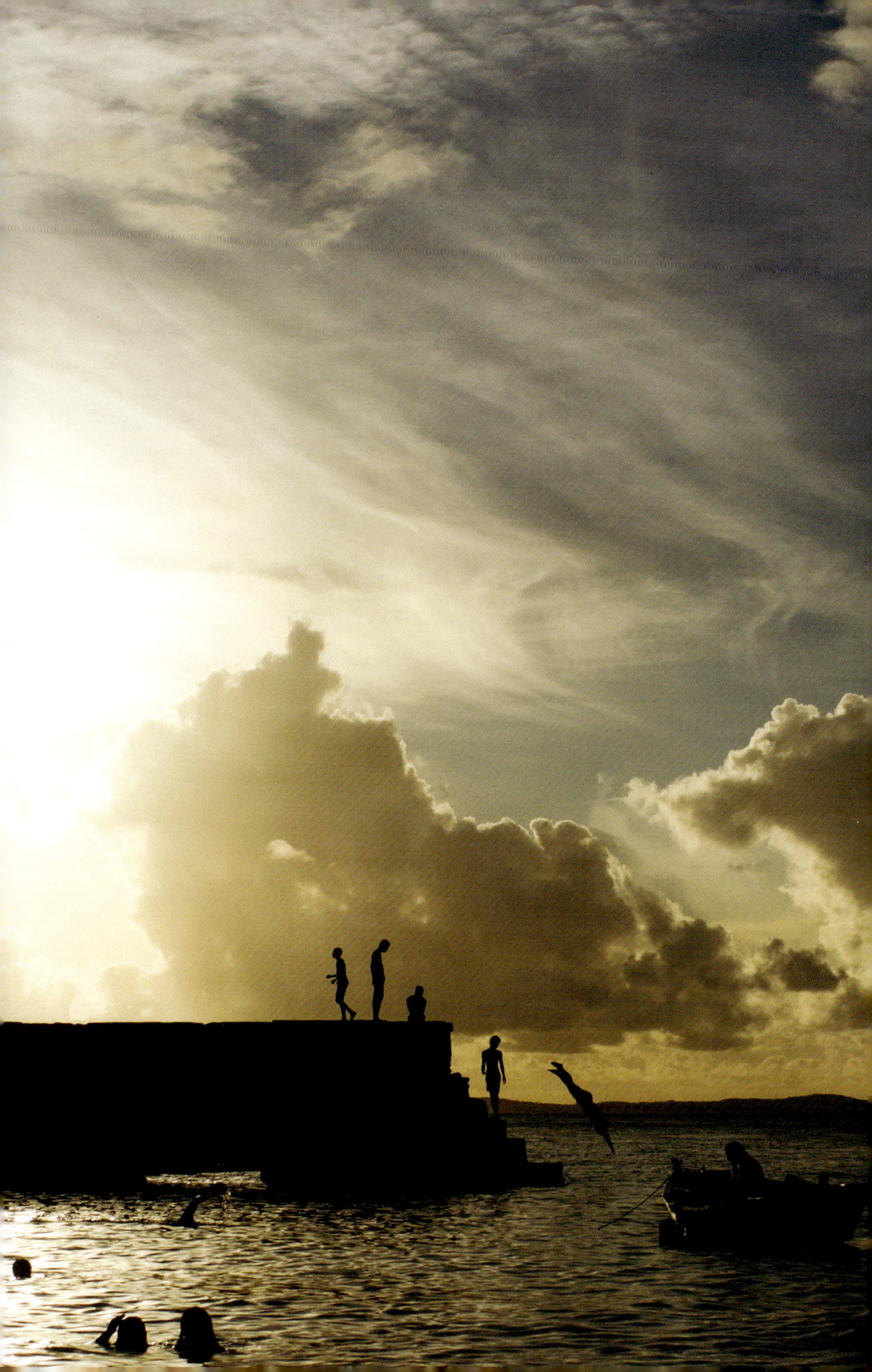

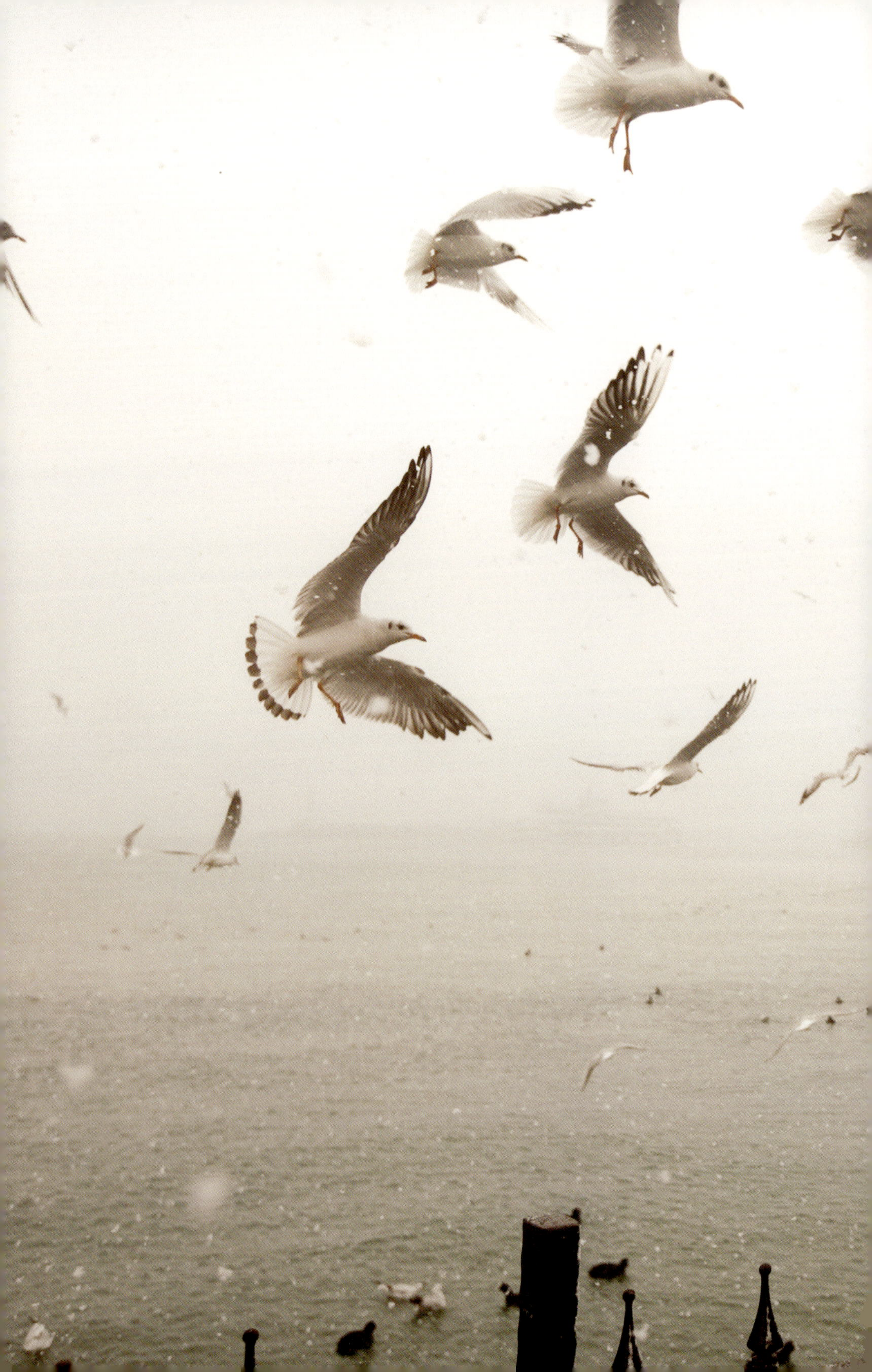

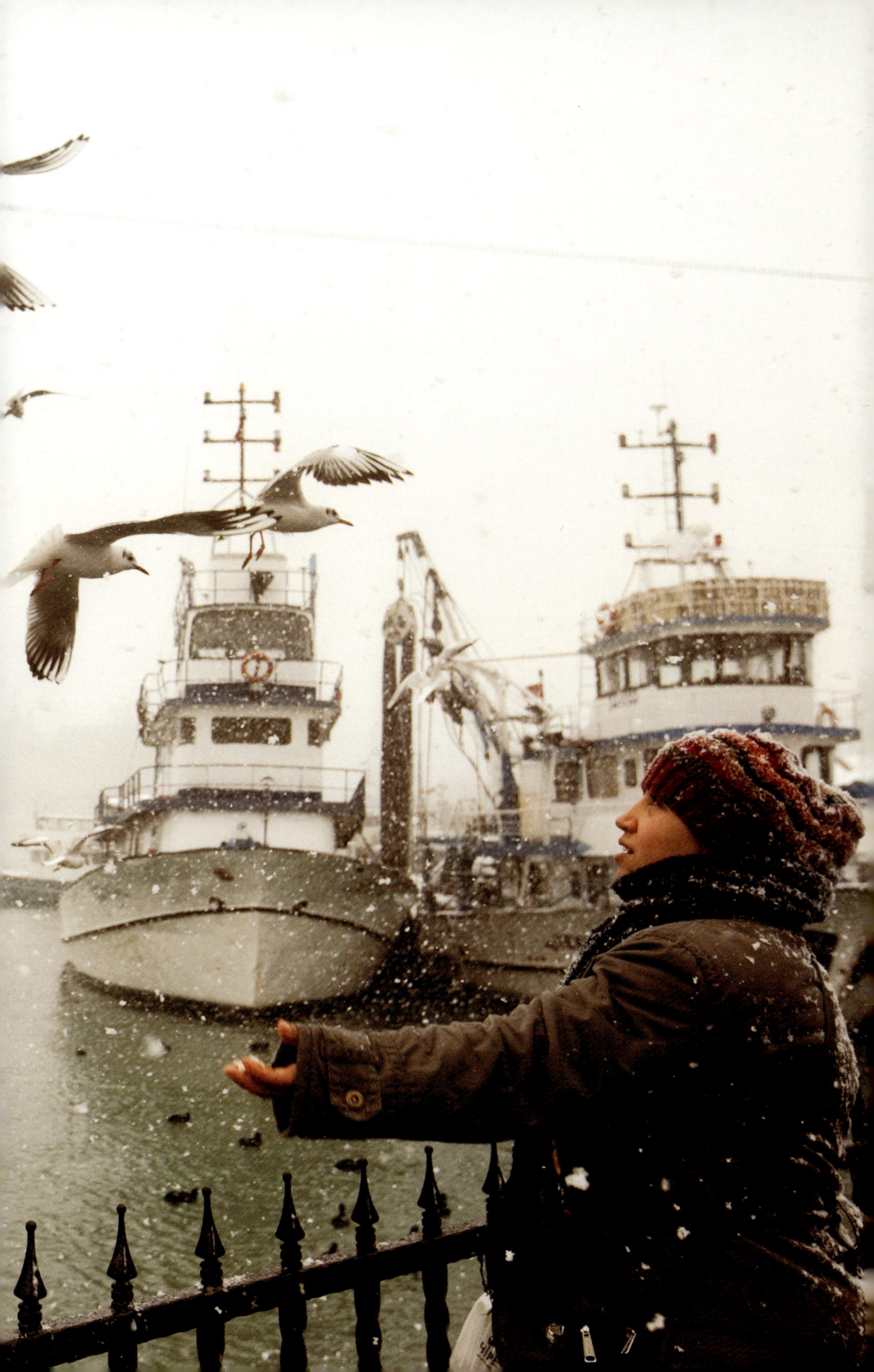

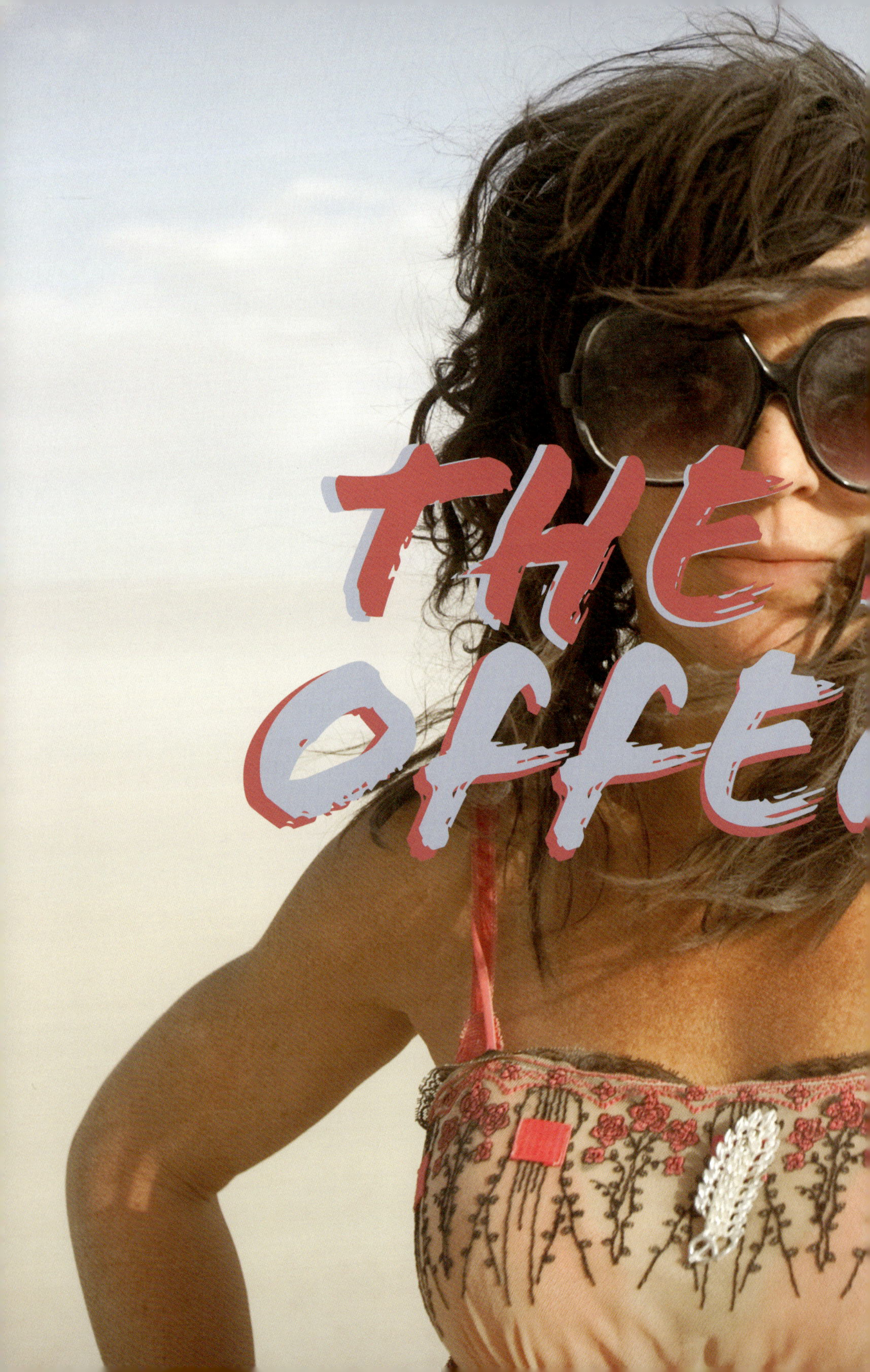
THE

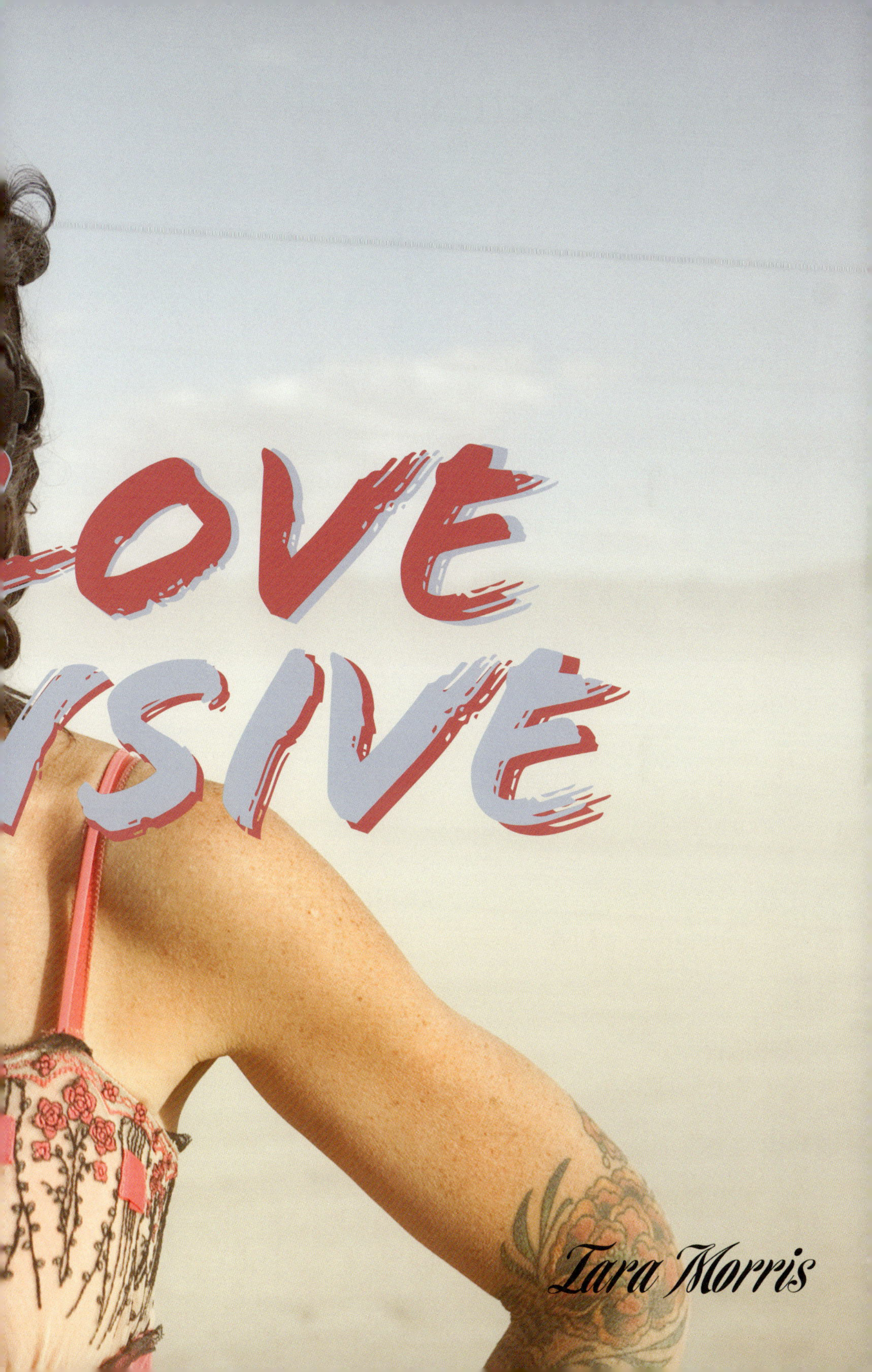
OVE
SIVE
Tara Morris

Table of Contents

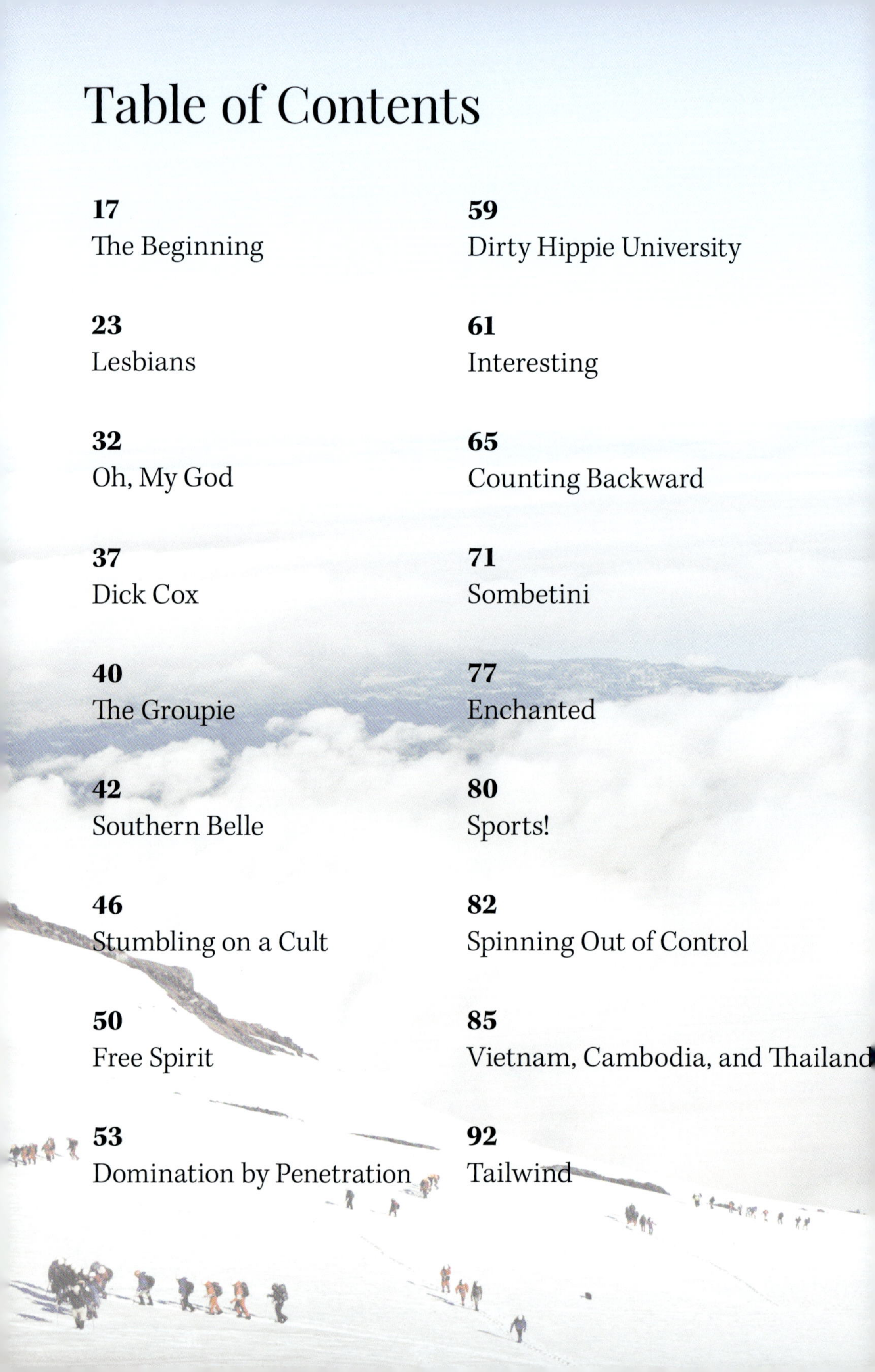

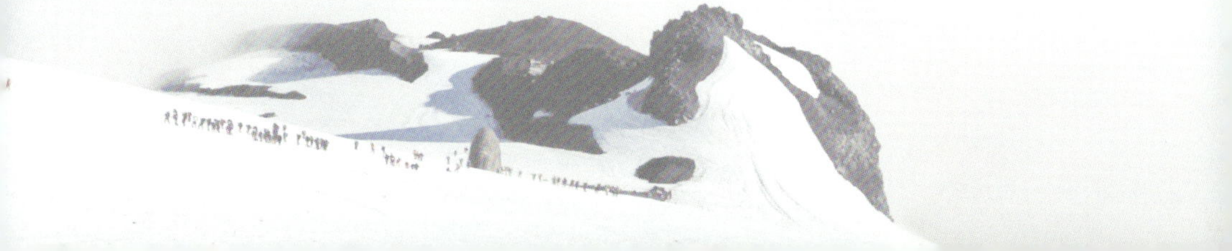

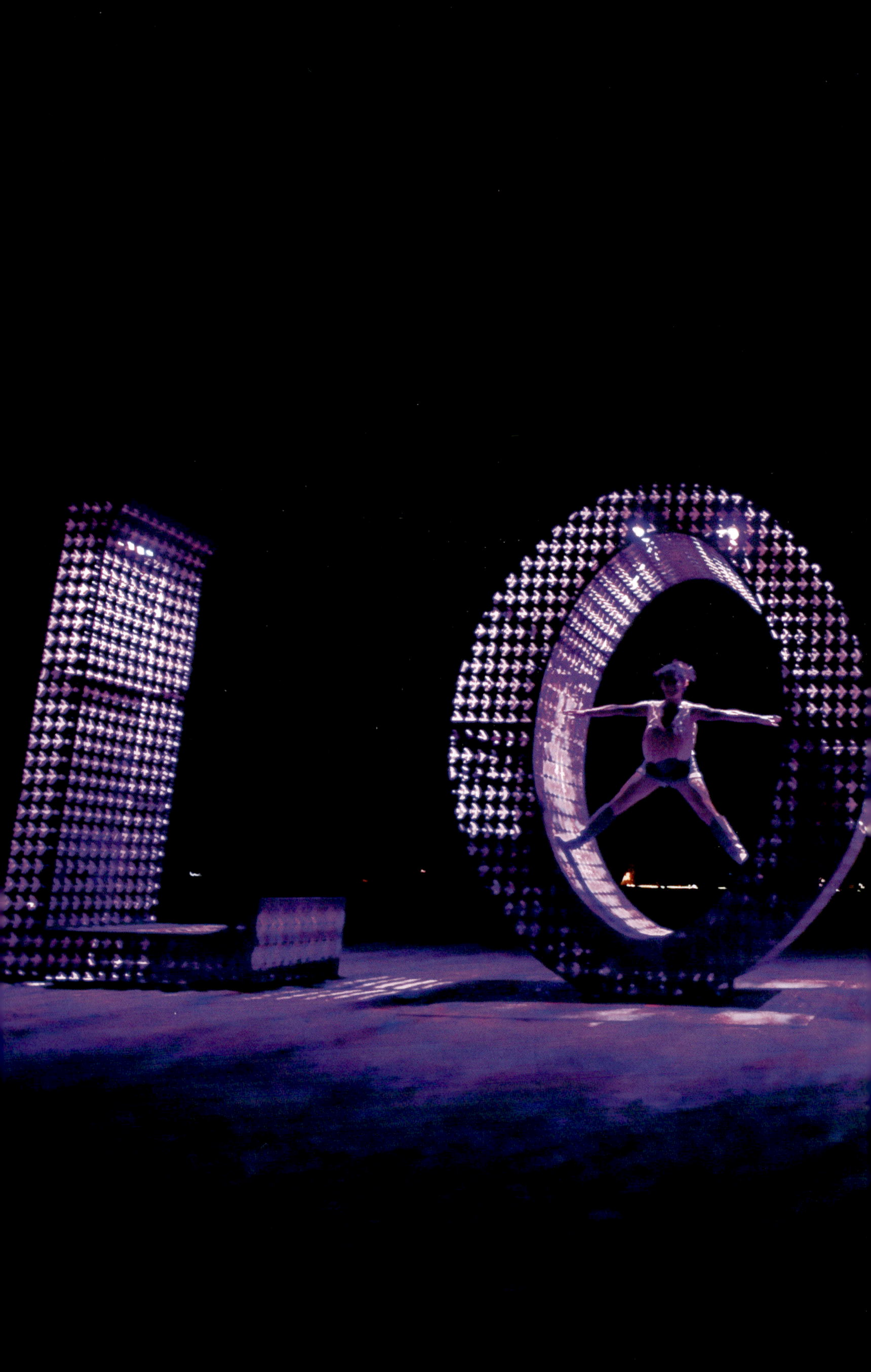

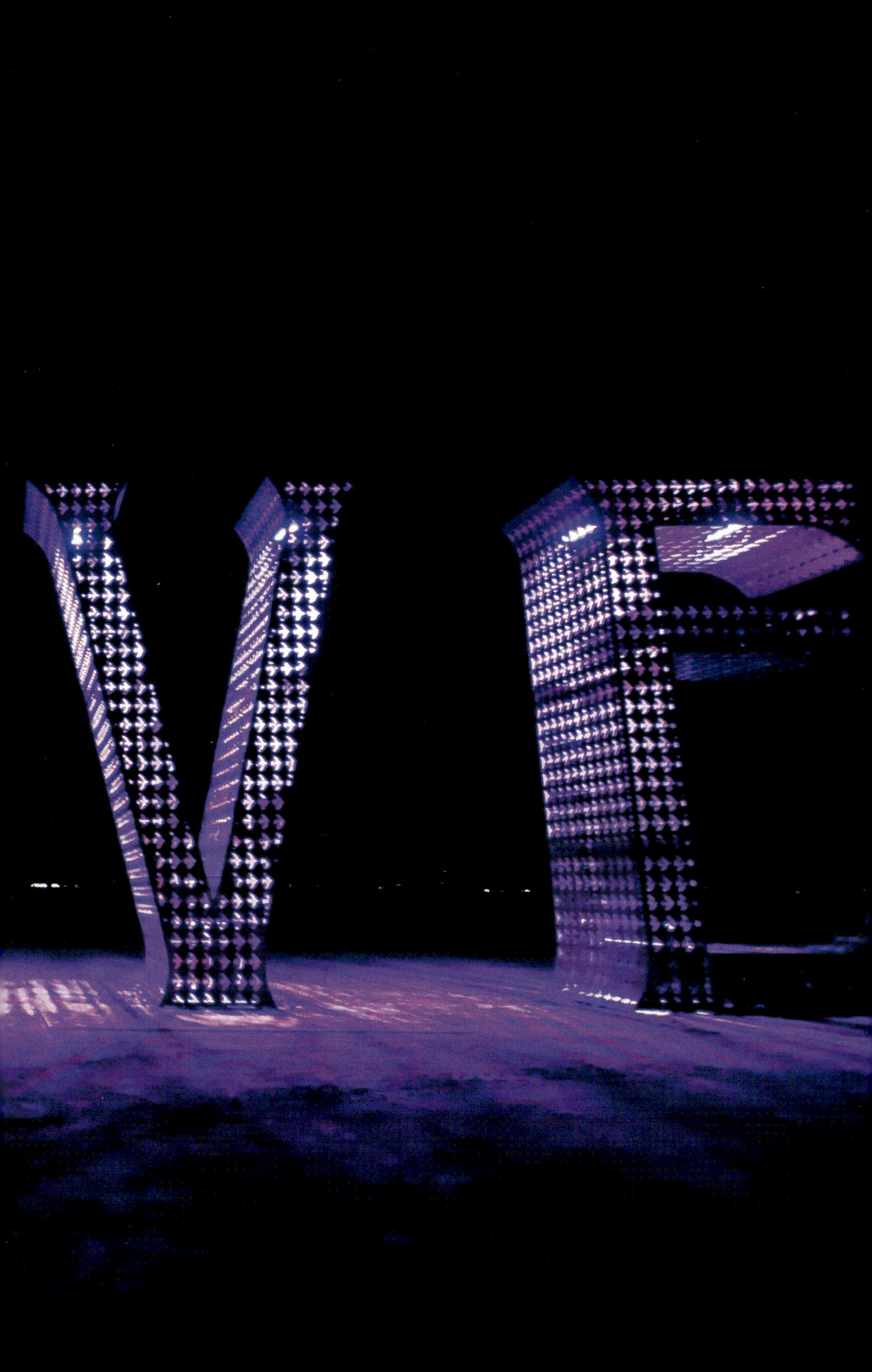

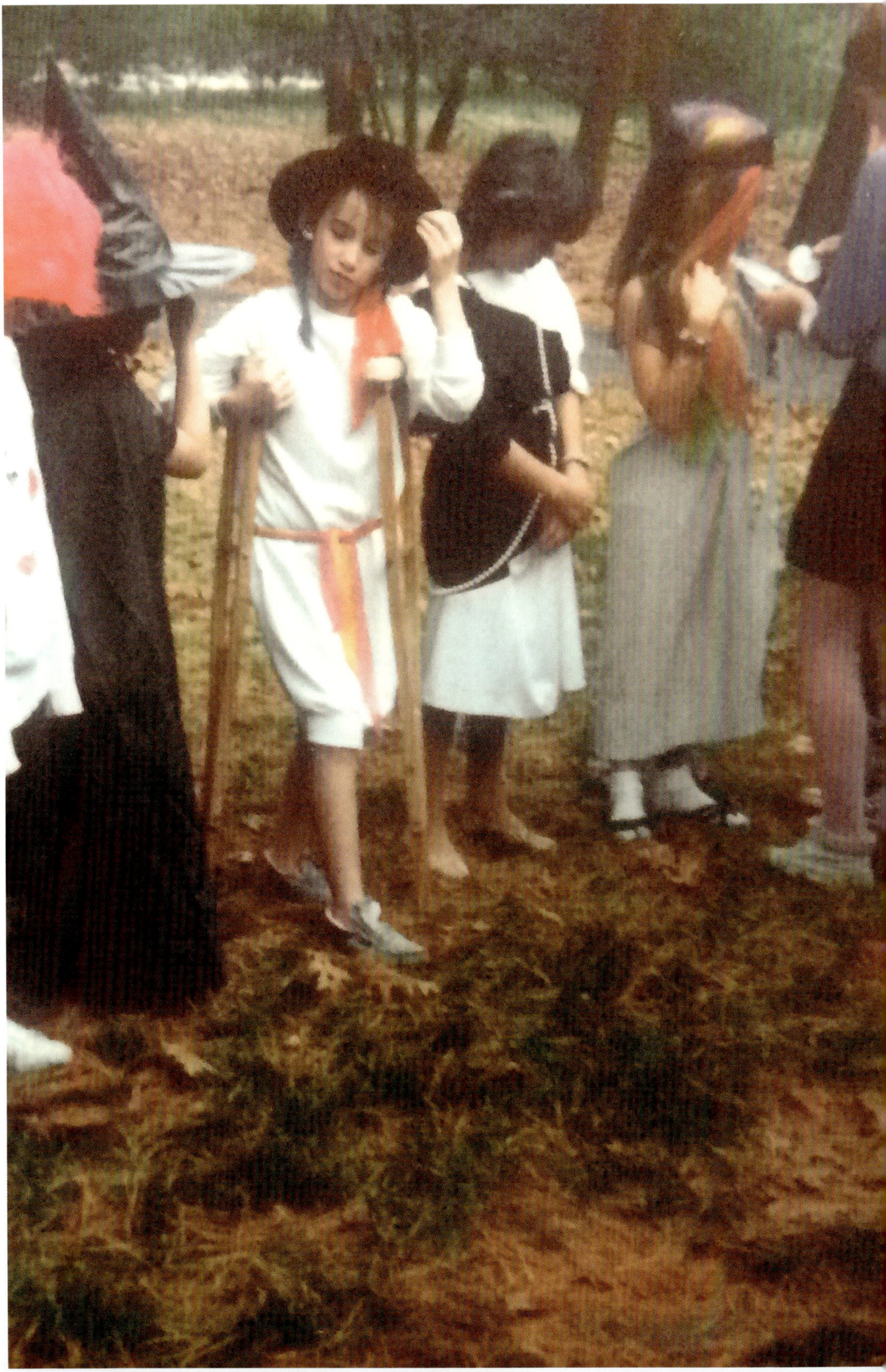

The Beginning

The day I finished writing this book—November 12, 2024—I went to Staples to print it, got it spiral-bound to make it look officially done, and splurged on a laminated cover. It was the eve of the three-year anniversary of the Love Offensive, my yoga studio, and I was absolutely fucking elated. That same afternoon, I had a mammogram that showed areas of concern in both of my breasts. After months of doctor visits, and more prayers and tears than I can remember, flanked by my two best friends, I arrived at the hospital for a bilateral mastectomy. I was absolutely terrified.

I chose this aggressive response to a Stage 1 breast cancer diagnosis because I will read the phrase "invasive ductal carcinoma" exactly never again. I did whatever it took to have many more worry-free years laughing with my friends, teaching yoga, and photographing the world. I am confident that the decision to get a double mastectomy was the right one. I know myself; if I hadn't removed all the breast tissue, I would've spent the rest of my life waiting for the cancer to come back. I did whatever it took to get free.

Losing my breasts is a life-changing and depressing adjustment, and I would be lying if I didn't admit that. But I absolutely cannot indulge in that thought. It's a bottomless, hopeless well of sadness, and if this crisis has taught me anything, I have learned—for the millionth time—that my thoughts are the pharmacy of my brain. I have to keep my head up. I have to keep noticing the good. I have to keep creating. I lost my "national treasure" breasts, but fuck, they had a good run.

I've always said that my gravestone will read:

Here Lies Tara Morris, Might've Overdone It

And now, on the other side of the scariest fucking shit I have ever gone through, with numb silicone balls attached to my chest, I have absolutely no regrets about that.

After my mastectomy people called me a warrior and told me I had "kicked cancer's ass." I want to be clear: I'm no warrior and I didn't kick anything's ass. I had a non-aggressive, well-researched, well-funded, slow-growing, removable cancer that had not spread. I was not brave, I was terrified in the months that I knew cancer was inside me, and if I hadn't found a surgeon to do the job, I would have cut off my own tits with a kitchen knife. *That* would have been some warrior-ass shit.

And obviously I'll never have a gravestone, but anyway, let's start at the beginning.

I grew up in the 1980s in a small beach town in Massachusetts called Marshfield. It was a workin' man's town surrounded by wealthier, fancier towns, and we liked it that way. We heard that being the scrappy underdog builds character, and our identity was in our grit. Plus, fuck those rich kids.

Growing up, Denise Huxtable was my fashion idol. Jo from *The Facts of Life* was my North Star. Julie from *The Love Boat* had my dream job. Smurfette had my dream home. I cut out magazine pages of Kirk Cameron, Ralph Macchio, and Alf and hung them on my walls. But the first three people I truly loved were Michael Jackson, Boy George, and George Michael, so when I first heard the word *gaydar* I knew I had none.

For most of my life I've tried my best to be honest. My dad was a salesman, and bullshit was his mother tongue, so I sided with my mom. I hear a lot about how authentic I am, and maybe this is why. My mom was raw, a big lady who grew up poor in New Hampshire, unable to lie about who she was even if she wanted to. After high school she went to finishing school, where apparently students learned skills necessary to attract a good husband and become interesting socialites and wives. Nice try, mom. I'm not even sure she knew how to use a fork and knife her whole life. I surely don't.

I watched that strong, honest mom of mine get very sick for most of my life. It broke my heart, then it became my tailwind. In her forcefield, I've built careers that brought out the best in me and traveled the world alone, searching for what it means to be human, what it means to suffer, and how to become a better version of myself. I hope you've found something that brings out the best in you, and that you've been able to spin your sadness into a life that is exciting, honest, and brave.

My sister, Shannon, is a hilarious, smart, and beautiful friend of mine, and no matter how much time and distance we allow to get between us—one of the many aftershocks of being raised by a drunk—we always find our way back to one another, mostly by making fun of our parents and reflecting on what assholes we are.

I have chosen not to partner or have children, and sometimes I think that's because I didn't want to, and sometimes I think it's because I was afraid to. Either way, this is not a story of independence where I search long enough for myself, then find a man and everything finally makes sense. That's not what I'm looking for so it's not what I find. Sometimes I regret not being a mom, but I don't dwell on it because it's hard to prefer a life you aren't living, and making a choice inherently means you forfeit all other choices. I once heard a guy explain the paradox of choice like this: you can't read a book while you snowboard. It's either one or the other. Maybe I just wish I could have had it all: one life lived the way I did it, full of adventure and romance, and another life lived as the mom of a big, funny Irish family where Sunday dinners start at 3 p.m. and last all night. Instead, I have filled my life with friendships. At every stage of my life, all my time and energy has been spent fortifying deep, lifelong relationships with the best people I know. My friends are the kaleidoscope of my life.

For the last ten years I have shared my life with dogs. This means—for me—that I have spent a lot of time outside, witnessing the rhythms of nature. I have learned that when I use the word *god*, what I mean is the word *nature*. I believe the "thing in charge" is the natural course of life: season after season, the cycles of life and death wait for no one in a relentless, unfair, brutal, beautiful march forward through time. Someone we love dies too soon, and we ask, how could it go so wrong? Maybe a better question to ask is, how does it ever go so right?

The enormity of it all—terrifying and freeing all at once—has helped me to relax and enjoy my life. I have no control. I'm just part of the rhythm. I might as well dance.

This is *The Love Offensive*.

This is the story of my life.

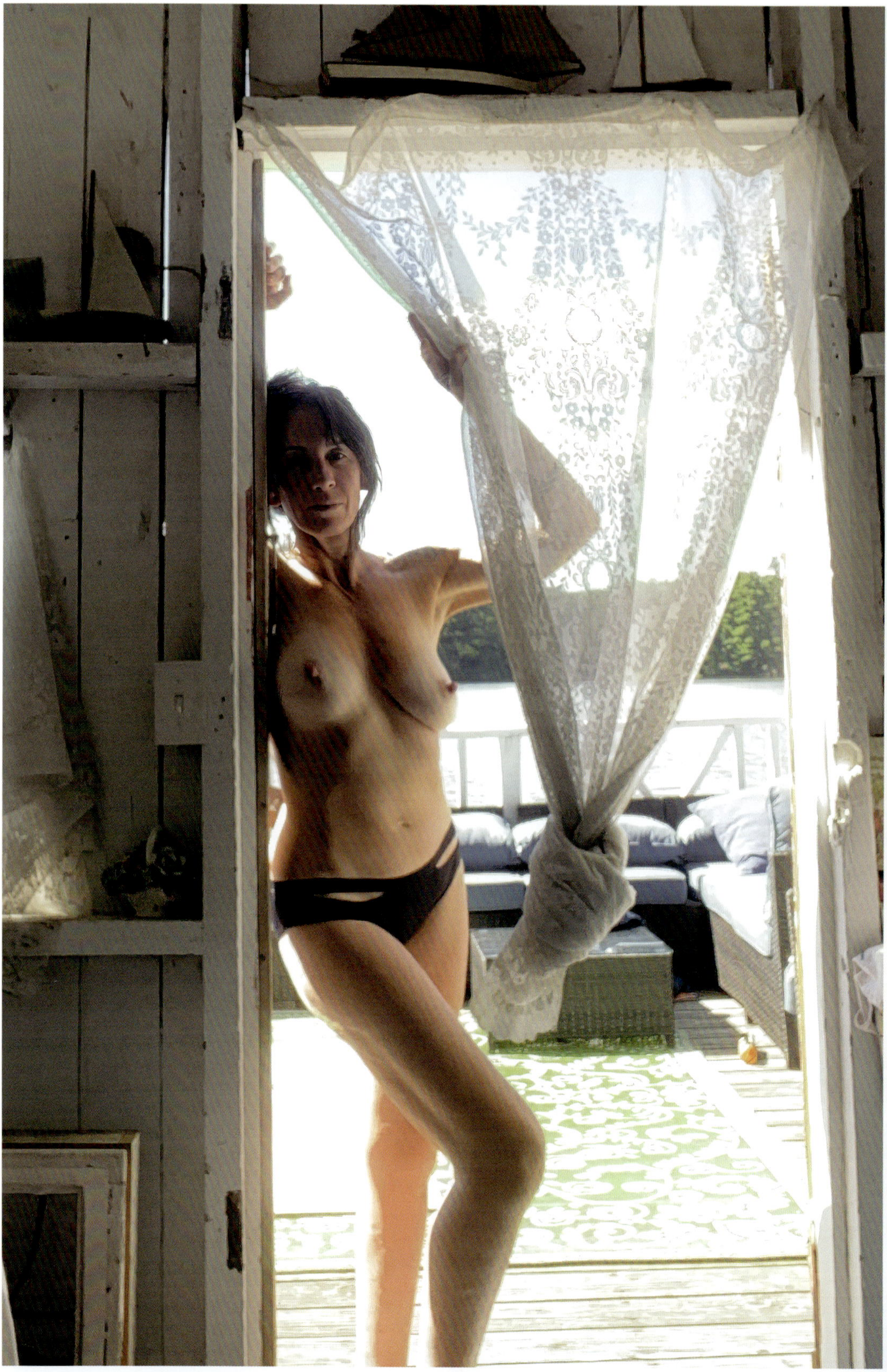

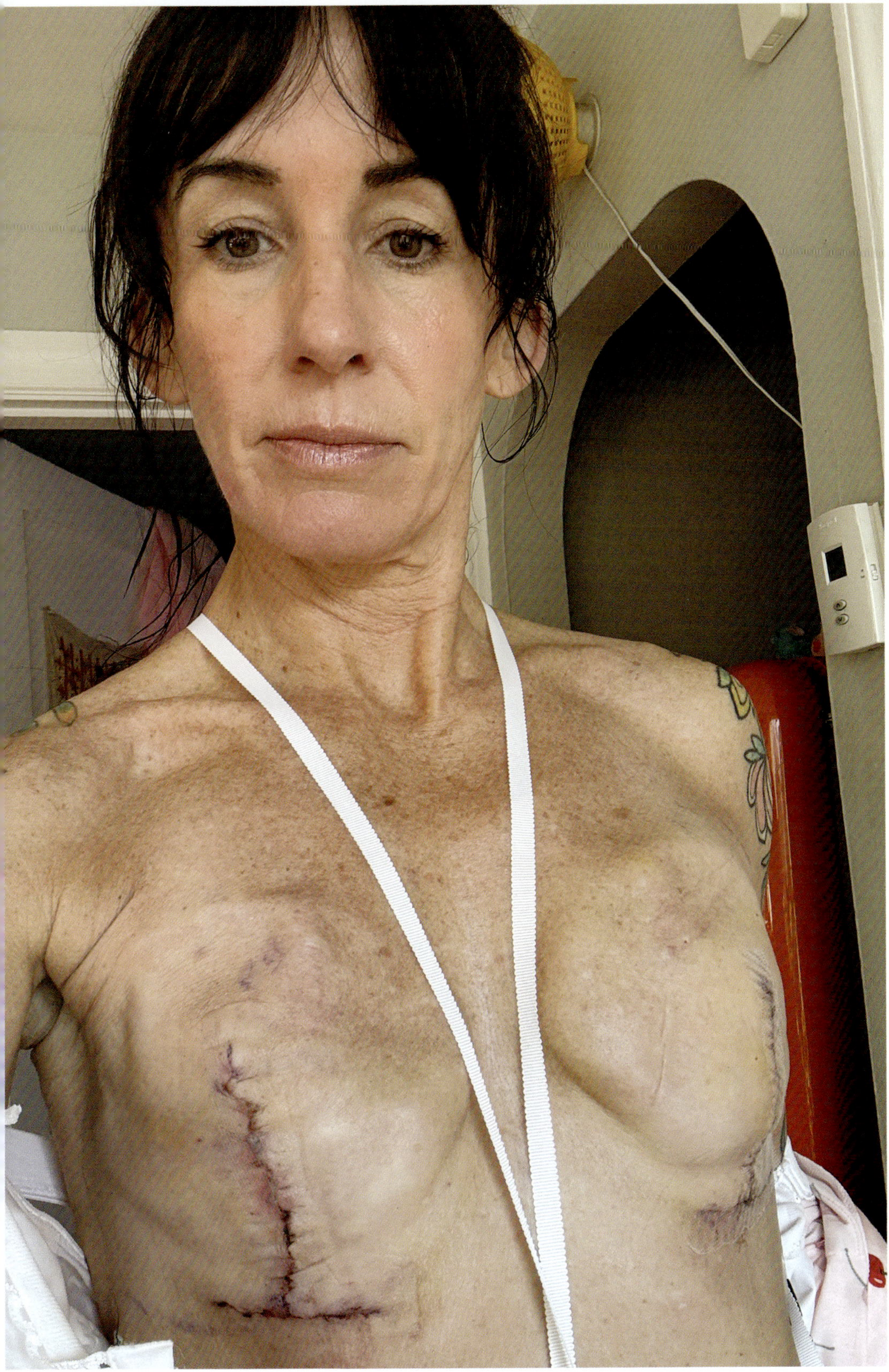

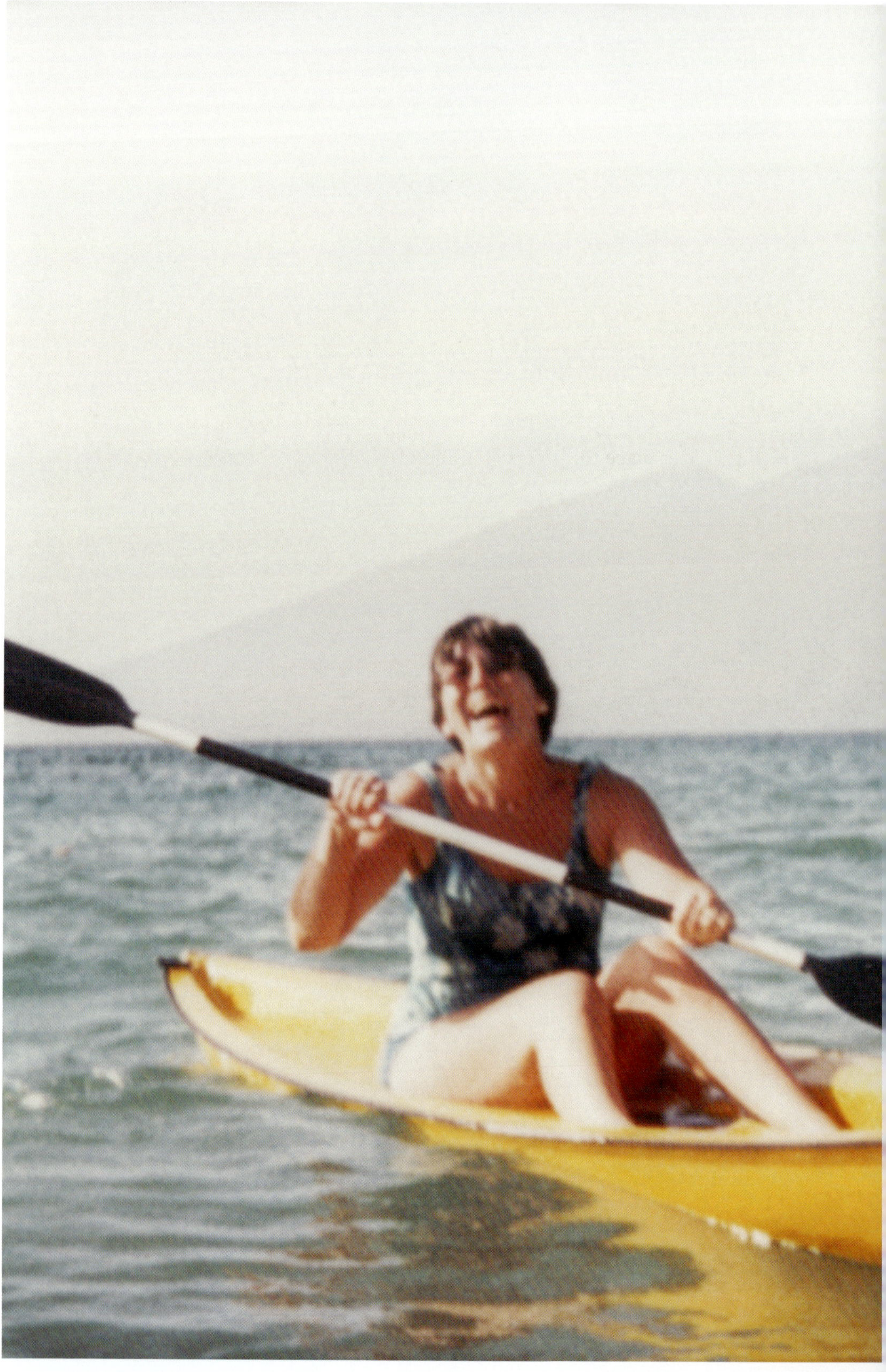

Lesbians

In the summer of 1980, my mom bought a station wagon at a yard sale for $200. We were in Bennington, New Hampshire, visiting her mom, and I don't know what she drove to get us there, but my mother paid cash for a 1968 Chevy Caprice Estate Wagon, and then we drove off a guy's lawn in it. It was brown with wood-grain paneling, had automatic steering, and an AM/FM radio. My mom put scraps of old carpet in the wayback, where Shannon and I liked to sit backward and wave enthusiastically at strangers, and she thought the bumper sticker was poignant, so she kept it: "Don't criticize farmers with your mouth full!" it warned. Resilient, tough, crafty, and honest, my mom found no better place to captain the ship of our family than from behind the wheel of that enormous land yacht.

My mother, Maryann, was born in Newton, Massachusetts, in 1940, the third of three girls in a family of five. As the story goes, seven years later, when her little brother was being born in the same city, her father's mistress was giving birth to *their* son in a nearby hospital. In what I assume was a desperate attempt to save her dignity, my grandmother, Blanche, moved her family from the thriving city of Newton, population 85,000, to Bennington, New Hampshire, population 655. Sure, there weren't bright futures in rural New Hampshire in the 1940s, but at least her son didn't have to go to school with his half-brother with the same birthday named after the same man.

Maryann's childhood was gruesome. Plagued by a father who sounded like a real son of a bitch—carrying generations of unregulated anger, resentment, and poverty—my mom rarely spoke of her young years. My grandmother eventually divorced the prick, married a guy named Ned, was widowed, and spent the last thirty-five years of her life as a perfectly content single woman.

As soon as my mom graduated Bennington High School in 1958, she moved to Boston and attended John Robert Powers Finishing School so she could bridge the gap between being raised poor in the country and attracting a man in the city. She met my dad at nineteen, at her first real job as a switchboard operator at a toilet bowl company where he worked in sales. They dated for a decade, and judging by their photographs they had a really great time and smoked a bunch of cigarettes indoors. They got married in 1969 on the campus of Boston College, bought their first and only home in Marshfield, Massachusetts, and had two daughters in the 1970s. Like lots of women, as soon as my mom gave birth, she dedicated her life to motherhood. She was obsessed with her two daughters and did her very best to give us a childhood she only dreamed of.

One afternoon on our way to ballet class, I looked out the window of the station wagon, trying to make sense of what I had learned about love that day at recess.

"Do you love me?" I asked my mom from the backseat.

"Of course, Baby T. Very much," she answered, smiling at me in the rearview mirror.

"That makes us lesbians!" I concluded, proud to use my new word so quickly after learning it.

My mom tried her best to swallow her laughter, and when we arrived at Duval Dance Studio, she suggested I not tell everyone about her and I being lesbians quite yet. There were many different kinds of love "between two girls," and we could talk about it over dinner.

In my first few months of first grade, Shannon had to walk me to the classroom doors because all I really wanted back then was to stay at home with my mom. When I eventually arrived at my desk, my bottom lip still quivering, I'd open my Winnie-the-Pooh lunch box just to make sure her note was there. "I love you so much! Love, Ma" was written on our lunch napkins every day of our school-aged years. And when I stopped bringing lunch, she wrote it on my breakfast napkin. Not once did she forget.

Though her priority was tending to me and Shannon's every whim, my mom also needed to make money, which, like for every mom in this dilemma, forced her to get creative. First, it was Tupperware parties, then Avon, once the word got out that Skin So Soft body oil doubled as mosquito repellent and sales went through the roof. For many years she worked as a secretary and bragged about her typing speed when typing fast was something to brag about. And though she always had a bottle of Wite-Out on her desk, she swore she never needed it. But the best job my mom ever had was teaching ceramics at the YWCA in Marshfield throughout the 1980s. She probably didn't make much money, but she turned an army of women on to their own talents, and she was also a beautiful artist. She eventually had her own kiln at our house, and once she made enough inventory, she'd open our home to the public so people could buy her pieces right off the mantle.

The next phase of my mom's life was tough. Her nest was empty, her marriage long gone, and after I left for college, her first signs of Parkinson's disease arrived. After those initial symptoms she had almost a decade of decent years. She saved her money and visited me all over the country, learned to use this thing called email, and lived vicariously through shows like Gilmore Girls and Queer Eye. She fearlessly underwent brain surgery in 2004, hoping it would help her symptoms, but the disease marched on. Eventually it was impossible to ignore, my mother was unable to live alone and needed full time care. She went bravely into life in a nursing home in one of the nicest towns in Massachusetts, if not on the planet.

When people asked where my parents lived—my dad lived in low-income housing around the corner—I'd answer, "My parents live in Duxbury."

"Wow!? So beautiful!" they'd reply, impressed.

"Totally," I'd agree.

In a desperate attempt to keep creating with her, I started bringing my camera to our visits and setting up photo shoots in every corner of the facility. She looked like such a bad ass, staring at the camera from her wheelchair, knowing that the strength of the photos lay in the two generations of disagreeable women daring you to stare back.

Forty years after my mom made her mark on the Marshfield YWCA, in October 2020, Shannon and I held her funeral there and scattered her ashes in the South River. Pandemic restrictions meant we could only gather outside, so we did just that on an unseasonably warm day, which we credited to my mom. These days, every time I enjoy anything beautiful in nature, I credit my mom.

It turns out that people die but love never does. My mother is a force now, the unstoppable momentum of time, the unavoidable reminder of fate, and the power of love that pushes me gently from behind, forever whispering in the wind: *I love you so much! Love, Ma*

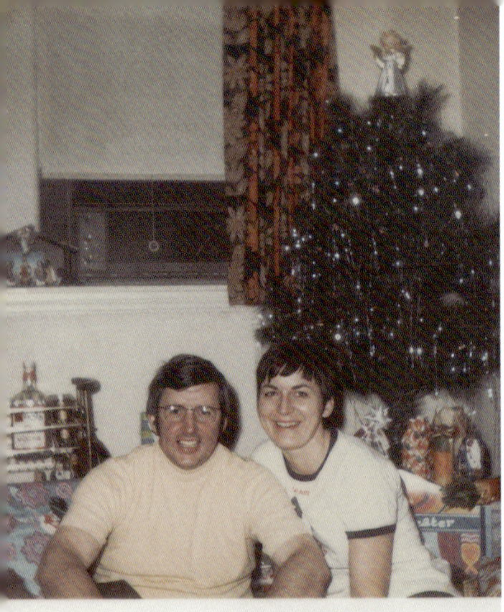
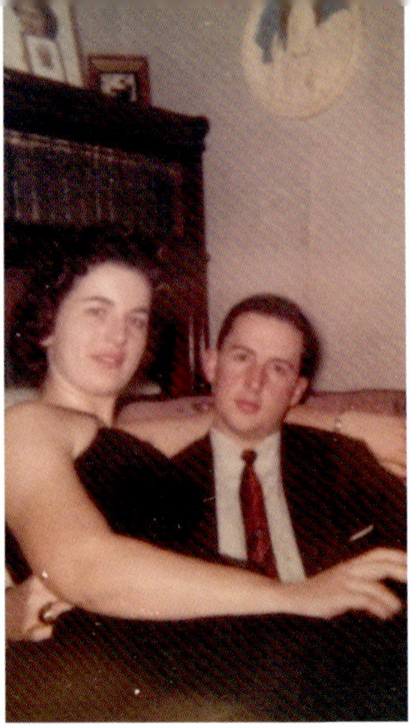
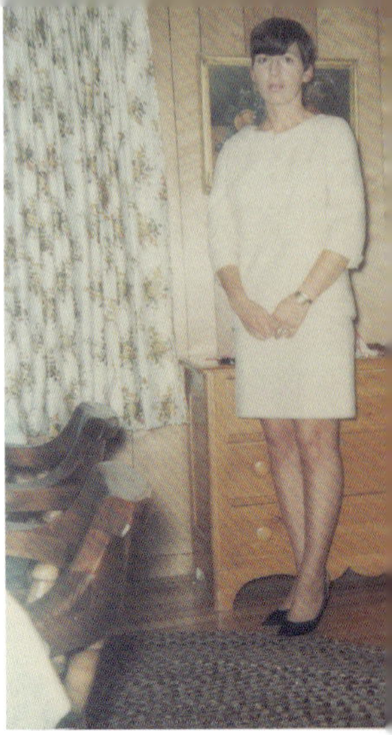
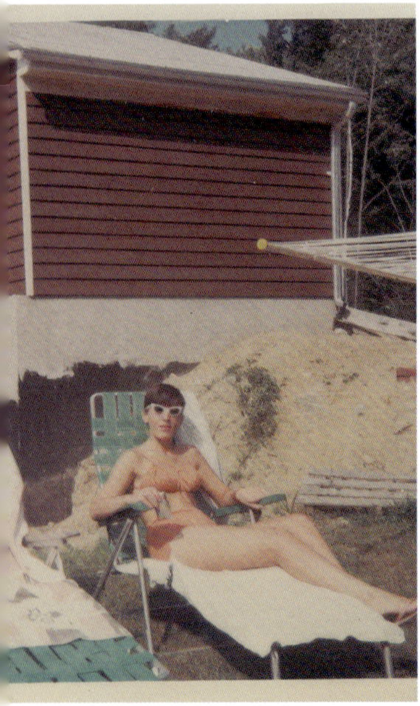
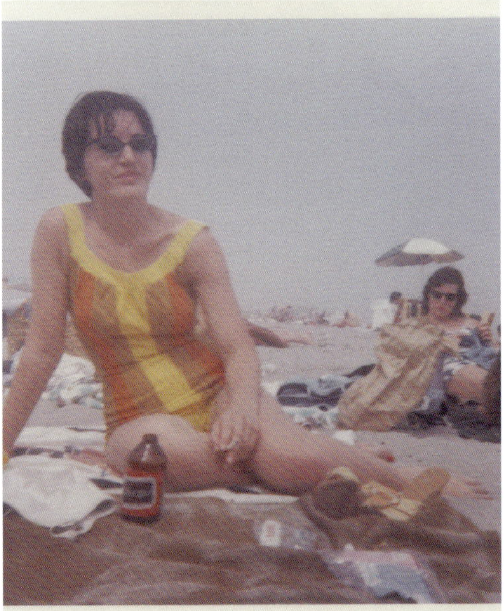
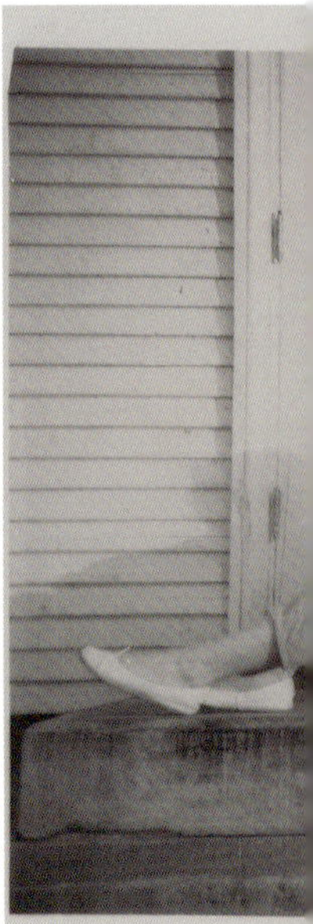
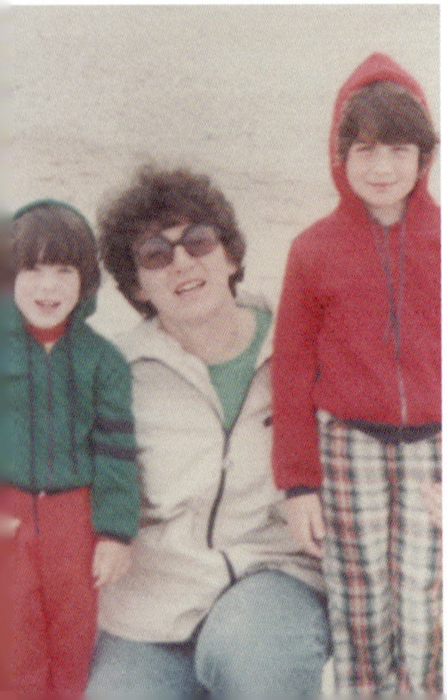
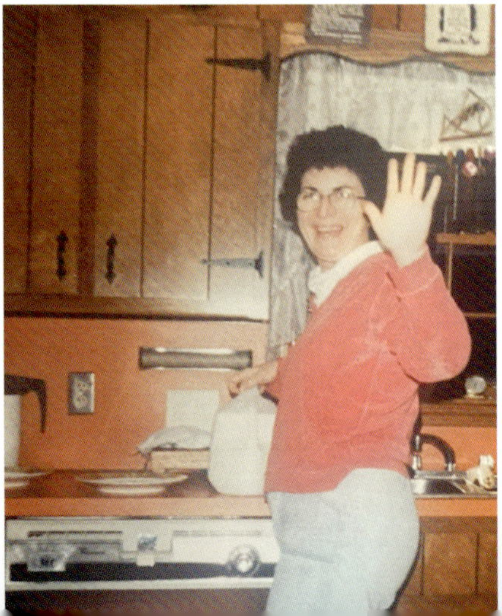
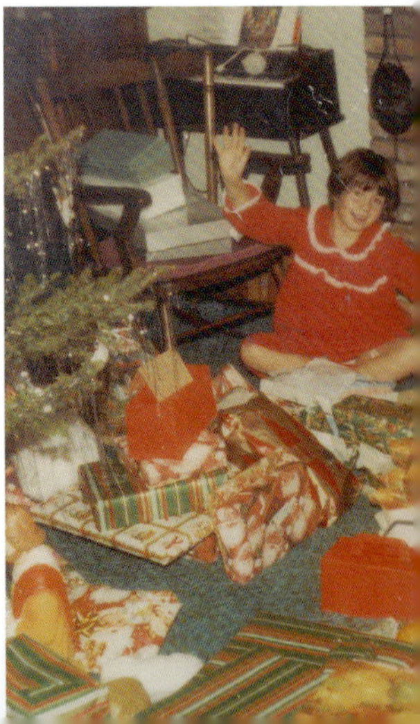

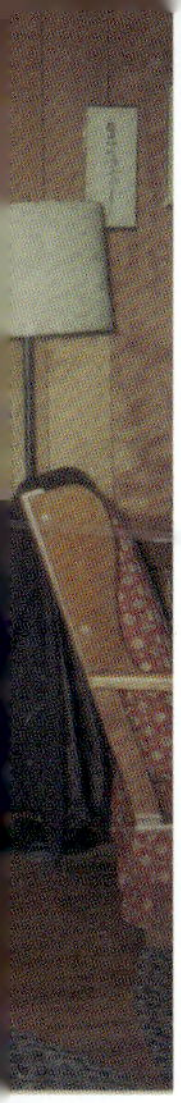

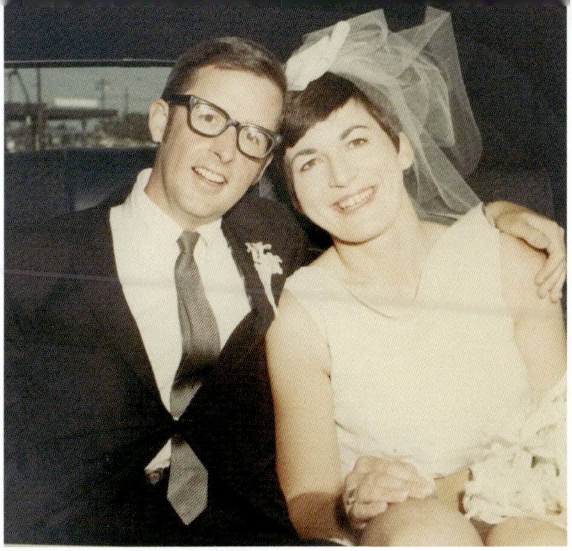

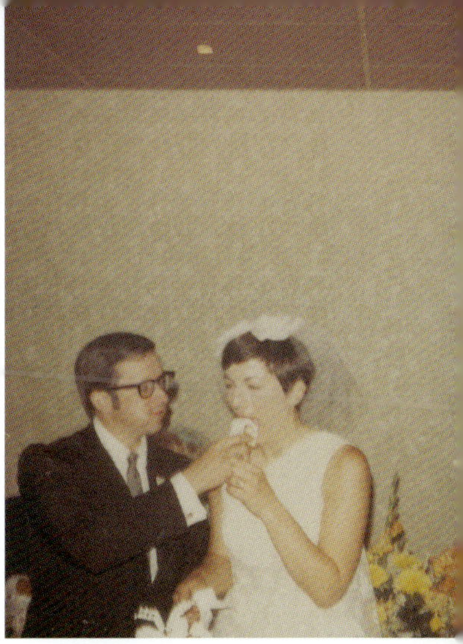

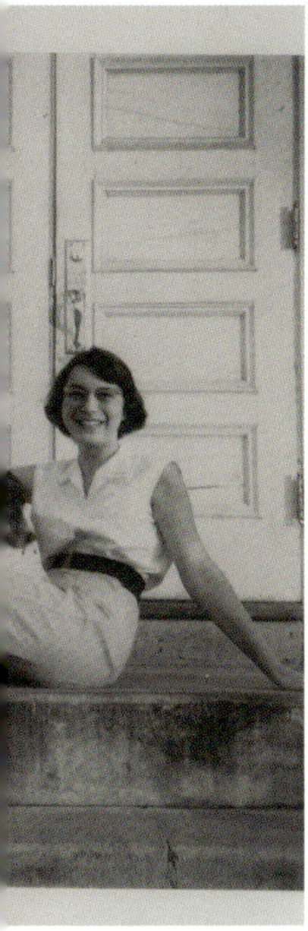

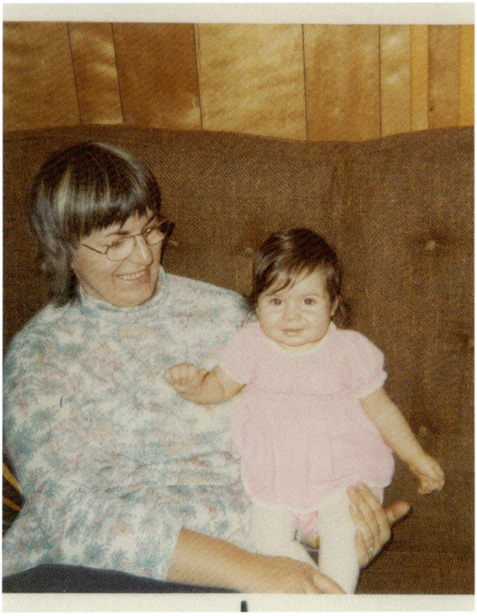

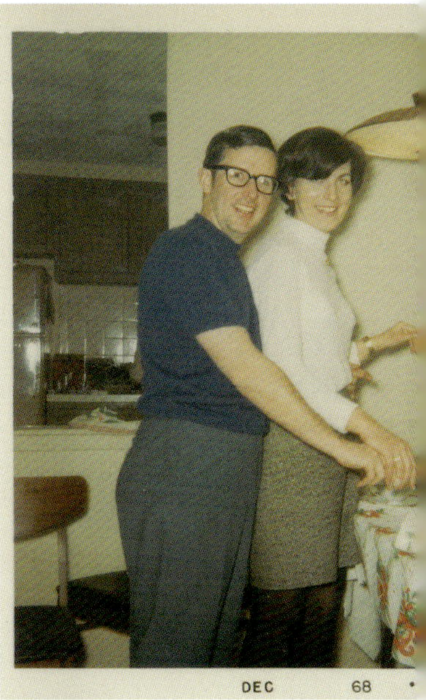
DEC 68

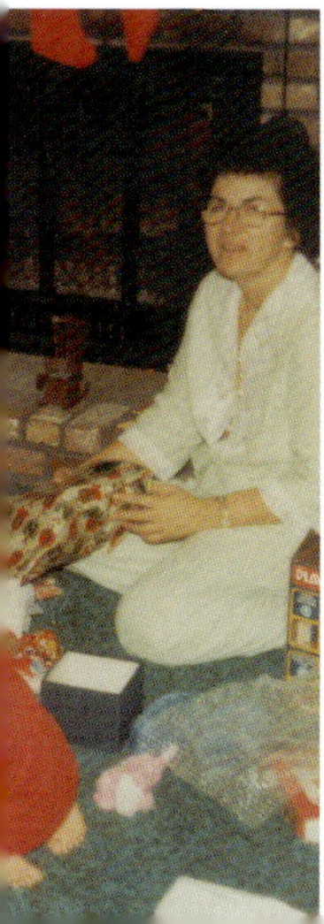

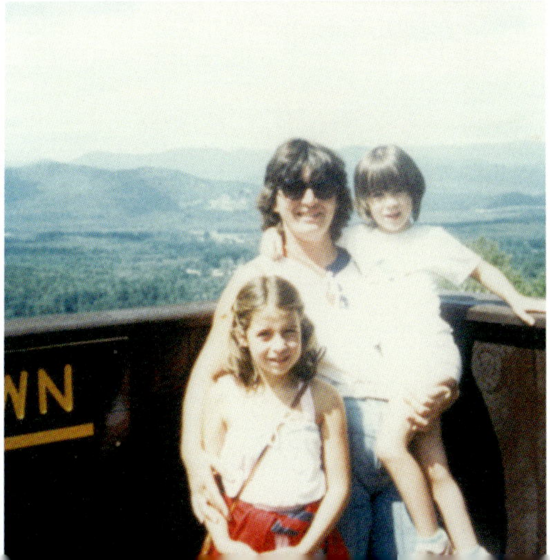

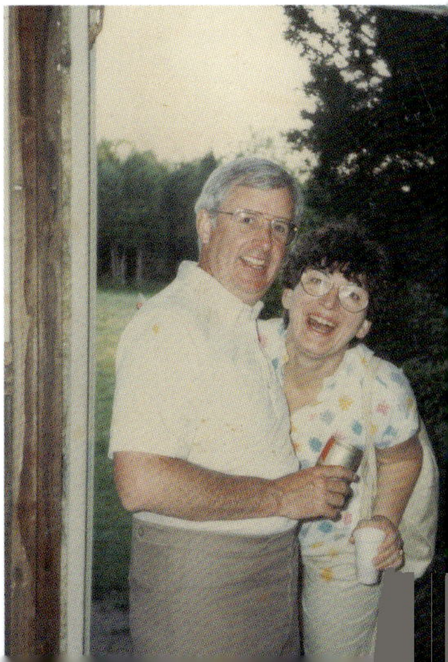

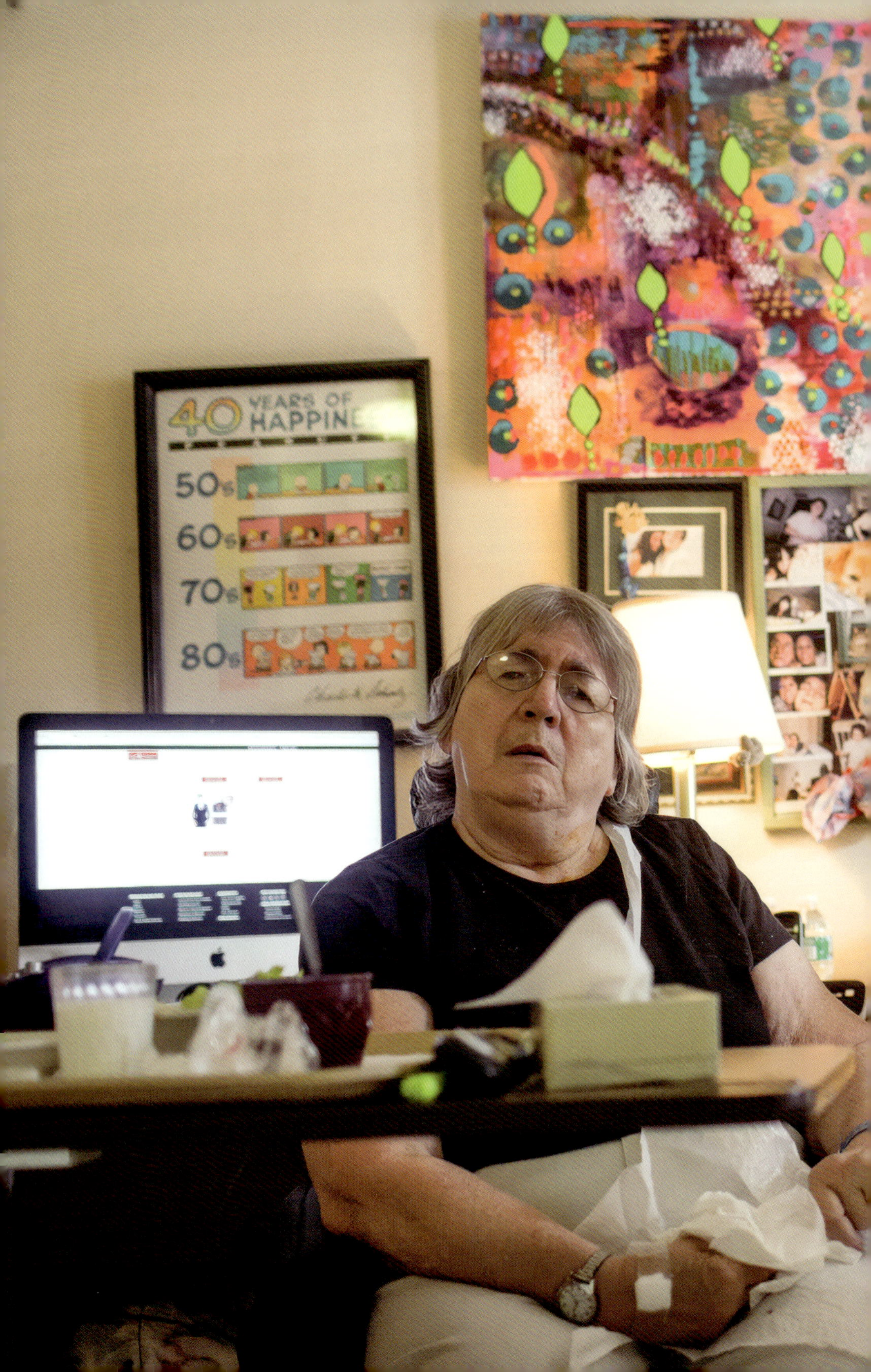
40 YEARS OF HAPPINE
50s
60s
70s
80s

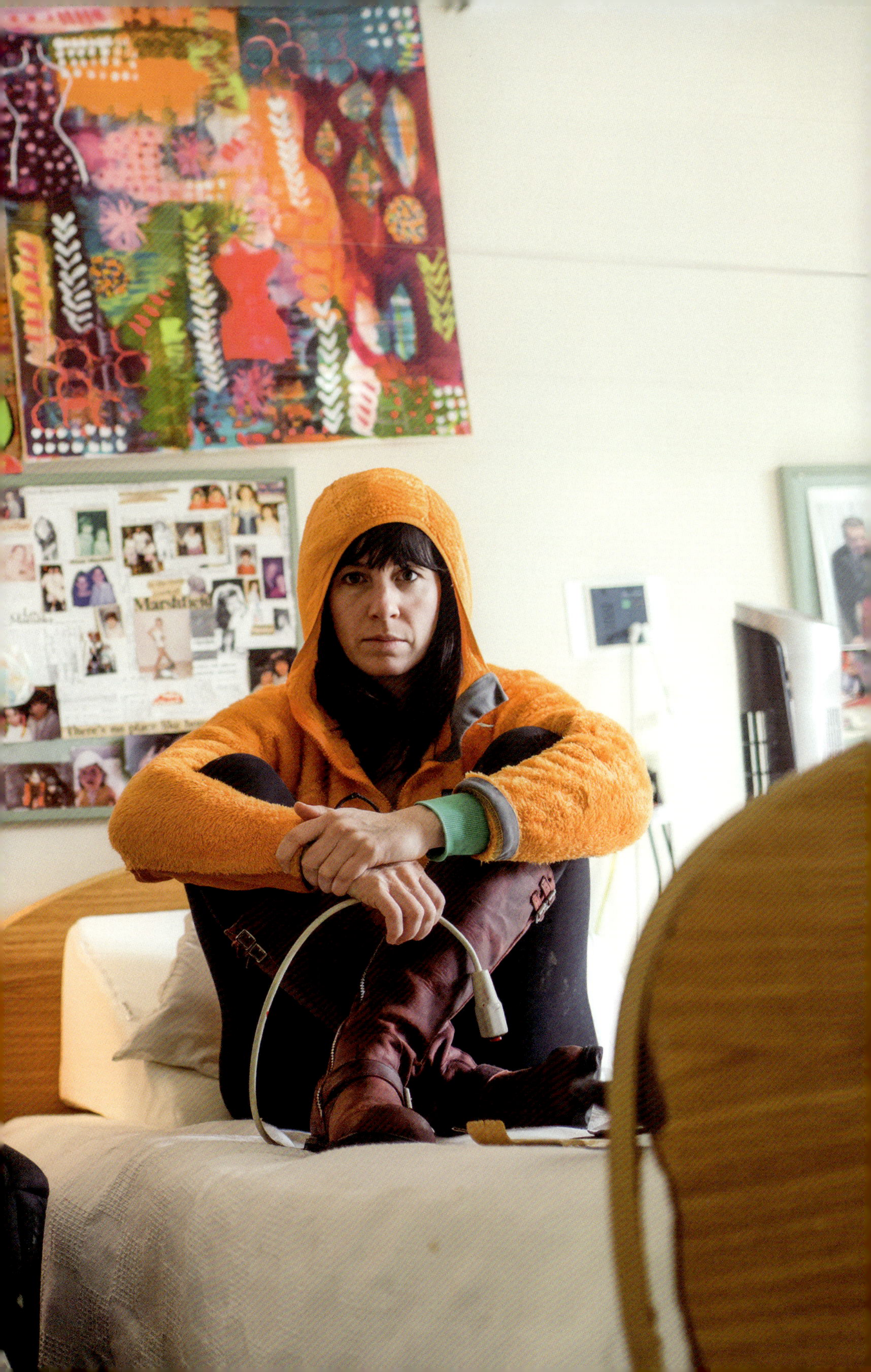

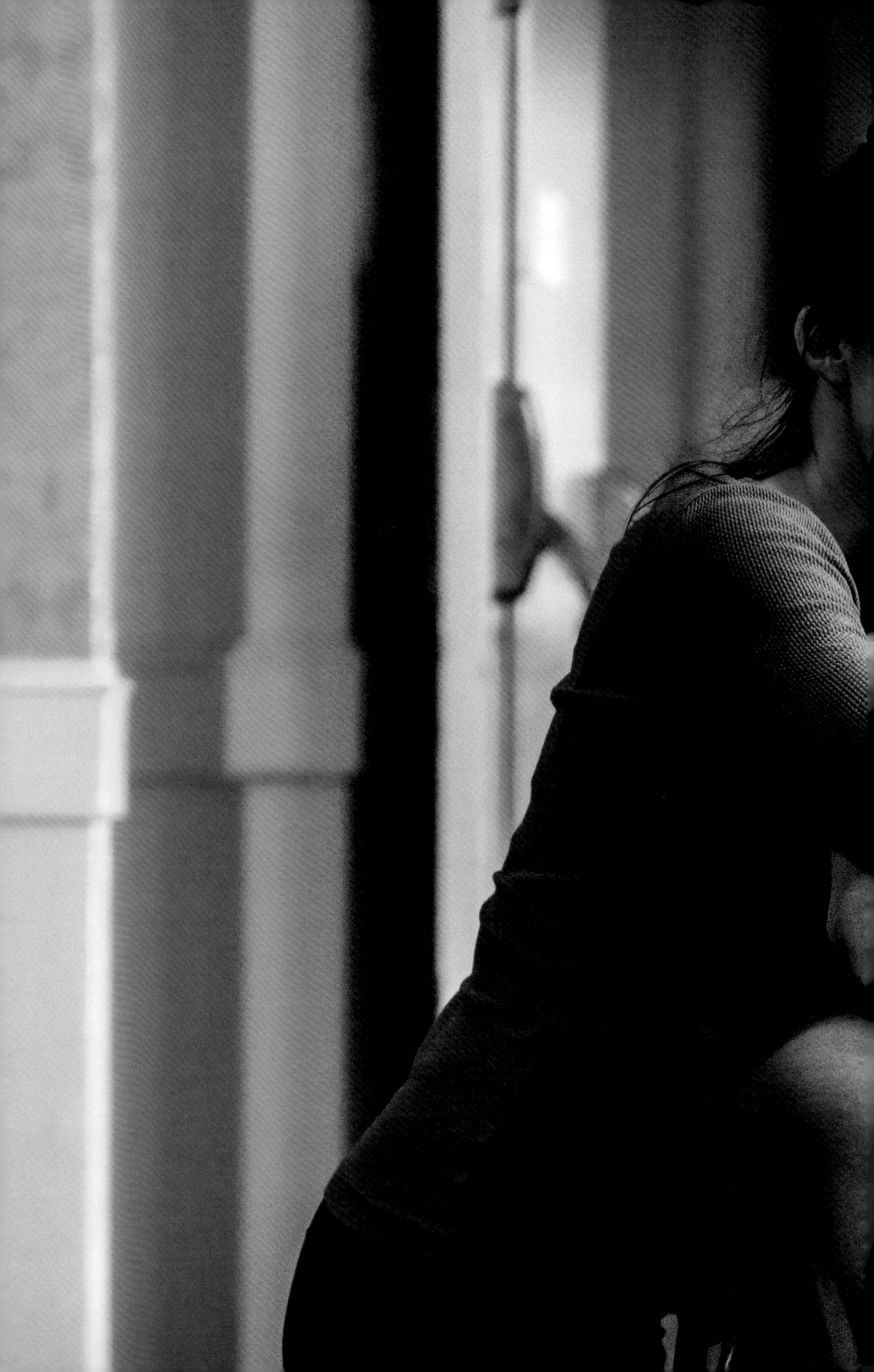

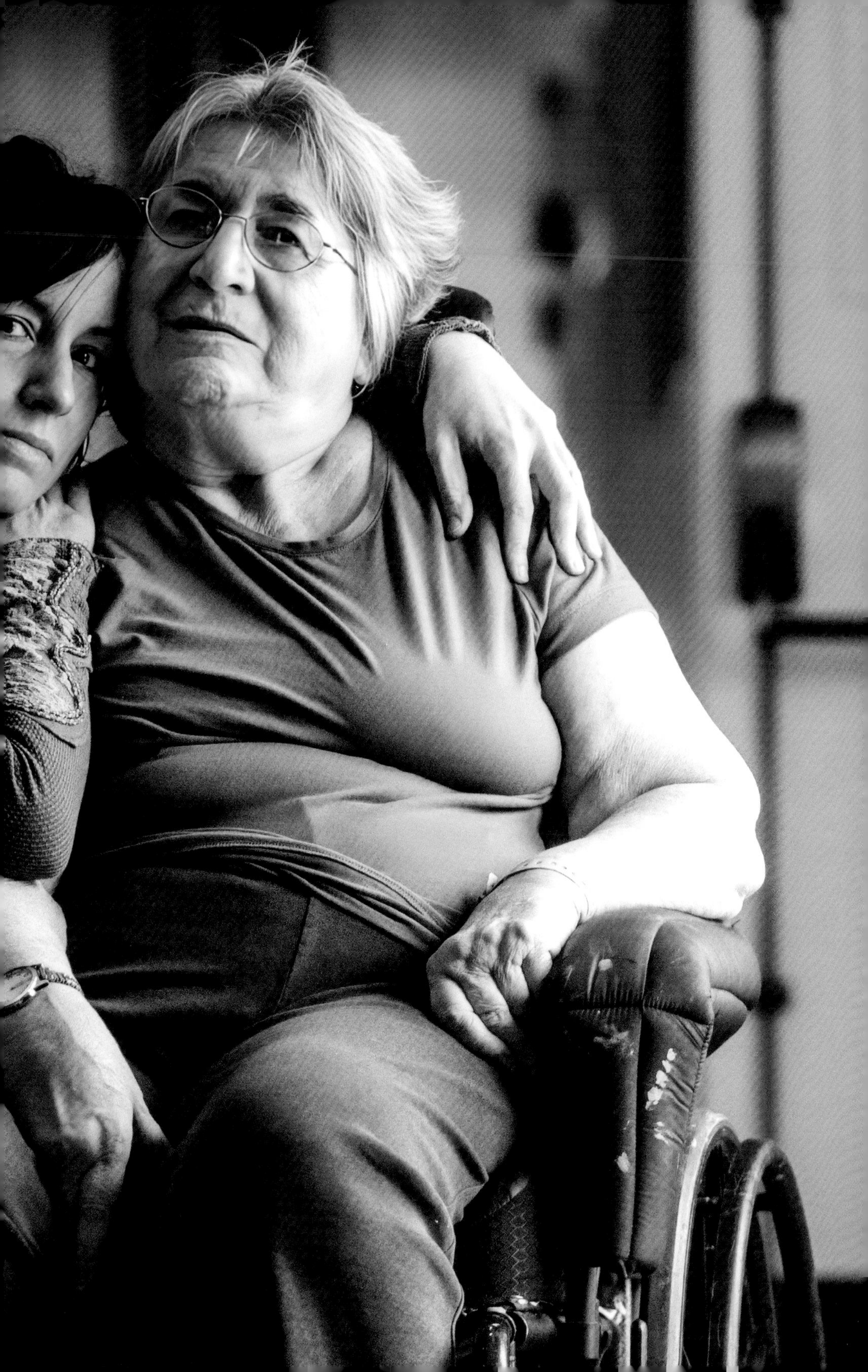

Oh, My God

There were two Catholic churches in the coastal New England town where I grew up, and as far as I knew, every family in town went to either one or the other. One church sat on the edge of the nicest part of town, so if you said you went to St. Christine's, I knew you were rich. Needless to say, my family went to the other one. Saint Ann by the Sea stood steps from the Atlantic Ocean in what was then the rundown part of town. It smelled like salt water, frankincense, and guilt, desperately needed a paint job, and offered a four o'clock Mass on Saturdays.

In 1983 we did two things really well as a family: we went to church and we went out to dinner. If we went to the four o'clock Mass on Saturdays, we could do one right after the other. My sister and I couldn't have cared less about lessons from the altar so church time was our time for shenanigans. Shannon—who I was not allowed to sit directly next to—would get my attention by leaning forward and flashing a mouth full of "fake braces" made from the paper clips she pulled off the community announcements. I'd stare back at her cross eyed until we cracked. My mom would pretend not to notice, staring ahead and biting the inside of her cheeks to stop herself from choking on silent giggles.

My dad, monitoring the throngs of parishioners seated behind us, would lean across our laps to whisper-yell, "Ted O'Toole and his son Teddy Juniah ahh heeh." My mom would tap him on the thigh, letting him know that we could hear him and encouraging him to stop talking. But he couldn't. "Great hockey playah. Funny bastihd."

After Mass, once my dad had found Mr. O'Toole to tell him a dirty joke, we piled into his silver Chevy Caprice Classic with the red interior and headed to dinner. My dad could practically taste the martini waiting for him. We were off to the Fairview Inn. He drove slowly for the one mile along the ocean that separated obligation from joy, singing at the top of his lungs to the new Lionel Richie tape the whole way.

As he sang every lyric of "Penny Lover" before Lionel did, pounding percussion on the steering wheel and pointing at the ocean over his left shoulder like it was full of adoring fans, Shannon and I would sway side to side and yell the chorus from the backseat, trying our best to be his ideal backup singers.

My adoring mom, living a life beyond her wildest dreams with her funny husband and two healthy kids, would smile at us while the cigarette lighter in the dashboard got hot. When it was ready, she'd flip open the ashtray, put a long cigarette between her lips, and light it. Benson & Hedges Menthol 100's soft pack was her choice. I don't know if she ever smoked an entire cigarette, but she also never ran out because my dad gave her a couple cartons every year for Christmas. Wrapped and under the tree.

The Fairview Inn was, and still is, a Marshfield landmark that sits not just on the edge of town but on the edge of the Earth, in a neighborhood called Brant Rock. Towering storm waves are infamous for destroying that strip of road, and in classic Marshfield style, the Fairview sits so close to the Atlantic she's practically daring it to swallow her whole.

As soon as we would pull into the parking lot—six spots on a cliff with a rotting wooden guardrail and a $10M unobstructed view of the water—we'd sprint from the car trying to outrun the salty spray of the ocean and tumble breathlessly through the doors of our favorite place. Womblike in comparison to the conditions just outside the door, the busy Fairview Inn in the 1980s, with its dulcet sounds and warm orange glow, made me feel like everything was going to be okay.

"Hi, Kev!" our hostess would cheer, making it obvious she saw him more often than she saw us.

"Mr. Wonderful is here," he'd announce half-heartedly as he peeked around the corner to see who was at the bar.

When we got to our table, Shannon and I always slid across the wide leather booth on our knees and immediately started to color our paper menus. We were giddy. Though Suzanne, our favorite waitress, knew our dad's drink choice by heart, Shannon and I would order it in unison nonetheless:

"AN - EXTRA - DRY - VODKA - MARTINI - ON - THE - ROCKS - WITH - A - TWIST!" We'd squeal in laughter as my mom raised her eyebrows, silently urging us to finish strong.

"PLEEEEAAAASE!!!," we would add, summoning our parents' applause.

As Suzanne turned away from the table, my father would follow her back to the kitchen so he could deliver a punchline too vulgar to say in front of his children, who had just ordered his anesthesia over ice.

When the bill finally arrived my dad would wave his arm in the air to call Suzanne back to the table, gesturing at the bill with a shit-eating grin. "Looks like we have a problem here, Suzanne. Who ordered the tax?" He'd fall sideways from laughter into my mom, whose eyes were already rolled to the very back of her skull.

On the way home we'd pass a dark and empty Saint Ann by the Sea, not a single car in the parking lot. Our dad would then drive slowly through town until we got to the final song on the tape, all of us singing "Hello" in four-part harmony as we pulled safely into our driveway on Whiffletree Lane.

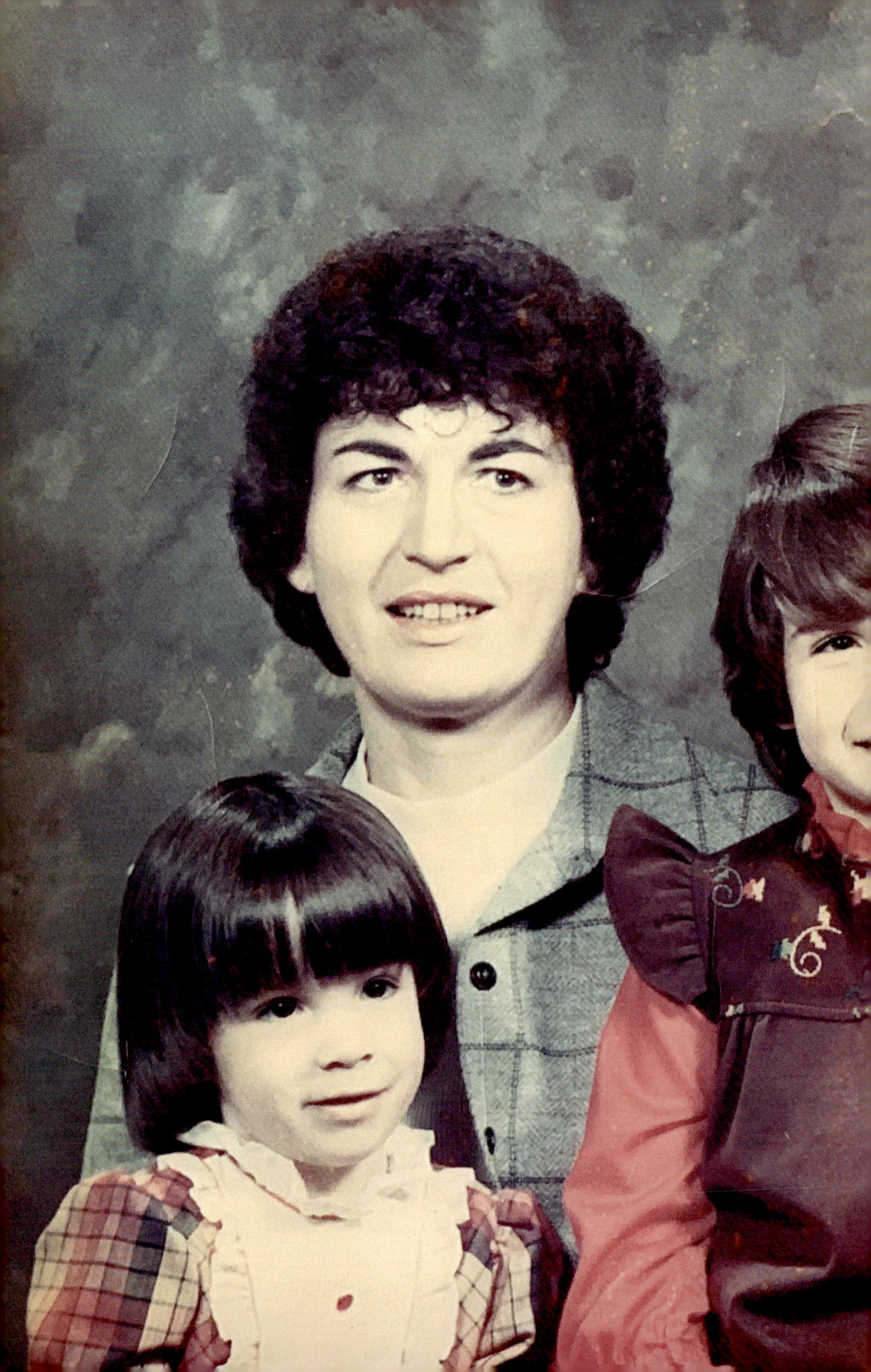

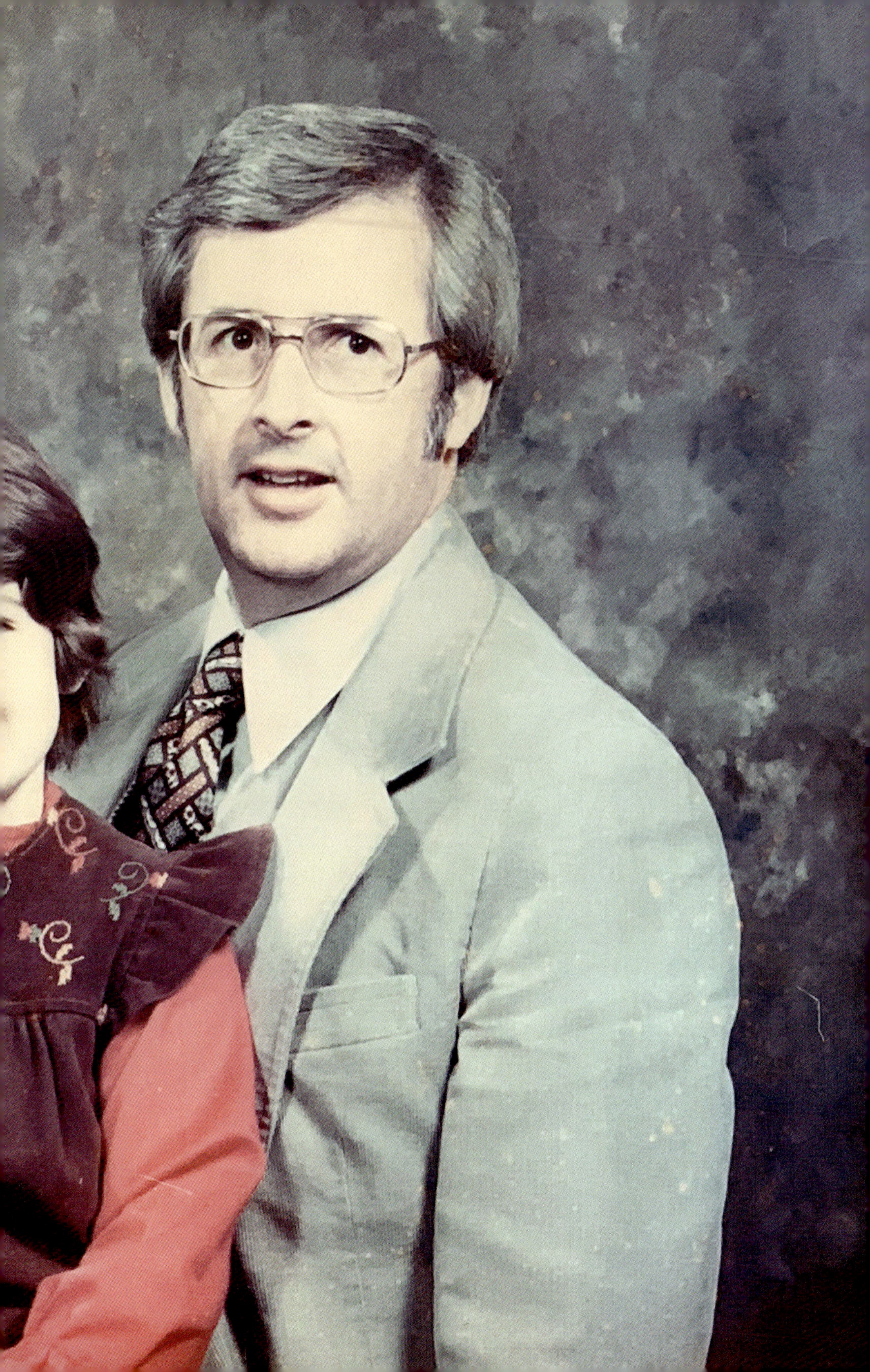

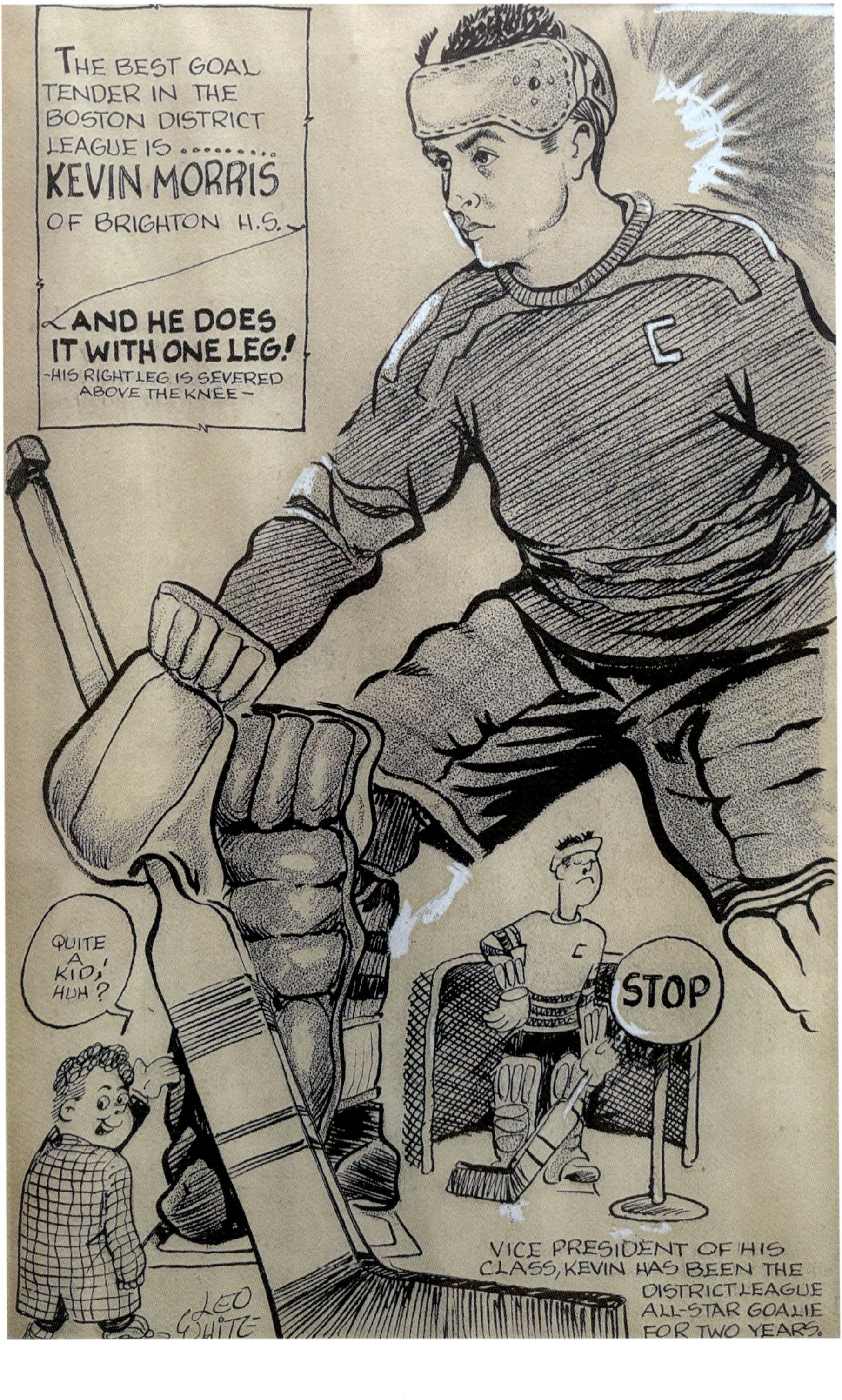
THE BEST GOAL TENDER IN THE BOSTON DISTRICT LEAGUE IS ....
KEVIN MORRIS
OF BRIGHTON H.S.
AND HE DOES IT WITH ONE LEG!
-HIS RIGHT LEG IS SEVERED ABOVE THE KNEE-
C
QUITE A KID, HUH?
STOP
VICE PRESIDENT OF HIS CLASS, KEVIN HAS BEEN THE DISTRICT LEAGUE ALL-STAR GOALIE FOR TWO YEARS.
LEO WHITE

Dick Cox

My father was just over five feet tall and had one leg. Being an alcoholic was more of a requirement than a choice.

In 1945, when he was just 7 years old, he attempted to jump onto a moving train with his friends in Brighton, the Boston neighborhood where he lived with his older brother and their parents. Jumping onto moving trains was what kids in Brighton did for fun back then, and no doubt he made that jump successfully many times. But this time, on March 27, 1945, he went to jump, slipped on ice, and fell under the train.

His right leg was severed at the ankle; gangrene eventually set in, and his leg was amputated to mid-calf. He spent the rest of first grade in the hospital, and his own father—humiliated that he now had a handicapped son—never visited him once. My dad eventually played hockey for Brighton High School as their famous "one-legged goalie," and then played one minute of one period as a freshman at Boston College. Apparently, he let in a goal immediately, so was pulled off the ice, never to play college hockey again—though it never dampened his love of the game.

When you're a small, one-legged guy you survive by making people like you. And no one did that quite as well as my dad did. Funny and charming, friendly and smart-enough, Kevin Morris had lifelong friendships and more friends every year. My dad's sense of humor was, let's say, pre-Me Too, and his best friend was a guy named Dick Cox so he was never without a punchline. He met my mom when she was 19 and he was 22, they dated for ten years, then got married in 1969. When I asked my mom how she knew he was "the one," she shrugged and said because he was an altar boy as a kid and went to college. I suggested she work on that answer.

My dad was always looking for a good time, and his answer was always yes, so he was famous for being a great chaperone. On our fifth-grade field trip to the New England Aquarium in Boston, as soon as we entered the building, my dad looked at the five ten-year-olds in his charge and asked, "Wanna get ahta heeh?" We spun on our heels and headed for Faneuil Hall, where we spent that whole afternoon doing fun shit we weren't supposed to—eating ice cream, watching street performers, and window shopping. We returned to the Aquarium as the rest of the class was lining up to get back on the bus. We had our own Ferris Bueller afternoon a whole year before that movie came out.

A bullshit artist to put 'em all to shame, my dad would tell you anything you wanted to hear. A salesman through and through, he peddled toilets in the '70s, dental equipment through the '80s, and then struggled professionally for many years until he finally got a job delivering foreclosure notices during the mortgage crisis of 2008. He wasn't from the bank that foreclosed, he was the guy who handed you the notice from the law firm. We were raised on bad checks and credit cards he didn't pay, so this was an ironic swan song for my father.

My dad's love language was gift giving, but back then we just called it being spoiled rotten. During the height of the Cabbage Patch Kid craze, in the mid-'80s when people stood outside Child World for hours to grab one of those dolls, I had thirteen of them. I mean, he did punch Dianne Evonne—my first and favorite Cabbage Patch Kid—in the face to make his friends laugh, but ya know, I had a dozen more in my room to cry into for emotional support.

With absolutely no example of a father himself, my dad did his best. He numbed himself with alcohol long before he became a father, and when I reflect on his childhood, I know I would have, too. In bars laughing with his friends was where he felt most appreciated, so that's where he spent his time. He would leave the house on Saturday morning, telling us that he was going to the post office, and we wouldn't see him again until he came home from the eleven o'clock Mass on Sunday.

My dad was inept at emotional availability, but the love was there. When we cleaned out his apartment after he died, cards I had written to him over the years were framed and hung on his walls next to countless photographs of Shannon and me. I used to think that he should've remained a bachelor his whole life, but he insisted that the best thing that ever happened to him was me and my sister. And every time Shannon and I make each other laugh harder than anyone else can, I know for certain that we are mighty grateful for the gifts he gave us.

Recently, I asked ChatGPT: "What are the long-term effects of being children of alcoholic fathers?" It listed, almost word-for-word, everything I've ever written as a warning to men on dating apps. But it ended with this gem:

> Resilience and Growth: Despite the challenges they face, some children of alcoholic fathers develop a high level of resilience. They may grow stronger through their experiences, develop a strong sense of empathy, and learn to navigate difficult situations effectively.

Thank you so much, Dad. For all of it.

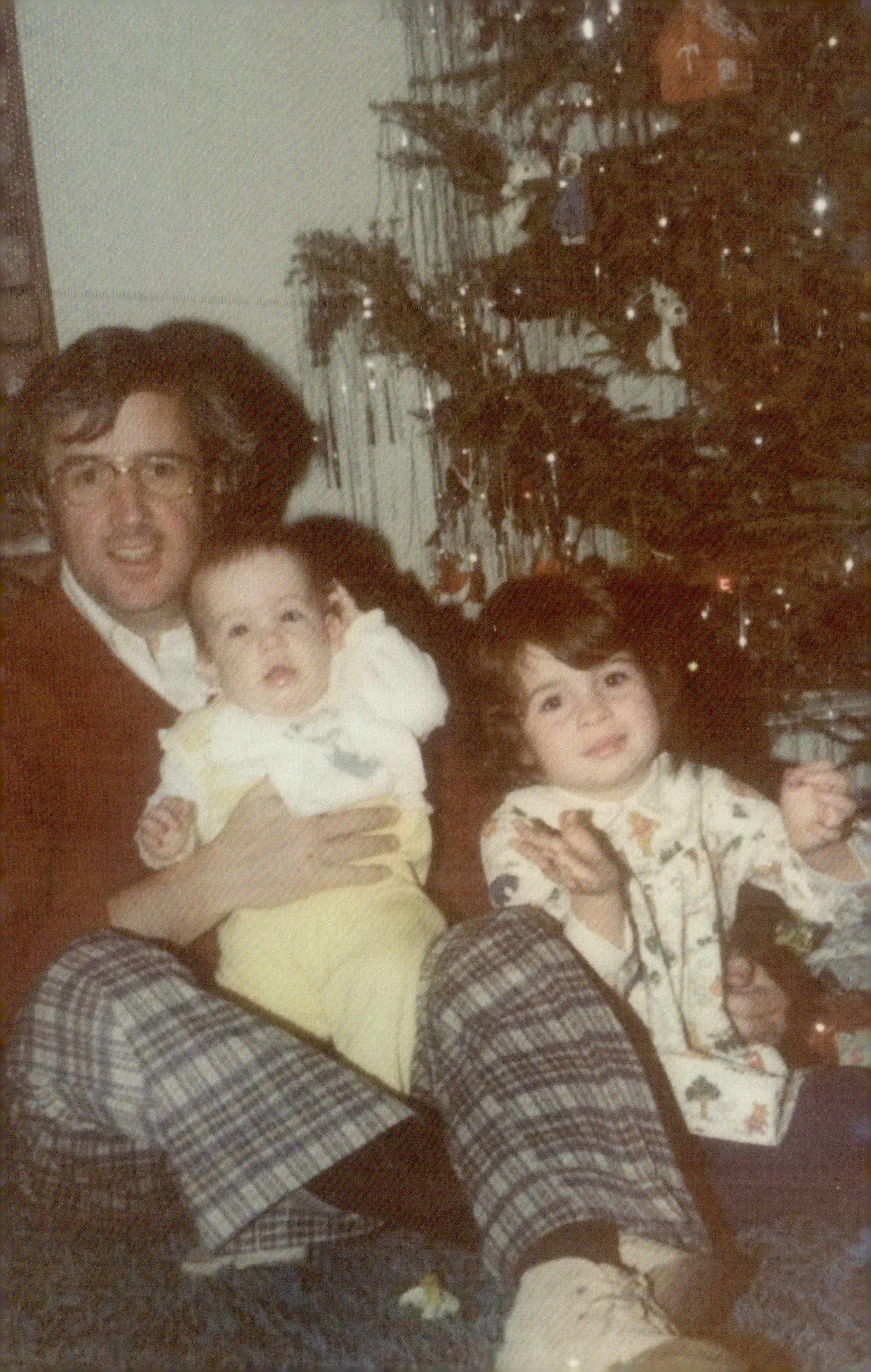

The Groupie

Shannon stretched the kitchen phone cord all the way down the hall and stood in my bedroom doorway with the phone in her hand.

"Are you seriously making people take a test to be your friend?" she demanded.

"Why?" I volleyed back.

"Because this is Kerre on the phone and Suzy [Kerre's little sister] is crying because she's so nervous about some test she has to take to be your friend!?"

When I was in the fifth grade, I started a group called The Groupie, and you had to take a test to get in. The Groupie was for girls only, and it had no purpose besides just being a group and making shit up to do as a group. The test to get in had two questions, and if you got both right—which everyone did—you were in. The questions were:

1. What's your favorite clothing label?
2. What's your favorite store?

The question about labels had two possible correct answers: Outback Red or Forenza. In a pinch we'd accept Esprit. The question about your favorite store could also go one of two ways: The Limited or Banana Republic. Benetton worked for either label or store.

Once you got in—and *again*, for the record, everyone got in, not a single person was turned away—you were given a new name. Your Groupie name was a hybrid of the first two letters of your first name and the first two letters of your last name. As chance would have it that method worked perfectly for my name, and TaMo was born.

Our first Groupie activity was to make the Groupie uniform. I brought in a pile of my dad's old undershirts, threadbare and yellowed with sweat, that my mom said I could take from his dresser. During recess we adorned each Fruit of the Loom undershirt with our new Groupie name in bubble letters with Puffy Paint dipped in glitter. Puffy Paint was a relatively new invention, and this activity exploded the group's popularity. We proudly wore our uniforms over our clothes like pit-stained capes and enticed anyone ready to join to take the test.

Next was the Groupie haircut, which turns out was just my haircut on everyone else's head. This timeless look consisted of very short hair parted on the side with a twelve-inch rat tail down the back. I offered to give each girl their new coiffure behind the school during recess, but girls wanted to at least ask their moms first. Turns out not a single mother allowed me to cut a rat tail into their daughter's hair. Well, besides Tracie's mom. Tracie's mom let Tracie get a very short haircut that was parted on the side with a very long rat tail. In my opinion Tracie pulled it off really well. Plus, that was the kind of enthusiasm I liked to see.

The greatest teacher of all time, Mr. Renaud, my fifth-grade homeroom teacher, lovingly referred to me as Tarabul for my antics, and may have been the one to turn me into administration for lording too much power over my classmates. The Groupie was disbanded by Mr. Devitt, our principal, and my reign ended as quickly as it began.

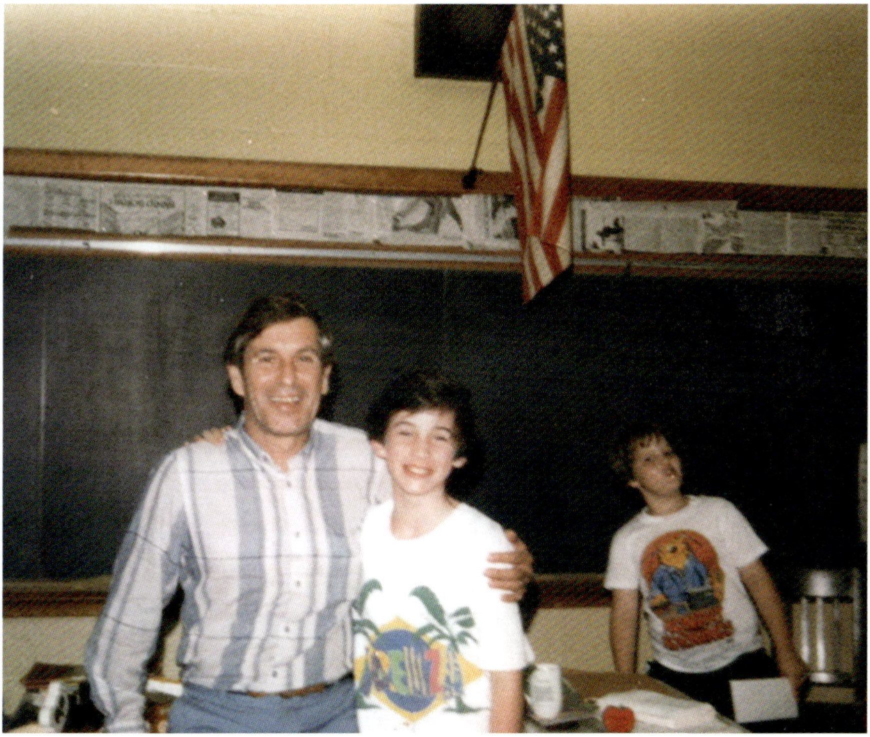

Southern Belle

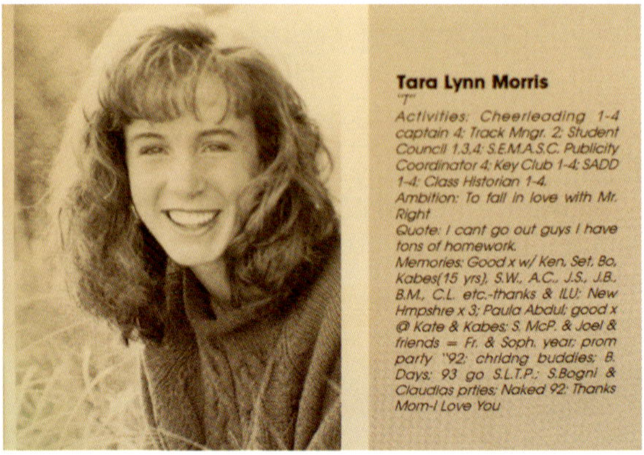

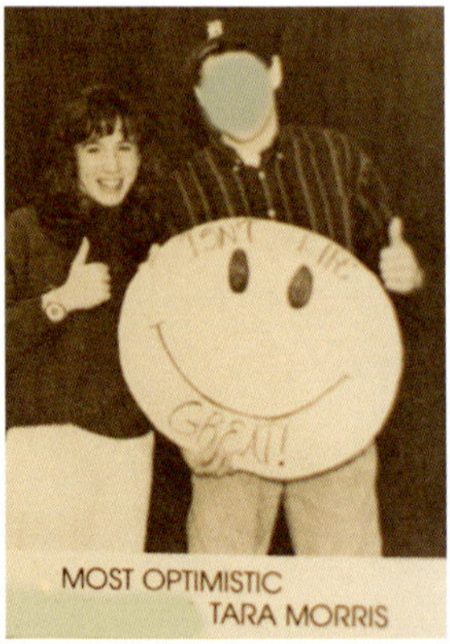

In high school I was a depressed anorexic faking it so well I won Most Optimistic my senior year. I was the captain of the cheerleading team but couldn't cartwheel. I read cookbooks but wouldn't eat. I was afraid of boys, but my yearbook ambition was "to fall in love with Mr. Right." I was so eager to leave Marshfield and finally be honest about who I was that I toured colleges during my sophomore year—a full year earlier than most kids.

Like many young people who didn't know much outside their hometowns, I wanted the full college experience. As a teenager in Marshfield, that meant: Big! Sunny! Far away! And, of course, football! California was too far, so the Southeast it was.

My mom worked at a storage facility in those years and saved every penny so we could visit every school I was even moderately excited about from North Carolina to Georgia during April vacation. That whole trip was so special. I still remember little details like the way the candle wax in a restaurant dripped all over the tablecloth and how we marveled at how beautiful it was. She brought her camcorder and followed me walking across every campus, and together we dreamed of my future.

When it was actually time to apply—a year and a half later—I was accepted at all the schools I didn't want to go to anymore and found myself with nowhere to go and not much time to decide. I asked one of my best friends, Kendra, to help me troubleshoot. She reminded me that a girl named Nikki was at the University of Alabama and loved it. Nikki had graduated a couple years ahead of us and was always good to me. It seemed like a safe bet: if Nikki liked it, I could probably like it. She'd be a familiar face, but I wouldn't feel confined within a former version of myself. I went home that day, called to request UA's single-page application, sent it away, and got in. Sight unseen, having never thought about this college once before, having never set foot in the state of Alabama, I accepted their offer. I was heading to the University of Alabama. Big, sunny, far away football school, here I come. Roll Tide.

The first time I saw the University of Alabama was in June 1993 during freshman orientation, and from the moment I set foot on the campus I hated it. No one and nothing seemed familiar, which was exactly what I was looking for, but when I got it, I was so regretful of my decision I was panicked. Teenagers were driving Mercedes and not only were there no Latino or Asian folks, there weren't even brunettes. There seemed to be only blondes and Black folks, and these two groups weren't hanging out together. Like, at all. The campus-wide disdain for "Northerners" was also obvious, but nonetheless, two months later me and my parents set out on the twenty-two-hour drive from Marshfield to Tuscaloosa. They dropped me off, we cried our eyes out, and I began my transformation into the genteel Southern Belle you know me as today.

My roommate in the freshman, girls-only dorm was Shelly Nealums, a quiet and kind Black girl from Tuskegee, Alabama. We got along immediately and had the most important things in common: we were homesick, out of our league, and totally intimidated to be at such a huge school. Shelly and I were paired together randomly, but we chose our floor purposefully: the 14th floor, which was the Quiet Floor. Choosing the Quiet Floor in the freshman dorm at an enormous college known for its parties let me control my surroundings and safeguard my anorexia, but it also guaranteed the inevitable: that I would remain homesick and unhappy for the year. That first day Shelly and I helped each other get settled, went to dinner together, and somehow fell asleep on our completely silent dorm room floor. Sorority rush started the next morning.

Rush at the University of Alabama in 1993 was a well-oiled, five-day machine, and everyone knew where to be and when. On day one, hundreds of nervous, white, teenaged girls (the Greek system at UA remained segregated until 2013) gathered in the middle of Magnolia Drive. Magnolia Drive was a bucolic yet surreal street. It looked like an everyday neighborhood in the middle of campus, only this neighborhood was lined with ornate, twenty-bedroom, antebellum-style mansions with Greek letters over their front doors.

At 9 a.m. the rush coordinators stood in the middle of Magnolia Drive and blew a whistle that prompted every door of all sixteen sorority houses to slam open at the exact same time. At that moment, every sorority sister of every house shot their heads out the front doors and yelled their "door songs" as loudly and as cheerfully as possible in hopes of getting our attention, winning our affection, and drowning out the other fifteen door songs. We, the rushees, were then shuffled through the front doors to spend ten minutes talking to a stranger while we both judged whether we wanted to spend our college years as sisters. We did this sixteen times in a row.

As I learned the following year, the sisters of each sorority arrived on campus weeks before all the antebellum mansion doors flew open for a boot camp of memorization, rehearsals, and role-play—all designed to eventually entice a mix of strangers, younger siblings, and friends-of-friends to join their sorority. Rush was showtime.

Every afternoon of rush had a "party," and every party had a name: Ice Water Tea, Ten Party, Six Party. These were not parties at all—they were more like twenty-minute open houses named for the number of houses each rushee was invited back to. And then there was Serious Night—held in the morning, of course. We lit candles, wore dresses, and bawled our eyes out (!?) as we got very serious about which sorority we'd choose. No more fucking around, girls.

The sorority I chose was Nikki's sorority: Zeta Tau Alpha. I was sort of open to others, but with my Boston accent, colorful outfits, and habit of cursing every fourth word I was not asked back to many places during rush. Oddly I *was* asked back to Tri Delt—surprising because that was one of the houses for rich, beautiful, Southern girls.

When the girl assigned to get to know me at the Tri Delt house asked what my father did for a living, I answered, "He's an alcoholic. He has a really fucking hard time keeping a job."

That kind of matter-of-fact honesty isn't welcome anywhere really, but definitely not during sorority rush at University of Alabama. I never heard back from the sisterhood of Delta Delta Delta.

On my very first day as a member of Zeta, my name tag still on as part of Bid Day celebrations, a respected sorority sister a few years older than me asked to speak to me privately and sat me down on the couch.

"I heard about your roommate situation," she said quietly, referring to Shelly's Blackness. "We'll get you out of that as soon as we can."

Horrified, I told her there was nothing to fix and walked away. I couldn't believe the horrendous reputation of Alabama was true—and that I saw it so quickly. I hated it here. I wanted to go home. I didn't want to be anywhere near people who thought like this.

The University of Alabama was so steeped in segregation it was hard to tell what century it was down there, but by the time the calendar read 1993, the dialect of our beloved staff—all Black Alabamians—was completely different from the Southern lilt of the pageant winners they took care of. Though it was hard for this Northerner to parse out exactly what was being said in the kitchen it didn't stop me and every decent girl in that house—of which there were many—from trying. Annie Pearl was my favorite cook. No taller than five feet, with a body shaped like a hug, you could hear her and Lizzy, the main cook, laughing their asses off twelve hours a day. Clearly all the fun was happening just behind those kitchen doors, so we'd hang out with Lizzy and Annie Pearl as much as we could to try to get in on their fun. Every time I talked to my mom she'd ask about Annie Pearl and Lizzy. I talked about them that much.

I remember watching the O.J. Simpson verdict in the Zeta living room in the fall of junior year. The entire staff, all Black Alabamans, and the rest of us, all young white girls in Patagonia shorts, sat motionless, staring at the TV. The whole world was upside down about this trial. It was obvious that O.J. was guilty, but since Rodney King's beating a few years earlier, racism and injustice by the police against Black people was also obvious. The verdict was called in a country, in a state, in a town, in a living room so tense with racism, I didn't know where to look, so I closed my eyes. The whole room, maybe twenty of us, choked. I heard crying, I heard clapping, I heard gasps. I felt the air leave the room and then I left the room. I walked upstairs and crawled into bed fully dressed and cried.

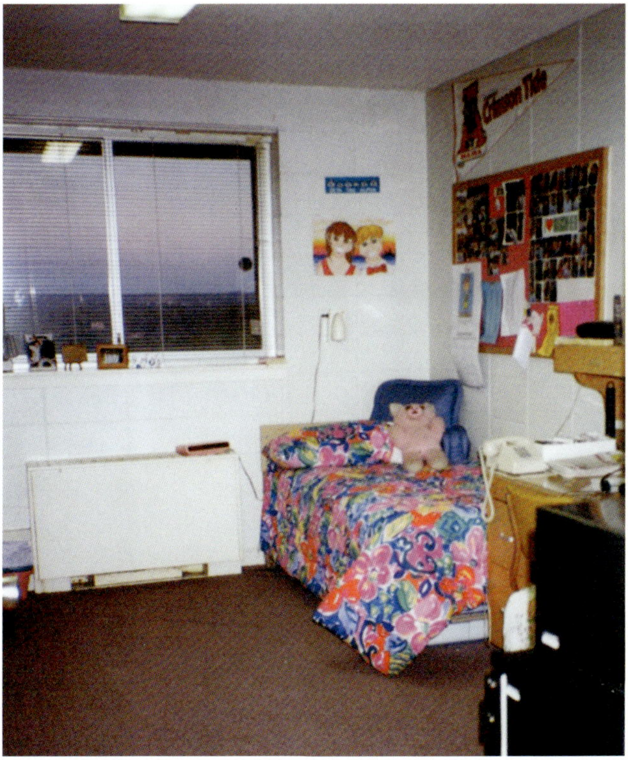

Stumbling on a Cult

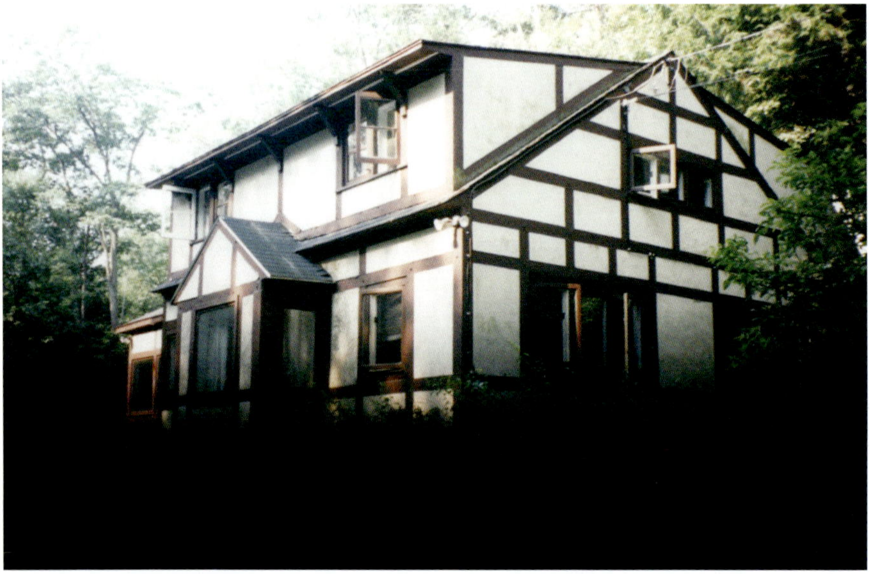

The summer between my freshman and sophomore years at Alabama I wanted an internship, but I found a cult instead. My major was Communications, but what I really wanted to do with my life was own a health spa. I had never even been to a health spa, but nonetheless I was constantly sketching the blueprints for the one I wanted to own: a place where people could do step aerobics, lift weights, barely eat, and get a facial. So I pored over the health spa classified sections in the back of fitness magazines to learn what existed and where. That's how I discovered Canyon Ranch in Lenox, Massachusetts, the fanciest health spa on god's green Earth. I sent away for their brochure, and when it arrived I read it so many times I memorized its glossy extolment of the Ranch lifestyle. I didn't want to just go to Canyon Ranch, I wanted to *live* there.

I soon wrote more or less a love letter to Jennifer, the general manager of Canyon Ranch, which landed me a meeting with her over Christmas break. I borrowed my mom's car for the three-hour drive from Marshfield to Lenox, and my dad wrote me four pages of directions in cursive. He never mentioned so much as a single exit number but instead described the landmarks I'd see and which ones to turn at. Over a ridiculously light lunch in the main dining room of the Gilded Age estate that is Canyon Ranch, I proposed my idea to Jen: "For my entire life (more like the last six months, but whatever) I've wanted to own a health spa," I told her. "Canyon Ranch is where I'd like to learn how to do that."

Moved by my own passion, I began crying. I told her I would live on the premises. In a guest room. Just like a guest. I'd do every exercise class, even the one called Feldenkrais, which looked lame, and even low-impact aerobics, which I hate. In the dining room I'd try everything on the regular menu as well as the new, groundbreaking, low-calorie menu. I'd start smoking now just so I could attend smoking cessation classes. I'd eat granola bars and walk around in a robe and slippers. Every seminar on how to lower your cholesterol I would attend. I'd learn How to Cook Fat Free at Home and try every spa service. I'd be Jen's little soldier, her eyes and ears of the Ranch. Insider shit. I'd report every detail back to her, and together we'd make this place even better. Basically, I told her, I'll be like your personal spy-consultant.

"Wowwwww," she said after a long pause, clearly more offended at my audacity than impressed. "No," she concluded. Instead she gave me an internship in Guest Services. I would welcome guests, pass on any real problem to properly trained folks, and walk, young and smiling, down the hallways.

"Do you babysit?" Jen asked.

"Constantly," I lied.

She found me free housing. I would stay with Doug, the yoga teacher at Canyon Ranch, and his wife, Danielle, in exchange for babysitting their daughter, Rena, while also interning at the Ranch. I was in.

My parents dropped me off at Doug and Danielle's home in Lenox on a Sunday afternoon in June 1994. My dad was still pulling out of their driveway, giving me a thumbs up and laying on the horn in support of my bravery, when Danielle turned to me and said with weight in her voice, "We're not really Doug and Danielle. We're Arnav and Aadya, the Sanskrit names our leader has given us."

I spun around to see how far my dad's car was to gauge if they would hear me when I yelled for help. They were completely out of sight. I turned back around and answered Aadya with enough enthusiasm to hopefully convince myself, "Oh, my god, that is so cool!"

"Well, let's get ya moved in," Aadya offered, as she took the suitcase from my hand and began walking toward the house. "Your bedroom is right across the hall from ours."

So, Doug and Danielle met each other through a guru-centric spiritual yoga society (a cult) at the then-ashram-now-yoga-retreat-center Kripalu, which was right around the corner from their house in Stockbridge, MA. In 1994 their cult had recently dissolved due to—god knows no one saw this one coming—revelations of sexual and financial improprieties committed by their leader. By the time we crossed paths they had mostly found their way through that chapter, married one another, and had a daughter, then two years old.

These people were classic hippie-yogis from the '80s, and a world away from anything I had ever seen. I was a suburban kid who went to Cape Cod for family vacations so my dad could drink at a new restaurant. This family walked around naked and slept in the same bed. On their windowsill sat a row of rotting garlic and avocados. Our sill had chicken collarbones to make a wish on. Mason jars full of wheat germ sat on Danielle's kitchen counter. Ours had a scale so my mom could weigh her Weight Watchers–approved food. Danielle did Ashtanga yoga in her living room. My mom smoked butts and watched *Guiding Light*. I had entered a new universe.

Three days after my parents dropped me off for the six-week internship, I was already regretting my decision. Never one to consider the details, I immediately realized I had no way to get to the Ranch for work. I borrowed Doug's expensive bicycle and struggled through the three-mile commute of undulating hills, practically crying in anticipatory dread every time I swung my leg over the crossbar. When I eventually arrived at work I provided absolutely nothing of value. I was unprepared and unqualified. This wasn't fun at all. I wanted to go home.

I had been there less than a week when I decided I had to tell Danielle I was leaving. I was particularly nervous about the conversation because, just a few days earlier, I told her how I hastily chose to attend the University of Alabama and how unhappy I was there. "I accepted Alabama's offer without ever even visiting the place!" I bragged, without the slightest awareness of how ignorant that sounded. So I was sheepish when I peeked my head in her office and broke the news that I wanted to go home.

Without taking her eyes off the computer screen, unsurprised by my announcement, she answered, "Start watching the pattern in your life where you jump into things with both feet and then wonder why you're drowning." Then she turned to me and smiled.

Embarrassed by the truth of Danielle's words and the transparency of my shortcomings, I knew I had to stay. I told her I'd make it work. Pretty soon riding a bike through the bucolic towns of Western Massachusetts felt like freedom to me, which is how riding a bike has felt ever since. I went to Doug's impossibly boring yoga classes at the Ranch and wondered how anyone could ever like yoga. I found my groove at Guest Services and tried to make people laugh to compensate for my ineptitude—a strategy that has a lifespan of exactly six weeks.

Back at Danielle's home I was happily being indoctrinated into a life I was meant to live. From her I learned about naturopathic medicine and veganism. She showed me a world of co-op grocery stores, farmers markets, and eating from the Earth. She gave me a book called *Diet for a New America* by John Robbins, and I didn't eat an animal product again for many years. Danielle showed me around Kripalu, pointing out how it had already changed so much, and we ate brown rice and steamed spinach for lunch in the silent cafeteria. I was introduced to books and authors in the natural health movement, which piqued my interest in the Pacific Northwest, where it seemed everyone was into this shit. I pored over recipes in the *Kripalu Cookbook* like chapters in a novel and started to see food in new ways. By the summer of 1994 I had been living with anorexia for three years and food had become my enemy. In the radiant glow of Danielle, food was medicine, and she shared with me her healing and healthy way of life. I'm still so grateful to Danielle for her life-changing wisdom, but I've never once taken her advice to not jump into things with both feet and then wonder why I'm drowning—not a single time. But every time I make it safely to the shore, I think of her and smile.

Free Spirit

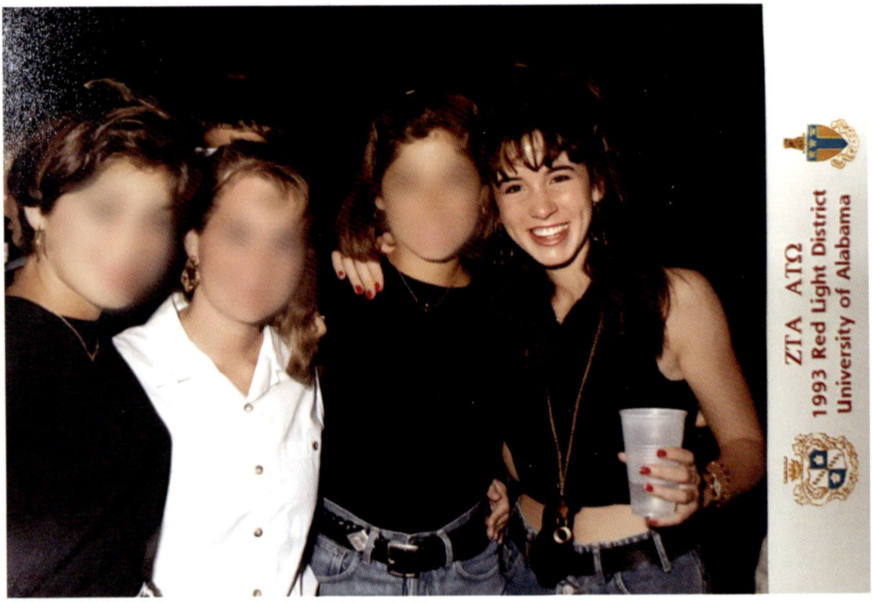

My mom and dad came to Parents Weekend in the fall of my sophomore year, in 1994. By that time I was starting to enjoy school. I had made a handful of great friends during freshman year and had a crush on almost every member of ZBT, the Jewish fraternity on campus. I was awarded Best Pledge from my sorority, and I absolutely loved my classes. Obsessed with exercise and weight control, I realized that most career options in the major I chose, Public Relations, required sitting in an office all day. Two things I could not imagine for my life were offices and sitting, so I called my mom in tears from my room in the Zeta house.

"If I get a real job, when will I exercise?!" I sobbed helplessly. I could almost hear her eyebrows raise as she assured me this was nothing to cry about.

I soon joined New College, a liberal arts program within UA, where undergraduates design their own majors. I combined the curricula of nutrition, exercise science, and psychology and called my major Personal Wellness. Though I absolutely loved being part of New College I was already dreaming of the next thing: going abroad for a semester. I made an appointment with the International Center during my parents' visit and soon we were sitting in their office. Queensland University of Technology in Brisbane, Australia, was the study abroad program the furthest away, so that's where I wanted to go.

"Baby T.Spoon going DOWN UNDAHHH!" My father cheered rhetorically as he perused the brochure. "What's the academic rigahh like in this country?" he asked the counselor insincerely as he winked at me. My dad didn't care about the academic rigor of anything, he just liked to ask people questions to make them feel important. A salesman till the day he died.

The counselor winked back and told me to start packing my bags.

"This wouldn't be until *next* spring semester, though, right?" I asked nervously. Every study abroad program I had ever heard of happened in the spring of junior year.

"Nope. You're ready to go now! *This* spring! Classes start in January so don't forget your bathing suit. January is summertime where you're going, and it'll be *hot*! You! Are! Ready! To! Go!"

Nineteen years old and absolutely *not* ready to go, I looked at my mom.

"Will financial aid cover this?" she asked, adding up how many pieces of ceramics she would have to sell to make this work.

"Same tuition. Same financial aid. No difference at all. You'll need to pay for living expenses, but that's it," the counselor answered.

"We'll make it work," my mom confirmed, clearly more scared than I was.

Ten minutes later we had signed official documents that said I would leave for Australia in ninety days. "G'day to you, mate!" my dad said to the counselor as he shook her hand and left the office.

As the three of us walked across the quad to the Carrot Top show, my dad was the only one who could speak. "Guess you'll have to get used to the taste of vegemite!" he quipped.

I stared at the ground, wondering what the fuck I had just done.

My Econ101 teacher bound up the auditorium stairs on the last day of classes that semester and put his hands on my desk. There were hundreds of people in the class, and I was unaware he even knew my name, which I'm sure he didn't, but he asked if I could meet him in his office. "Can you TA for me next semester? I like the questions you ask," he said as I sat in his office for the very first time.

"I'm studying abroad in Brisbane, Australia. I leave in a month," I answered.

He pivoted immediately, "Even better. Listen to me, do not work so hard! Just go there and have fun. Don't study, just enjoy yourself."

Shocked at the whiplash of the last two minutes, I agreed, stood up, and walked out. As I shut the door behind me, he repeated, "DO NOT WORK HARD IN AUSTRALIA!"

And I did not. I went from straight As to straight Fs. Barely even went to class. Instead I summited Ayers Rock at sunrise when people were still allowed to do that, sang karaoke in a cowboy bar in Alice Springs, and snorkeled through the Great Barrier Reef when it was still stocked with coral and vibrant sea life. My friends and I hitchhiked barefoot to a surfing competition in Byron Bay, got picked up by a guy who had machetes in his front seat, and tried to make him laugh so he wouldn't kill us. That tightly wound anorexic who skipped out on every fun thing for the previous five years just so she could study and exercise? The one determined to be utterly miserable? She may have signed up for this trip, but she was not the person who came home. A free-spirited, world-traveling, pot-smoking, beer-drinking 19-year-old came home, and there was no turning back.

My time in Australia was as silly and fun and adventurous as any rich kid's semester abroad could be, but I would have no idea how drastically my first time abroad would change who I am. I, of course, was masquerading as a rich kid. I'm not the demographic who studies abroad, I shouldn't have even been there. I should have been working three jobs and studying in Tuscaloosa, but somehow my mom made everything I ever wanted to do happen. After spending five months in a country that prioritizes travel and freedom, I saw how happy I could be, and I wanted more. My experience in Australia taught me that I could no longer just endure college, I wanted to enjoy it. I had a decision to make: Should I finish the last two years of college at Alabama, or should I drop out and start over somewhere else? Unsure, I returned to Alabama.

In the fall of junior year, a sorority sister, Karen (the same one who told me she'd get me out of my roommate situation with Shelly) knocked on my bedroom door at the Zeta House. She sat down on my bed and told me she had heard that Stephanie, a drop-dead gorgeous and wonderful member of our sorority, was planning to bring her boyfriend—a handsome and talented football player—to the winter formal happening in a few weeks. He was not allowed to attend the formal, Karen said, because he was Black. Because Stephanie and I were friends, Karen asked me to deliver the news to her. Absolutely fucking appalled, I refused. A few months later, halfway through my junior year, I dropped out of the University of Alabama and didn't set foot in that state again for thirty years.

Domination by Penetration

As soon as I left Alabama, in December 1995, I came home and got a waitressing job at a sports bar in the coastal town of Scituate, MA. Shannon was a bartender there and got me the job, and I was one of five Taras who worked there that season. Though I had just dropped out of college, I learned a universal truth that spring: working in a restaurant should be a prerequisite for being allowed to dine out.

I had a plan: work until August, then move to California and finish college at San Francisco State. A friend I'd met in Australia was moving to San Francisco to start her career and encouraged me to join her. I toured the campus of SF State, loved it, applied, and got in. I didn't give a shit that I left Alabama halfway through my junior year, or that I didn't know what I would study at SF State, I just wanted to be with people who inspired me in a place that excited me.

San Francisco State is absolutely fucking awesome and the furthest thing from Alabama I could have imagined. I remember walking into my very first class and meeting the teacher. She was this super smart, funny, queer, Black woman with a shaved head and an addiction to caffeine that made her exhilarating to be around. Her class was on fire with discussion, debate, and emotion, and when she referred to herself as a feminist dike I almost fell out of my chair. One girl in that class identified as—her words—a "red dot and curry Indian," and when another girl identified herself as Laotian, I had to look up what and where that even was. Most students were Latino and Asian, and everyone seemed fearless, passionate, and stoked to be in college. There were daily protests on campus about things I had never even thought about. Sitting in the corner of the quad, I'd try to learn what everyone was fighting for. I remember thinking, "What the fuck is Fair Wages for Farm Workers?" I was in awe that people gave such a shit about people they didn't know. I wanted to give a shit like this. I wanted to be someone who cared about the world and its underdogs. I had never even heard of social justice, never been around anyone who cared about things that don't affect them, but here I was in San Francisco right in the heart of it all. The year before I worked with four Taras. Now the people I was surrounded with were so different from me. My friends in San Francisco gave a shit about the underdogs of the world because many of them were the underdogs. Like millions of people lucky enough to spend a chapter of their lives in San Francisco, I found a place that built my confidence to be unapologetically liberated, raw, outspoken, and bold.

I was still a virgin when I took a Sex Ed class that semester, and my final paper was about sex, a topic I obviously knew nothing about. I titled it

"Domination by Penetration," which doesn't get a lot of points for a fun little title, but it must have been half decent because the teacher asked me to TA the next semester. I was so nervous I said no. I lived in a studio apartment in the Cole Valley neighborhood of San Francisco and after a guy gave me my first orgasm I was phenomenally interested in giving myself one. I would run home from school or my job at the coffee shop leaving a trail of clothes across my apartment just to get naked and masturbate. Better late than not at all, but TA-ing a Sex Ed class felt like a big jump from learning how to finger myself.

After school I worked as a barista at a coffee shop called Pier 40 Coffee Roaster. It overlooked the Bay Bridge, and the fog sat so heavy and low every morning we couldn't see our own signage until the afternoon. My coworkers at Pier 40 are still some of my favorite people, but there was one in particular who will always be one of the most important people in my life—my favorite California kid of all, Jonathan Gray.

I had been in San Francisco for forty-eight hours when I applied for this barista job, and Jon and I were hired on the same day. It was August 1996, and our friendship was fast. Or maybe it just escalated quickly.

"At first I hated you," Jon admitted when I was dropping him off after work one night. It was one of our many multi-hour conversations, this time in my car, parked in front of his house. I could tell there was something else he wanted to say. "At first I hated you, but now I think I'm in love with you," he said, like he wished it wasn't true.

"I love you, too," I answered, and we had our first kiss.

Jon was tall, lanky, and handsome, and the coolest motherfucker anyone could ever know. He spun disco records in his room, smoked cigarettes, and read entire books in two days. He loved women, his friends, his foster mom, who he just called mom, and his brother, Will. He knew everything there was to know about music and could speak philosophically about Prince, Stevie Wonder, and Donna Summer, among countless others. Jon was the smartest guy I had ever met, and we'd get so lost in conversation at the café we'd forget to notice the line of customers trying to get our attention. When I arrived at work, he would look up at me walking across the room and fake that his knees went weak at the sight of me. He was that nice, and he made me feel a way I had never felt before. For the next fourteen years Jon and I were in love. We'd write letters and poems, sometimes confessing our love, sometimes sharing our torment that our feelings for each other felt impossible. We'd then go on many-year sabbaticals from correspondence because one or both of us were in a relationship, and when we were finally both living on the East Coast—me in Boston and him in Brooklyn—he'd take the bus to visit me or I'd visit him. Fourteen years is a long time to be in love with your dear friend even if it's not straightforward or easy or the right thing to do.

On April 21, 2011, weeks before Jon was finally about to graduate college, he died alone in his Brooklyn apartment from complications of pneumonia. He was 35 years old. I got the news from Paul, an incredible friend from our days at the café in San Francisco. I already knew it was bad news when I saw a text from him, so I sat down to open it. When he didn't show up for work his boss suspected something was wrong and she got access to his apartment and found Jon on the floor. The cause of death was a pulmonary embolism.

Jon's memorial was at the bar where he was a beloved bartender, and the celebration was exactly what he would have wanted. All the friends I had heard so much about over the years were there, and it felt like I was meeting characters from my favorite book. So many people stood up to share great stories of a great guy. I shared one of my favorite pieces of advice from Jon. Years earlier, when he was visiting me in Boston, he asked me where my condoms were. After I answered, he paused, thought about it, and finally said with kind wisdom, "Tara, when a guy asks you for a condom don't say you 'ran out.' Just say you don't have any."

Sage advice from my favorite guy of all time.

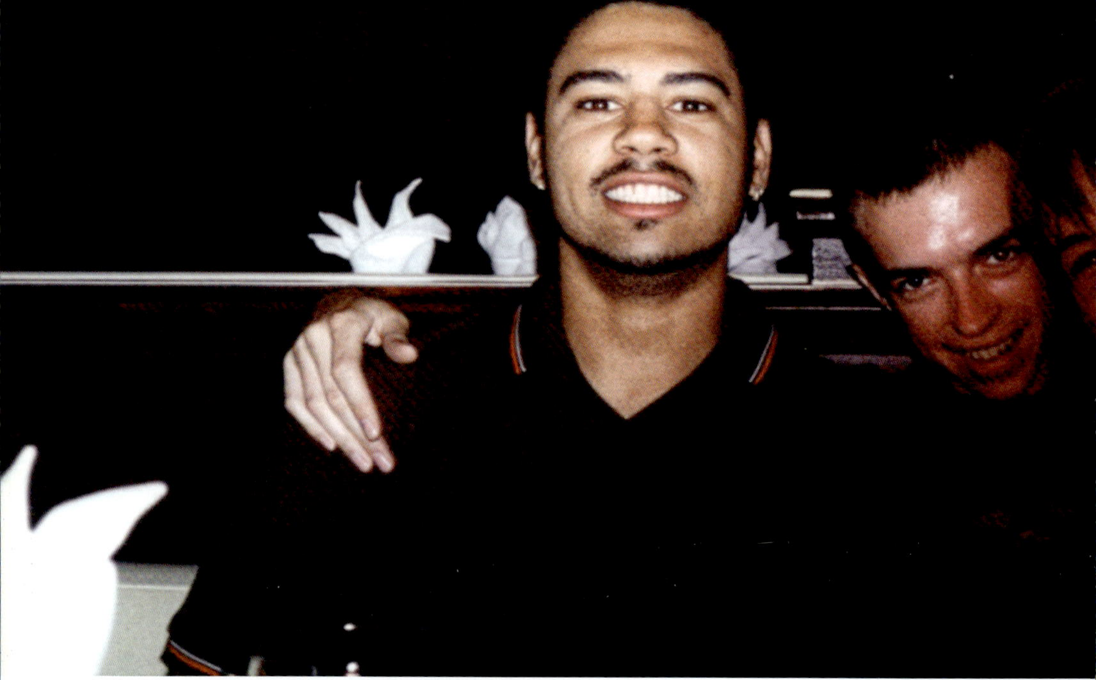

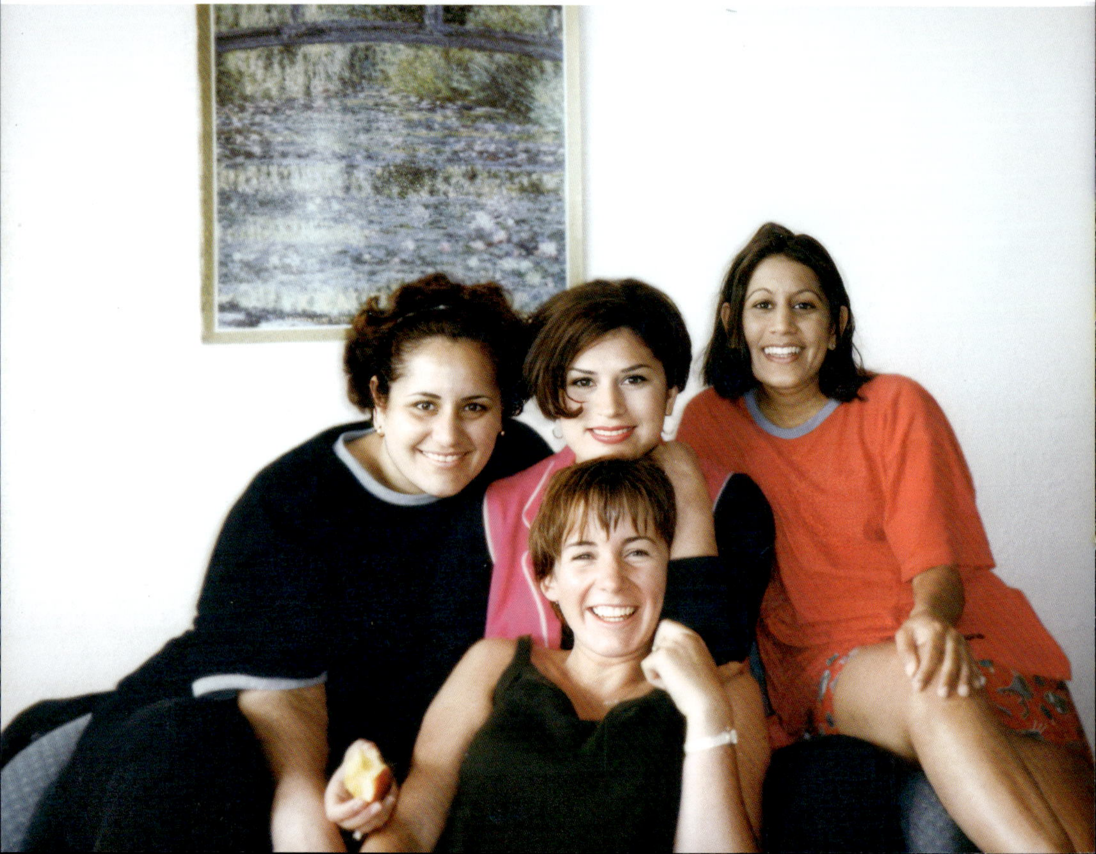

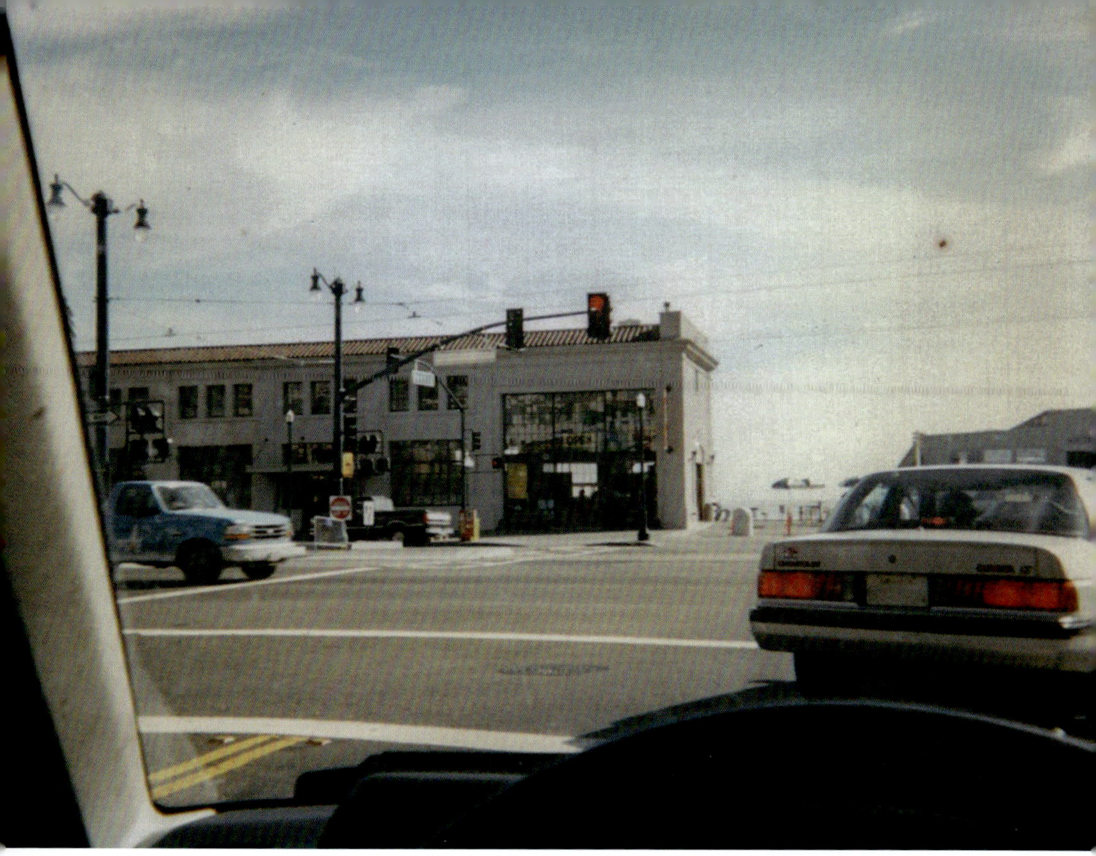

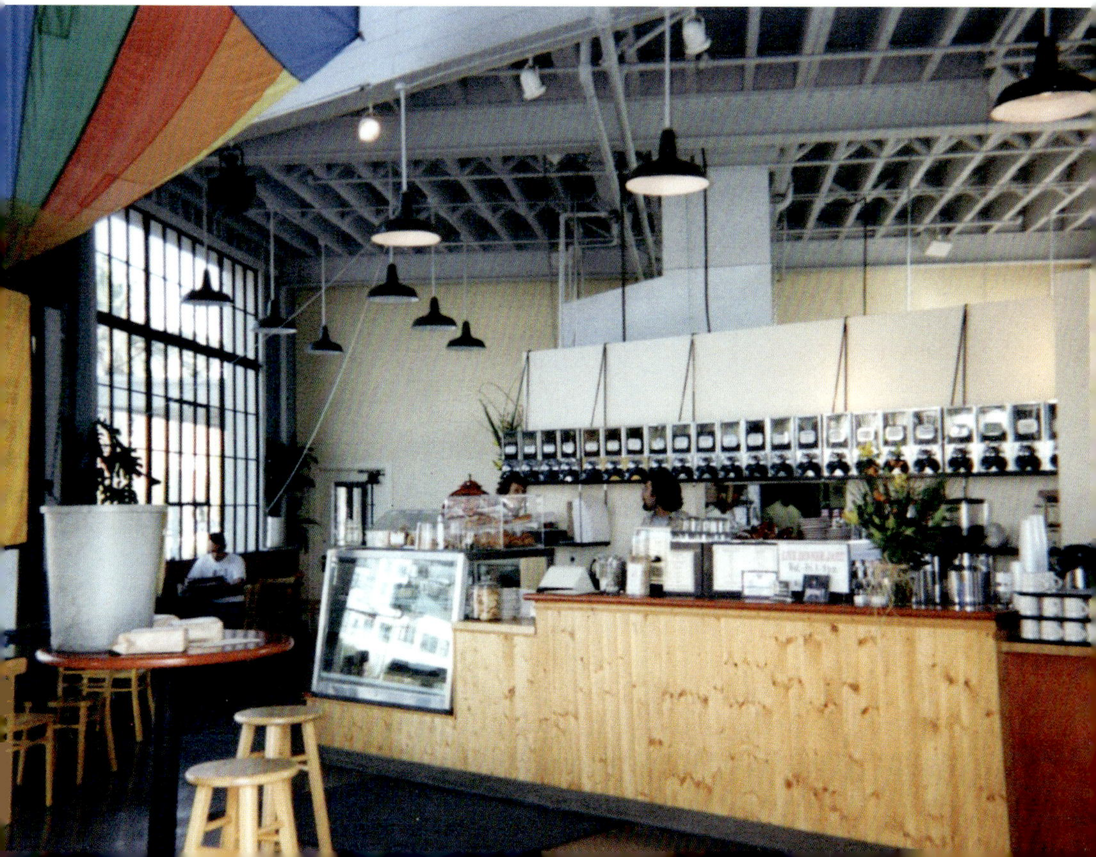

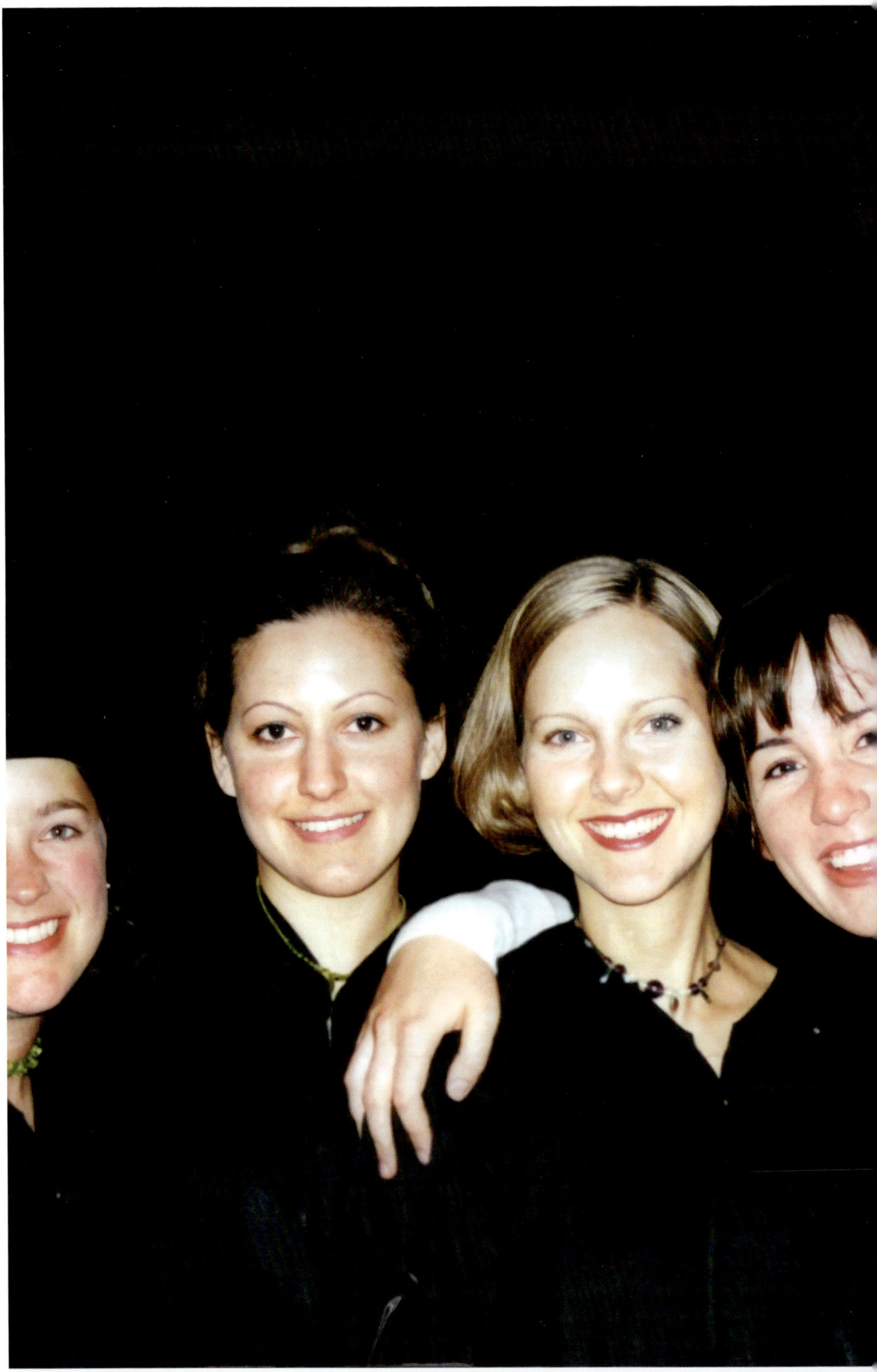

Dirty Hippie University

At SF State I read in the back of some magazine about a Holistic Health Conference taking place in Seattle. God knows what credit card I funded this trip on, but a month later I flew from fairly sunny San Francisco into the pouring rain of Seattle and wondered how anyone could ever live there. On the last day, on my way out of the conference center, I walked by a kiosk that said *Bastyr University* and grabbed their brochure. As I read about this school on the bus to the airport, I couldn't believe a place like this existed. Tucked in the outskirts of Seattle, Bastyr seemed like some sort of dirty hippie nirvana, and I wanted every part of it.

Bastyr is a Naturopathic Medical School that, in 1997 when I was discovering it, offered three majors: Naturopathic Doctor, Acupuncture, and Nutrition. Their nutrition program was revolutionary—at least to me. Far from the simplistic food pyramid mindset we'd been raised on since elementary school, this was a whole major dedicated to the healing nature of food, the benefits of eating from the Earth, and to cooking classes that took nutrition from theory to practice. I was more than intrigued.

My mom came to visit me in San Francisco weeks after I learned about Bastyr, and because she was truly the best mom ever, she bought us two round-trip, same-day flights to Seattle so we could check out the campus. Bastyr didn't have even a thousand students enrolled at that time, and they had just moved to their new location on the site of an old Catholic seminary. The entire campus was just one building, and coming from University of Alabama and SF State the size of the place mixed with the leftover religious iconography made it the weirdest college I had ever seen. I loved it. Transferring schools again felt reckless, and San Francisco State was incredible, but Bastyr felt like such a perfect match I had to jump.

In July 1997 I packed my car and drove north to Seattle to attend the school I eventually got a BS in Nutrition from. I hoped silently that sunlight wasn't required to sustain life.

Bastyr was a trip. The college was so small and so new it almost felt like an experiment. Every time something went wrong—which was basically every single day—my friends and I would look at each other and ask, "We're sure this place is accredited?"

All but two of the thirty-two people in my graduating class were women, and for hard-core college fun we had potlucks. We gorged ourselves on vegan shepherd's pie and "muscle muffins" until we were all plump enough to last a day or two without Janelle's homemade trail mix, if and when things ever got so dire. Though a degree in Nutrition is essentially a degree in organic chemistry—which almost buried me alive—my friendships and the nonstop laughter and love we shared made up some of the best years of my life.

Our cafeteria felt like the dining room at a yoga ashram, and that's where we could mingle with folks from the other two majors. Once, as I sat down for lunch, I went to shake a guy's hand when we were being introduced. He crossed his hands behind his back and refused my handshake, saying, "No thank you. I don't cross-contaminate with others." He was a white guy with dreadlocks, so I half wanted to ask how many Dead shows he managed to attend without cross-contaminating, but I figured I'd just hold a grudge and write about it in my book twenty-seven years later.

One day I sat down at a dining table with two people I hadn't met yet. They were discussing a club on campus they were thinking of joining.

As the founding father of The Groupie, I was curious. "What's the club?" I asked.

They paused for too long. I knew they didn't want to tell me.

"Oh ... we were thinking about joining SFB," one of the girls finally said.

"Oh, nice. What's that?" I asked, bringing a spoonful of broth to my mouth.

"Students Against Forced Bathing."

I lowered the spoon. "Forced bathing? Like, being forced to take a bath?"

"Ya. We'll talk about the societal pressures of bathing every day. How it ruins our natural bacteria. Weakens the immune system." She was bored with how obvious it was.

"Plus, bathing wastes water!" her friend chimed in.

"Fuck being clean," I answered in solidarity, and picked up my bowl and drank from it. I was late for class. But damn, I love Bastyr.

Interesting

In the summer of 1999, I was 24 years old, living in Seattle, and working several jobs that took a lot of time and energy but paid shit. A brand-new BS in Nutrition gave me few career options beyond becoming a registered dietitian, but people warned me, "Go down that route and prepare to be handing out Ensure to old people for the rest of your life." Though that did sound inspiring I decided to go with my old standby: act confident and appear qualified at something I know nothing about. And so began my Nutrition Coach career.

"Gotta watch out for the whites," I told my clients, who paid me $100 to teach them the basics of whole foods nutrition. "The whites" were white flour and white sugar, two things I binged on privately but told others were off limits. I met with each client three times. Our first meeting was strictly informational. I explained the benefits of eating from the Earth and staying away from processed foods. "If you can't picture it growing, don't eat it," I'd say. For our second meeting we'd meet at the local co-op, where I'd tell them what tempeh, tofu, and kale were and how to shop in the bulk bins. On the clock with clients, I'd point out the virtues of buying quinoa by the ton, on my own I'd buy chocolate-covered almonds by the pound. For our third meeting I'd go to their home and teach them how to cook all these new foods. Besides the one cooking class at Bastyr and the fact that I'd been an avid cookbook reader since the onset of anorexia in 1991, absolutely nothing qualified me to teach someone how to cook. There I was, though, wearing an apron in a stranger's kitchen, demonstrating sauté methods.

One day I was teaching a busy and successful single mom named Erin how to season her collard greens with Braggs Amino Acids, and she turned to me in her enormous kitchen and asked, "How much do I have to pay you to just do this for me? You plan the meals, you go to the grocery store, you cook the food. All I have to do is eat it?"

"I charge $200 a week for that," I answered, like I was reading from a menu of services. My personal chef business started the next morning.

Quick back-of-the-envelope math will reveal that $200 a week for all of someone's meals purchased, prepared, and delivered, even in 1999, is not enough money. But when you're broke, hustling, and unqualified, $200 sounds like a lot of money. At the height of my two-year side hustle as a personal ~~chef~~ cook I had seven clients and was exhausted, broke, and bloated. Luckily the career fizzled after a couple of years, mostly because I'm not a great cook.

Alongside my cooking gig I was also a personal trainer, a Spinning instructor who yelled at people in the dark before that was a popular way to ride a stationary bike, and I cleaned houses with my friend Thomas. One afternoon to make Thomas laugh I flashed my tits at him down the hallway of someone's home in the suburbs of Seattle. He asked me to come into the room he was standing near, and we sat down on the bed I had just made. He was older than me and we had a sibling-like relationship so it wasn't creepy, but he told me that my breasts were a national treasure and should be treated as such. I hesitate to use the phrase "signature move," but encouraged by Thomas's reaction, I believe I have flashed every person I know, including my own mother, for the last twenty-five years. And if the cover of this book does not feature me topless it's not because I didn't try.

Thomas also introduced me to Robert, a well-respected acupuncturist who suffered a stroke while in surgery for something minor a few years earlier. The stroke left him unable to care for himself, confined to his bed, barely able to speak, unable to read, but still able to listen. I cooked and cleaned for Robert two days a week while he devoured books on tape. He played these books—on spirituality, consciousness, the meaning of life, and the benefits of cold therapy—at full volume every day I was there. Though I was supposedly there to help him, Robert's quest to heal himself and appreciate life no matter the circumstances healed me just the same. Robert defined what it meant to be generous, and I used what I learned from him and his audiobooks to help myself and others in my Spinning classes. Through garbled speech, he also gave me quite a bit of Yoda-like advice on relationships, which not only gave me a window into his life before the stroke, but helped me see that I was afraid to be loved.

I seemed to be only interested in three kinds of guys back then: gay dudes; dudes clearly not interested in me; and my closest male friends. (My friend Will gets points for being all three.)

Besides one boyfriend who I lived with for a bit, chasing disinterested boys defined my mid-20s. Well, that plus binge drinking, being mad at my dad, outrunning the sadness of my mom's illness, having emotionally unregulated outbursts, and flashing my tits. My friends from home were getting married and starting families, and I was totally and utterly unhinged. I felt like an outsider everywhere I went, so I overcompensated and acted like a fool for the pure shock value of it. Somewhere inside me I knew I had to make a change, but I didn't know how to do that or what exactly needed to change. I was lost.

One weekend in the summer of 2001 my roommate was hosting three handsome friends of hers who were hiking the Pacific Crest Trail (PCT) from Canada to Mexico. They had come off the trail for a couple of days, did laundry and showered at our place, and slept on our floor. We stayed up all night as they told us all these wild stories about the things they saw and survived on the PCT. They were so interesting and alive with adventure, so different from anyone I had ever met. I was fascinated.

When I finally went to bed that night I walked down the hallway to my room still laughing from their stories. I lay my head on the pillow and knew one thing for certain: I wanted to be just like these guys. I thought to myself, *I want to be interesting.* I decided then and there, staring at the ceiling in the dark, that though I had neither experience nor skill, I would hike 100 miles of the Pacific Crest Trail by myself. Then, when I got home from the hike, I'd join the Peace Corps. This life of chasing boys and embarrassing myself had to end. I had to become an interesting person.

This plan absolutely terrified me, so I had to start telling everyone about it. Being raised by a bullshitter like my dad made me obsessed with being good on my word. If I said I was going to do it, then I would.

I was so psyched. I was going to be interesting, not someone who lived a normal life. A "normal life," as I saw it then, meant spending all my energy finding a man to marry, having his children, and moving to a cul-de-sac where I would fold socks and cook dinner for this man while he chased his dreams. It felt like a trap. I didn't want it. I had so much more growing to do, so much more to become. I wanted to live a life of adventure and experiences. I wanted to live a life where I could become the best version of me.

I talked about my new life that I was unprepared for in every way to a guy I had never met while out with friends that night. "I'm gonna hike 100 miles by myself and then come home and join the Peace Corps!" I shouted over the music at a bar in Seattle.

"Don't do that," he warned. "You don't want to travel overseas as part of the US government. Go get the book Alternatives to the Peace Corps. Find ways to volunteer abroad without representing the Bush administration!"

"Fuck the government!" I answered, unsure what else to say.

The next morning I walked into Barnes & Noble and asked the guy sitting at the help desk, "Do you have *Alternatives to the Peace Corps*?"

"We have lots of alternatives to the Peace Corps," he said quickly with a wry smile, and walked me over to the book on its shelf.

Alternatives to the Peace Corps listed all kinds of non-governmental organizations offering volunteer opportunities around the world. I could search by area of expertise (none), country (no idea), or desired length of stay (same). Everything looked exciting, but I knew I wanted to go as far away as possible. I wanted to go where only the most well-traveled and interesting people would go. I wanted to go to Africa.

But first: that 100-mile hike on the Pacific Crest Trail.

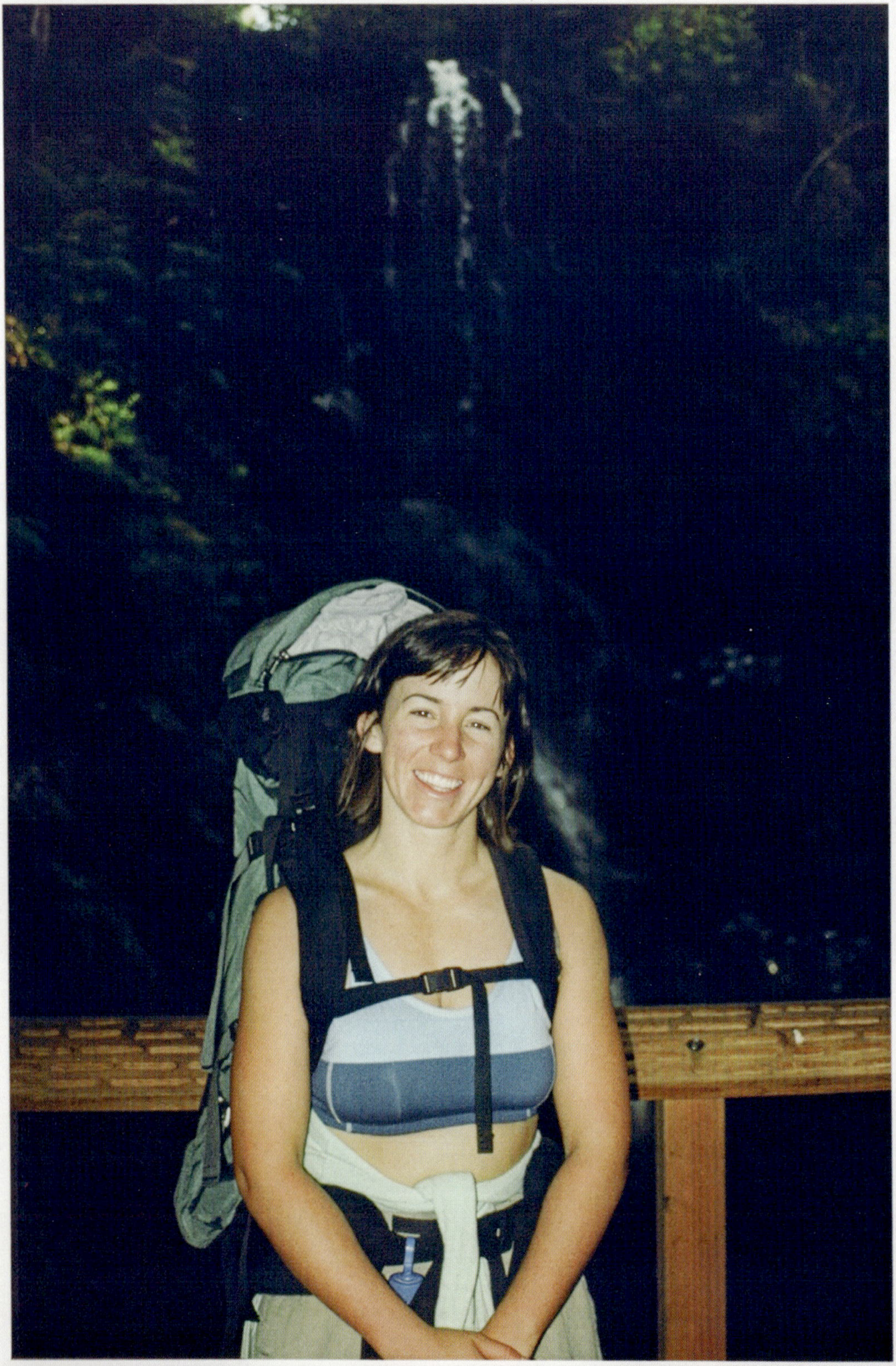

Counting Backward

I devoured a book called *The Pacific Crest Trail Hiker's Handbook for the Long Distance Hiker* by Ray Jardine. "Long-distance hiker" was a stretch, but for the first few years I lived in Washington state, I spent at least one day a week discovering the stunning beauty of both the North Cascade and Olympic Mountain ranges by myself. I found a therapy in hiking I couldn't describe. Even though my hikes only ranged from 6-12 miles round trip, they were long enough that getting to the summit always made me feel truly confident in ways I didn't find anywhere else. I wanted to be strong and healthy and comfortable in my own skin, but everywhere in my life there was no limit to what I wouldn't do for a laugh, and I was hurting myself in the process. I was raised by a guy whose superpower was his humor. Funny guys with one leg don't hike mountains, they drink martinis and overcompensate, and I was heading down the same path. I saw my patterns, but I felt like I couldn't stop. I was constantly searching in self-help books, weekend empowerment workshops, and with therapists in a relentless pursuit to be better than I was. It was sitting alone on mountain tops that helped me trust that I was capable, resourceful, and strong.

I wasn't fast or particularly good at hiking, but I figured 100 miles, if all I had to do was hike all day, would take seven or eight days. Easy.

In the back of the book was a suggested packing list. Jardine encourages hikers to pack lightly for an easier time on the trail. I took his word as gospel, brought his book into REI, handed it to the guy in a uniform, and told him, "I need everything on this packing list."

"Everything?" he asked.

"Everything," I confirmed. "And an REI credit card," I added.

I remember dumping out the enormous bag of light, but not really that light, camping equipment in the driveway of my beloved house in the Green Lake neighborhood of Seattle. Pots, pans, and sporks lay next to aerosol bear spray (!), a one-man tent, and a portable water filtration system. I was so fucked. I had never even set up a tent by myself, and when I went to light my new propane camp stove I stood back like I was setting off fireworks in my backyard.

I distracted myself from premonitions of getting eaten alive by a bear and setting fire to Yosemite by planning my route. I was fucked on that, too. I realized that because I had one car the route would have to begin and end at the same spot. I finally mapped out a 100-mile out-and-back trip that began and ended in Half Dome in Yosemite. I'd climb Half Dome on day one, then venture through Tuolumne Meadows, then Ansel Adams Wilderness, and finally into Inyo National Forest. Then I'd trace my steps back to my beloved Honda Civic waiting to take me to San Francisco to hang out with my friends, which is all I really wanted to do anyway.

I set the date to start my adventure: September 14, right after my mom's visit. My mom's visit to Seattle that year was both incredibly special and insanely difficult as 2001 marked her eighth year with Parkinson's. Because I lived 3,000 miles away for most of the years she had been sick I hadn't seen the slow progression of her illness, but during this visit I saw how much she was suffering. Every day, as her medication wore off, her body went into what's medically referred to as dyskinesias though it looked like she was having an exorcism. My mom didn't want me to see her suffer like this so she asked to be alone in my room. When I heard her struggle I walked in on her. She was being thrown around my room from the momentum of her limbs violently thrashing while trying to whisper to me that she was OK. Sweating and gasping, barely able to breathe, this seizure-looking episode took place every single day of her life for years, but this was the first time I saw it for myself. A long-term illness reveals its decline in definitive markers—ones that are clearest in hindsight. This stage: this 4pm-spastic-fits-stage was a big one. I started to appreciate how sick my mom really was.

Knowing that my invincible mom would continue to get worse made my plan to "be interesting" feel not just necessary but urgent. Panic stricken, I felt I had no choice but to live an enormous life all by myself far outside my comfort zone. I had to do it all. Right now. While I was still healthy enough to move my body and breathe my breath on my own terms. My mother's illness brought a relentless intensity to the way I would live my life from those days forward.

My mom took the last plane ride of her life on the afternoon of September 10, 2001. Her flight from Seattle to Boston landed safely sometime around 9 p.m. and almost twelve hours later, at 8 a.m. on September 11, out of the same terminal at Logan, the hijacked planes became airborne. The news hit Seattle as I backed out of my driveway just after 6 a.m., heading to work as assistant manager of Westlake Athletic Club. We all spent the day stunned and huddled around the lobby TV.

With even greater conviction, I set off for my trip three days later, driving thirteen hours to a hotel in California, then getting up the next morning and driving the rest of the way to Yosemite. I parked my car near the trailhead to Half Dome on the morning of September 15, strapped my pack to my back, and, without a clue, began my 100-mile journey.

The hike to Half Dome, even days after a national disaster, was filled with a steady stream of people from all over the world marching up the long, steep climb—sixteen miles round trip. The final section of the path to the summit is a sheer, granite-faced wall with steel cables mounted to the rock for hikers to hold on to. I chatted with a group of people on the hike up, and we enjoyed the view and peanut butter sandwiches together before starting our descent. Despite my fitness résumé and fearless façade, I have absolutely no athletic ability outside of a dance floor, and this becomes immediately obvious when I'm engaged in literally anything that requires my limbs. On the way down I held up the line of hundreds of people as I gripped the cables and took slow, tiny little baby steps sideways while still trying to make everyone laugh.

A guy behind me, clearly frustrated by my pace, yelled loudly enough so that everyone could hear, "You might move faster without your ice axe, buddy. How long do you plan on taking to get down this thing?"

The line of people looked up to notice the ice axe strapped diagonally across the outside of my backpack and laughed. Ray Jardine suggested packing an ice axe for self-arrest on glacial conditions while hiking the PCT. The average daily temperature in mid-September in central California is 80 degrees, and I was scheduled to be gone for a week. I never even questioned it while packing.

When I finally made it to the bottom of the sheer granite face, I took off my backpack and unstrapped the axe. The group I had spent the day with was headed down to their cars in the parking lot, and I asked if they wouldn't mind taking my axe with them. "Remember me," I joked, as I handed it over, then pressed on toward the trail marked Tuolumne Meadows. I walked alone for hours, wondering how the fuck I would have stopped myself from sliding down a glacier with an axe.

The first night in the open wilderness of the John Muir Trail turned out to be an open-eyed panic attack until sunrise. Sometime in the middle of the night, multiple bears showed up and roared—a lot—very close to my tent. I don't know how many were out there or what was on their minds, but I was absolutely fucking terrified lying alone in a nylon tent waiting for them to tear me apart. That night was exactly 1,000 hours long, and I can't believe I didn't go home in the morning, but the brisk beauty of daybreak inspired me. I boiled water for coffee and oatmeal, packed up, and headed out with everything I needed to survive balanced on my back. *I'm doing this,* I thought, *I'm a fearless, outdoorsy athlete.*

Hiking almost twenty miles a day with no training and no athletic prowess was hard. Sometimes it was good because Yosemite is insanely gorgeous, but hiking alone for ten hours a day was not that fun. Actually, it sucked.

I started counting my steps backward … 100, 99, 98 … to distract myself from my own shitty thoughts. I promised myself I could quit, sit down, and feel bad for myself if I could just do a hundred more steps. But every time I got to one, I started again at one hundred. Little by little I chunked off sections of something that felt impossible by distracting myself from my thoughts. Even now, so many years later, when I'm super frustrated and kinda gonna lose my shit, I start counting backward. When I get to one, I start again.

Something like 40,000 steps later, mostly counted backward in sets of one hundred, I landed somewhere on the John Muir Trail for sunset in the rugged, breathtaking beauty of Tuolumne Meadows. Less scared of my propane stove than I was even a day ago, I made split pea soup and crawled in my tent, exhausted. I slept for the first time in two days, woke to the dewy spectacle of a new morning surrounded by glassy lakes and violet mountain tops, and set out again.

As I walked through the beautiful alpine meadow, I heard, then saw, two rock climbers hanging off the side of a mountain face. As my eyes adjusted, I noticed men hanging off *every* rock face of Tuolumne Meadows—small, vibrant specks of color dangling precariously from a network of ropes. It was a rock climber's paradise.

An hour or so later I started to see signs for the Tuolumne Meadows Grill, and I became singularly focused on getting there. This store/post office/grill smelled like hamburgers and felt like a mirage. Inside it was miraculously full of everything you just ran out of, and on the outside it was surrounded by countless gorgeous, rock-climbing men loitering in the sun.

The moment I walked up to the place I noticed I was the only female around. In the same way that hunger makes the best sauce, being the only female in the wilderness worked well for me. A particularly filthy guy named Ben was the first lion to approach. To my sheer horror he held my hand after I told him my first name. For months before this moment, I had imagined bears ripping my limbs off and sucking my bones dry, and never did I fathom being scared of a dude in the woods on this trip. But here we were.

Ben was heading inside to pick up a package he had mailed to himself months earlier and told me to wait for him. I promised I'd be right there—wouldn't move a muscle—then ran away to the parking lot and hid between two parked cars for an hour. I didn't know what else to do, he would have found me on the trail no matter which way I went. I needed a time-out anyway. I weighed my options.

Hiking a hundred miles by myself sounded exciting and interesting, but now that I was here it felt reckless and stupid because of my sheer ineptitude.

Yes, I wanted to be an athletic outdoorsy athlete, but I'm not, and I wasn't even halfway to my turn-around spot. Once I got there, I'd just have to trace my entire route back for fifty miles. I also packed like an asshole and didn't have enough food to last me. Sitting by a main road that runs all the way through Yosemite—meaning it runs from where I was sitting to where my Civic was parked—I had an idea.

I stood up and started hitchhiking. The first car to drive by stopped. A harmless looking guy in a pickup truck nodded when I told him I wanted to get back to my car parked at Half Dome. I took a giant step onto his bumper and threw myself in the bed of his truck, leaned against my backpack, and stretched out my dirty legs. I enjoyed the two-hour drive through Yosemite while the sun went low enough in the sky to turn the whole place gold.

The guy dropped me off and I slept in my backseat that night. The next morning, I drove straight back to the Tuolumne Meadow parking lot and headed out with a new plan. I would go on a 20-mile hike with one more night sleeping in my tent, this time in the Ansel Adams wilderness. My new plan suited my actual skill level, and I knew I had made the right decision by my relaxed confidence on the trail. I spent the whole day walking alongside waterfalls and sky-scraping jagged spires, then fell asleep in my tent that night in the middle of nowhere with absolutely no skills—survival or otherwise.

I woke up that final morning, retraced my steps for ten miles, threw my pack in my backseat, realized I had plenty of gas but no money, and headed to San Francisco.

Almost four hours later I rolled up to the guy in the tollbooth at the Bay Bridge. I told him about the bears on the first night, about hitchhiking, and about how Ben was the real predator! We laughed and laughed, and then I told him I didn't have any money. Not even a dollar.

Someone behind me honked their horn. I smiled. He rolled his eyes, lifted the gate, and waved me through.

"I LOVE YOUUUUUU!!!" I yelled out the window and sped ahead toward the city.

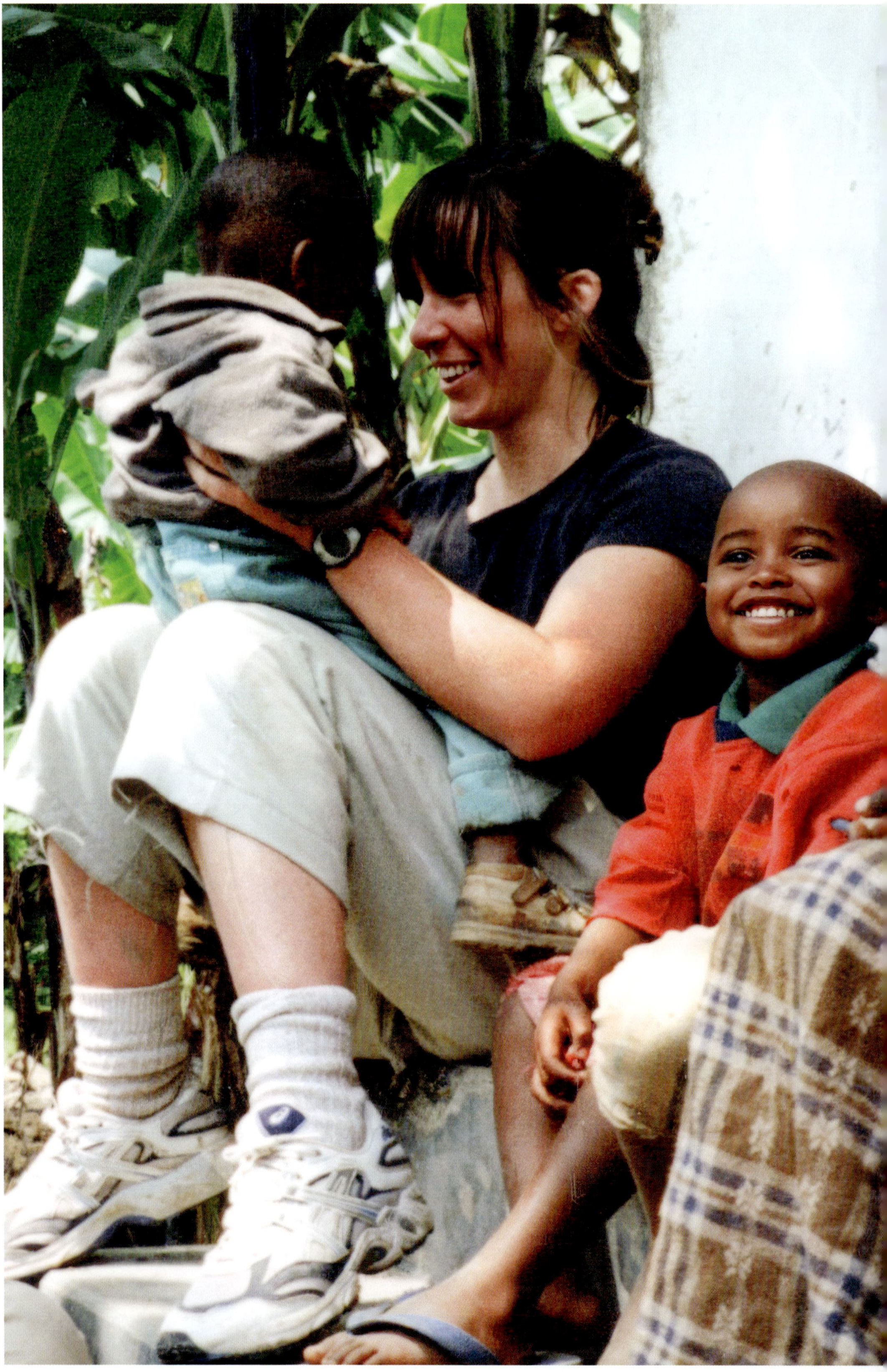

Sombetini

A few days later, back home in Seattle, I was still not interesting. My not-quite-a-hundred-mile hike was plenty difficult, but it was also too easy. I needed something riskier, further away, longer. I needed some life-changing typo shit.

I picked up the *Alternatives to the Peace Corps* book that still lay dogeared on my nightstand and found an organization called Visions in Action that brought volunteers to a village outside of Arusha, Tanzania, for three-month stays. It said that we, the volunteers, would help folks living in this village build a community center and hub for micro-entrepreneurship opportunities. Local folks would learn soap making, oil extraction from seeds, and how to start small retail shops selling housewares out of wheelbarrows. The very last line said, "Contact us for fundraising ideas." So I did.

I had been a personal trainer and Spinning instructor at the Redmond Athletic Club (RAC) in a suburb outside of Seattle for years. I asked Dan Lehr, still my favorite boss of all time, if I could hold marathon Spinning classes to raise funds for my trip to Tanzania. He said yes immediately, adding as I left his office, "I'll match every dollar you raise."

Between Dan and the many generous people who took my classes and trained with me at RAC, I raised $9,000 and left for Tanzania in June 2002. I remember landing in Arusha at night, stepping onto the tarmac and into the sweet-smelling air, knowing instantly that I'd never be the same. I was one of seven volunteers with Visions in Action being met by our trip leader, Regina Galang. A native San Franciscan and UC Berkeley grad, Regina was my age but vastly more traveled, brilliant, sensible, gorgeous, hilarious, and even-keeled than anyone I had ever met. In short, she was absolutely everything I could have wanted in a fearless leader.

The night we arrived was pitch dark and perfectly warm as we drove through Arusha and turned onto the dirt roads of Sombetini, the village where we would work and live for the next nine weeks. Sombetini is a vast network of dusty roads and gigantic jungle plants. The houses are simple structures made of mud walls and corrugated tin roofs, and there are gravestones in every yard. In the daylight hours the place absolutely teemed with people. Sombetini is two square miles, and almost 50,000 people call it home. Adorable little kids outnumber adults three to one.

The headlights of our taxi minivan, our *dala dala*, cut through the darkness of the dense jungle in a strobe-like first impression that shook me alive. Enormous Jurassic leaves, then pitch darkness. A candlelit face of a man sitting on a stool selling onions. Darkness. Two toddlers with no shoes holding hands on the side of the road. Darkness. Three young men all leaning on the same tree. Darkness. I was on a different planet. I felt honored to be there. I fucking loved it.

The family I got to live with, the Mangana family, had a cement house and reliable electricity, so relatively speaking they were rich. The patriarch of the family was Don Mangana, and this guy was a fucking G. Living among thousands of people wearing T-shirts handed down from Salvation Armies around the world (a friend told me that an old man in her village wore a Baby on Board shirt with an arrow pointing to his stomach), Don dressed in monochrome jogging suits, a cell phone tucked in his waistband and gold chains hanging from his neck. If Sombetini had a king, it was Don Mangana.

On our first evening in Sombetini, the volunteers gathered at the Mangana home for an official welcome ceremony. After we met the key players of the village and sat down in the living room, ten little kids singing in perfect harmony and making complicated percussion with their feet on the sandy floor turned the corner and entered the room in song. The volunteers burst into tears at the absolute talent and grace of our tiny welcoming committee.

At daybreak the next morning the roosters announced the new day, and the backyard was already teeming with ladies. The procurement and preparation of water was an all day, every day job done exclusively by women, starting before the sun was up. In the middle of our backyard was an enormous cauldron of water, heated all day long and used to bathe, cook, and clean. On the side of the yard were two stalls made of sticks—one to stand in for a bucket bath, the other to squat in and shit into a hole.

The women of Sombetini also took care of their children, their husbands, each other, and their fathers. They turned practically nothing into a feast for many, pristinely cleaned their homes, and then sat down with each other and laughed until nightfall. And when dawn struck the next day, they did it again. We learned quickly to be both conscious and grateful for every drop of water we used and conscious and grateful for every morsel of food that was made and served to us.

The money each volunteer raised paid for the families to host us, for the materials needed to build the community center, and for daily Swahili lessons. Our presence in Sombetini was an economic boon, but damn did we look fucking weird in there. A few of us liked to exercise in the morning so every day we'd turn a corner in a light jog and spot a little kid on early lookout, hiding in the bush. He would yell back to the rest of his crew, who were poised and ready further down the path, and within seconds we were swarmed in a dusty cloud of giggling, joyous little kids running circles around us barefoot or in sandals five sizes too big. We'd stop jogging not just because we were surrounded, but because we couldn't stop laughing.

Our daily routine fell into an easy rhythm. After exercise, bucket baths, and breakfast we'd catch a *dala dala* to Swahili lessons. We tried to learn the language, but mostly we just tried to make each other laugh, and if I learned two different curse words a day, I was happy. On our way home we would occasionally stop in the bustling city of Arusha and check our email in an internet café. Then we would head to the work site, where we were supposedly building the community center but were absolutely useless. The Tanzanian guys quite literally ran circles around us—in flip flops—and built this community center right before our eyes. We would offer to help and they would sort of let us dig a ditch or make a cement brick, but because it's just easier when talented people do things, they encouraged us to go back to playing with all the kids.

Toward the end of our stay the volunteers went on a three-day safari to the Serengeti. Of course it was an incredible trip and I hung out the top of the jeep taking photos, dreaming of one day being a professional photographer. Each night, one of our guides cooked dinner while the other set up our tents and outdoor shower. One evening I pulled the shower rope and let the hot water dump onto my dusty head just as hundreds of wildebeest migrated across the field right in front of me. As the ground shook beneath me and plumes of dust and dirt lingered in the air I stood awestruck and naked. I promised myself I would never forget that moment.

On our last day in Sombetini we had a joyful but tearful ribbon cutting ceremony for the community center, and our nine-week stay was over. My friends left for the airport as I headed to a hotel in Arusha. The next morning I would be picked up at 5 a.m. to start the hike up Mt. Kilimanjaro.

Every day about two hundred people leave for the summit of Mt. Kilimanjaro, so I know this is not unique, but it felt like a challenge to me, so I had to do it. We—my guide, Eric, and I—headed out on a five-day hike that kicked my ass while Tanzanian porters ran by us in sandals with several dozen raw eggs balanced on their heads. I read *The Alchemist* by Paulo Coelho, smoked weed with my porters, and applauded the hundred tiny rainbows that scattered across a waterfall. On the final push to the summit I got altitude sickness, lost my mind, and begged Eric to let me take a nap on the side of the trail.

"You cannot nap here, Tara," he said solemnly, lifting me to my feet by the back of the jacket. We made it to the summit—which felt like the top of the world in every sense—as the sun crested over the plains of Tanzania.

I remember getting back to a friend's house outside of Arusha filthy, grateful, and in absolute shock at what I had just done. I drank a beer as I packed my hiking clothes back into my suitcase. The next morning I'd catch a bus to Nairobi. I read in *Lonely Planet* about an island off the coast of Kenya called Lamu. They called it one of the most enchanted places in the world and compared it to Kathmandu in the 1970s. I didn't read another word. I didn't want to be just interesting. I wanted to be enchanted.

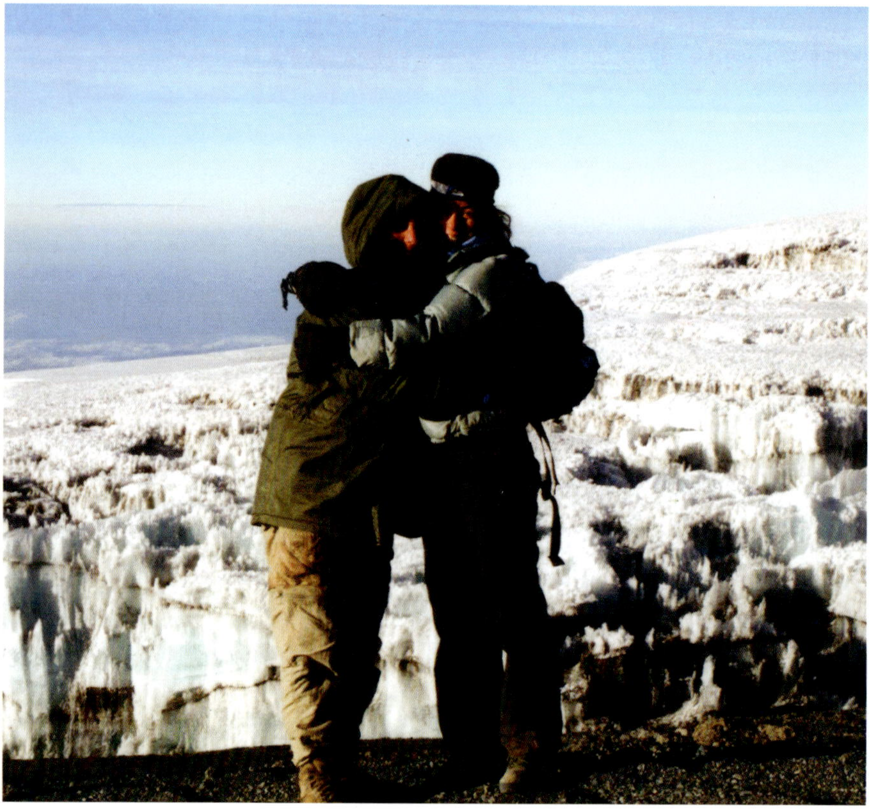

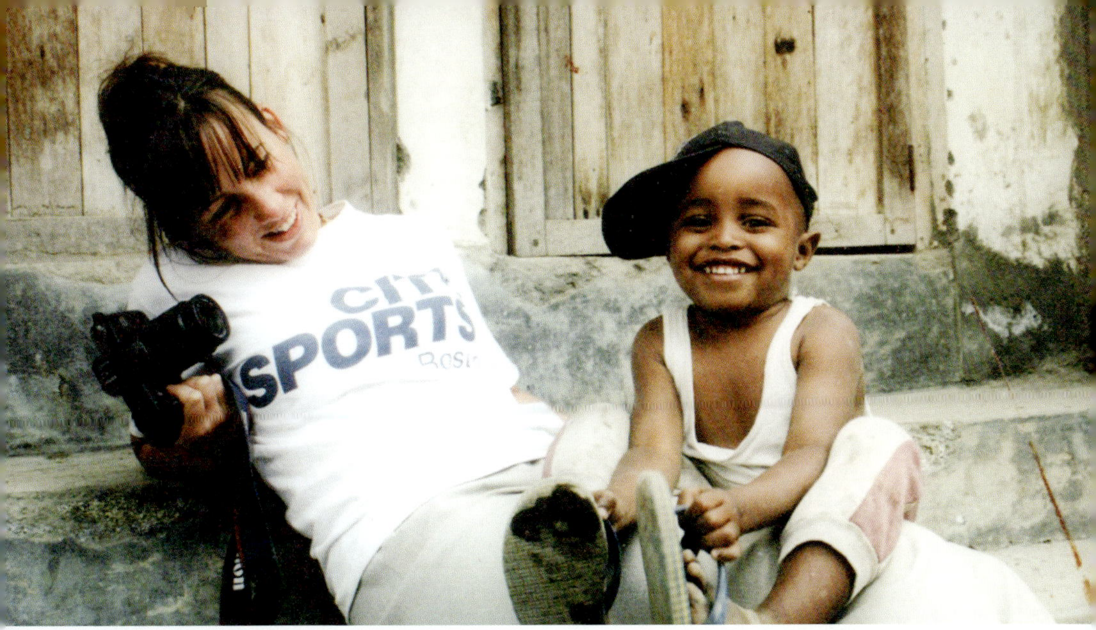
SPORTS

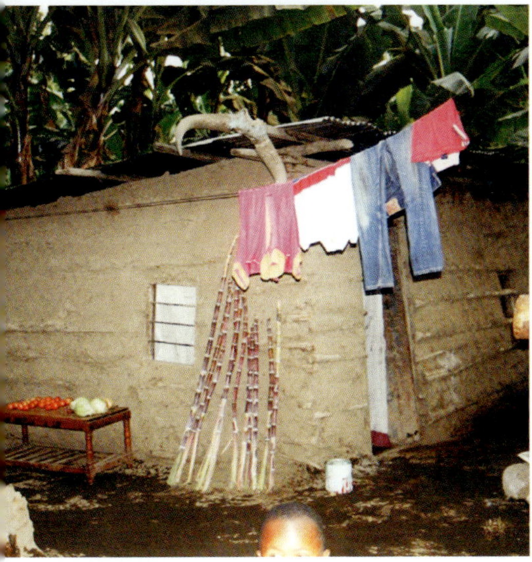

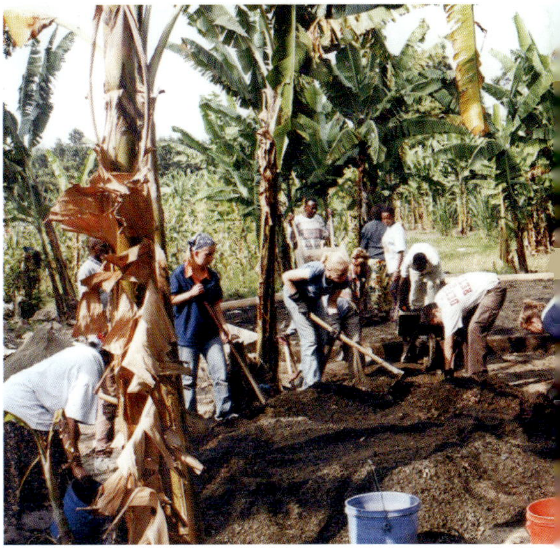

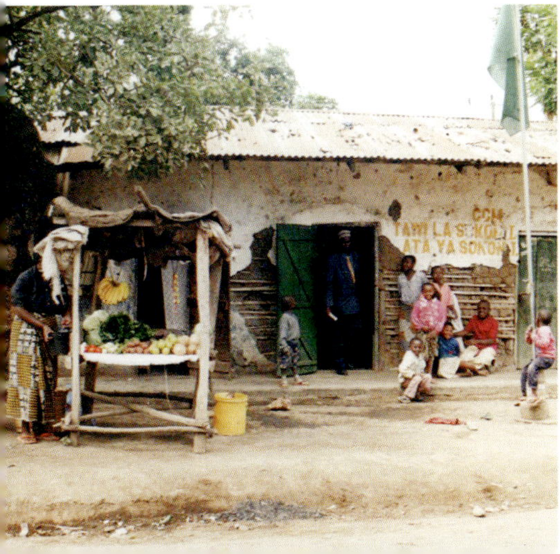
CCM

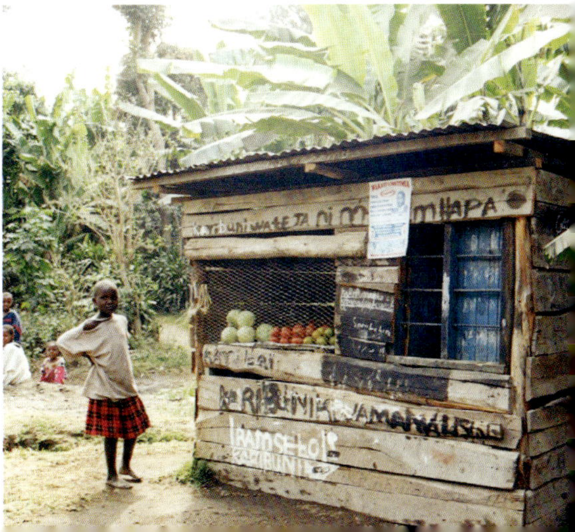

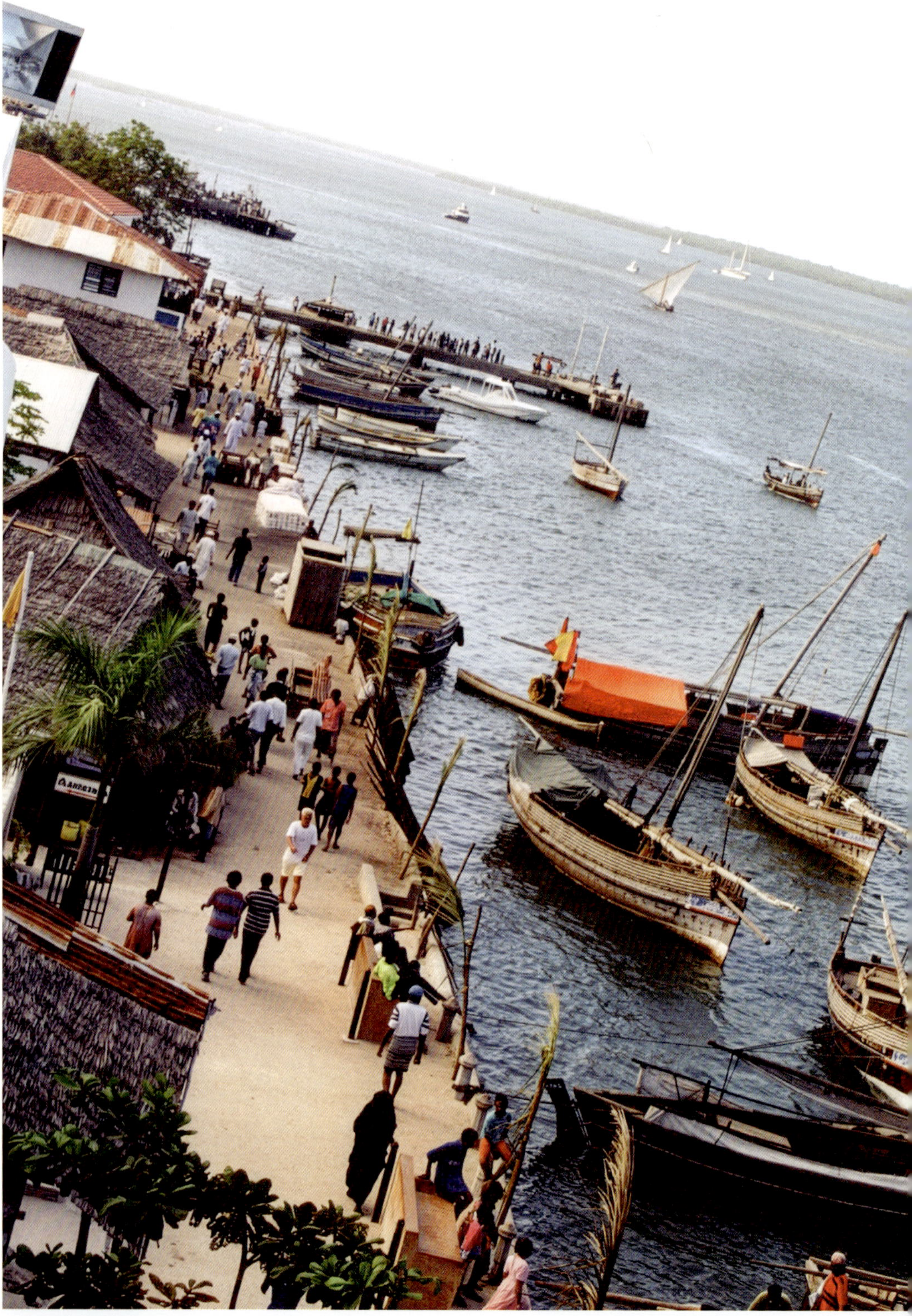

Enchanted

The bus depot in Arusha was teeming with fast-talking Tanzanians peddling snacks, bewildered young backpackers, and thousands of locals traveling to and fro. I jumped on the bus that said *Nairobi* and sat halfway back. I bought water and peanuts out the window from the guy scaling the side of the bus as we rolled out of the dirt parking lot.

Nairobi is an enormous city that felt intimidating to navigate alone so I stayed in my hotel until it was time to get a cab to the airport the next day. The flight landed safely in Lamu, the enchanted island in the middle of the Indian Ocean near the border with Somalia. There are no cars on the island, only donkeys, and the maze of ancient streets that make up Lamu Town are so narrow you have to turn sideways to let someone walk by. I checked into my beautiful hotel, put my stuff down on the bed, grabbed my camera, and headed out to the waterfront, where everyone seemed to be. The moon was full that night, and the best way to enjoy it, I was told, was a harbor cruise on a dhow—a small, traditional wooden sailboat—with a captain. Approaching the harbor I immediately caught eyes with a dangerously handsome man sitting on his dhow. Within seconds he took three big steps—one on the side of his boat, one on the dock, and a third on the dirt ground right in front of me.

"Hi," he said as he brushed dreadlocks off his face, smiling. "Welcome to Lamu."

Siadi Omar stood well over six feet tall and wore baggy pants, no shoes, and no shirt. He was lean and strong and his skin had the depth and sheen of melting chocolate. His huge bright smile took up half his face and when he asked if I'd like to go on his boat to see the full moon, I could only say yes. That night, in the moonlight, he sat next to me on his boat and grabbed my hand and placed it on the tiller, wrapping his hand over mine and squeezing it. A tiller, by the way, steers the boat, and Siadi called it a "thick, strong stick" as he moved my hand there. I wish I was kidding, but I'm also pretty stoked I'm not.

We kissed goodbye and made a plan to meet the next day. I lay in bed amazed at how an Irish girl from Marshfield can seem exotic if the plane flight is long enough—an exhilarating realization that I have taken full advantage of since.

Saidi was waiting for me at exactly noon. We took a walk through a palm grove on the beach, then sat in the shade of a coconut tree. Within seconds Saidi scaled a twenty-foot-high tree, took a machete out of his pocket, chopped down two coconuts while he hung from one hand, and scaled back down. He opened each coconut with one swift machete hack and together we drank from them on the deserted beach. I looked up to notice we were sitting under a treehouse. He saw me notice and we smiled. He leaned in to kiss me.

"Hold up," I said, ruining the mood. "I gotta take a picture of this shit. My friends are never gonna believe me."

When I was done photographing, I told him there was no way I'd be able to scale the tree to get in the treehouse. He agreed.

He knelt down and asked me to step into the palm of his hand. Before I could put my hand on his shoulder he stood up and pressed me over his head and into the treehouse. He was sitting beside me before I even had time to turn around. The floor of the tree house was completely covered with rice bags filled with sand: the entire thing was one big bed. Outside the little windows coconuts hung at eye level, and we could hear waves crashing onto the beach. It was the most romantic place I had ever been. Saidi lit a joint and passed it to me, took a condom from his pocket, and smiled.

"My passport," he declared.

And there I was: having sex with the hottest guy on the planet on top of a coconut tree inside a treehouse on the Indian Ocean. Enchanting.

Saidi and I spent the rest of the week together. He worked on his dhow every day, then would inevitably find me around some narrow corner and pull me into his house or someone else's house, where I would live out a chapter of a romance novel I had never read.

One night we ate at a busy local restaurant where no one in the whole place used utensils; I scooped food in my mouth with my hands and felt liberated. We went on a sunset sail in his boat to a remote beach and stared up at the sky together. We watched a crab scurry beneath the sand, and Saidi whispered to me, "Isn't God great?" and I still say that to myself every time I see crabs scurry on the beach. It was such an incredibly romantic and sexy week with Saidi that I just let myself fall in love with him until the very last moment when we kissed goodbye.

When the week in Lamu was over, I returned to my life in Seattle. I didn't care about being interesting anymore because the three months in East Africa was life altering and shifted my focus. I knew what I wanted to do with my life: *see the world and make people feel good.* I didn't want to vacation to see the world, I wanted to *travel.* That was non-negotiable. I loved the perspective traveling gave me, how it taught me what it meant to be human, and what it meant to be alive. I didn't know exactly how I'd be able to afford it, but I was going to see the world.

And *make people feel good*. I didn't know how I was going to do that either, but I was excited by the broad scope of it. I knew I had a way of connecting with people. I could make people laugh without language. I could make people feel good wherever I went. By no means had I figured everything out, but I had a North Star: see the world, make people feel good. I had to get creative. I still had years ahead of me filled with drinking too much, chasing boys, and acting like a fool, but I was getting closer to becoming someone I could respect. If I could just survive my twenties.

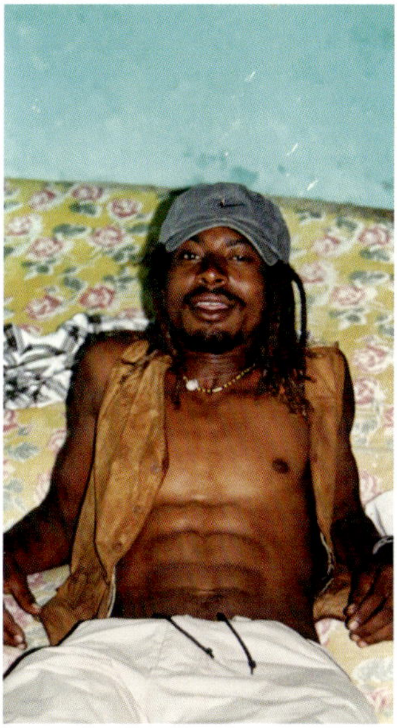

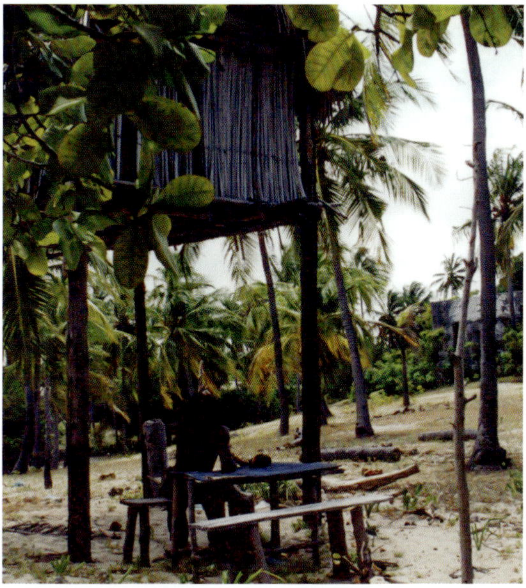

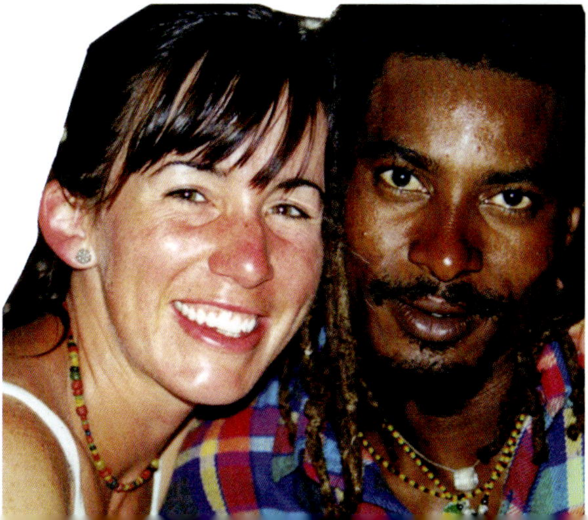

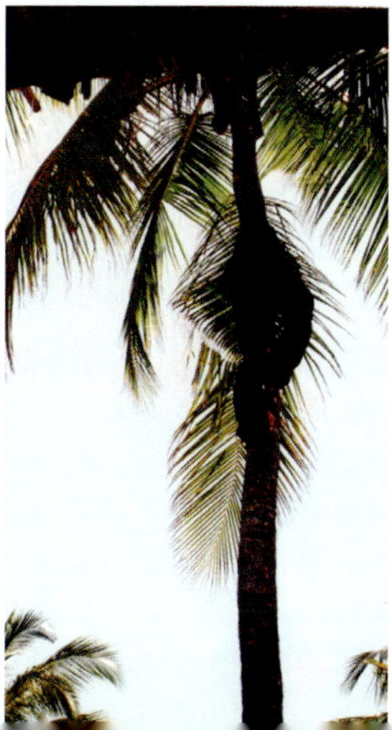

Sports!

I attended the Landmark Forum, a three-day personal development course, in 2003 at the urging of my friend, Ed. Ed was a polished, painfully gorgeous man who modeled for REI, among other accolades. He was also a member at the Westlake Athletic Club, the rundown gym I managed on Lake Union in Seattle. And by *managed* I mean trolled for handsome men on the basketball court who might be interested in funny chicks with daddy issues. Of which there were plenty. Ed was openly hot for me, which made me nervous, so I swore a lot, drank too much, and acted like an immature fool until he stopped wanting to fuck me and instead gave me advice on expensive self-improvement courses.

If you're one of the 2.4 million people who have attended the Landmark Forum you probably got something really good out of it. If you've heard of the Landmark Forum but haven't attended, you think it's a cult. The main lesson I squeezed out of that weekend was that my dad gave me my best traits—my sense of humor and friendliness. Those traits, I surmised, heavily outweighed the student loan debt and utter inability to have an intimate relationship—traits I have also spent years attributing to my father. One exercise of the weekend was to reach out to the people you've decided to forgive to let them know as much. They want you to make amends right then and there, get over it, and start living in love. So I did. I stepped out of the conference room and made the call to my dad. I'm not sure I had called my father even once in my life, so this was more awkward than it should've been.

When he picked up the phone he was shocked, "T.Spoon? Are you calling your dear old dad?!" he asked rhetorically with his trademark cheerfulness.

I went on to describe the weekend and why I was there, leaving out the fact that I may have some emotional issues to work through, at least in part because he was either not around or drunk throughout my childhood, but I skipped all that and went right for the good stuff.

"Dad, I want you to know how grateful I am for you. I can make people laugh, I can make people feel good, and I know for certain that's 100% thanks to you. It's been the trait that has opened every door in my life and it's all thanks to you. I love you."

There was a very long pause. The sound of my childhood—New England sports on TV—blared in the background.

Finally, he spoke, "The Red Sox won yesterday."

Another long pause.

"The Bruins won last night."

He could barely go on, "And now the Pats are up by three."

"And now *this* phone call. You just made my day, T.Spoon. You just made my whole day. I love you."

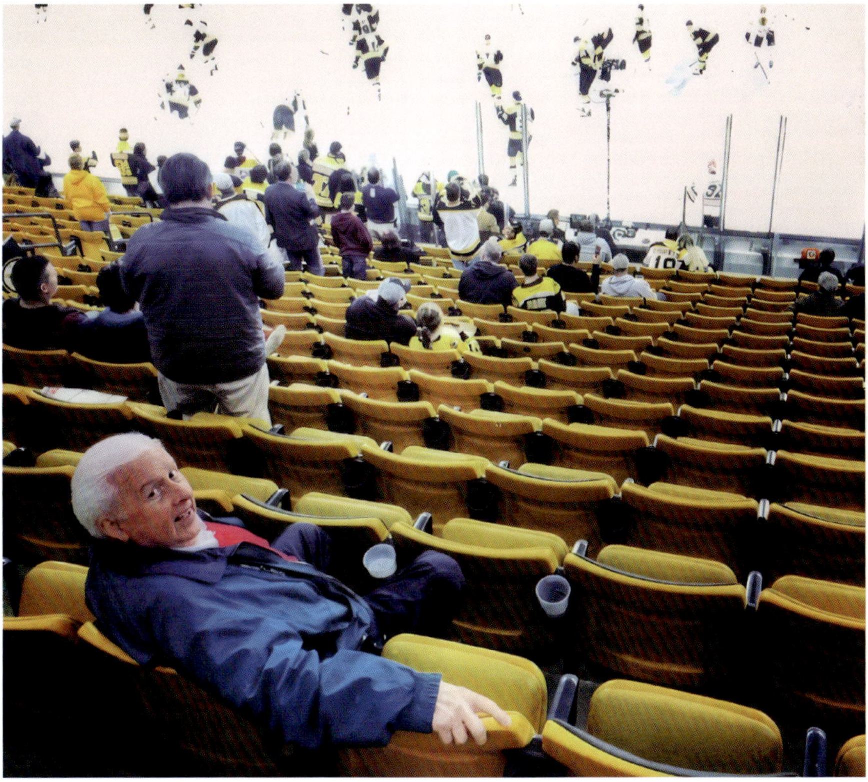

Spinning Out of Control

In July 2003, ten years into our mom's disease, my sister asked me to move home to help out with her care. In response, Dan, the owner of RAC, offered to fly me from Seattle to Boston every other week just so I wouldn't have to move away. The first weekend I flew home, when my mom answered the door, I tried not to gasp at the sight of her. The lazy eye she had in childhood had returned for the first time in her adult life, and she was uncharacteristically thin and sickly. Shannon was right, it was time to come home. I returned to Seattle on a Sunday, and on Monday told Dan I was moving back to Boston.

The Pacific Northwest, particularly Redmond, was booming with Microsoft's success, and my clients and Spinning students shared their good fortune and showered me with support when I told them the news. They came up with the idea to have a Spinning class that raised money for me to move back East, and just as he had for my Tanzania trip, Dan matched every dime. I thought I'd live my whole life in the Pacific Northwest, but after seven years in Seattle, at 28 years old, in October 2003, I was heading home.

A Spinning student at RAC named Greg told me about a new health club in the Ritz-Carlton Hotel in Boston, the Sports Club/LA. You'd have to see it to believe it, he told me. If I were going to continue to be a personal trainer and Spinning instructor I'd want to work here, with Boston's wealthiest clients. He told me it was impossible to get an interview there, but he knew people, he could help me out. Then he started sending me unsolicited dick pics, but that's neither here nor there. I got the job and was handed a pile of new member intake forms for people who eventually became my clients and lifelong friends.

This chapter of my mom's time with Parkinson's disease was fucking brutal. She was sick in ways that would have been hard to believe if I weren't there to see it myself. When I moved out at 18 my mom was a big, strong woman and now, a decade later, I was watching her crawl to the bathroom because her legs didn't work. Some days she'd walk halfway across a room, freeze mid-stride, and crash into a wall. Whenever she'd get upset, her tremors got so intense it looked like she was purposely flapping her arms. She was still having the same violent reaction to her medication that I first saw years earlier in Seattle, and as soon as those spasms began, she'd get on the ground so she wouldn't be thrown there by her own force. Her limbs thrashed and she gasped for air in agony like someone was holding her face underwater. And then, forty-five minutes later, it was over. She'd lay on the floor soaked in sweat, exhausted, and whimpering in pain. Every day I watched my mom struggle like this and every day I went to work as a personal trainer and helped the wealthiest folks in town ride stationary bikes up imaginary hills. It was an insanely painful and bewildering time.

Somehow my mom and I never spoke about how sad and terrified we both were about her illness back then, and I had no emotional skills to navigate these waters. I wasn't just angry, I was enraged, as I witnessed my strong mom lose her ability to move or live independently. I know lots of people would have handled those years with more grace, kindness, and compassion, but I was already unhinged. I was already a reactive and broken person; I was already being rattled inside a rattling cage. I had never seen anyone as sick as my mom was in those years, and I didn't know where to turn. I was terrified, heartbroken, and resentful. And then I was given a microphone and an audience.

I worked around the clock from 2003 to 2006 with dozens of personal training clients and three Spinning classes a week. This was before students could reserve a bike ahead of time, so folks lined up around the building before dawn to get a bike for my 6 a.m. classes. Whatever enthusiastic no-bullshit pep talk I was giving in Seattle was now on a different level. My Boston classes were insane, and I let my massive emotional pain spill out at the front of the room.

I want to exaggerate and say that I was abusive and awful, but I'm still friends with many of my students from back then and they assure me: Wild? Yes. Abusive? No. Honest? Yes. Rated G? No.

The wilder and more honest I became in class, the more people liked it. The classes where I felt I had gone too far or said too much were people's favorites. They showed up to the next class, and this time they brought their friends.

Seeing my mom's struggle juxtaposed with such fortunate people was very difficult for me to square. I would call for more resistance on the bikes, close my eyes, and try to find the words to encourage, but I was really just screaming out for help. I would remind my students that riding a stationary bike up a fake hill was luxury, not hardship. It was someone's *lack* of true hardship that attracted them to my classes, and we all knew it. These classes were so raw and physically challenging that people accessed something gritty inside themselves they didn't find otherwise. They felt powerful, like they could do hard, gnarly shit without disintegrating. I would think of my big, strong mom, my artist mom, my fearless mom crawling on all fours, and I would cry out. We all would. I said things in that room that people from polite families don't say in public. I said hard, ugly things that are true and that often involved the word *fuck*. I swore all the time in those classes because I swear all the time because I like to swear. I know what I'm doing. I mean what I say.

The people who loved those classes are still my friends. The people who didn't, well, they wrote letters to management about how downright offended they were. I was warned twice and then fired on the third time I was reprimanded. My students and clients went *nuts*. Dozens of people cc'd me on their complaint emails to my managers, and I printed every one. I read them every few years when I come across them while looking for something else. When SoulCycle eventually hit the scene, past students reached out to tell me how much those classes reminded them of our time together: good, raw, honest, gritty energy in a dark room with loud music. Every time I take a SoulCycle class I'm still the one yelling at the top of my lungs, but now I'm in the back row yelling in joy, more grateful than ever to still be able to use my strong, healthy body for even one more day.

Vietnam, Cambodia, and Thailand

It was 2004 and I was determined to find creative and helpful ways to see the world and make people feel good. I wanted to continue to travel to places that felt intimidating and witness the reality of the human experience. I wanted to understand, as best I could, the unfairness, chance, and beauty of life on this planet. I wanted to go to places that changed me. I wanted to go to SouthEast Asia.

I found an organization called Kids First Vietnam, which provided wheelchairs and prosthetics to landmine victims. As volunteers, we would ride our bikes across Vietnam to raise $10,000 for the cause. I hit my fundraising goal, and in March 2005 arrived in Hanoi with a group of volunteers to begin riding our bikes across Vietnam.

Okay, so when I say "riding our bikes across Vietnam" I mean that loosely. We rode like twenty-five miles a day, drank beer at lunch, stayed in mid-level hotels, rode in vans occasionally, and took a full-on plane flight for part of it. So it's more like we rode our bikes in Vietnam. Even still, countless unforgettable moments happened against the beautiful backdrop of Vietnam, and it was a magical trip. We rode our bikes next to little kids riding on the backs of water buffalo and past bright green rice paddies for as far as you could see. We peddled alongside toothless elderly people squealing in laughter and through tiny villages with schoolhouses full of adorable little kids. We cheered each other on as we summited big hills and raced each other across long straight-aways. The friendships I made on that trip were instant and are still with me today.

For Christmas that year my clients bought me gift certificates to a local camera store, and I was able to purchase my first digital camera. I was just figuring out how to use it on this trip, and while I was posing a line of Vietnamese school girls for a picture it dawned on me: I should be a professional photographer.

Ever since my mom gave me my first camera for my 14th birthday, I tried to celebrate the people I love through photography, but I never thought it was a career within my grasp. I thought there were only two paths for photographers: *National Geographic* or fashion photography, and both seemed out of reach. But there I was at 29 years old setting up a photo shoot with a row of strangers in Vietnam when I decided that I should go to photography school. Being a professional photographer seemed like the perfect way for me to see the world and make people feel good. I could spend part of the year traveling the world, donating my time and photographs to the kinds of organizations I had been fundraising for. The other part of the year I could photograph families, kids, and weddings back home. As soon as I got back to Boston, I thought, I'd start my new life.

When the trip through Vietnam was over and the rest of the crew went home, I jumped on a tiny speed boat with ten strangers and rode down the Mekong River to Cambodia. Four hours after I left Vietnam, now sunburned and parched, I felt my dreams coming true as the boat docked in the capital of Cambodia, Phnom Penh. The people of Phnom Penh were so insanely nice to me, and I encourage anyone reading this to bring your love, energy, and money to Cambodia, but my week there in 2005 was grim.

My first morning in Phnom Penh I went to "grab a coffee and people watch." That's when a person with no arms and no legs on a skateboard followed me all the way to the café and parked next to my chair and looked up at me and said "please" over and over again until I emptied my entire wallet in the can he had taped to the front of the skateboard. I was almost in tears when I noticed the large, middle-aged German man sitting at a table ogling a 12-year-old Cambodian girl and rubbing her back. I walked out to the street, horrified, and tried to reset. I didn't know what to do with myself, so I hired a mototaxi to take me to see the sights, which was fun for a minute until we crashed. That's okay, just some minor cuts and scrapes so we switched bikes and headed back out. It turns out the "sights" of Phnom Penh are all memorials of the genocide of the Cambodian people by the Khmer Rouge in the 1970s. Even the mototaxi driver was crying at the Killing Fields. I headed back to my stifling-hot hotel room, which was right around the corner from the skyscraper of trash with children picking through it for food. I lay motionless and heartbroken in my room until morning.

The next day I took a five-hour taxi ride to Siem Reap to see Angkor Wat and Ta Prohm, the incredible ancient temples of Cambodia. These are stunningly gorgeous and inspiring places, and I photographed from sunrise to sunset, pretending I was on assignment as a world-traveling photographer. But fuck, that was lonely. After two days I flew to Bangkok.

Forever trying to be an athlete even though I'm not, I signed up for an eight-night kitesurfing camp on the lush and beautiful island of Koh Phangan in the Gulf of Thailand. If you've ever seen someone kitesurf I hope it didn't look easy *at all* because it's not. Maybe for someone who surfs or sails it might be fun, but I'd never even flown a kite. So there I was with no ability or experience, hoping I'd just get the hang of this massively difficult sport in eight days. It did not go well.

Besides me, every person staying at the kite surfing camp was a male model from Belgium. I mean, I don't actually know that, but this place was literally the sexiest place on the planet. I do know that. And I was the only female staying at this place. I definitely know that.

The first morning at the camp I took an introductory lesson on the beach in front of all the Belgian models having coffee and it went so poorly that the instructor never let me take another lesson. He told me I didn't have the strength to hold the kite at an angle that would be considered kitesurfing. He made the sound of a champagne cork popping and said it would be considered suicide. But he said it with a French accent, and the models were watching so I laughed like we were flirting.

What to do when you land in a sandy surf camp full of male models, but you don't want to be there anymore? Maybe I could try being myself. Tits up, girl, big smile. Turns out there's plenty to do as a single woman on a Thai beach besides fly a kite.

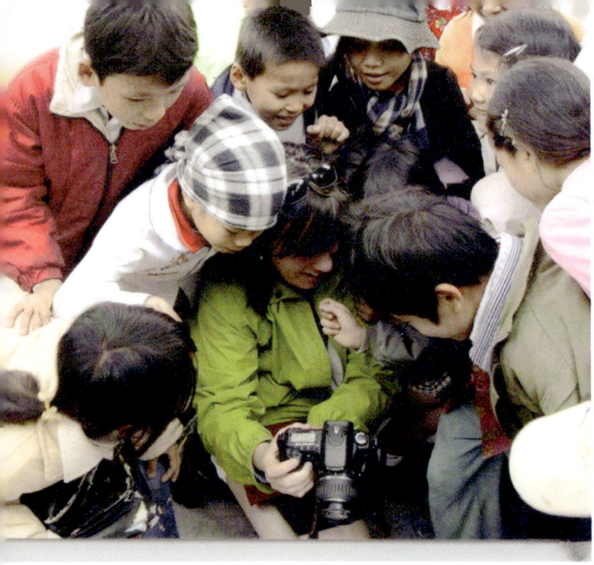
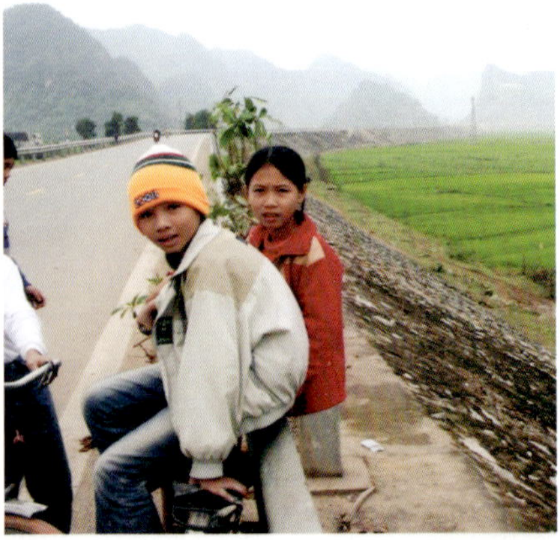

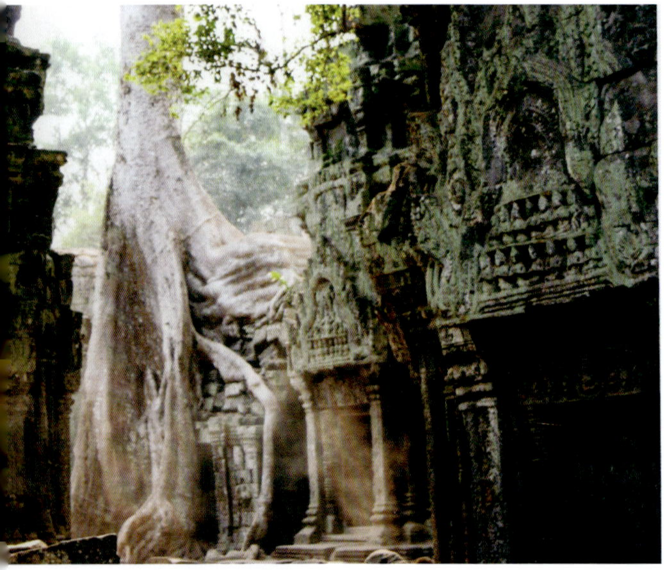
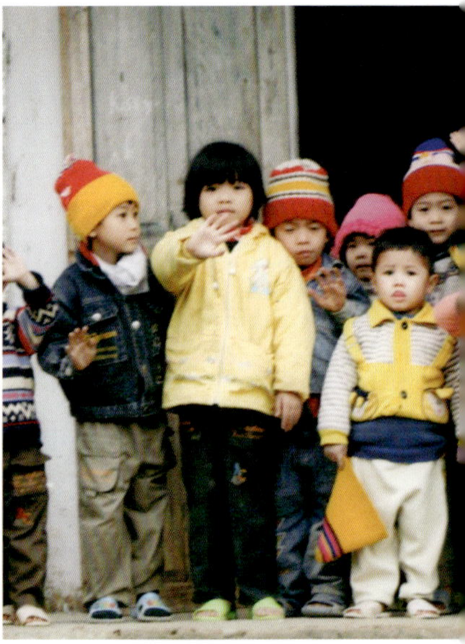
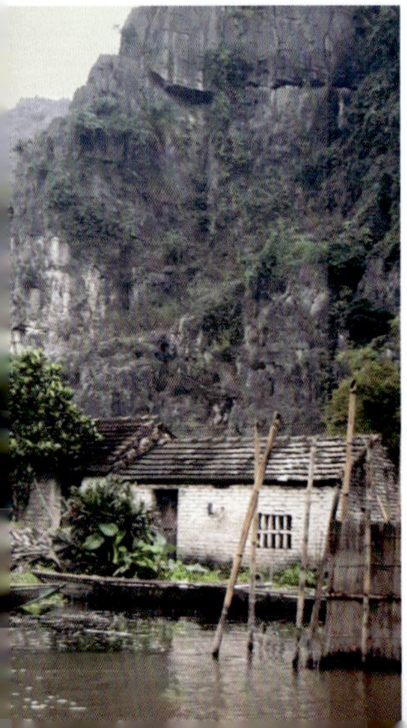
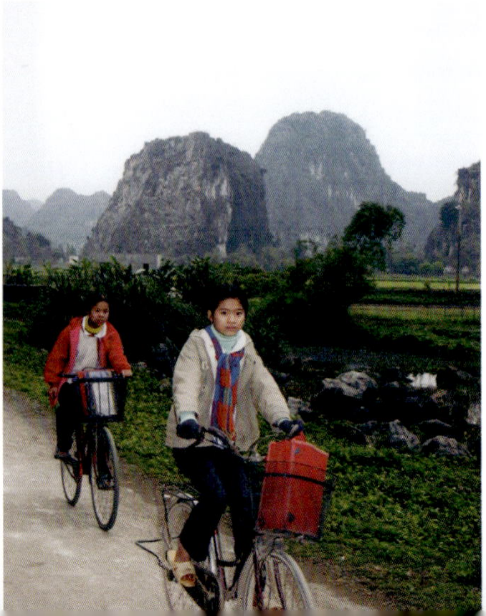
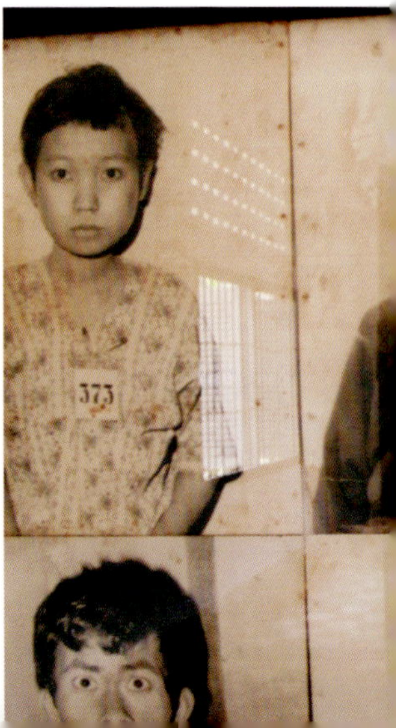
373

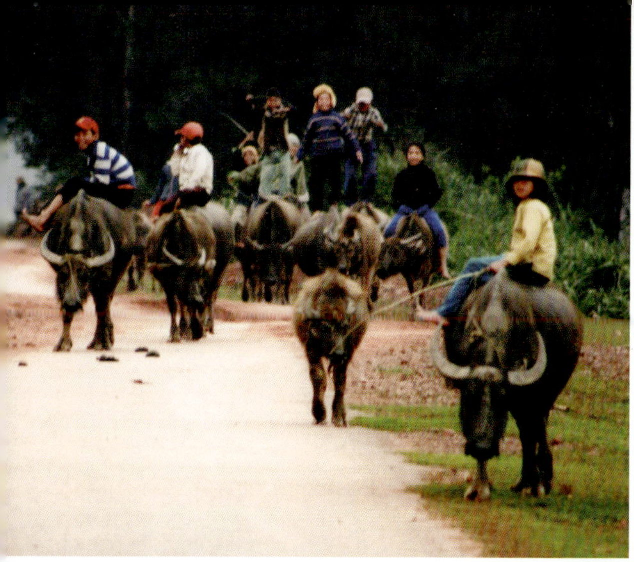

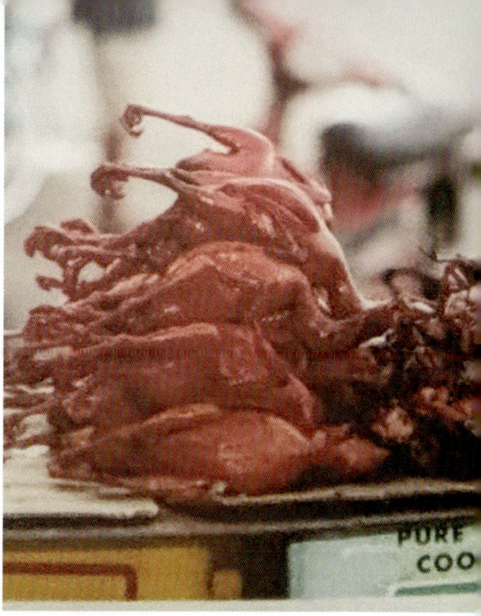
PURE

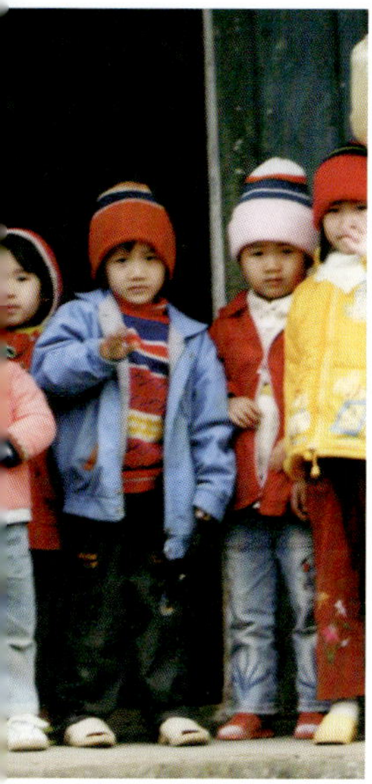

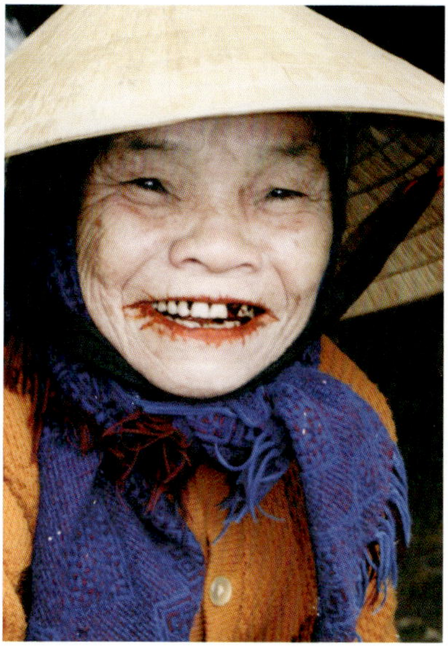

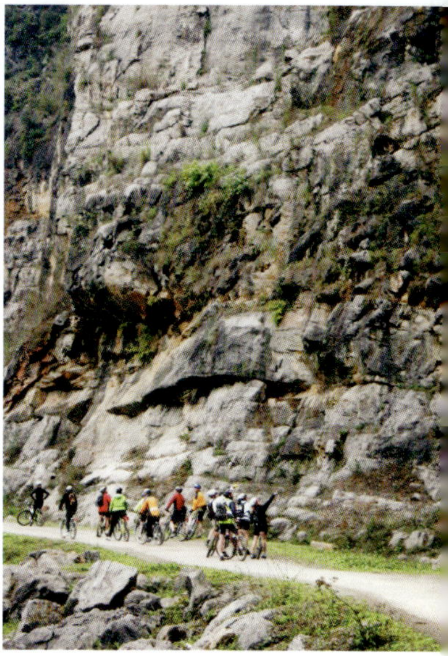

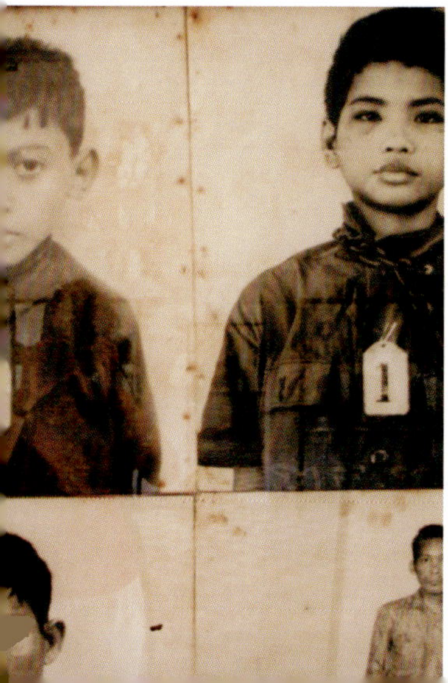

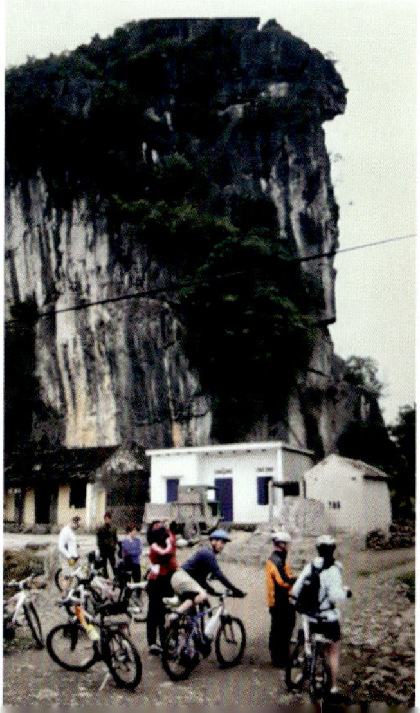

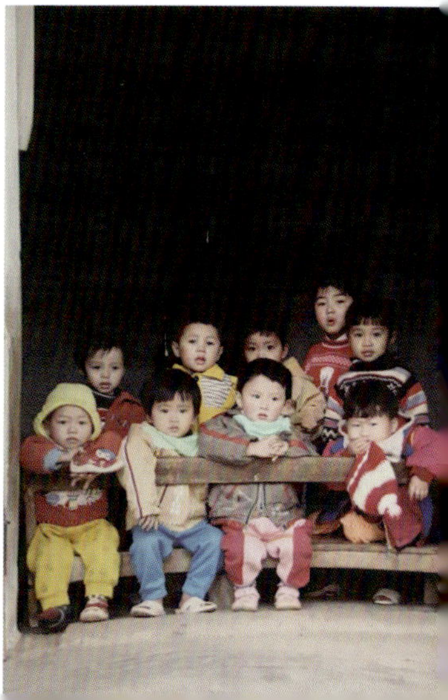

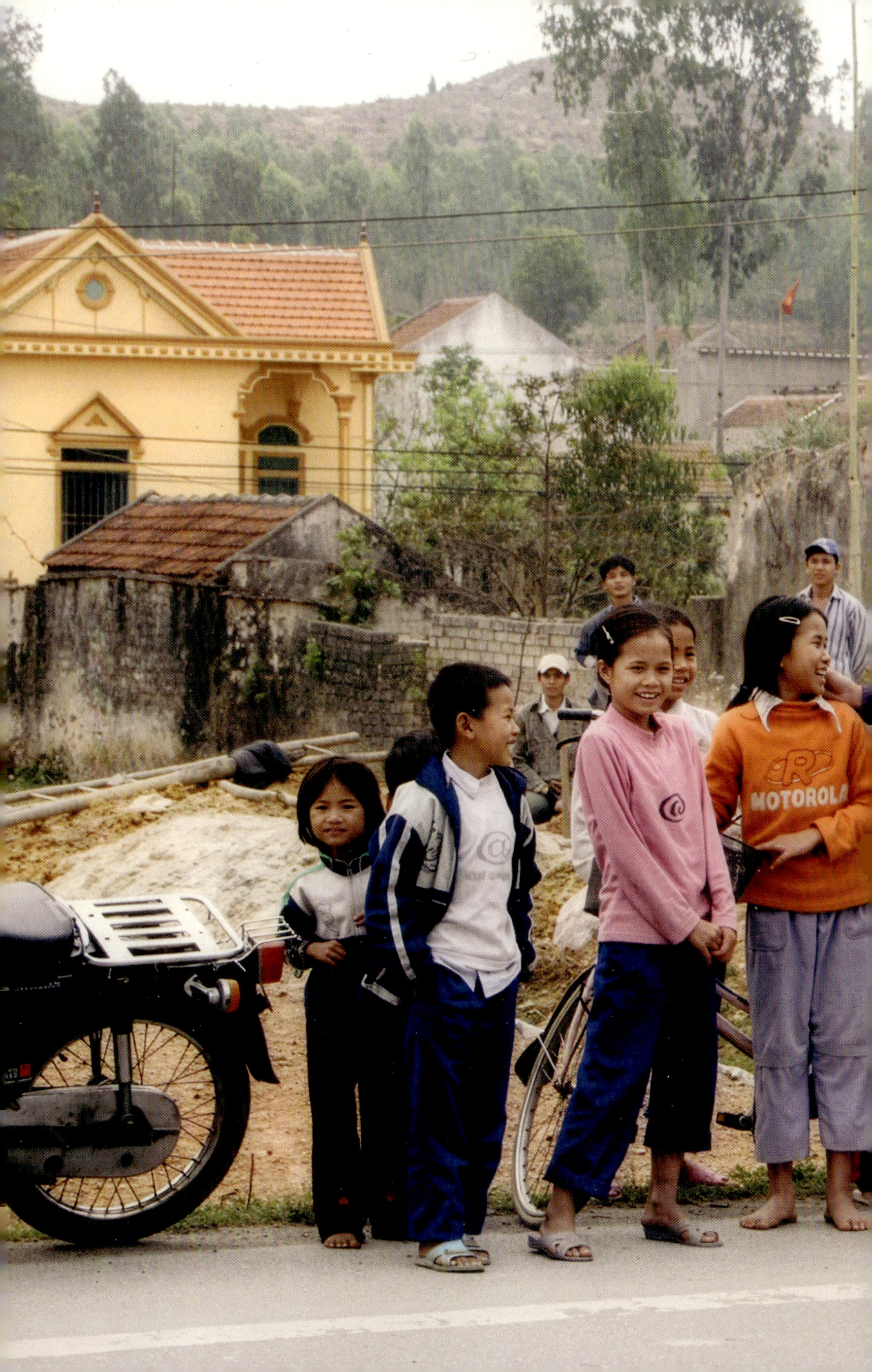
MOTOROLA

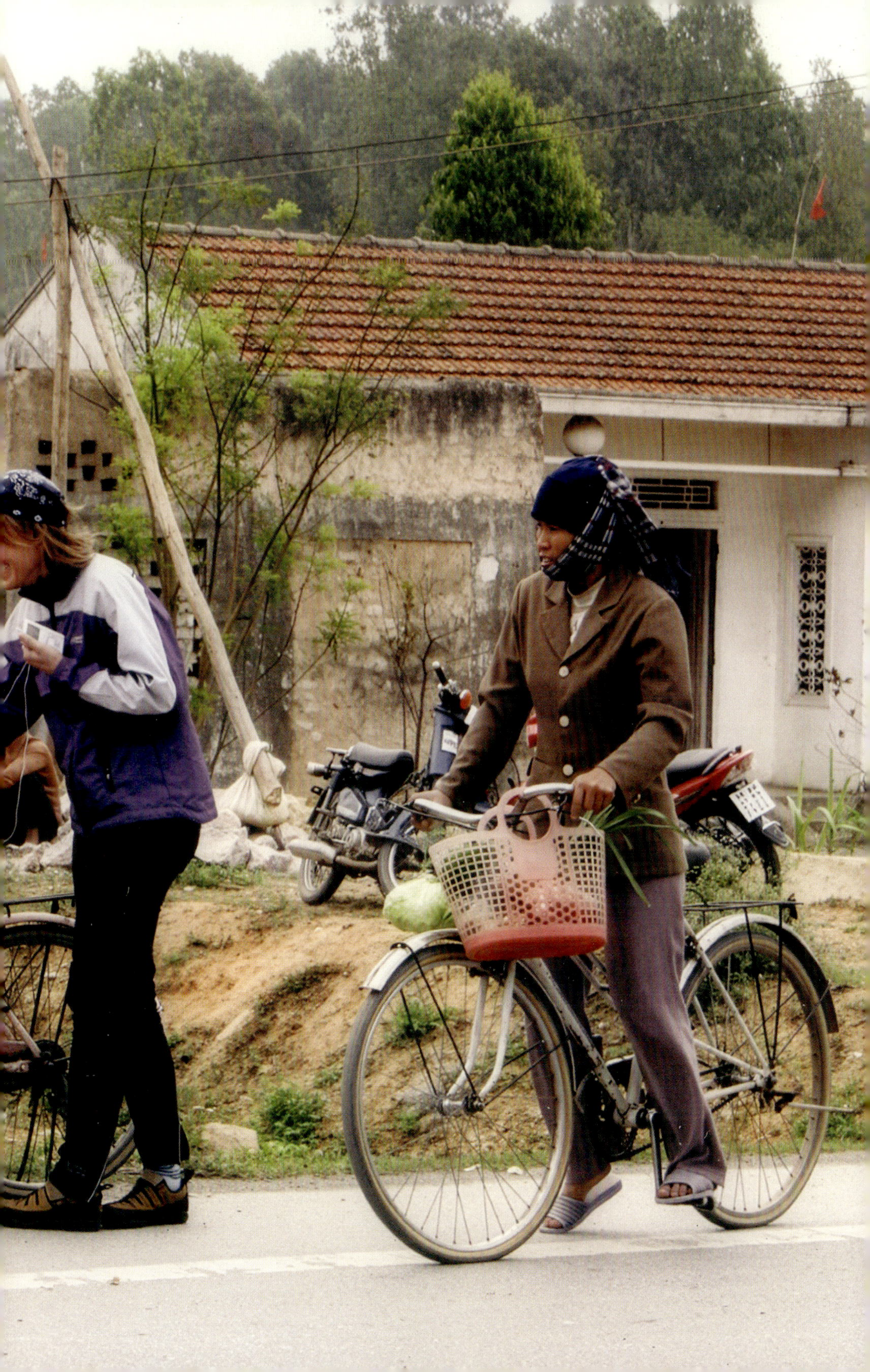

Tailwind

When I returned from Southeast Asia, hell-bent on changing my life and becoming a professional photographer, I immediately applied and got accepted to New England School of Photography (NESOP) in Boston, but I couldn't afford it. I was denied financial aid because of my existing student loan debt, and I was heartbroken. My personal training clients were along for the emotional ride because they bought me my first digital camera and knew how desperately I wanted to become a photographer. They were always trying to help me troubleshoot.

One Tuesday morning, after our 7 a.m. weekly session, my client Sandy pulled me aside and said she wanted to discuss my predicament. Sandy was my very first personal training client in Boston. We had been working together for a year and a half at this point.

"Listen," she said. "I've had a lot of breaks in my life, and I want to give you one. I'm going to pay for you to go to photography school."

I was stunned. A woman who was not related to me and owed me absolutely nothing was about to completely and totally change my life.

"And," she added, "You can live with me while you go to school."

Sandy wrote me a check for $30,000 and I moved in with her and Frank—her soon-to-be husband—a month later. I lived in the guest bedroom of their beautiful home in the suburbs of Boston for a year while I went to photography school.

Soon after that, at the Sports Club/LA, Ted Winston, an owner of the Boston-based Winston Flowers, one of the biggest floral companies in the world, overheard me telling someone I was going to photography school. I had seen Ted at the Sports Club but had never spoken to him, nor had I heard of Winston Flowers. He asked if I took photos of flowers. I didn't, but I said I did. He then hired me to photograph mind-blowingly beautiful events around Boston created by a genius named Marc Hall who worked for Winston's at the time. My first check of my photography career was for $100 from Winston Flowers, one week after my 30th birthday. Photography school hadn't even started and already I was feeling a tailwind.

A few months later, in September 2005, Hurricane Katrina ravaged the Gulf Coast, leaving such devastation that people from across the country desperately wanted to help in any way they could. One of my dearest friends from Seattle, Flora Bowley, temporarily moved to New Orleans that October to lead volunteers for Emergency Communities, an organization that formed in response to Hurricane Katrina. They served 1,400 meals a day to relief workers from a geodesic dome in a parking lot in St. Bernard Parish, affectionately called the Made with Love Café. Flora told me they could use all the help they could get, so I signed up. In late December I landed in New Orleans.

Most of the volunteers at Emergency Communities were members of the Rainbow Gathering, which, if you haven't heard of it, defines itself as "a temporary, loosely knit community of people who congregate around the world for one or more weeks at a time with the stated intention of living a shared ideology of peace, harmony, freedom, and respect." They were a free-spirited crew. Lots of hula hoops, a fair bit of LSD. One guy legally changed his name from Justin to Just Chillin', which feels like a real, respectable commitment to the lifestyle.

The Made with Love Café experience was unforgettable, and it felt so good to help. I met a fireman from Austin who I dated for a year, but most importantly I got my feet wet as a documentary photographer. In our time off I borrowed a car and photographed the ravaged neighborhoods of New Orleans. The photographs were just for me, but my camera made me feel brave, like I had a purpose, like I was supposed to be there. Between working with Winston Flowers and documenting the Katrina disaster I was already in full stride as I entered New England School of Photography in February 2006.

The first day of class we were paired up with another student and took turns talking about ourselves for five minutes. Then our partner had to introduce us to the whole class. When a woman named Maria Luisa stood up to introduce her partner she began with, "Everyone get to know this guy. He's the nicest guy you'll ever meet. His name is Ben Wight." So the next day I spotted Ben in an otherwise empty classroom and sat next to him. We spent those years in photography school forging a best friendship, and we created Hitched Studios, our wedding photography company, the day after graduation.

I had incredibly high hopes for photography school, and the reality surpassed my dreams ten-fold. I loved the teachers, the classes, the homework, and the people. At 30, I knew this was my chance to go for something I had dreamed about since I was a child, so I worked my ass off. What I lacked in talent, I made up for in hard work. By the time I graduated I had ten wedding photography jobs booked as well as countless other shoots that paid next to nothing but gave me work to put on a website. I saw personal training clients in their homes while I got T.Spoon Photography, my family photography business, and Hitched Studios off the ground. Then I pulled my financial safety net out from under me. For better or for worse I stopped training and forced myself to fly with photography.

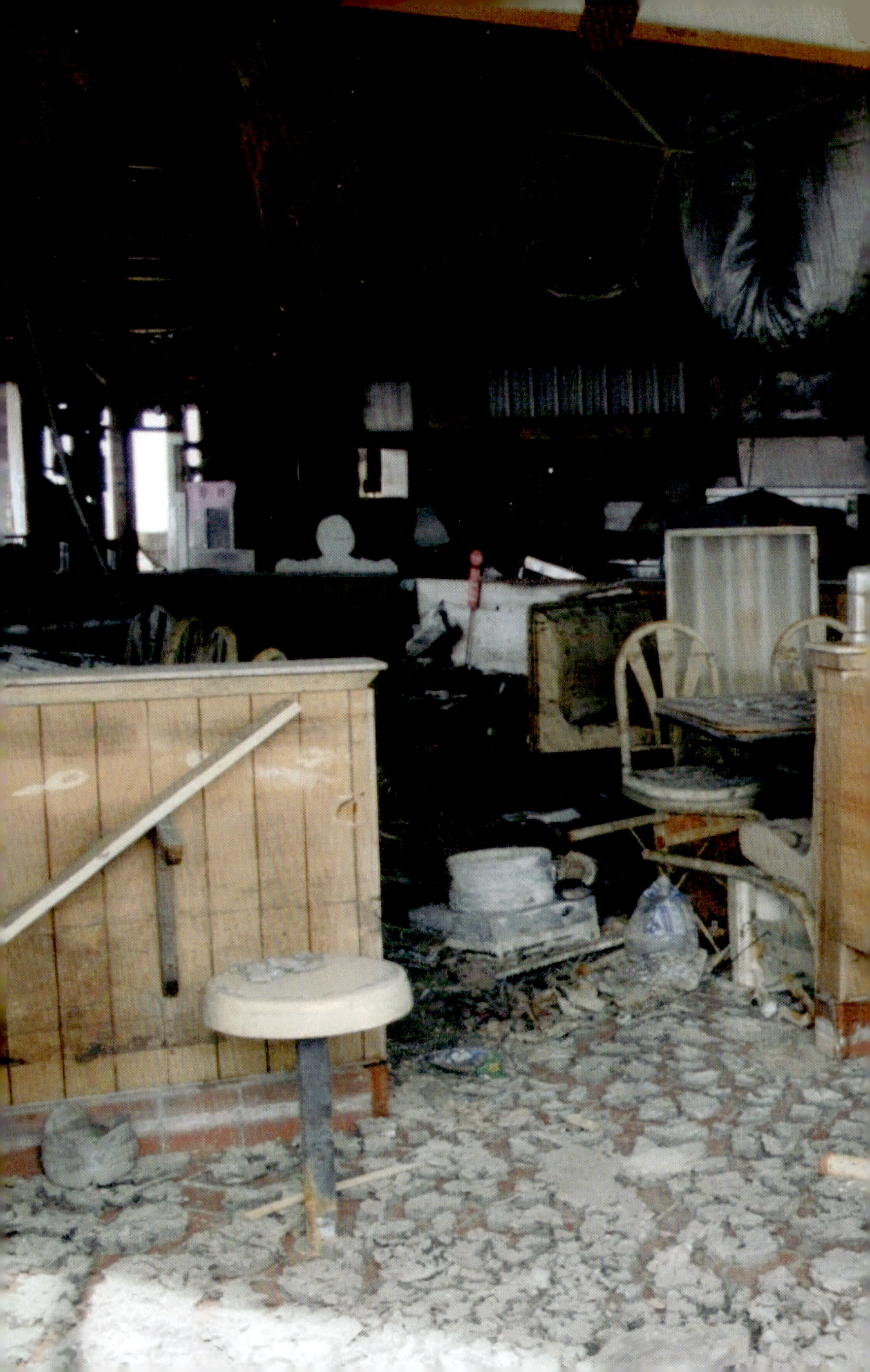

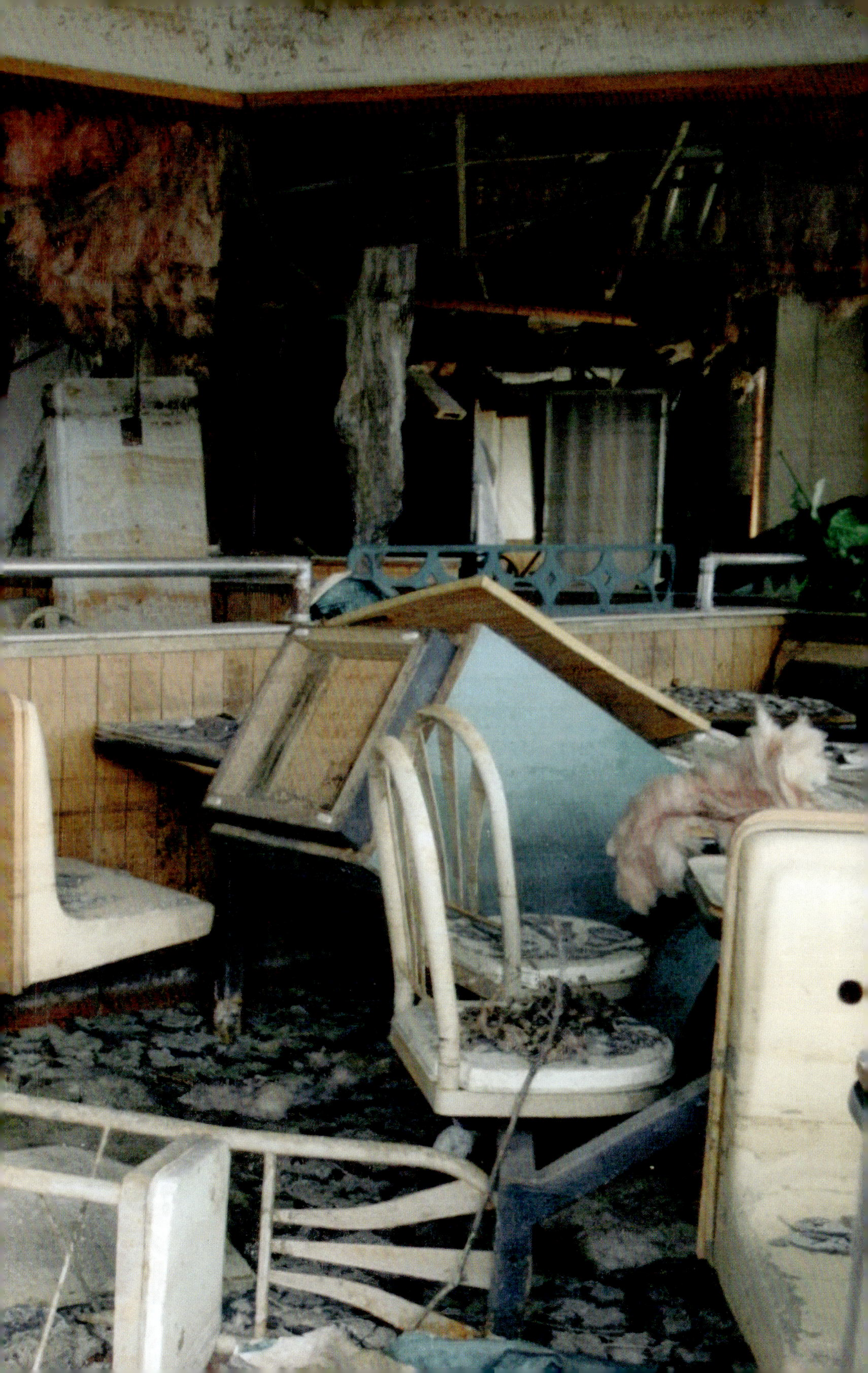

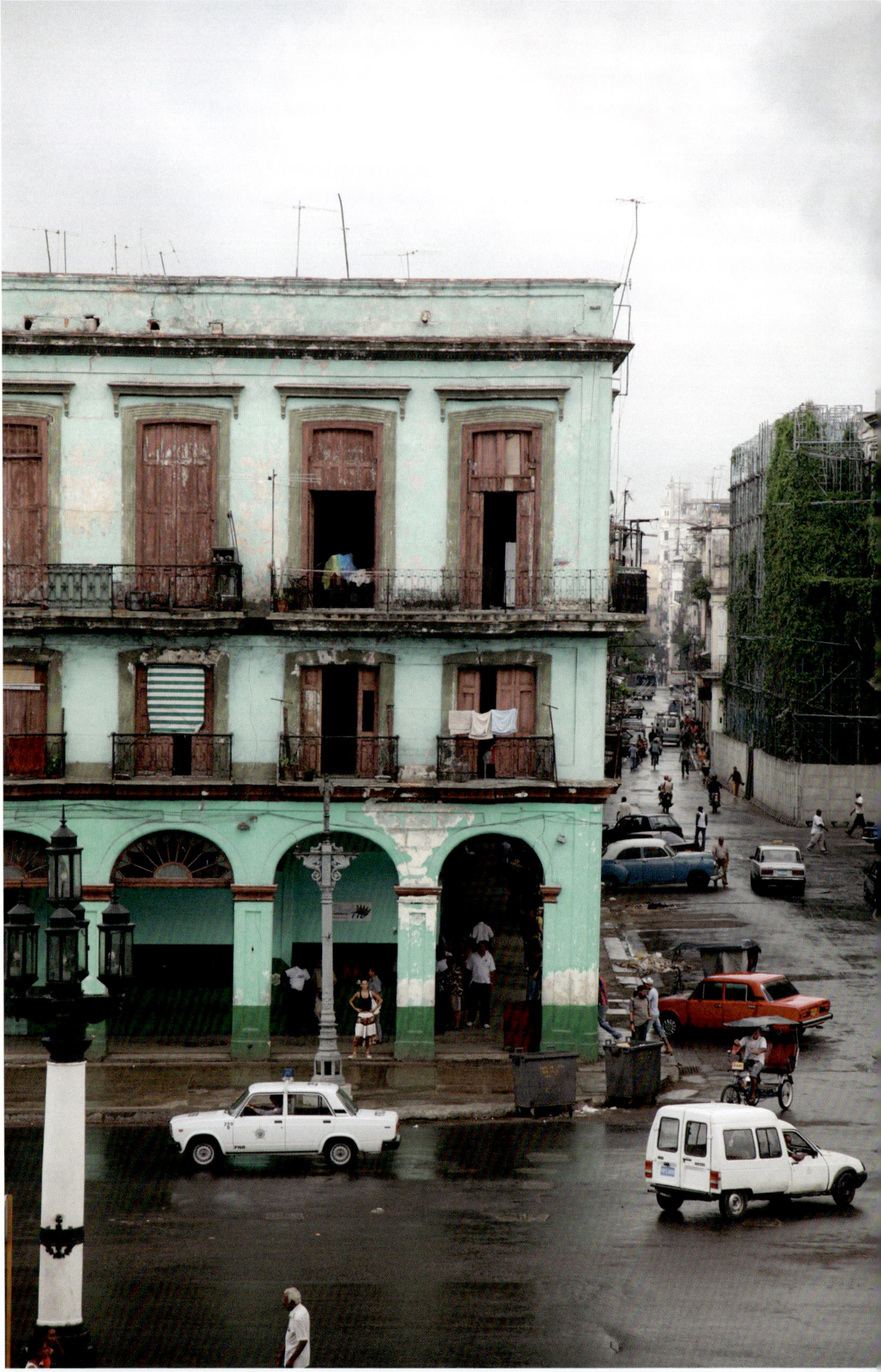

Cuba

As soon as I graduated, I wanted to start my life as the world-traveling photographer I promised myself I would be. Naturally I started with a place no one was allowed to go: Cuba. One of my favorite teachers at NESOP, Wayne Colter, told me about the times he had snuck into Cuba without getting caught. He assured me that if he could do it, I could do it, too.

"I wanna sneak into Cuba this September," I told him a month after I graduated. Just hearing the words come out of my mouth made my stomach turn.

It was 2007 and Cuba was still suffering under the travel ban that President Kennedy put into place in 1963, which meant, among other things, that no planes left the US heading to Cuba. To get into Cuba, Americans had to fly in from another country, pay in cash, and hope they didn't get caught. Cubans didn't give a shit, they welcomed the dollar. This was an American ban.

Over the next two months Wayne helped me get my head around the trip and set me up with email introductions to his Cuban friends. I planned to spend my first afternoon in Cuba with his friend Juan, a blind tour guide in Havana.

I flew from Boston to Cancun with a carry-on, took a golf cart to another terminal, and walked up to the Cuban Air counter. I paid $14 for a travel visa and $58 in cash for a plane ticket to Havana. Boarding the flight thirty minutes later, I felt like I was doing something totally illegal. I was absolutely terrified, and I loved it.

The old Russian airplane looked more like a flying submarine—I don't even think it had seatbelts—and it was raining so hard in Havana that the pilot nose-dived for the landing, missed, and tried again, three times. By the third attempt even the flight attendant was crying. Everyone was yell-praying in Spanish, and every time the plane tried to land but didn't, we all screamed like we were being murdered.

AirBnB, then airbedandbreakfast.com, launched in August 2008, eleven months *after* this trip, but Cubans already had a longstanding tradition of hosting travelers in their homes for extra income. Juan set me up with his friends, Gloria and Pedro, in their spare bedroom, in a sweltering-hot, mid-century apartment in the center of Havana. I tried to take a shower as soon as I got there and was electrocuted by the initial stream of water so decided against it. That first evening I mentioned this to Juan, and he shrugged like I should have expected it.

My first full day in Havana had me awestruck. The whole city felt like a 1959 movie set with a Buena Vista Social Club soundtrack, and my camera never left my face. The buildings, all in some stage of decay, were shades of pastel pinks and greens and adorned with clean laundry drying in the breeze. The cars, pristinely maintained, were the ones my mom told me about from her childhood, and I kept hoping to see her and her high school prom date drive by and wave. Seven-piece bands played at hole-in-the-wall cafés, and the gorgeous people dancing to the music spilled out onto the streets. Everywhere I looked I was inspired. All the faded decay, the vintage cars, and the nostalgic feeling that came with them are direct results of the trade embargo with the US. This was, and is, horrible for the Cuban people, but for a freshly graduated photographer it felt like I entered a dreamworld. I photographed Havana and the people who bring it alive from sunrise to sunset that first day, stopping at restaurants for Cuban sandwiches and pretending to read a book.

Wayne reminded me many times before I left that because of the travel ban my ATM and credit cards would not work in Cuba. Whatever money I was going to need had to be brought with me in cash. Without a moment of research, I decided $500 for a four-day visit to Cuba would be more than enough. What I didn't know—and this is written in every travel guide about this place—was that there are two working currencies in Cuba. Local Cubans use pesos, which run around ten to the dollar. Tourists use convertible pesos, exchanged at one-to-one with the American dollar. It was day one of the trip, and I realized I had only a tenth of the money I thought I did. I was gonna run out of money.

Juan had given me an address for a place he suggested for dinner so on the second night in Havana I decided to check it out. When I got to the doorstep, I realized it wasn't a restaurant, it was someone's house—and the whole family was home. A young boy, maybe 12, greeted me at their wide-open front door and invited me in. The lights were off in the living room, and two sisters sat in the dark, braiding each other's hair. I walked through the kitchen, where the boy's mom was cooking, then out to the back porch and sat alone at the only table. The boy came out and asked if I wanted chicken, and when he served me the enormous pile of chicken and rice, he told me, in English, that I had beautiful eyes. He was so proud of himself that he walked back into the kitchen and hugged his mom in celebration.

"Trinidad, *por favor*," I said to the guy at the bus depot in the center of town the next morning. I was referring to the colorful and cobblestoned colonial town in the center of Cuba. I had heard it was an incredibly photogenic place with a great nightlife, so I wanted to go.

The trip to Trinidad was supposed to take seven hours, but it took nine because the bus driver pulled over at his friend's house and had a formal sit-down lunch while the bus full of people sat in silence, watching him out the windows. When he was done eating, he grabbed a toothpick, said a pretty lengthy goodbye, got back onto the bus, and began driving again. Never even acknowledged it.

My twenty-four hours in Trinidad was dicey. I salsa danced (got thrown around a dance floor like a ragdoll) with a guy who pretended that he couldn't speak English suddenly—after speaking English to me all night—when the conversation turned to whether or not he had a condom. Then, after photographing for hours the next morning, I missed the bus back to Havana. Though I caught the next bus, I had officially run out of money. Luckily, I sat next to an incredibly kind and generous English guy who was traveling through Cuba during his year-long trip around the world. When we got to Havana he hailed a cab, spoke perfect Spanish with the driver, rode with me to the airport, bought my plane ticket in cash, then kissed me goodbye. Later I lay down in a bed in an oversized Cancun resort hotel and didn't stand up again until it was time to take a flight home. By afternoon, safely on the other side of customs in Boston, I sat in a cab in total disbelief that I had just pulled that shit off. If this was my first trip after photography school, then I picked the right career.

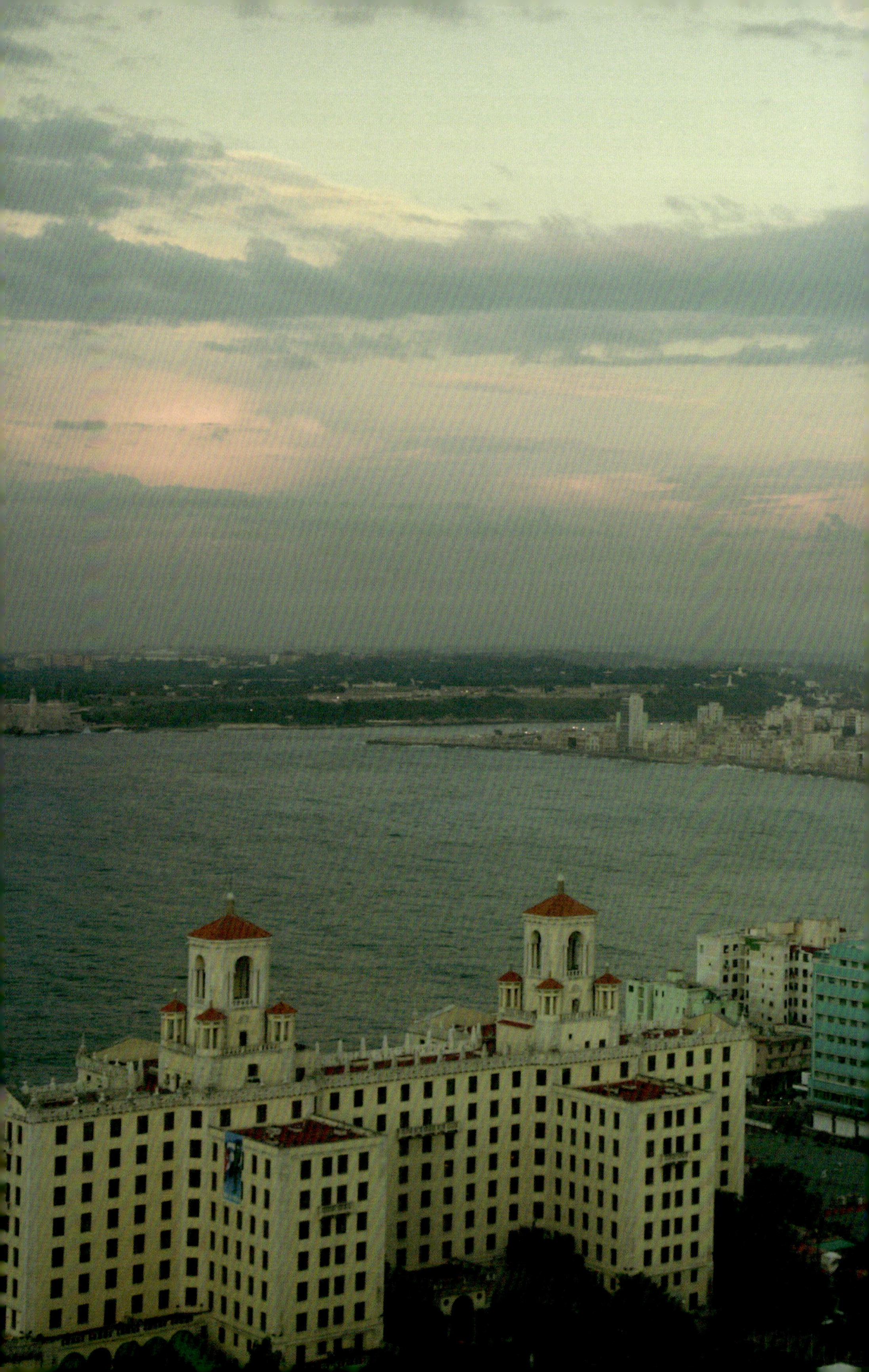

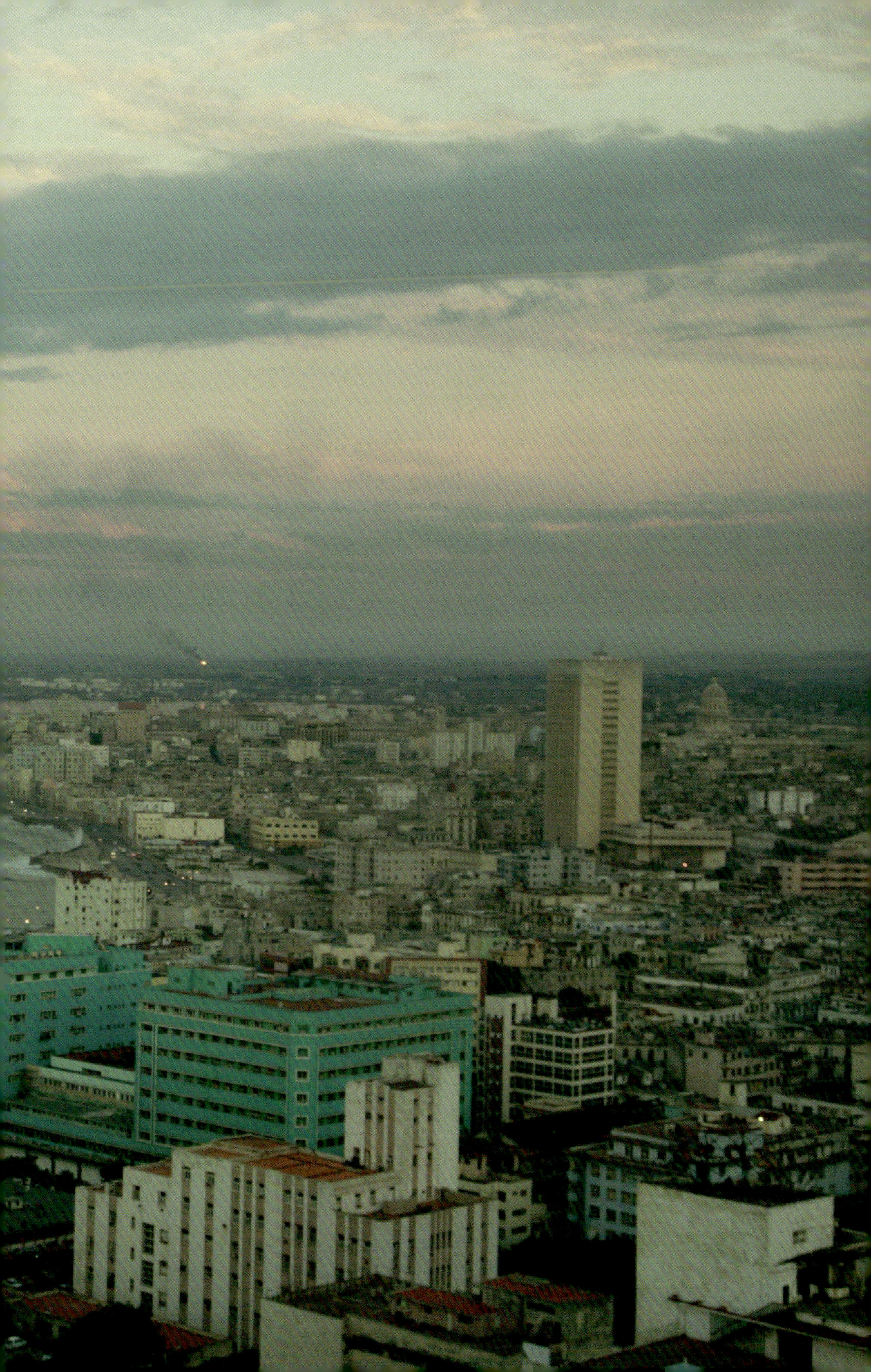

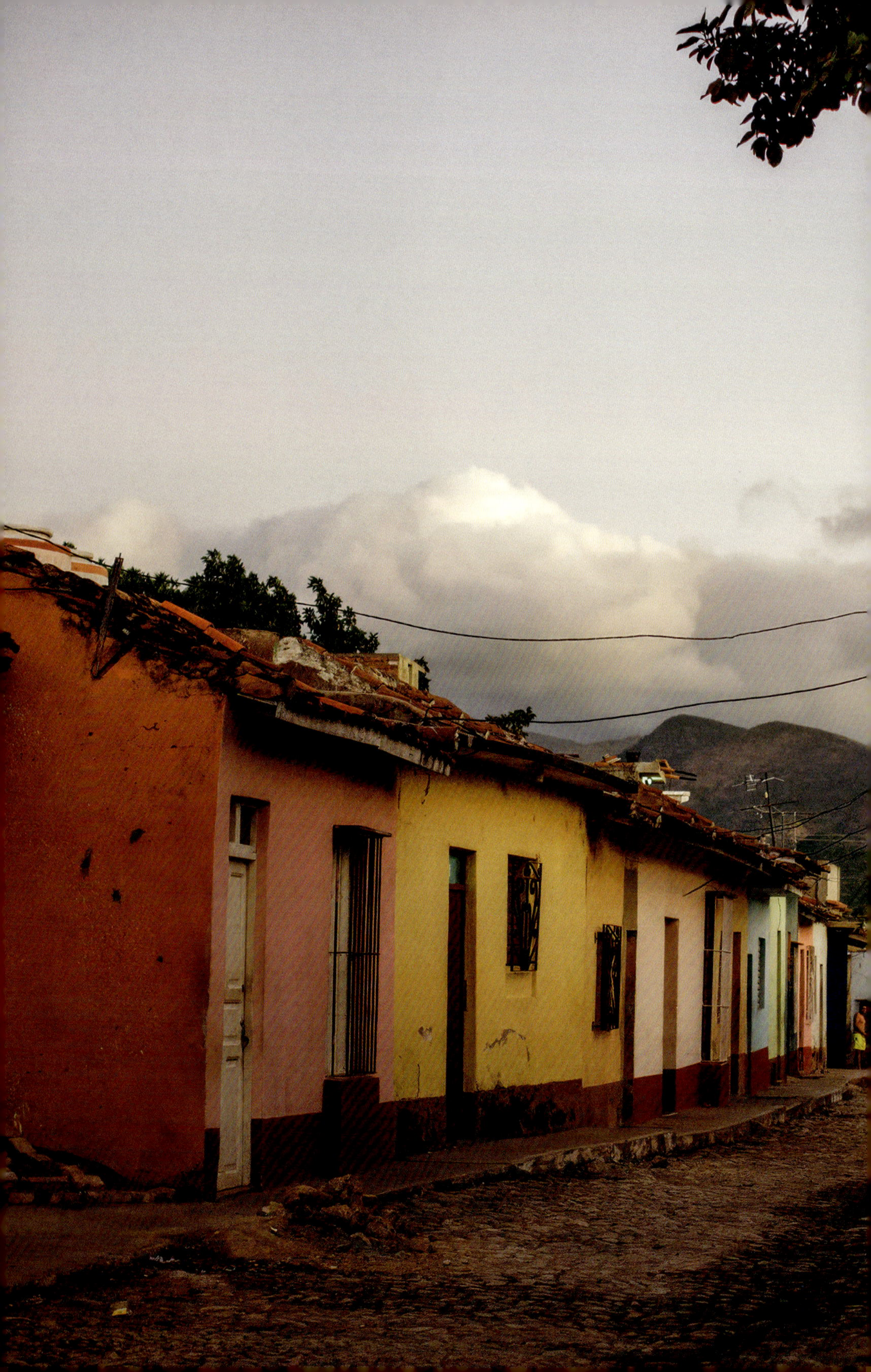

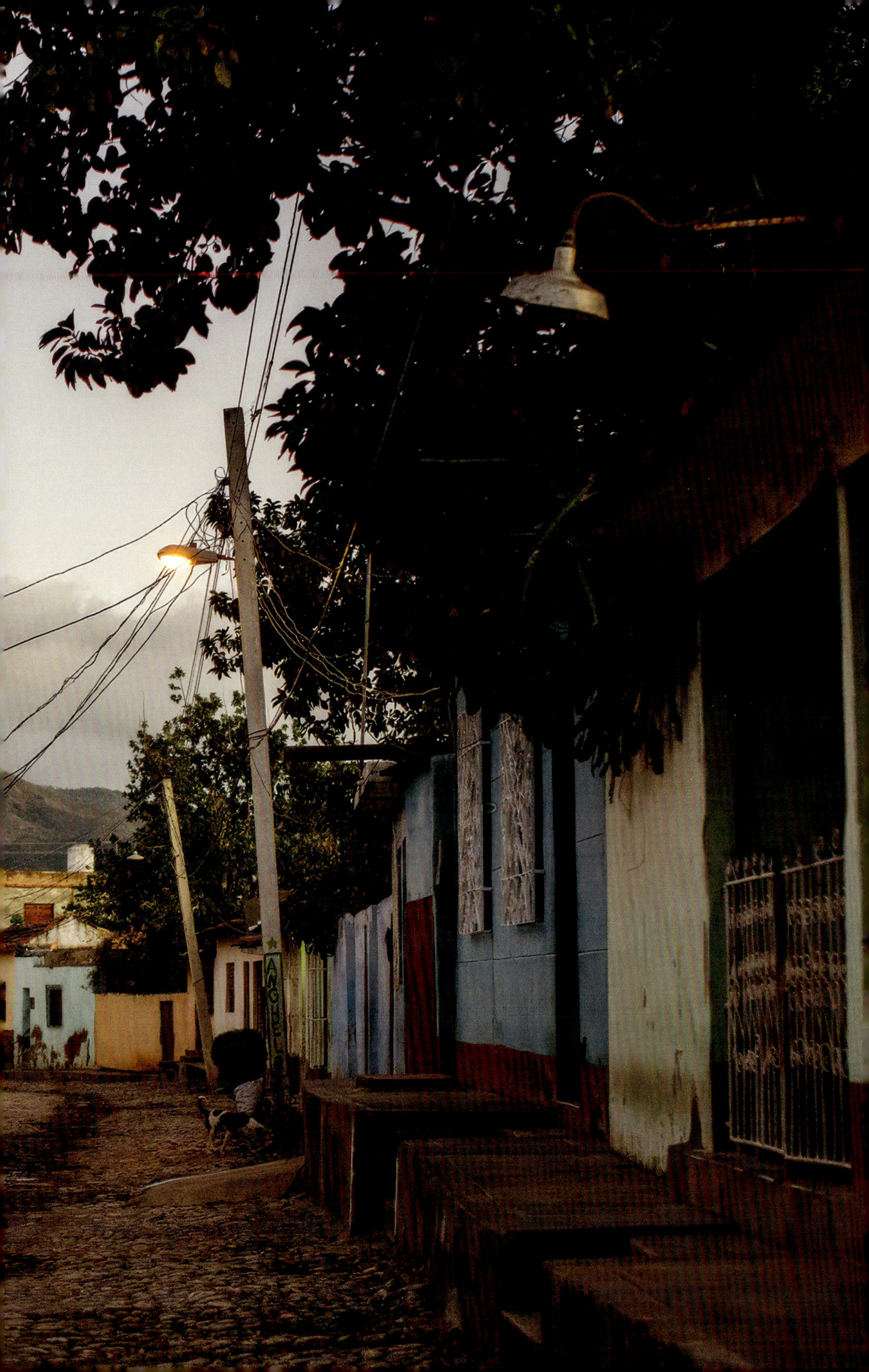

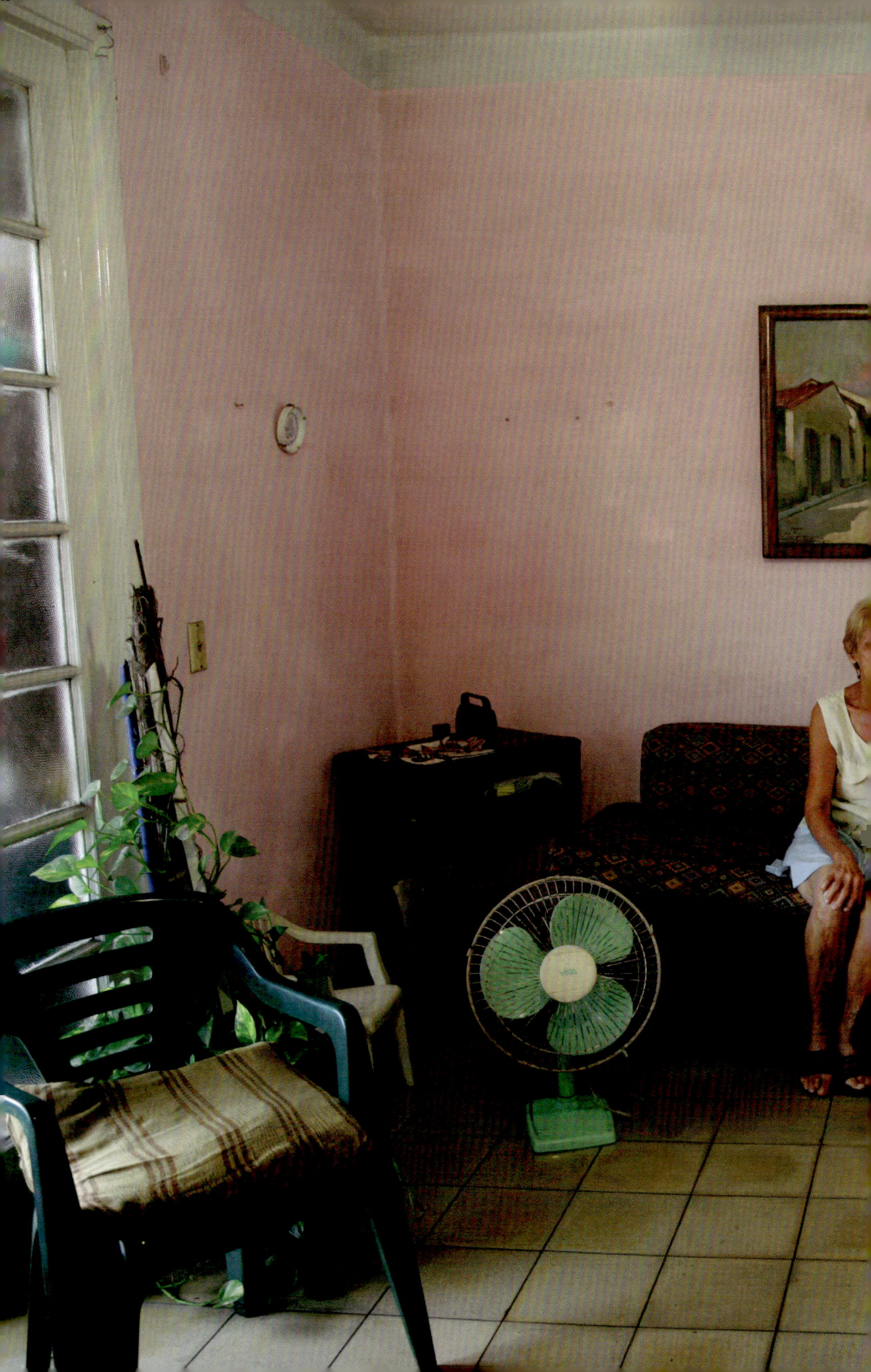

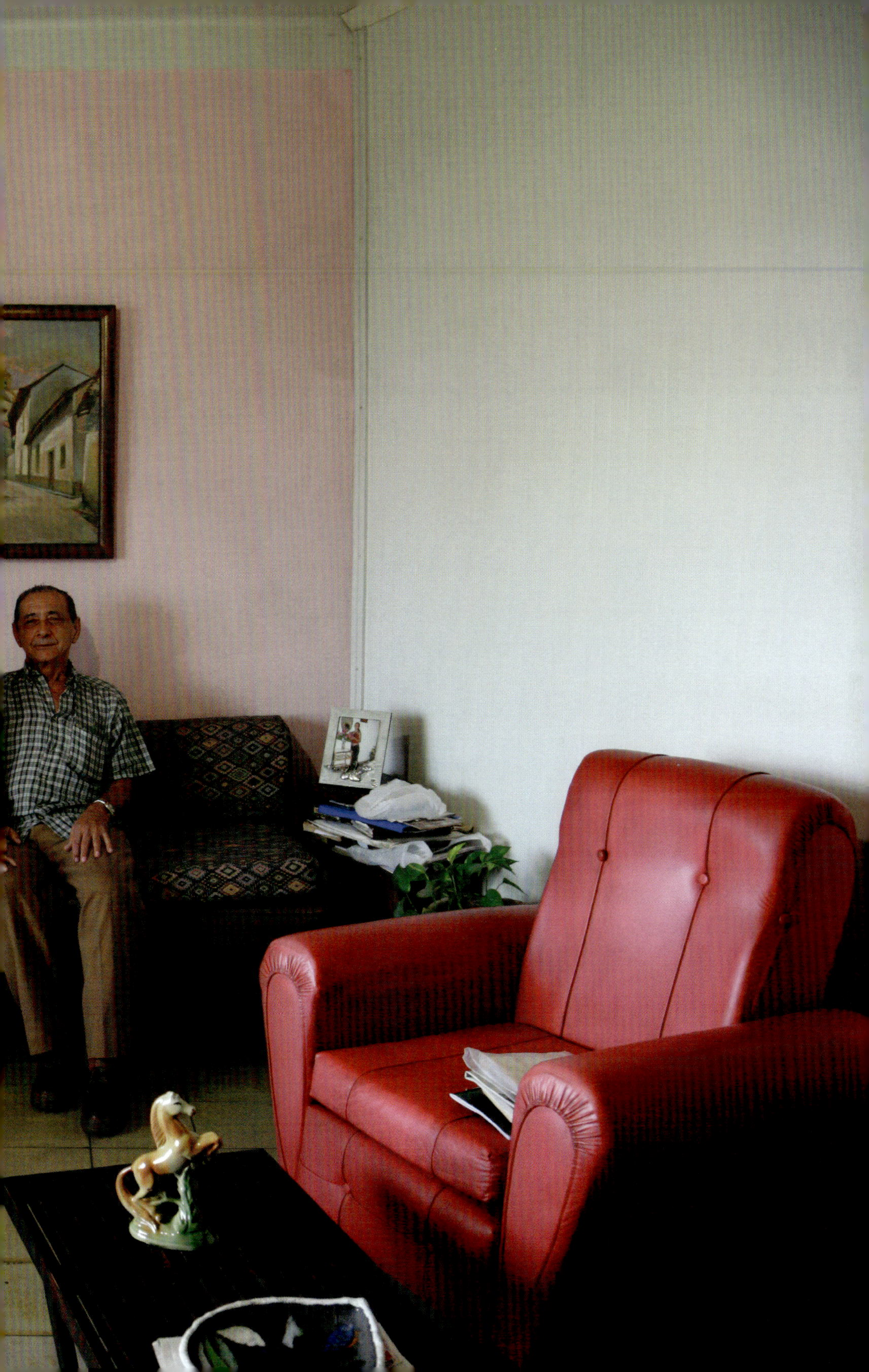

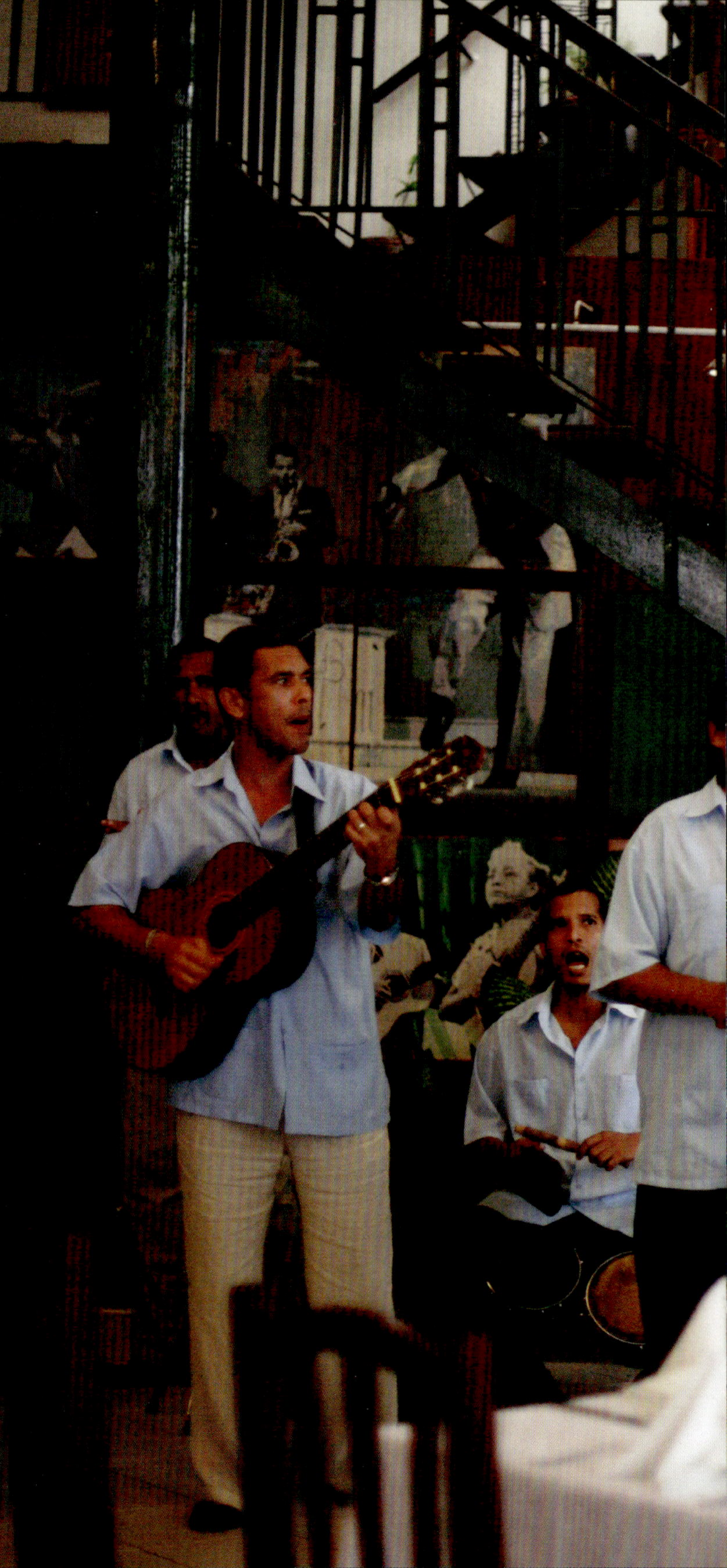

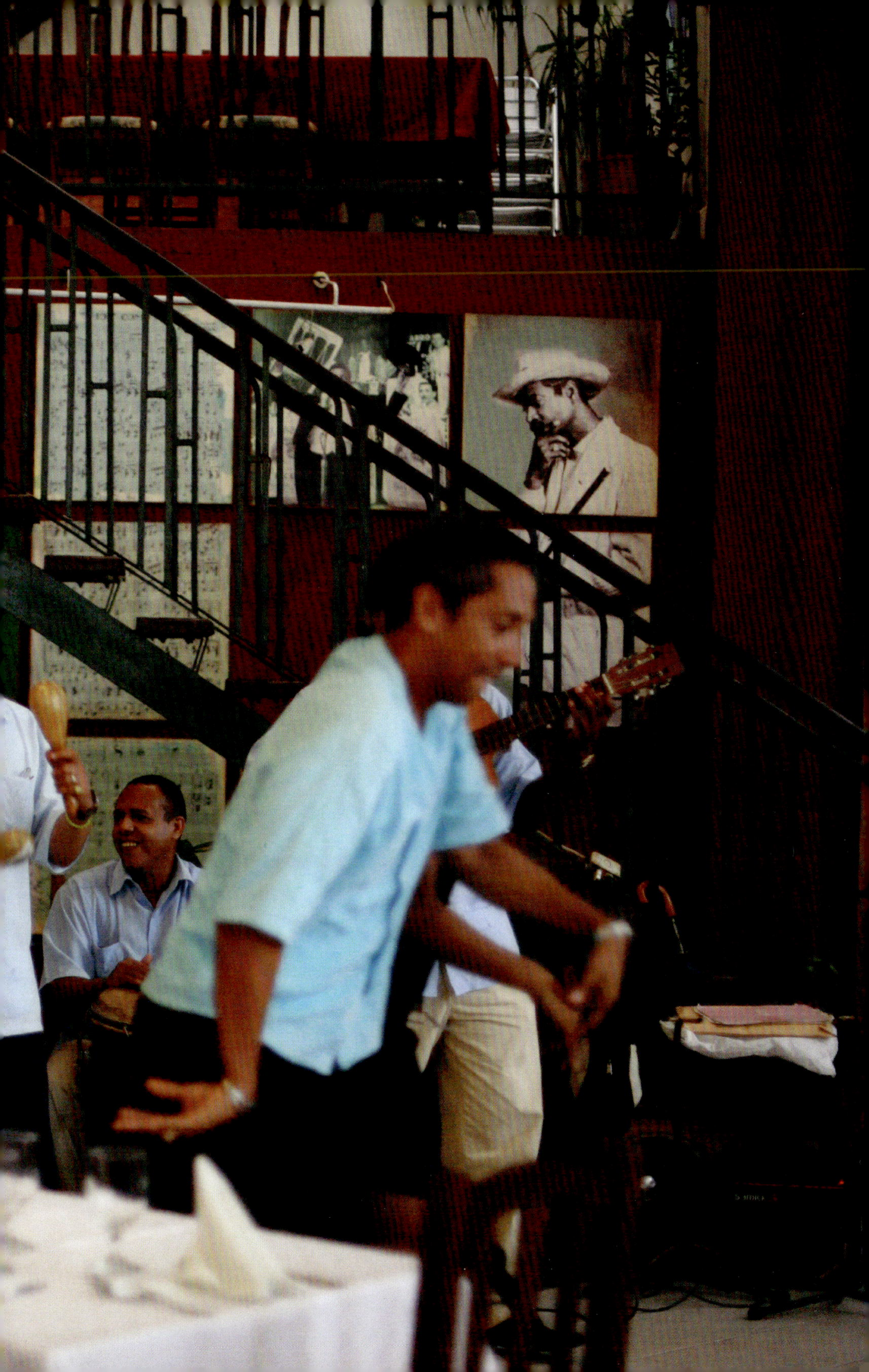

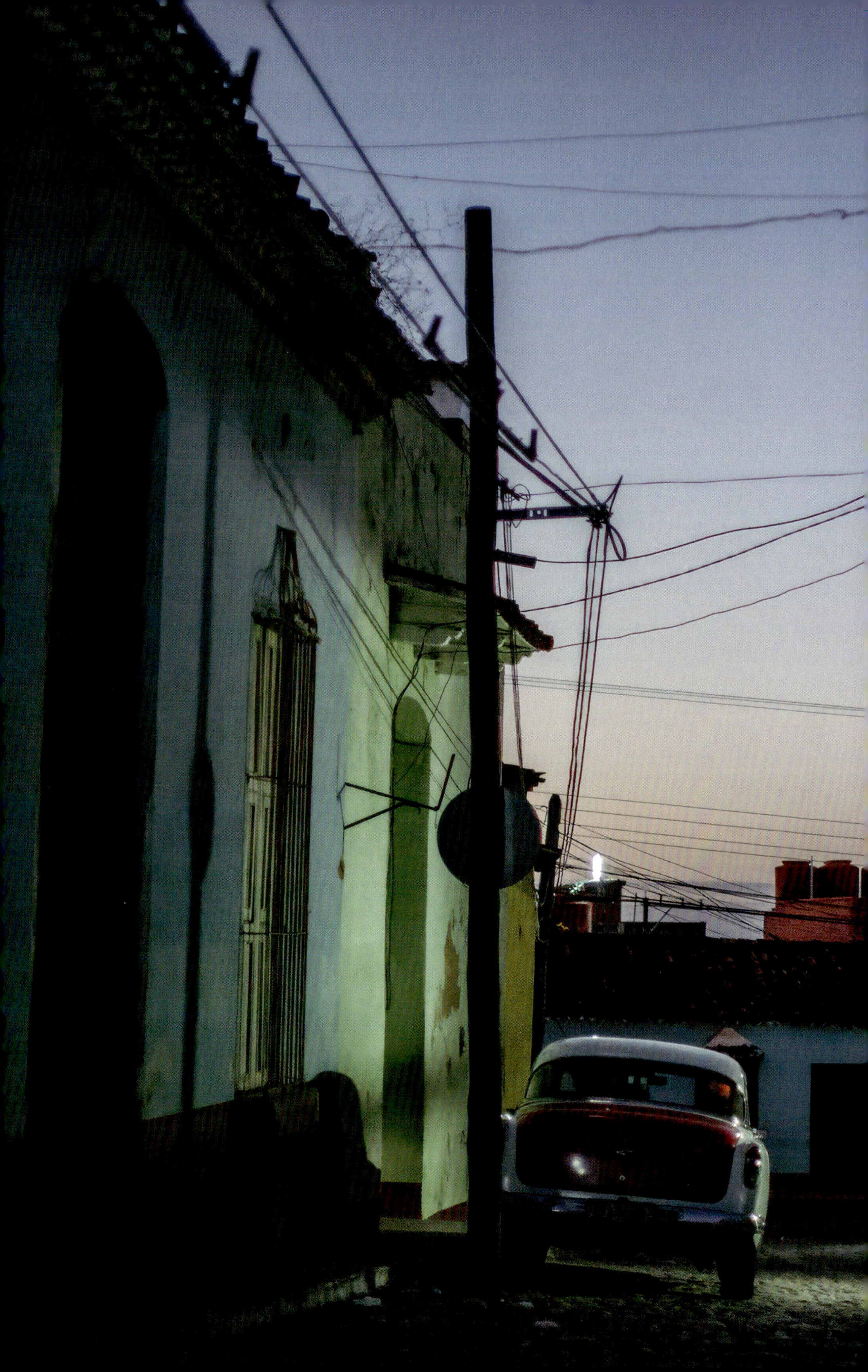

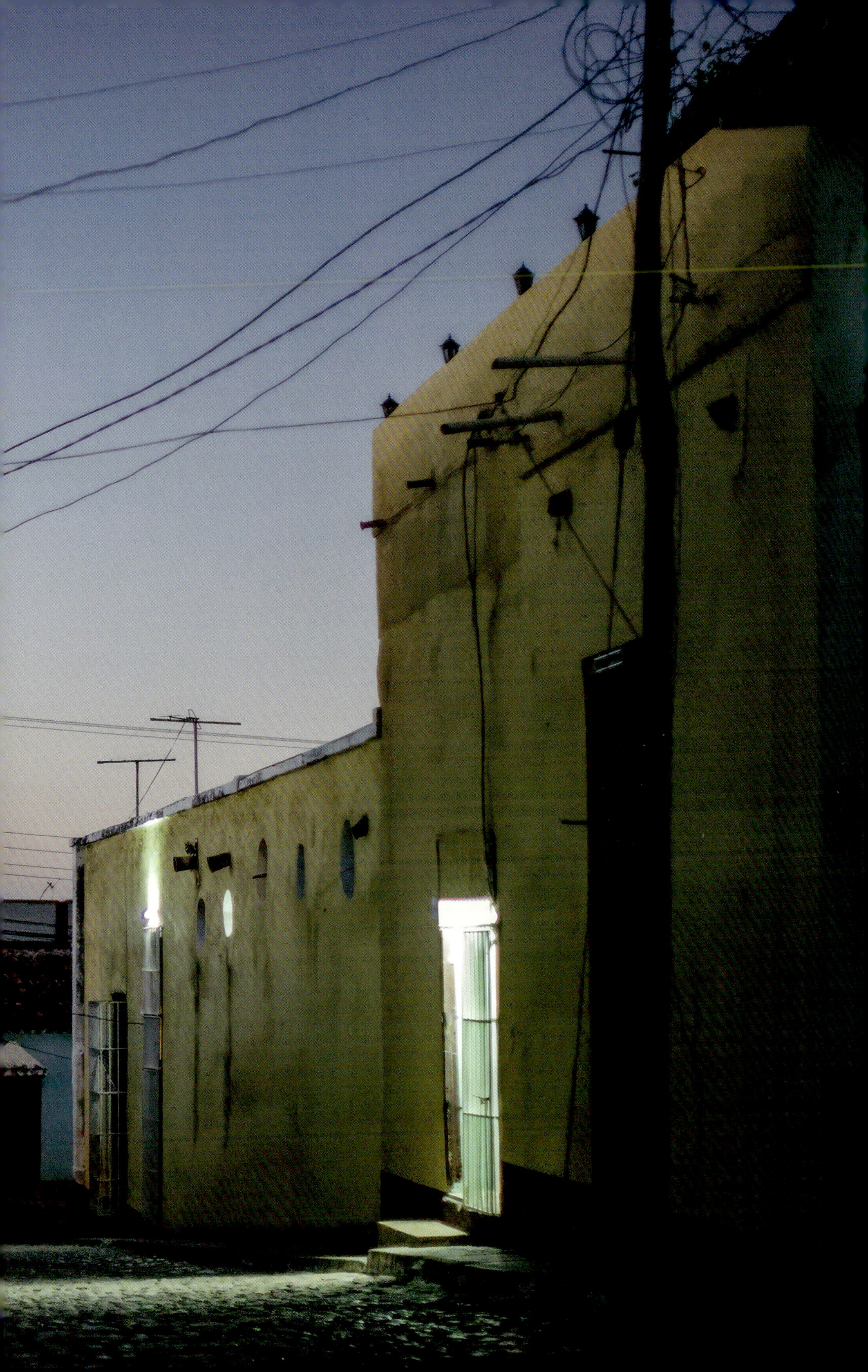

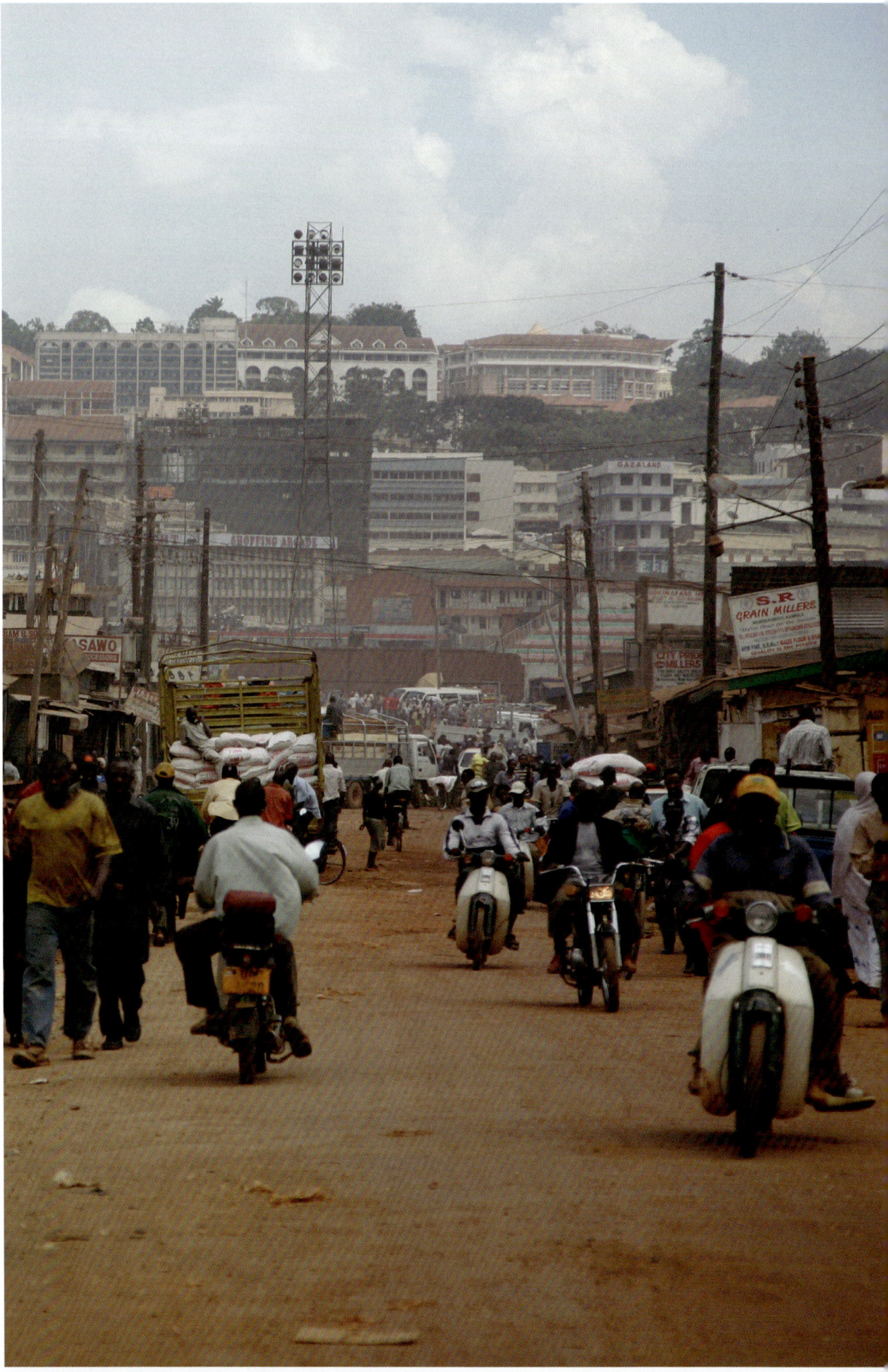
S.R
GRAIN MILLERS

Uganda

In fall 2007, fresh off the clandestine trip to Cuba, trying to get my photography career off the ground, I saw a workshop called something like "Learn How to Photograph International NGOs in Kampala, Uganda," and knew I had to go. Terrified as always but determined as ever, I signed up, and on December 7, 2007, I landed in Kampala.

The last time I had been on the African continent was five years earlier in Tanzania, where we had to boil water for food and bathing, shit in a hole, and walk a mile to an internet café. Kampala felt "downright modern in comparison," I wrote to my mom in an email sent from my pretty luxurious hotel room on the first afternoon. Kampala is green and lush, with tree leaves so big and lilies so orange that I made twelve *Jurassic Park* references that first day. It's also *very* crowded: 1.5 million people live in that town—about the same population as Manhattan, but one-third the size—so it's absolutely overflowing with humanity and traffic.

On the first day I arrived in Kampala—before the photography workshop officially started—I asked the hotel manager where I should go to photograph the people of the city. He wrote "Owino Market" on a piece of paper and told me how to walk there. With over 50,000 vendors crammed into twenty acres, Owino Market is a masterpiece of commerce and chaos. It is the crown jewel of Kampala, not to mention a photographer's dream.

More than 300,000 people shop at Owino Market every single day, and it would have taken weeks to comprehend the dizzying display of plywood shanties selling everything anyone could possibly need to survive. Gorgeous women wrapped in bright sarongs shucked beans into red plastic bowls next to their fathers who peddled spices imported from Asia. Walls of fresh produce in every color of the rainbow stood ten feet high, and the women standing in front of it laughed at the sight of me. Thousands of yards of stacked fabric formed shady forts where dozens of women napped in the heat. A teenager sold baby carriages and all the supplies you'd need to clean a house. His grandfather roasted maize beside him. A man crossed the street with forty-eight raw eggs balanced on his head just as two kids raced motorbikes through the crowd and no one even noticed.

Totally inspired and completely overwhelmed, I brought my camera to my face and began photographing through the awkwardness. Street photography has a gut-wrenching mix of nervousness and exhilaration for me. Taking someone's photograph on the street is legal, but it feels bold, possibly dangerous, and maybe even rude. I love doing it, though. It's one of the reasons

I've come all this way. I can travel alone without getting lonely because I have my camera with me. My camera gives me purpose.

When the workshop finally began, each of the six students spent two days photographing local organizations in Kampala that we had found on our own before we arrived. The NGO I found didn't work out the way I hoped, and the guy who ran it turned out to be a fraud. He was some Bible-thumping bullshitter from Texas who had a fish farm and wanted to feed fish to the people, he told me, just like Jesus did. I photographed him and the ten fish in his pond for an afternoon, sent him the photos, and thanked him for his time.

The best part of the workshop was when we traveled north to the town of Soroti to photograph in an Internally Displaced Persons (IDP) camp for an organization called Right to Play, an incredible organization whose mission is "to protect, educate, and empower children to rise above adversity using the power of play." These people were saints and tried so hard to help. They had a vaccine-awareness game modeled after "duck, duck, goose" that drew throngs of little kids. Their squeals and laughter broke up the hopelessness of the place and we happily chased them around the circle with our cameras.

IDP camps are like refugee camps in that they shelter and protect people displaced by life-threatening circumstances, but an internally displaced person doesn't cross a border; they find protection within their own country. Thousands of families live in this IDP camp because they were forced to flee their homes due to the longstanding violence and mutilation brought by the LRA, the Lord's Resistance Army, a rebel militia that has been terrorizing their own people in Uganda since the 1980s.

Along with photographing for Right to Play, each student was paired with a family who lived in the camp. We spent two days documenting their lives, then gave them the photographs as a small token of gratitude. I was lucky enough to photograph a family of nine with a boy named Daniel as the eldest son. Daniel, his six siblings, and their parents—who I called Mama and Papa—lived in a thatched-roof hut the size of a garden shed among thousands of other families living just like them. Photographing this family and witnessing the reality of life in an IDP camp was easily the most profound experience of my career.

Mama started her day at dawn, walking a half hour to a barely-there river to scrape its bottom for water. With one bucket on her head and more in each hand she walked back to her family, humming the same tunes she sang in church. Along the way we passed a young woman sitting on the ground breastfeeding twins, one on each breast, in front of a man with elephantiasis selling goat heads from a chair. A gang of children, twenty deep, chased a little girl with clubfoot as she stumbled past a toddler cradling her newborn sister in her arms. Soccer balls made of socks, rags, and garbage bags were kicked around all morning, and discarded inner tubes of old bike tires became hula hoops and jump ropes. Mama smeared a paste of cow dung over the floor of her hut to protect it from snakes. A woman walked to church in a turquoise prom dress. The priest, an hour late the Sunday I was there, promised a hundred people gathered in a hut that their next life would be better than the one they were living now. Heart-wrenching, beautiful, horrifying, inspiring—life in the IDP camp in Soroti was raw.

After two days photographing Mama's family, it was time to go back to Kampala. As each volunteer piled into the bus after saying goodbye to their families Daniel pulled me aside out of earshot of his parents. In perfect English—learned when there was still a primary school for him to attend—he said to me, "Christmas is coming, and we have no money. Can you please give me anything you can spare so I can buy my family presents? We have nothing."

We were advised, repeatedly, to not give or promise money or gifts in any way. We were told that a family with money and toys in a sea of others who have nothing is unsafe—a gesture like this would cause more pain than healing. Heartbroken, I apologized and told him I couldn't help. Daniel did not say a single word in response. Instead, he broke down sobbing, turned around, and walked away.

Seeing smart, strong, and resourceful people suffer so much due to no fault of their own is a humbling and humanizing experience. I realize that so much of the ease and success of my life is because I was born when and where I was born, no more deserving, just lucky. I'm so grateful that the people I met in Uganda let me into their lives, into the heart of an existence so drastically different than mine. They have changed me forever.

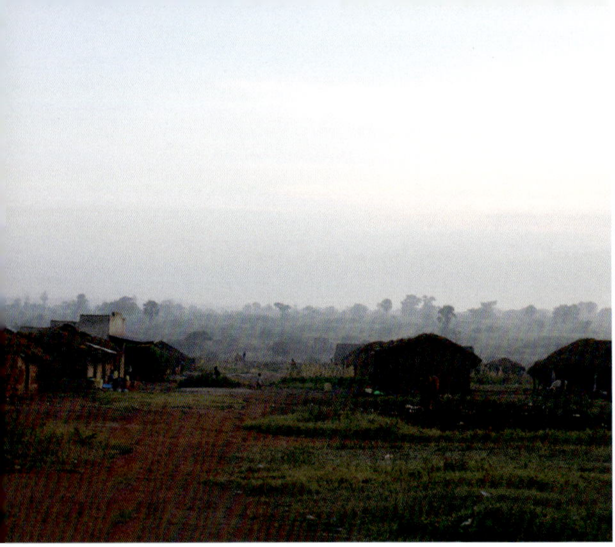
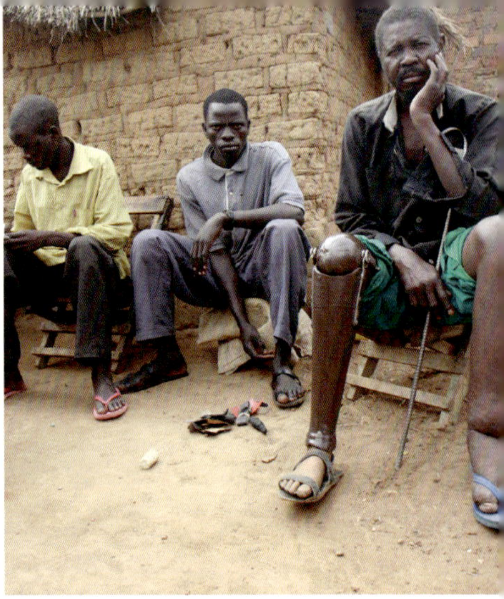
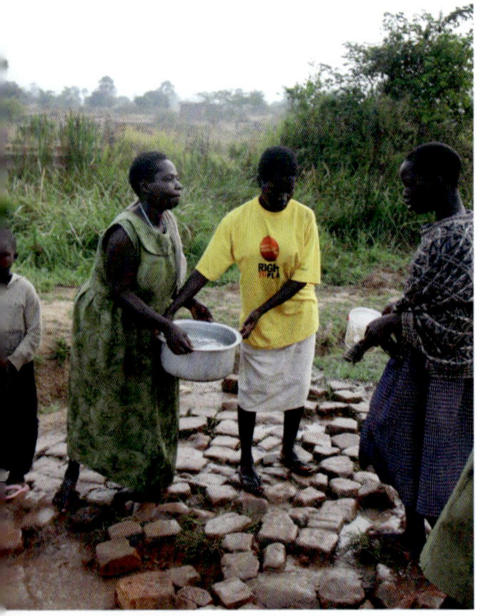
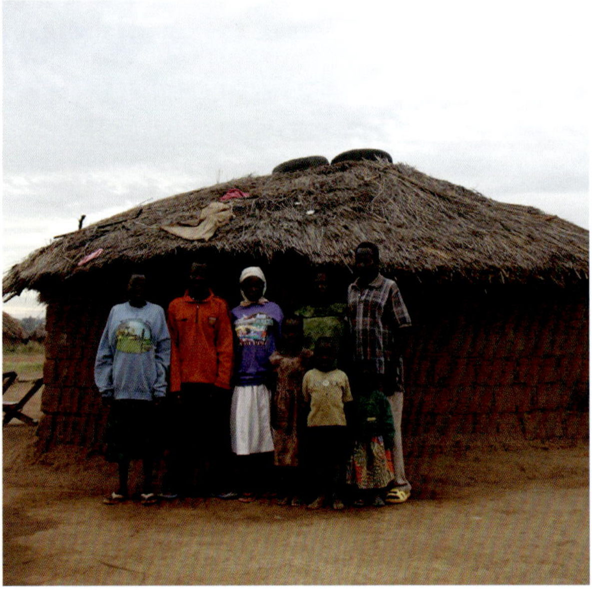
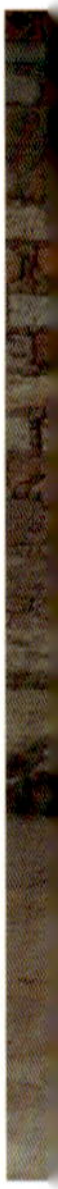
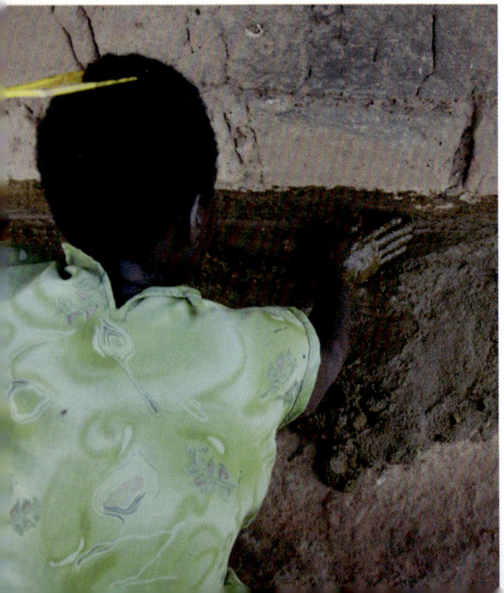
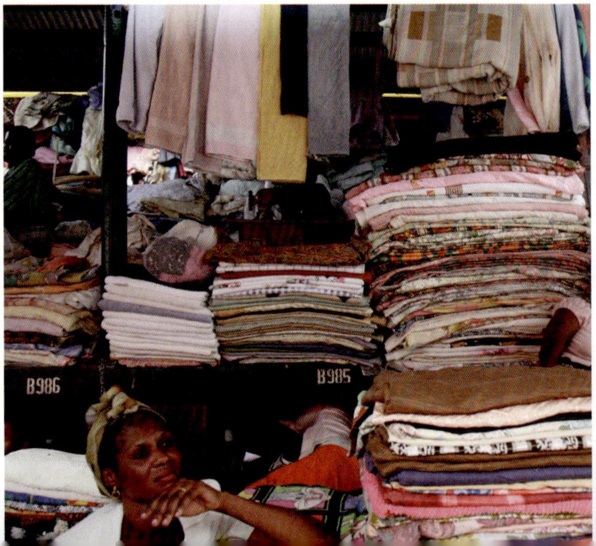
B986
B985

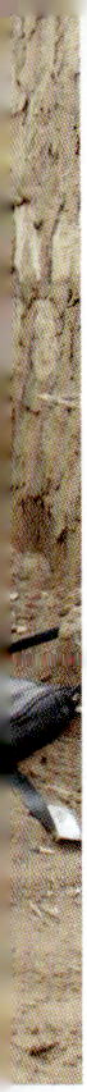
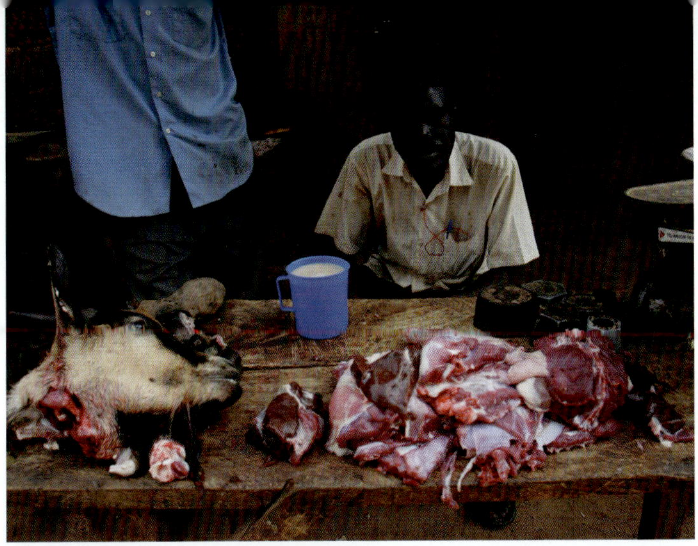
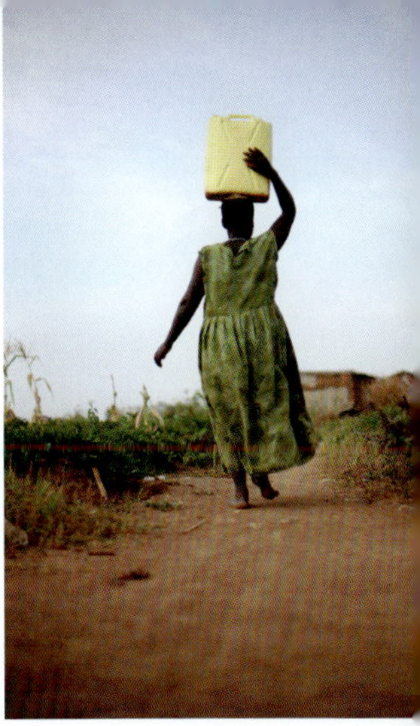
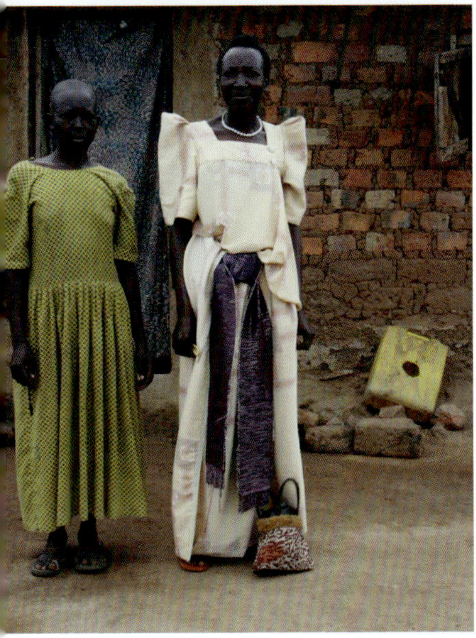
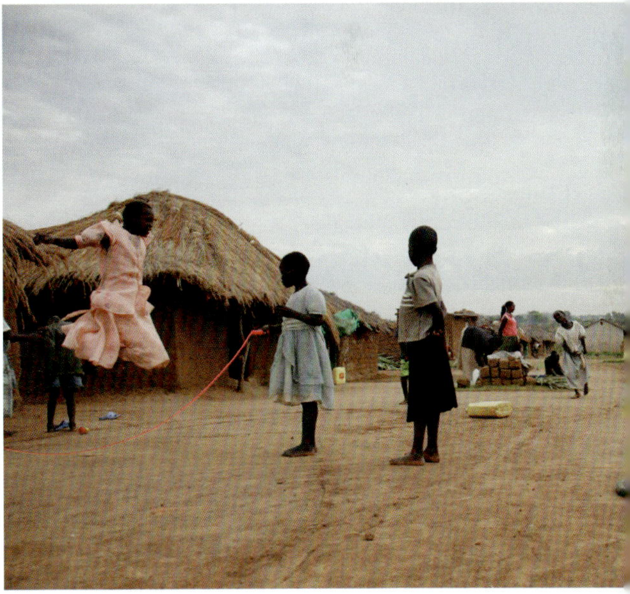
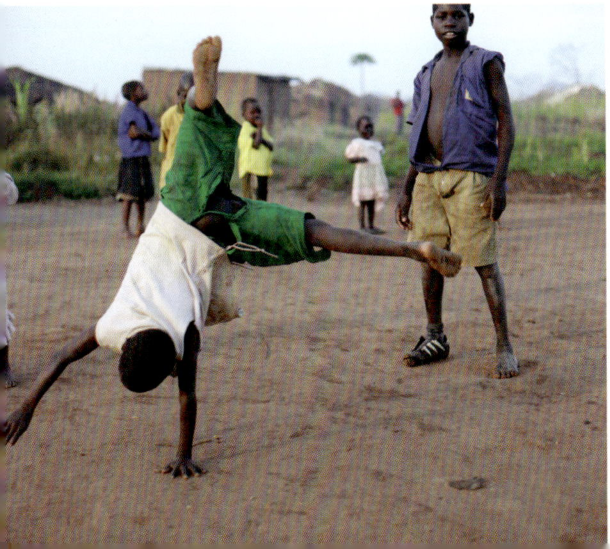
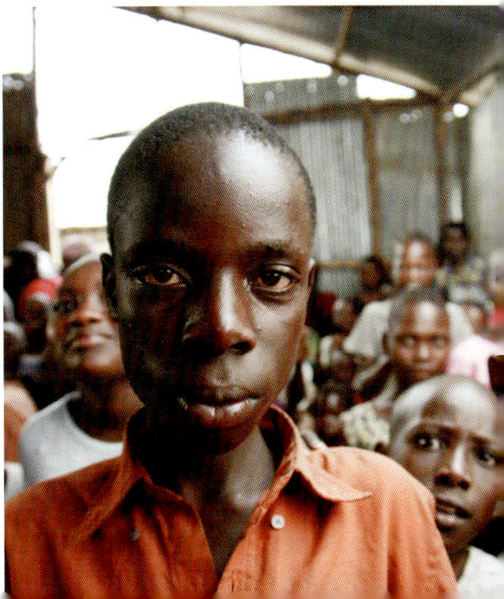

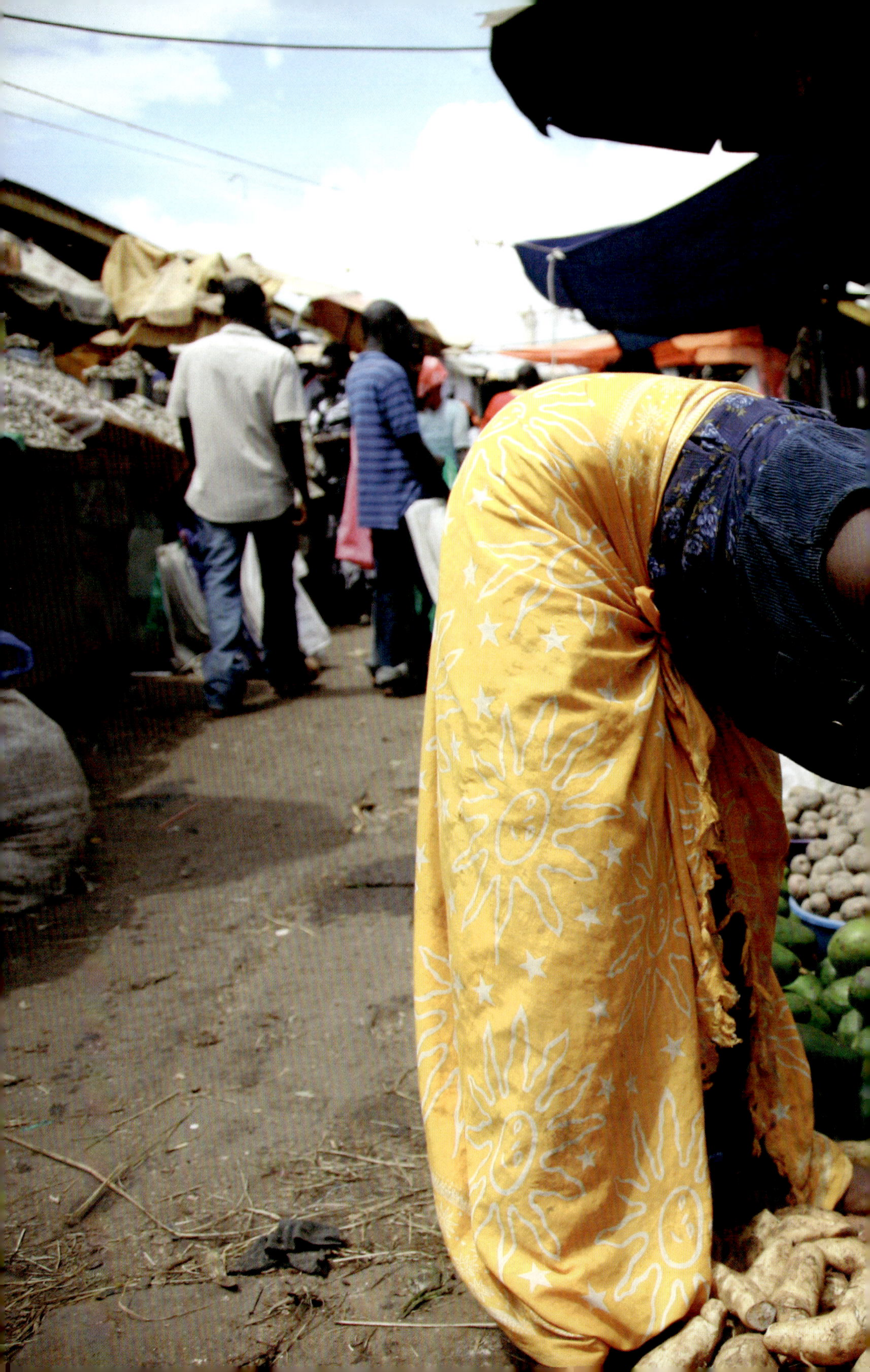

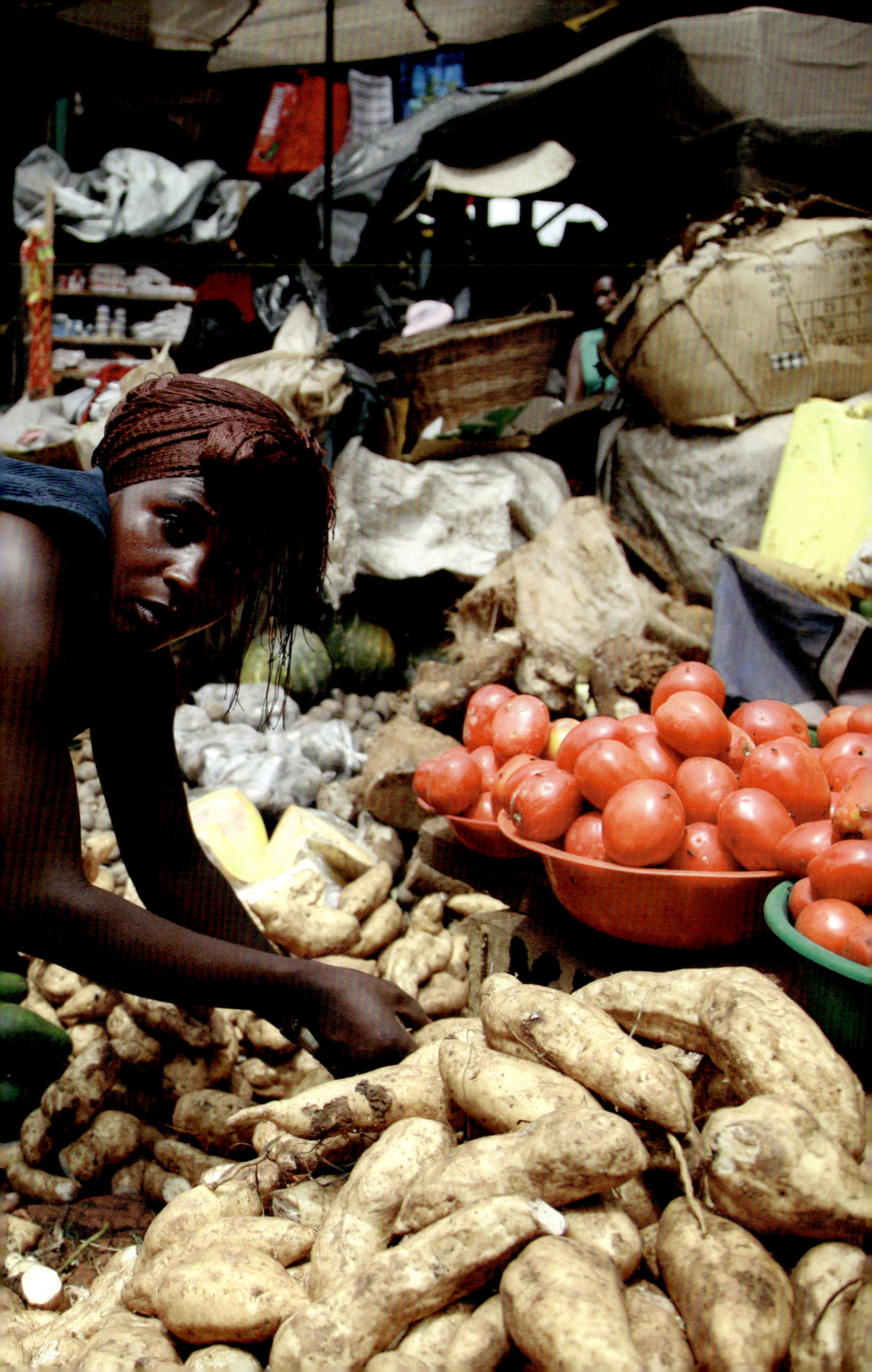

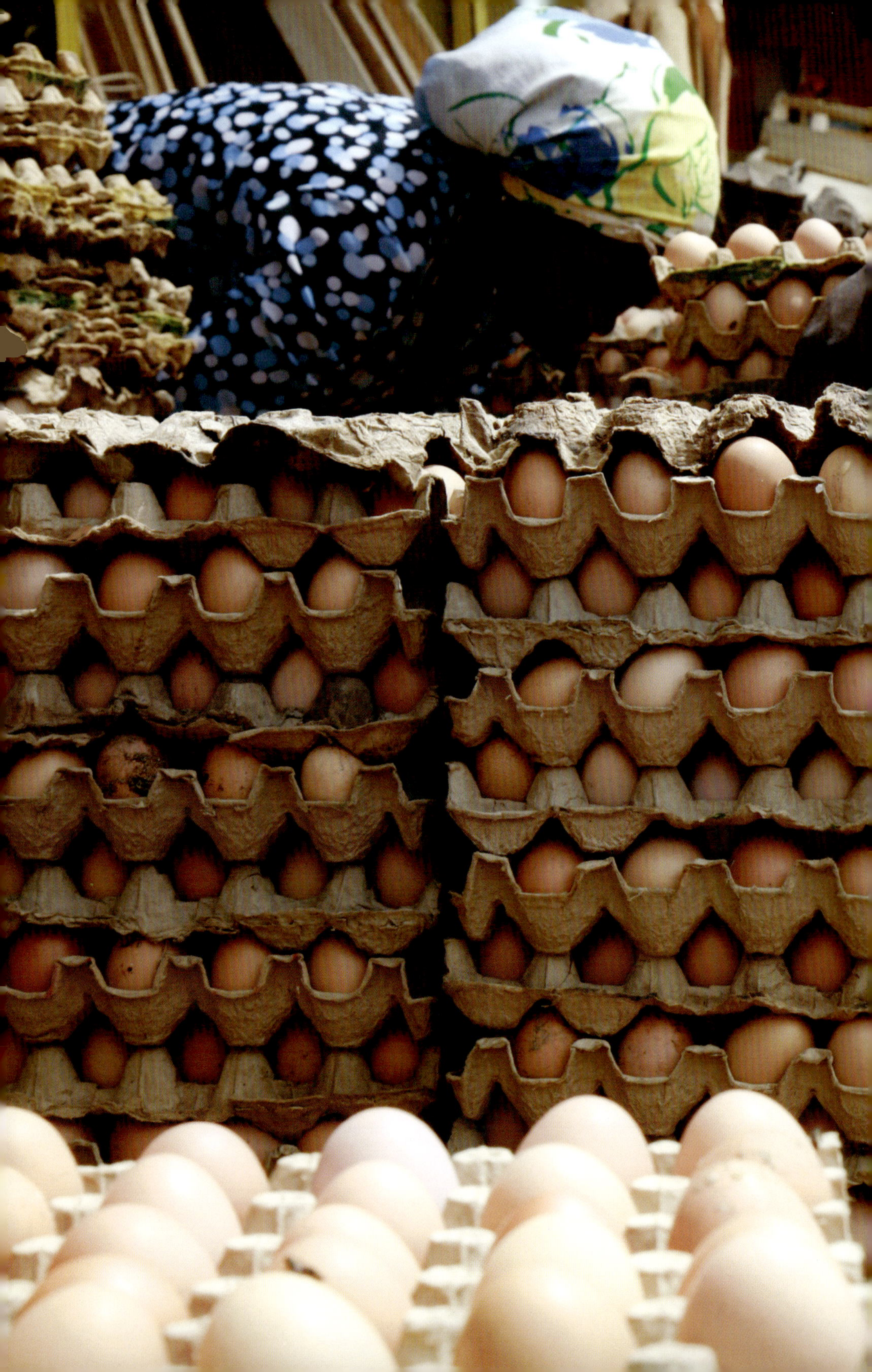

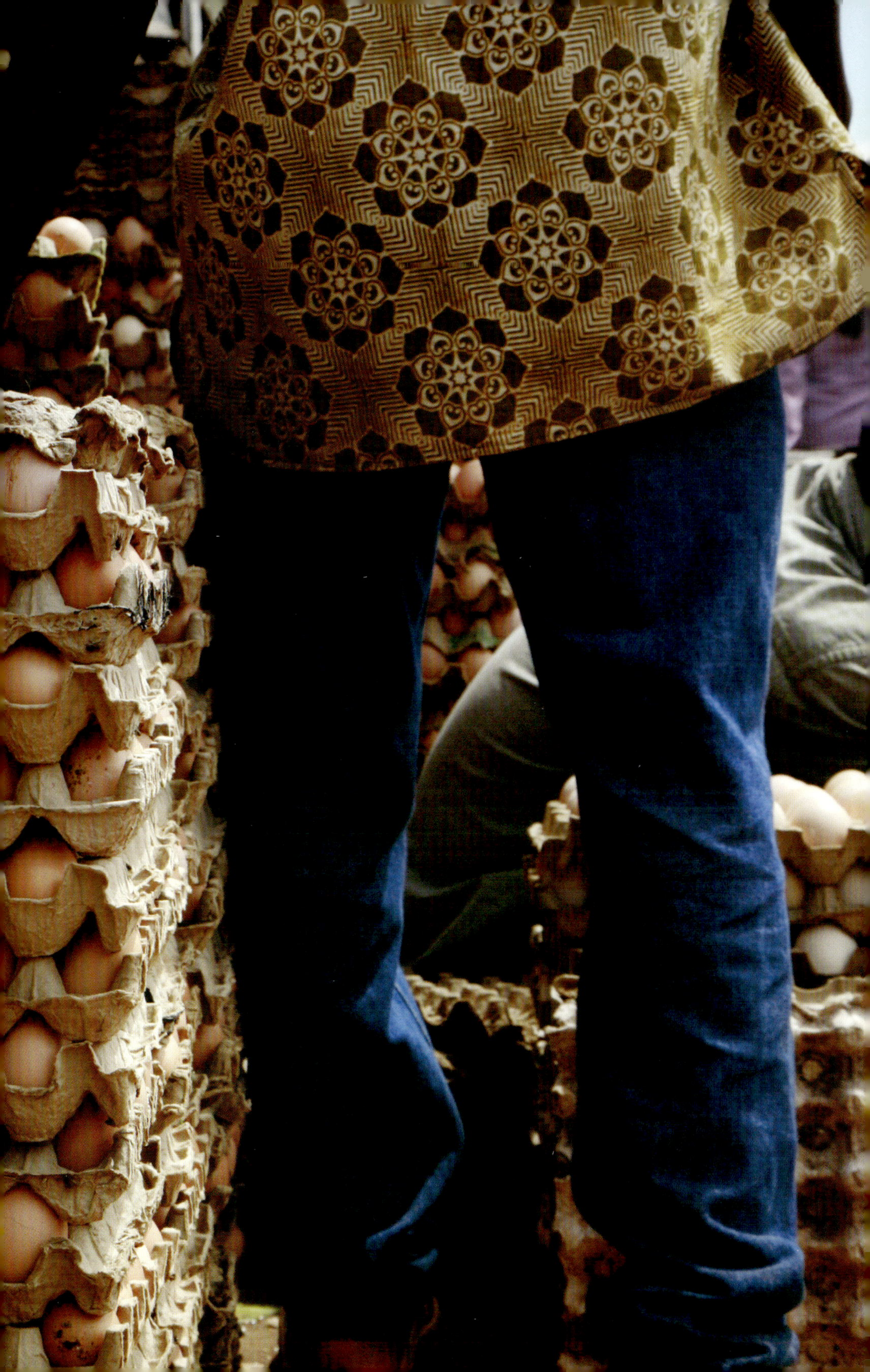

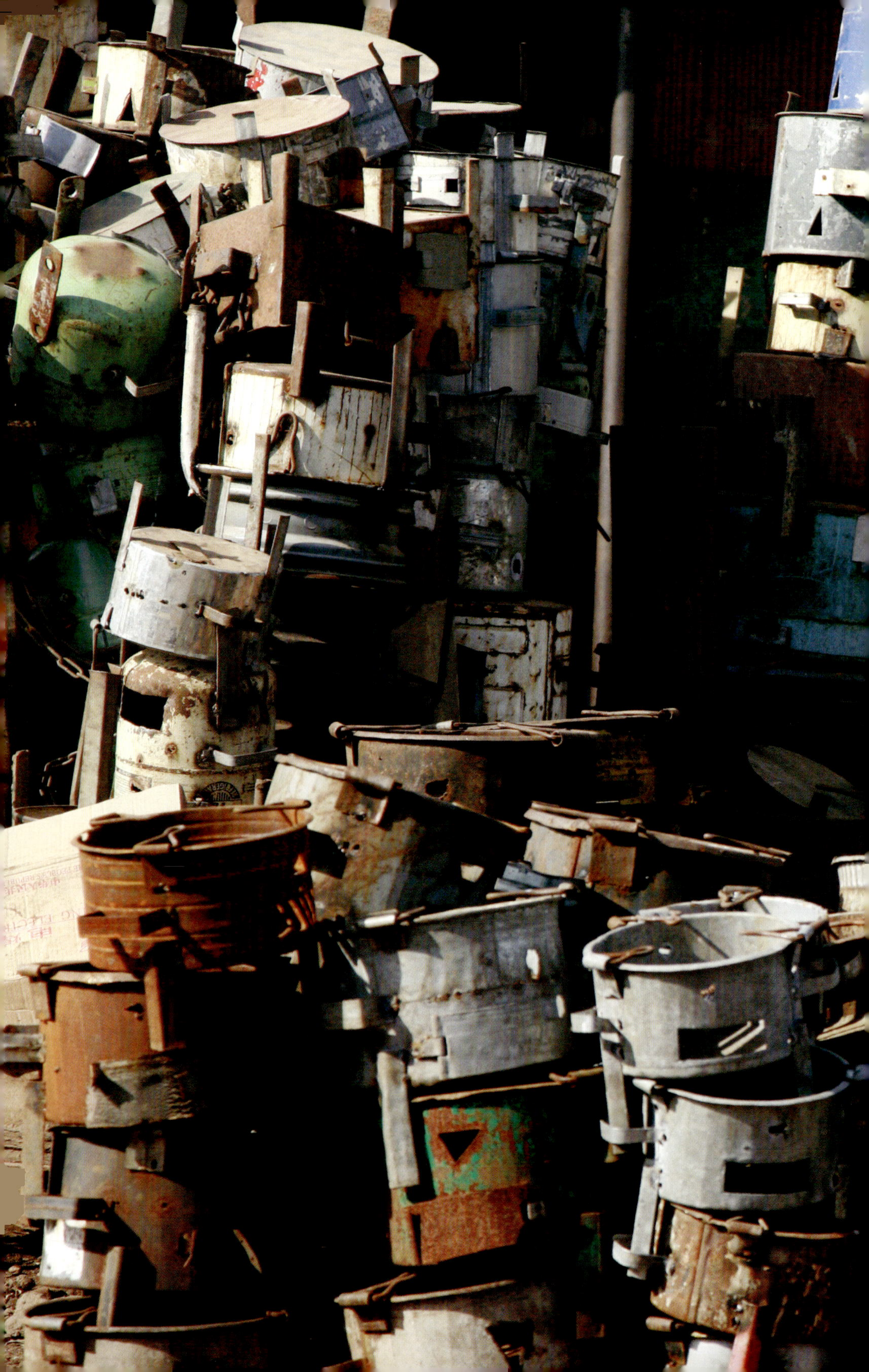

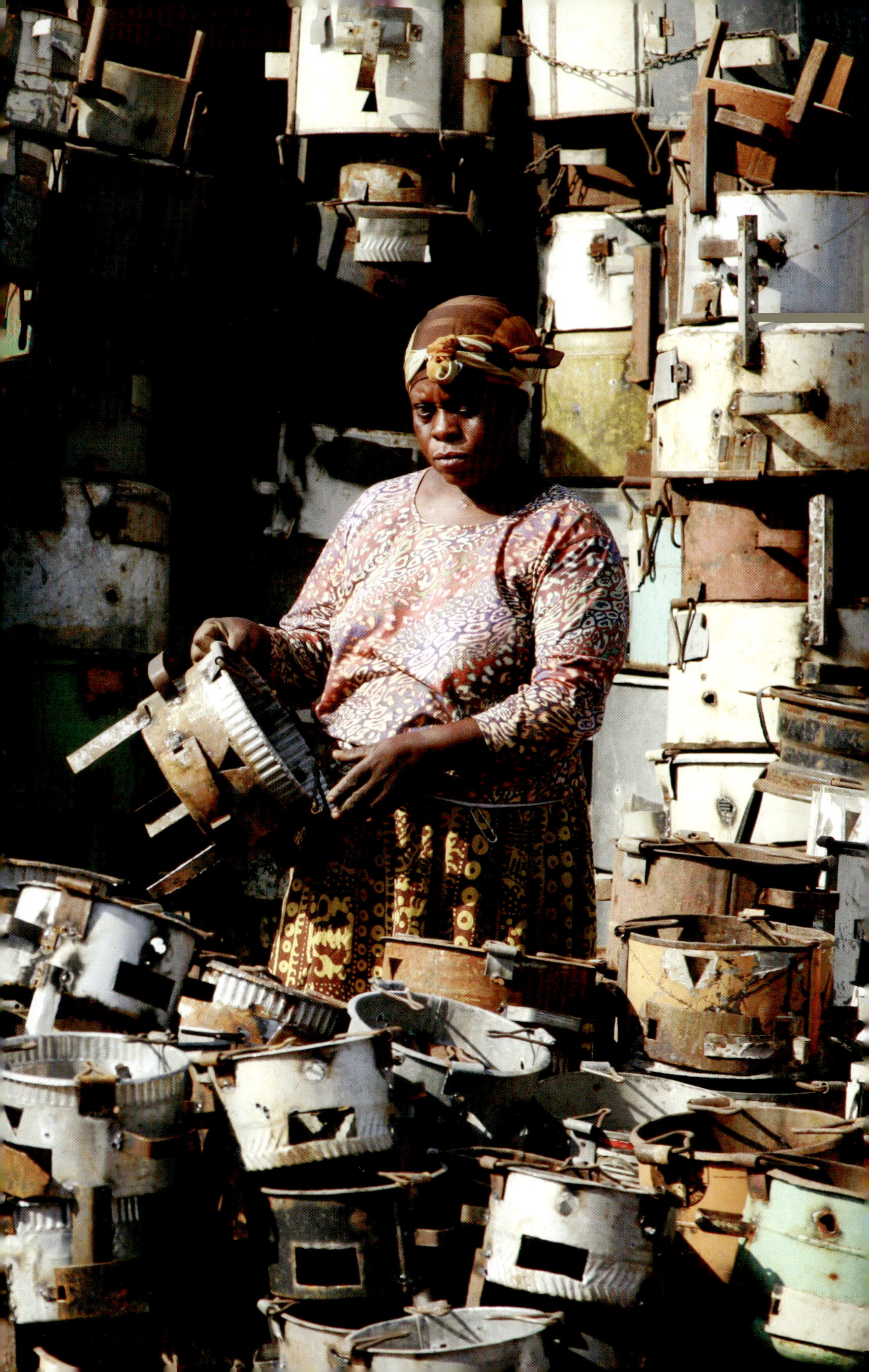

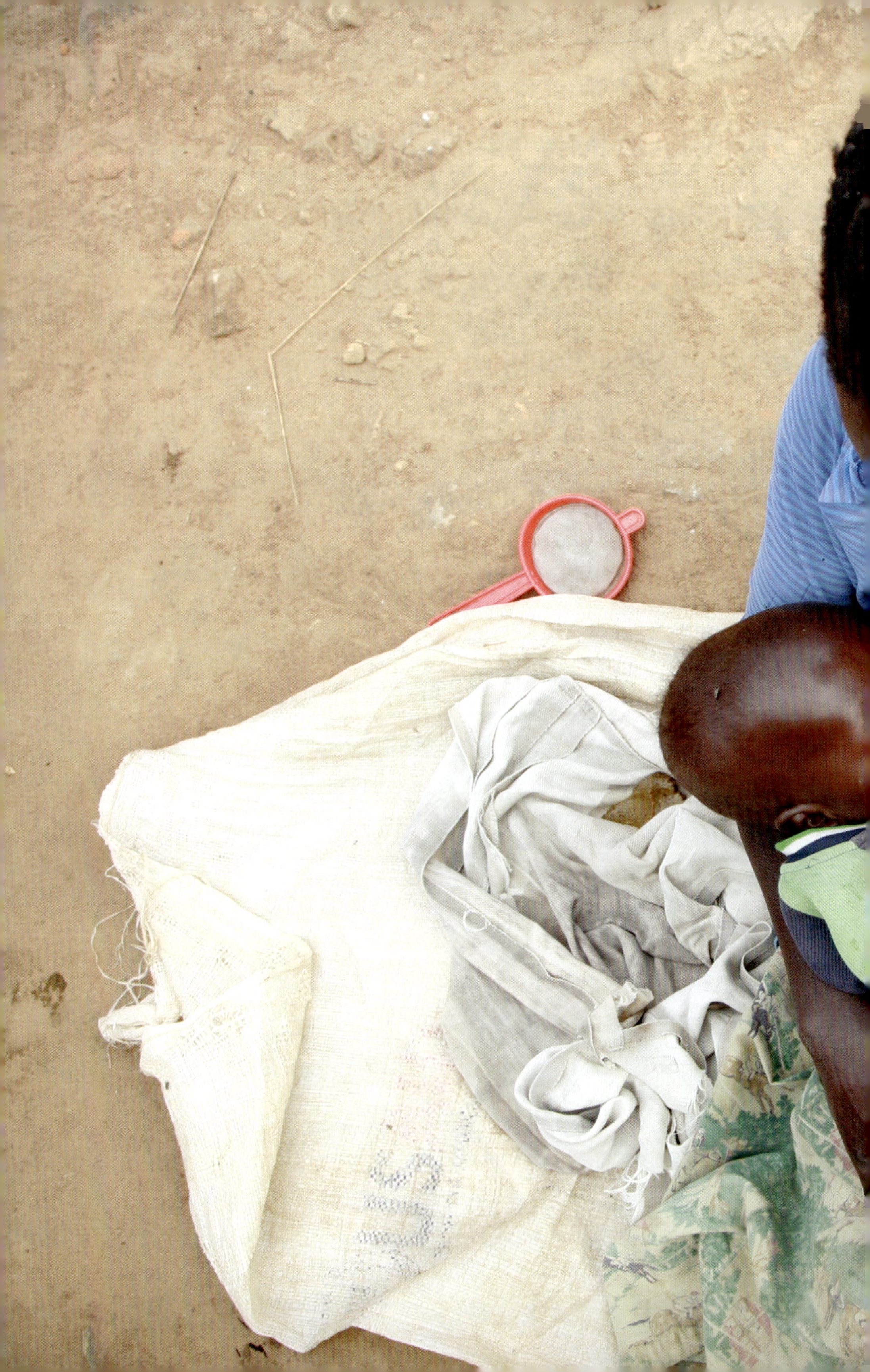

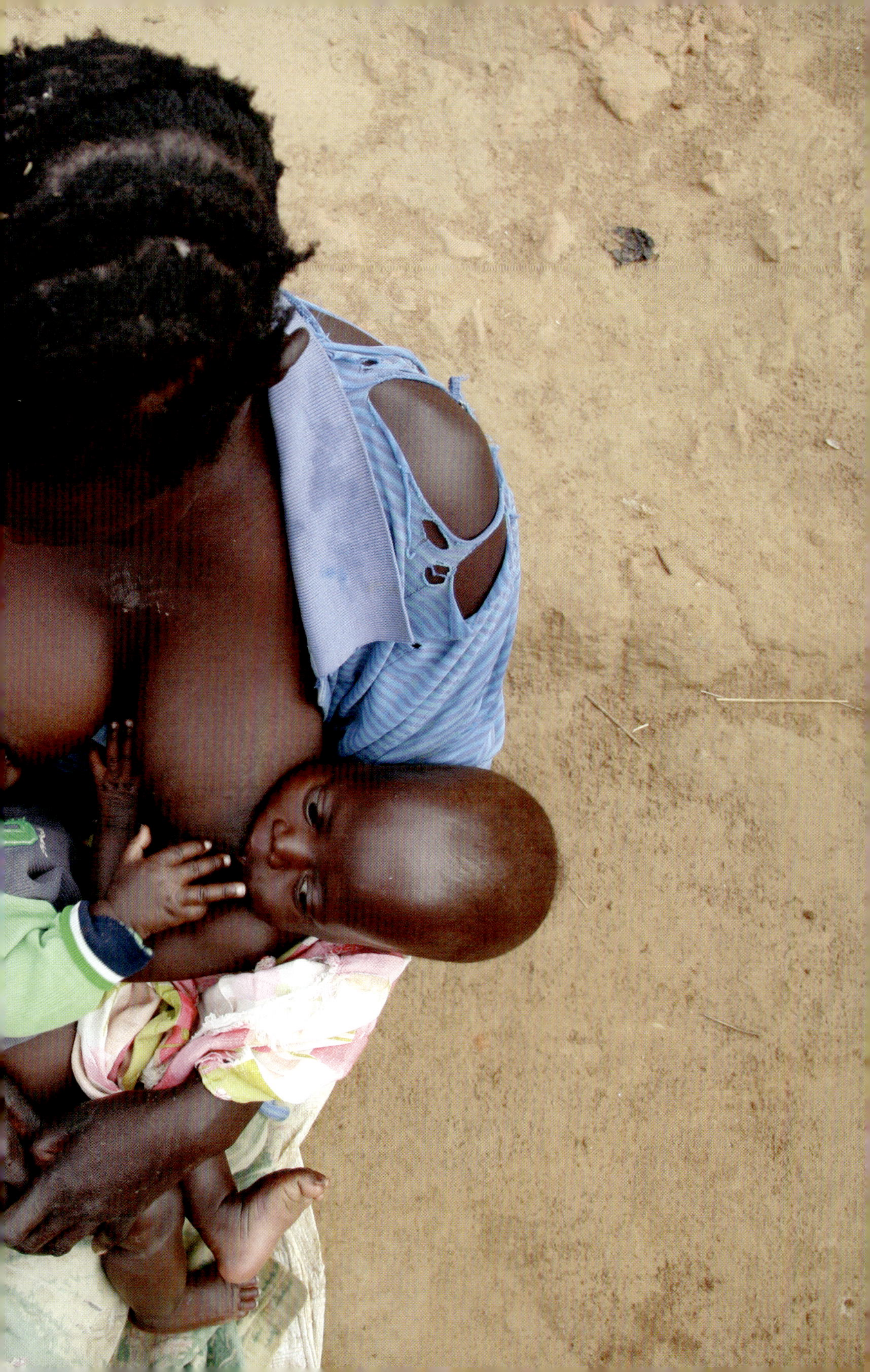

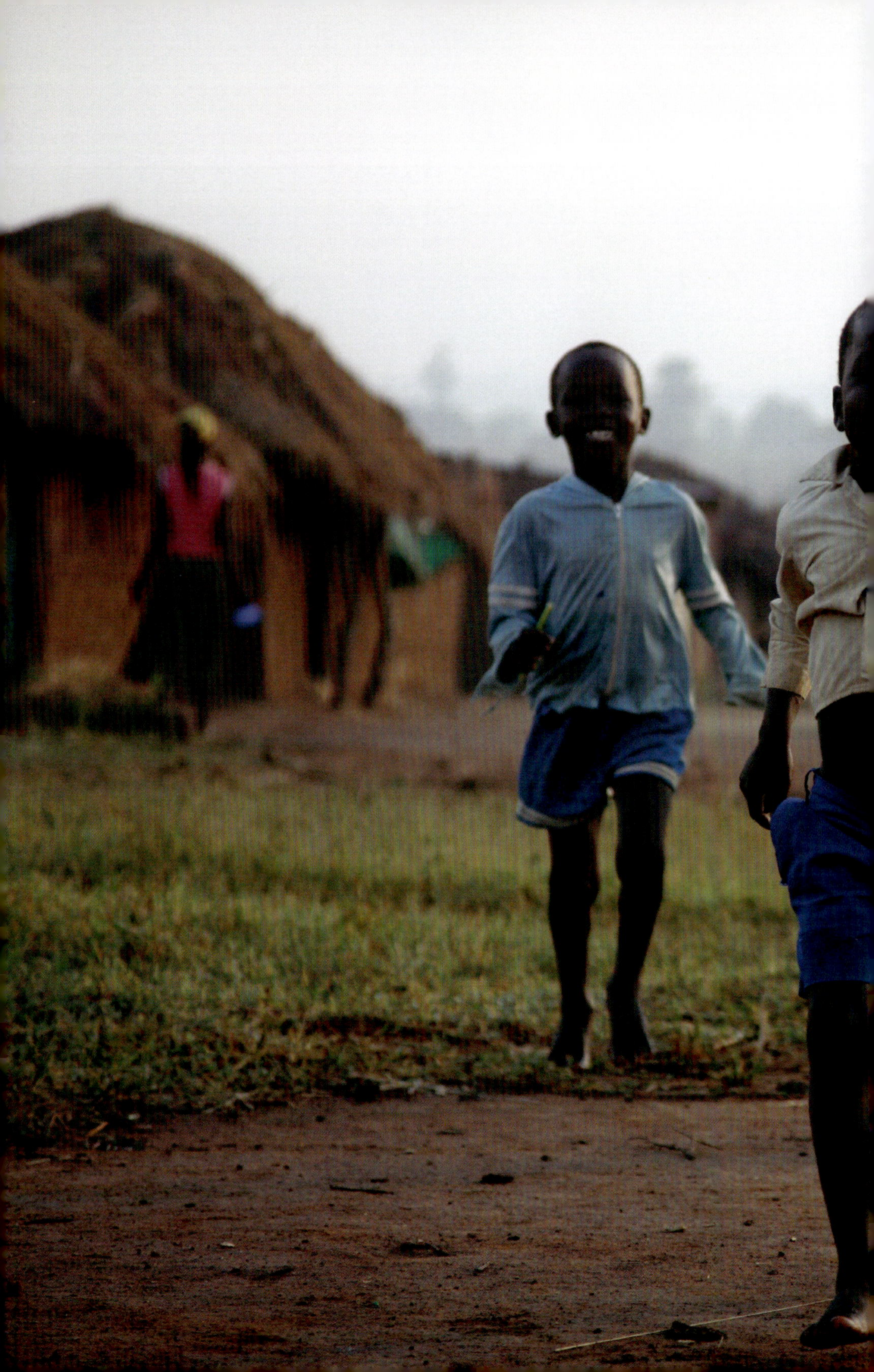

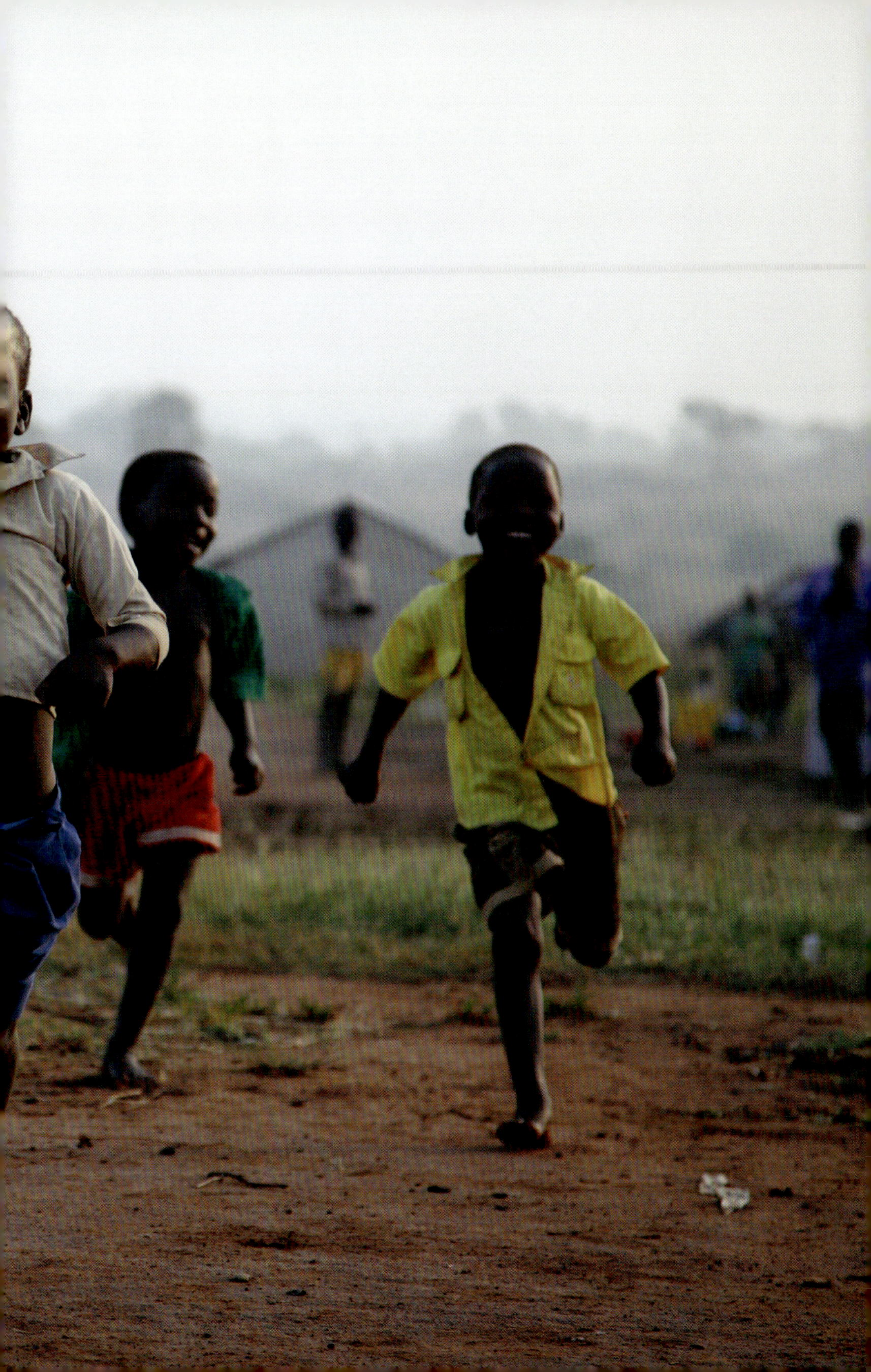

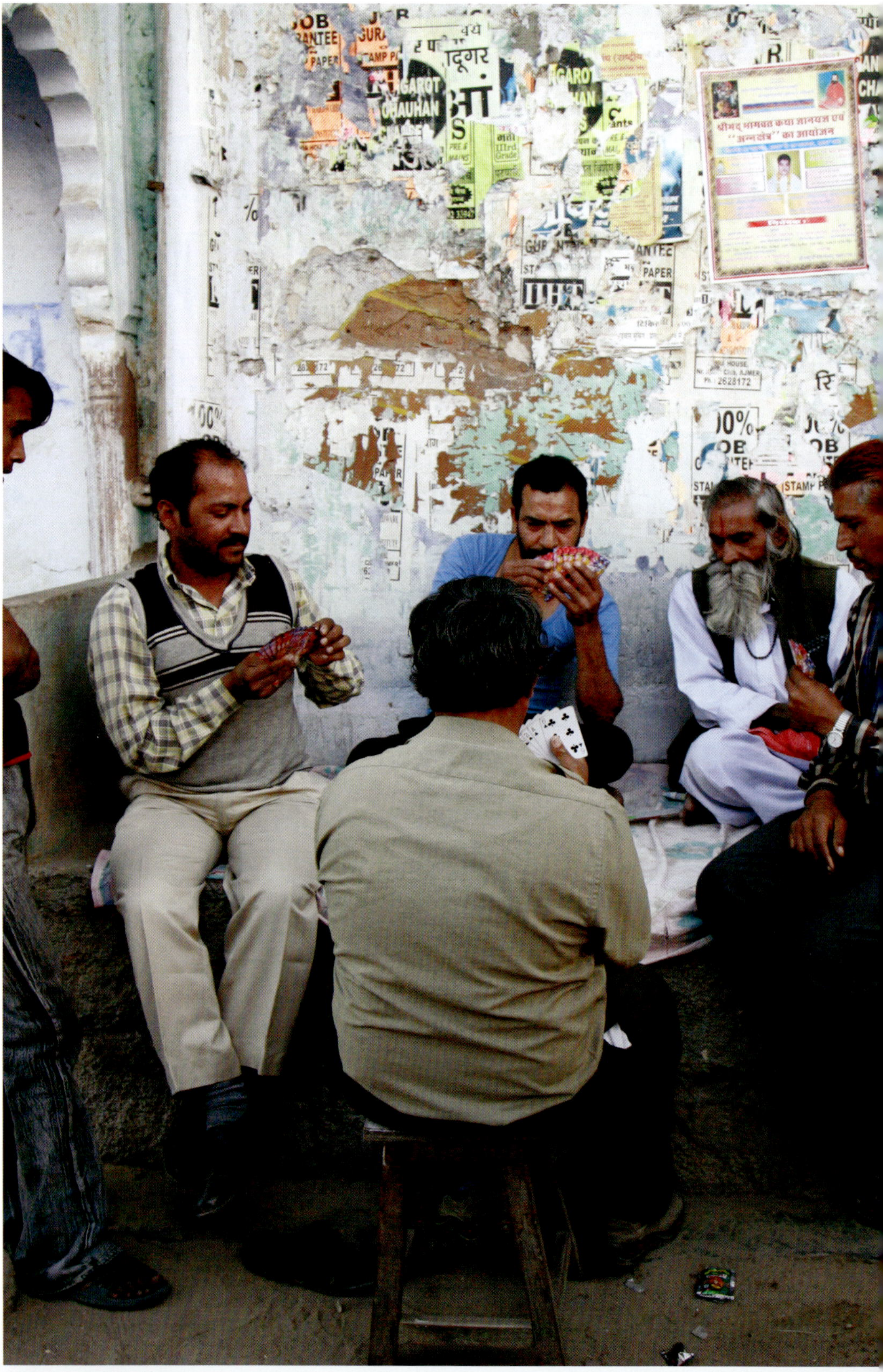
CHAUHAN
PAPER
Ph : 2628172

India

From Uganda I flew to India, landing midmorning in Delhi in a haze, and met my two friends, Aaron and Caitlin, at baggage claim. The three of us planned this adventure as Aaron and I were graduating from photography school five months earlier and we were thrilled that the trip had finally arrived.

Our taxi dropped us off at the door of our hostel in Paharganj, a neighborhood known, at the time, as Delhi's backpackers' district because of its cheap hostels and restaurants. As soon as we arrived, we took a walk down the main drag into what felt like an impromptu circus colliding with abject poverty spilling onto an overcrowded sea of people. We immediately passed an elephant that was sauntering down the street with a little boy standing on its back, juggling. A girl, maybe 8 years old, tried to hand us her newborn sister as she made the universal sign of needing food. Then a young kid did one back flip after another through the middle of the crowd until we lost sight of him—still back flipping. Adult men were pissing in the middle of the street. The smells vacillated from body odor to clove to feces to grilled meat to sweet jasmine with every step we took. If Uganda felt chaotic, India was an assault—and still, I absolutely fucking loved it.

We planned to spend two weeks in India, all in the state of Rajasthan, known for its desert castles and pink and blue cities. The hostel manager in Delhi suggested a private driver for our trip. He promised it would be the safest, most efficient way to see such a huge state in such a short time. Plus, he added, splitting the price three ways would make it super affordable. We jumped on the offer without much thought, and after a quick phone call, he turned to us and said our driver would arrive at 7 a.m. the next morning. We would pay him at the end of the trip.

A middle-aged man named Malik picked us up as planned, and for two weeks the four of us spent eleven hours a day in a car driving across the vast, tan expanse of the Rajasthan desert. Occasionally we'd pass through a bustling little town with an explosion of color, and we'd press our faces against the window to try to take it all in, but mostly it was stir-crazy nonsense. Between the heat, Malik's short temper, and playing chicken with the infamous Indian garbage trucks, it's incredible we got out of this trip alive.

We spent Christmas in the stunningly beautiful lakeside town of Udaipur, in a former palace turned hotel called Fateh Prakash. Our room was inside a turret perched above a makeshift cricket field, and every morning I'd hear the crack of a bat and young boys yelling to each other in Hindi. On Christmas morning in Udaipur—a decidedly Christian holiday in a Hindu town—a small and skinny teenager was dressed up as Santa Claus in a red suit so absurdly large that when he tried to say "ho, ho, ho" we just hugged him.

We stopped in both Jaipur, known as the Pink City, and Jodhpur, known as the Blue City. Jodhpur was where we spent New Year's Eve and rang in 2008, but we bought a brick of hash off our rickshaw driver earlier in the evening and got so high we were in bed at 10 p.m.

Our final destination before we turned around and headed all the way back to Delhi was the city of Jaisalmer, which sits at the edge of India only seventy miles from the border with Pakistan.

The jewel of Jaisalmer is the sprawling, massive Jaisalmer Fort, which looks like a gigantic version of the Fisher Price castle from my childhood. We heard we could stay *inside* the fort instead of in the crowded, hot desert city surrounding it, so we looked for cheap accommodations for our two nights in town.

We chose a hostel called Hotel Desert, which gets points for straightforward branding if nothing else. After checking in to one room for the three of us we headed upstairs to the rooftop terrace. A handsome, tall, kind guy, no older than 25, named Sawai stood up from the table to greet us as we walked onto the terrace. He was the night manager of Hotel Desert, drove a hot-pink moped, and was suave as hell. I told him I was traveling with my two friends—making sure to mention they were a couple—and that we hired Malik to drive us from Delhi to Jaisalmer. I planned on going to bed soon, I told him, so I could get an early start on photographing the fort the next morning.

The next day my alarm went off before dawn and I creeped out of the room with my camera around my neck, trying not to wake Caitlin or Aaron. Closing the door gently, I stood on my tiptoes as the door latched, let go of the handle, and turned around, breathless. Sawai was standing in silence five feet from me at the stop of stairs with his arm outstretched. Without saying a word, he took my hand and confidently led me down the main flight of stairs to the lobby, and then down another staircase to the basement below. This fort was built in 1156 AD and Sawai had set up blankets and candles in a romantic makeshift nest on the ancient basement floor. He sat me down on a blanket, said nothing, leaned in, and kissed me. Then he ejaculated all over himself—fully dressed, not even twenty seconds into the kiss.

Luckily he spoke first so I didn't have to. "Indian men are hot blooded," he explained. "Sometimes just the thought of a woman gets us horny."

"Makes sense," I confirmed.

Not sure what else to do I stood up and grabbed my camera. I reminded him that I was heading out to photograph the fort. Maybe we'd meet up again later.

When I returned from a morning of photography, Sawai was sitting in the lobby crying. He told me he was still sad about what had happened that morning but had called a friend for help. Sawai never told me how his friend helped him, but I suspect it was the procurement of Viagra because every time there was a vacant room in the hostel, Sawai and I snuck into it. On the last night in Jaisalmer, we made our way up to the rooftop terrace to have sex one last time. A few minutes in, I suggested doggy style, and though he had never even heard of such a position, when I turned around on all fours, he figured it out. As I looked at him over my shoulder, beneath the Indian sky bright with stars above us, he threw his head back and yelled out, "I don't know what heaven is, but I hope it's just like this!"

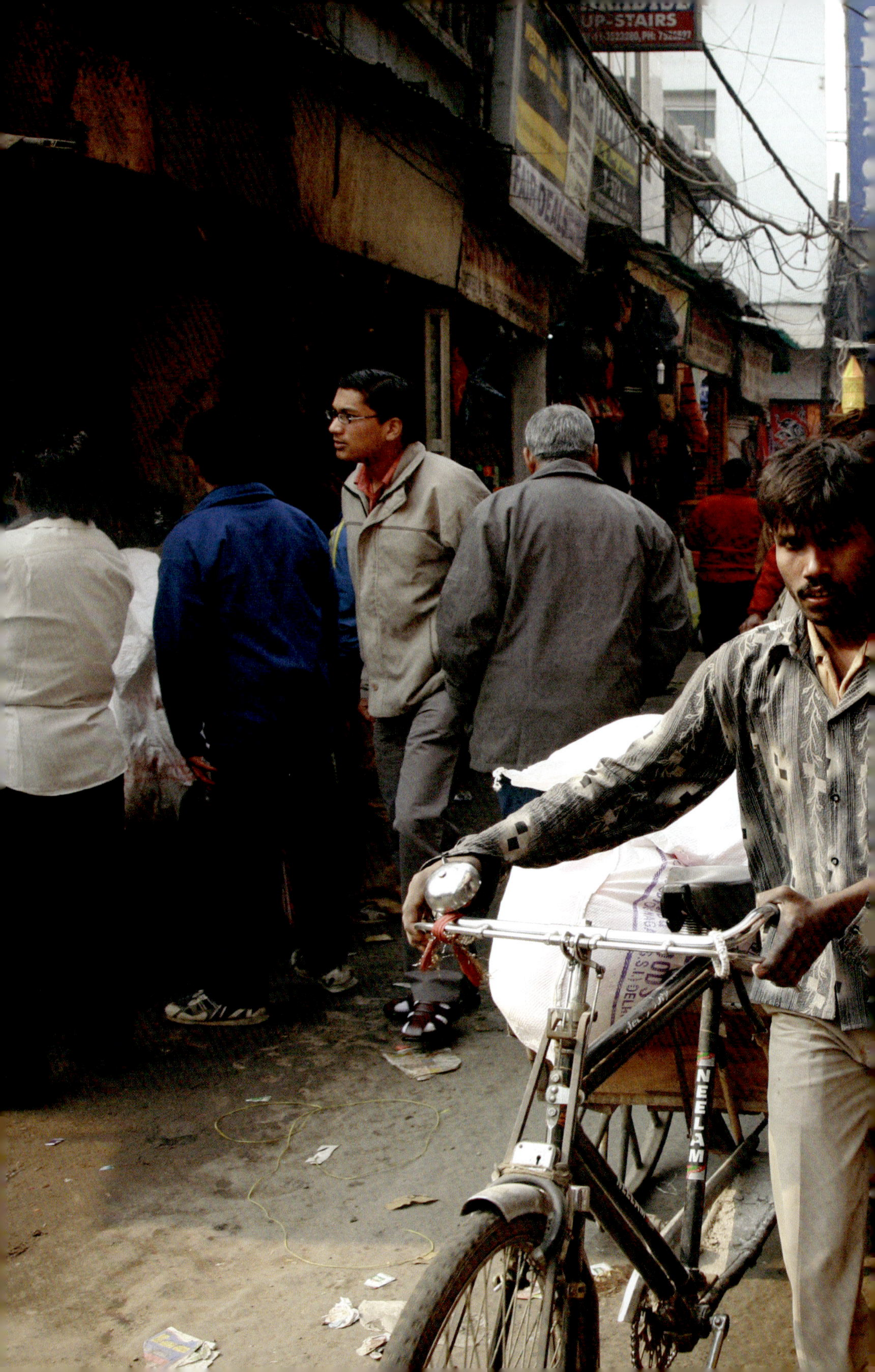
UP-STAIRS
NEELAM

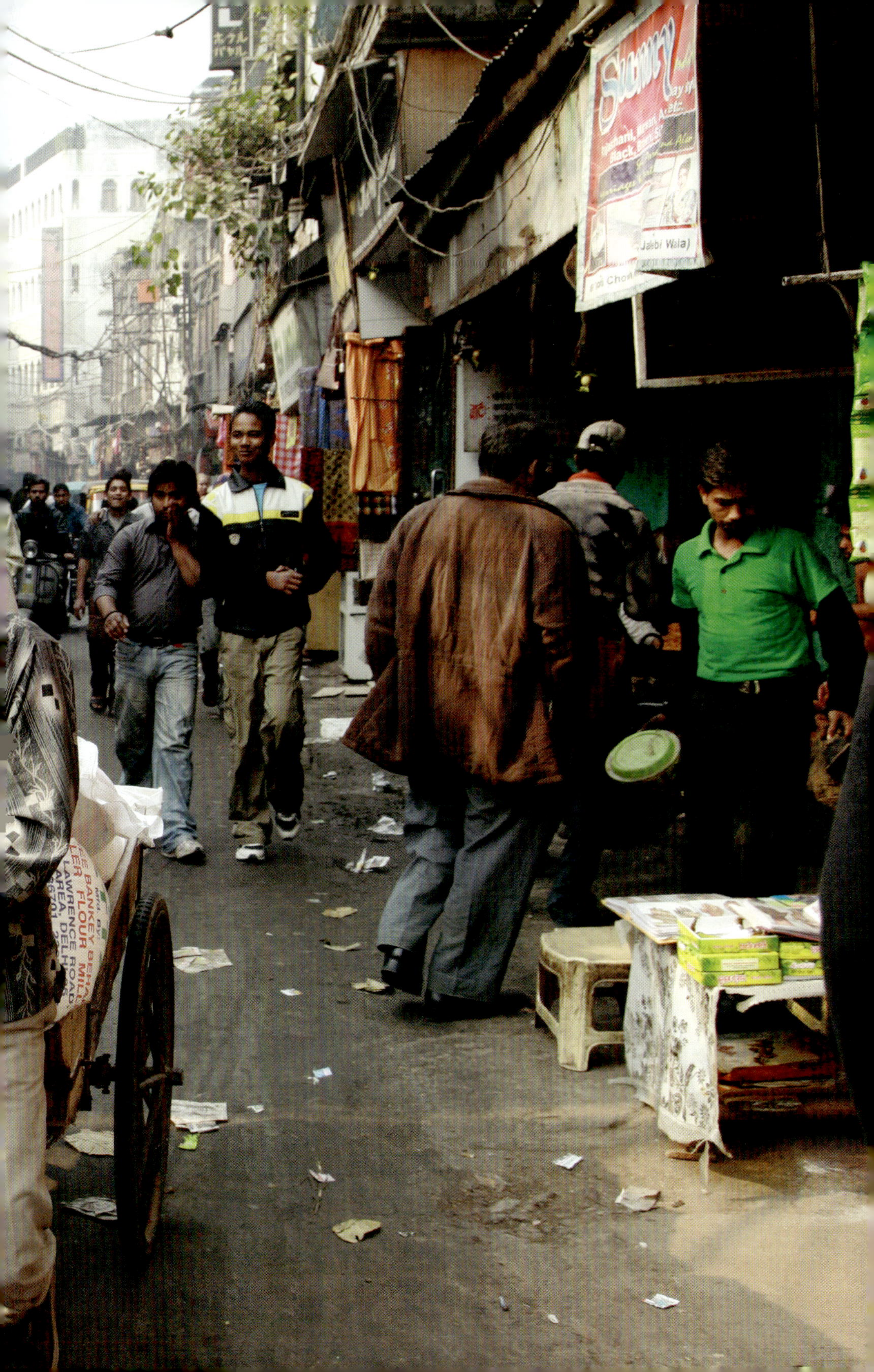
Jalebi Wala)

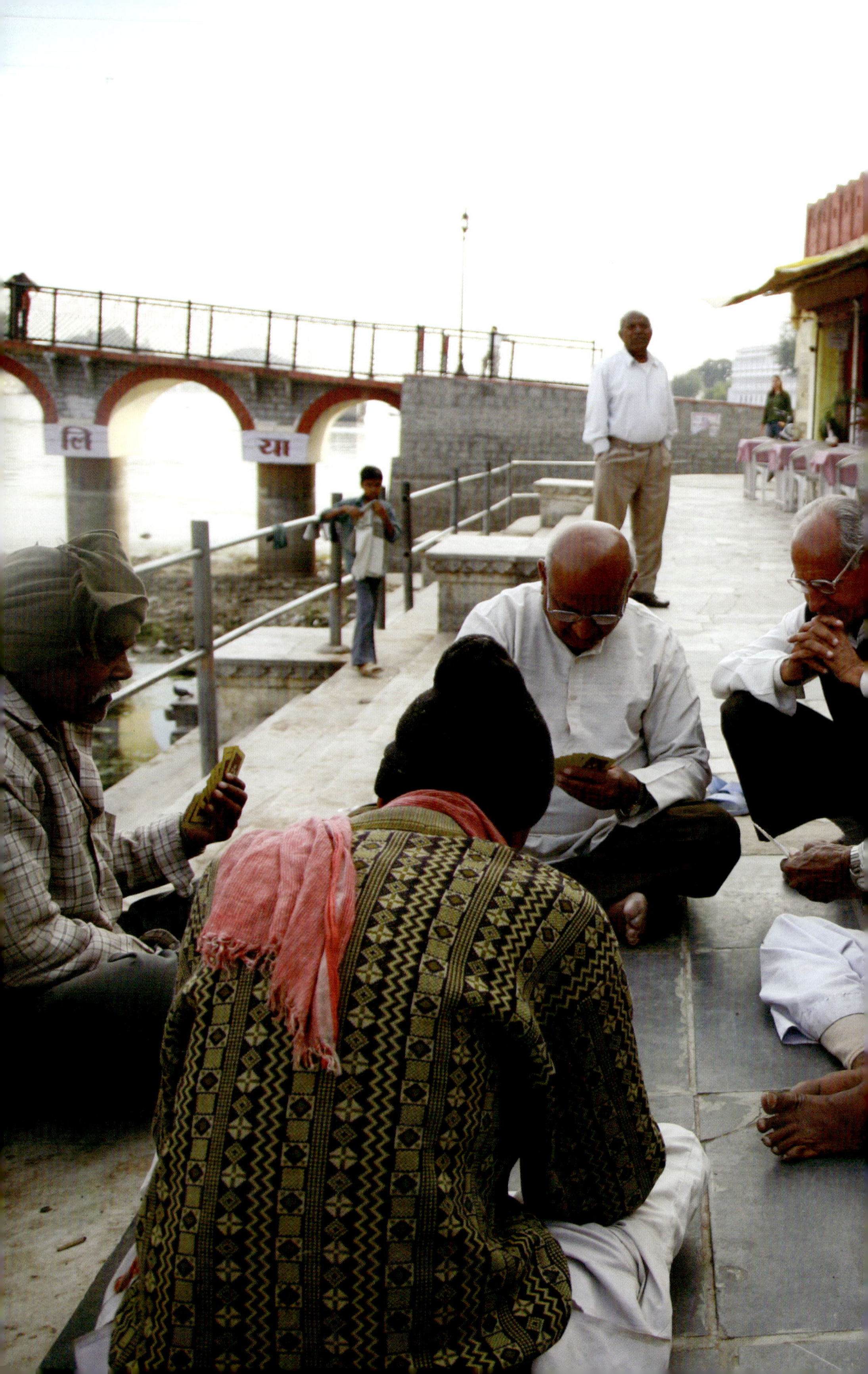
लि
या

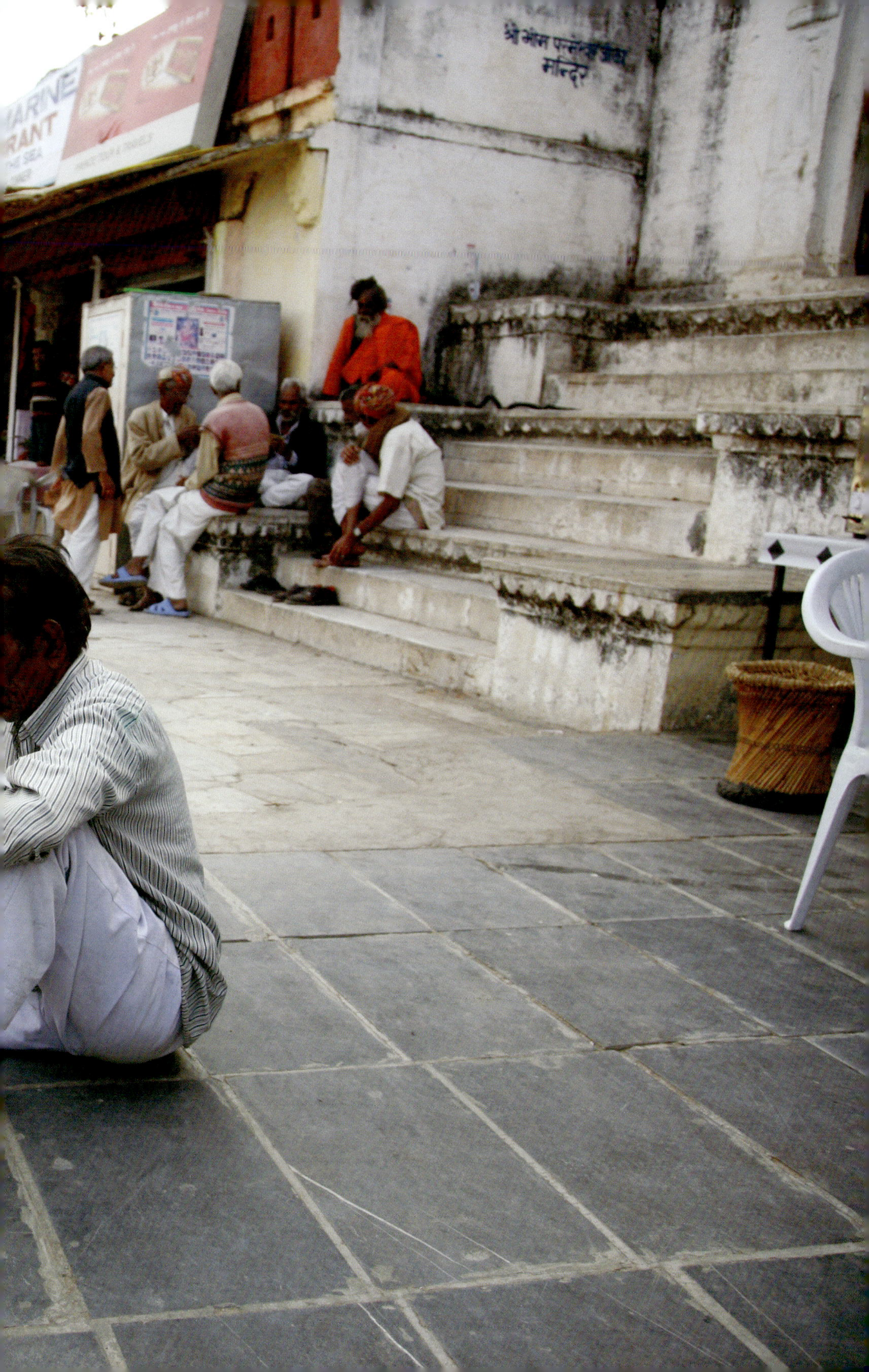
ARINE
RANT
THE SEA
मन्दिर

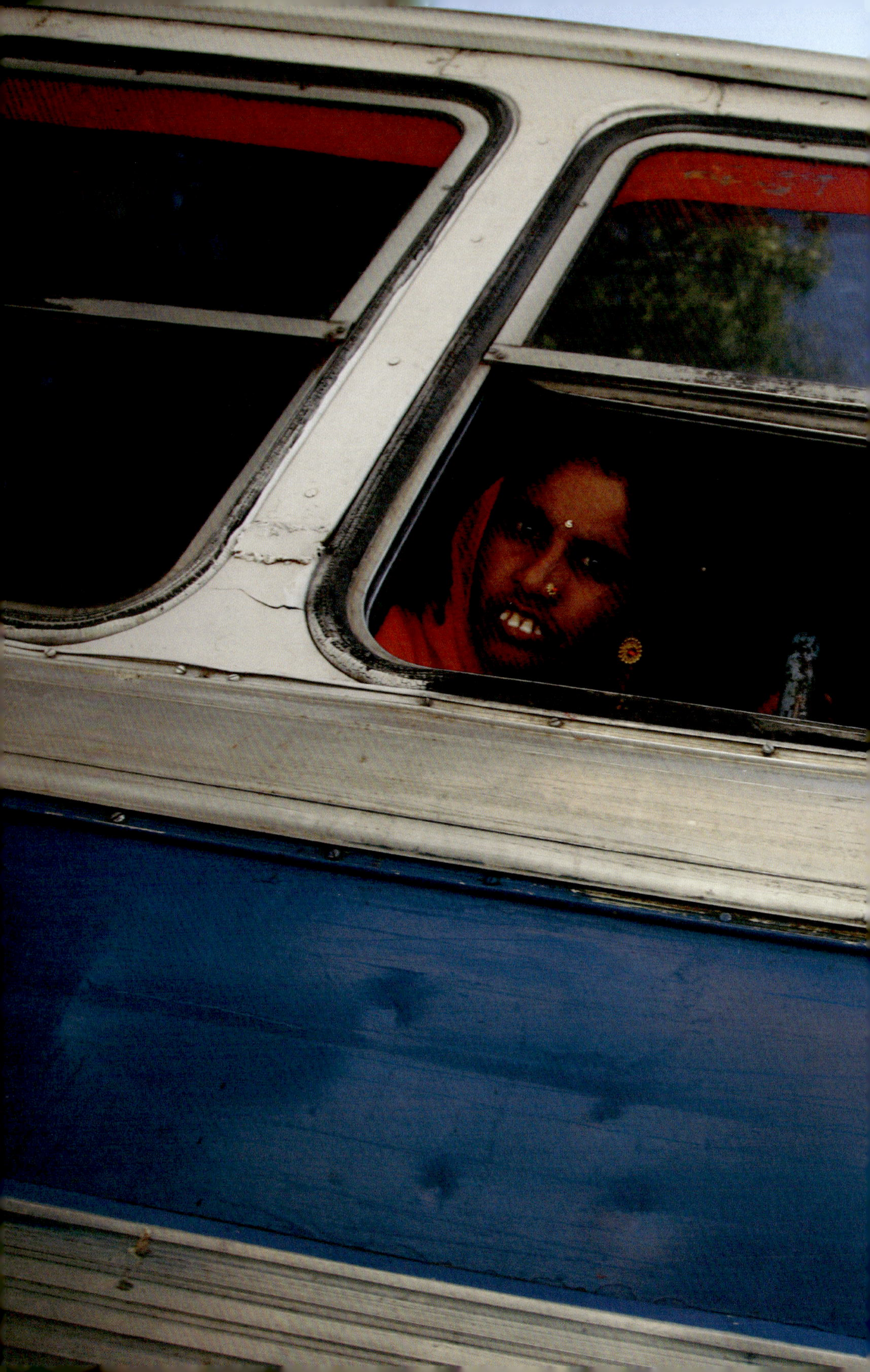

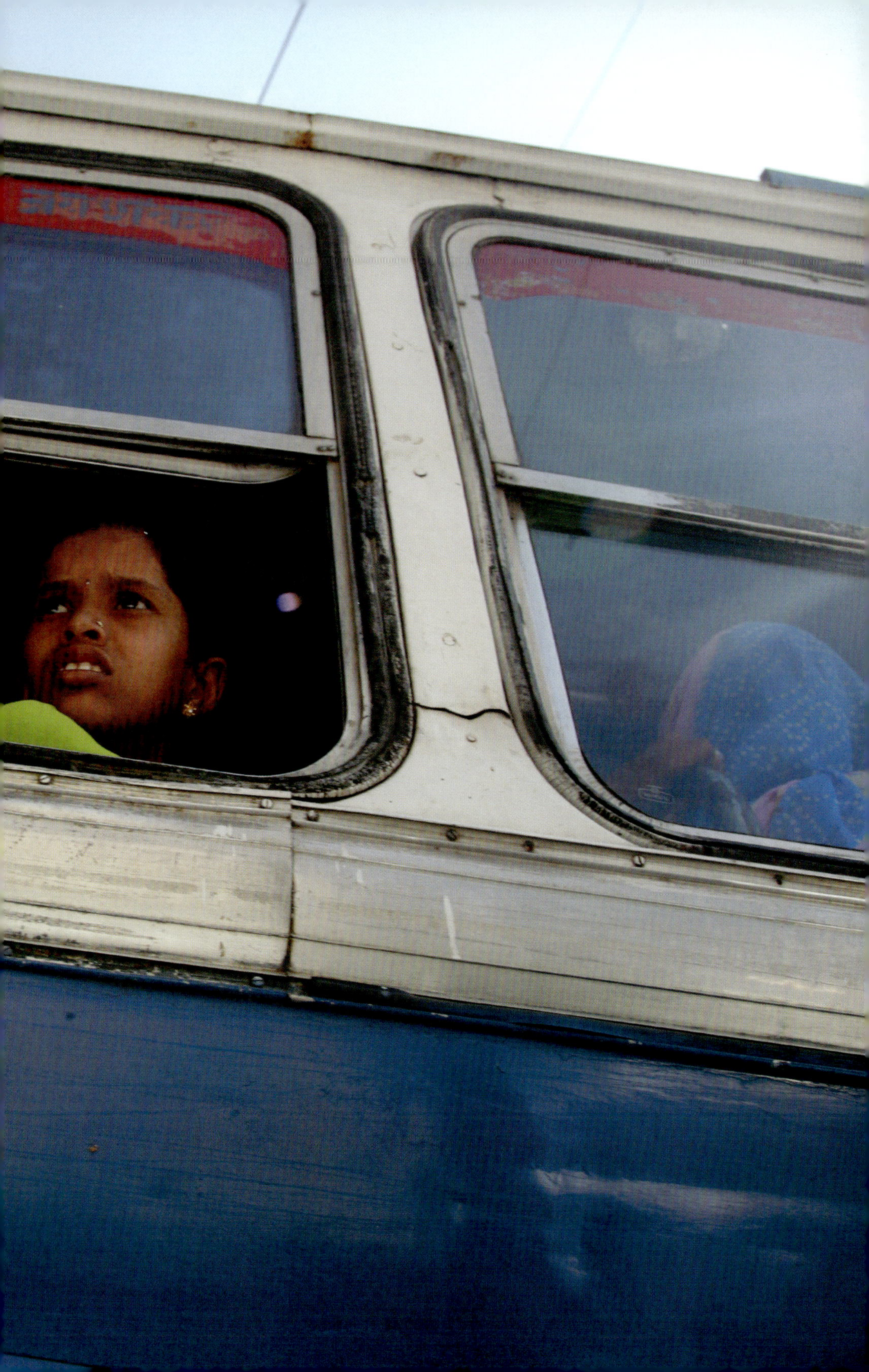

Far from Alone

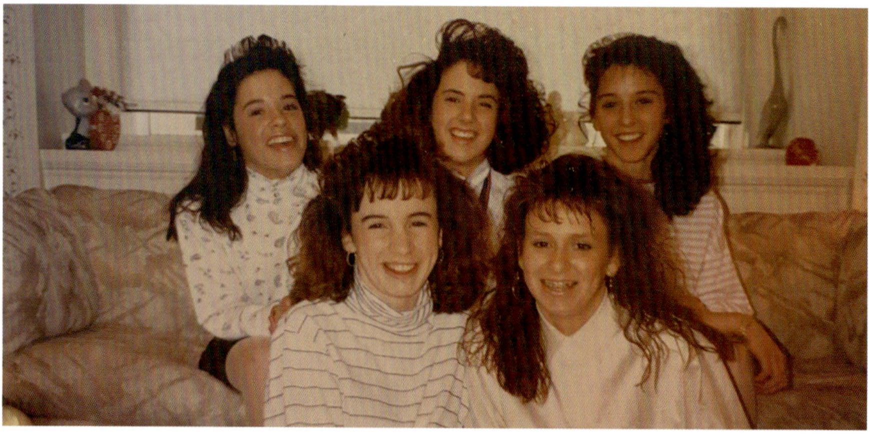

When my mom gave me a camera for my 14th birthday, I immediately used it to idolize my four best friends. I would schedule elaborate photo shoots with each of them, orchestrate outfit changes, and pose them in every corner of my home. Sometimes I'd have them look over their shoulder at me in a *who's there?* sexy kind of way, and sometimes I'd just have them pout. But my favorite photos were when their bangs made a giant rainbow arch and they'd flash me a huge smile full of braces. I remember getting those prints back from the FotoMat in the Marshall's parking lot and promising to "send them to a modeling agency," as if I knew where or how to do that.

I fell in love with being a photographer immediately. I loved the creativity of it and the collaboration between photographer and subject, but most of all I loved making my friends feel as beautiful as I saw them to be.

Fifteen years after my mom gave me my first camera, the same four friends—Kate, Kristen, Sara, and Kendra—who were my original muses were now starting families. Once again they were my biggest inspiration. Through photographing their young families I was able to develop a style of family photography that was candid, honest, and messy and T.Spoon Photography was born. T.Spoon was my childhood nickname. Candid, honest, and messy are the only things I do.

A couple times a week throughout photography school I would sit in the middle of Kate's living room floor with her children, Ben and Anna, and fulfill assignments. Kate would set up their snack station by the sliding glass door so I could capture different directions of light as it spilled onto their tiny bodies, and I learned how to tell a story through photography by recording Ben and Anna's every move. I spent so much time photographing Kate and her family that I was able to catch the countless little moments of love that happen all day, every day, between a mother and her children. No one posed for me, no one stopped to be something they were not. Entrenched in the utter chaos of two toddlers—and then three kids when Will arrived—Kate and her husband Jay would unselfconsciously live their lives while I had a front row seat with my camera. I honed the craft of stopping time with a photograph while childhoods went by in an instant.

Kristen, who moved next door to me when we were 3 years old, is as much a sister to me as she is a best friend. She lives in Wisconsin with her husband and three kids, and for ten straight years I photographed them on the third weekend of November in a "day-in-the-life" style of candid photography. One year my visit conflicted with their trip to Disney World, so Kristen suggested I join them in Orlando and do the shoot there. Kristen and I had been dreaming of going to Disney together since we were four so I all but wore mouse ears on the flight down. Mark and Kristen deserve a Medal of Courage for that trip, and if you have taken three children to Disney World then you do, too. We went to three theme parks *a day*, and I photographed every single meltdown except my own. When we arrived at EPCOT Kristen and I actually raced each other to the restaurant in Germany to see who could get to a beer faster. Of all the family photo shoots I have ever done, that weekend in Disney with the Lasky family is still my favorite of all time.

Sara's mom, Linda, felt like a second mom to me and even cosigned my student loans when my parents didn't qualify. In 2010 she was diagnosed with cancer and somehow she was gone ten months later. Later that same year I photographed Sara's daughter, Nora, at her first birthday party in hopes that Sara could see her own mother reflected in the way she now looked at Nora. And if Sara couldn't quite see it then, it would be hard not to see Linda in every part of who Sara is today.

I would not be able to live with myself if I wasn't able to photograph Kendra's family, so I flew to Atlanta to surprise her and capture the sweet and silly love of hers and Wade's family when their kids were still little. I also spent the first Christmas without my mom with Kendra in Atlanta, and if ever there was a family-sized shot of pure joy it is Christmas with the Hugues/Pope family.

Photography and friendship feel like the same thing to me. I know that's where it started, and I think that's why I've been successful at it. I go into every shoot like I went into those first ones when I was 14. I'm there to celebrate you, I'm there to show you how beautiful you are. I'm your hype man. And if you're my friend, I'm your hype man for life. My friendships are almost the only thing I care about, and at 50 years old I still use the words *best friend* to describe no less than twenty people who make my life worth living. My sister is one of my best friends, as is her husband, so when I say friends, I'm also referring to them.

I know there's a mad dash in this life to find a romantic partner and start a family because I've made a living photographing that finish line, but I don't know where any of us would be without the love and loyalty of our deepest friendships. Personally, I think lifelong friendships are even more remarkable than romantic partnerships. We are not in a contract with our friends. We didn't have a ceremony, and we made no promise. We stay because we want to. Both of my grandmothers were single my whole life, my favorite aunt was single, and my parents clearly preferred their friends over one another. I did not see a romantic relationship I wanted to emulate a single time anywhere in my family when I was young. I saw friendship. So friendship is what I've done. And taking care of my friends, being their hype man, and showing them how beautiful they are is what I'll continue to do.

'Til death do us part. I promise.

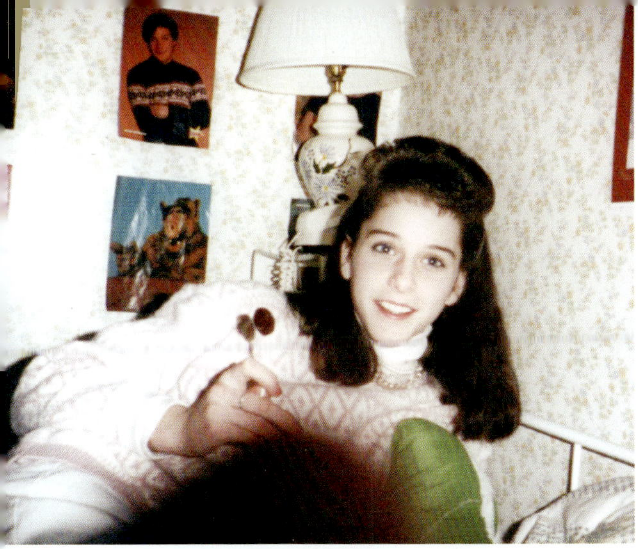
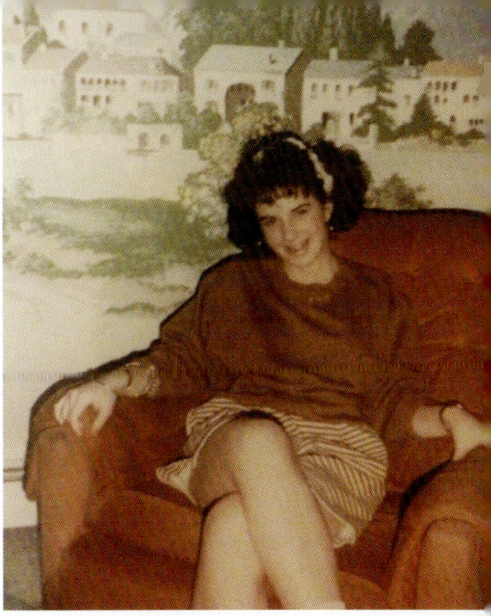
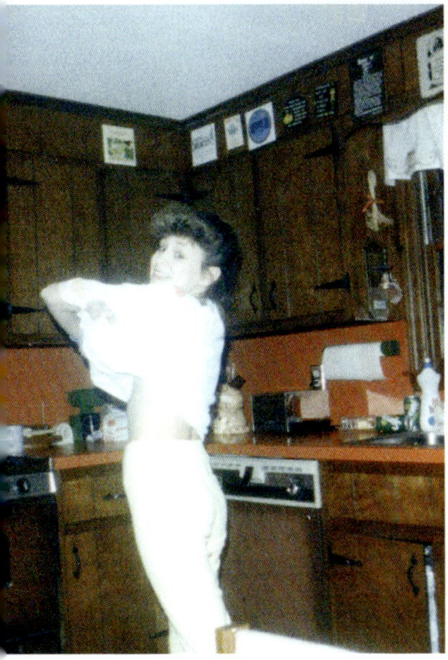
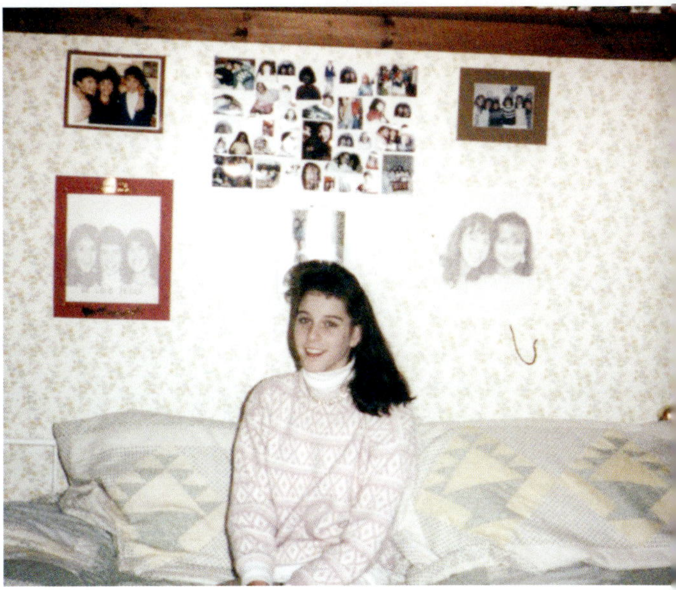
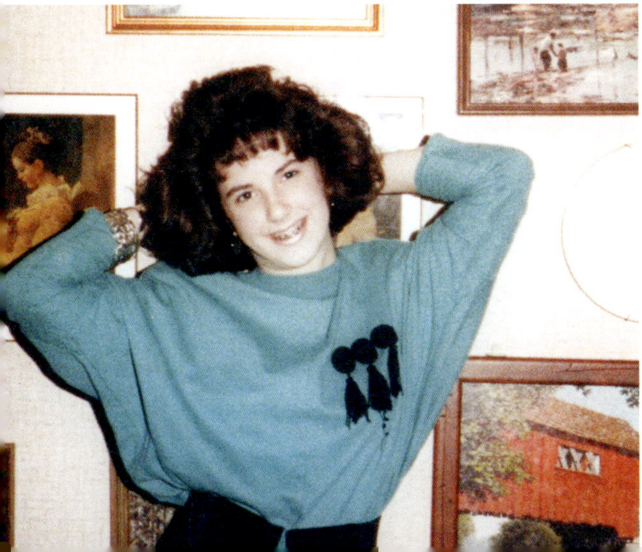
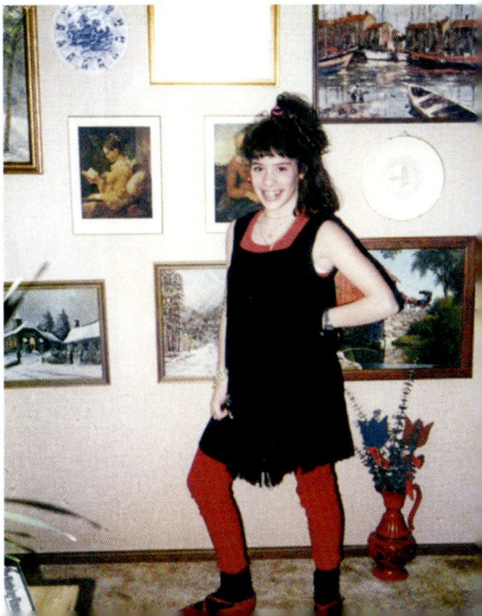

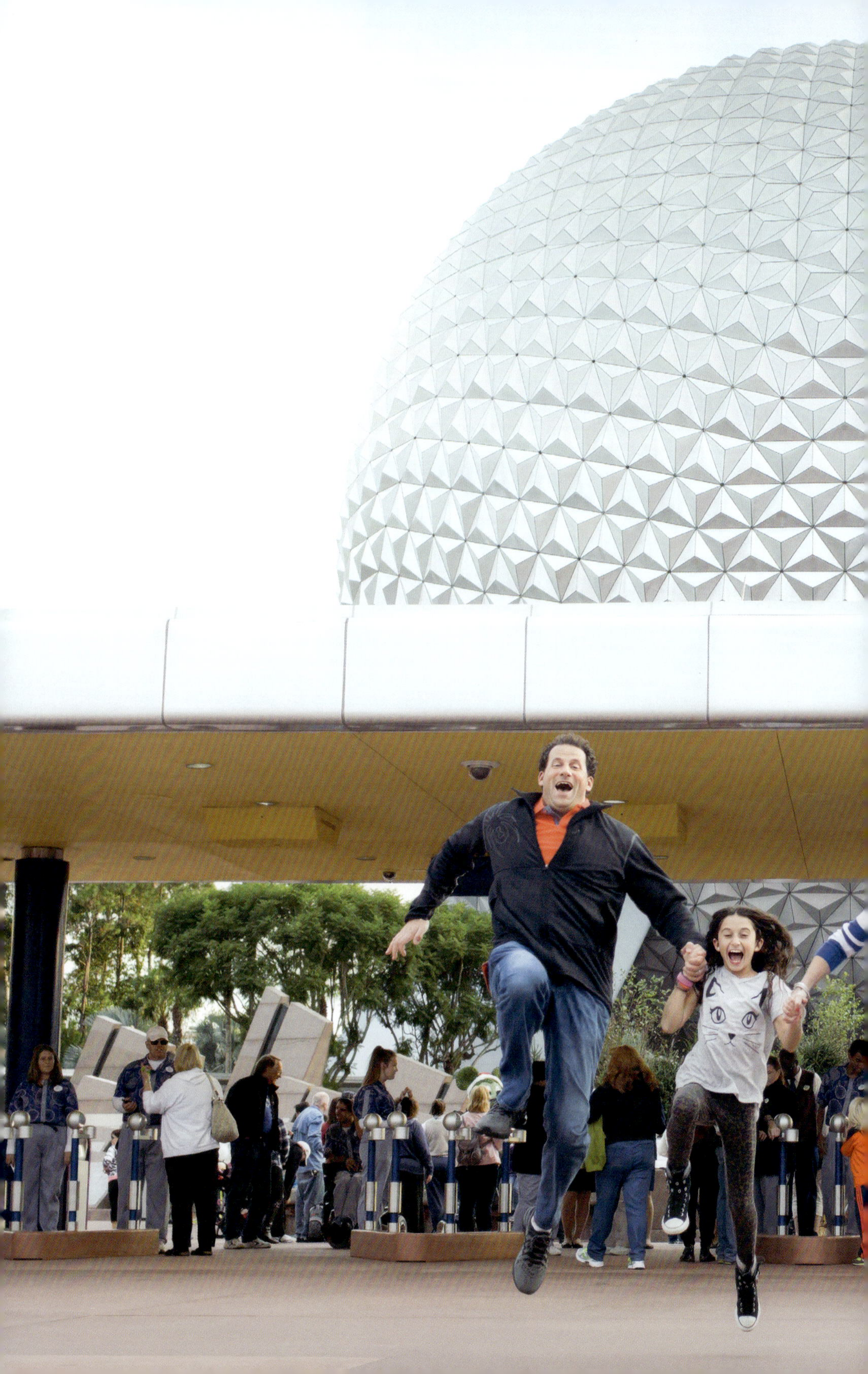

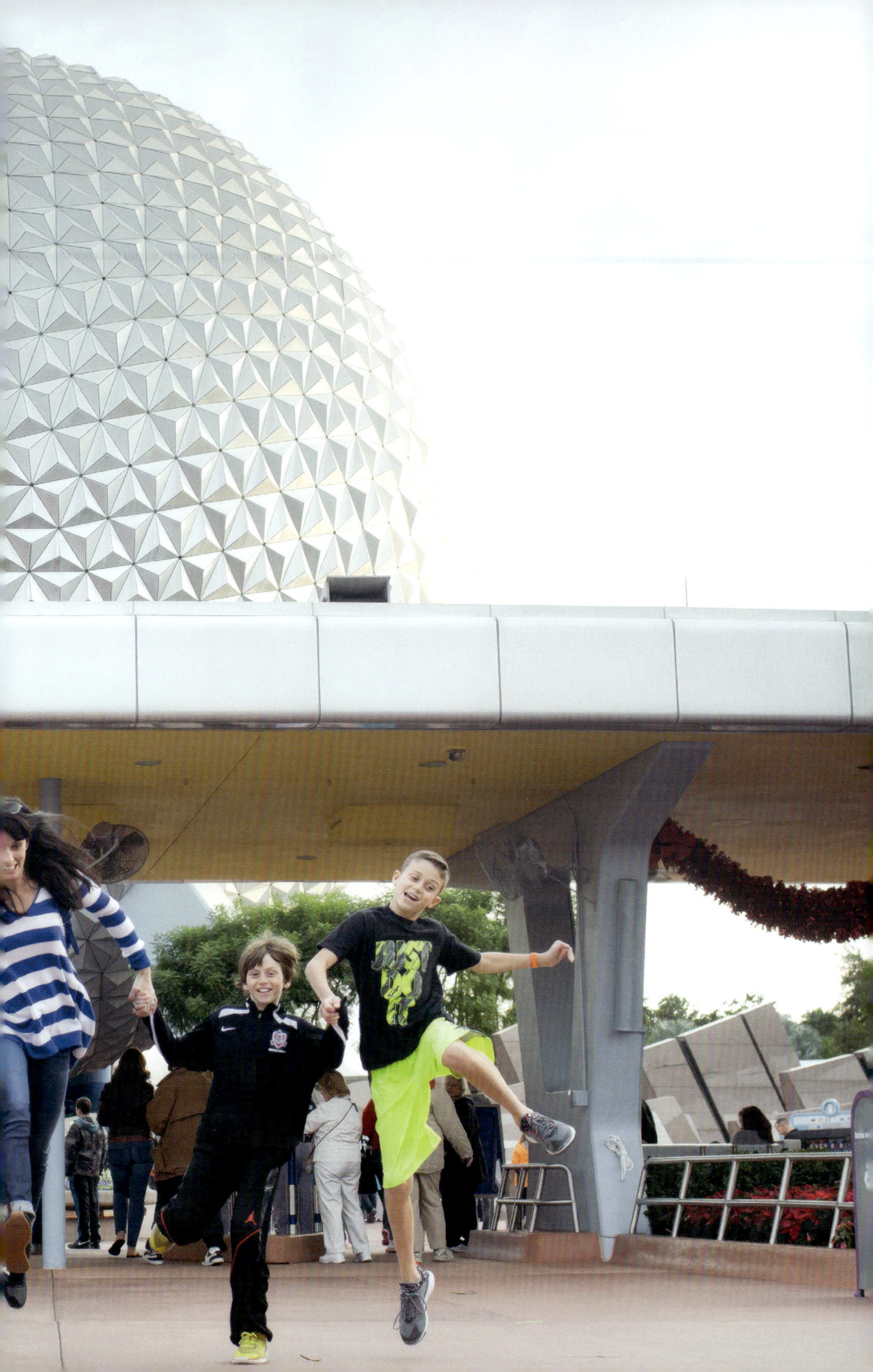

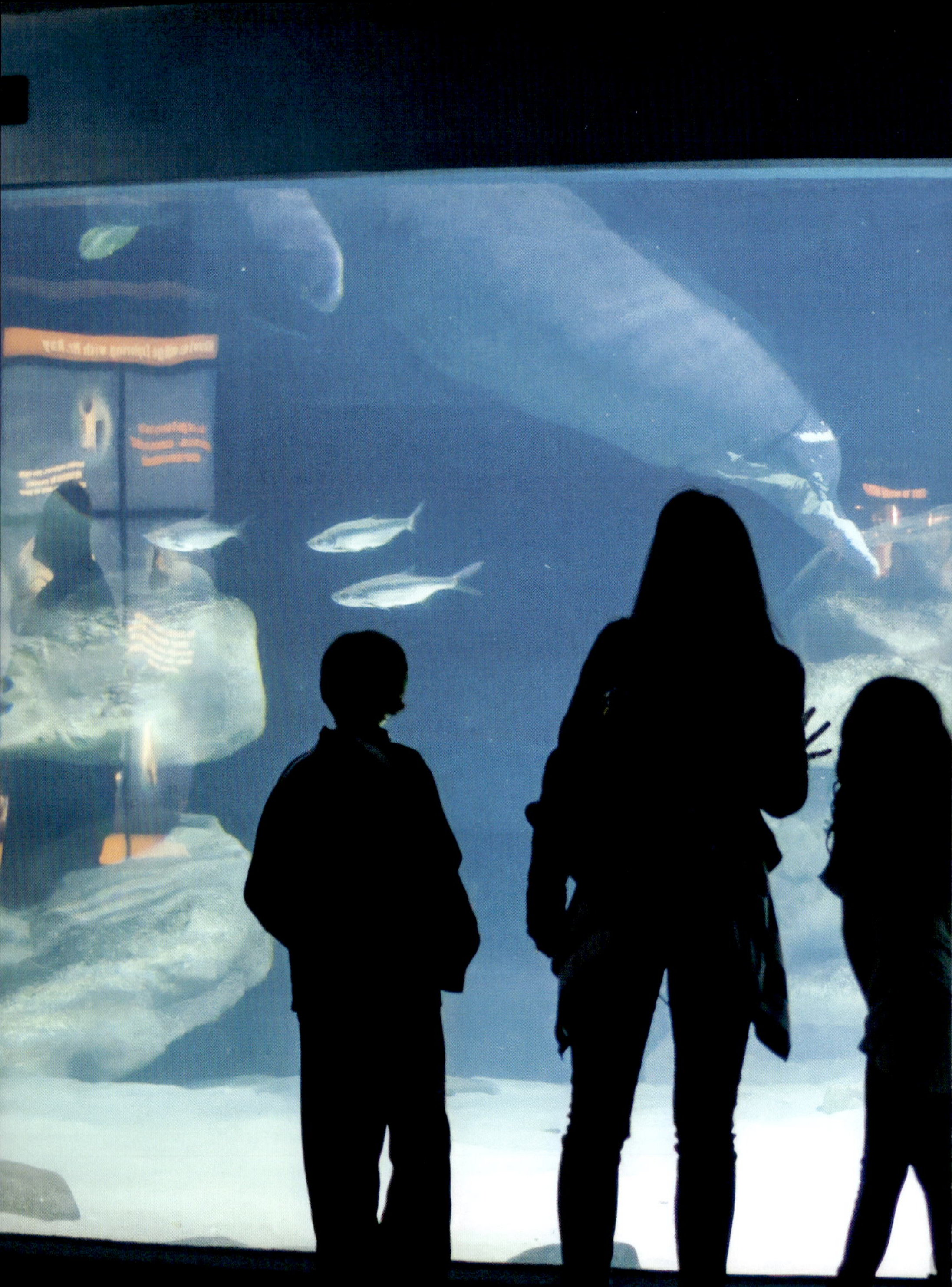

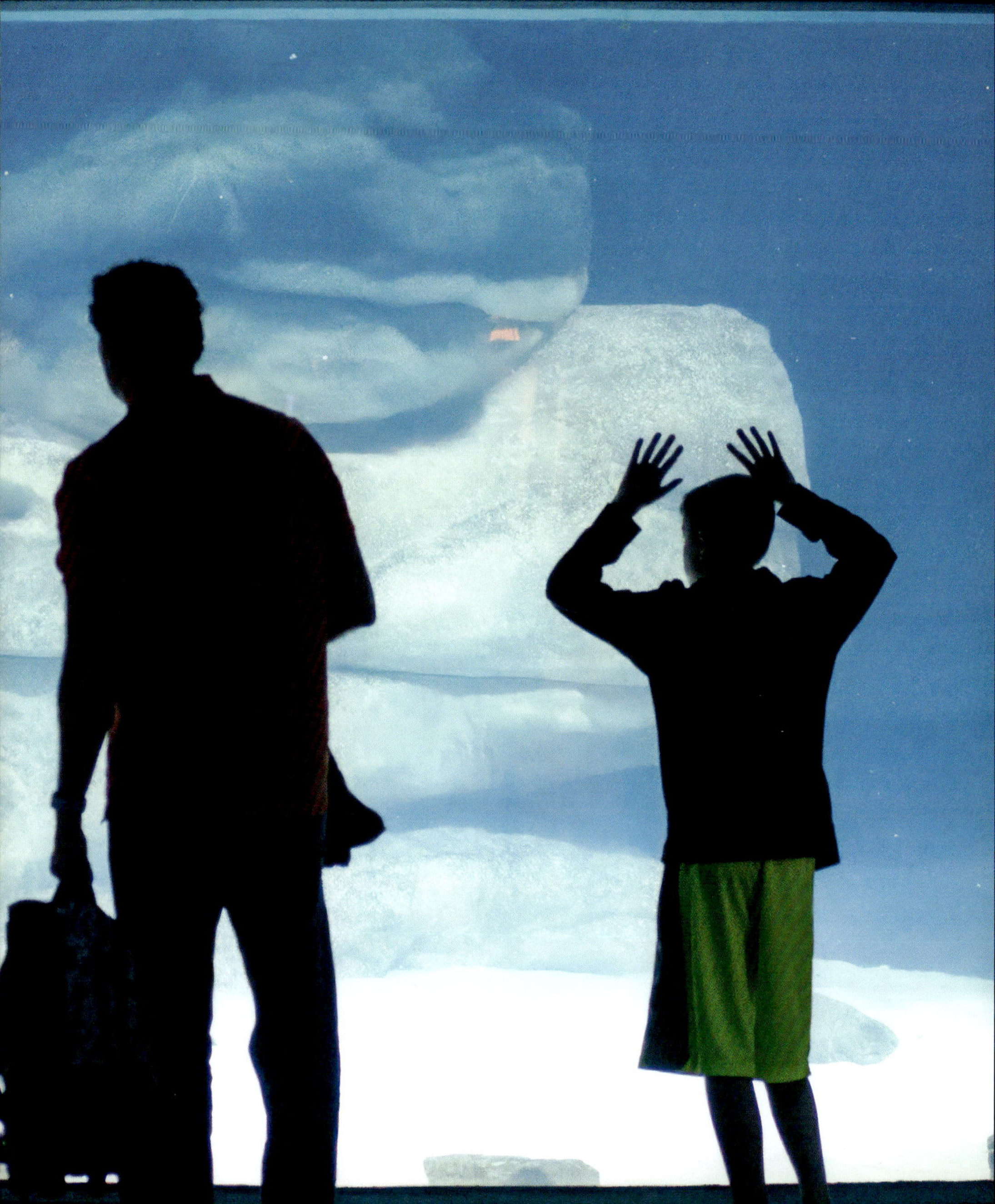

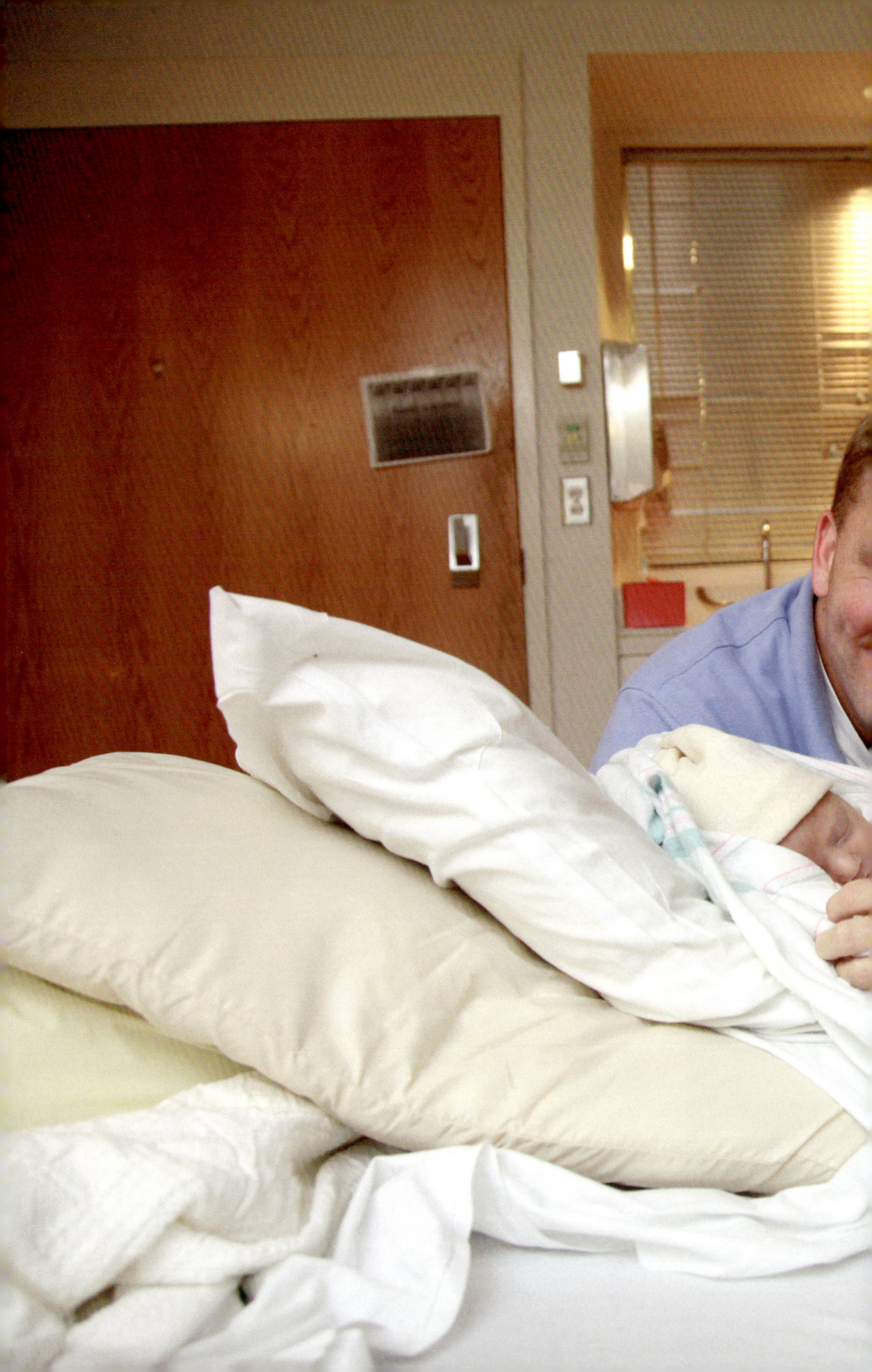

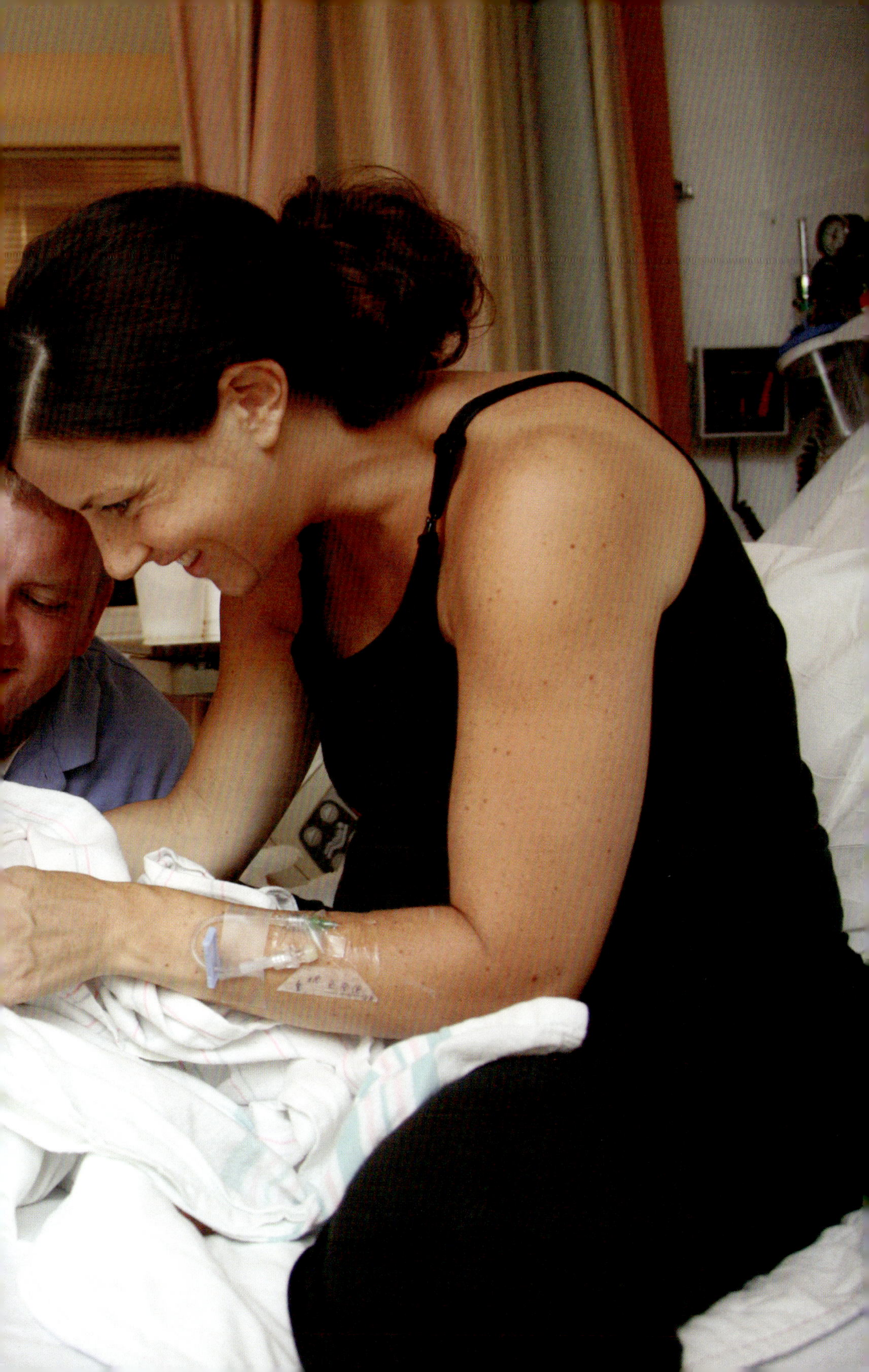

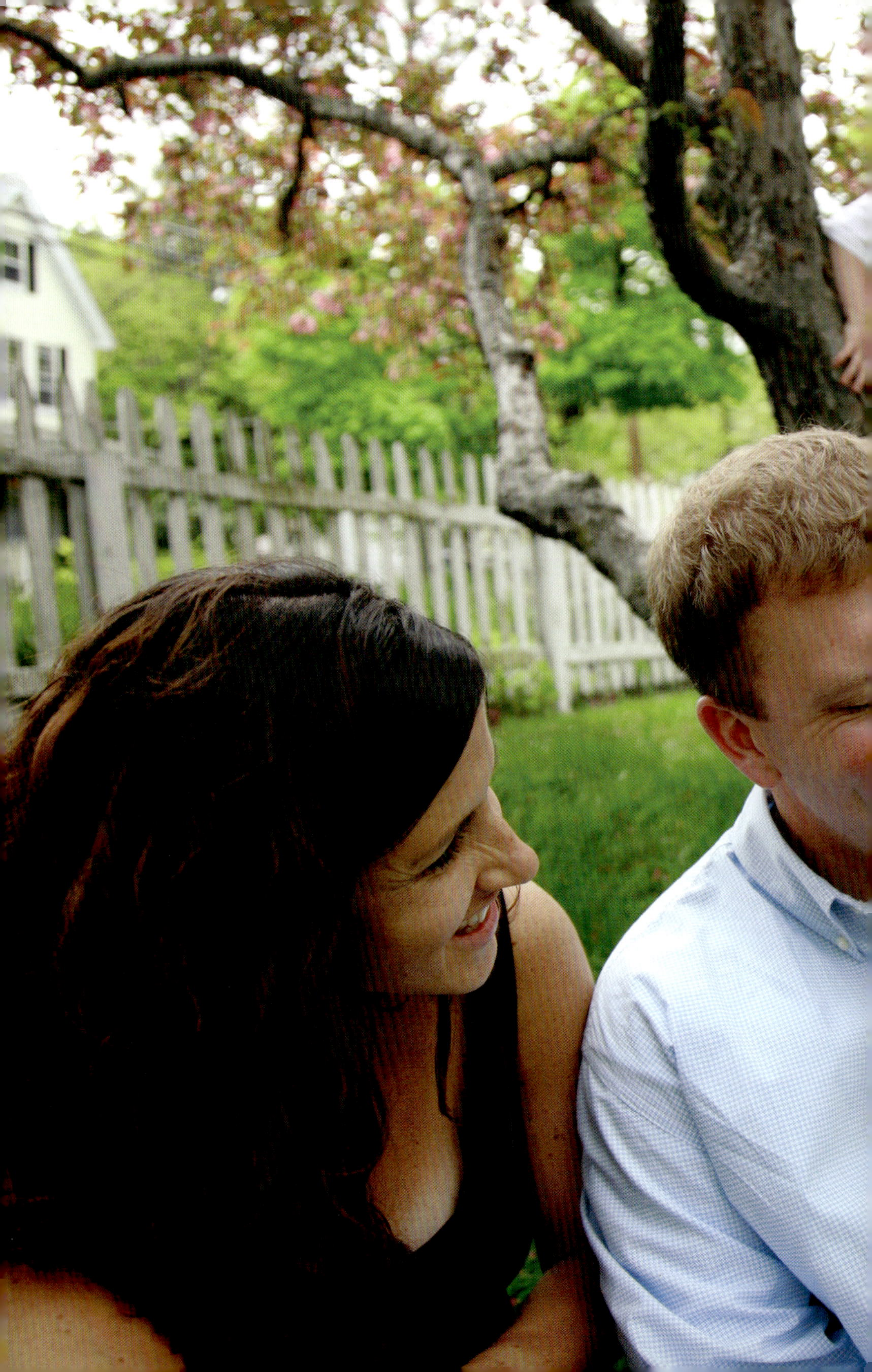

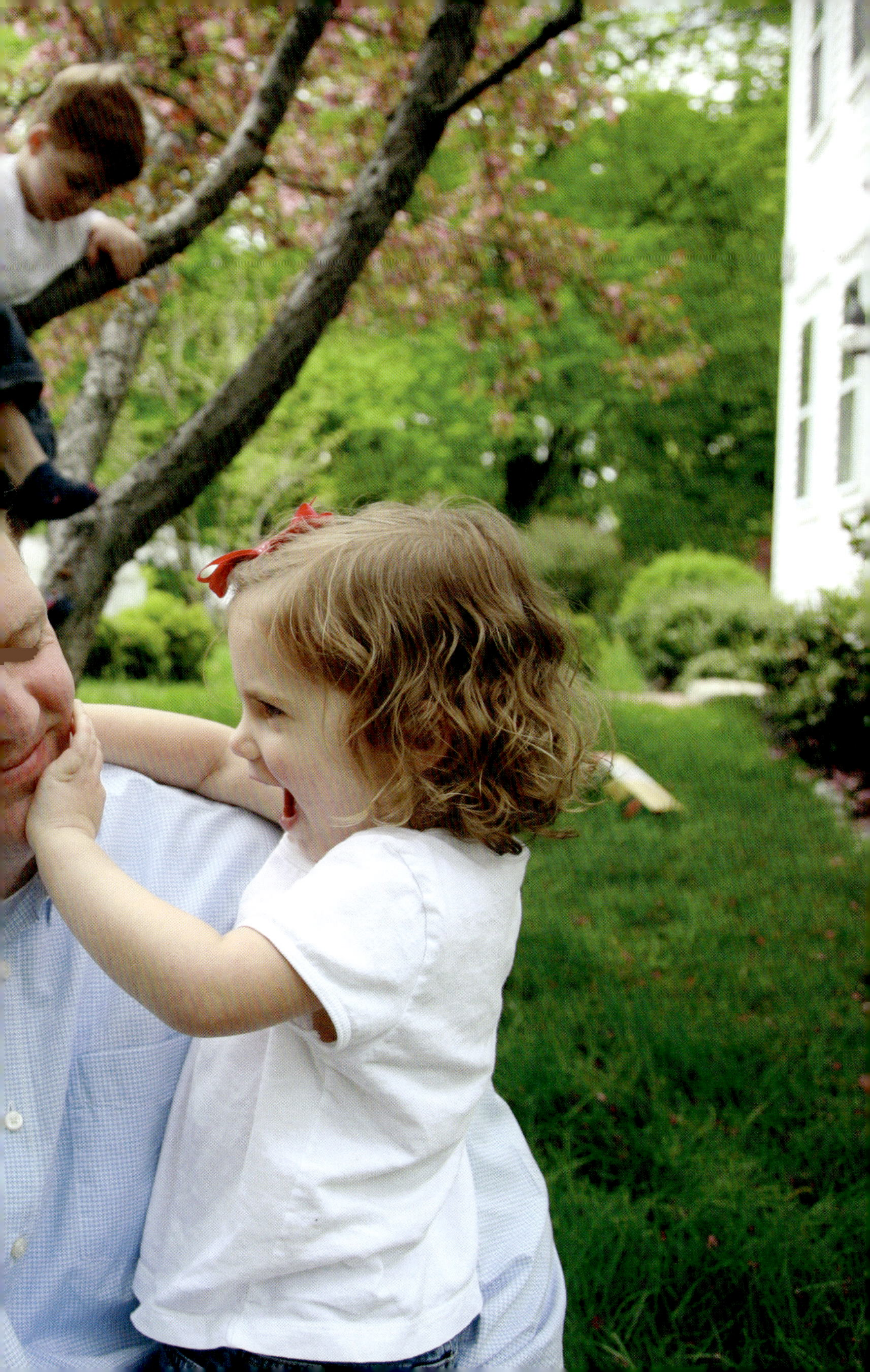

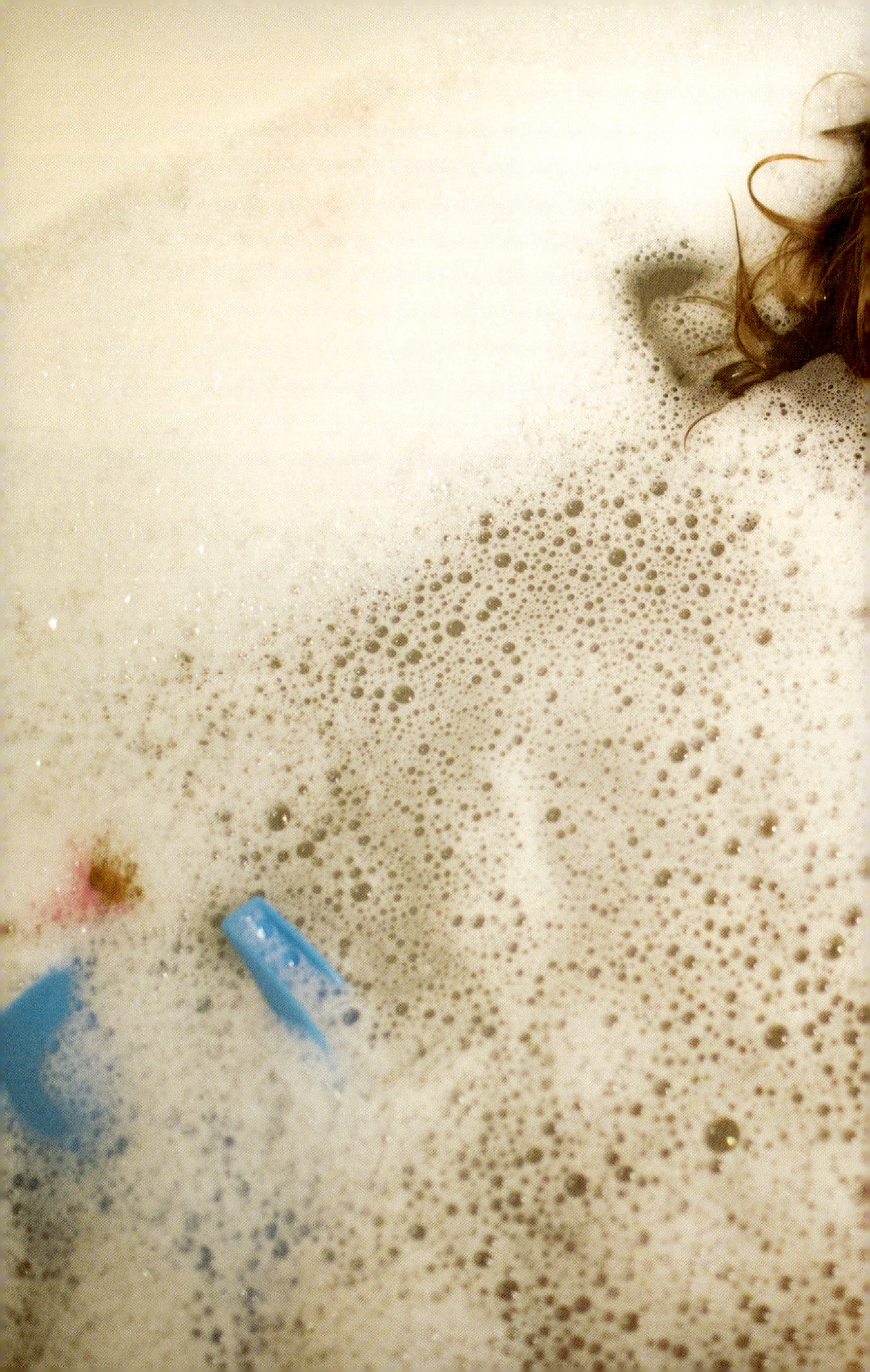

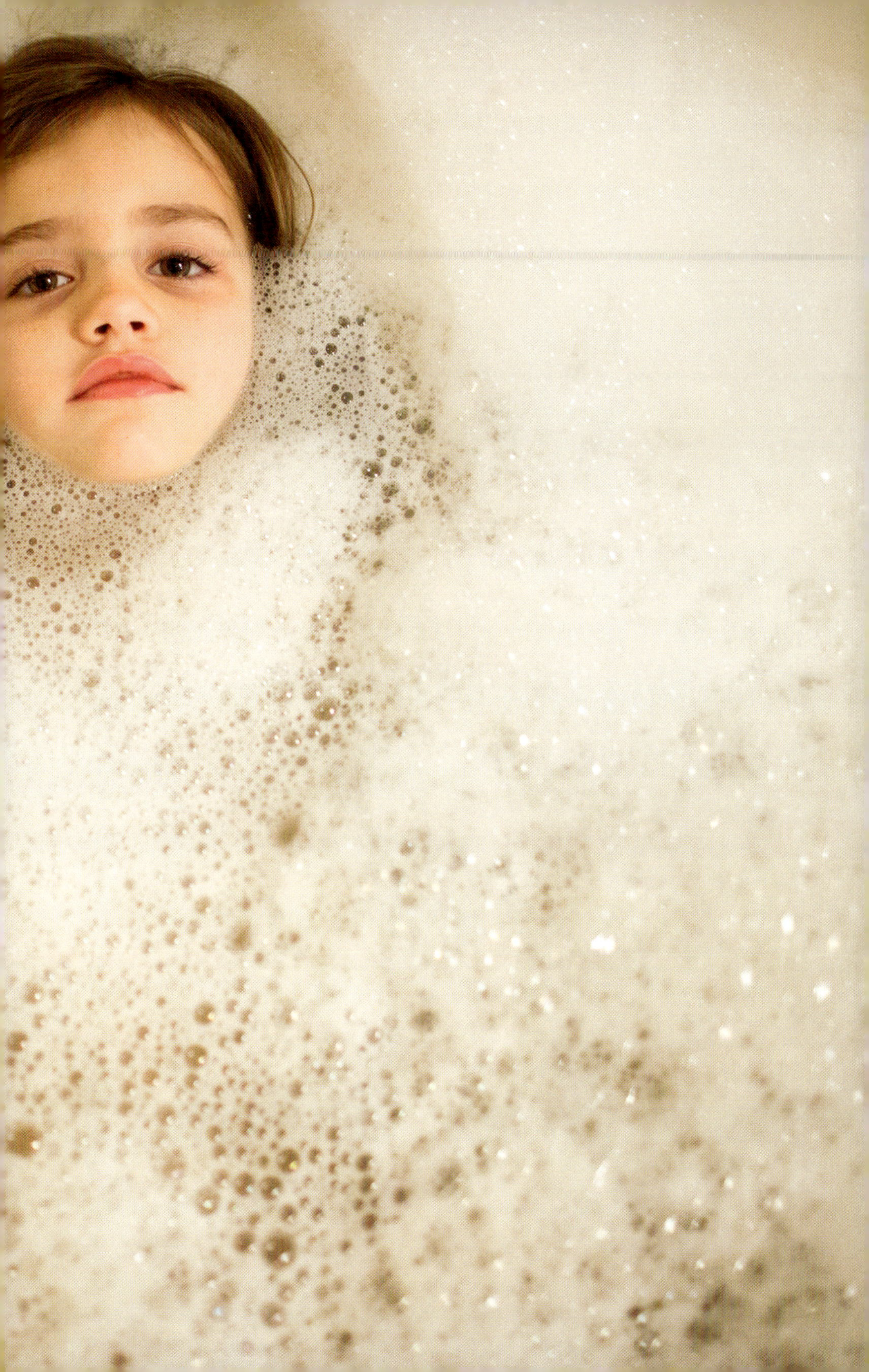

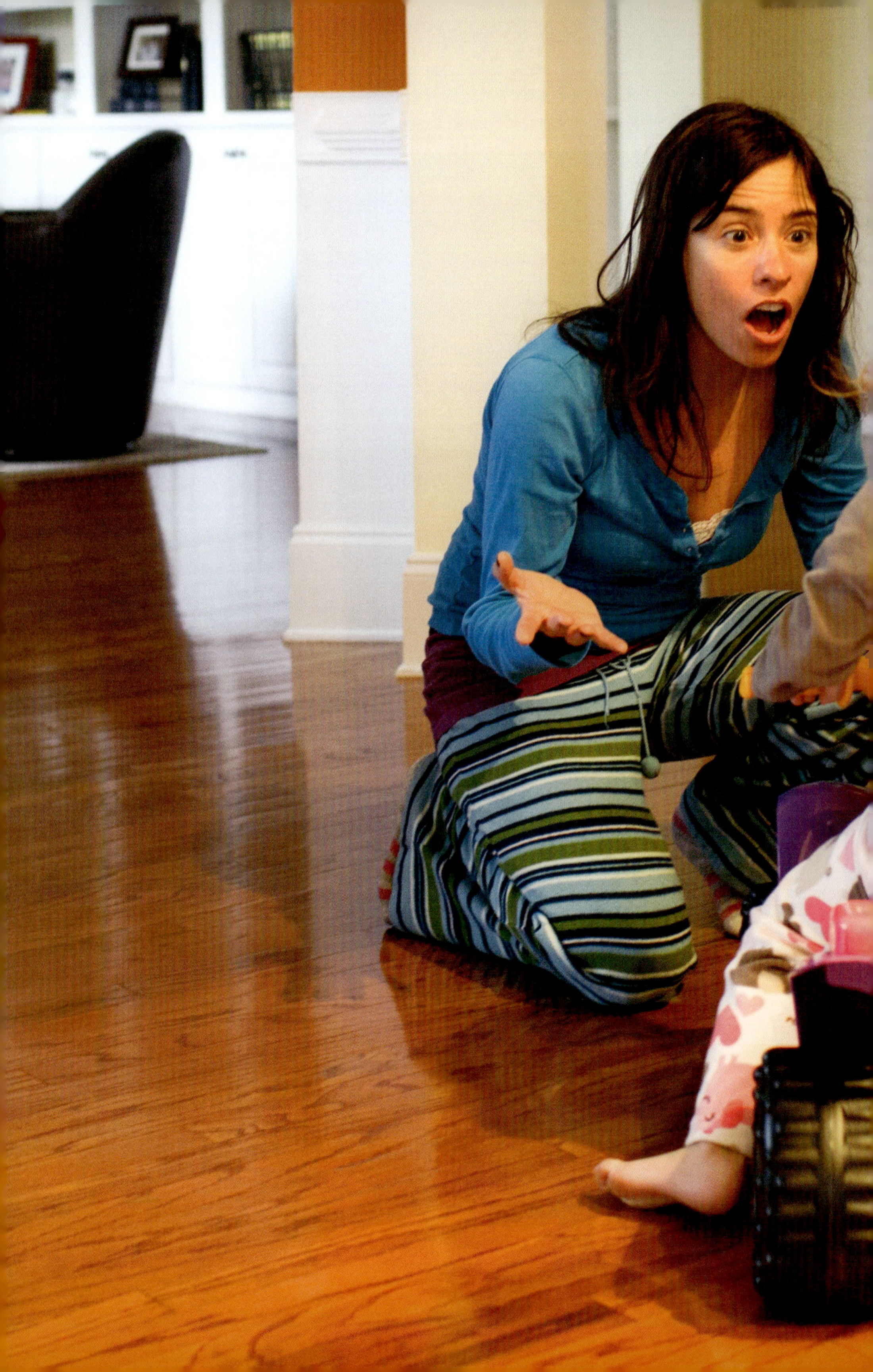

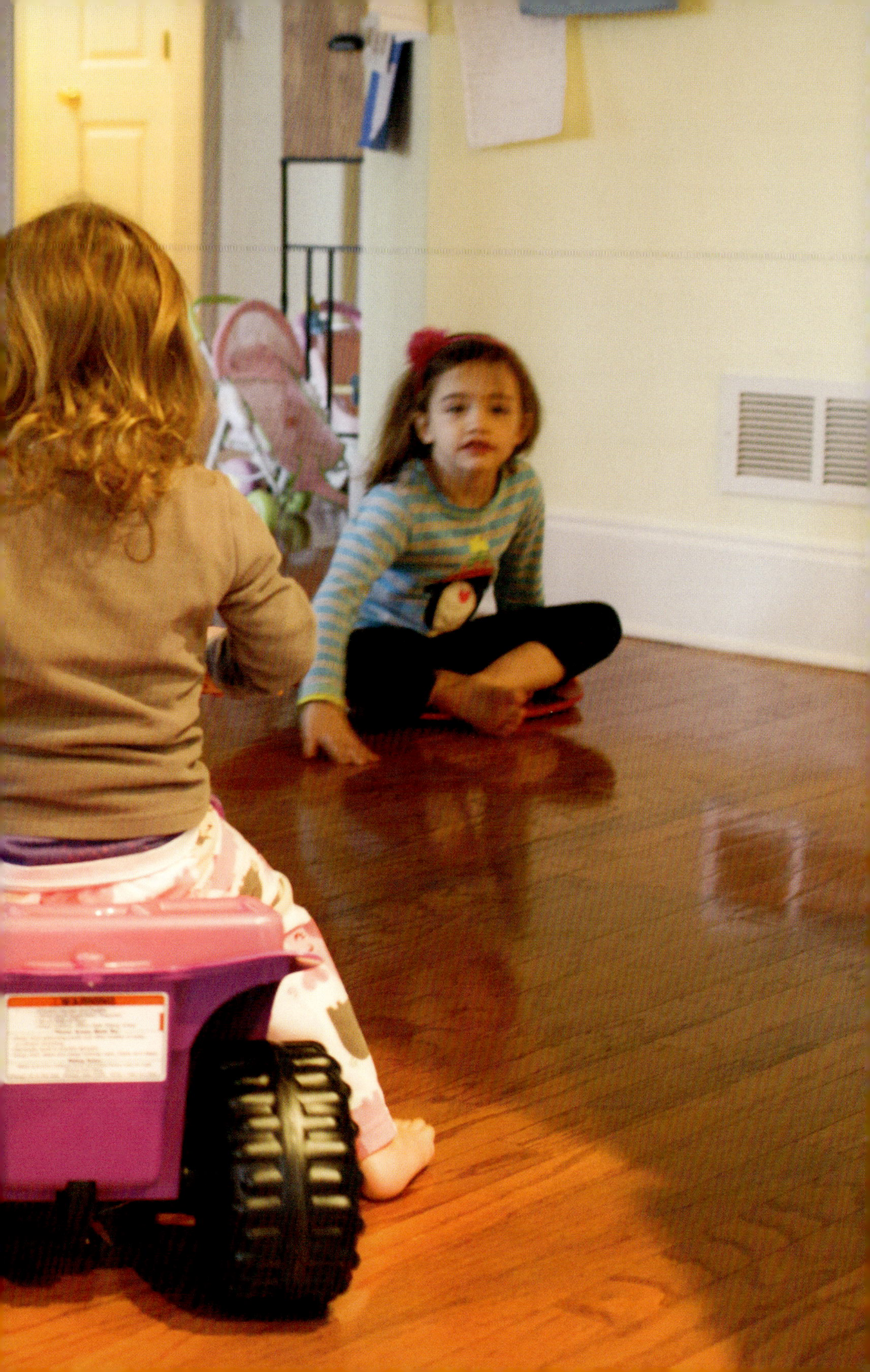

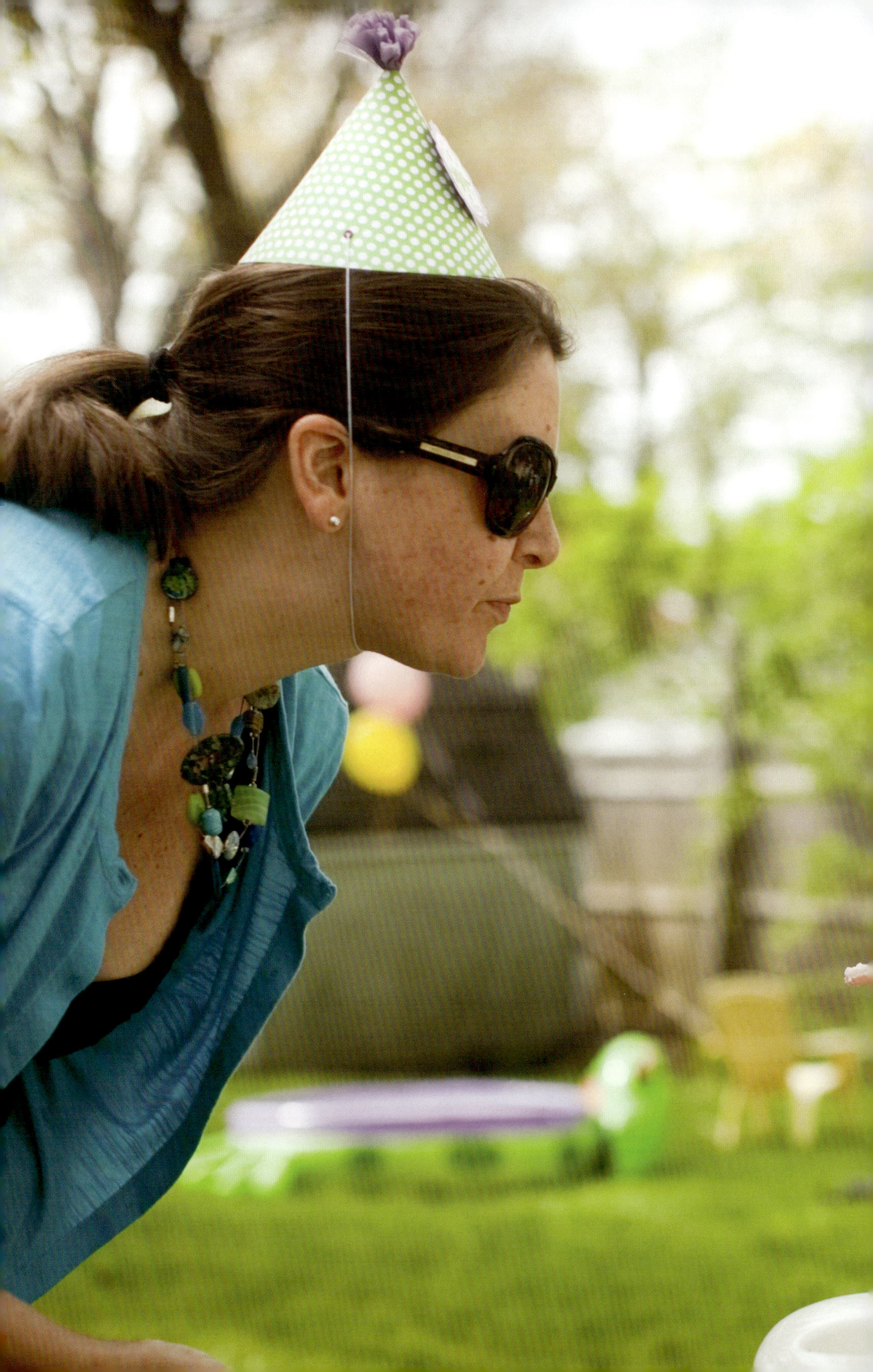

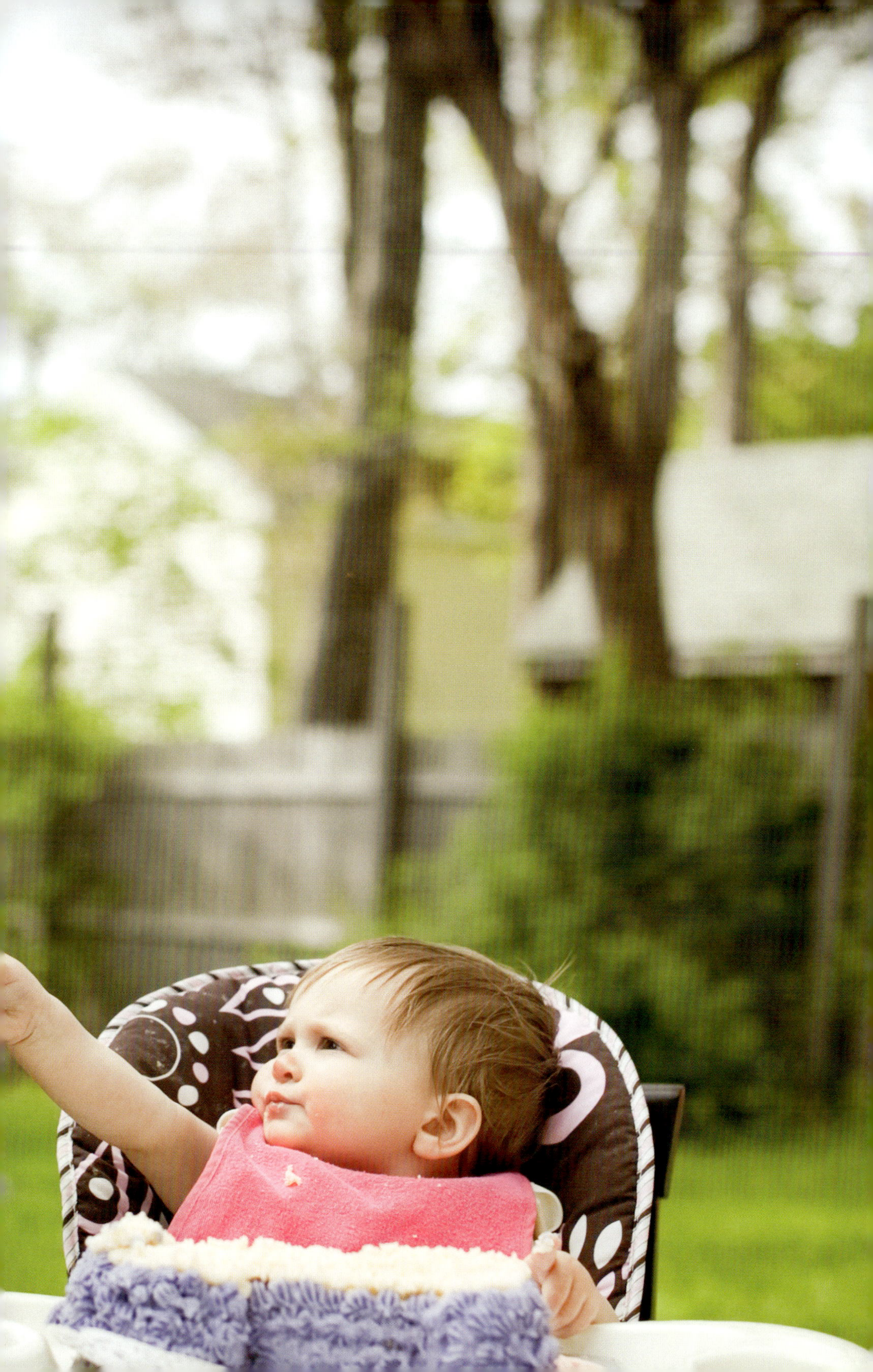

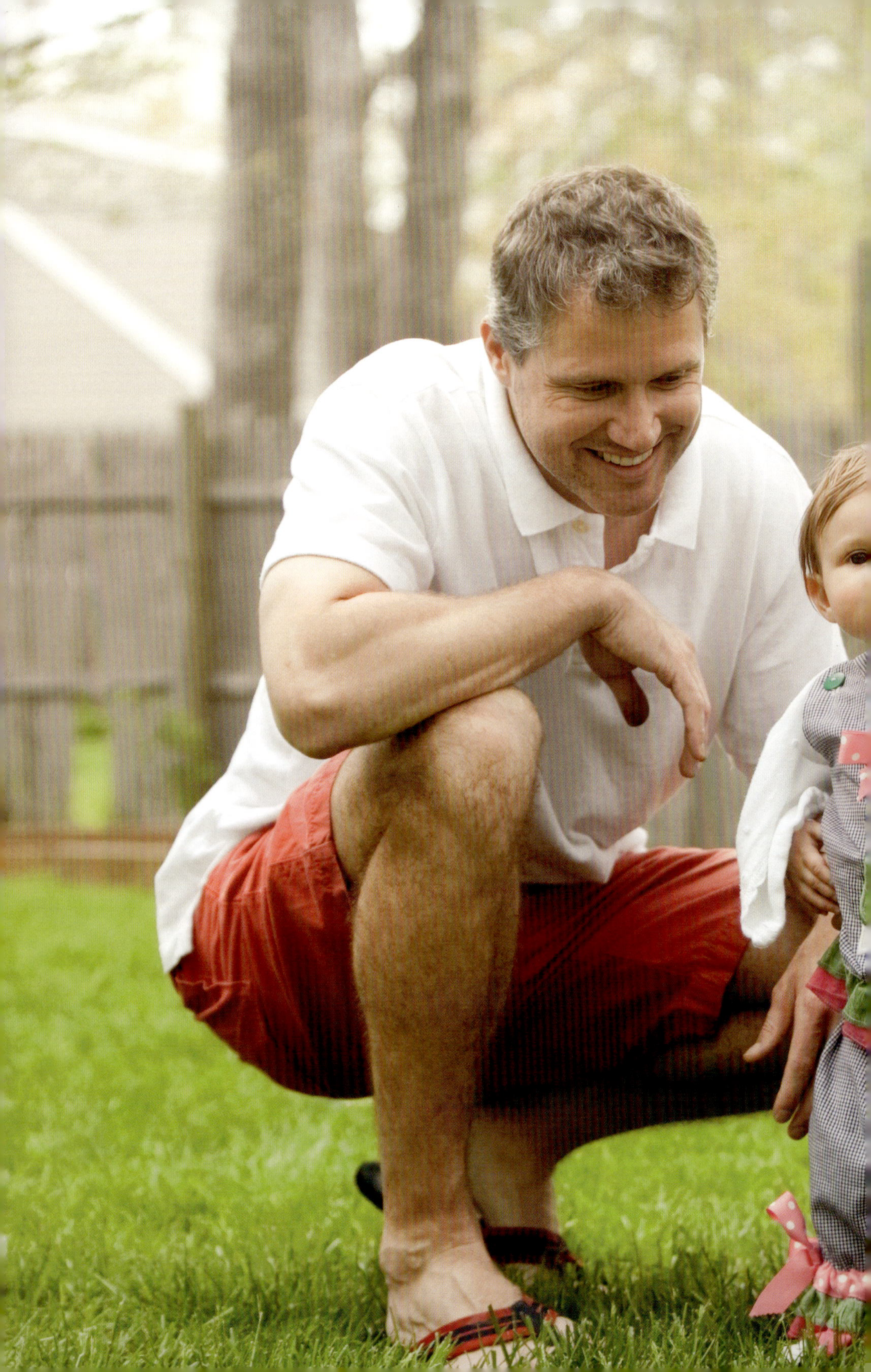

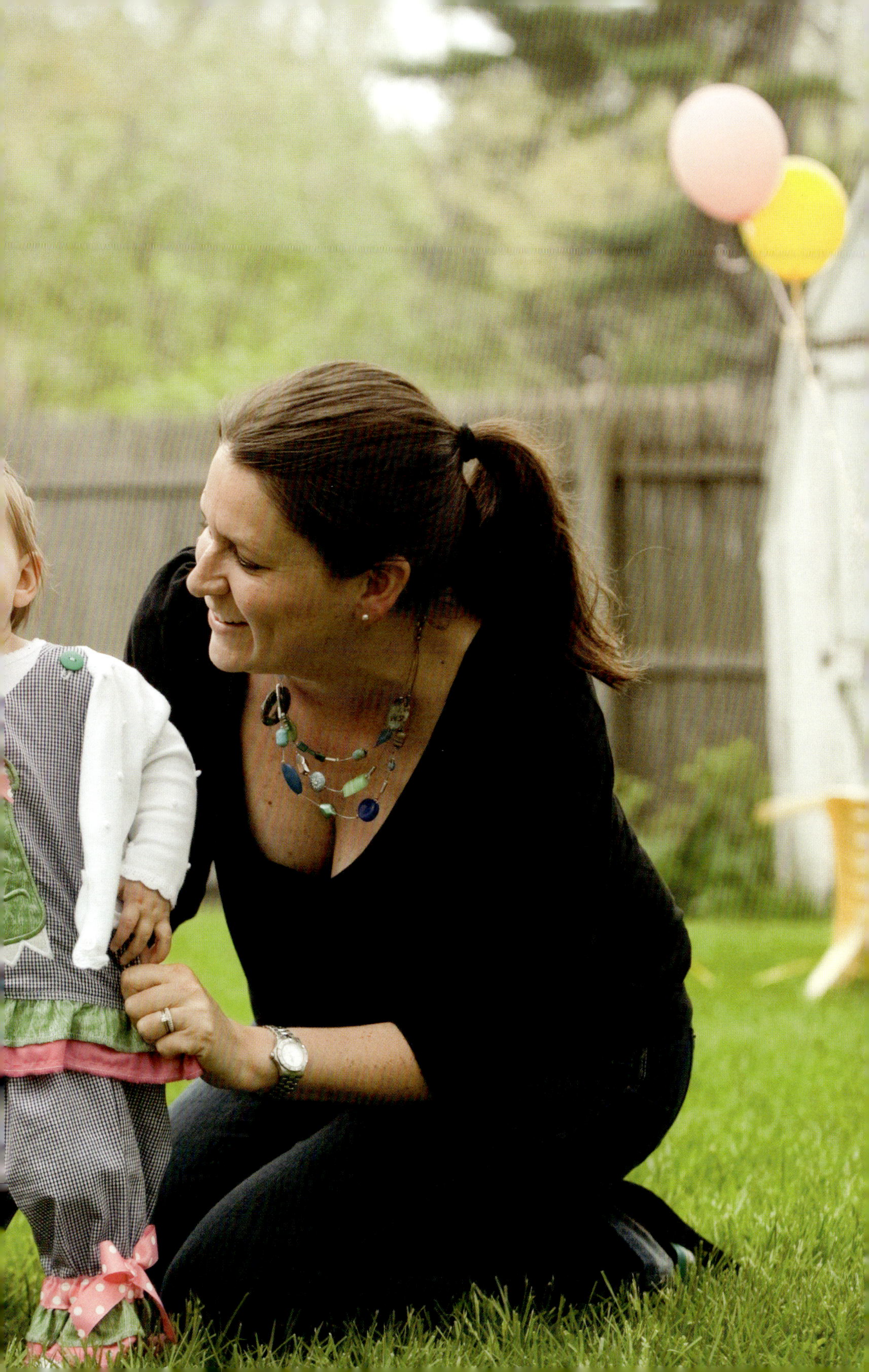

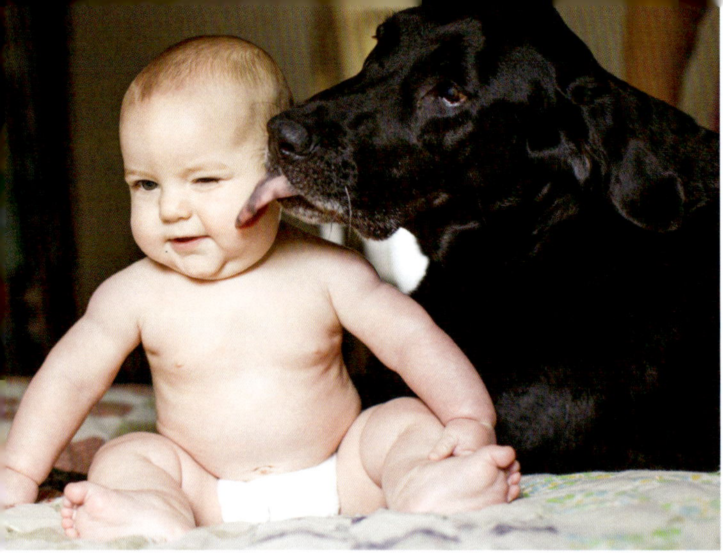

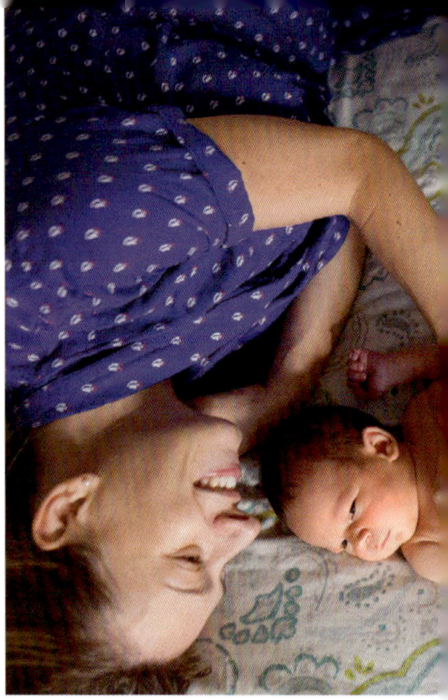

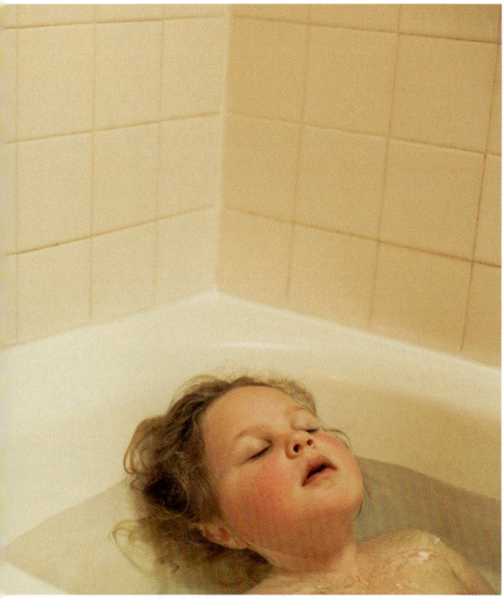

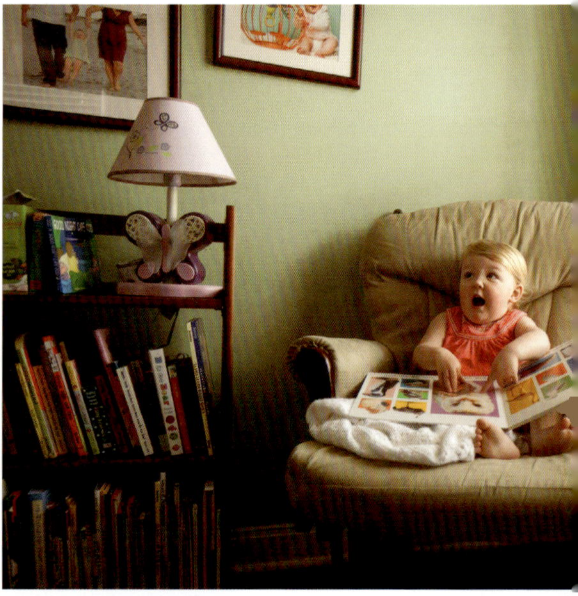

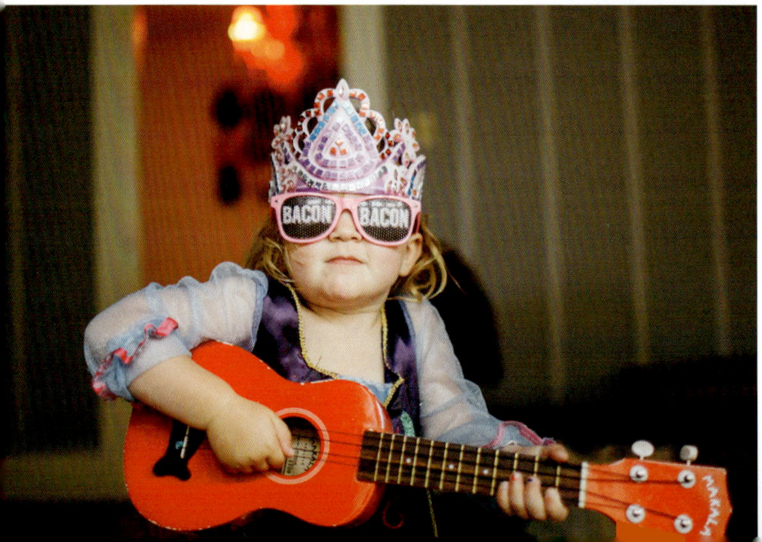
BACON
BACON

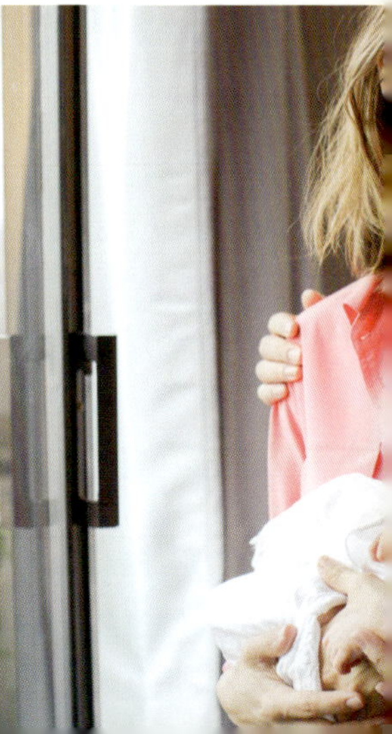

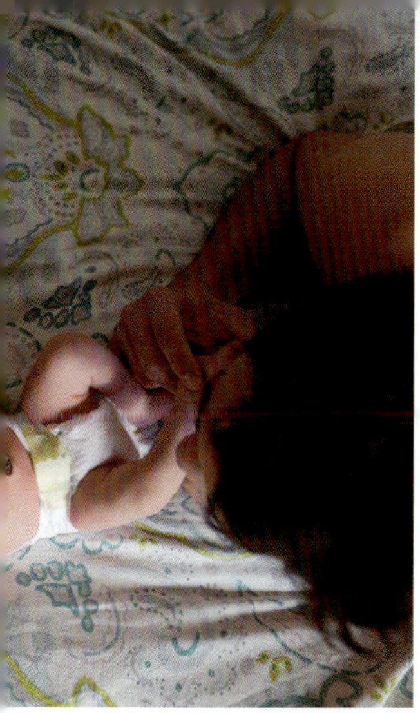
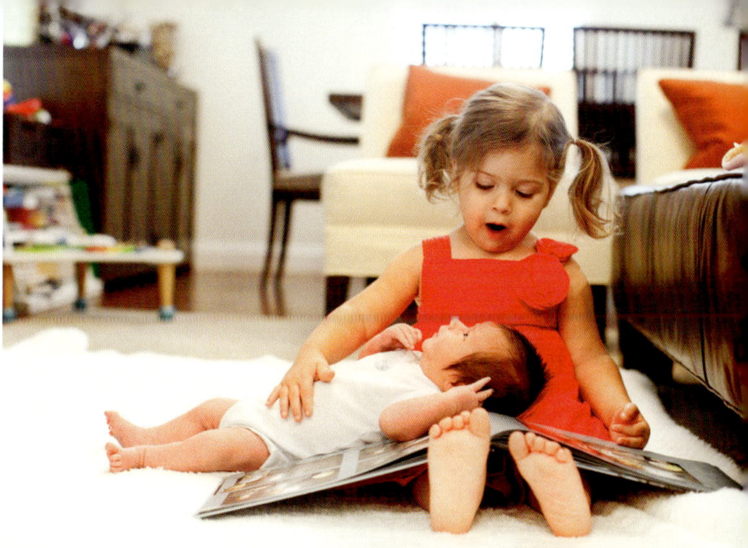
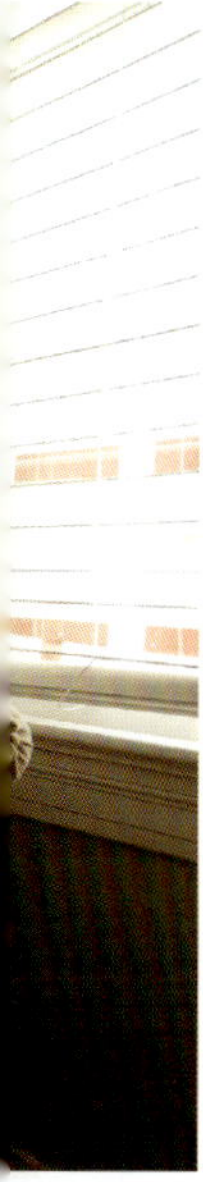
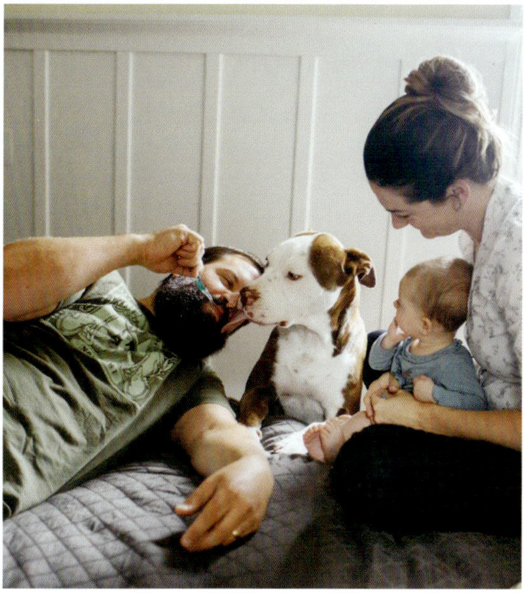
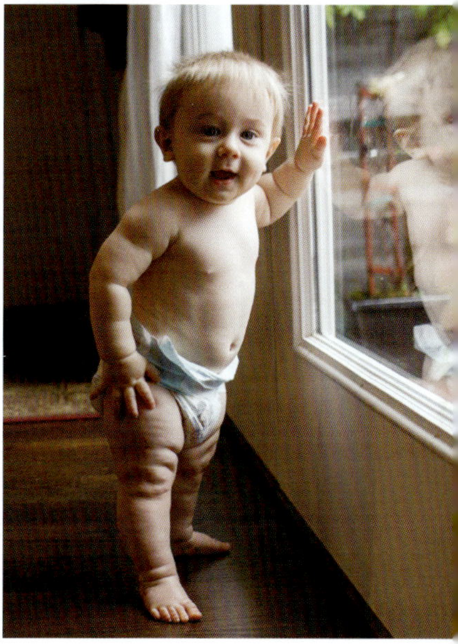
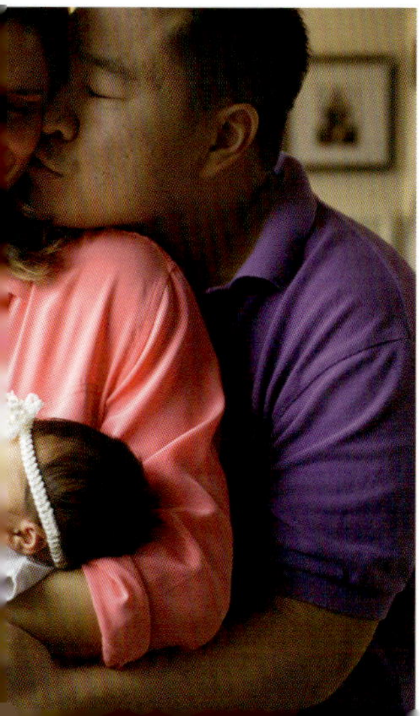
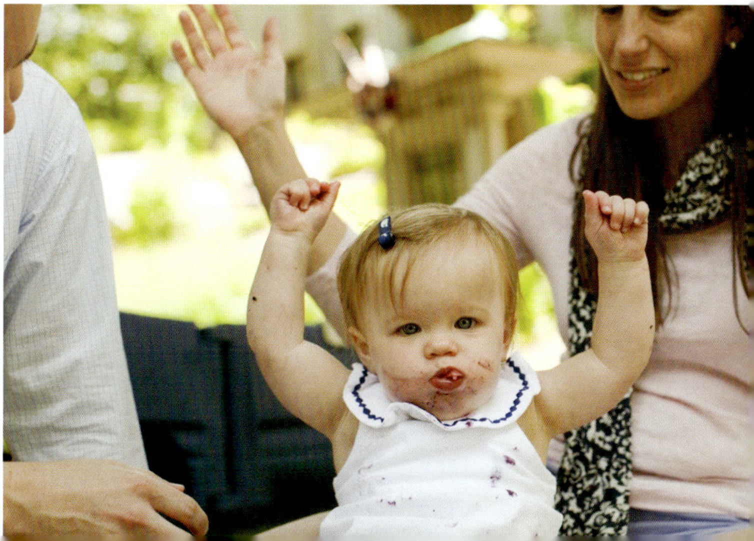

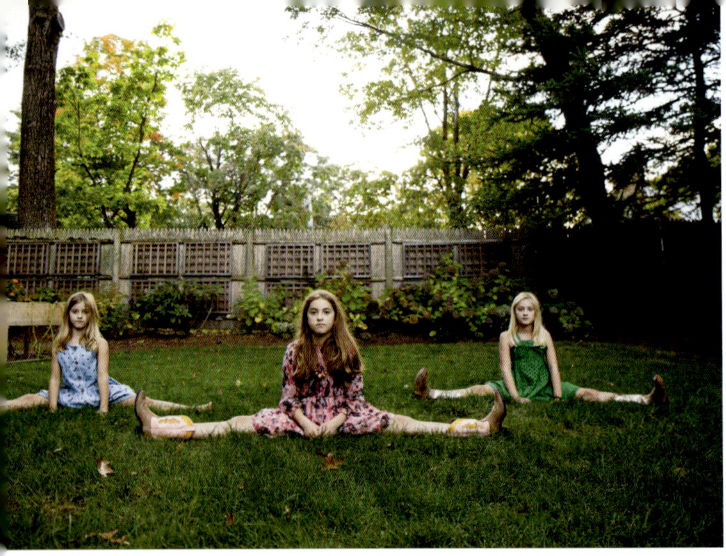

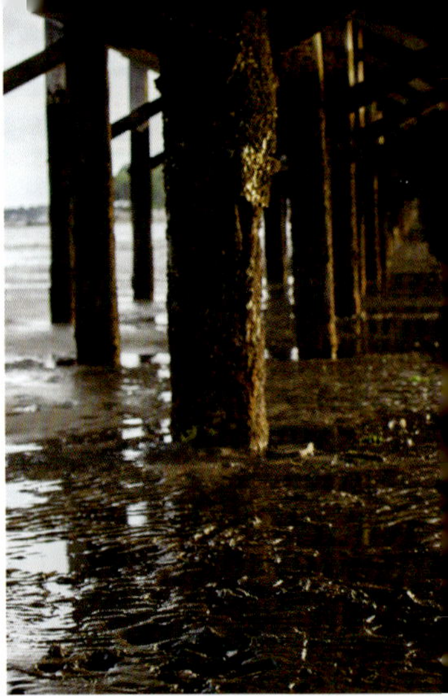

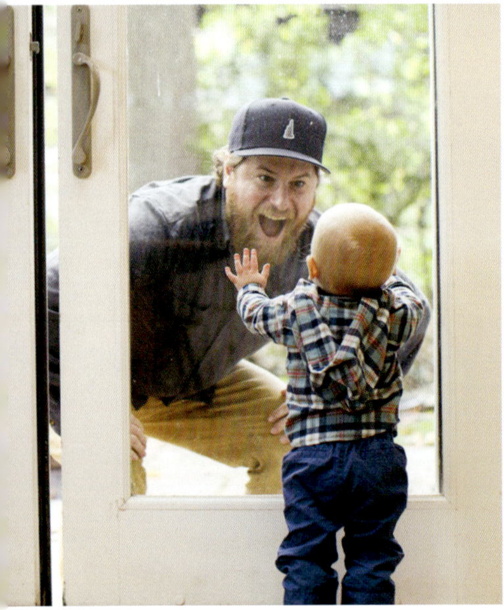

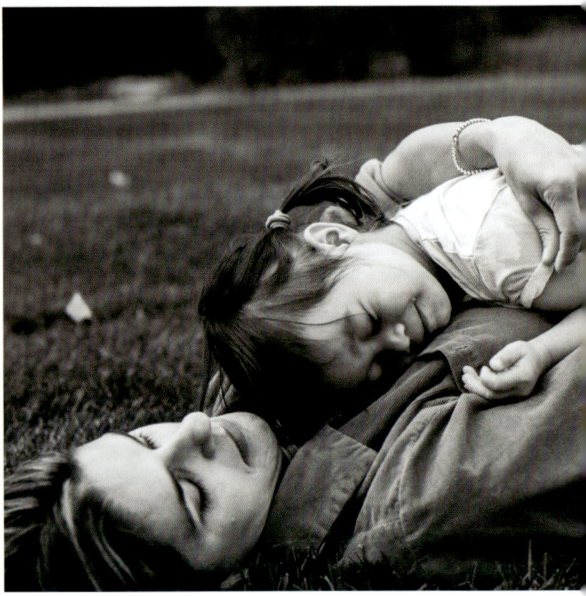

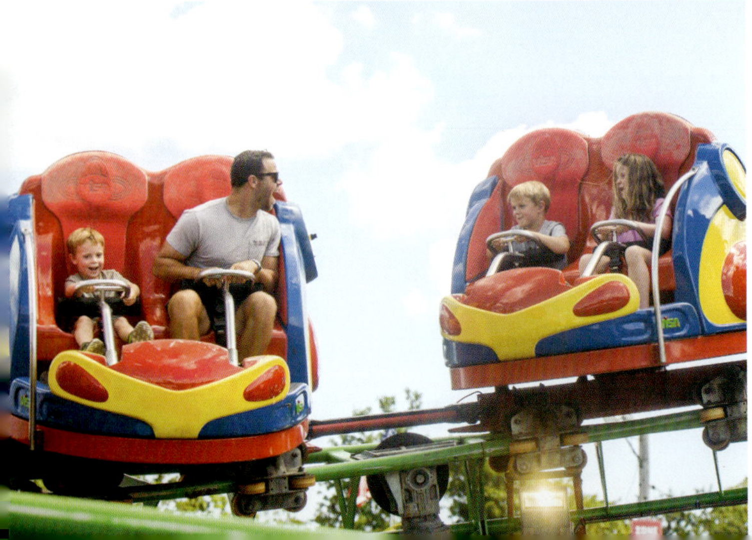

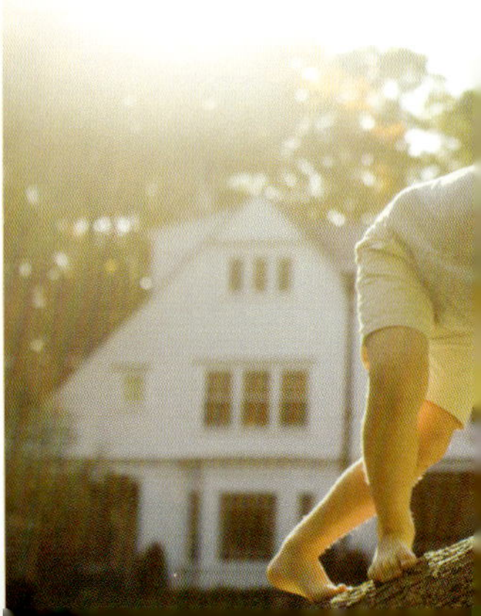

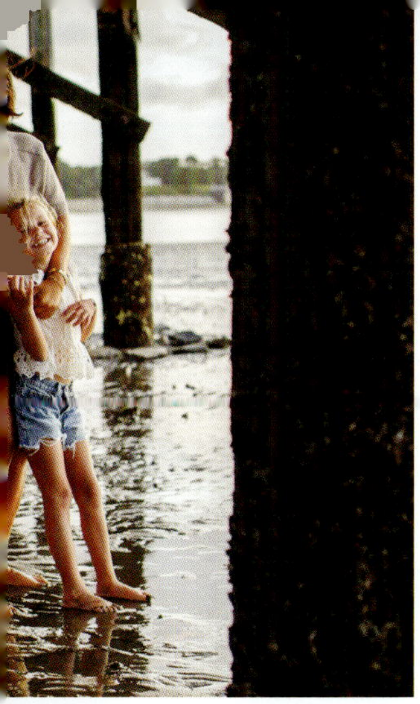
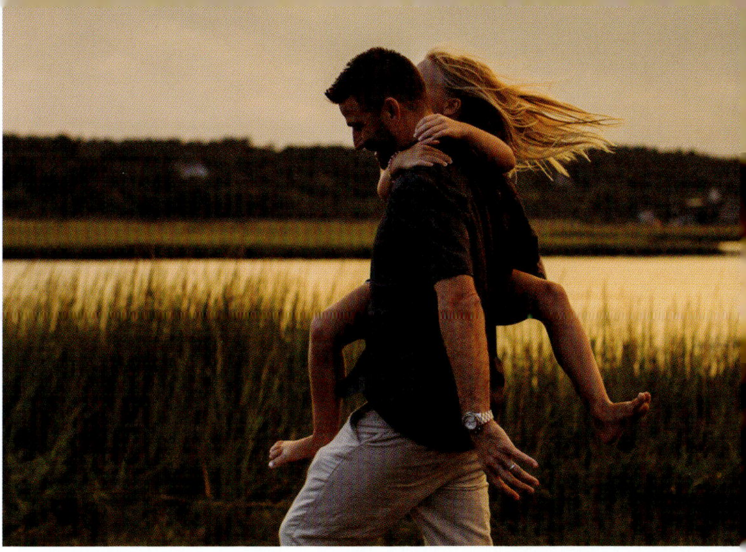
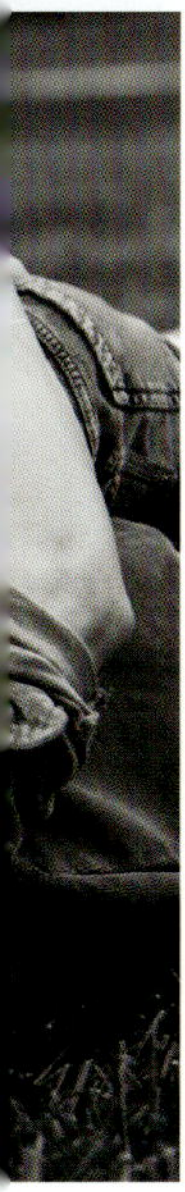
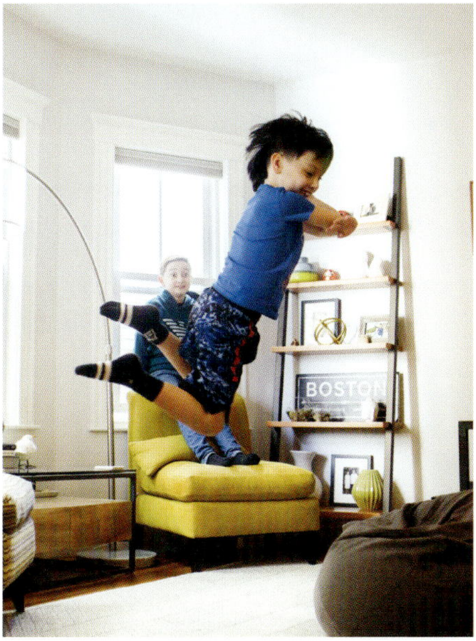
BOSTON
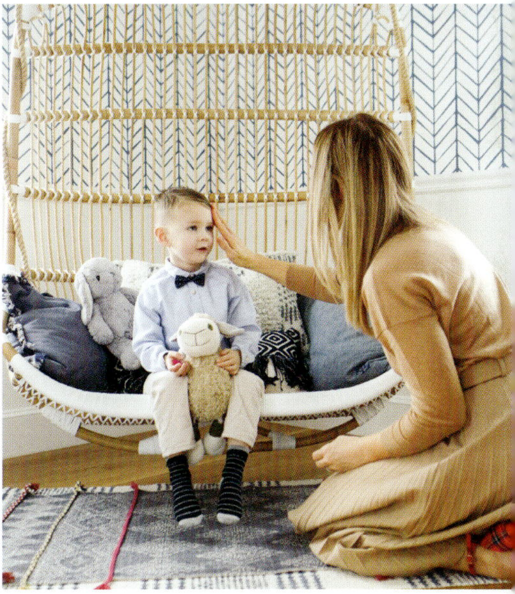
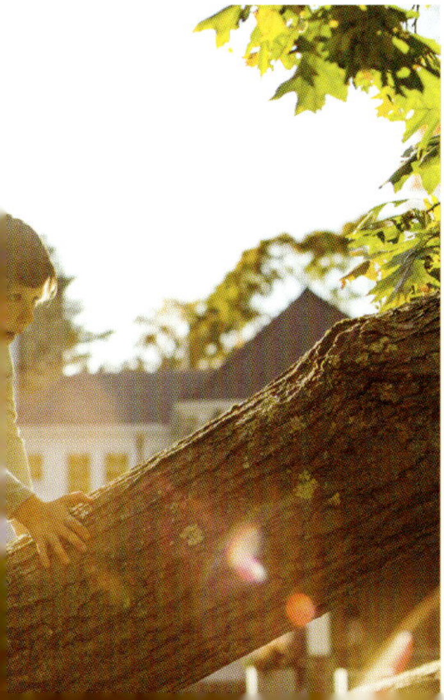
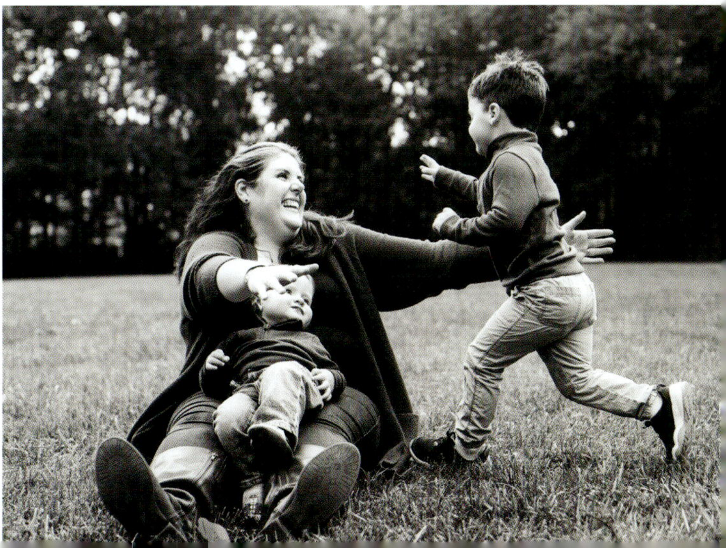

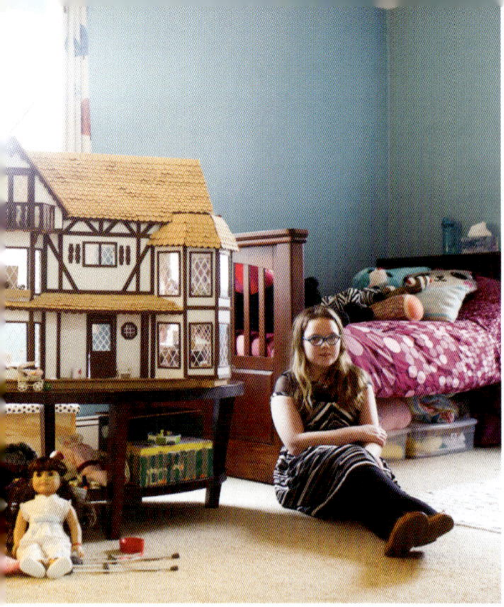

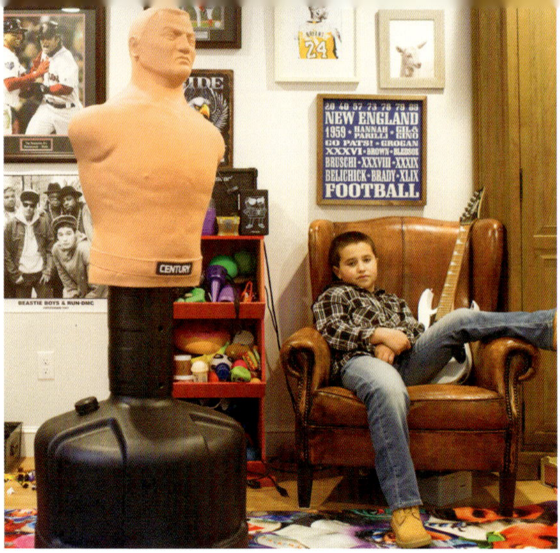
NEW ENGLAND
FOOTBALL
CENTURY

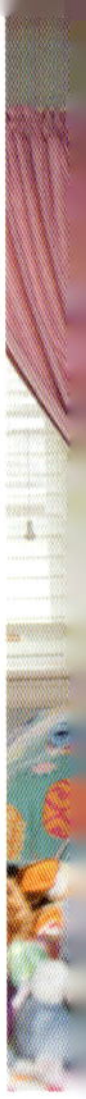

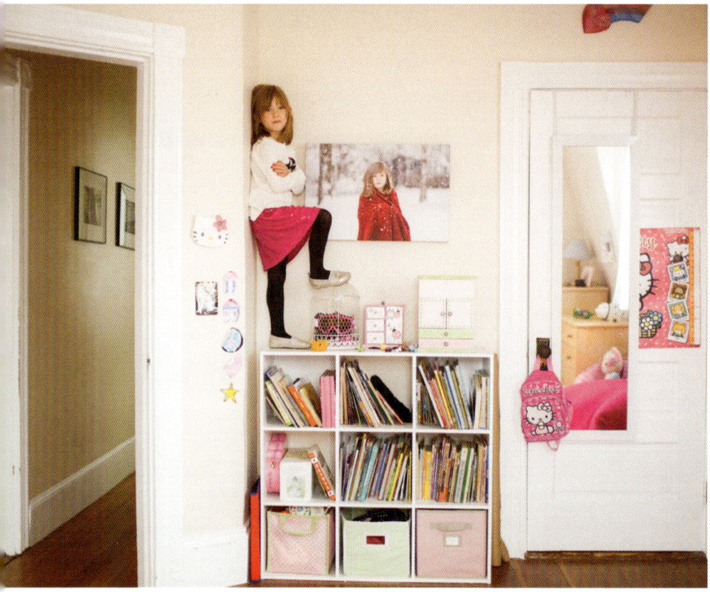

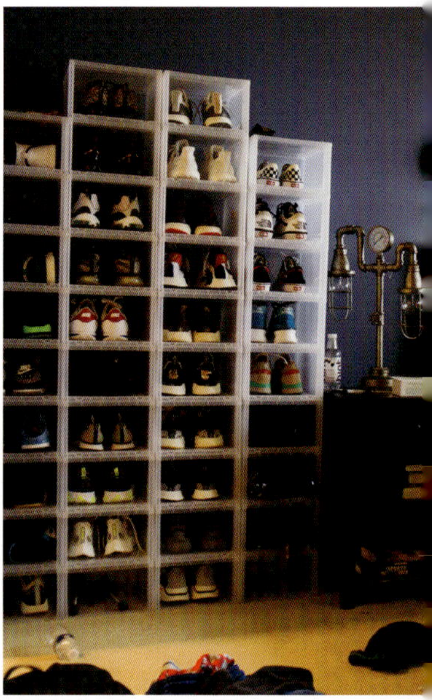

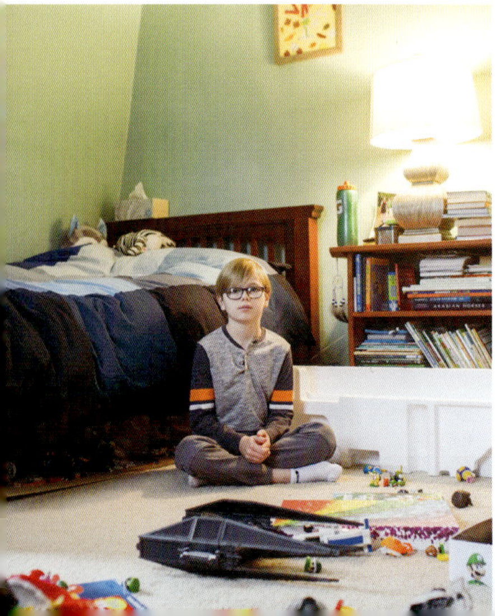

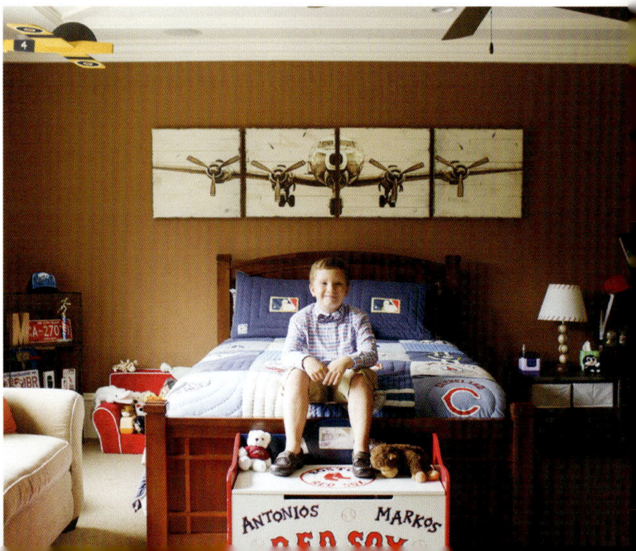
ANTONIOS
MARKOS

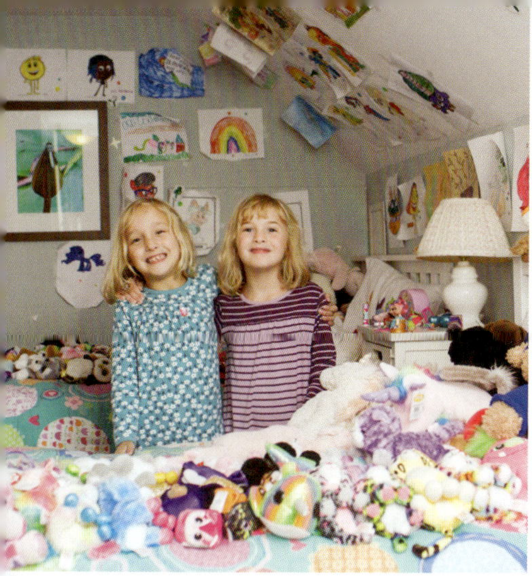

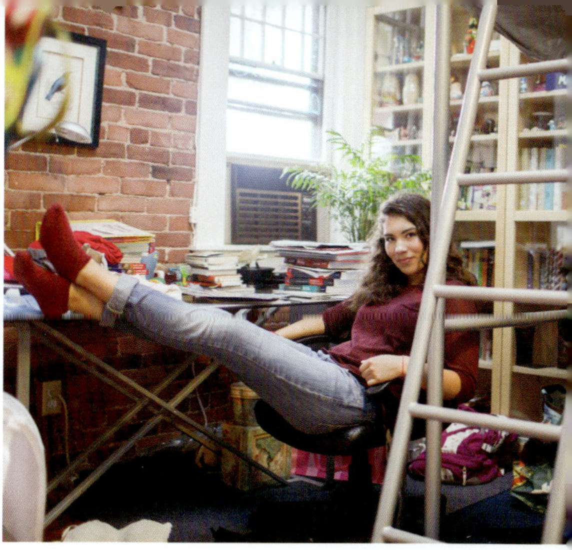

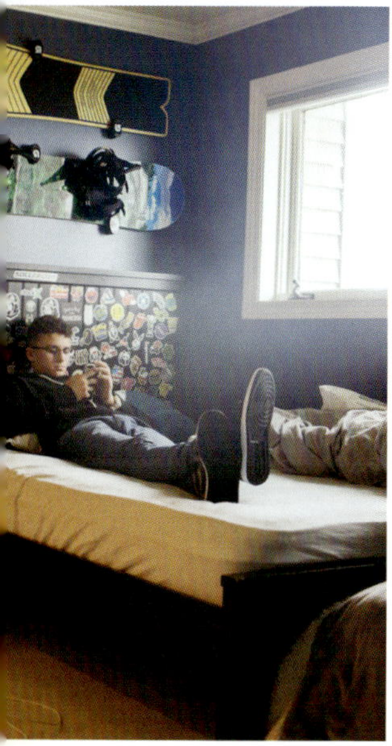

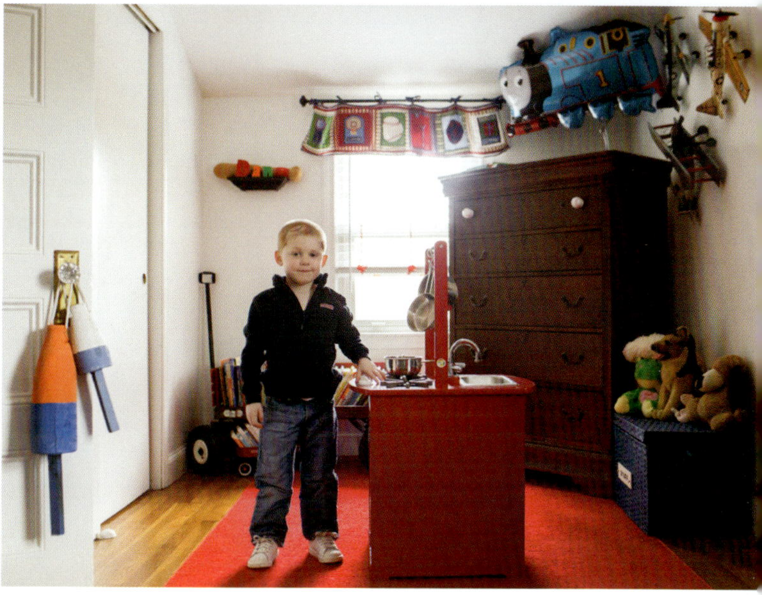

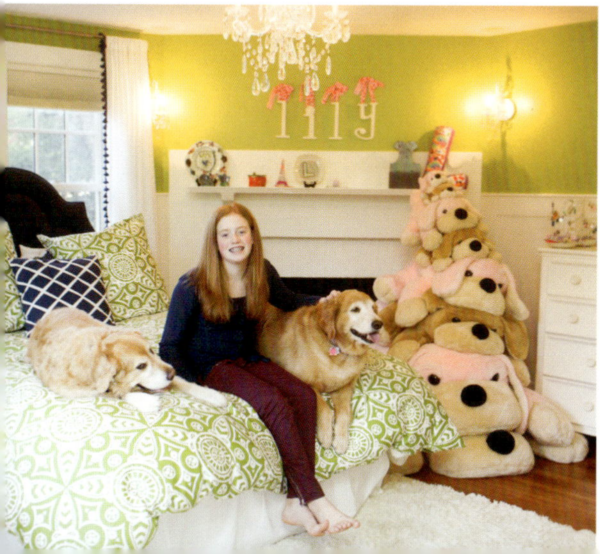
lily

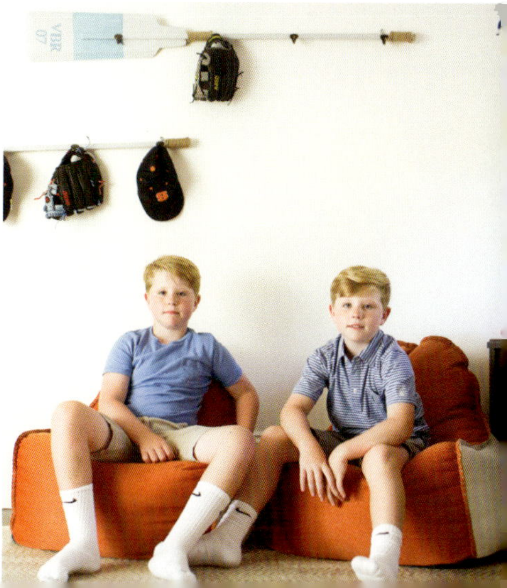

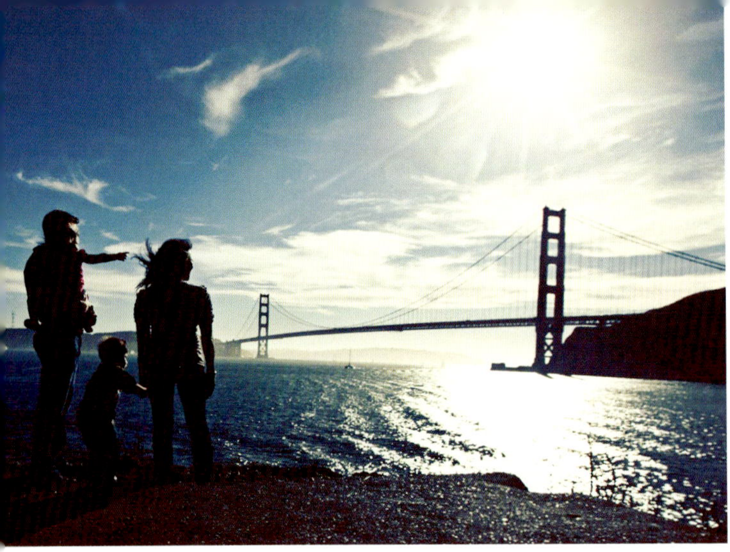
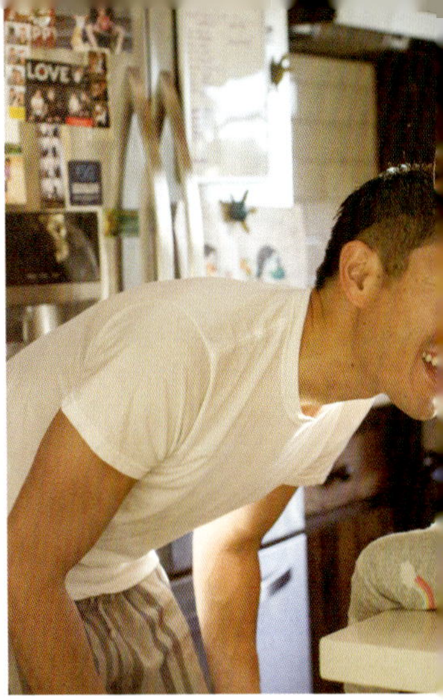
LOVE
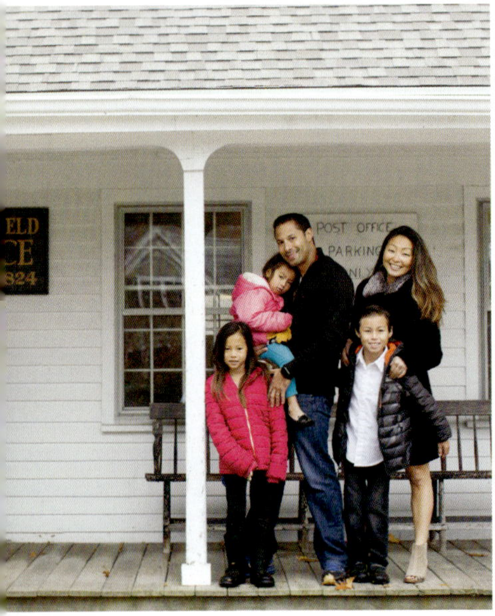
POST OFFICE
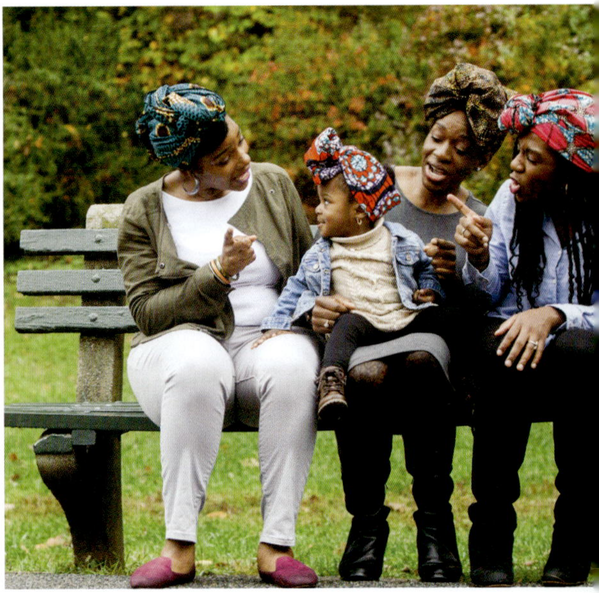
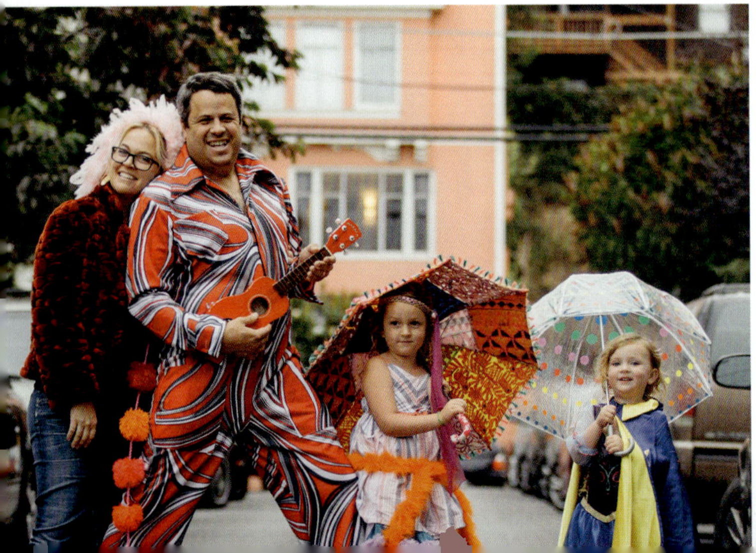
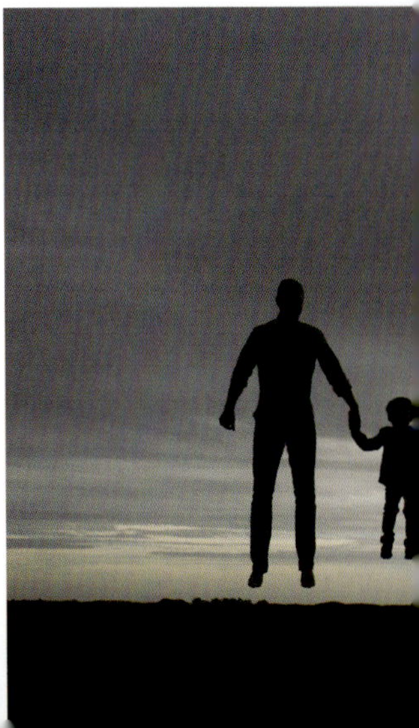

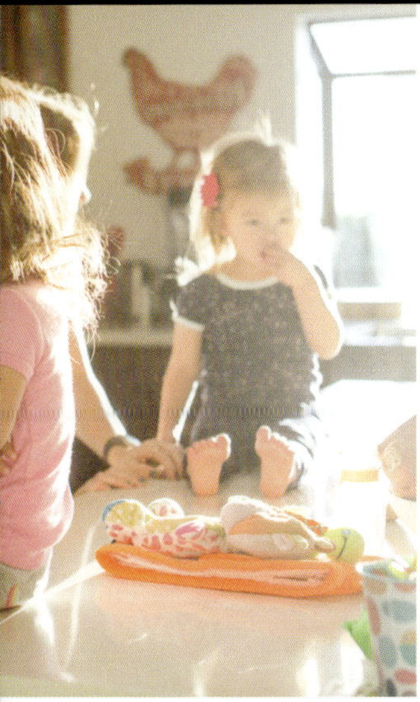
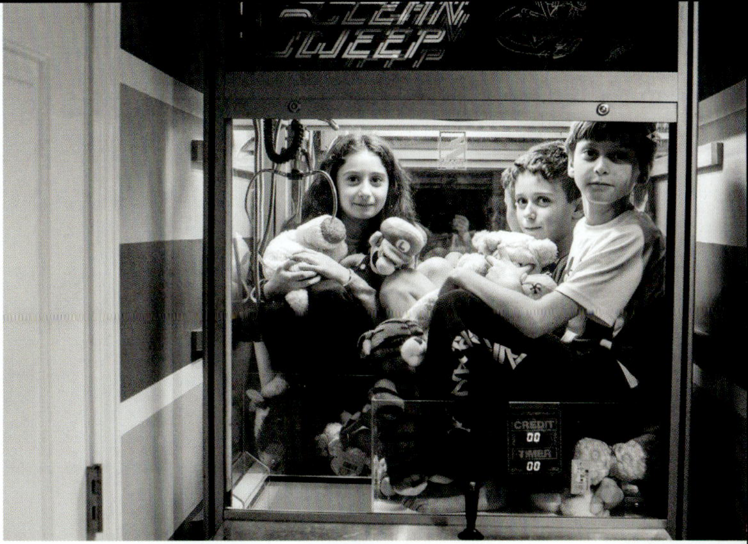
CREDIT
TIMER
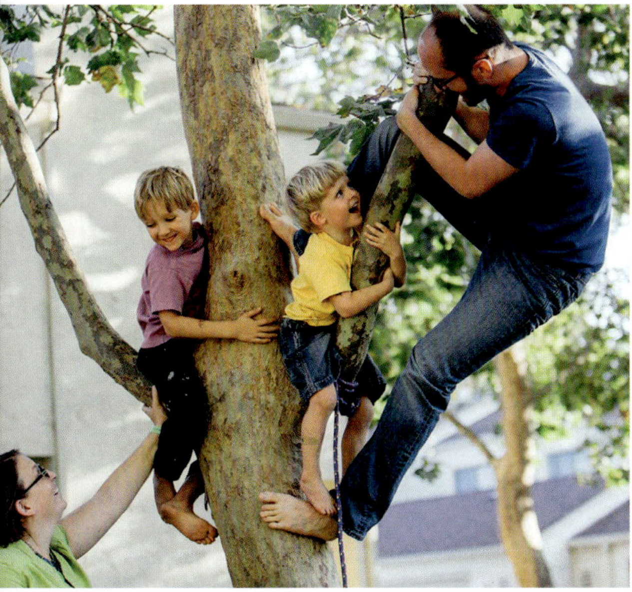
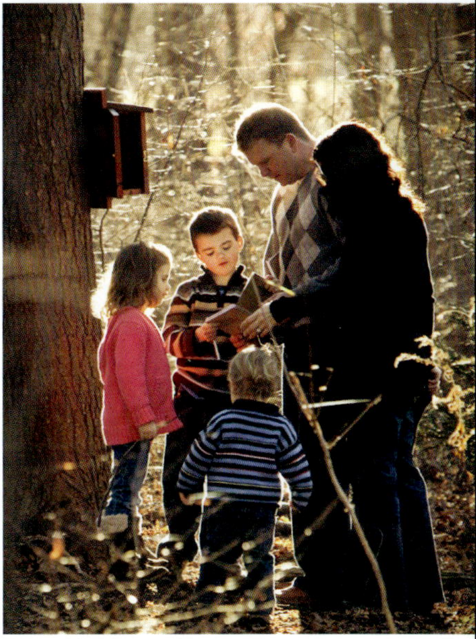
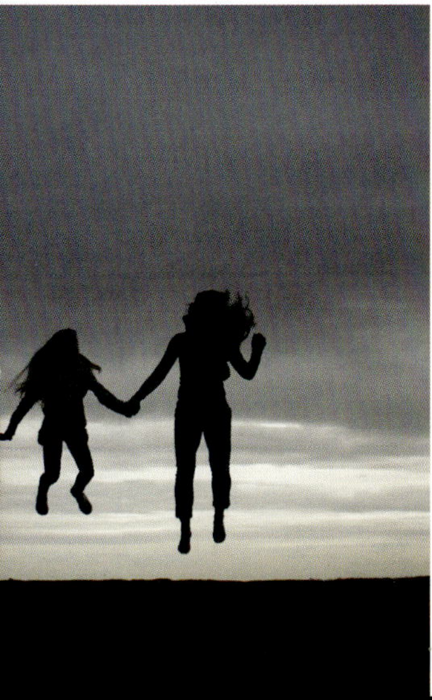
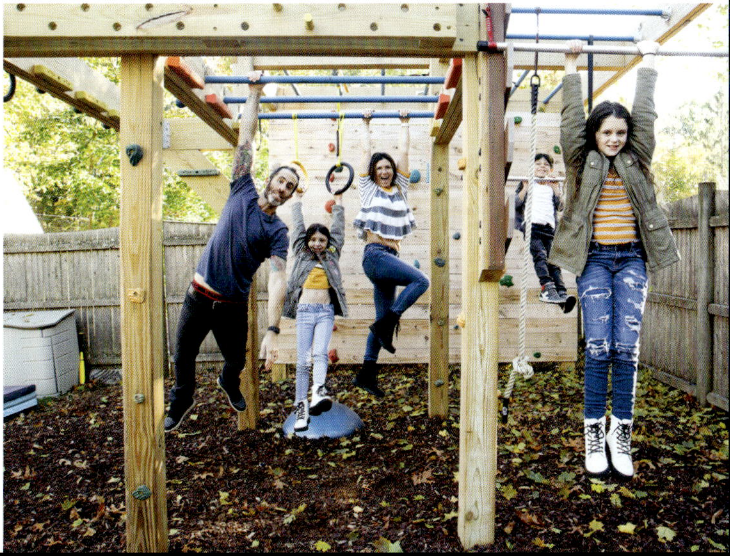

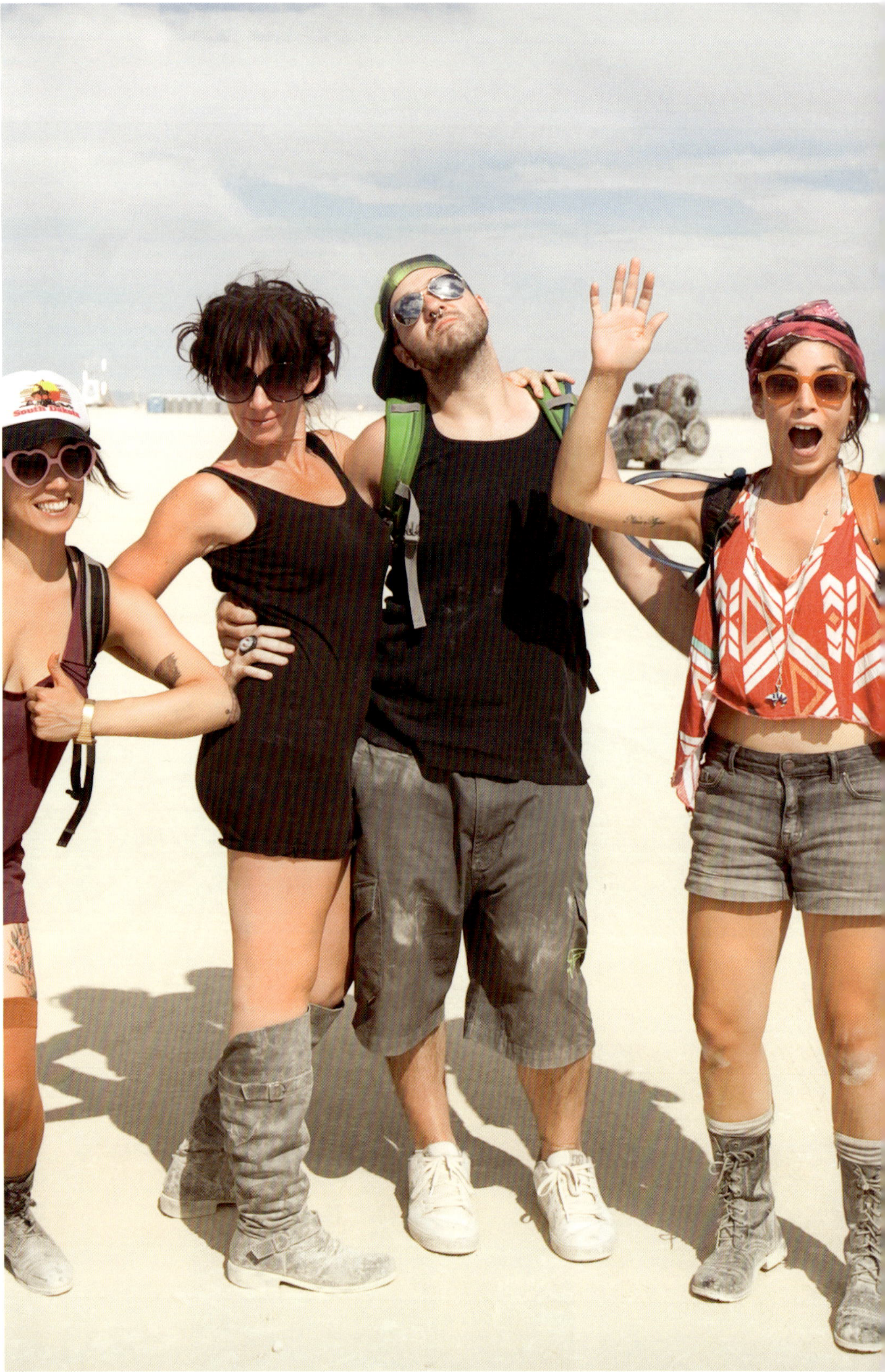
South Dakota

Never Been the Same Since

A concerned friend took me out to lunch one day to tell me about his new therapist, Harry. He said that Harry made him feel completely transformed—like a new person. He strongly suggested that I hire Harry to start my own transformation into a new person. I immediately made my first appointment and met with Harry once a week for five years.

Harry helped me slam the brakes on binge drinking and come to terms with my mom's illness. He helped me stop destructive behavioral patterns and find ways to emotionally regulate. The people close to me noticed such a 180-degree turn in my personality that more than one friend also saw Harry for many years.

In addition to lots of therapy, Harry gave me two life-changing pieces of advice.

One day I was sitting in Harry's office, 34 years old and four years into my photography career—you know the one, my dream job, the one I always wanted—lamenting that I loved the work, but I was lonely. Turns out that wedding and family photography is a lucrative, creative, ultra-positive career with no community.

"Go to Burning Man," he said, like it was the most obvious thing in the world. "I'm sure there's a whole community from Boston that goes every year. I bet they're all artists. It'll be fun."

Flora, my dear friend who I volunteered in New Orleans with, had been going to Burning Man for many years at that point, and every year she'd get home, call me, and urge me to come with her next time. "Trust me!" she promised, "You'll love it!"

I had heard enough lore about Burning Man that the thought alone overwhelmed me. I pictured doing too many drugs, being too hungover, getting too depressed, not being sexy enough, and then feeling trapped there. I didn't want to go. But with Harry's urging on top of hers, I was in. I called Flora and asked if I could camp with her. She told me she'd take care of absolutely everything. All I needed to do was get there.

Eight months later I flew to Reno, rented a car, and drove to the middle of nowhere: Black Rock City, Nevada. I arrived on a Wednesday, and the 50,000-person party was already three days in. As far as I could tell I had either just arrived on the set of *Mad Max* or on the surface of the Moon. I stepped out of my squeaky-clean rental car wearing jeans and someone in a tutu covered in white dust rode by on their bicycle and yelled, "Welcome home! You're beautiful!!"

The reason Harry wanted me to go to Burning Man was so I could find people in the Boston area who were artists and creatives not living traditional lives. The reason, or one of them, that Flora wanted me to go was because she wanted me to feel the difference between being traditionally beautiful and feeling attractive. She hoped that going to Burning Man would be a way I could learn to celebrate who I was, not who I wished I was.

Both of their hopes came true. I found lifelong friendships with kindred spirits and felt sexier and more confident than I had in my life because of Burning Man. Back in Boston I began dressing in a way that felt truly expressive. I wore big boots every day for years, which made me feel like a superhero, and I wore clothes that were unapologetically sexy. I had just gotten my first tattoo and told the artist, "I want something that says I'm a strong, confident female artist." Now, with Burning Man in my blood and those flowers wrapped around my elbow, I was finally stepping into the confidence and self-expression I had always hoped for. At 35, I finally felt awesome in my own skin.

I've been to Burning Man a total of four times, which is nothing for lifetime Burners, but it was enough for me to learn the lessons I needed to learn. Though I camped with Flora's friends from Portland, Oregon, I immediately, and have consistently, met other people who have gone. This is- in part- how I met the large crew of people I have spent the last 15 years calling my best friends. I have an incredibly strong community with creative, expressive, beautiful human beings who are in my life because I went to Burning Man. Harry was right: I found my community, in one degree of separation or another, through making that leap. I have never been the same since.

A couple of years later, I was sitting in the chair across from Harry and told him I was looking for a second job that fostered community. I had friends outside of work, but I wanted friends at work. "I'm thinking of becoming a bartender," I told him.

He spit his coffee across the room. "No," he said immediately. "That is not a good path for you. That's not smart. You do not want to do that."

I assume he was thinking about the long line of alcoholics who have come before me and what would happen to my life if I had an endless supply of booze at my fingertips.

"Orrrrr ..." I continued, floating the other idea I was toying with, "a yoga teacher!" I chirped with a hopeful grin.

"Better," he exhaled. "Much, much better."

When I set out to find a community through teaching yoga, the only style I wanted to teach was Baron Baptiste's power yoga. Ten years earlier, I had stumbled into Lisa Black's Power Yoga class at 8 Limbs Yoga in Seattle and fell in love. Sweaty, athletic, and dance-like, power yoga had me hooked.

Soon after I found Lisa's class in Seattle, I learned that I was moving back to Boston. When Lisa and I were saying goodbye to each other she told me that her teacher, Baron Baptiste, who invented the sequence she taught, had not one but two studios in Boston. The first morning I arrived home in Massachusetts in 2003, I walked into the Cambridge Baptiste studio, and for nearly a decade I practiced there every day before finally considering teacher training.

I signed up for Baron's iconic Level One: Journey into Power in Hawaii, and I absolutely loved it. The whole training I sat uncharacteristically quiet during the group sharing exercises as others got up to share their personal stories. The week before this I had done ayahuasca for the first time, so I was calm, steady, and observant for the first time ... ever? But at the end of the training I finally stood at the mic to speak. I explained how I was recently at a crossroads in my life and had asked my therapist which path I should take to cure the loneliness of professional photography: bartending or teaching yoga? I elaborated on how Harry practically fell out of his seat at the thought of me bartending, and I'm sure I overdid it in every possible way because when I finished speaking, the room erupted in a standing ovation.

From the stage, Baron asked, "Can everyone feel how much heart she has?"

Right then and there, hoping people *could* feel how much heart I had, I knew I would build the rest of my life around teaching yoga. I have never been the same since.

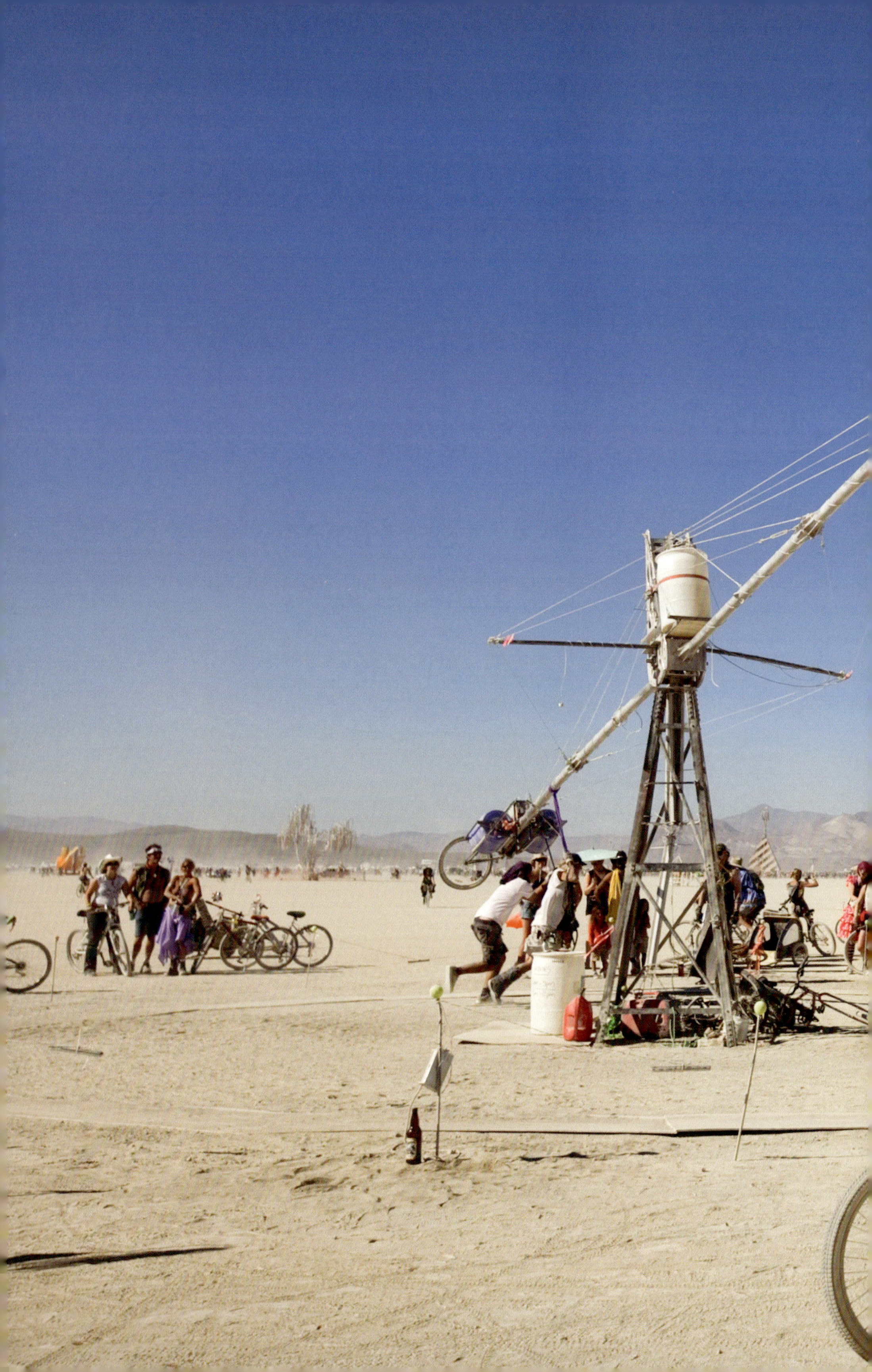

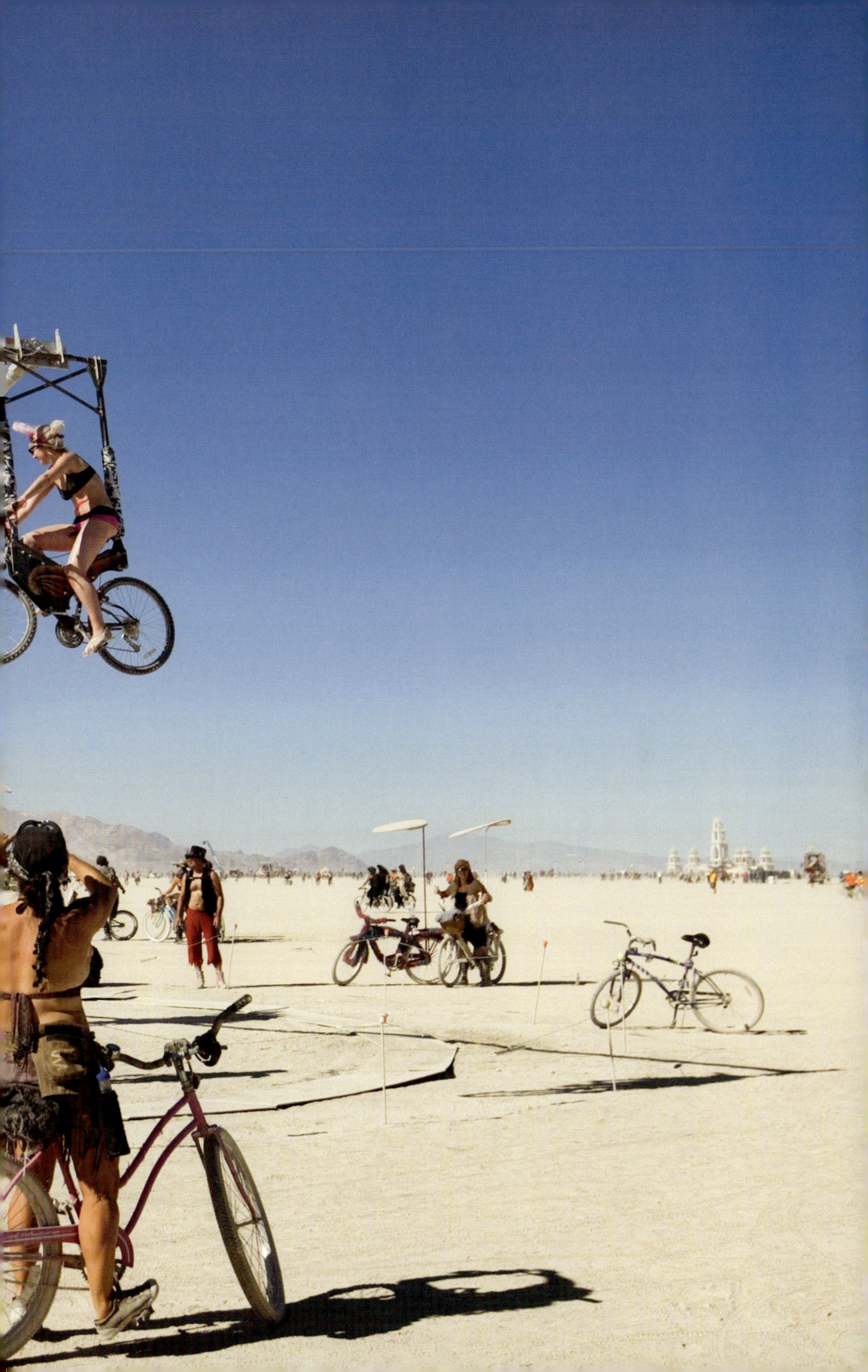

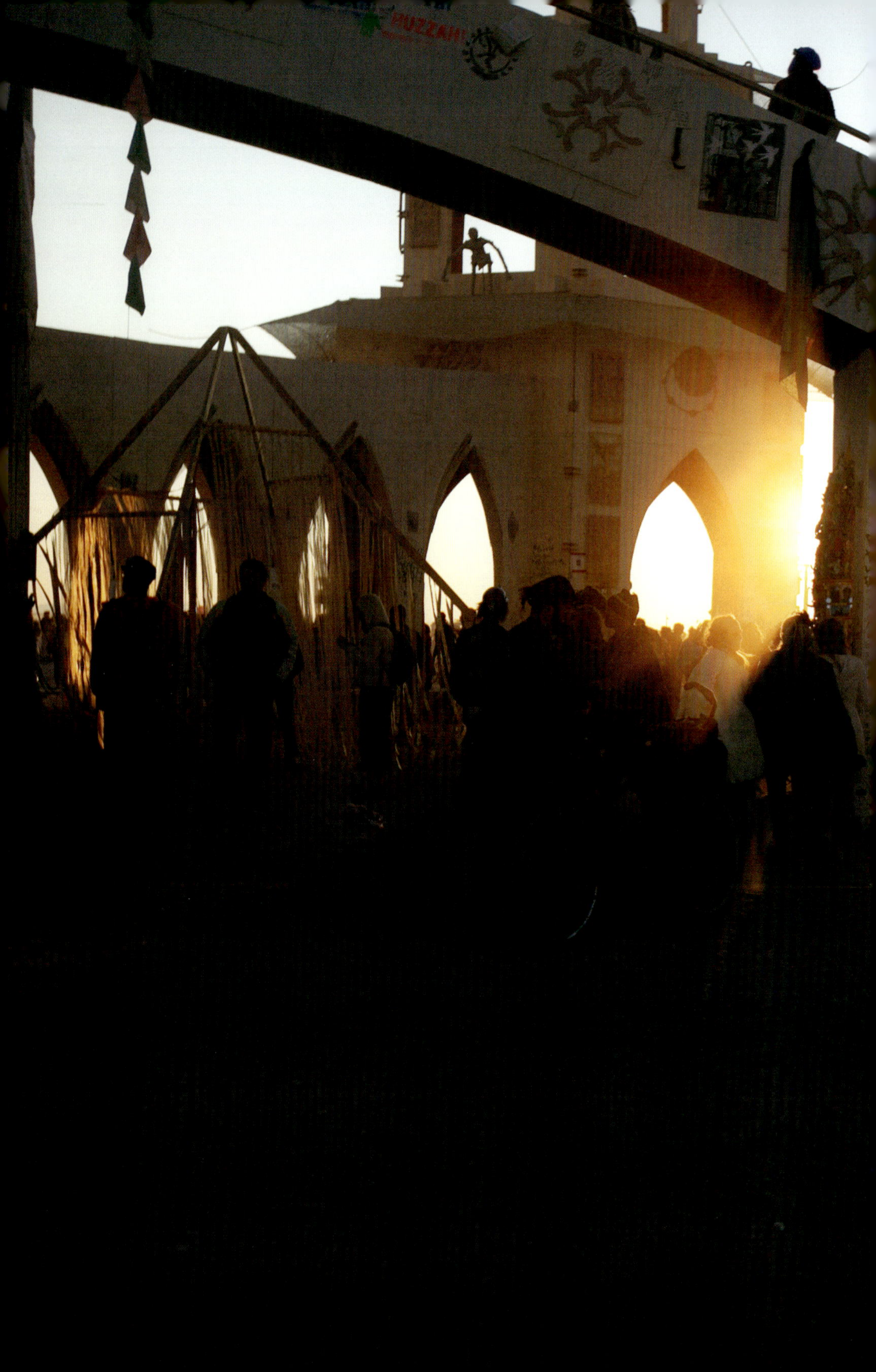
HUZZAH!

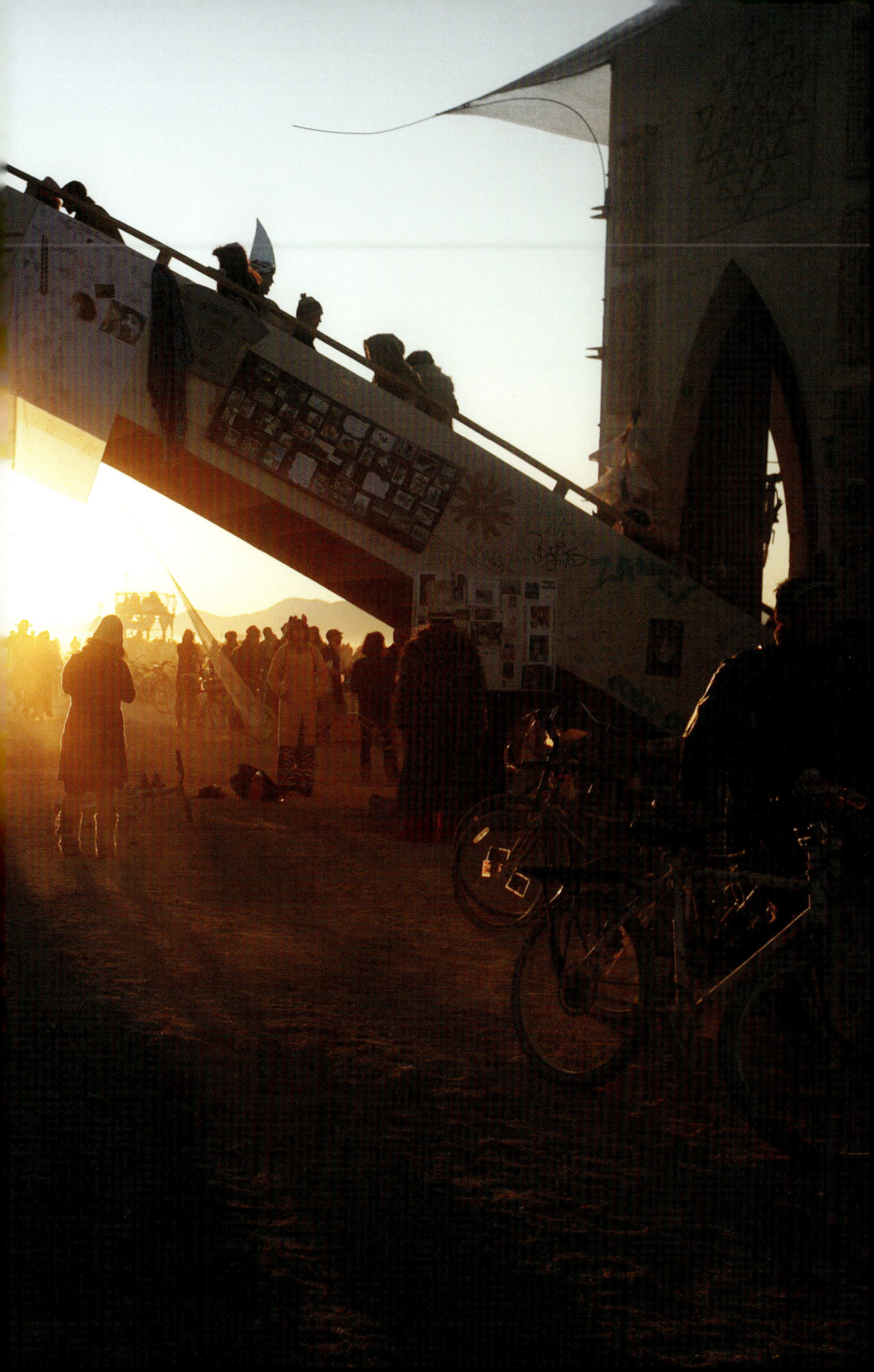

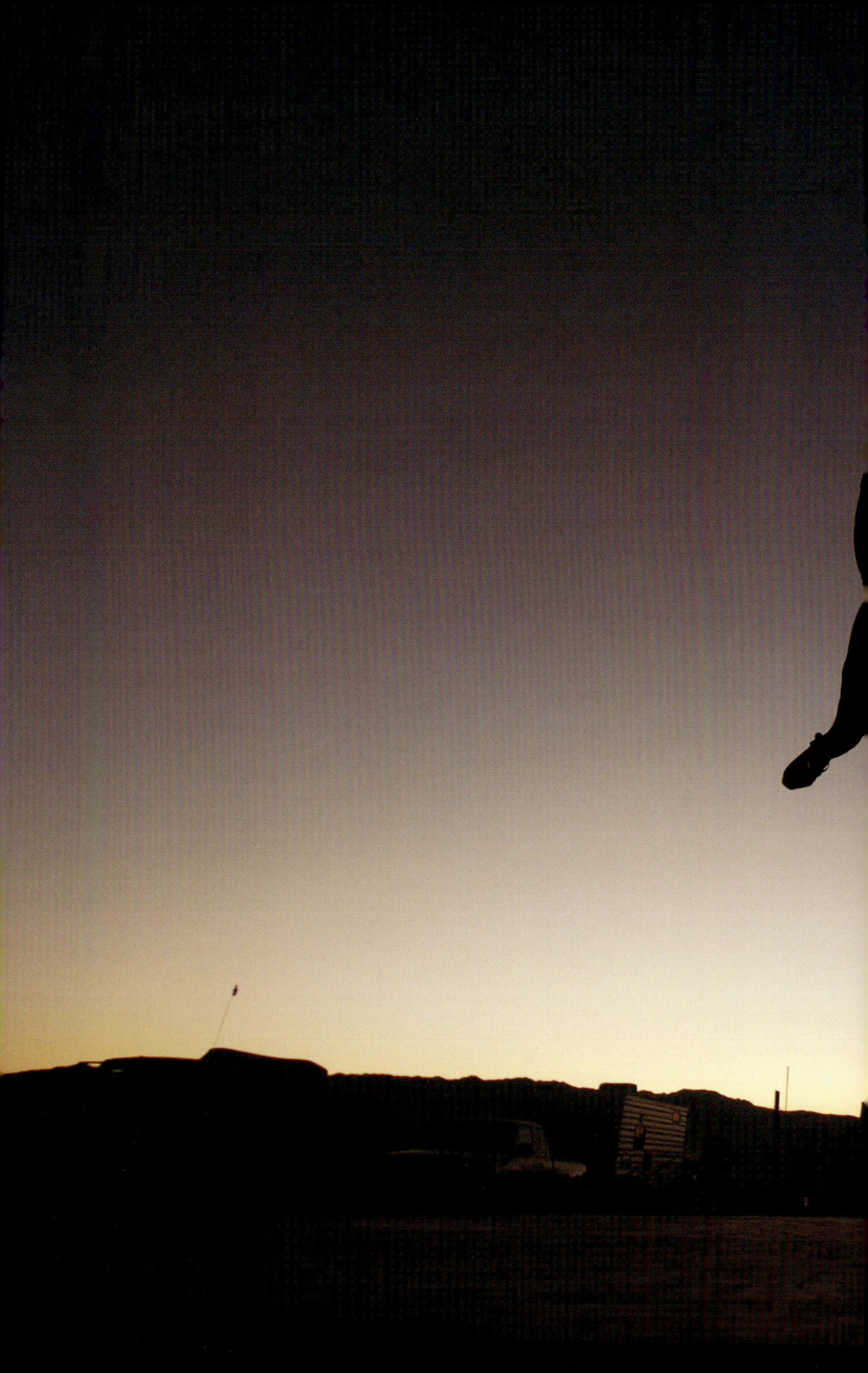

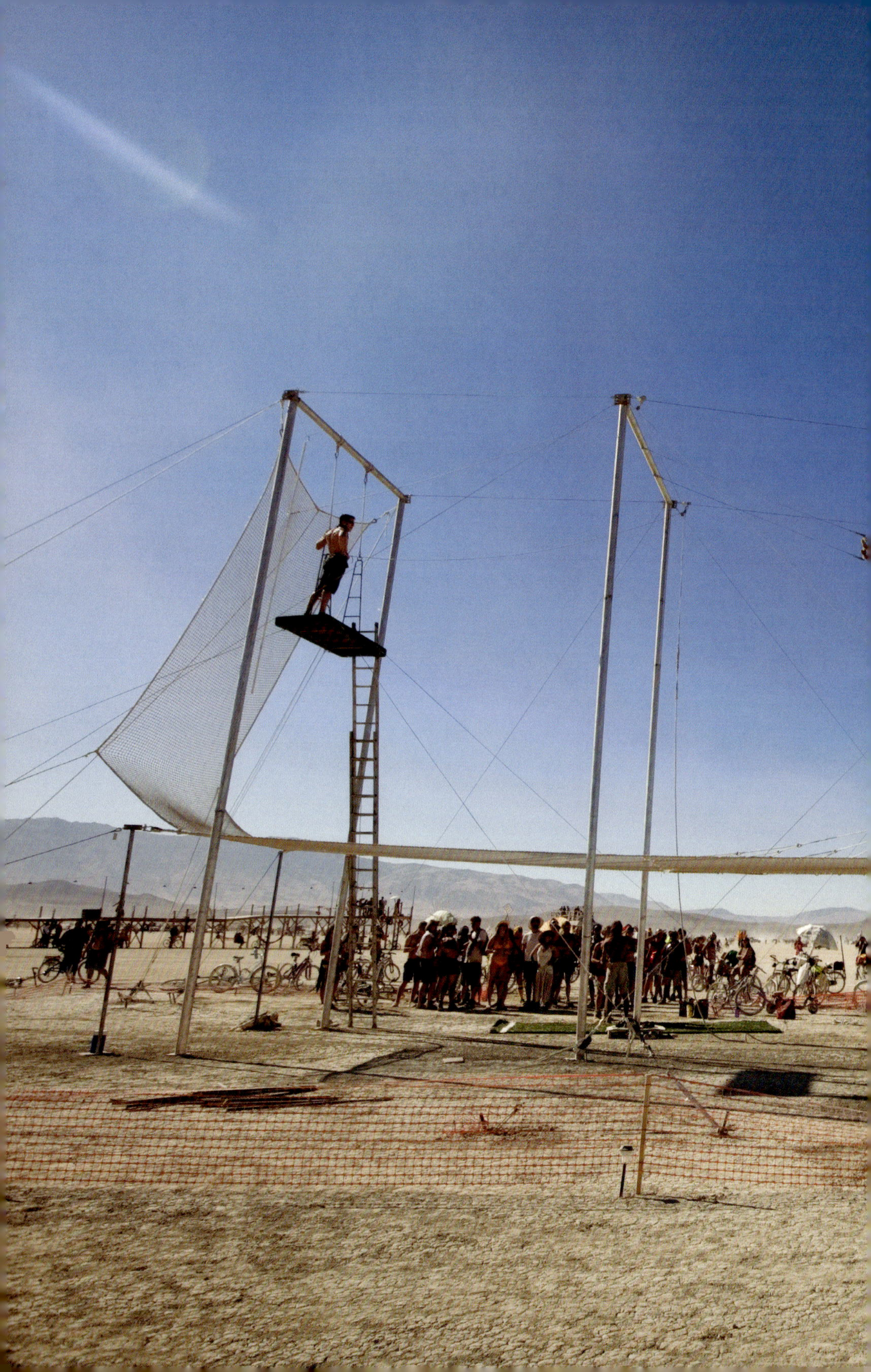

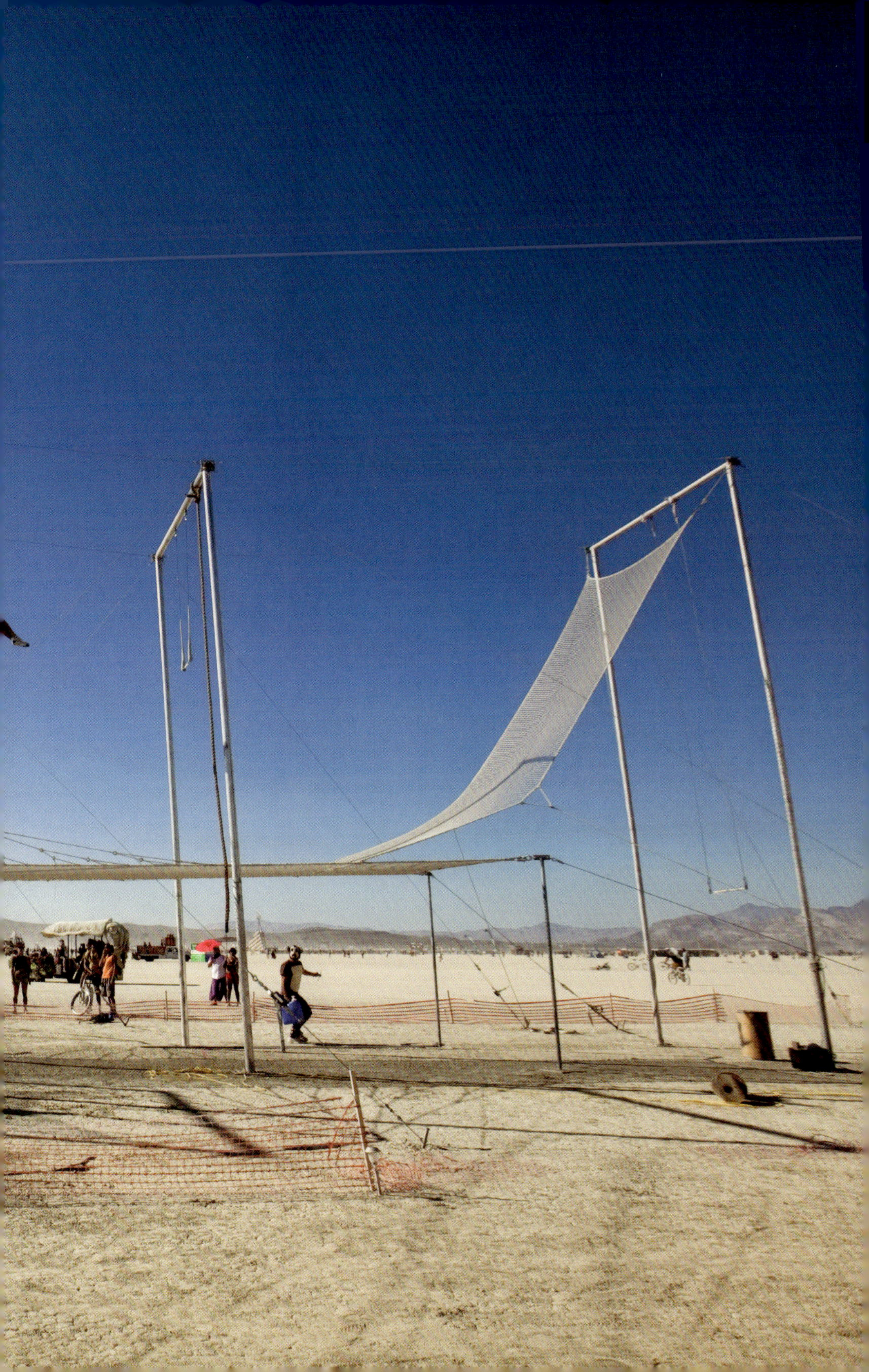

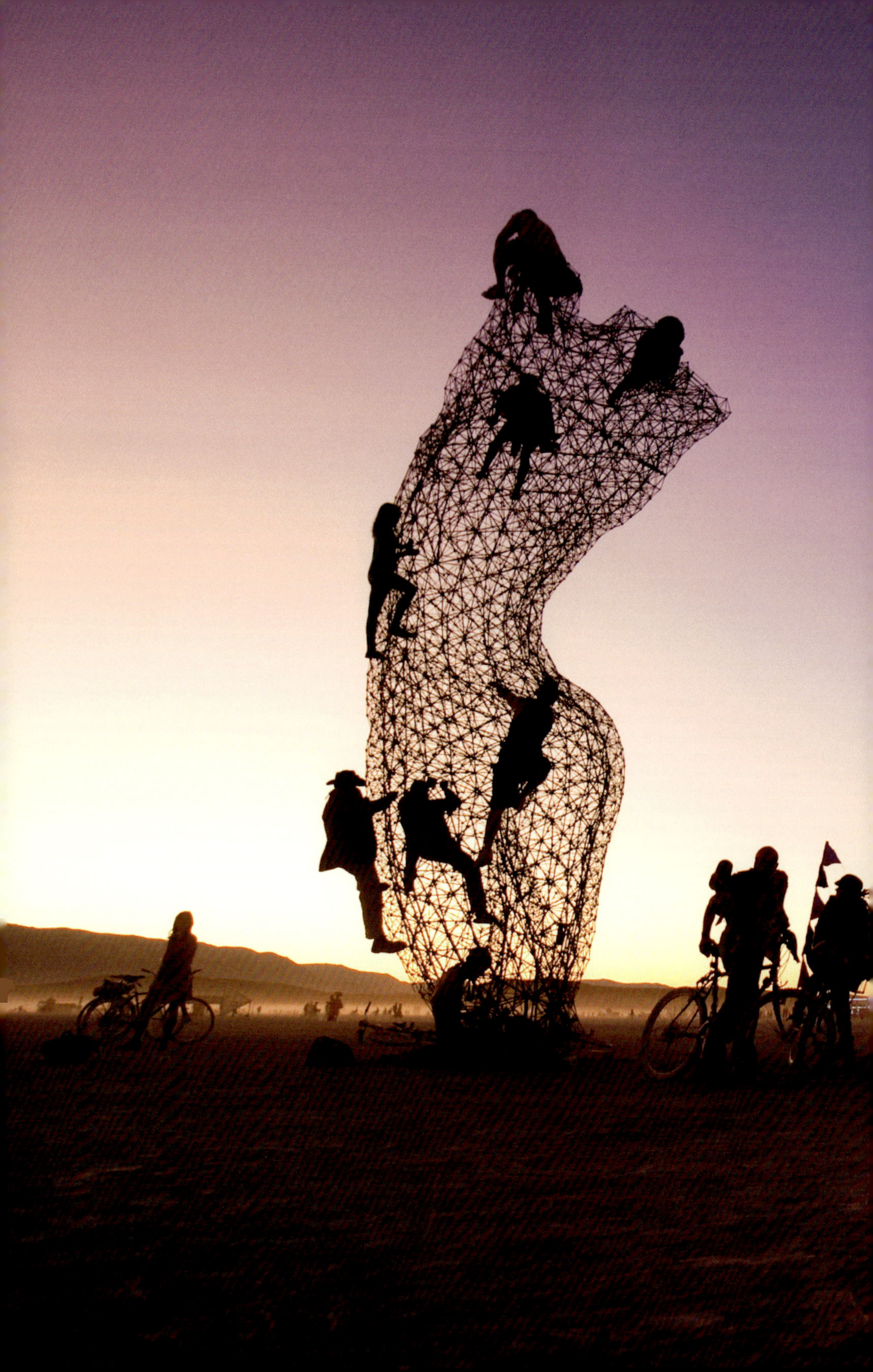

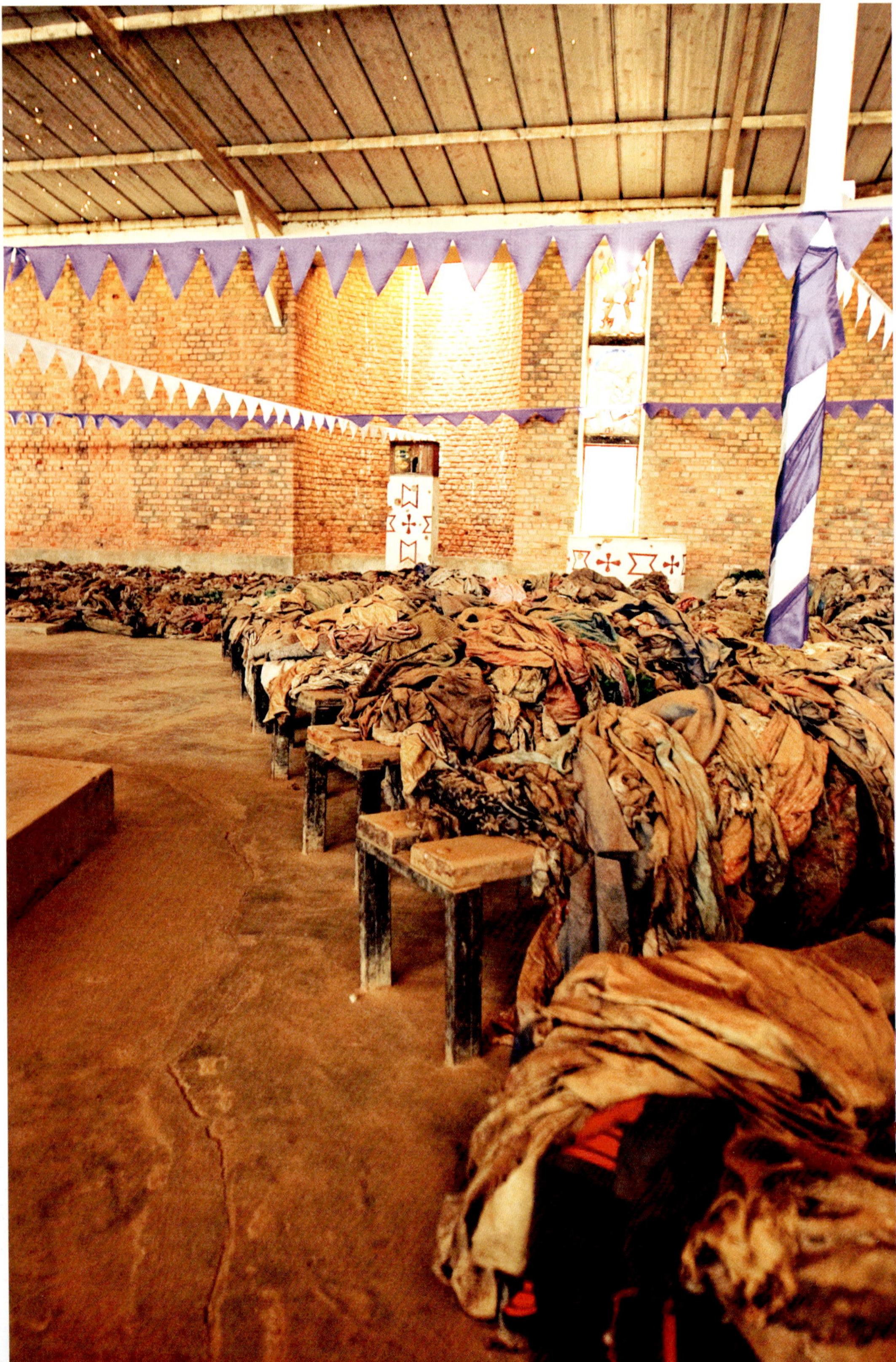

Rwanda

On a boyfriend's suggestion, I read Philip Gourevitch's *We Wish to Inform You That Tomorrow We Will Be Killed with Our Families: Stories from Rwanda.* The book, about the 1994 Rwandan genocide, absolutely rocked me in its haunting retelling of the massacre. The details that Gourevitch describes, like so many conflicts we hear about in faraway places, felt almost impossible to believe. After reading the book, I had to see Rwanda for myself.

With a few exceptions, from 2007 to 2015 I was interested in traveling only solo and only to places that scared me. If the thought of going somewhere made me nervous then I went. Rwanda is a lush and gorgeous place full of beautiful people, but I wanted to do two things there that sounded intense and scary to me: visit their genocide memorial sites and go gorilla trekking. I know lots of people have done both things but doing them alone felt terrifying, so in February 2011 I spent a week in Rwanda by myself.

I visited two memorials in Rwanda, both Catholic churches in two quiet and otherwise ordinary neighborhoods in the suburbs of Kigali. Each were sites of major massacres because thousands of people hid there thinking they'd be safe from the violence. I hired a driver to pick me up at my hotel and take me to both churches. He sat in the car while I went in alone.

Nyamata Church was the larger of the two. Within its walls 10,000 people were murdered over three days in April 1994. The victims' clothes, still dark and stiff with dried blood, are piled high on pews, and a bloody machete still sits on the altar. The ceiling and walls are littered with bullet holes from soldiers shooting indiscriminately into the chaos inside. Blood is splattered across every inch of this place.

A crypt beneath Nyamata Church holds row after row of human skulls next to thousands of leg and arm bones of the people who died here. A single coffin lies alone to symbolize how women were killed in the massacre too brutal to repeat in this book. A young Rwandan woman gave me the tour of the crypt and practically whispered as she recounted the details of what happened in April 1994. It was so harrowing I could barely speak so I nodded to let her know that I understood what she was saying.

My driver then brought me to Ntarama Church, which was much smaller but equally as gruesome. This one had human hair still matted in the dark blood stains on the walls. It was one thing to read a book about a massacre, it was another thing to smell the blood.

I traveled to these places to understand the extremes of the human experience, to feel the truth of what really happens on this planet. But when I sat in my hotel room later, I imagined the terror of the innocent people inside those churches and sobbed. I hope their passing was fast. I hope they knew love and friendship and laughter when they were still alive.

Seeing gorillas in the wild was a relief, profound in a very different way. Only a handful of permits are issued each day, allowing just one hour with the animals, and I went two days in a row. On the first day I was with a group of people who all raised our hands when asked, "Who wants to go on the longest and hardest hike to see the most gorillas?" We trekked for four hours in the pouring rain through the dense jungle with no trail. Our guide was in constant radio communication with the trackers ahead, and when we caught up with the gorilla family, I looked up to see an enormous animal with his back to me sitting eight feet away. He casually turned around, his mouth full of bamboo, and looked directly into my eyes. He flopped onto his back, scratched his armpits, yawned, and stood up and strolled past us. I hid behind my camera, pretending it was protection and desperate to capture proof that this moment actually happened. The rest of the hour was spent in awe as fifteen gorillas moved around us—climbing trees, peeling bark, grooming one another, and playing like little kids. We were so close we could smell their body odor.

The next day, two teenage sibling gorillas tumbled down a mountain toward our group, twisted in a headlock, then chased each other in circles. Moments later, a baby gorilla no bigger than a kitten climbed off his mother's back and tried to walk, wobbly and unsure. His mother reached out, gently grabbed him by the scruff of the neck, then lay on her back and fed him as he sat on her chest. Ten minutes later she stood, placed her son on her back, and disappeared into the trees. We were all in tears.

Of all the places I have visited alone, Rwanda was the hardest for me. When I was younger, traveling alone just meant arriving somewhere alone, photographing all afternoon, and then inevitably hooking up with a group of strangers who became my friends. But in Rwanda I hired a private driver and arrived alone to exclusive tours, never mind the haunting nature of what I was seeing. My loneliness felt heartbreaking. I needed to figure out a way to still see the world in a less lonely way. Maybe I could travel in a group, maybe South America would be fun. Maybe I could lead group travel. I could figure it out later, I was heading to Morocco. Surely, I'd have fun there.

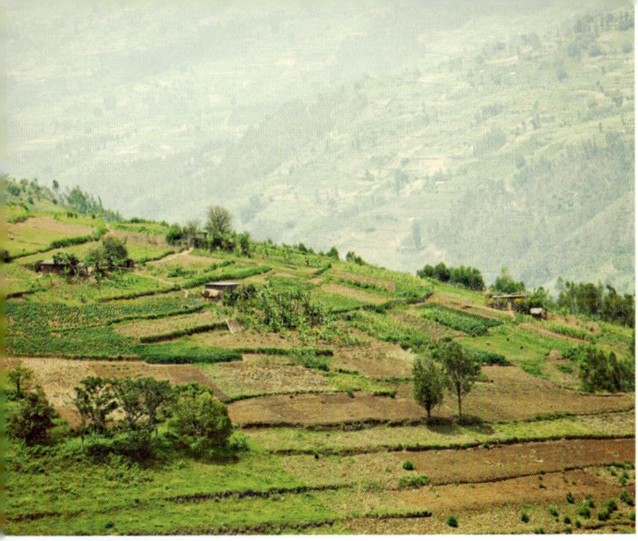
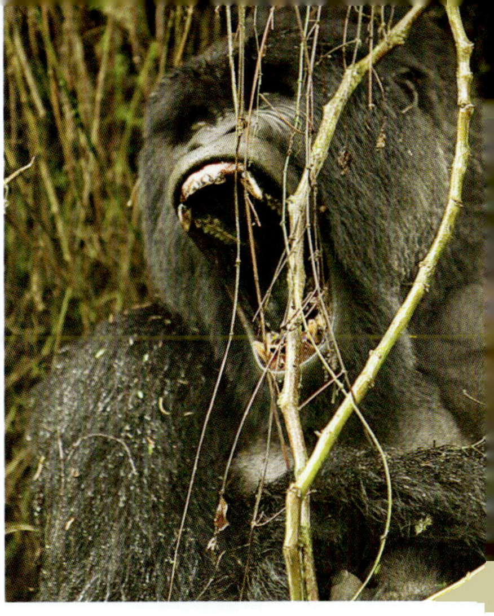
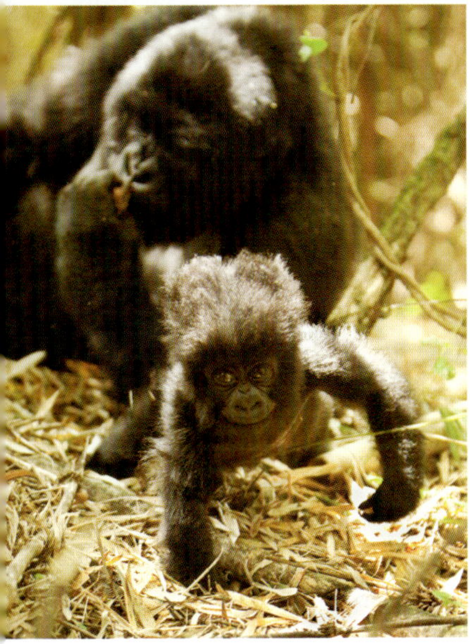
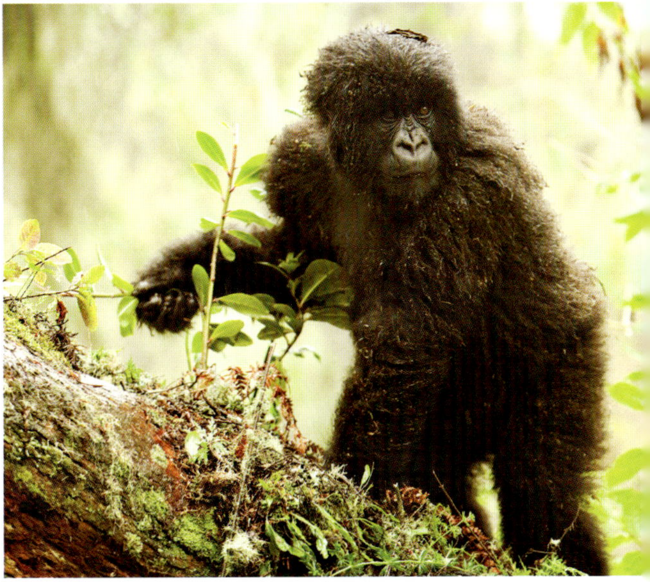
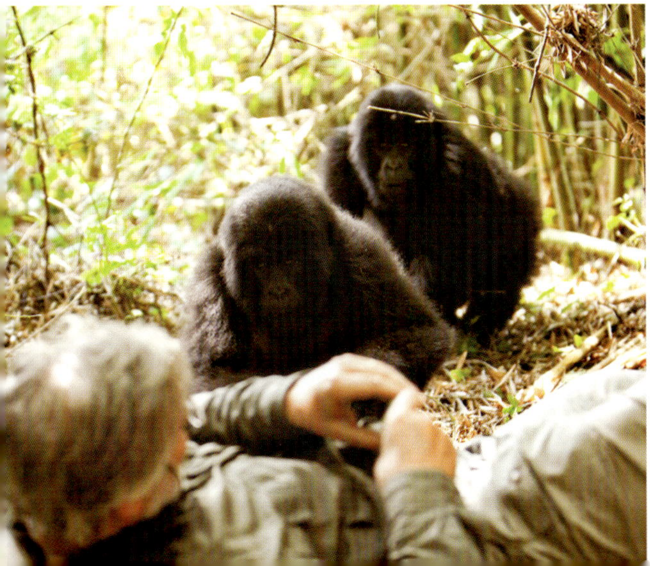
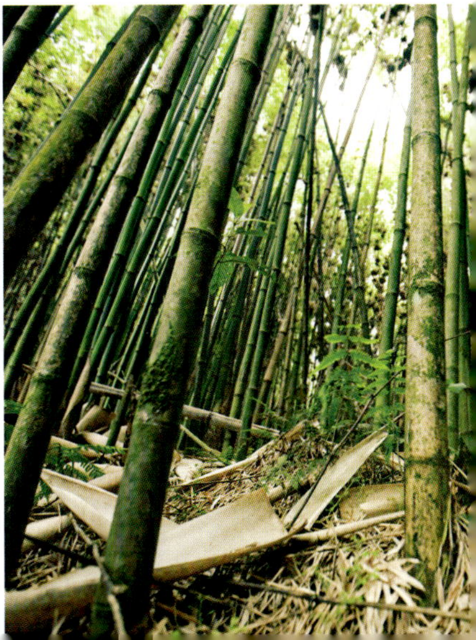

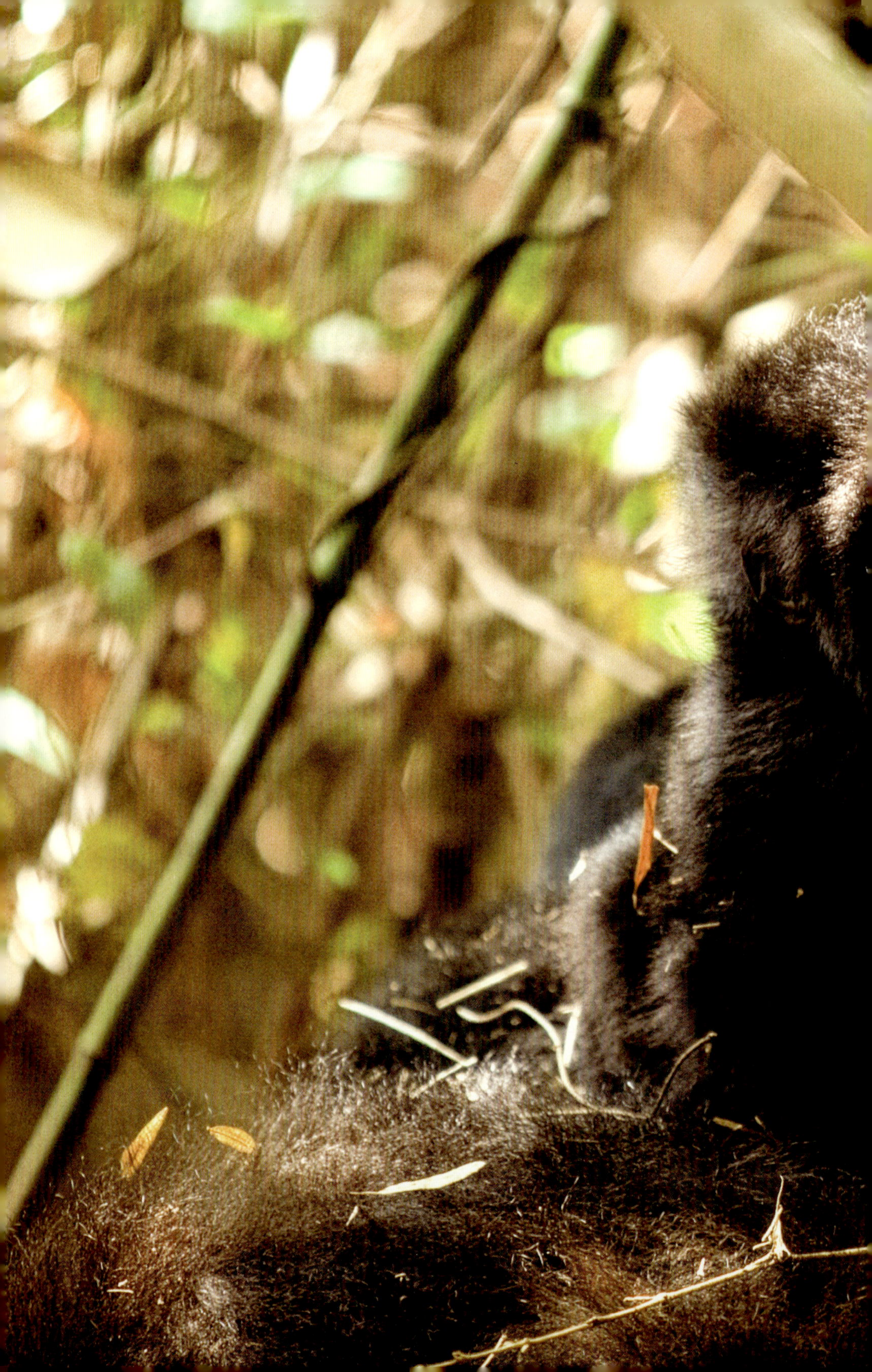

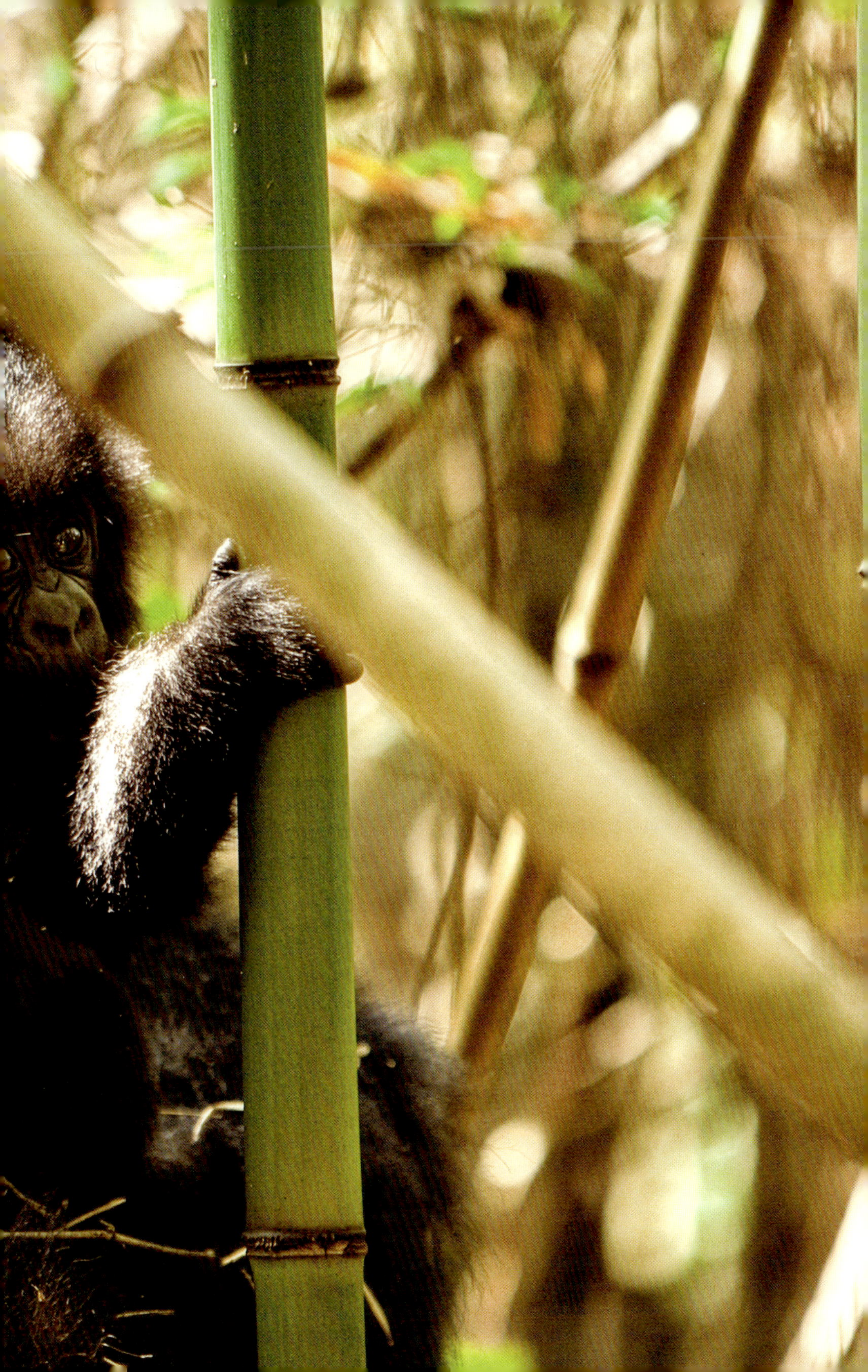

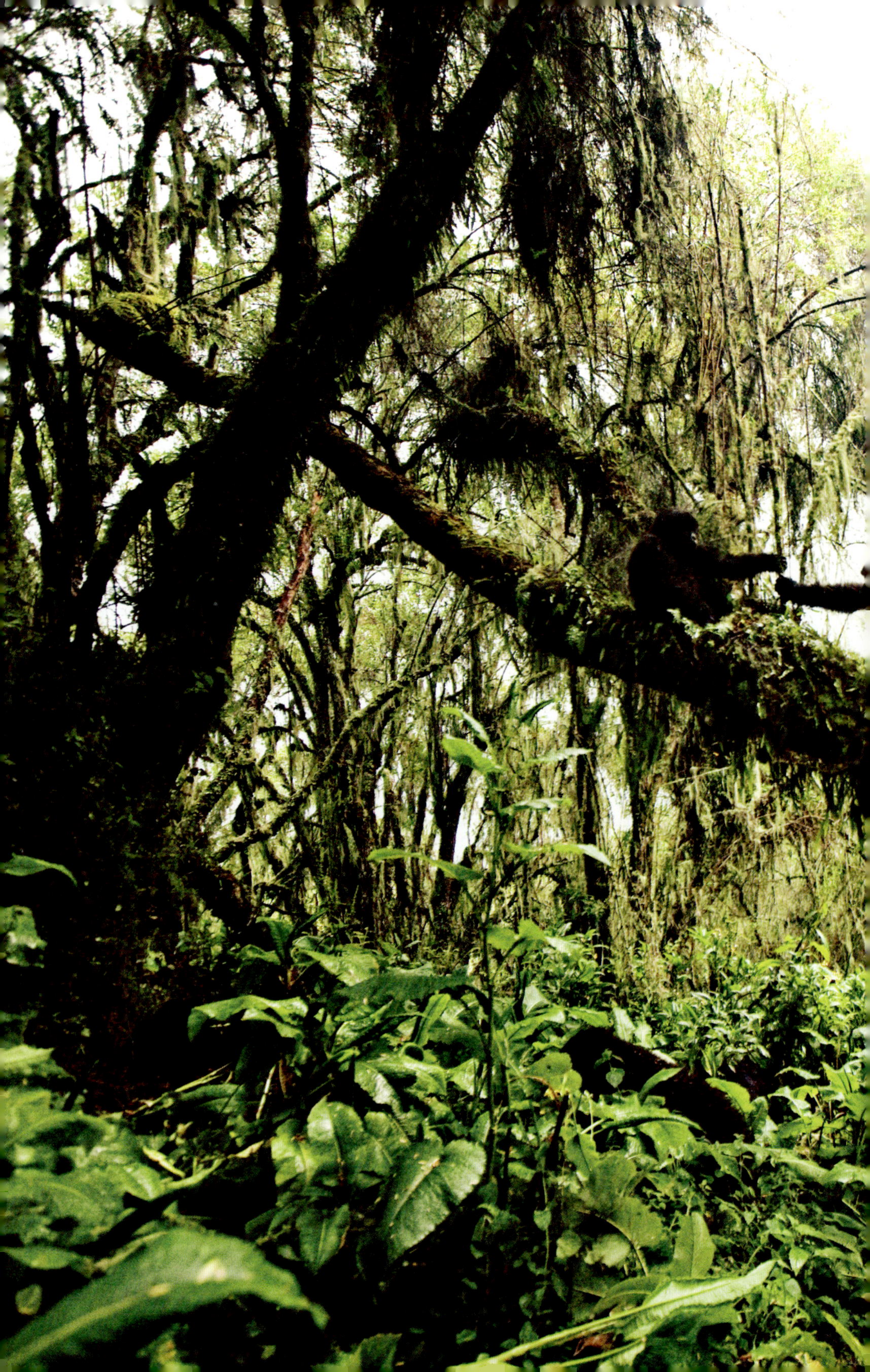

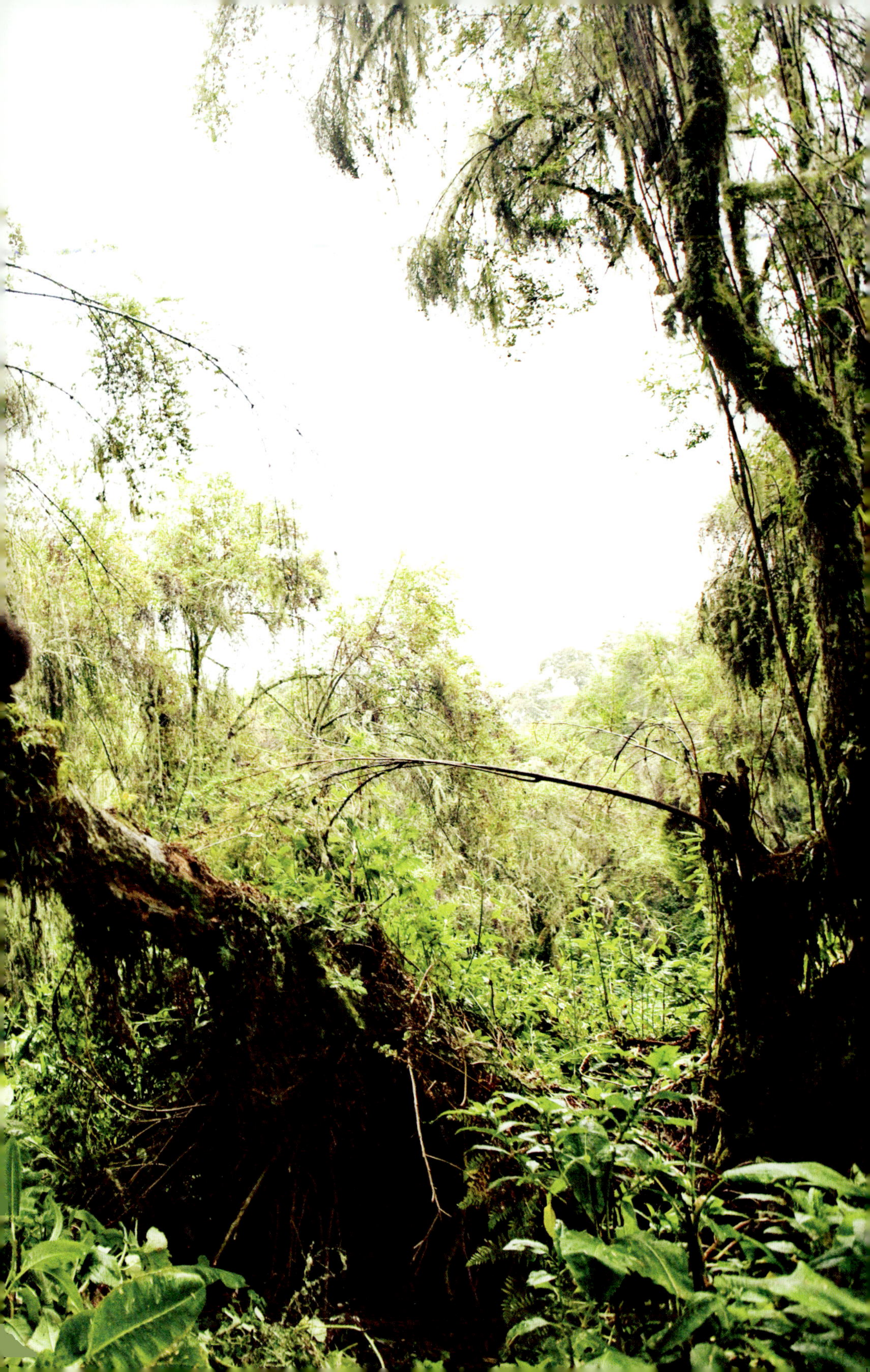

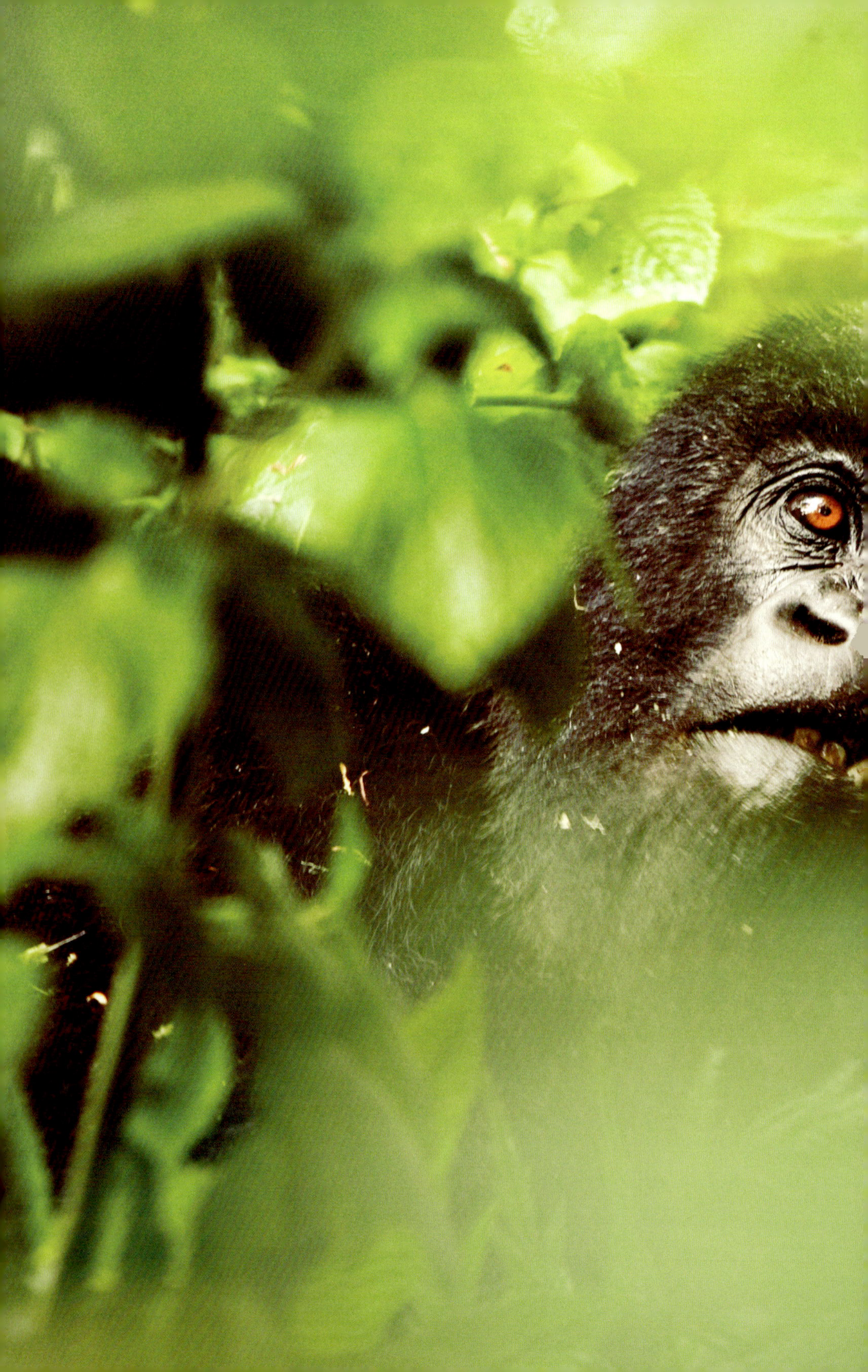

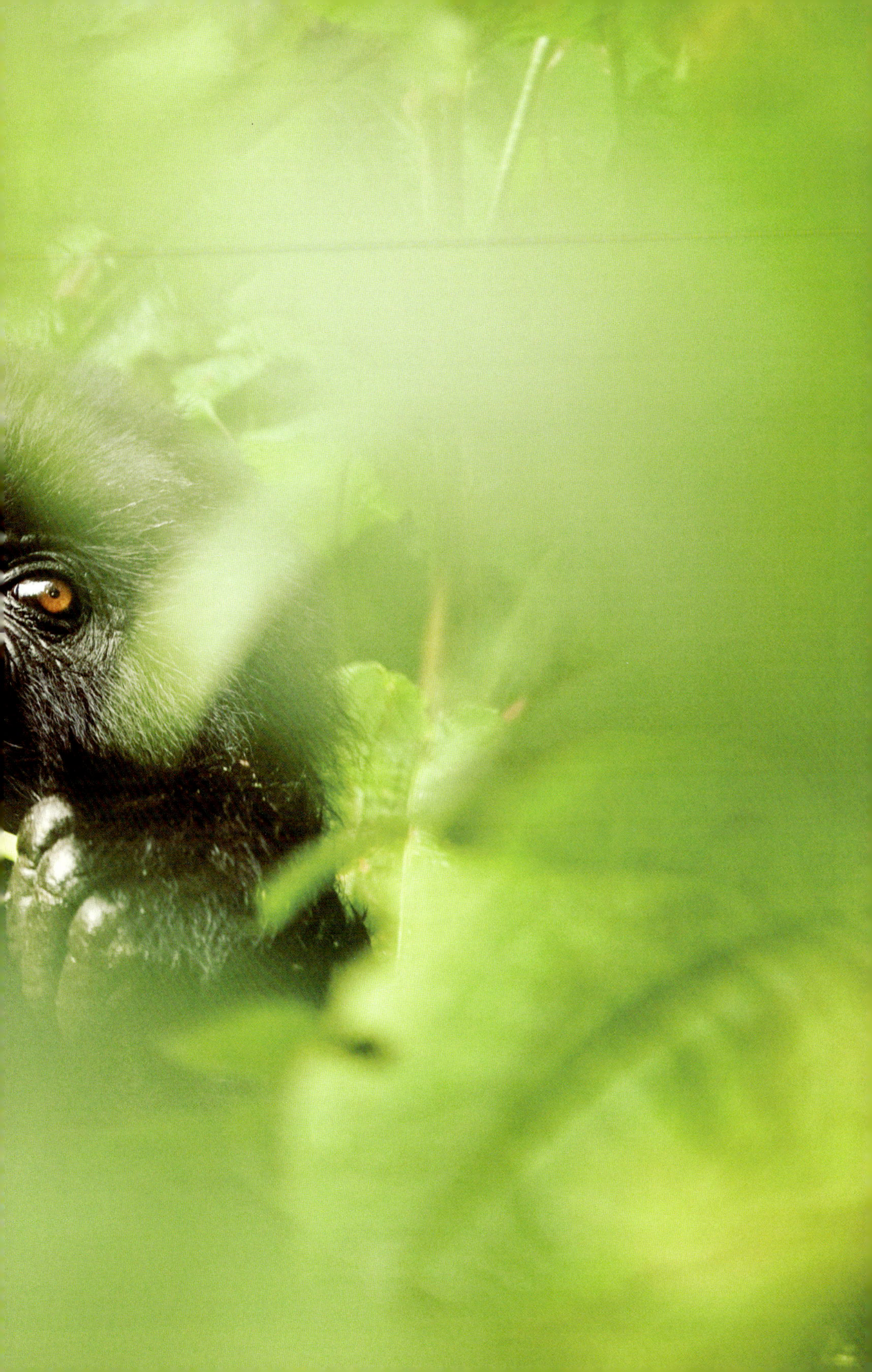

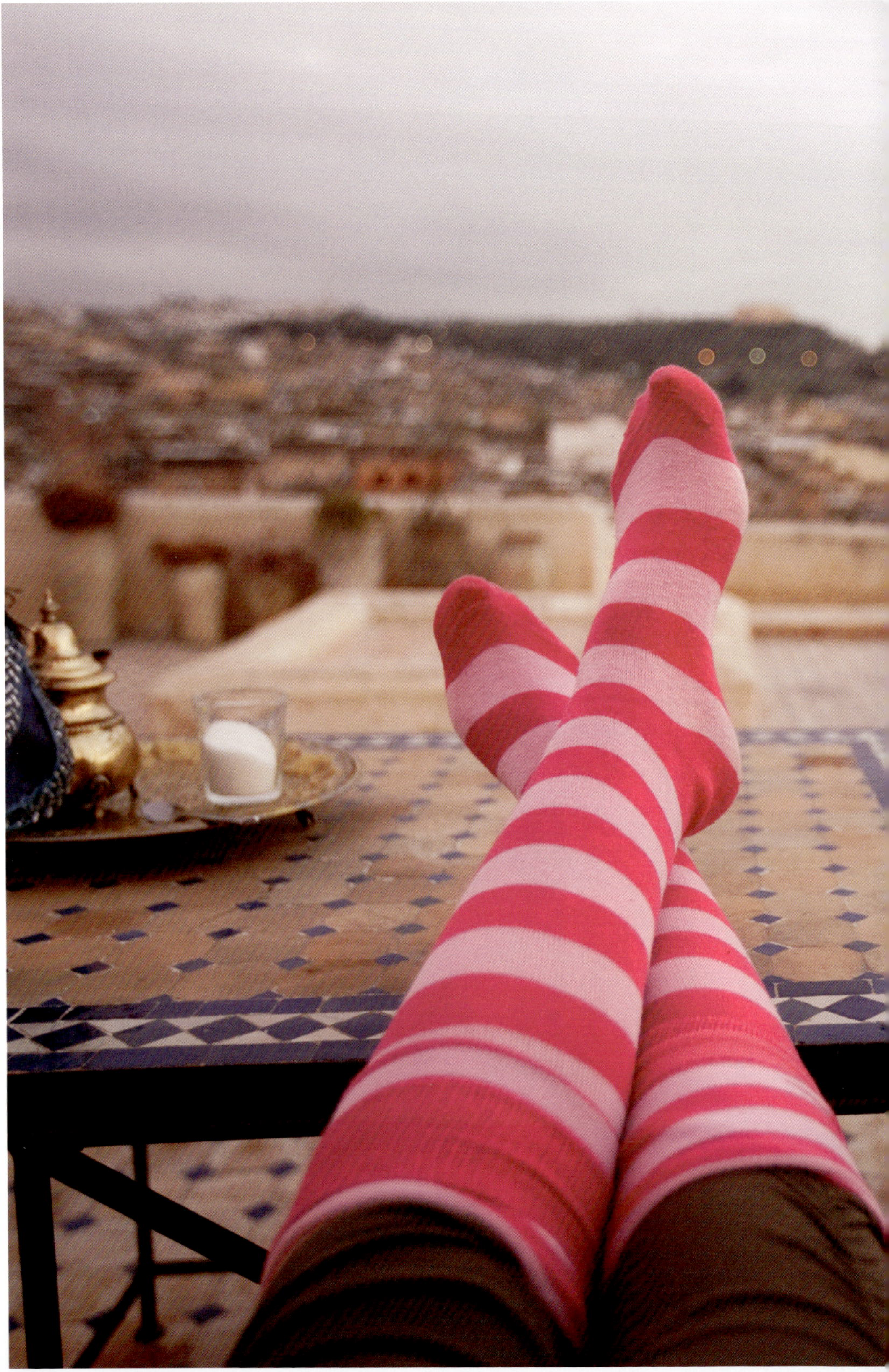

Morocco

An email to Harry, my therapist, dated Thu, Feb 24, 2011.

hi

I absolutely need to talk to you on the phone today. i'm still in morocco and i'm having lots of anxiety. i had a romance with a guy in the city of Fez and we had unprotected sex. Afterward he told me that he has had sex with a prostitute. I now have a rash and a sore throat. I thought it was a heat rash from the 8 hour train ride yesterday and I thought my throat hurt from the insane pollution.

A rash and swollen glands are two of the initial signs of HIV (that show up immediately after infection).

Harry, I need to hear that even if I have HIV that I'll still have a wonderful life, full of friendships and success and beautiful things.

I have to get out of this hotel room. I'm absolutely mind fucking myself and it's useless. I want to enjoy my last five days here, breathe, relax, and enjoy. I'm really hoping you can help me with this. What is your skype name? Maybe we can set up a time to talk?

thank you so much,

love

t

Nothing from Harry, but that night I got an email from the guy referenced above.

Thu, Feb 24, 2011:

Hi sweety

I really miss you darling. How are you Tara? I hope you are fine. How is Marrakech? I wish you like the stay and everything is going well with you.

I know you are in deep sleep now but im still thinking about you and the lovely time we had in Dar Saffarine.

You are amazing Tara and you have to know that i still find your lovely smell in my body. you are such an attractive crazy woman.

I hope to see you again baby.

Best Tara

Zouhir

I had initially planned to go to Egypt after Rwanda, but plans changed. By January 2011 the Arab Spring—the wave of pro-democracy protests and uprisings in the Middle East and North Africa—was moving into Cairo, which meant visiting Egypt was no longer an option.

Though Morocco was suffering from the same political corruption and economic stagnation that started the demonstrations, and would also see protests, it was a relatively safe destination. I flew from Kigali to Casablanca. Or really I went to bed on a plane in Rwanda, leaving the lush jungle where women walked with piles of sticks on their heads, had a dream called the Dubai Airport, which might as well be one of the seven wonders of the world, and woke up in ornate, bejeweled Morocco.

After one night in Casablanca, I was on my way to the city of Fez. My friend Abby had studied abroad in Fez a few years earlier and loved it. I had been intrigued ever since. I booked a room for three nights in a guest house called Dar Seffarine.

The Fez medina is a medieval dreamworld—a 1,200-year-old walled city with 4,000 dead ends and 9,000 alleys so narrow you have to turn sideways to pass. It's an ancient, enchanted, filthy, exhilarating maze of markets and humanity, where even a short walk demands skill and audacity. For a single woman with a camera, it felt almost unsafe, so I took most of my photos without even raising my camera to my face.

When I first arrived, I was met at the gates of the medina by Mohammed, one of the managers of Dar Seffarine, who led me effortlessly through the maze to the massive, ancient wooden door that told nothing of what was behind it. Mohammed used his full body weight to budge the door open and over the threshold was a palatial courtyard that served as the centerpiece of Dar Seffarine. Three stories high and open to the sky, the courtyard was a work of art and I would dare anyone not to gasp at the sight of it. Seven rooms, each more stunning than the next, were available, and I was one of three guests staying there that night so I felt like I had Aladdin's castle to myself. Dinner and breakfast were served on the rooftop terrace overlooking the medina. Mohammed told me that he'd be gone the rest of my stay, but Zouhir, the other manager, would take good care of me.

On my first morning, I headed out early to photograph the glory of Fez. As the city came alive, I peered over the balcony of a leather tannery as it began its daily production, then sat cross-legged on the floor of a rug shop while three generations of men—all named Mohammed—tried to sell me a carpet bigger than my apartment. I photographed merchants selling mountains of saffron next to stacks of ceramic piled six feet high and watched a line of women in burkas haggle with a butcher. Everything in the medina was magical, everywhere I looked felt like another world.

I returned exhausted and satisfied to Dar Seffarine and sat down in the corner of its majestic courtyard to read. A tall, lanky guy, maybe 27 years old, with huge brown eyes and an even bigger smile walked out of the kitchen and across the courtyard toward me.

I sat up straight.

"You must be Tara," he smiled, "I'm Zouhir."

I felt his voice in my vagina.

He offered to give me a tour of the guesthouse, and by the time we were in the kitchen, which was the first stop on the tour, he turned around and kissed me. We made out in every room and were having sex within minutes. He was the manager on duty for the next forty-eight hours, which was exactly how much time I had left in Fez, and we made the most of it. Both mornings he snuck out of my room at 6 a.m. after having sex all night and began serving breakfast to guests.

"Good morning, Tara," he'd say as I entered the dining room while pouring tea for someone. "How did you sleep?" We'd meet eyes and smile.

"I slept very well, Zouhir. How about you?" We held our gaze long enough to give our secret away if anyone had even thought to be suspicious.

"I had a very good night sleeping, Tara," he'd answer as he pulled a chair out for me, and I sat for breakfast.

On my last night with Zouhir I started to wonder how young guys in the Islamic world had sex before marriage. I knew that lots of people weren't getting to 27 without having sex no matter what a religious text told us to do. But if the girls here were chaste, which seemed easier for me to believe, then who was obviously-not-a-virgin Zouhir having sex with? So, I asked.

We fumbled through a conversation about prostitution, AIDS, paying for sex, and condoms. Between a language barrier and waiting until day three of a love affair to bring up this topic the conversation was a disaster. When I asked if he had ever been tested for an STD he thought I was telling him that I got

AIDS in Rwanda, the country I had just left. We went around and around like this until we were both frustrated and scared. My bus heading to Chefchaouen was leaving in an hour and we were both glad I got on it. We kissed goodbye and lingered in a hug.

Chefchaouen is a small village in northern Morocco near the Atlas Mountains just hours from the Strait of Gibraltar separating Europe from Africa. It's known as the Blue Village because the entire town is painted in guess what color. Local folks used to say the blue color kept the mosquitoes away, but they eventually came clean: it was for tourism. I heard that it was a town worth seeing so I booked two nights in a gorgeous B&B right in the heart of the place. The owner greeted me at her door, and when she was showing me her rooftop terrace—every place I visited in Morocco had one—we walked by an ashtray with a joint and a lighter. She made sure she understood my situation.

"Traveling alone?"

"Yes," I answered in hopes of where this was going.

"This is really good hash, want some?" she asked, pointing to the joint.

"I do," I answered.

After she had taken a few hits she handed me the joint and told me to finish it. She walked downstairs to tend to the inn. Within ten seconds of taking a hit I was overlooking Chefchaouen's main square from outer space.

Higher than I wanted to be (the working title of my next book), I found the technicolor beauty of the town from a bird's-eye view eclipsed by gut-wrenching paranoia. Arab Spring demonstrations broke out right below me the moment I leaned over the railing and throngs of enraged men began setting off small explosives and furiously chanting in a language I did not understand. I had heard about the violence in Tunisia and Libya, and my hash-brain told me I was about to be part of the violence here. Then I remembered I also had full-blown AIDS. I only had one course of action: When they kidnap me, I'll tell them about my communicable disease, and they'll cast me aside. I hugged my knees to my chest in the corner of my room, certain of my foolproof plan.

The demonstrations stopped within twenty minutes because Chefchaouen is a tourist trap, and everyone's dad probably came out from behind their pushcarts and told their sons to go home. Nothing happened, no injuries, no damages, just a little yelling and fireworks.

I spent my one full day in Chefchaouen photographing all the blue stuff, then realized there was nothing else to do there so I caught the bus back to

Fez. The nicest room in Dar Seffarine was vacant and over email Zouhir asked me to come back for one more night on my way to Marrakech. So, I guess I didn't regret having sex with him that much.

The eight-hour train ride from Fez to Marrakech the next day had no running water in the bathrooms and no air conditioning. As I sat on the sunny side of the train with all my luggage on my lap and stared out the window, I let my thoughts throw me back into terror before arriving overheated, filthy, dehydrated, and afraid. As soon as I got to my hotel room, I looked in the mirror and saw that I was covered in a rash all over my abdomen. Maybe I also had a sore throat. Against my better judgment I googled "initial signs of HIV" and then—fully over the edge—sent that email to my therapist.

Instead of pacing my hotel room, I forced myself outside with my camera. I know Marrakech is beautiful, but in my horrendous state of mind it felt like an outdoor mall with snake charmers. I didn't like it at all until night fell when Jemaa el-Fnaa, the main square, exploded into a frenzy of food stalls and travelers from around the world. For the first time all day, I felt happy as I sat at a picnic table in the middle of the chaos for dinner.

"Hey, can I sit here?" An insanely handsome blonde guy with an English accent asked me as soon as I sat down.

"For sure," I said, scooting over to make room. He introduced himself as Thomas.

Thomas was also traveling alone, and when he asked me where I was from, and I answered Boston he reached into his pocket and handed me his Massachusetts license. He had just moved back to London after graduating from Boston University and still had his MA license on him. When we were both done eating, he stood up.

"Let's go get in trouble," he said, grabbing our paper plates and tossing them in the garbage.

"I have some hash from Chefchaouen back in my room!" I called out to him as I fumbled with my camera bag and tried to keep up. So much for writing my own obituary.

We ducked in and out of hookah lounges, got lost in alleyways, and stopped in little bars, all without my feet ever hitting the ground. When we found ourselves back at my hotel—wait for it: on the rooftop terrace—we smoked that leftover hash and laughed so hard the manager came up and told us we had to leave. Because of the AIDS I tried to avoid his kiss and instead gave him a hug and tried to walk him out. As we passed the door to my room, he kissed me, took off both our shirts, wrapped my legs around his hips, and walked me into my room in his arms. In under one second, I was on my bed shirtless, and Thomas was taking off both our pants.

"I HAVE AIDS!" I yelled.

No, no I didn't actually say that, but I wanted to. I made up some bullshit story about why I couldn't have sex with him, and he was a total gentleman about it. We got dressed, wished each other the best, and he left.

In the morning a driver picked me up to go to the Erg Chebbi dunes of Morocco for the obligatory camel trip through the sand. The dunes are insanely photogenic and we, a group of international travelers, stayed overnight with a Berber family who made us tea and cooked us dinner.

"Just two more days until I can go to an STD clinic," I whispered to a woman who didn't speak English as we took in the night sky.

"Very nice," she whispered back.

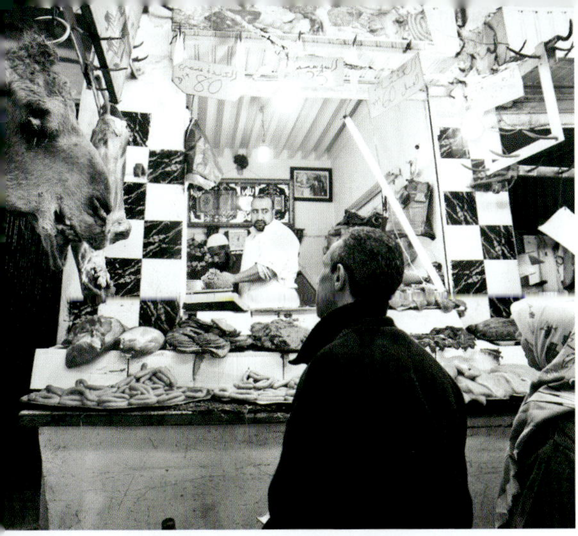
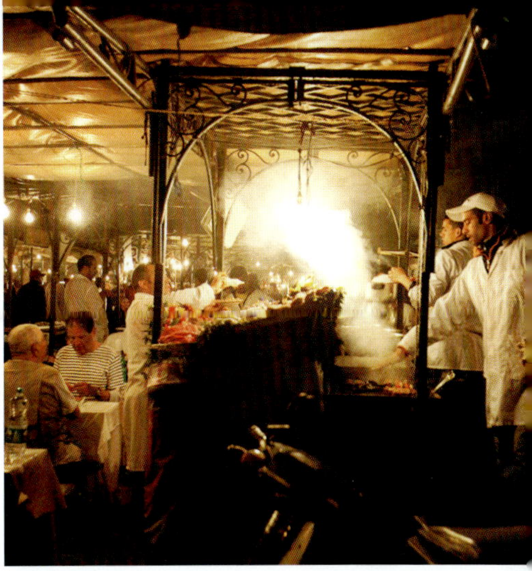
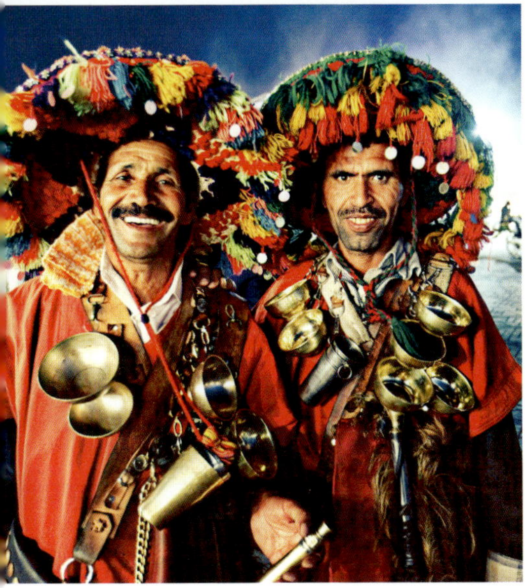
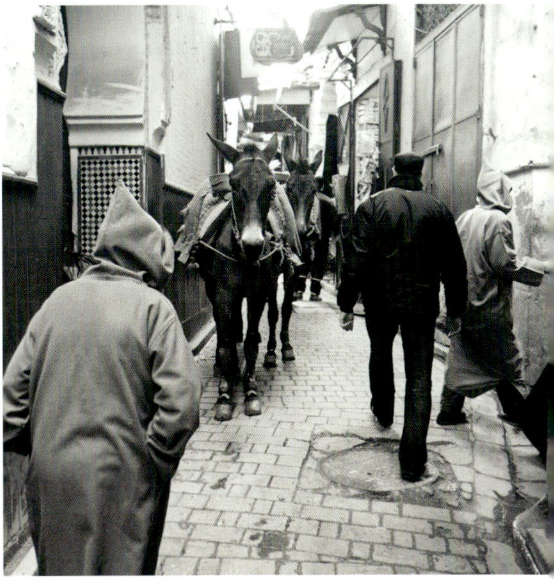
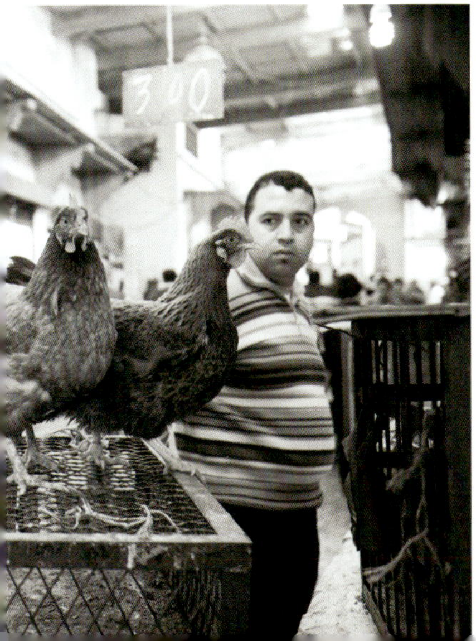
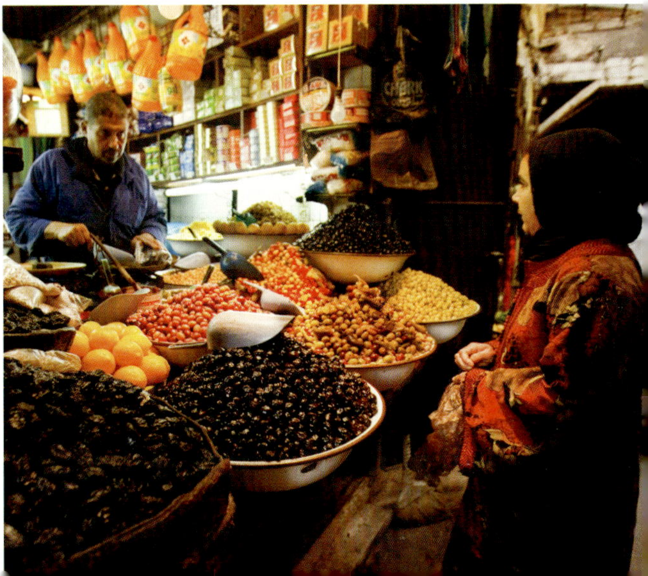

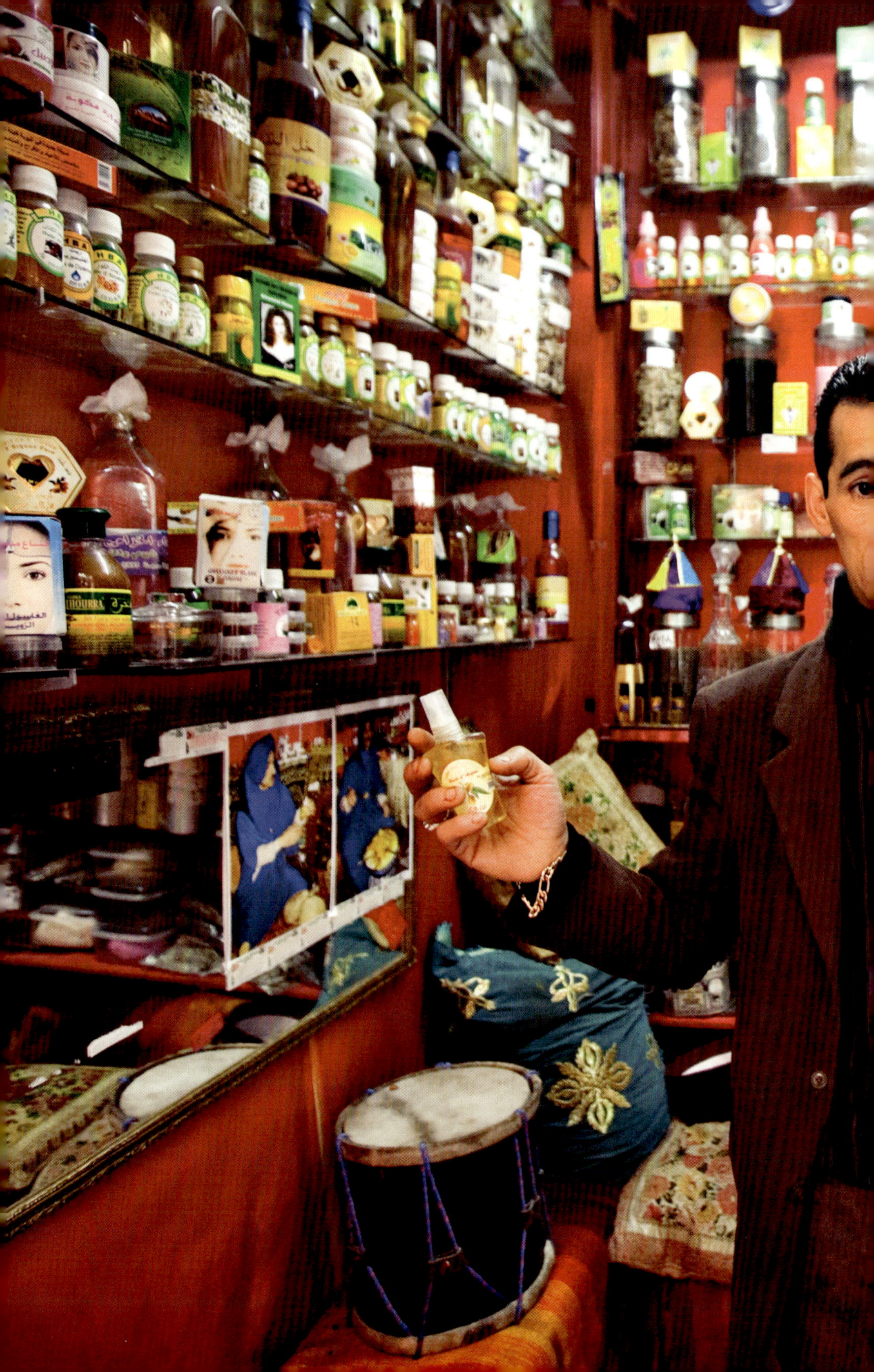

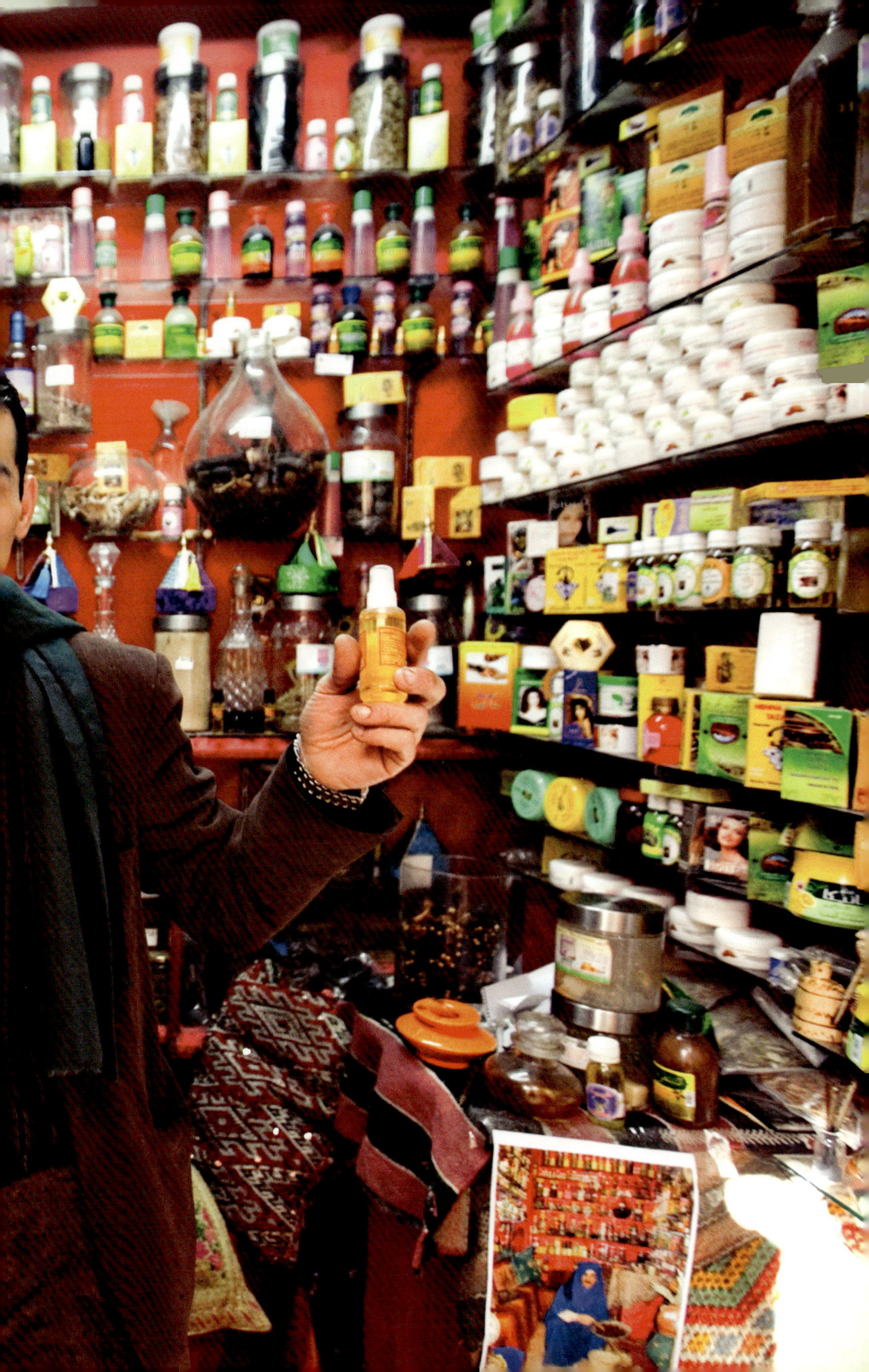

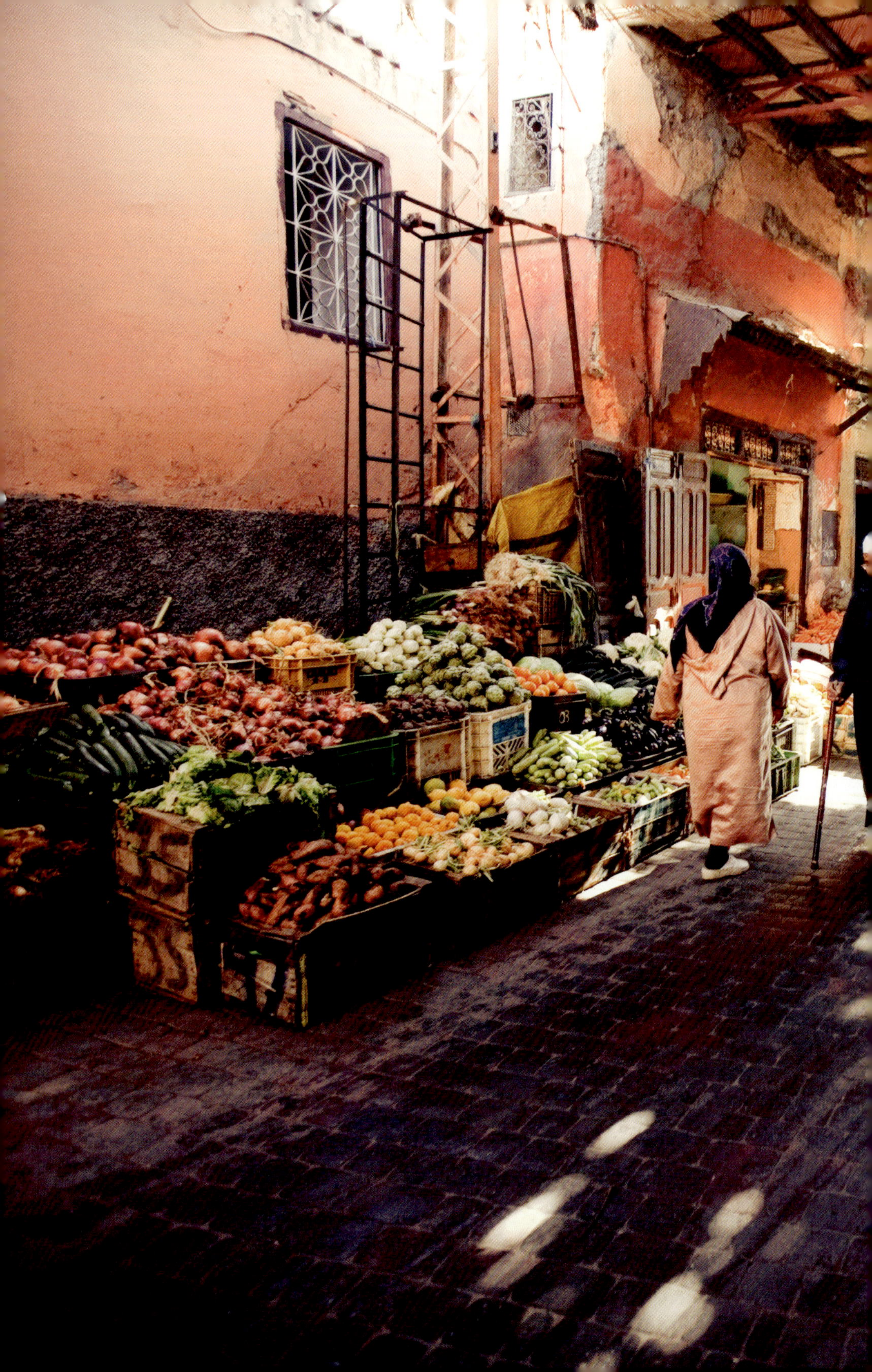

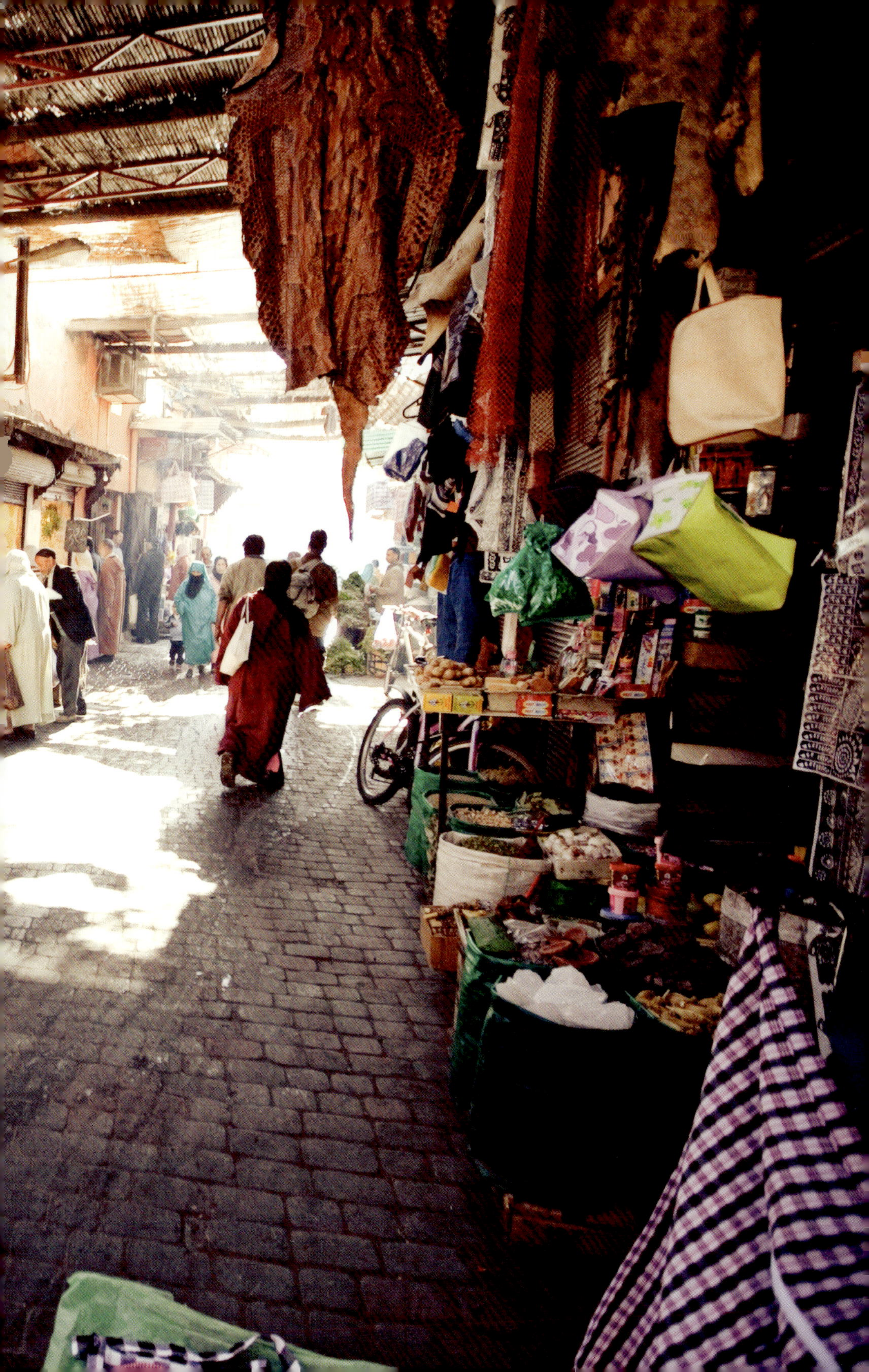

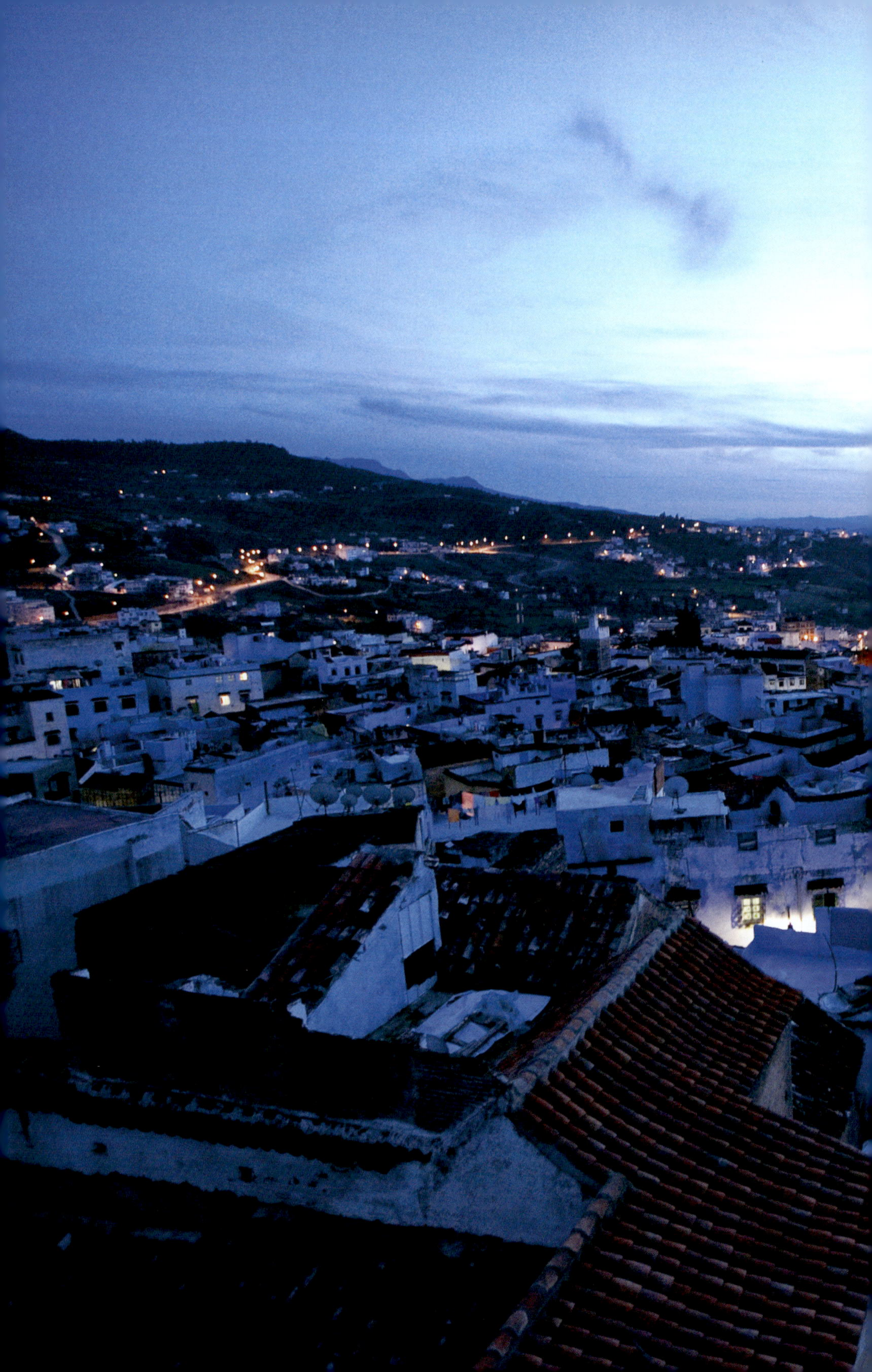

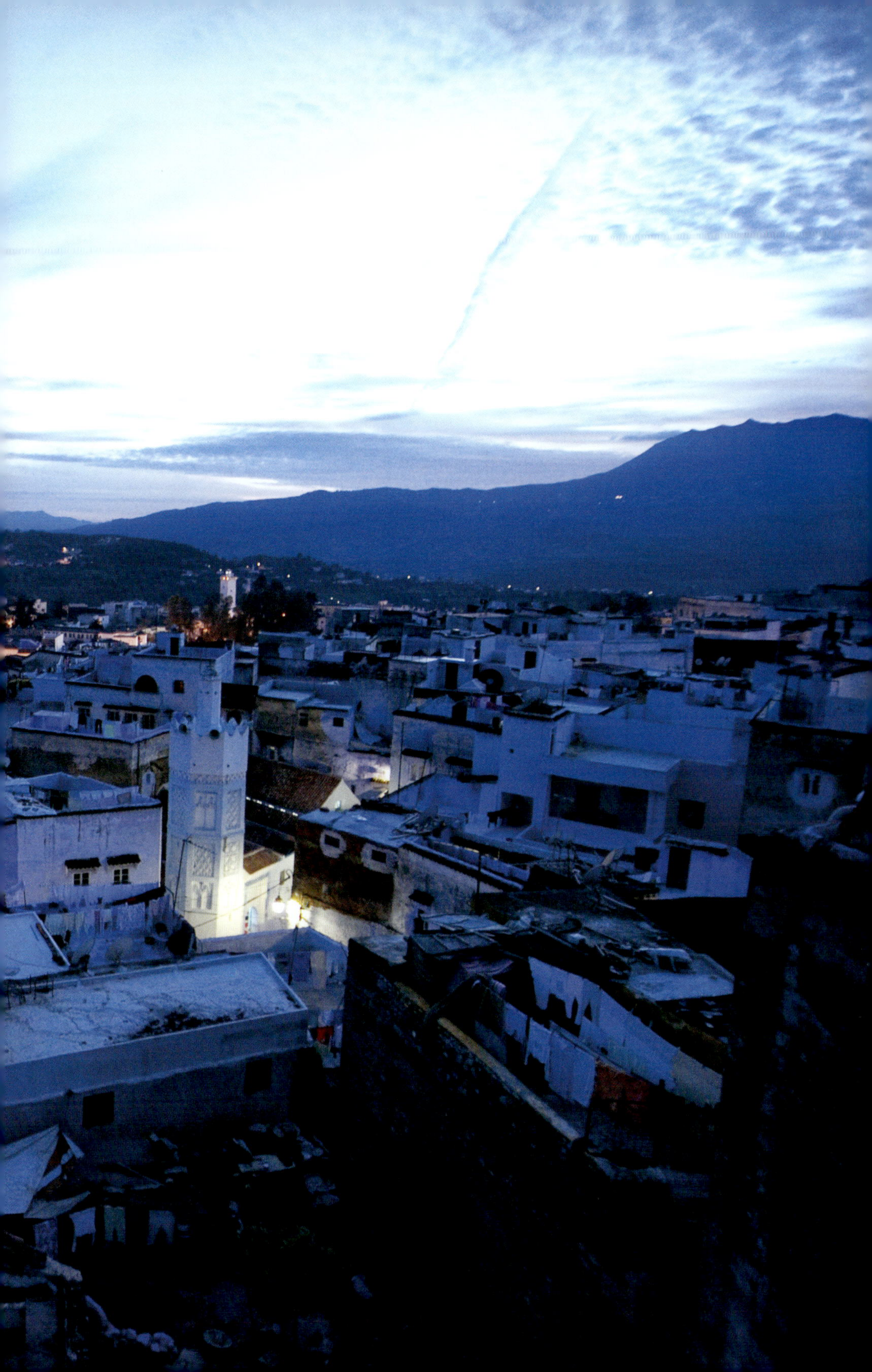

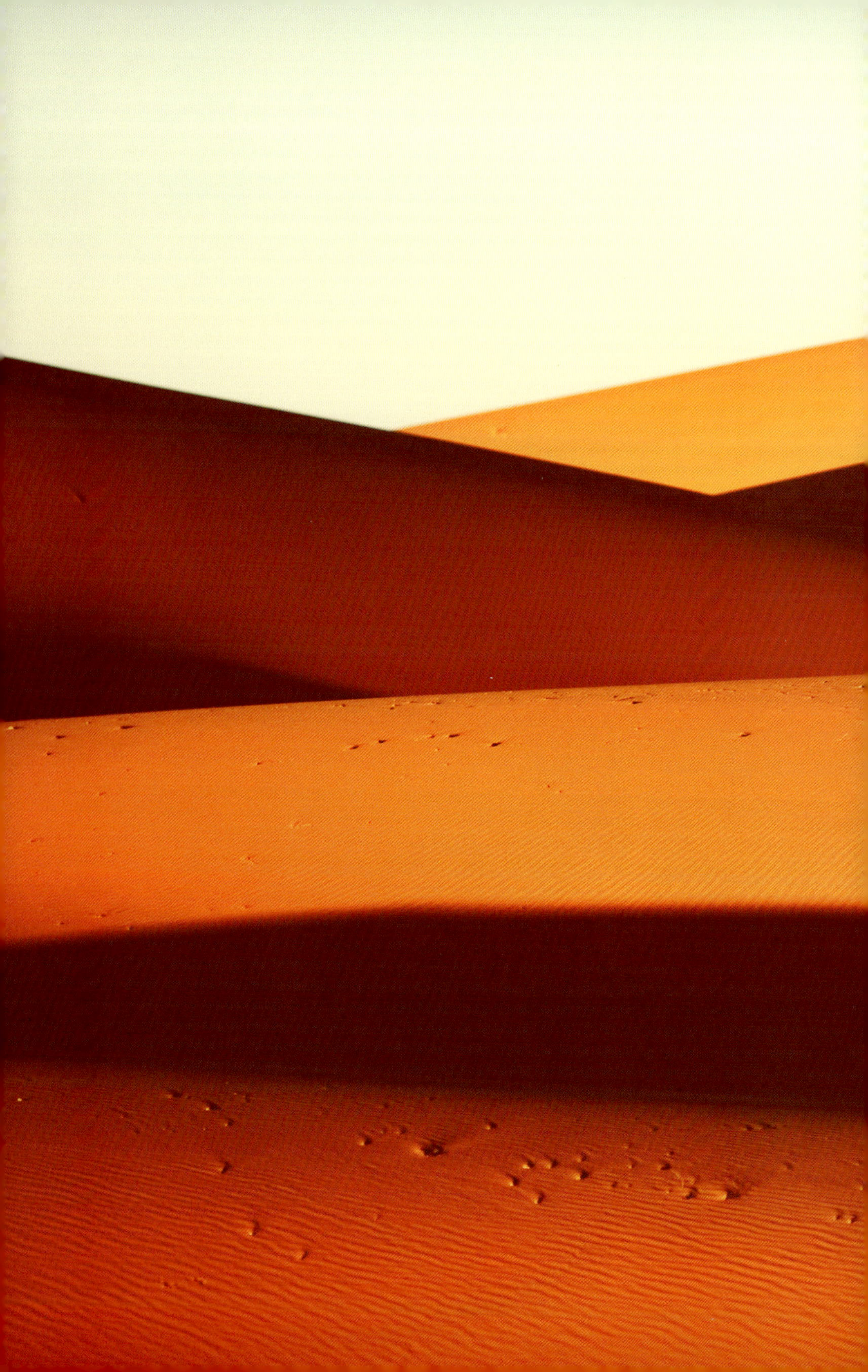

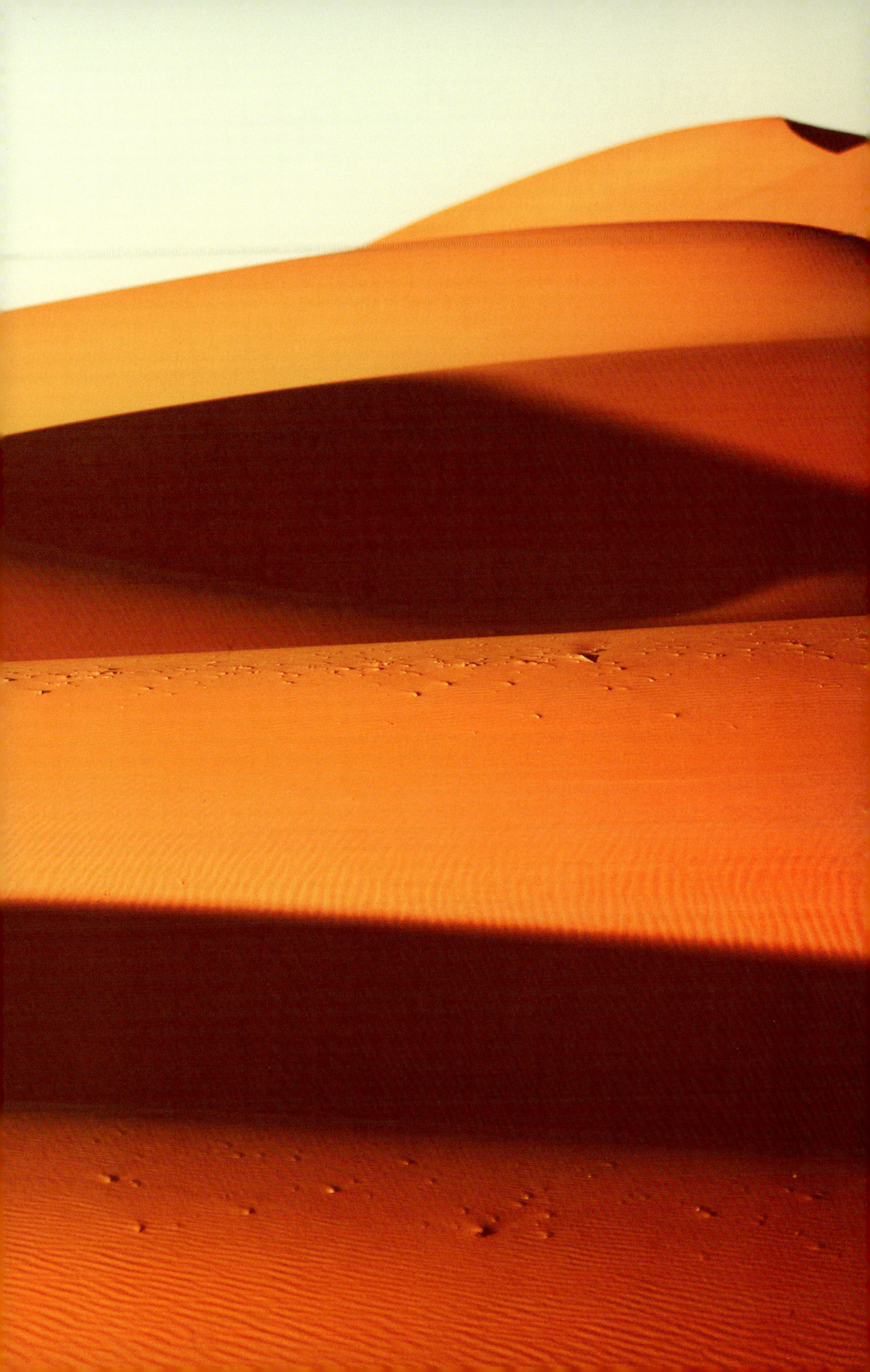

Front Row Seat

When I tell people I've been a wedding photographer for almost twenty years, they always want to hear the horror stories, but believe it or not, there really aren't that many. What I do have is a front row seat to some of the most beautiful days of people's lives and a career that's insanely rewarding.

Ben Wight and I started photographing weddings in 2007, when wedding photography was having a bit of a renaissance. Just then, tastes turned from cheesy and over-posed moments to candid and emotional moments—right as we were hitting the scene. We shot our first wedding together the day after graduation from NESOP on a Saturday in June and called ourselves Hitched Studios by Monday. When I look back at my life, Ben Wight is my life partner. Working side by side, building something beyond our highest hopes, and remaining best friends along the way is a feat we're both very proud of. Ben is a brilliant artist, the best friend anyone could ever hope for, and a reliable, honest, trustworthy business partner. I count myself very lucky to be spending my life with Ben.

Guests often assume I'm an old friend of the couple because I'm bawling my eyes out through their vows, but really, I'm just moved, every time, by the promise of a life built together. If I had to pick my favorite vows of all time, they'd be Allen's. His parents had both passed by the time he got married, and when he spoke his vows, he sounded like a reverend at the pulpit. When he ended in a full crescendo with a rousing, "And when I meet my mother and father again at the *gates of the kingdom of heaven...*," I was crying so hard I was hyperventilating.

Please don't make me tell you about the butterfly release that went awry—the one where, on the count of three, all the guests opened their little origami pouches holding live butterflies, but all the butterflies were stunned dead. The screaming was so intense it felt like a horror movie.

How about the time a newly engaged couple came in for their initial meeting and when they arrived at the studio we said, "Hi Danny!" to the groom-to-be. We had photographed this dude's first wedding two years earlier. He must not have recognized our studio name when she booked the appointment. We spent the whole meeting suggesting other photographers and wished her luck.

One time Ben and I were having a snack for *five minutes* during a cocktail hour (guest total: 12) and the very drunk bride leaned into us and furiously said through clenched teeth, "When you're done eating my *shrimp* why don't you get back to photographing my *wedding*?!" Ben said he smoked so many joints after that wedding he can't remember her name.

Once, an estranged family member didn't eat all day, so she passed out during the cocktail hour right next to the cheese tower. Toes up, out cold. When the EMTs arrived, they put her in a five-point restraint and wheeled her out like Hannibal Lecter in *Silence of the Lambs*. She ended up returning to the wedding with her hospital bracelet still on and jumped right in the conga line. I thought that was bold.

We were shooting weddings pretty early after the legalization of gay marriage. Everyone was so happy and emotional during those ceremonies even the valets were crying.

I've had romances with a handful of wedding guests, a band member, and two different groomsmen—all at separate weddings—so we eventually had to stop saying, "We're flies on the wall, you won't even know we're there."

Ben once bumped into the urn of hot frankincense and had to keep shooting the ceremony with burning oil running down his arm. I might have found that funnier than he did.

Once we photographed an outdoor ceremony during a hurricane. Pouring rain. High winds. Guests shivering under their umbrellas. It was such a photogenic event that we won a national award for our photos of that ceremony. We have since encouraged everyone we meet to get married in the rain.

How about when Tim and Scott hired *actual* Cirque du Soleil acrobats for their reception? If anyone was even thinking of topping that wedding it might be better to just elope.

We photographed Cyndi's wedding when she married Mike and then again years later when she married Gienah. Somewhere in the middle of those two weddings she started working for us and we became best friends.

One of our favorite ceremonies of all time was held in the middle of a busy sidewalk in downtown Philadelphia. We mention this to people when they're worried that their ceremony venue isn't romantic enough.

We won Best Wedding Photographer in Boston in 2011 and the writeup called Ben and I a "Super Duo." For years we debated if SuperDuo was one word or two.

We started Hitched Studios in the spare bedroom of my apartment in Boston and eventually moved to a huge loft space on the other side of the city.

Ben made it the loft of his dreams, and I taught my first-ever yoga class in that space.

It was, and still is, a beautiful responsibility—photographing someone's wedding. This job is so wildly positive and fun, and I have loved every moment of being such a big part of people's wedding day. I feel like the luckiest person alive to be trusted to make an heirloom that will outlast us all.

Okay, so I do have this one crazy wedding photography story I could tell...

I met a bartender named Tim in Brooklyn in May 2013 when I was visiting my friends Tommy and Liz. Tim was super charismatic and confident, great at his job, handsome—everything a bartender should be. I saw him flirt with everyone, both guys and girls, and just to make sure, before I sat there any longer, I asked if he was gay.

"No. Why do you ask?"

"Because you don't want to fuck me," I answered with a confidence that left me long ago.

"That's not true," he answered, and the rest of the night was a blur.

The next morning we grabbed something to eat and I got on the bus back to Boston. We never kept in touch outside of social media. He's twelve years younger than me, it wasn't a relationship, or even a friendship, and I'm confident neither of us gave the evening much thought. Over the next three years I saw on social media that Tim met a girl, dated her for years, and eventually got engaged. He reached out to me in 2016 and told me about the backyard wedding they were planning at his childhood home in Pennsylvania. He asked if I would photograph it.

In July 2016 we arrived at Tim's house in a neighborhood that looked like a Hollywood set of suburbia. The backyard was decorated in what must have been a million dollars in flowers and decor. There were ornate rose archways and this little bohemian teepee moment in the corner and vintage crystal and fresh fruit everywhere. Even the water table looked dope. Ben and I saw Tim right away, but I was eager to get to Holly, the bride.

Holly was sitting by a window in what I suppose was Tim's childhood bedroom getting her makeup done. A gorgeous girl who looked like a young Rihanna, no older than 12, sat at her feet. A beautiful woman in a hot pink muumuu with tiny roses in her platinum blonde hair sat in a chair in the corner.

I took one look at the woman with the tiny roses in her hair and said, "Oh, my god you look fucking gorgeous!"

She smiled.

All of Holly's bridesmaids looked like models, but I'm not sure if they were actual models or if they just lived in LA. That's kinda the same thing.

As I photographed Holly getting her makeup done I made small talk with her, Baby Rihanna, and Roses in Her Hair. This sort of small talk and friendliness is part of the job. Ideally it helps make people feel more comfortable so we can capture more candid moments. It's how I take the pictures that I'm hired to take.

"So how do y'all know each other?" I asked casually.

Immediately, Roses in Her Hair answered, "Tara, why don't you back up so the people who actually know each other here can talk."

Totally caught off guard I backed up and continued shooting from the far corner of the small bedroom. One of the model bridesmaids eventually walked in. She said rhetorically to the room, "I feel like I look like a drag queen. Do I have too much makeup on?"

Every weekend at least one person at a wedding says something like this before they put their dress on. I've heard it hundreds of times. I said the same thing I always do, "You look gorgeous. Once you have your dress on it'll all come together."

Absolutely furious, Roses in Her Hair banged her fists on the chair. "That's it!" she announced as she shot up from the chair and marched across the room. "Tara, grab your camera and come with me!!" she demanded, and stormed down the stairs.

Confused and embarrassed I grabbed my camera bag and followed her out of the crowded room. No one even blinked.

"You can photograph details, or the boys, or ..." She suggested other things for me to photograph as we met up at the bottom of the stairs.

I interrupted her. "I've been doing this for nine years," I said standing face to face. "I'm 41 years old. What is going on here? What do you need to say to me? Just say it to me straight."

"Good," she said, "I'd rather deal with it straight on, too."

I waited.

"It's Holly's wedding day today, okay? If you can go up in that room and not speak *at all* then you can go up there, but Holly is not looking for her new best friend today."

"Got it," I answered, feeling like a perfect stranger just slapped me across the face.

She said she'd let me know when I could go back upstairs.

I found Ben and told him the story with tears in my eyes. He grabbed my shoulders, got right in my face, and said, "Don't you dare. Don't you dare let that get to you. You have made our careers happen with how you act at weddings. Fuck her, dude."

This moment is one of the many reasons you want to photograph weddings with your best friend.

For the next hour, after photographing all the details that Ben had already photographed, I asked people on their way upstairs to check if I was welcome up yet. Each person was super friendly on their way upstairs but couldn't even look at me when they came back downstairs. I was the enemy of these people, and I didn't know why.

I was never allowed upstairs again, but finally it was time to start the ceremony. Baby Rihanna was the flower girl, but instead of throwing flower petals she—I shit you not—set off a cloud of hot pink smoke and emerged from it. Models one through six walked down the aisle with teary grins, and Roses in Her Hair looked directly at me as she walked down the aisle with a smile that could light up a stadium. Lights. Camera. Action.

Sometime during the cocktail hour I looked over at the whole crew—the models, Baby Rihanna, Roses in Her Hair, plus a few other recruits—taking selfies near the bohemian teepee far away from the rest of the party. I finally asked a guest I was chatting with, "What's the deal with these people? They act like they're famous."

The guest looked at me. She could tell I didn't know. Finally, she answered, "Well… I mean… it is Sia."

Roses in Her Hair was Sia, the super-famous pop star known for her powerful voice and face-covering wigs and large bows. Baby Rihanna is the girl from Dance Moms who danced in her videos, I guess? People know her. I don't, but tons of people do. Sia sang her brand-new song, "Cheap Thrills," when the band took a break, and Baby Rihanna did the dance from the video. I watched from the side of the dance floor in total amazement.

By the end of the wedding Tim explained it all to me: Turns out Holly was Sia's former manager back in LA. She probably protected Sia countless times from paparazzi and other nonsense. And apparently Tim told Holly that he and I had slept together years earlier *three days before the wedding*.

Turns out I was enemy number one before I walked through the door. Holly must have been, not surprisingly, furious, and Sia was protecting her friend. I get it. It sucked, but I understand. I absolutely should not have said yes to photographing that wedding. I figured if he asked me then there was no baggage to be had, but I was wrong. And for whatever it's worth, Sia is gorgeous. I don't follow her story, so I don't know why she covered her face for so long and maybe it has nothing to do with her looks, but she's a natural beauty. Not to mention a fiercely loyal friend.

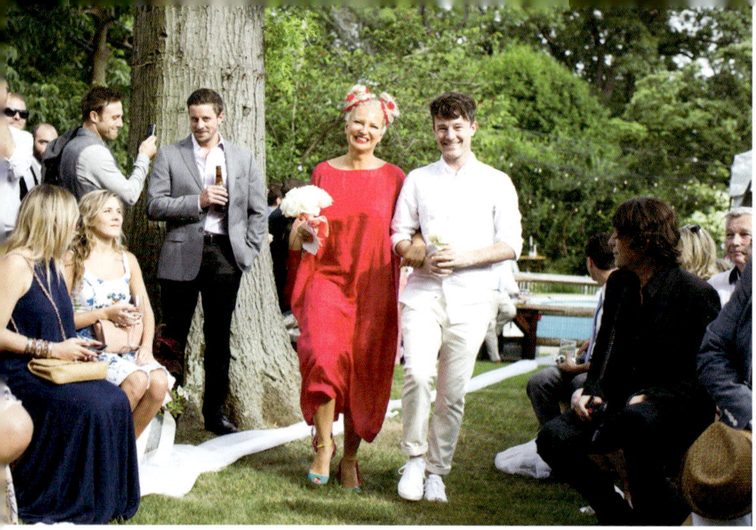
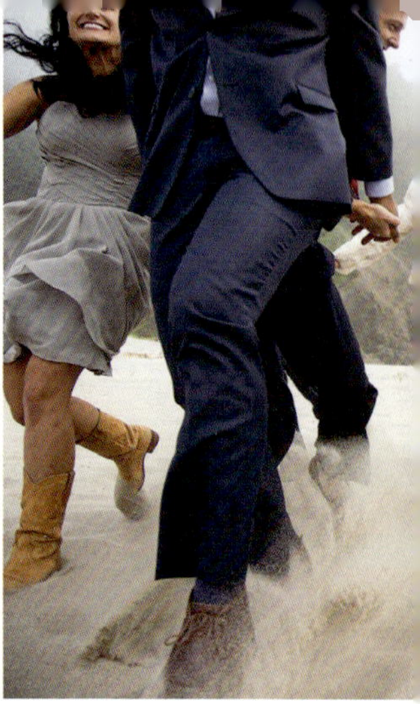
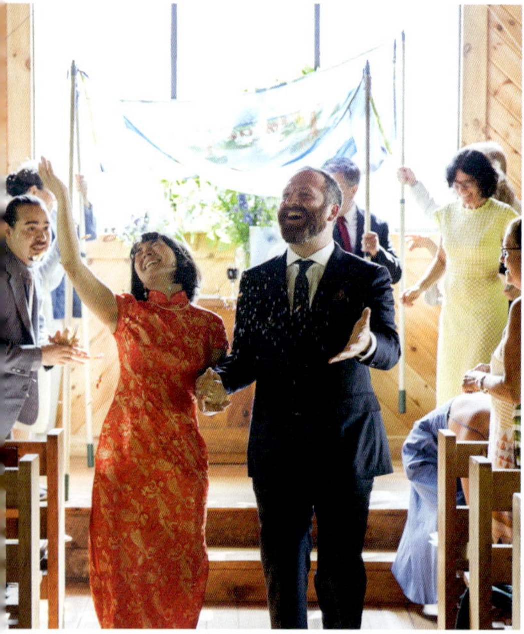
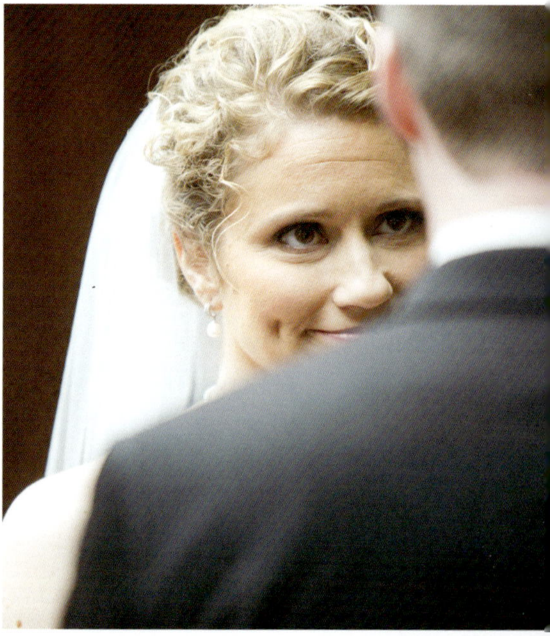
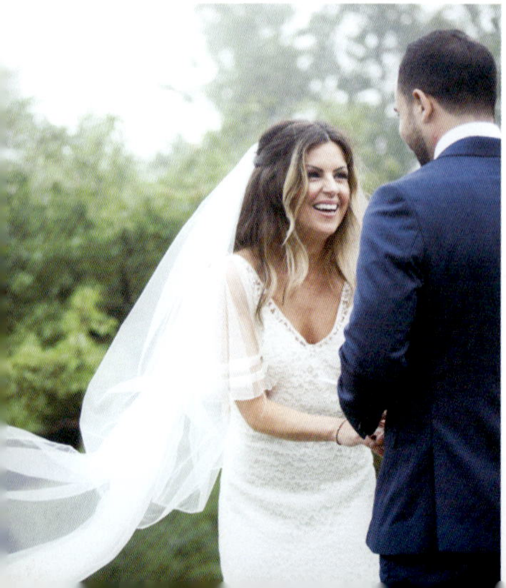
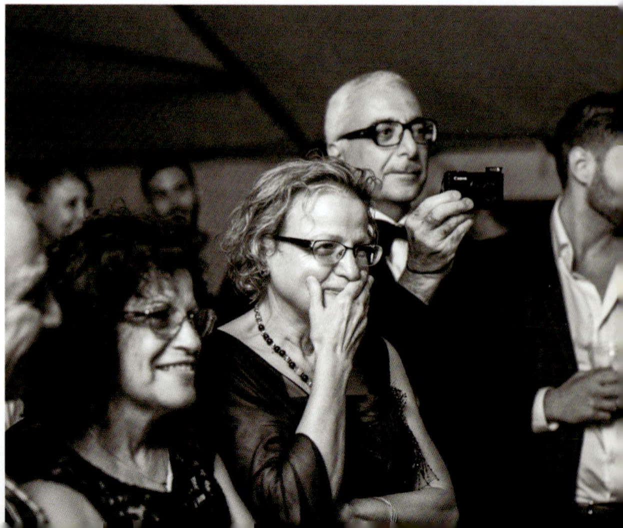

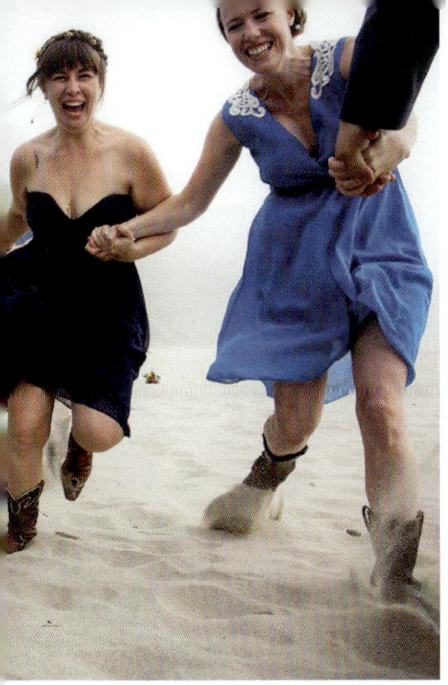

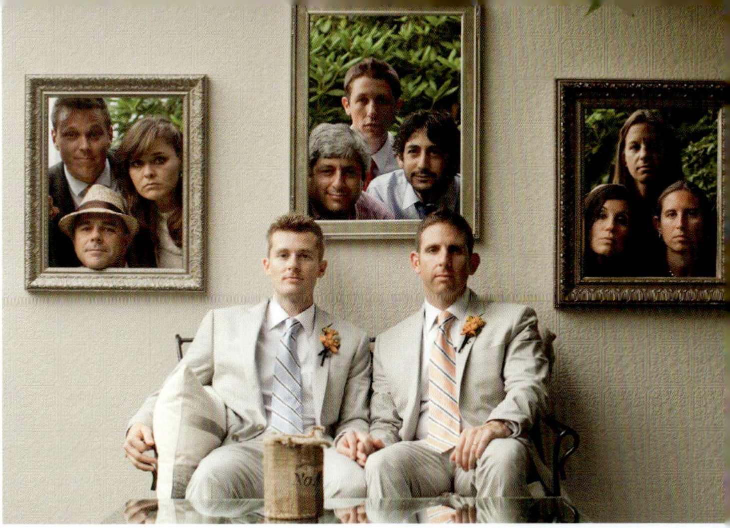

PHOTOGRAPHER

HITCHED STUDIOS

In a perfect world, your wedding photographer would be an ace professional *and* your best friend. In the real world, superduo Tara Morris and Ben Wight come pretty darn close. The pleasant pair transcend the typical shutterbug-client relationship not only by taking top-notch photos, but also by making you and your guests feel shockingly comfortable. Be forewarned: Before the evening ends, you *will* get attached.

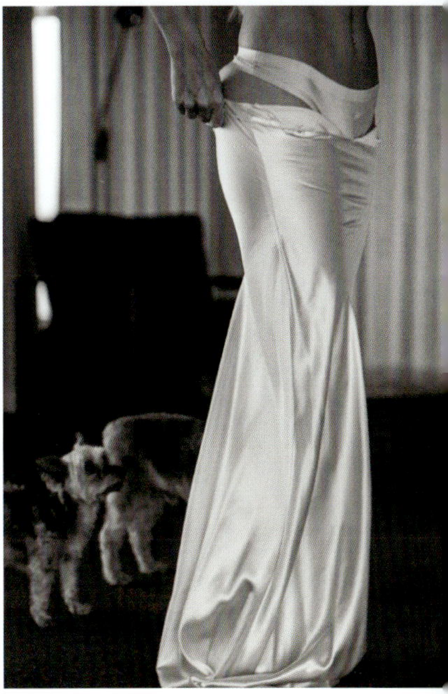

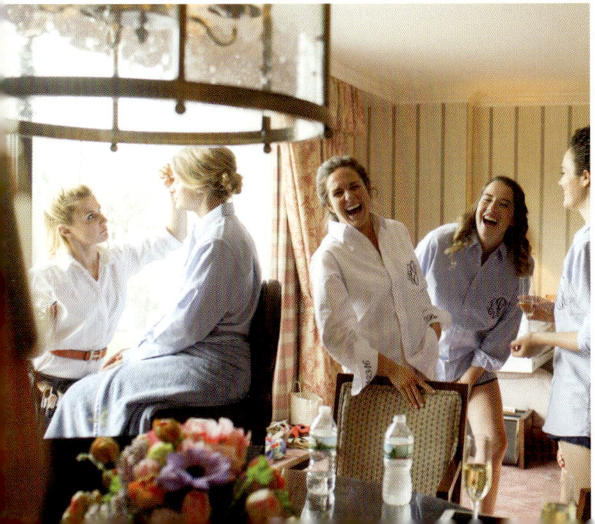

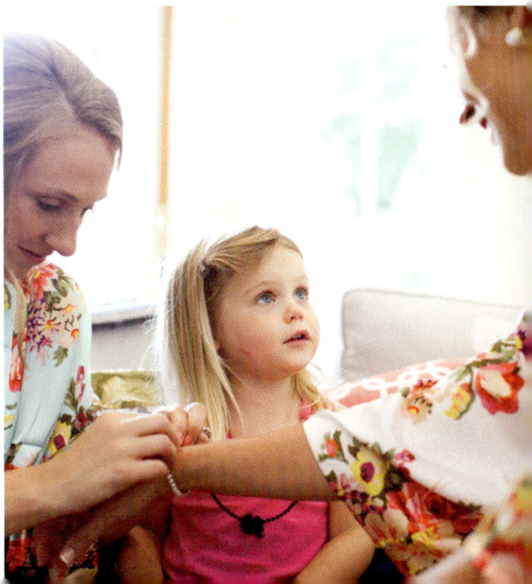

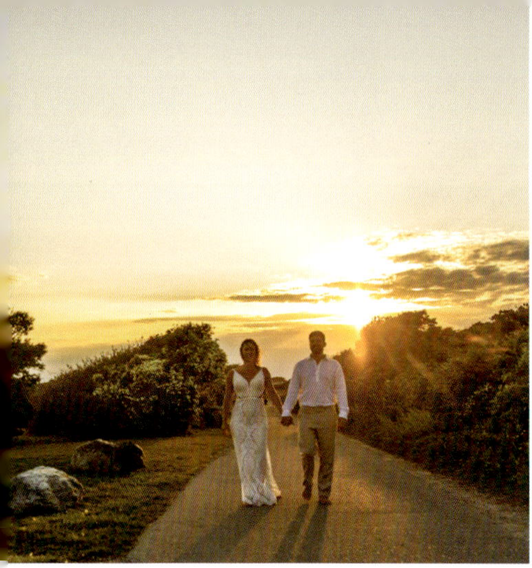
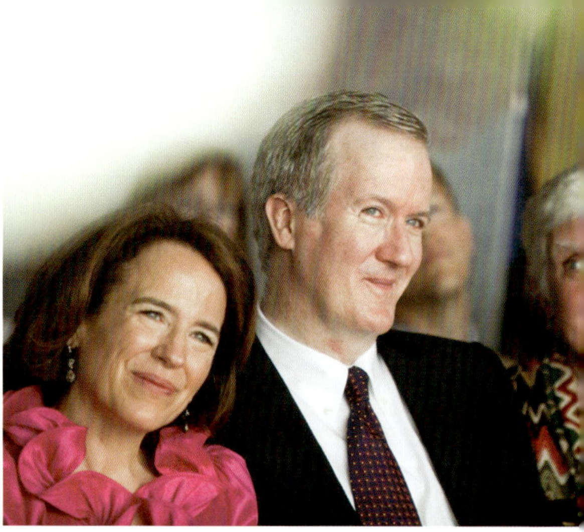
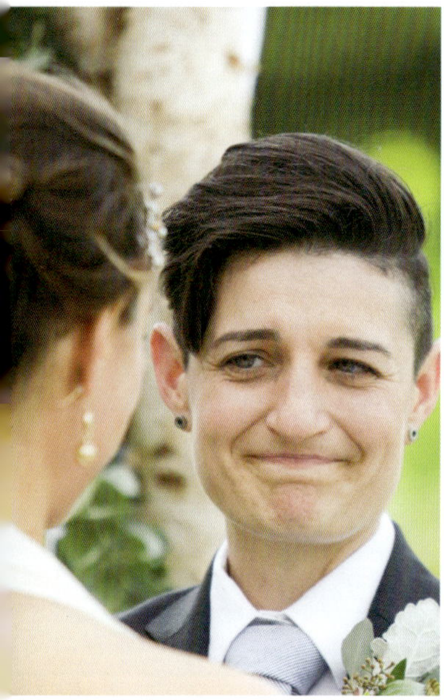
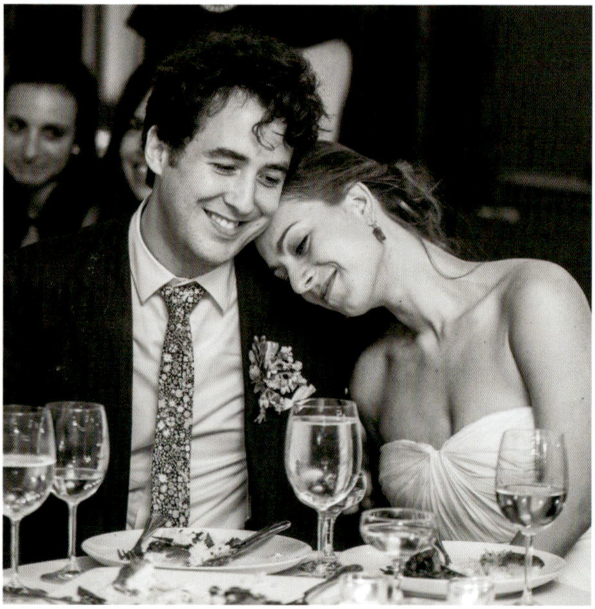

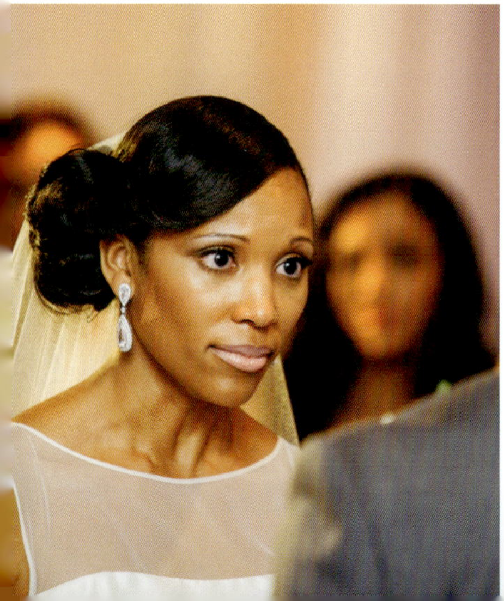
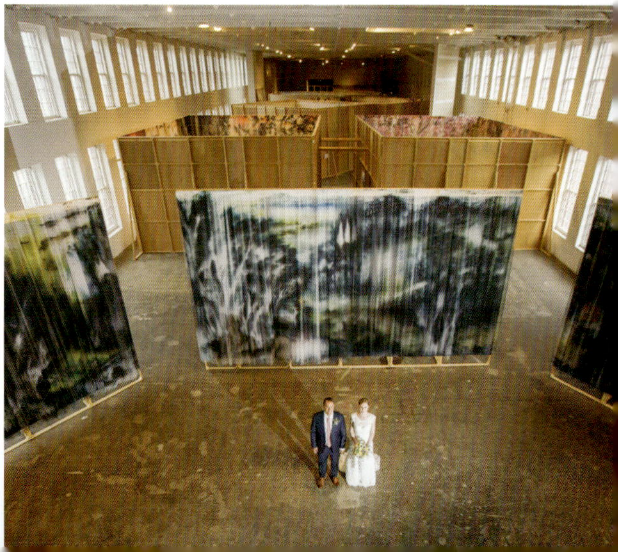

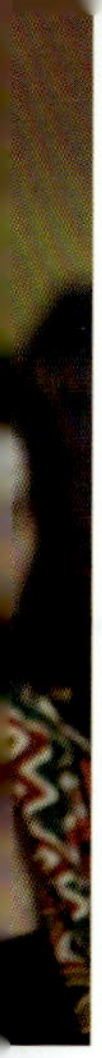
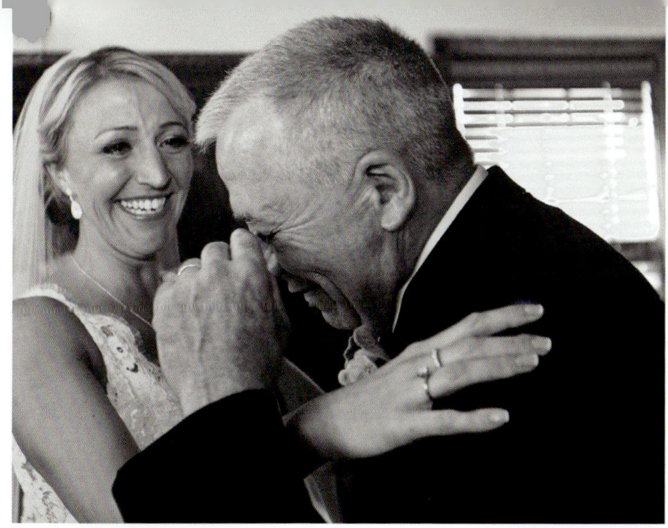
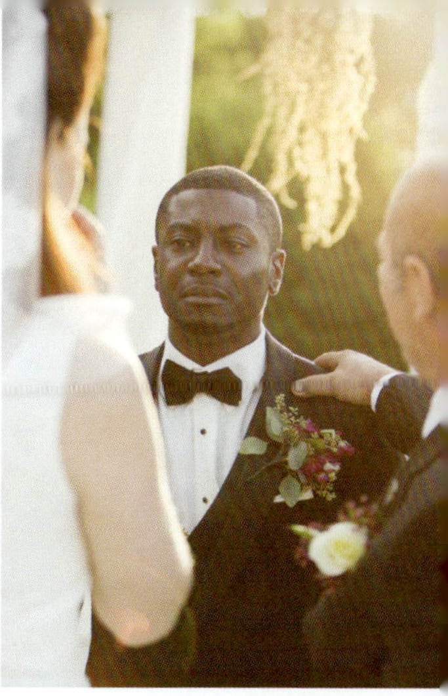
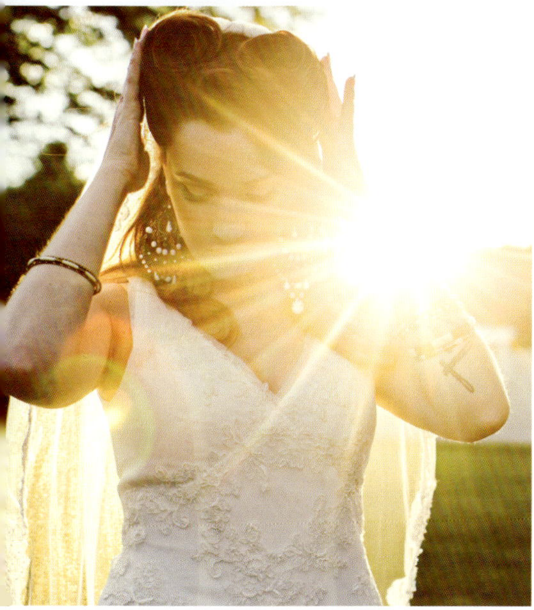
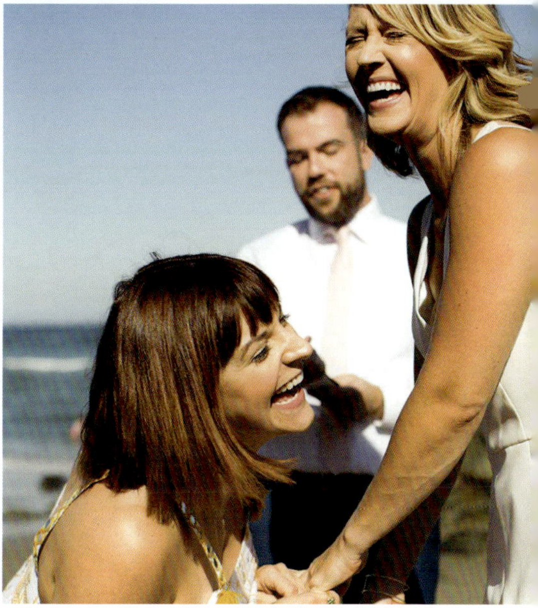
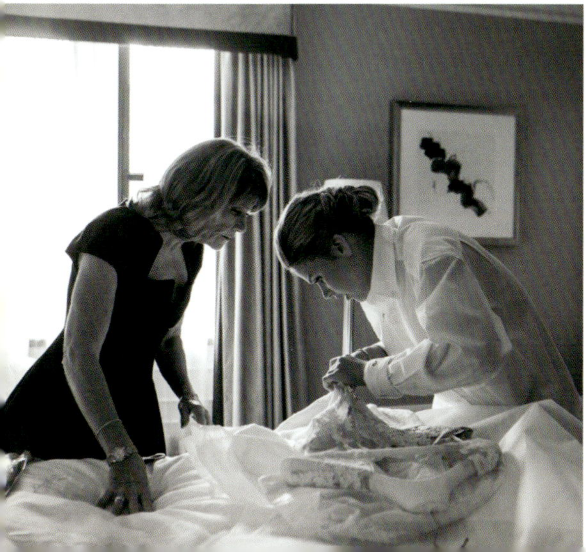
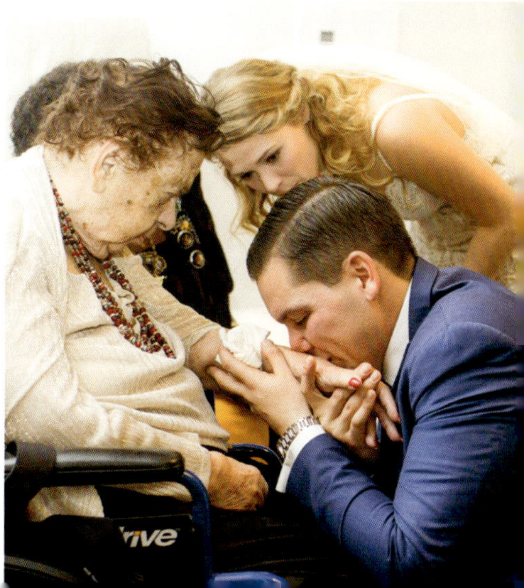

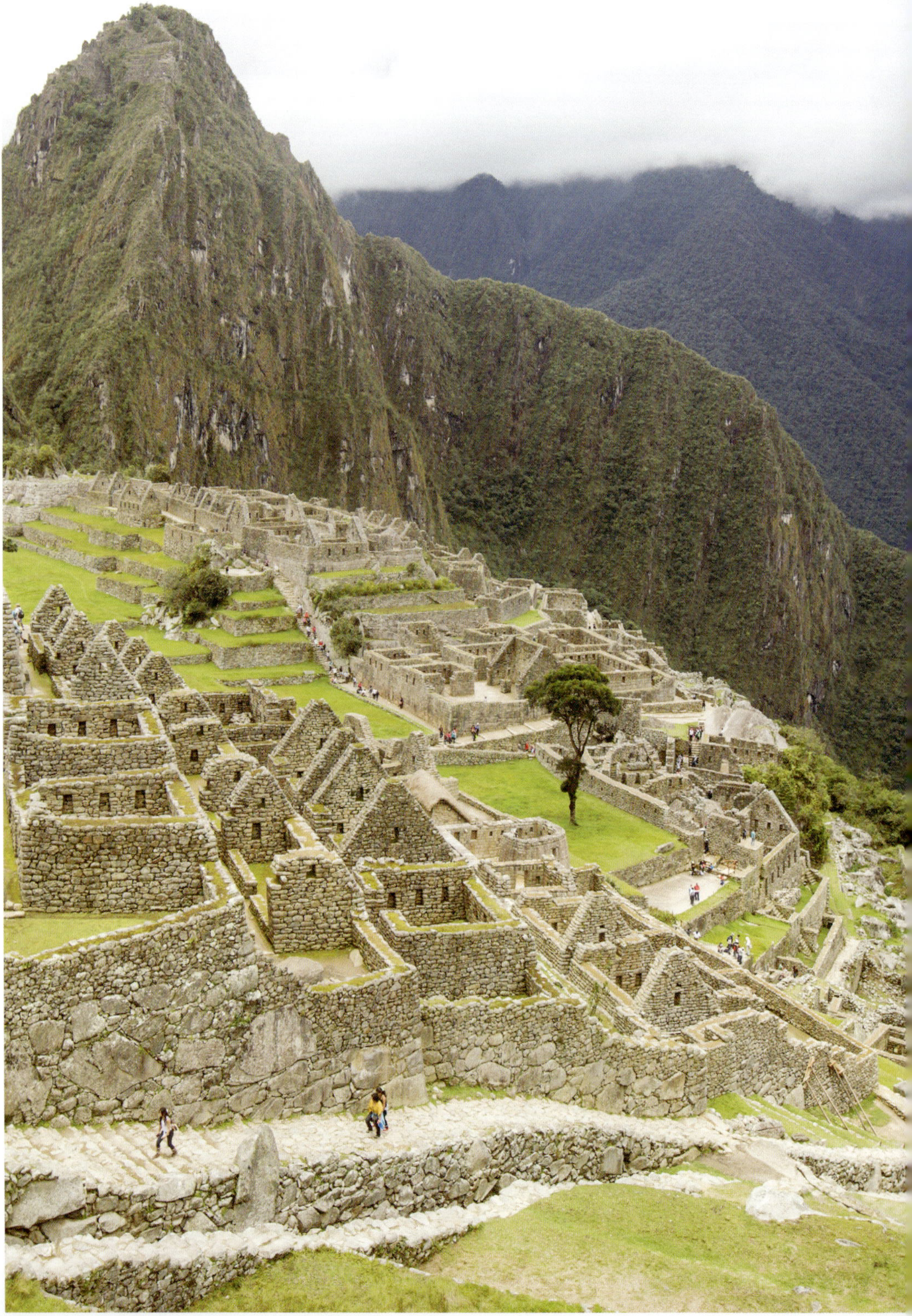

Peru, Bolivia, and Brazil

The Inca Trail is a well-traveled four-day hike to Machu Picchu, the ancient Inca city in the Andes Mountains. Almost every day of the year about four hundred travelers, guides, and porters set out on the journey from the beautiful Peruvian mountain town of Cusco. I figured it would be a fairly easy hike but did no research to confirm or deny that. Arriving in Cusco at 1 p.m. the day before the trek, I spent the day gasping for air, feeling flu-like symptoms and other telltale signs of mild altitude sickness. Guidebooks warn of such things and encourage travelers to allow several days for acclimatization.

I hiked with a trekking company who treated our group to things like three-course lunches, powdered milk mochas, and happy hours atop mountain peaks in portable dining rooms that men carried up on their backs. On the first day I noticed that nothing made me feel more like a loser than gasping for air and praying to god while someone ran by me in flip flops carrying my dining room table.

On our second day the guide woke us up by announcing, "There are many challenges in life. Today will be one of them." I assumed he was exaggerating. We hiked for eleven hours to a place called Dead Woman's Pass at almost 14,000 feet above sea level and I realized he was not. I spend a lot of energy trying to separate hard work from suffering, and deep down I know hiking doesn't count as suffering, but damn, it got close.

Shockingly, I didn't pack well. My camera gear alone weighed fifteen pounds, and that was just what was hanging around my neck. On my back was a change of clothes for each day, a couple of books (!?), and my journal. Every step of that eleven-hour hike I wondered how someone so well-traveled could remain so inept.

Day three of the trek is called the Gringo Killer, and it lived up to its name—it was thousands of tiny granite steps so steep we had to climb them like a ladder, in the pouring rain. It's not easy to throw a temper tantrum on a mountaintop on day three of a four-day hike, but I managed to get it done.

The fourth day started at 3 a.m., and we were scheduled to finally get to Machu Picchu by sunrise. We arrived at what we were told was Machu Picchu, but four straight days of hiking led us to a complete whiteout of fog and clouds. We could see nothing. The guides were saying things like, "It's usually right there," while pointing into a white void. Our whole group was laughing so hard we were crying. Or maybe it was the other way around.

Once the fog cleared, I took thousands of photographs of this mind-blowingly beautiful place, and not a single one does it justice.

I flew from Cusco to Iquitos, Peru, a small, steamy city in the Amazon rainforest in the northern part of the country. A moto-rickshaw picked me up at the airport and we buzzed through villages where families cooled off in rivers brown and thick with mud. I leaned out the side, taking photos in the hot wind.

I had come to the Amazon to do ayahuasca for the week in a shamanic center called Ninue Ta (NT). I had done ayahuasca with a shaman in LA three years earlier and had such a profound and life-changing experience that I was eager to do it again.

The first order of business when someone arrives at NT is to take a *vomitivo*, which is exactly what it sounds like. I drank a liter of liquid that smelled and tasted like fermented onion until it "cleared my system," which apparently makes it easier for the ayahuasca to work. I drank it, puked, puked again, had diarrhea, and was glad when it was over.

An 18-year-old girl, who looked like she was 12 and seemed terribly depressed, shy, and anxious, arrived the day after I got there. She told me she was there with her own money and her parents' blessing to find a way out of the depression she had been suffering with for years. She had tried everything else. Ayahuasca was her last resort.

During that evening's ceremony, after drinking ayahuasca for the first time, she got up off her mat, ran into the jungle, and sprinted back and forth in the pitch dark, screaming like she was either possessed or having an exorcism. We all listened to her blood-curdling cries until she stormed back into the hut and screamed, "WE'RE ALL DOOMED! EVERYBODY IS DOOOOOMED!" When the shaman began to sing his traditional songs, she yelled, "MAKE THE DEMON STOP!!" Meanwhile, the person next to me writhed in agony for an hour, whispering "fuuuckkk" over and over again.

All of this could be yours for only $100 a day.

My time at NT had a few beautiful realizations, but what it never brought me was the kind of clarity or insight that I experienced in LA three years earlier from ayahuasca. Three years earlier, heartbroken and on a friend's recommendation, I went to Santa Monica for two nights of ayahuasca ceremonies. The first night, I was visited by a parade of all my childhood toys, took a psychedelic tour through the house I grew up in, and had a vision of all my photography clients holding up the photos I'd made of their families while shouting, "You are everywhere!" The second night was six straight hours of question-and-answer with my subconscious. I asked myself why I acted the way I did and received brutally honest answers—all with my eyes shut, sitting in the corner of a room.

The experience helped me so much that I assumed going to the Amazon—where this stuff supposedly comes from—would be even more remarkable. It was not. Between the teenager's full-blown mental breakdown and the shaman at NT falling asleep and snoring through the ceremonies, I never really trusted the place.

People have all kinds of opinions about ayahuasca, often calling it "ten years of therapy in one night." I've done it enough times to know it deepens my appreciation for the beauty of life, but I don't think the wisdom comes from the plant. It feels more like it unlocks the books I've read, the lessons I've learned, and the truths I've known for years. Eleven ceremonies in, ayahuasca keeps shining a light on what I already know: that love is all there is, and I am the luckiest person alive.

My next destination was Salar de Uyuni, the salt flats in Uyuni, a town in the middle of nowhere, Bolivia. When planning the trip I googled, "What's the closest airport to Uyuni, Bolivia?" and the internet told me it was in Calama, Chile, so I booked a one-way flight there from Iquitos. Though Calama is the closest airport to Uyuni as the crow flies, there are no roads between the two places. So no bus, no train, no way to get from Calama to Uyuni. With my signature haste-makes-waste planning skills I solved the problem by making a last-minute reservation at a fancy hotel near the salt flats that could help hire a private driver from the Calama airport. One driver picked me up at the airport, and for eight hours we had an off-road experience through the volcanic wasteland of Northern Chile until we reached the Bolivian border, where he handed me off like a baton to another driver. This feat was coordinated by the hotel and an army of guardian angels.

The hotel in Uyuni was made entirely of salt—salt floors, salt walls, salt furniture, you get the point. It was such a fancy place it booked only private tours to see the salt flats, in contrast to the usual way people see the flats: with a gaggle of other people drinking beers, taking pictures, and having fun. So there I was at a really nice hotel for the sole purpose of needing to book the transfer from Calama, and I was a middle-class kid on the rich-kid solo track. The salt flats were stunningly gorgeous, and I loved photographing them, but after a couple days I was ready to go. I took the bus to La Paz, and for dinner had the llama medium rare.

The next morning I caught a flight to Brazil, landing in Rio de Janeiro at dawn. The city was hot, overflowing with beautiful people, and I felt more alive than I had the whole trip.

With full "when in Rome" logic, the first thing I did in Brazil was get a Brazilian wax. Turns out, it's not as common as the name suggests. I ended up pantomiming hair removal to three confused women at a salon before finally lying on my back with my pants off, repeating "all gone, please" like an imbecile.

Rio is fucking huge, and the whole city was pre-gaming for Carnival, which officially started the next week, so the place was going wild. I tried to join the fun and must have drunk a hundred caipirinhas from milk-crate bars at every little street party I found. I met a guy who asked me out, then stood me up, so I met another guy who took me samba dancing in a beautiful but condemned building. The next day, he took me to Ipanema Beach, pointed to a guy in a Speedo, and asked me what we call those in English. I told him we call them "banana hammocks," and when the translation landed, he laughed so hard he was drooling.

People *said* Salvador, Brazil, had a heavy Afro-Brazilian influence. I *heard* Salvador, Brazil, is full of super-hot dudes. I flew to Salvador and rented a room with a nice woman named Lili who lived in a little apartment near the beach. If you're wondering if renting a room in a 58 year old's apartment when you're 37 is a cool way to have a ton of fun in a big city full of hot dudes, then I can help you with that answer. It is not.

I flew from Salvador to Ilha Grande, an island off the coast of Rio with remote beaches and no roads—just mountainous jungle and protected nature reserves. It was beautiful, but also undeniably romantic, and my determination to do everything solo was starting to feel stubborn at this point. I could feel my time traveling alone coming to a natural end. Whether it was true or not, I felt like I was too old to stay in hostels, but all these nice hotels made me feel so alone. This six-week trip through Peru, Bolivia, and Brazil marked my last big solo trip. I needed something else in my life. I needed some roots. I needed a dog. I needed a community.

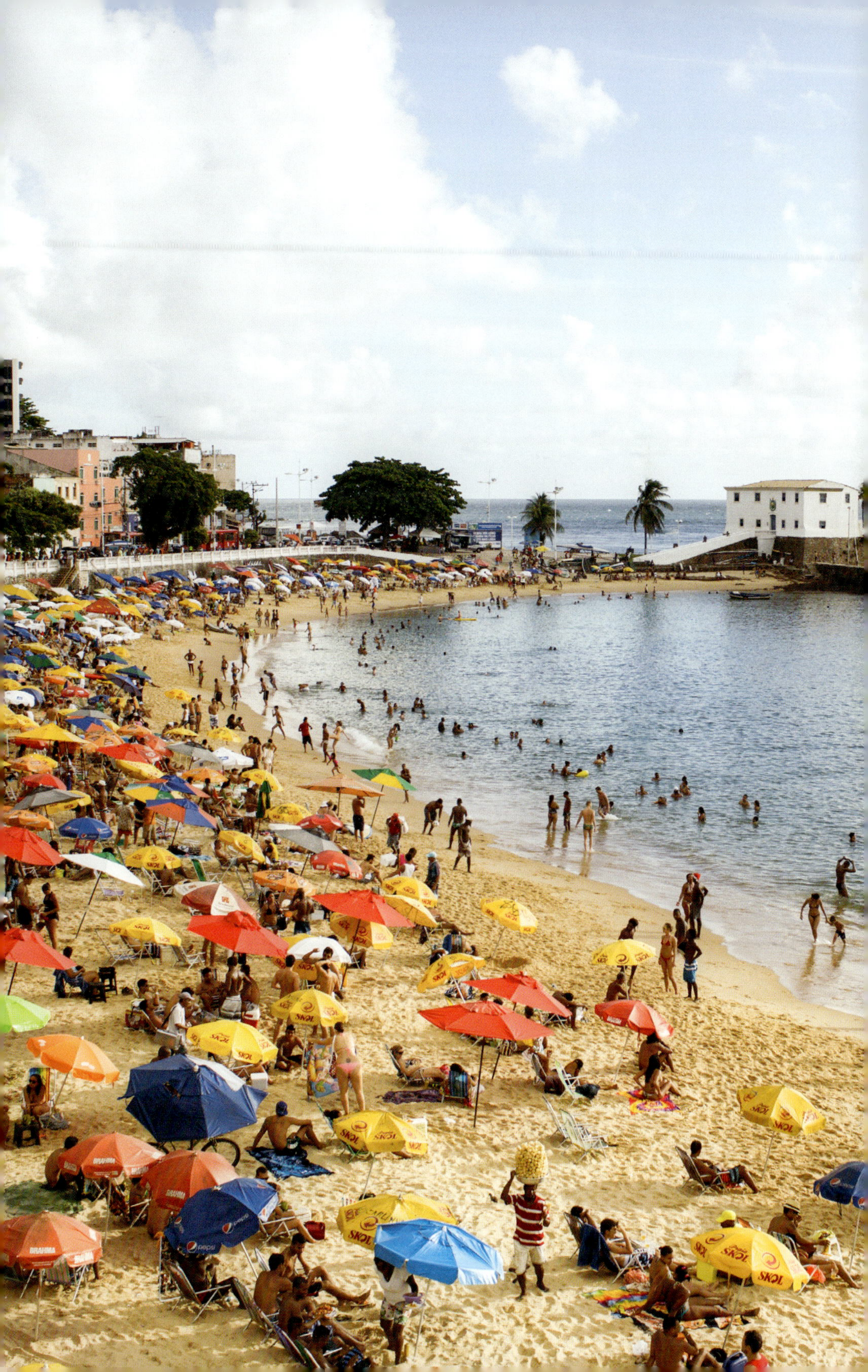
SKOL

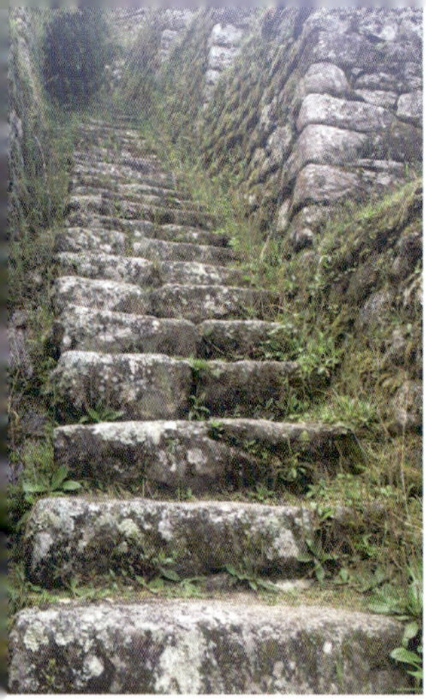
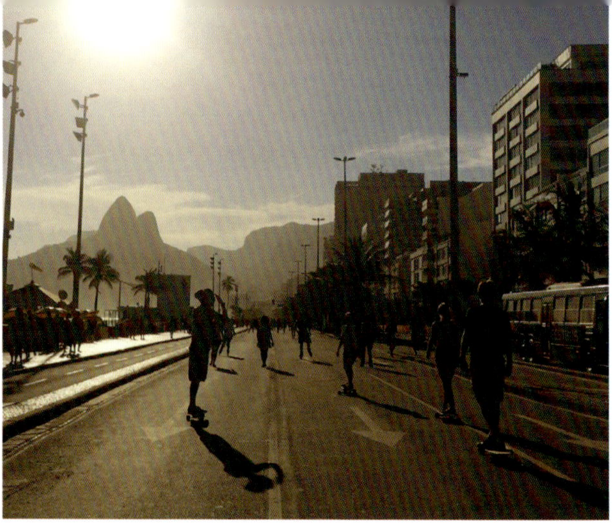

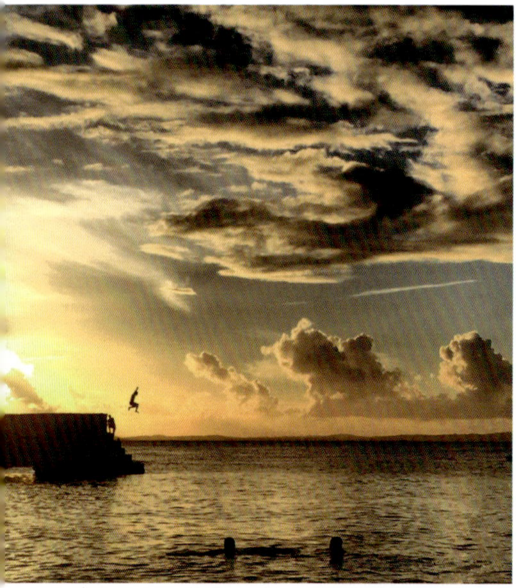
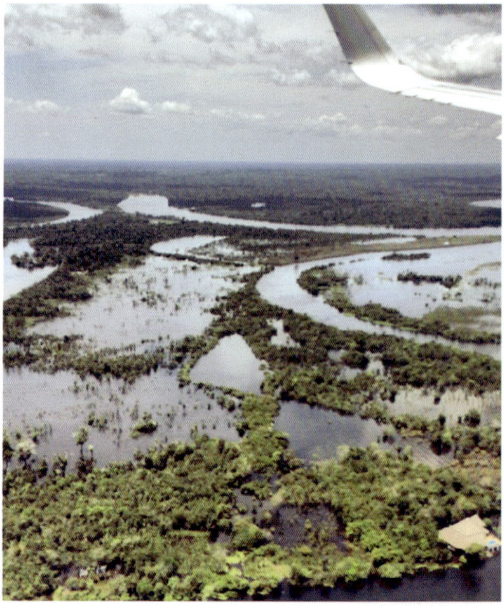
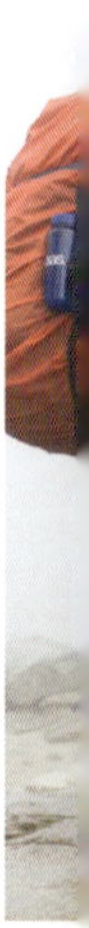
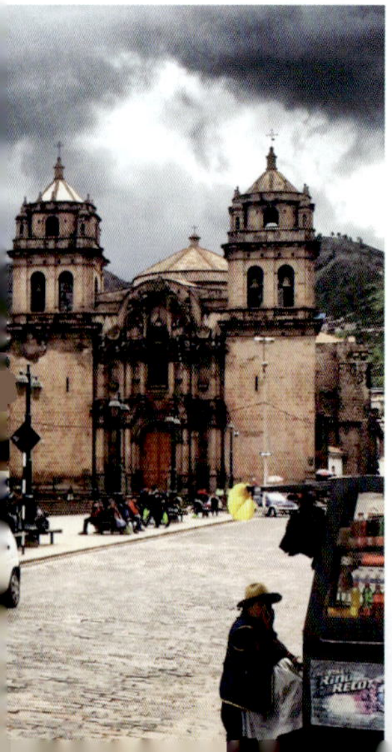
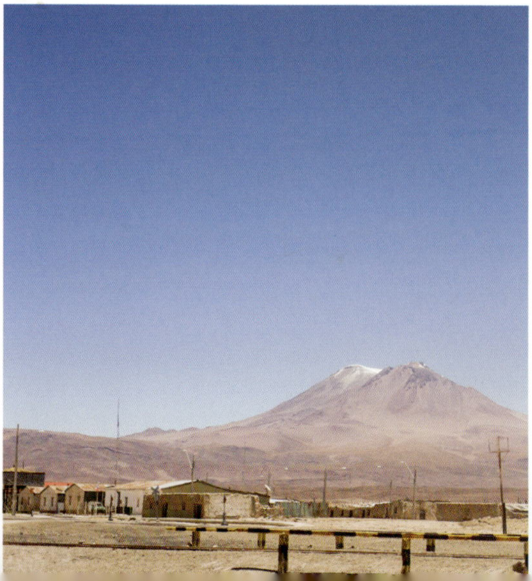
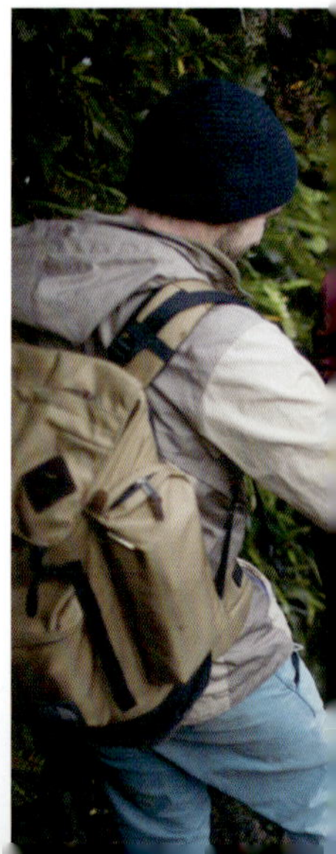

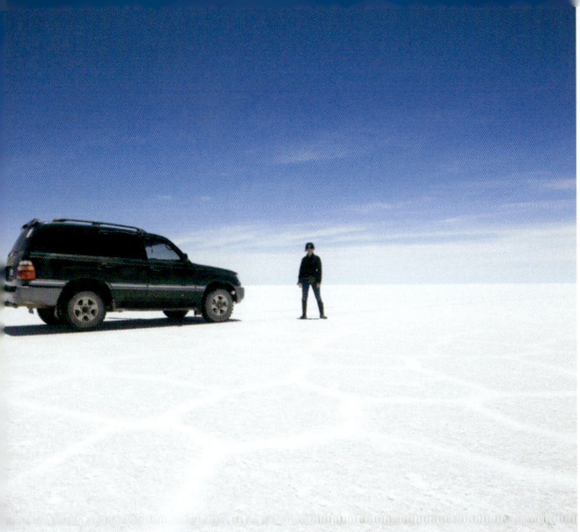

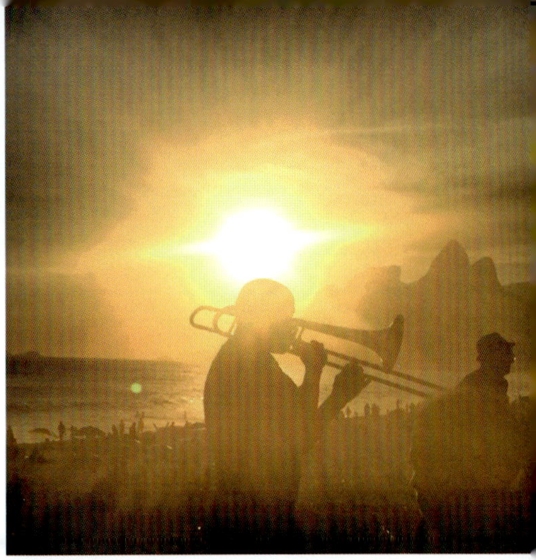

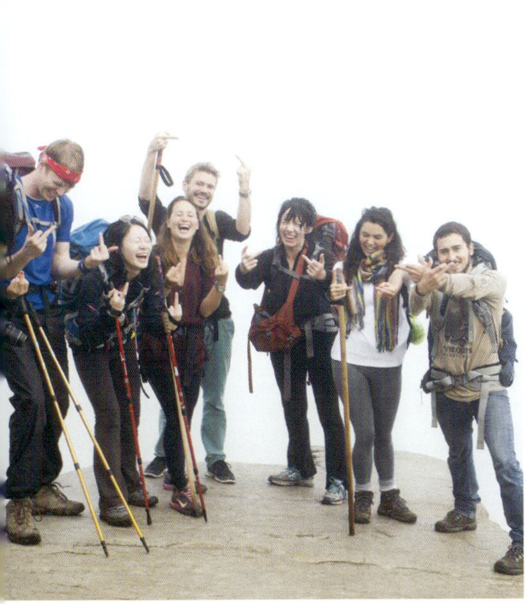

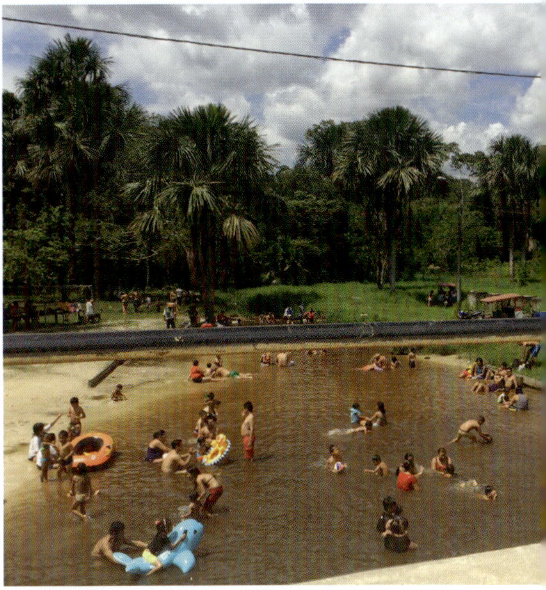

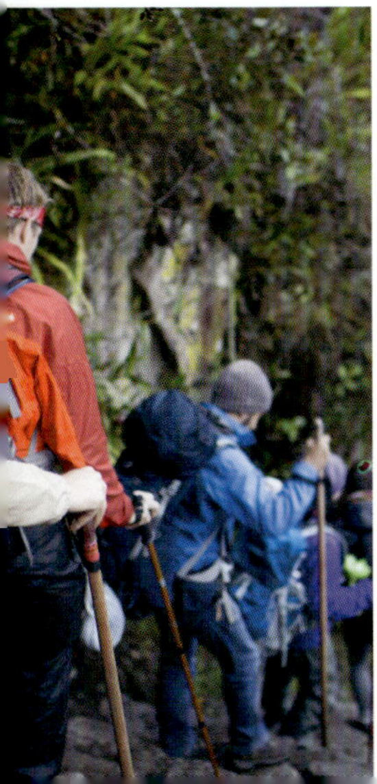

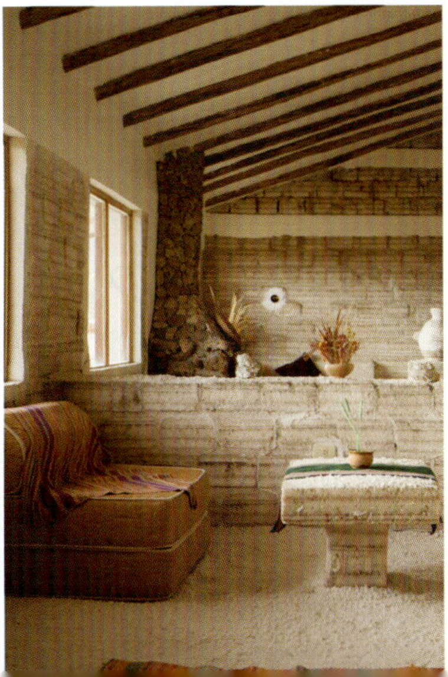

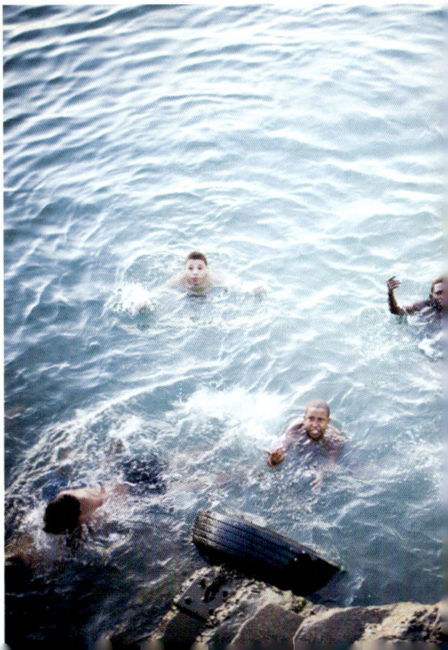

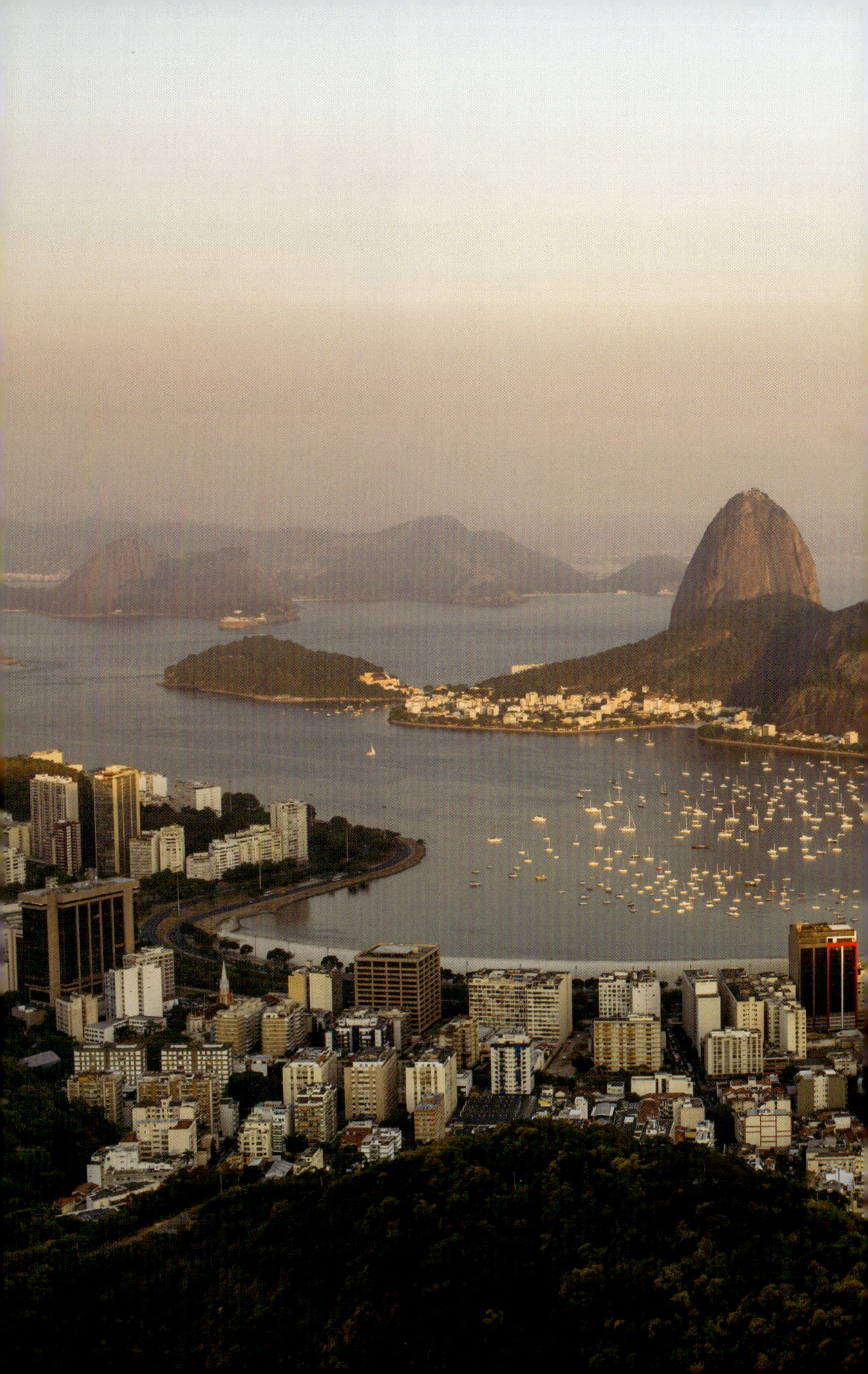

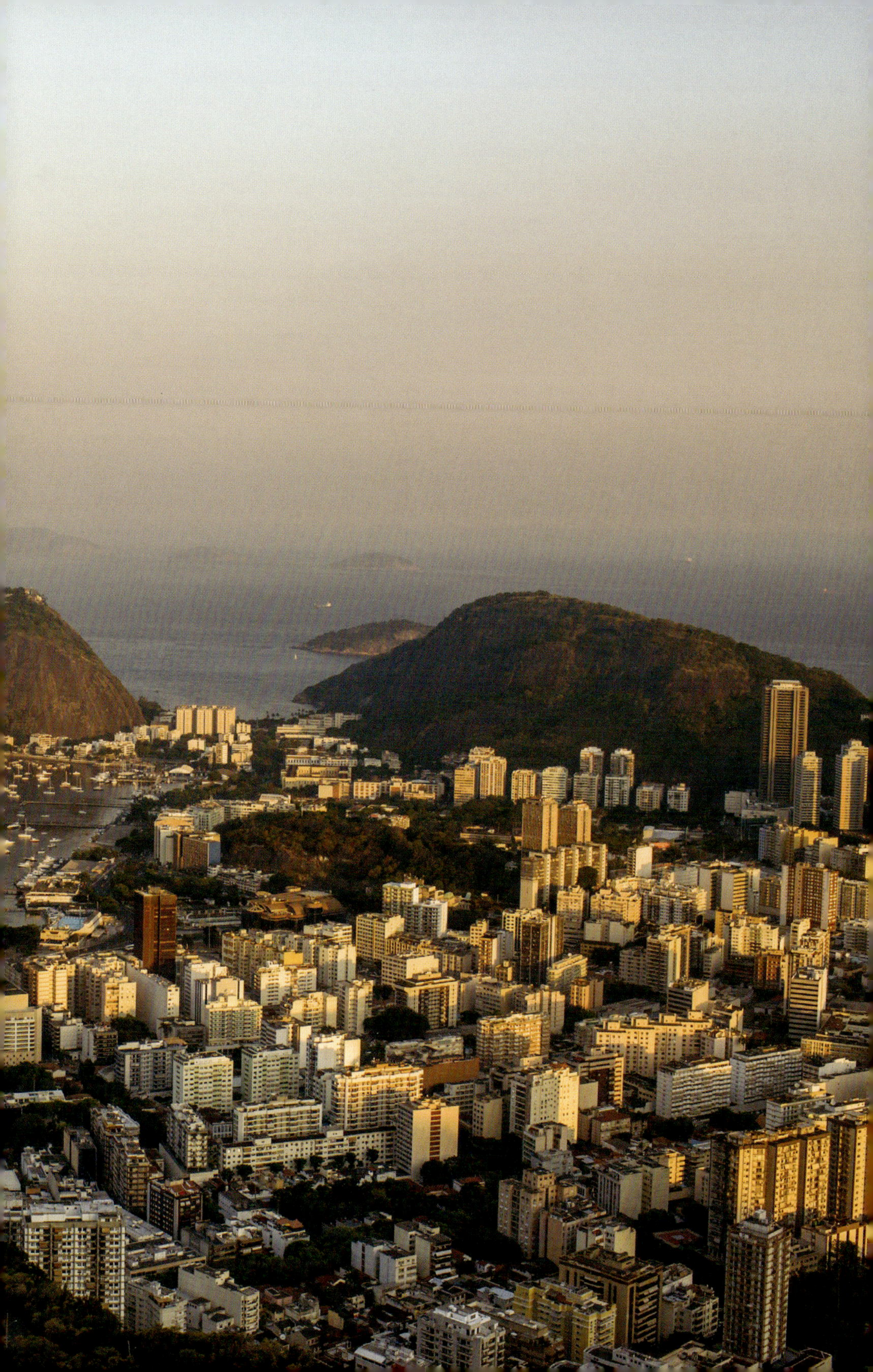

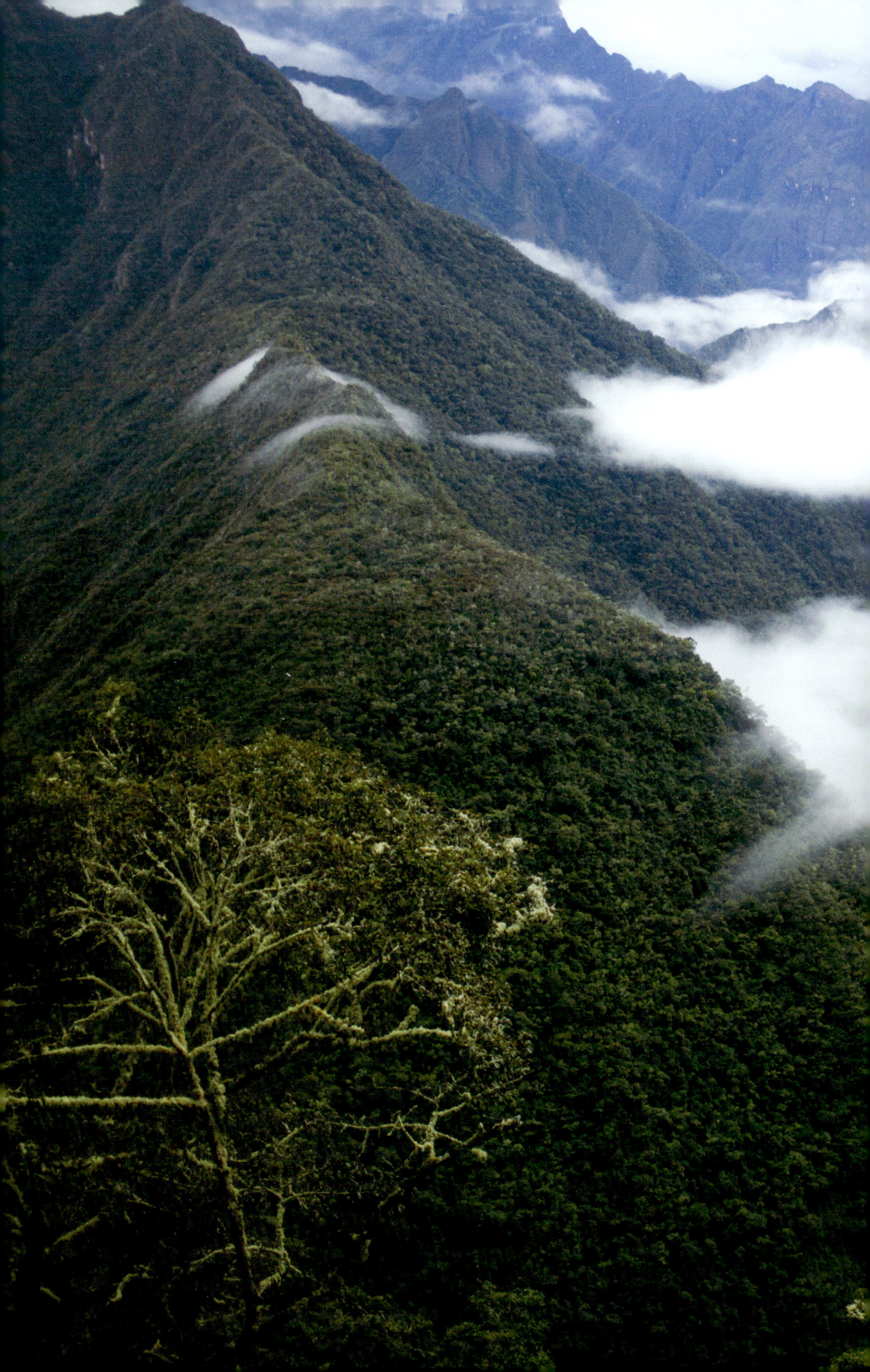

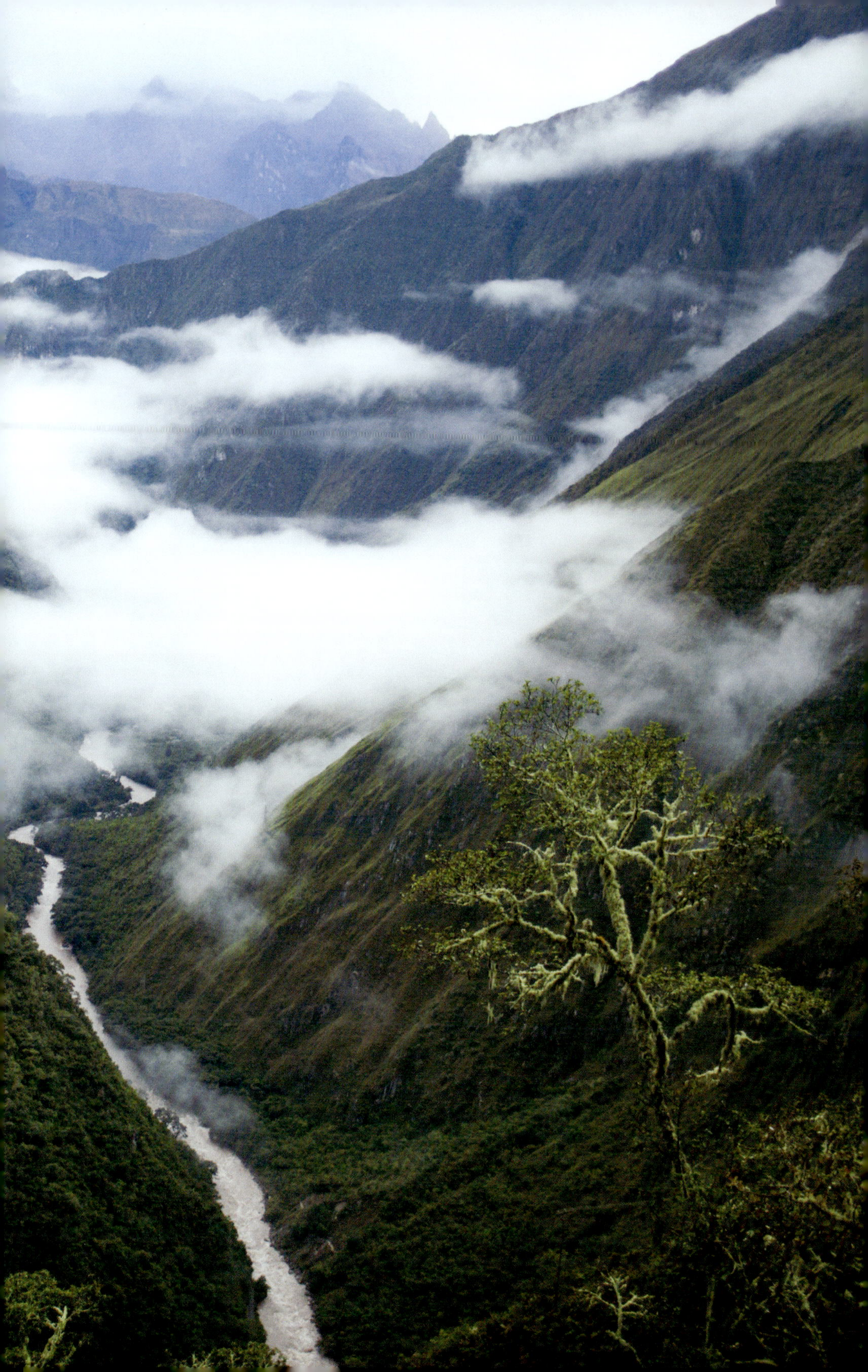

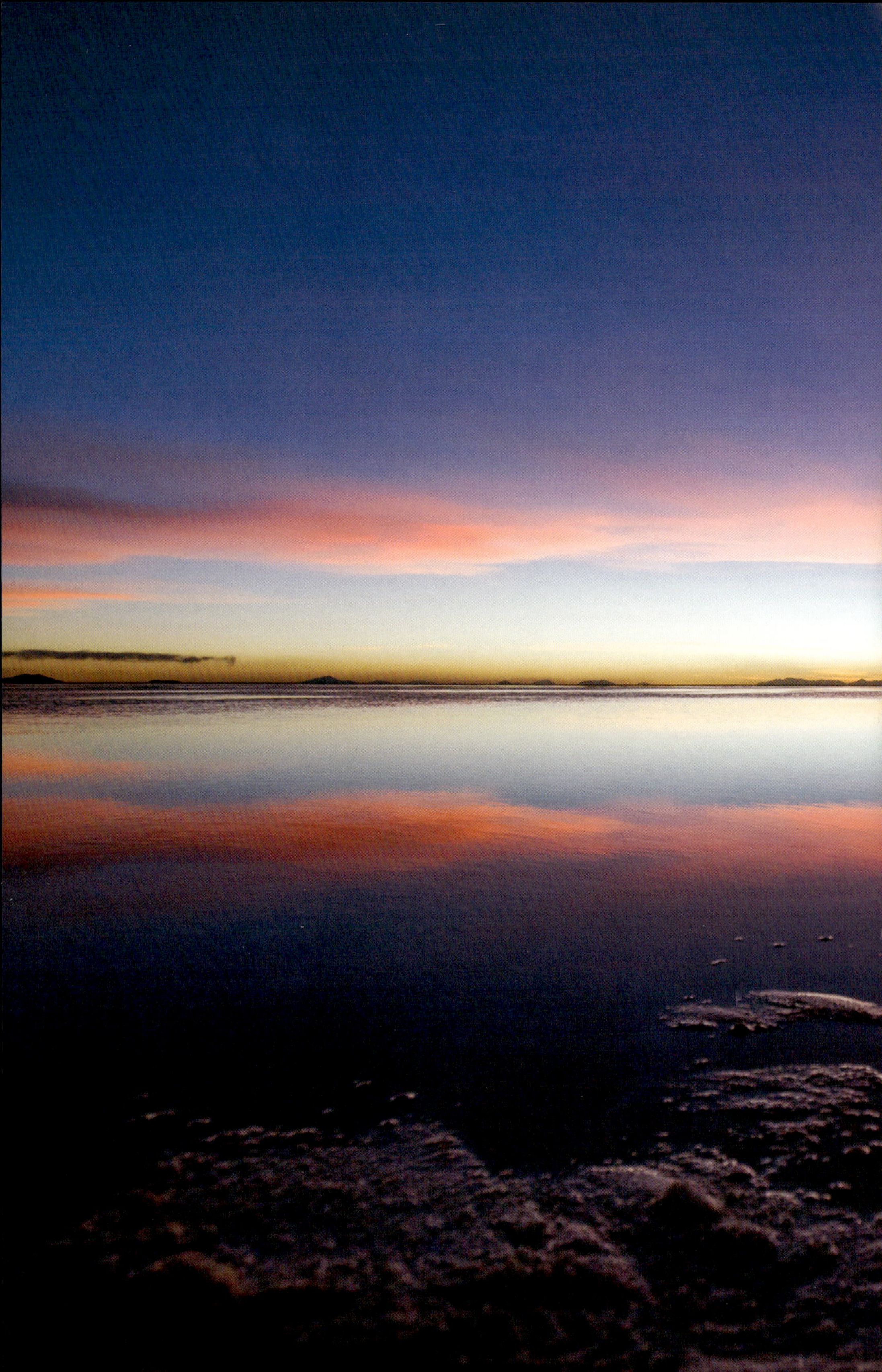

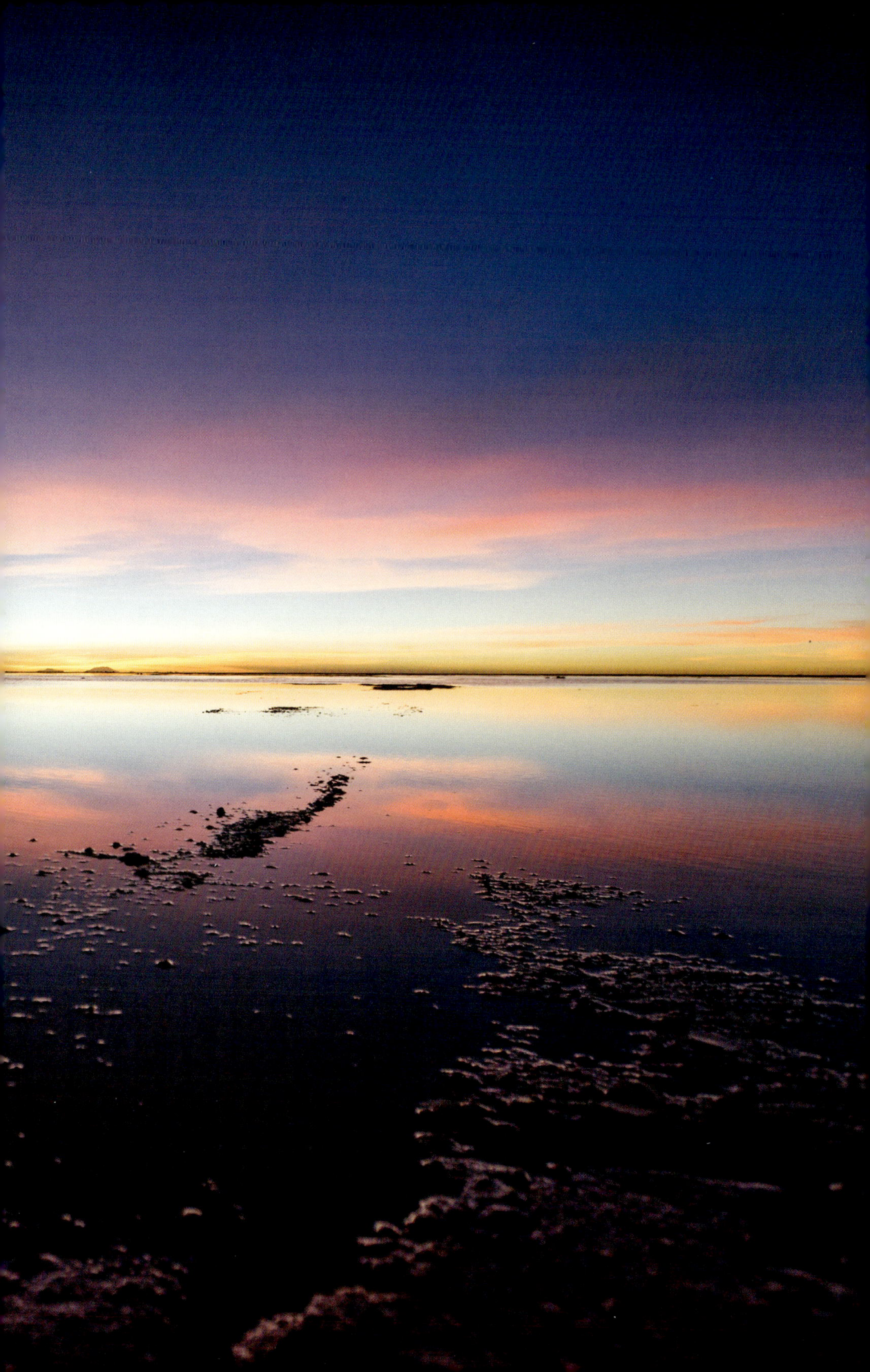

I'll Drive

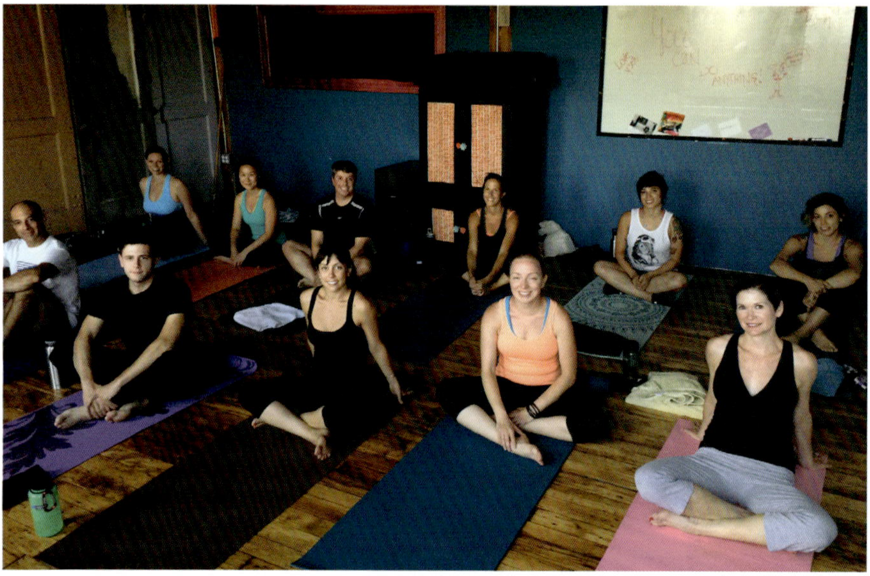

A couple of years after I started down the road to becoming a yoga teacher, I finally received my 200-hour certification with Rolf Gates. Rolf is a former student of Baron Baptiste, and I've always loved him as a teacher, so I wanted to get my certification with him. Rolf's training and his teachings on Buddhism and yoga felt like answers to questions I didn't even know how to ask. Both traditions teach impermanence, and something about their fearless acceptance of death put my life into perspective. When I thought about my own mortality, instead of obsessing over what I wasn't or where I'd gone wrong, I saw that none of it mattered. Only love did. Yoga has been steering my life in this way ever since.

To get my feet wet as an instructor, I memorized Baptiste's Journey into Power sequence and offered free classes at our photography studio in Boston in the summer of 2014. My incredible friends showed up to fill those classes as a show of support and—once again, terrified, as usual—I taught my first yoga class.

From the moment I stepped in front of the room, I loved teaching yoga. Years of personal training and Spinning gave my classes a strong coaching vibe, years of dance taught me rhythm and tempo, and after years of practicing yoga myself, I knew what a great class could offer. I vowed to teach a class that I would love to take, which meant a strong, athletic flow that felt like a dance.

I also wanted to be a better yoga teacher than I was a Spinning instructor. I was embarrassed that I let my sadness spill out as anger in those classes and wanted this chapter to be different.

By the time I taught my first public yoga class in January 2015 I had been all over the world just to learn what it meant to be human. I had met people along the way who had every right to suffer but instead found joy in just being alive. I had watched my mom's life crumble around her in a relentlessly cruel way but also watched her treat her fate as a mountain to climb. My heart had been broken and my worthiness tested countless times, but I had learned to stop my spiraling thoughts to save my own life. I had examined my reactions, opinions, and habits through many years of therapy—never mind eleven ayahuasca ceremonies—enough to know that I wasn't really mad about things, I was just really sad about things. I danced in the dust until I felt beautiful far beyond the reality of my appearance, took every self-help course, and read every book on how to heal. I was ready to teach.

One of the first yoga studios I taught at was in Wellesley, Massachusetts—a leafy suburb of Boston ranked the fifth wealthiest town in the country as I write this and surrounded by other towns equally as beautiful. Needless to say, I hadn't been there before.

I wanted to teach a challenging class. I knew folks in Wellesley wouldn't have it any other way, but more than that, I wanted to relentlessly remind people to notice, and be grateful for, how good they had it. In a town like Wellesley, where comfort and success are in abundance, I wanted people to feel grateful for the things that are easy to overlook until they're gone. I began with what we all had in common: a free hour, an extra $20, and legs that worked well enough to carry us down the stairs into the studio. Gratitude wasn't the only thing I talked about. My mom was really sick during those years, and I spoke often about the heartbreak of watching her die. I tried to be honest and vulnerable, but also helpful and encouraging. No more being mad instead of being sad.

I have always felt free to be vulnerable in a public way, to admit my pain and fear so that others who feel the same way might feel less alone. It's the bright side of not having great boundaries. The more we admit our deepest truths, the more we inspire each other to do the same, and the closer we become. Vulnerability is the bridge across the chasm that lies between each of us. We are all afraid. We all wonder if we're enough. We all do and say shit we wish we hadn't. In my classes, I was saying: I'll go first. You can join me when you're ready.

As a new teacher, I closed my eyes so I could find the right words without losing the tempo of the class. I didn't want to get distracted from what I wanted to do: inspire people to be grateful and let them dance. I know it's a bad habit, but I still teach with my eyes shut.

Recently, I overheard a girl tell her friend, "Tara closes her eyes to channel people in her class. I think she channels her mother." To that I will reply here: I'm from Marshfield, homie. I used to climb through my neighbor's kitchen window to smoke her mom's cigarettes. I don't channel people. I don't even know what that means.

Most of my students were mothers back then, and I would start my class by asking them to release the white-knuckled grip on their lives and trust me. "I'm gonna drive for the next hour," I'd assure them. "All you have to do is breathe."

Almost immediately, my classes began to sell out. People came for a good sweat and got a reminder of how much they had to be grateful for. My students began to rely on me for something that made the rest of their lives work, and I felt it. No matter how many classes I taught or how far I drove, I promised I would never drop the ball. I gave everything I had to every class I taught.

In return, my students asked how they could support me the way I supported them, so they filled my retreats, hired me for family photography, and became my friends.

Those first students gave me the confidence to teach in a raw and honest way and prepared me to do everything I have done in my yoga career. They were relentless in their appreciation, unwavering in their generosity. An army of support, they were, from the beginning, a Love Offensive.

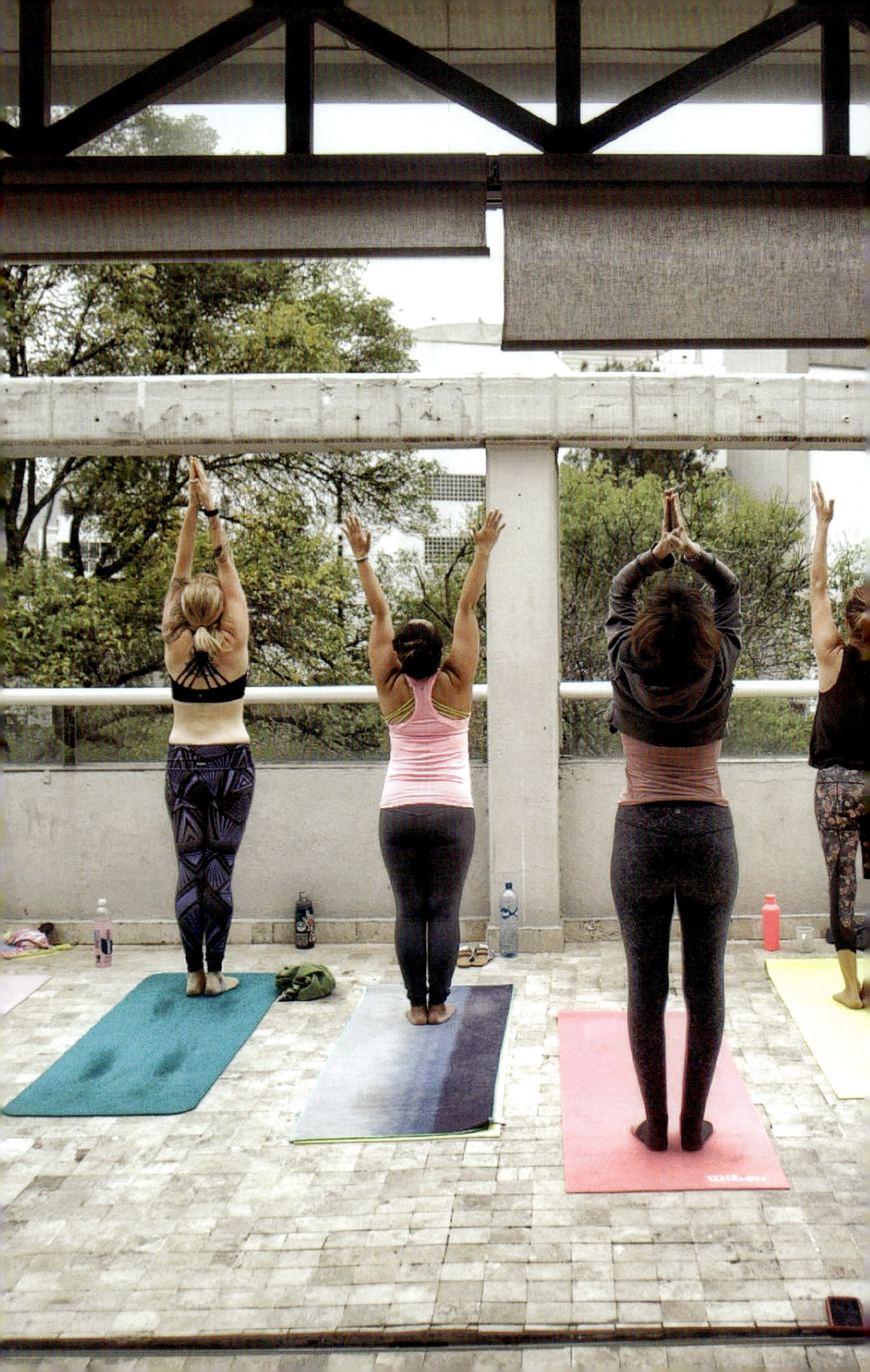

Aggressively Friendly

My friend Aaron once referred to me as "aggressively friendly," and I liked the oxymoron. Other people have remarked on the salty/sweet nature of my personality, and I wanted to capture that contrast when I was naming my online photography course in 2015. The Love Offensive was what I came up with.

The Love Offensive was an online portrait photography course where I taught folks the importance of a good photograph and how to take one. So many times we can let a bad picture confirm our worst fears about our appearance, and we often think a good one is just a lucky mistake. I wanted to teach people how to use portrait photography to make other people feel good—not in a vain way, in a real way. Out there with our cameras, taking beautiful photographs of one another, I saw us as an army of love on the offensive. The online course was only kinda successful, but I had fun making it with my friends. I kept the name.

After spending so much of my life learning the awkward lessons of world travel, finding peace through yoga, and honing the craft of photography, I was ready to combine these things and share them. Just as I was coming to this realization Jenn Ciplet entered my life. Jenn is a photography student turned dear friend whom I met at an art workshop. She told me she'd run logistics and translate on my trips in exchange for free travel. It took us one second to shake on it, and Destination Love Offensive was born.

We led our first trip in February 2016 to Nicaragua, to a town where the Pacific Ocean rolled in so gently that people with even a single athletic bone in their body could learn to surf. This counted me out, but I still rode the ocean kneeling on a surfboard and called it a win. We rented out a small but beautiful yoga retreat center in a rural and unsuspecting neighborhood and fell in love with the place. Each student spent an afternoon with a local family, photographing their beautiful lives, and as a thank you for their time, openness, and generosity, Jenn printed all the photos, and we gave them to the families.

Our second trip, to New Orleans, kicked off the morning after Trump won in 2016. Most of us still had our pantsuits on and were trying to scrape off the "I'm with Her" temporary tattoos when we arrived in the Big Easy, still in shock. One student was so outnumbered by us Lefties that she couldn't admit who she voted for. Poor thing told us she voted for her dad.

On our third trip, to Guatemala, in 2018, my sister called me on the first day. As I looked out over Lake Atitlan, she told me that our dad had fallen in his apartment, hit his head, and died. I was both the photography teacher and the yoga teacher and had absolutely no option to leave. My dearest friend, Nina, was on that trip—thank god—and without me having to ask, she crawled under the covers with me that first night so I wouldn't have to sleep alone. Halfway through the week, when my dad's death actually hit me, Jenn held my head in her hands for a full day while I cried my eyes out.

In 2019 we took a big group to one of the greatest cities on Earth, Mexico City, for Día de los Muertos. Ben Wight joined us so he could help teach photography while I led the yoga portion. The whole region was in full regalia for the multi-day holiday of honoring the dead. Carpets of orange marigolds and walls of sugar skulls were everywhere we looked. Elaborately decorated altars called *ofrendas* were in everyone's front yard. People dressed up as skeletons and joined a parade that wrapped around the city. In short, it was a photographer's dream.

We hosted two back-to-back yoga and adventure trips to Cuba in January 2020, and both were insanely good. Minus the chick who went home after one day because she needed to "lift weights every day." I suspect it had more to do with the crumbling infrastructure of the hotel, the terrible food, the uncomfortable beds, and the loud music from the neighbors all night, but I didn't ask.

The itinerary for our trip to Alaska went like this: we'd start in Anchorage, then head to a ski town called Girdwood, continuing to Seward, then Homer, and finally back to Anchorage. I would teach yoga every morning, give photography assignments and critiques all day, and drive a fifteen-person van. Jenn and I would also cook and serve breakfast, clean dishes, do laundry, and run logistics for seven days straight.

We sold out immediately, and Julia, a woman I had never met, signed up with her mom. If you run, or have gone on group trips, you know that the chemistry of the group, when good, feels like a dream you once had about how summer camp should feel. When the chemistry is off—and it's almost always off by just one—you take up smoking cigarettes for a week so you have an excuse to sit out back and talk shit.

By the time we got to Seward, an insanely photogenic town with a vibrant fishing culture, Jenn approached me with a problem. "Soooooo... Julia is gonna rent a car with her mom and actually follow the van in her own vehicle for the rest of the trip."

Turns out Julia is an actuary. She analyzes data to estimate the risk of shit going wrong. Julia saw that there were two large-bodied people on the trip and guessed how much each of them weighed. Then she guessed how much everyone else on the trip weighed. Then!… Julia looked up the weight rating of the year, make, and model of the van I was driving. Then!!… Julia added the trailer of luggage we were towing to her risk analysis. Then!!!… Julia deemed us unsafe and began taking each person aside to tell them just how unsafe we were.

Jenn read my facial expression as she delivered this news and confirmed, "I'll handle it."

Jenn must have convinced Julia to ride out the rest of the week with us because she did. On the last day of the trip we were in Homer, and Julia told me she'd be missing the final celebration but asked if I could still critique all of her work. Turns out she and her mom were catching a small single-engine plane back to Anchorage—and it would depart in an hour. Safe choice, I thought, as a John Denver song played in my head. Their taxi arrived and off they went, leaving Jenn and I wondering how she could have wreaked so much havoc without any remorse.

I've never seen Julia again though she signs up for almost every trip I have run since. Something always comes up that prevents her from joining and she cancels every time. I credit my mom for every serendipitous piece of luck I experience so every time something comes up to prevent Julia from coming on another trip, guessing how much I weigh, and testing my aggressive friendliness, I whisper, "Thanks, mom. I love you."

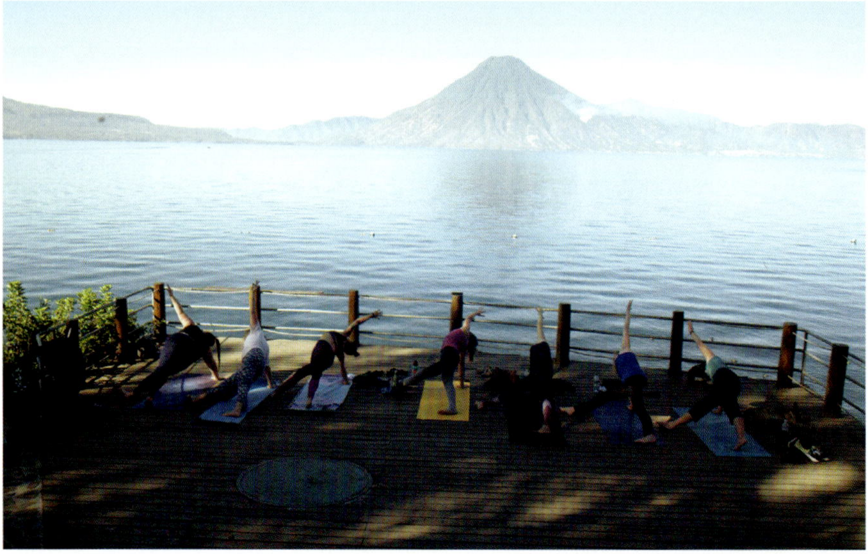

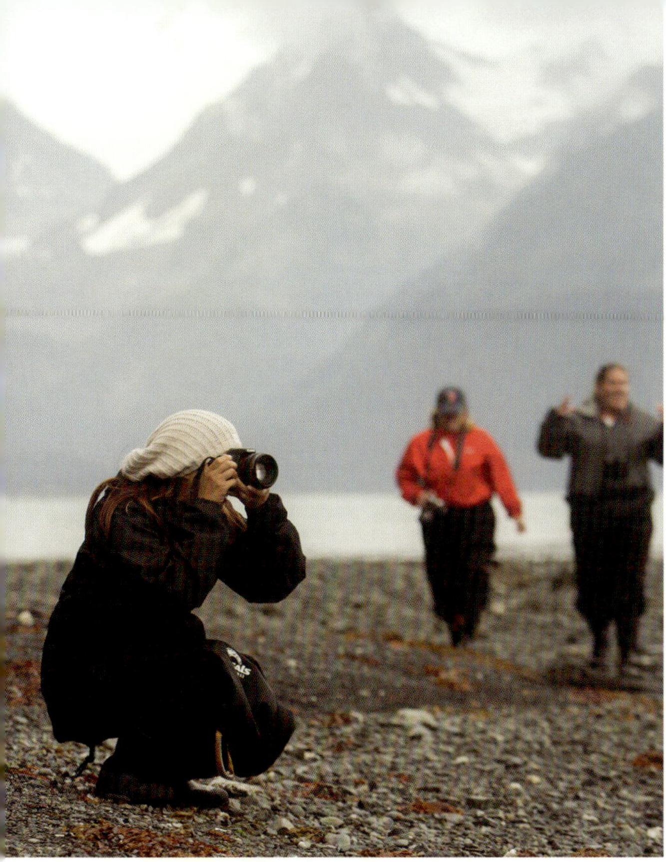

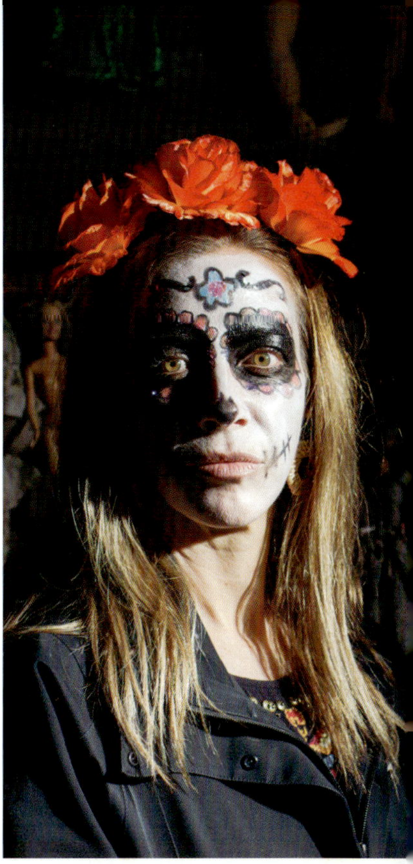

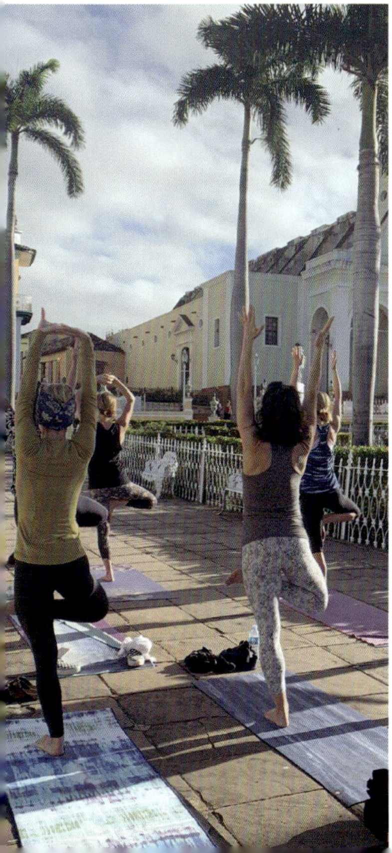

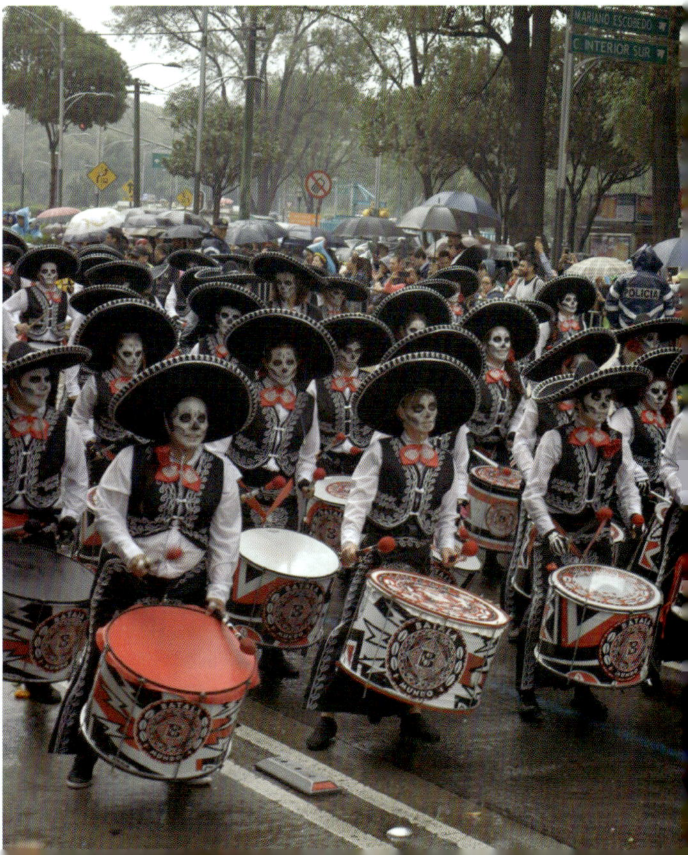
MARIANO ESCOBEDO
C. INTERIOR SUR
POLICIA

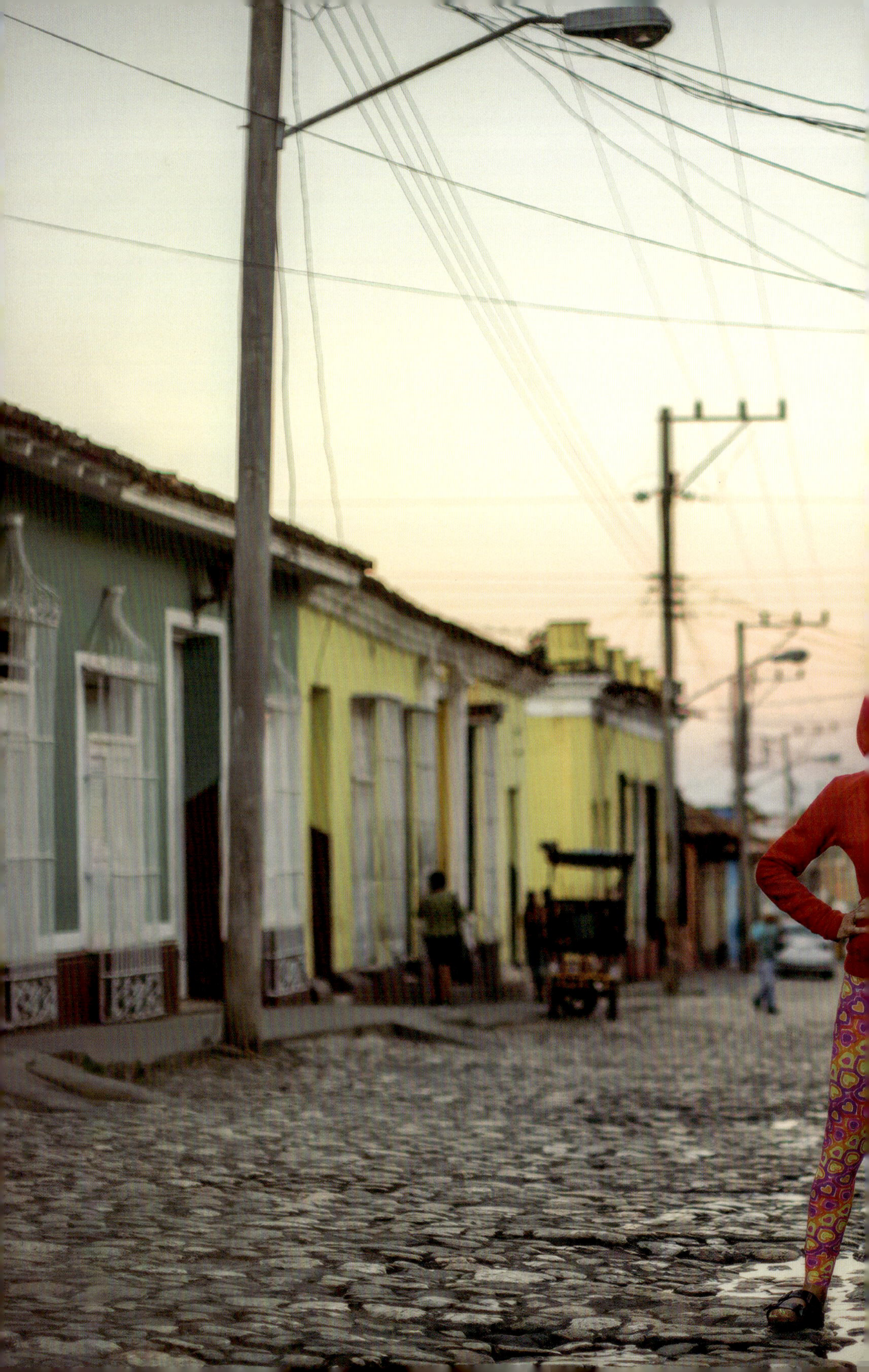

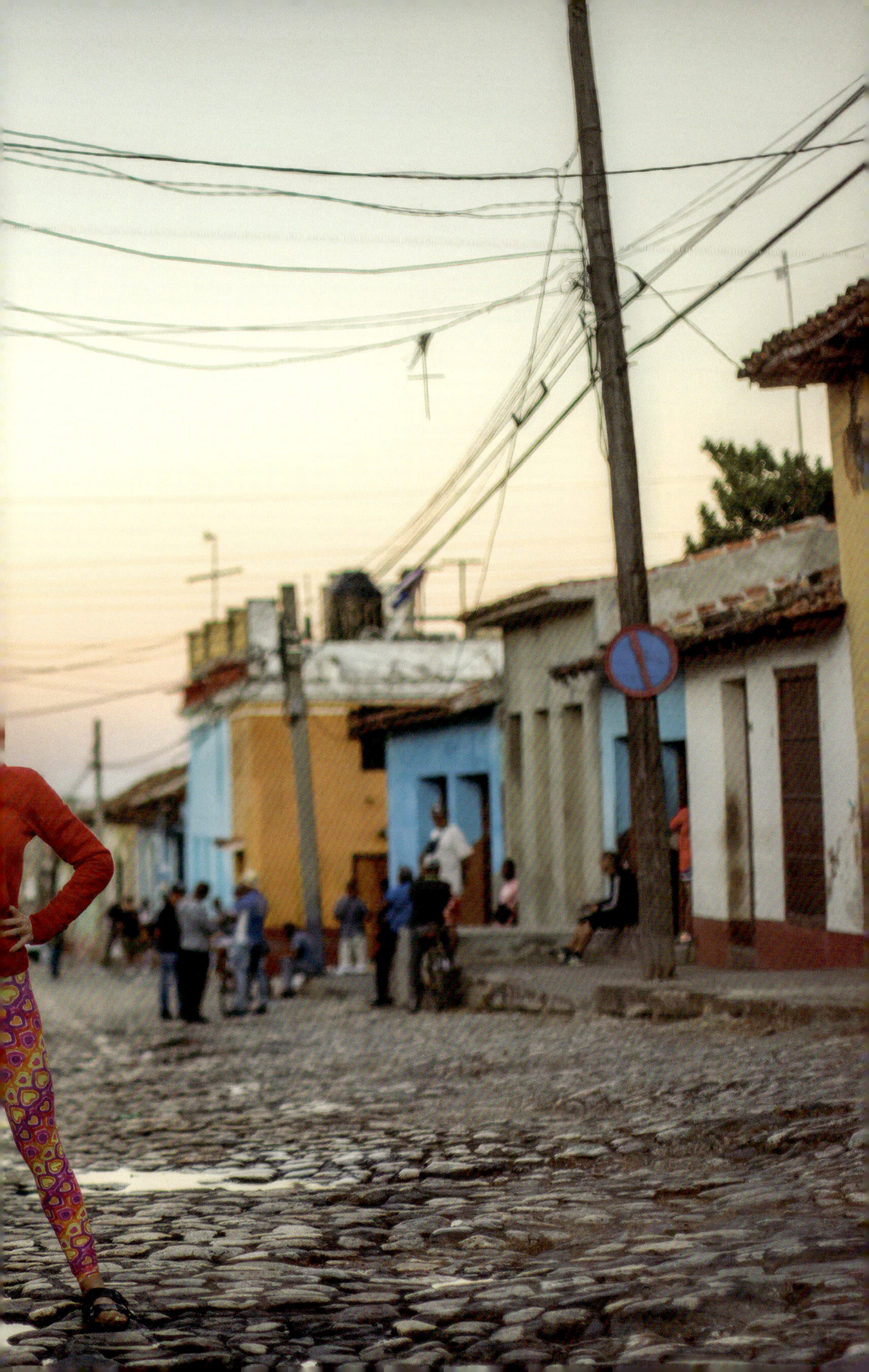

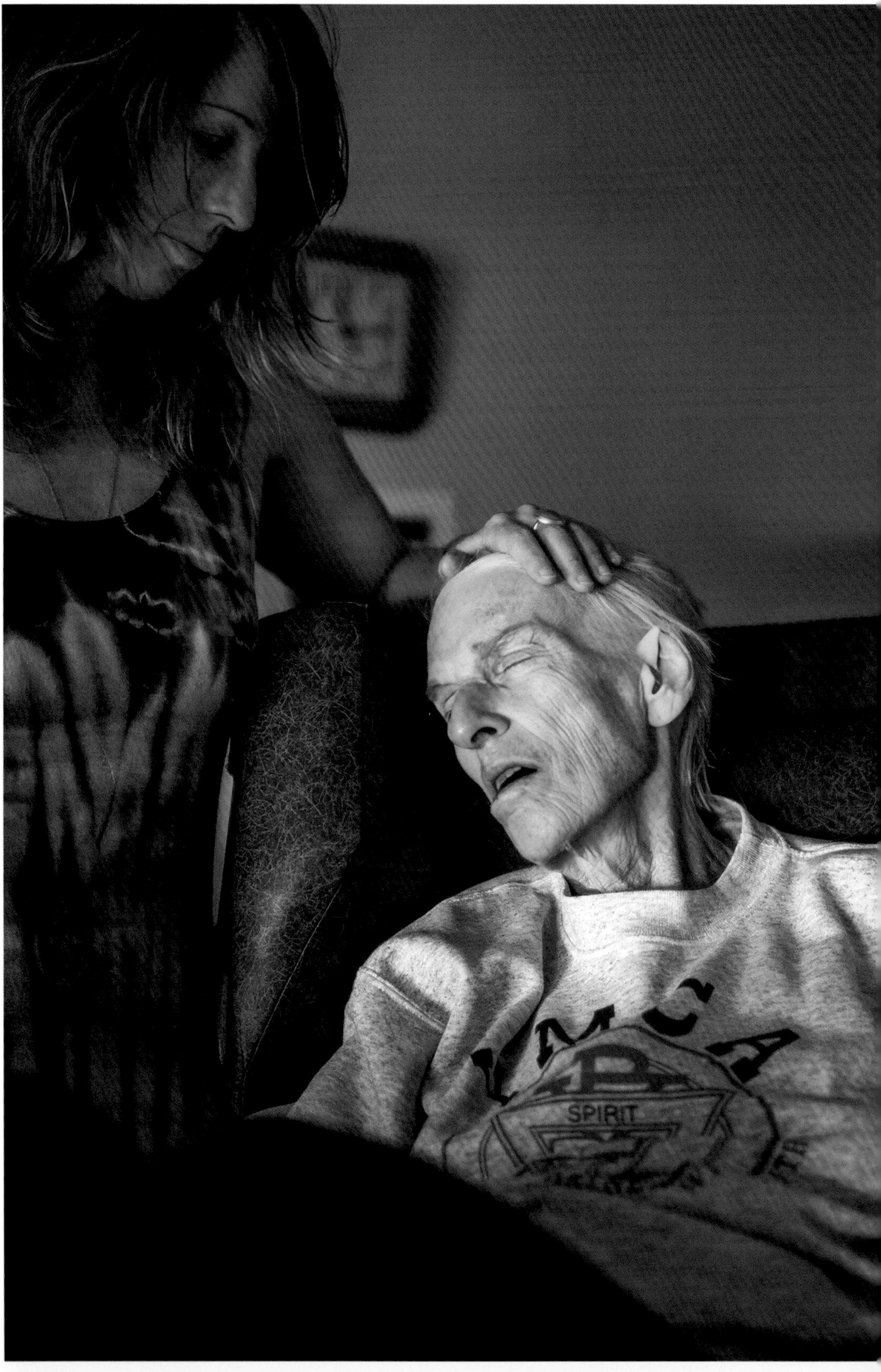
MCA
SPIRIT

Can I Get a Witness?

Over the last twenty years I've photographed hundreds of weddings and thousands of families. I've been trusted to preserve the moments that make a life, and in return my clients have made me feel like part of their family. It's such a massive honor to be someone's personal documentarian, and I'm grateful to be spending my life as a photographer. Over time, photographs fuse with our memories until we can't tell whether we recall the moment itself or the photo we've seen a hundred times. Photography, at its heart, is proof. Proof something happened. Proof we were here. Proof we loved and were loved in return.

Though I'm usually asked to photograph joy and milestones, twice I've been asked to photograph not the highlights of someone's life but the moments they knew would break their hearts.

When Flora first told me that her mom, Carol, had recently been diagnosed with Stage 4 ovarian cancer I immediately offered to photograph them together. Envisioning the shoot, I saw Flora and Carol cooking dinner together, maybe having a glass of wine, and telling stories on the front porch of a log cabin before falling asleep in peace. A month later I arrived in Green Bay, Wisconsin, to document Flora having her last days with her mom. Our time was not spent on Golden Pond like I pictured but in a rehab facility in Flora's hometown.

Carol Bowley was a smart, down-to-earth, selfless woman who spent her life running the YMCA of Green Bay and pouring her energy into other people. Even in her final days she introduced me to every nurse who came in the room, proclaiming, "This is Tara, she's a professional photographer. She won Best of Boston!" Not a single nurse cared about my awards, but the fact that she used what energy she had left to brag about me was wildly generous and completely in character.

Ovarian cancer is a brutal and haunting way to die, and I watched Flora care for her mother selflessly through the darkest days of both their lives. We cried a lot in those days, but I think we laughed even more. Carol loved that she had a project to do with her daughter—this photoshoot—and Flora loved that she had a witness. I'll never forget the love I saw from both of those women, and I'll forever be inspired by their strength. Anyone who has watched someone go through this ordeal will attest that words are terribly insufficient to describe the experience. Photographs can bear witness in ways words cannot.

My dear friends Kathy and Paul hired me as their personal trainer in 2005. When I left training in 2008 I became their family photographer. Over the years I have witnessed all three of their children's evolutions by photographing everything from senior portraits and birthdays to big celebrations like family reunions and weddings. Kathy and Paul have invited me into their lives and have treated me like family.

One April afternoon in 2023, Kathy called to tell me Paul had been diagnosed with terminal pancreatic cancer. He was given a year to live. She asked if I could photograph them one more time as a family, while Paul still looked healthy. Three weeks later I arrived at their summer home on Cape Cod to photograph a family that felt like my own. Trying to stay light in spite of their broken hearts, they built model rockets like they used to. They played lawn games like they always had. They laughed and loved their favorite person while I looked on with my camera.

All three kids, now adults, and their spouses, were so brave and so full of joy. They knew how much they—and especially Kathy—would treasure these images for the rest of their lives. Though Paul was a devoted father, a smitten husband, and a loyal friend, his best trait was his kindness, and I tried so hard to capture that in the way he looked at his family. Paul died nine months later and those photographs on Cape Cod are the last record of him in his full vitality, the last proof of the life he and Kathy built together in love.

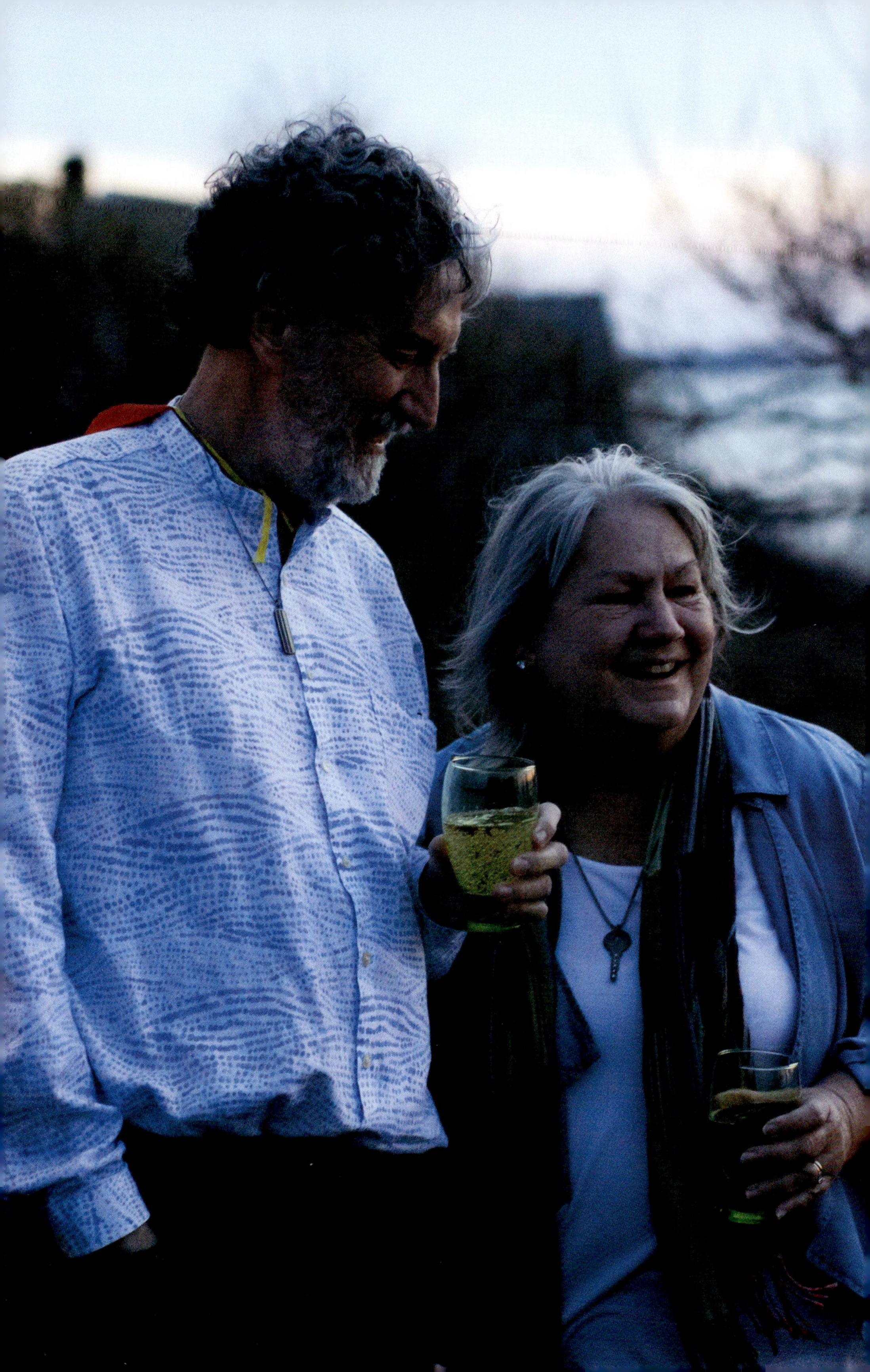

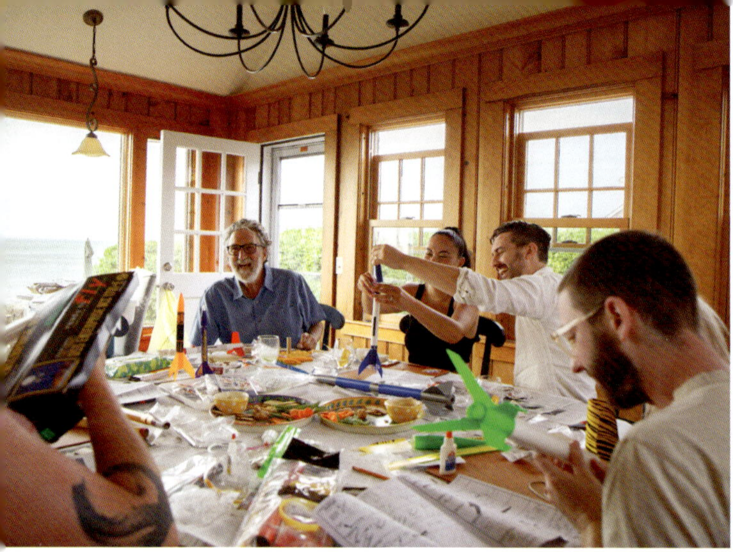
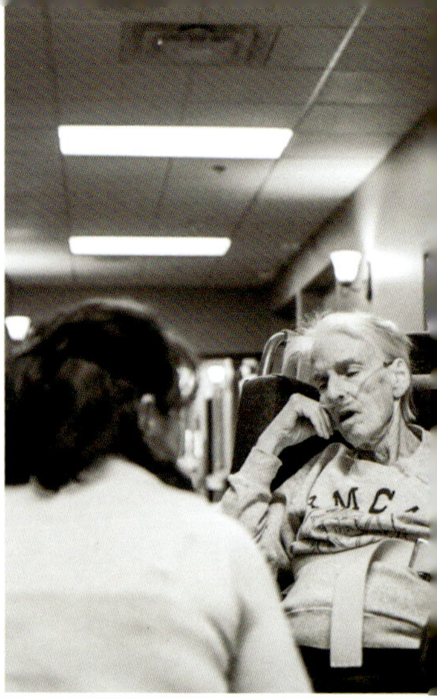
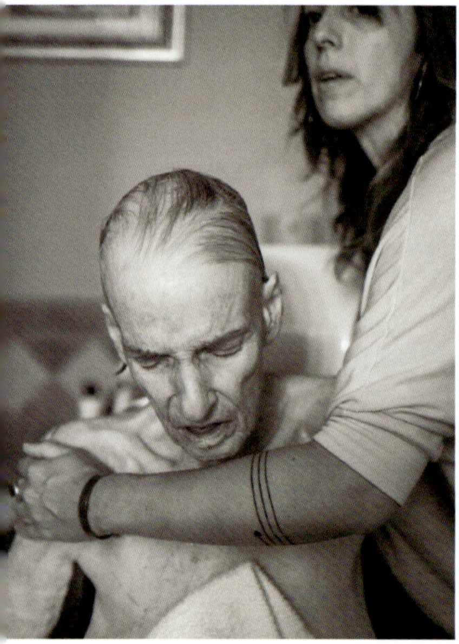
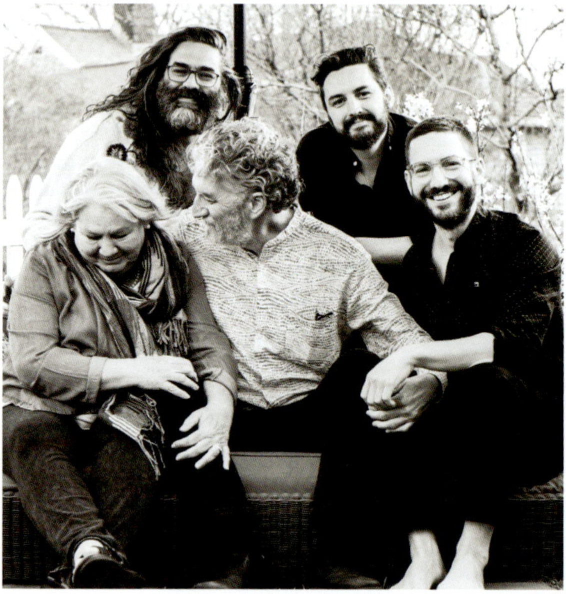
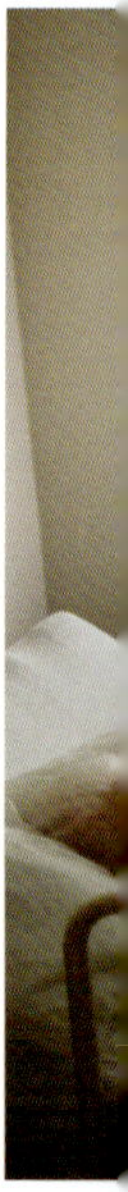
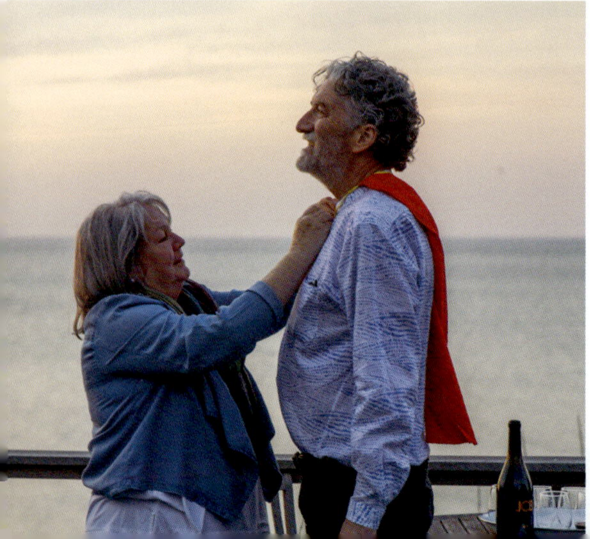
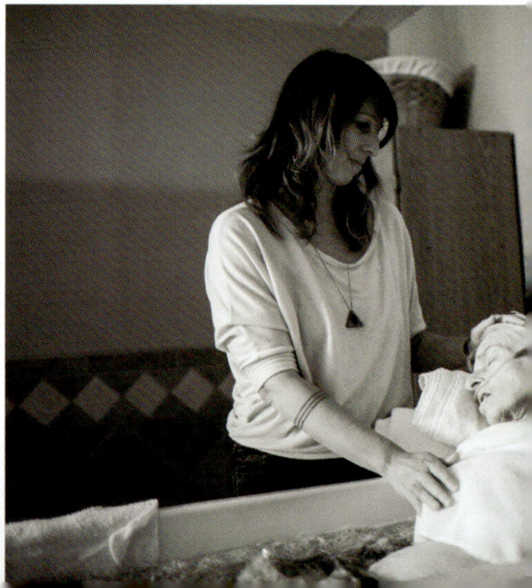

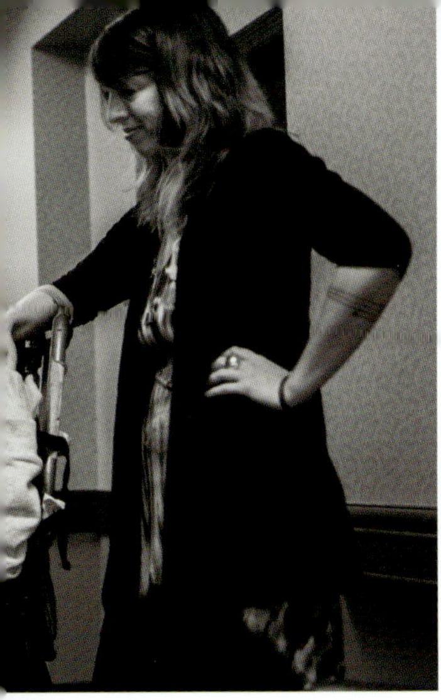
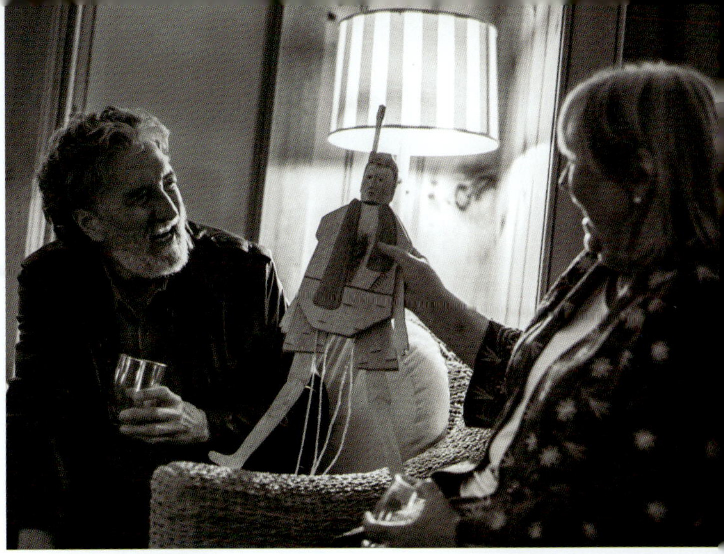
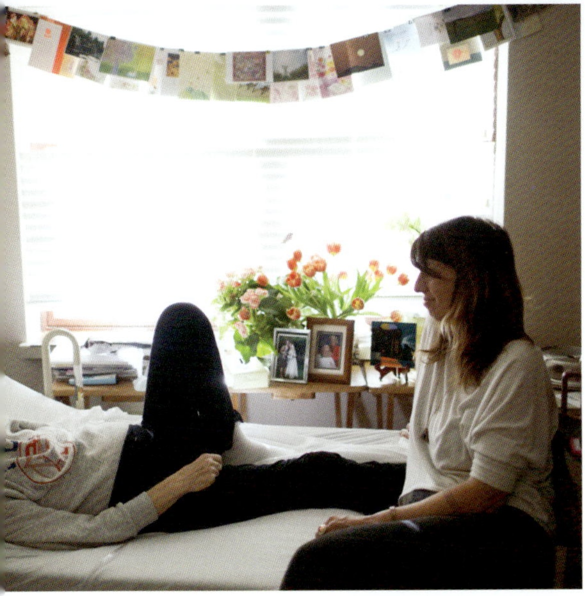
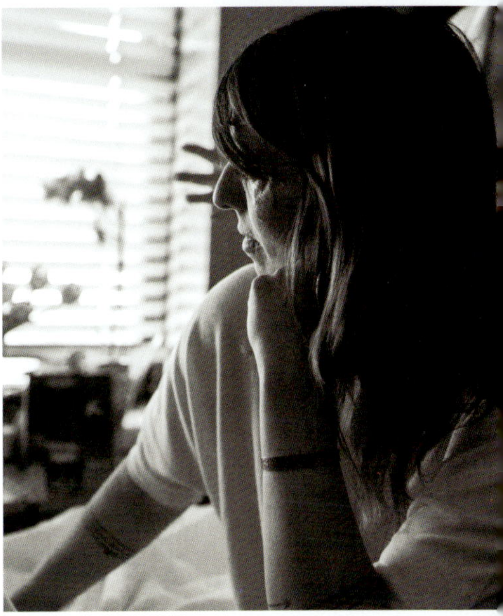
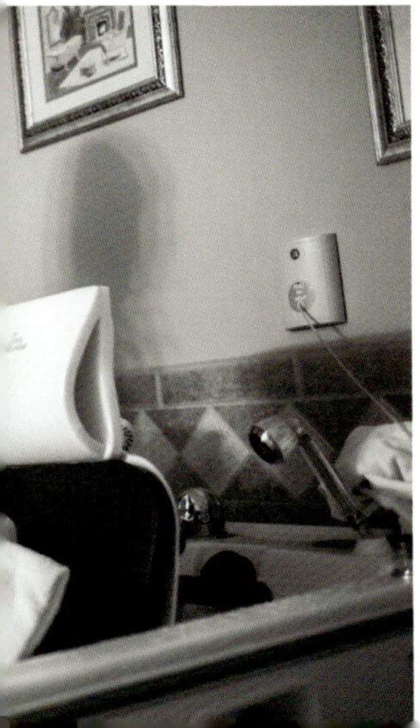
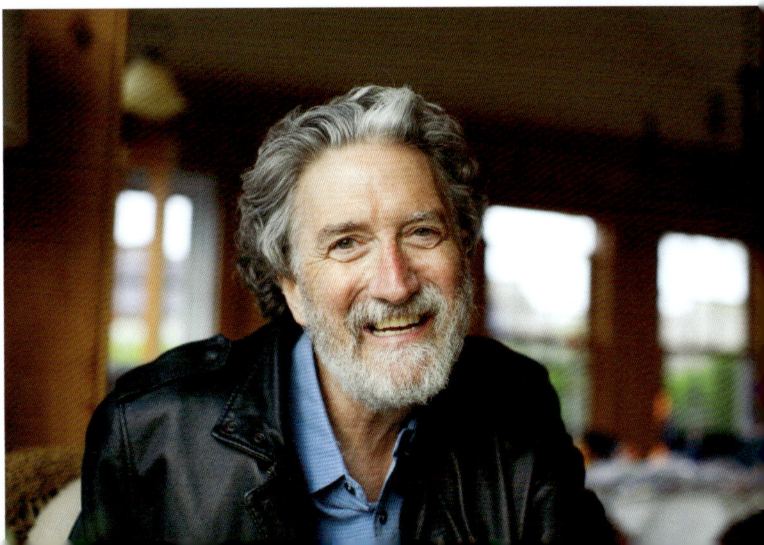

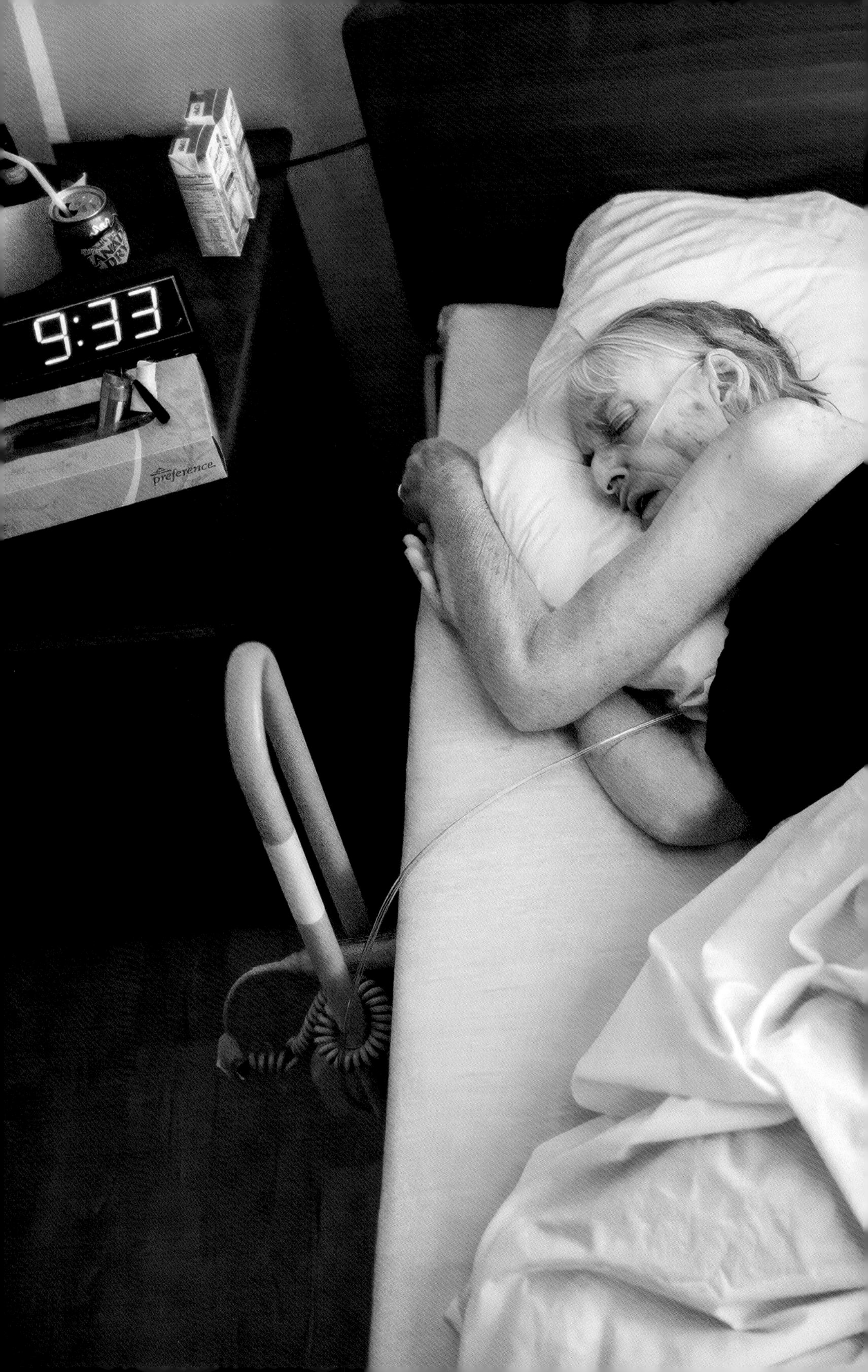
9:33
preference.

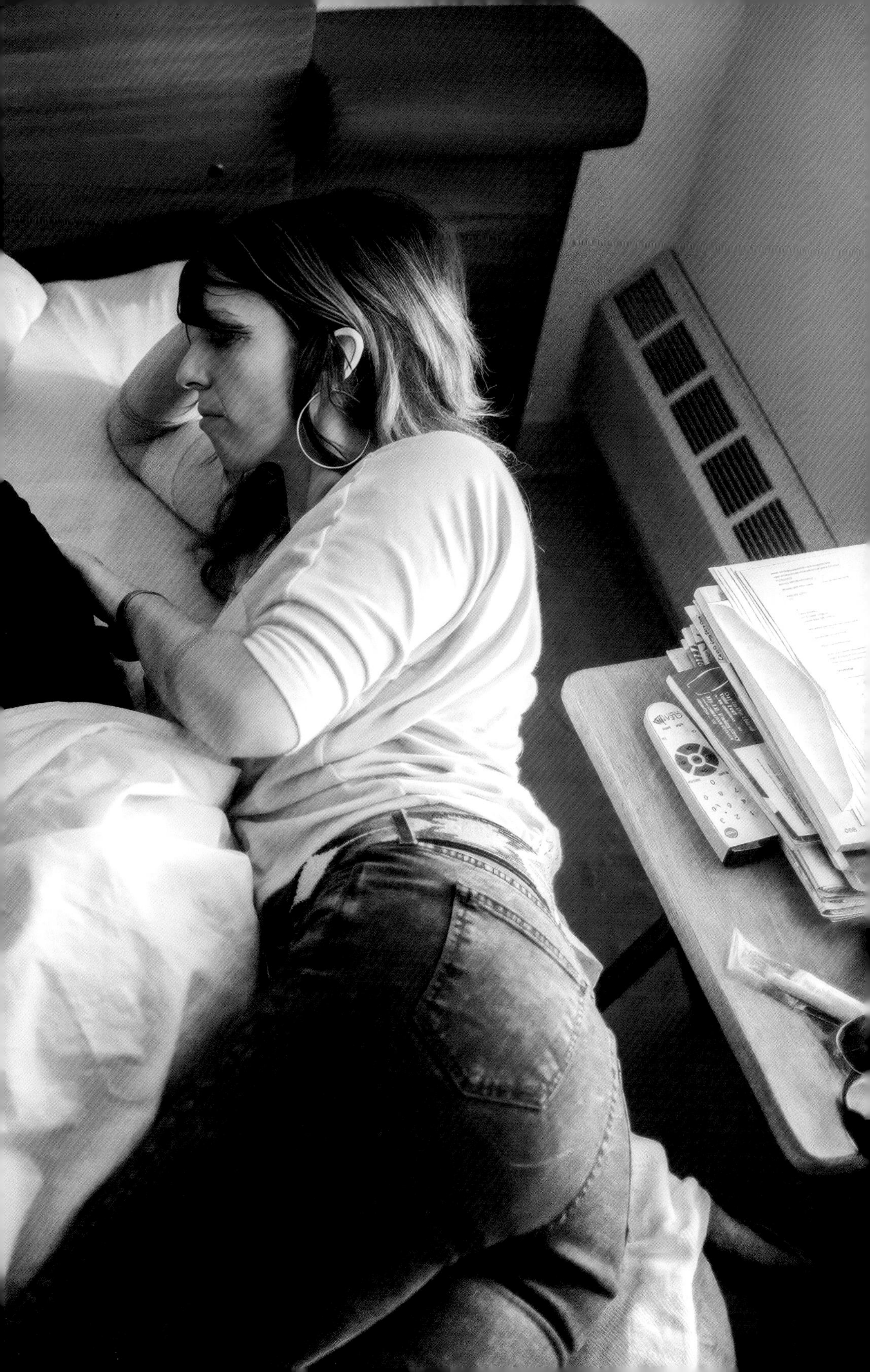

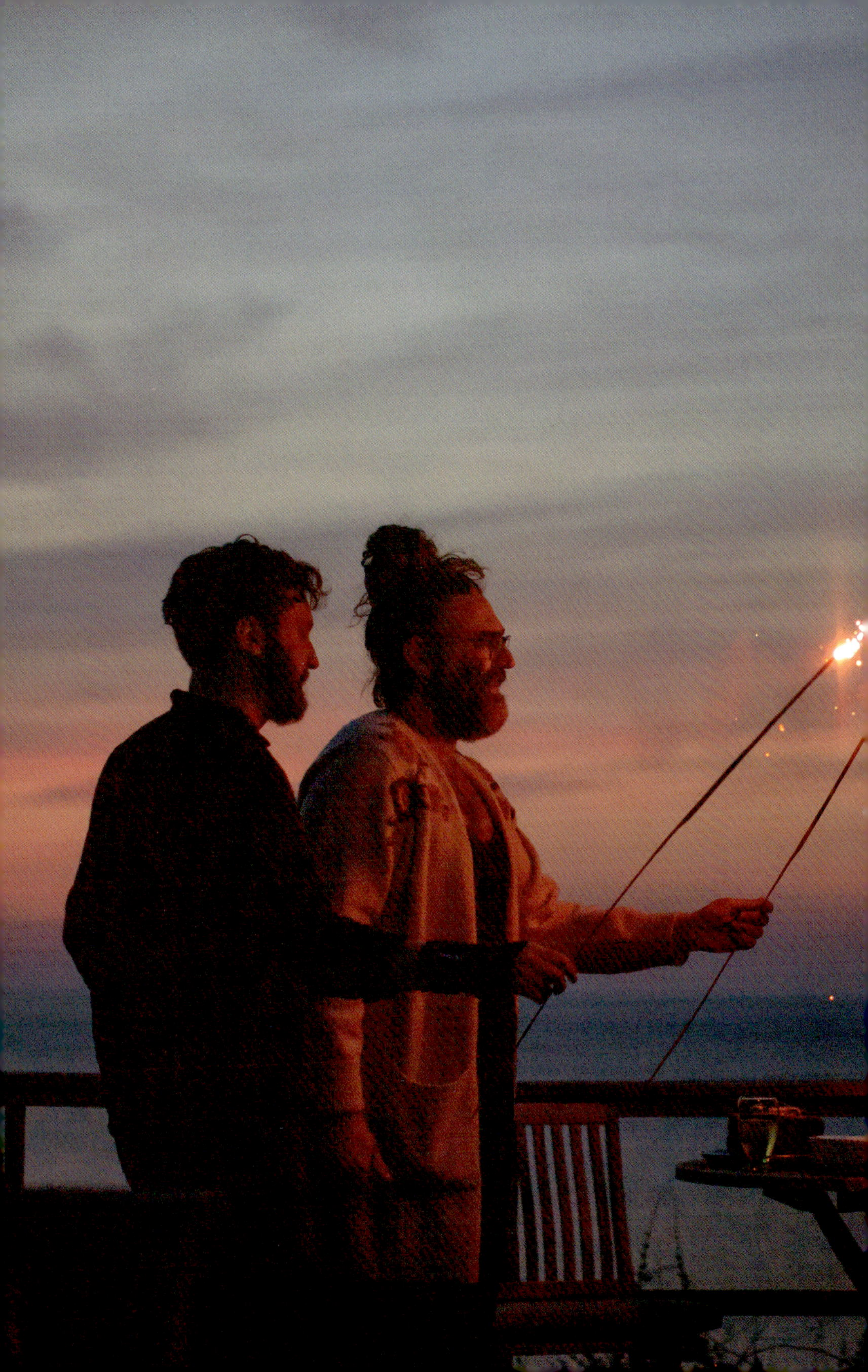

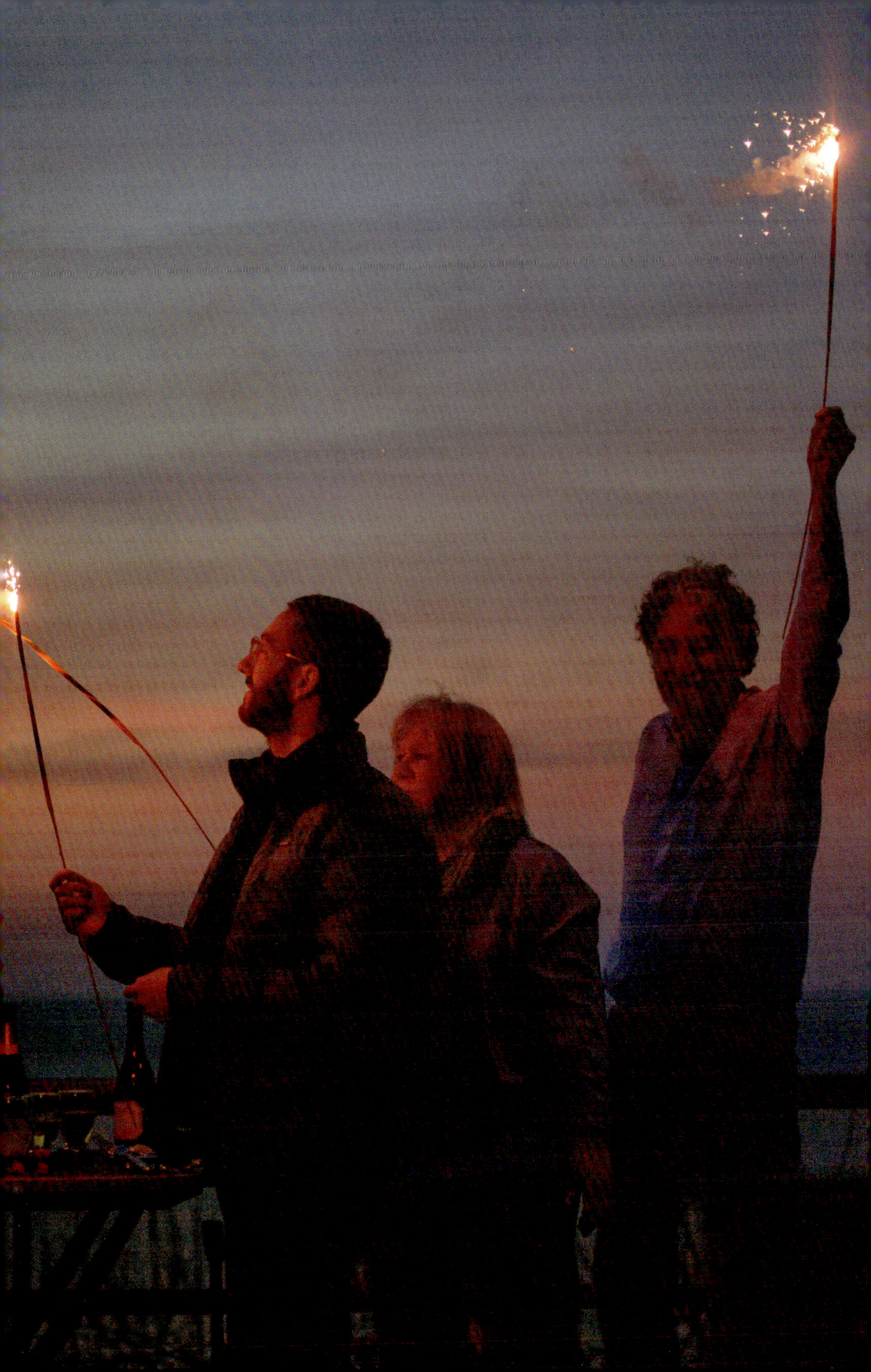

Crimetown

I moved to Providence, Rhode Island, five days before my 40th birthday in May 2015. A few months earlier I had decided to buy a house to celebrate my middle-agedness. It was time to make my debut as a woman indebted with a mortgage.

I had a false sense of my own wealth and borrowing power at first, but found out I had neither, which meant buying a home in Boston was not an option. Sifting through the real-estate bargain bin, I had some non-negotiables: no condos, no suburbs. I wanted a free-standing house. The suburbs make me nervous.

"You are so Providence!" Three different women said to me, which made me immediately suspicious but also intrigued. Providence, the capital of Rhode Island, sits about fifty miles south of Boston and was once nicknamed Crimetown for its mob ties, but has since enjoyed a rebrand as a city full of artists and great restaurants. I was curious enough to begin looking online at real estate.

I contacted an agent named Jess Powers, and the next day we met at a bakery in the city's West Side. We looked at a couple houses I had found online, but Jess wanted to show me one more place she thought might be perfect.

It was February and New England had just suffered a record amount of snowfall, so the entire neighborhood felt like the inside of a luge track. We climbed over a mountain of snow to get to the front door of a noticeably ugly two-family home on the corner of a quiet street lined with other noticeably ugly homes.

The place was even more gross inside than outside. Outdated, dark, and claustrophobic, it wasn't just soulless, it was kinda scary. I stood on the enormous dark stain in the middle of the wood floor that was probably dog pee, but also could have been blood, and told her to make an offer. I'd take it. The house was listed for $199K, but Jess told me to write a letter to the owner and offer $179K so that's what I did.

I went home that day and looked at the house online. Under the mountain of snow, the ugliest house on the planet also had a concrete parking lot that could fit at least twelve cars. I could take out the parking lot and build a fenced-in yard, I thought. I could put in sliding glass doors in that ugly kitchen and build a nice deck that could overlook the yard. What if we knocked down all the walls inside the claustrophobic shithole and made it like a tree house?

Lots of ideas, no money. I took a very wealthy friend out for lunch in Boston to ask if I could borrow a lot of money to renovate a house in Providence. Without hesitation, he said no. Another generous friend said yes, so I borrowed $80K and hired a horrendously dishonest, shitty construction company that I can't name, but they got the job done in six weeks. A stone mason named Tommy had recently left the union and was looking for work, so I called him. He turned that parking lot into a backyard oasis in six weeks. My friend Bobby and his dad, Bob, built the deck in three days.

On May 21, 2015, I moved away from the life I had built in Boston over the past twelve years into a beautiful tree house with a deck overlooking a fenced-in yard in a city I had never been to. The first night in Providence I could hear mice in the walls and the voices of people walking by the windows as if they were inside the room with me. I lay awake with my eyes open all night, wondering what the fuck I had just done.

Two days later I walked onto a fourteen-hour flight to Tokyo for a two-week trip through Japan to celebrate my 40th birthday. I remember I had an extra-long birthday that year because of the time zone change mid-flight. I pretended like that was a cool thing to notice while alone on an airplane on my 40th birthday. Japan was incredible. Tokyo and Kyoto are two of my favorite cities of all time, but I wouldn't suggest traveling abroad in the middle of a home construction project, in case you were considering it.

While contemplating the move to Providence I figured as long as there was hot power yoga and enough funny, cool dudes to date I'd be happy. Turns out there were neither and I did not like Providence at all. Afraid I would become irrelevant to the Boston photography market, I told none of my clients that I had moved, spoke nothing of it online, and immediately began commuting over an hour to yoga and dinner and jobs and haircuts and friend-dates every single day. I continued with life in Boston like I had never left.

Slowly but surely, though, this tiny little Crimetown grew on me. I started to love the never-ending list of great restaurants and bars and how easy it is to live in Providence. I found a boyfriend who lived with me for a few years, and we had fun discovering a new city within a new relationship. Three years later one of my best friends, Laura, moved to Providence, which made everything better. Then two more of my best friends, Nina and her husband, Neil, eventually moved to town. As long as I have my best friends around, I could live anywhere. Then I started to fall in love with the beaches of Rhode Island and the people and the energy of Providence. It's small, but it's cool, and I love it.

I still couldn't find any traditional hot power yoga in town so I thought if I stayed maybe I could open a studio of my own one day. It would be six more years of commuting to Boston to teach yoga, but eventually, I thought, maybe one day, I could make that happen.

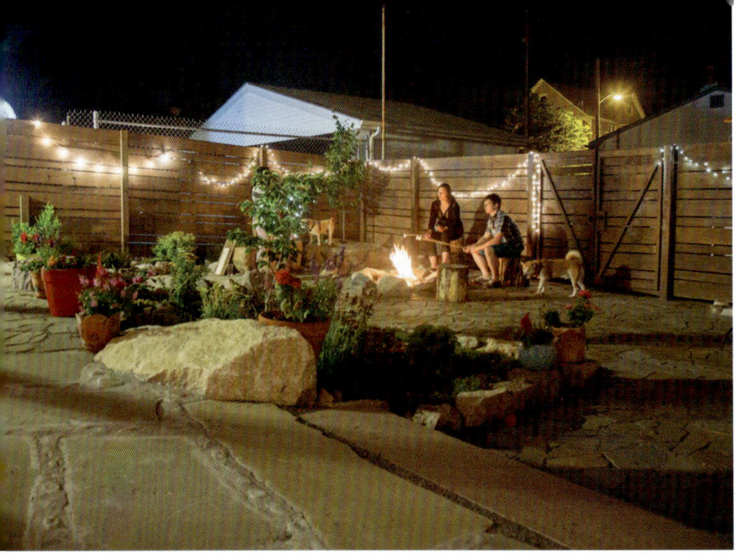

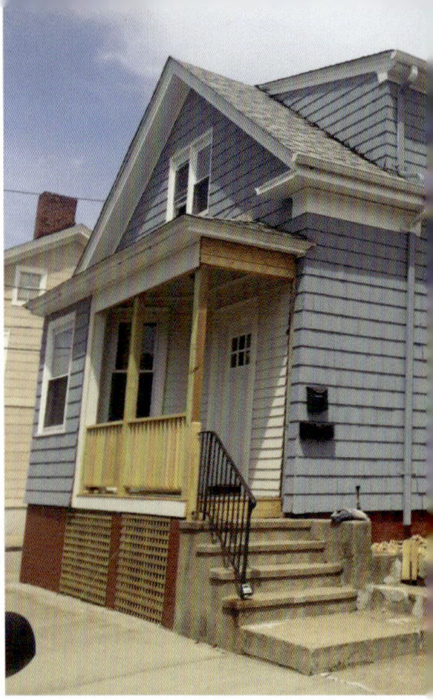

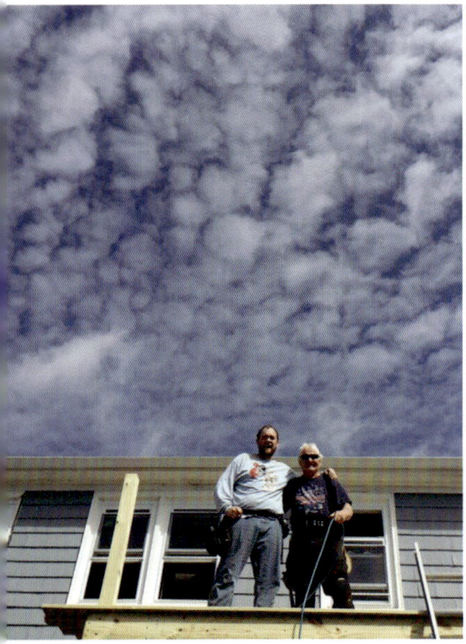

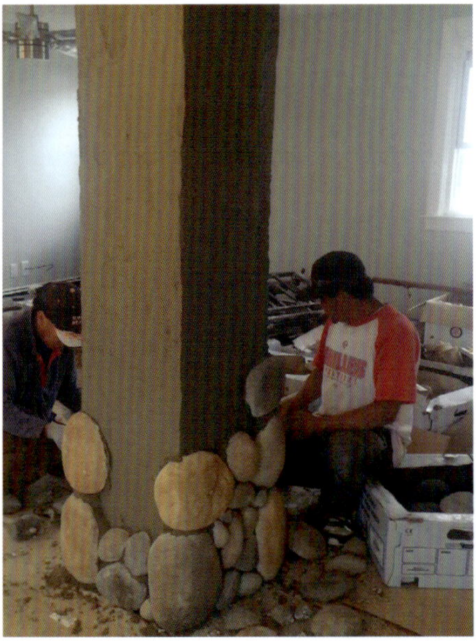

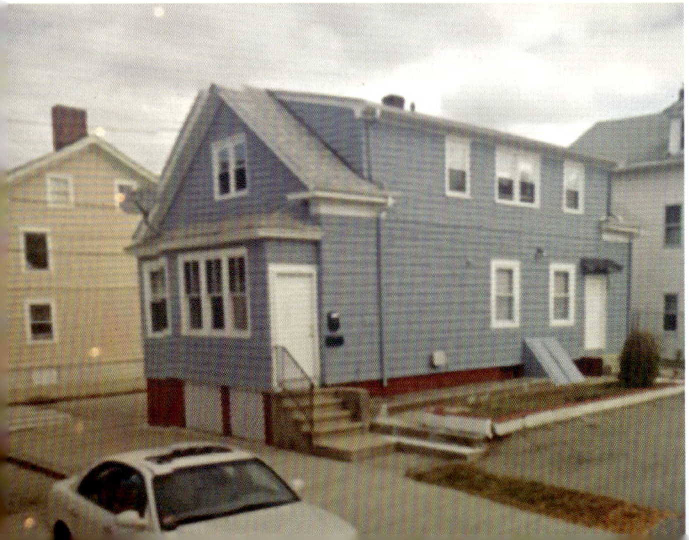

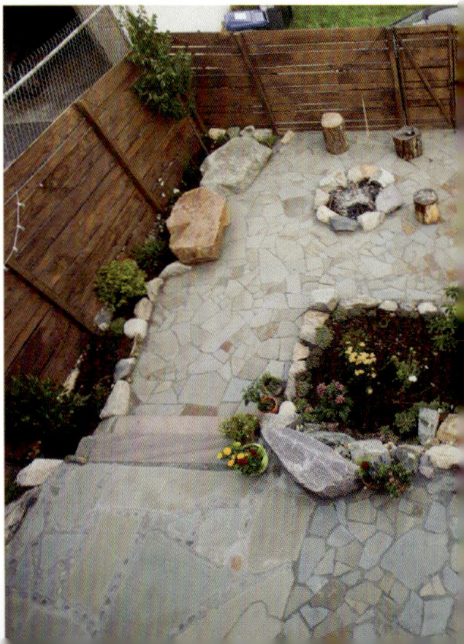

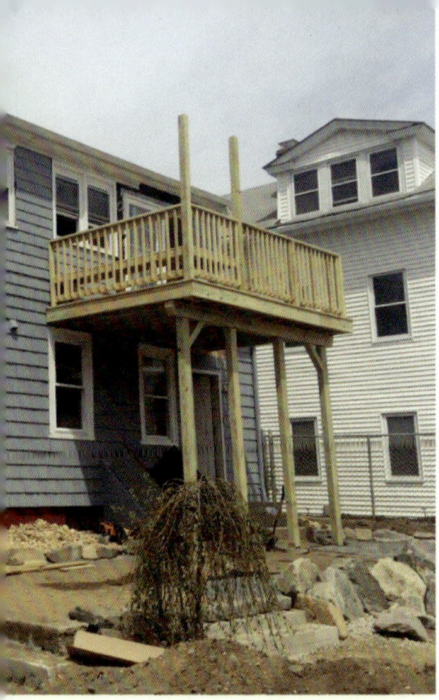
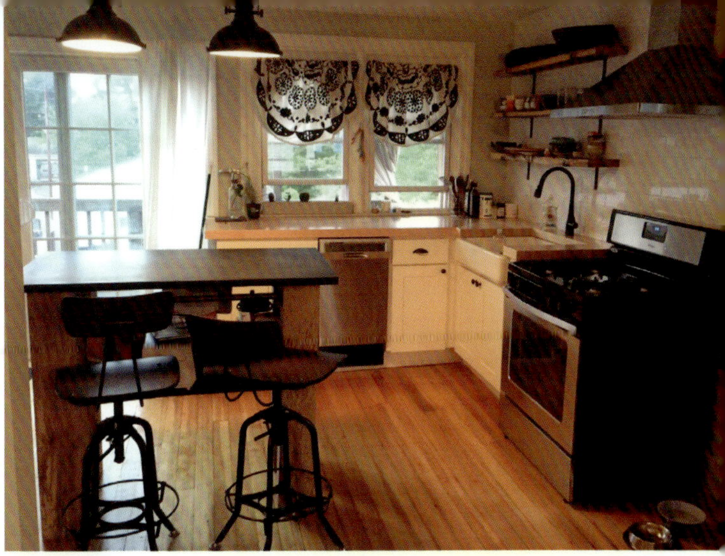
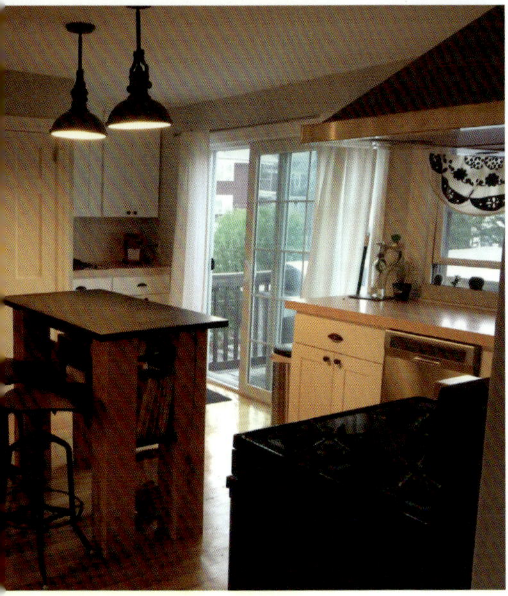
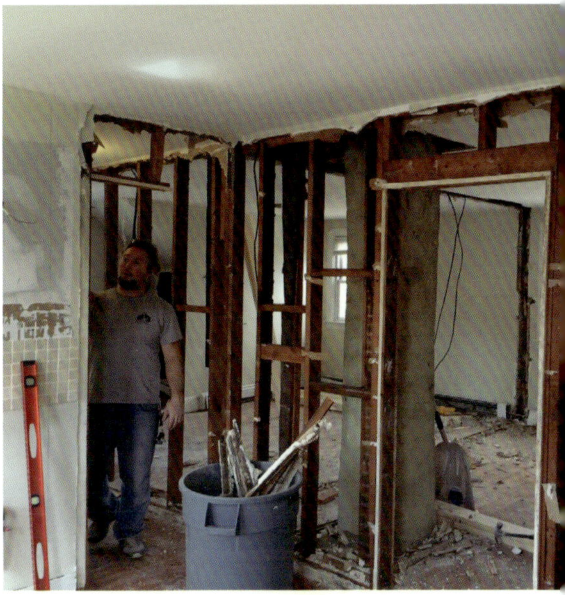
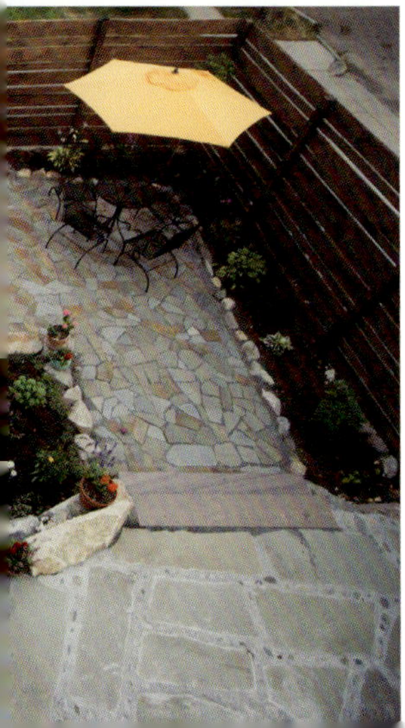
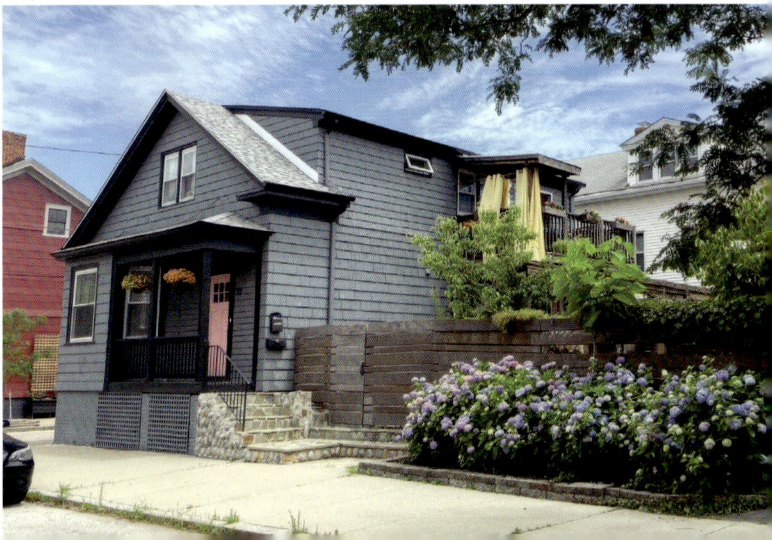

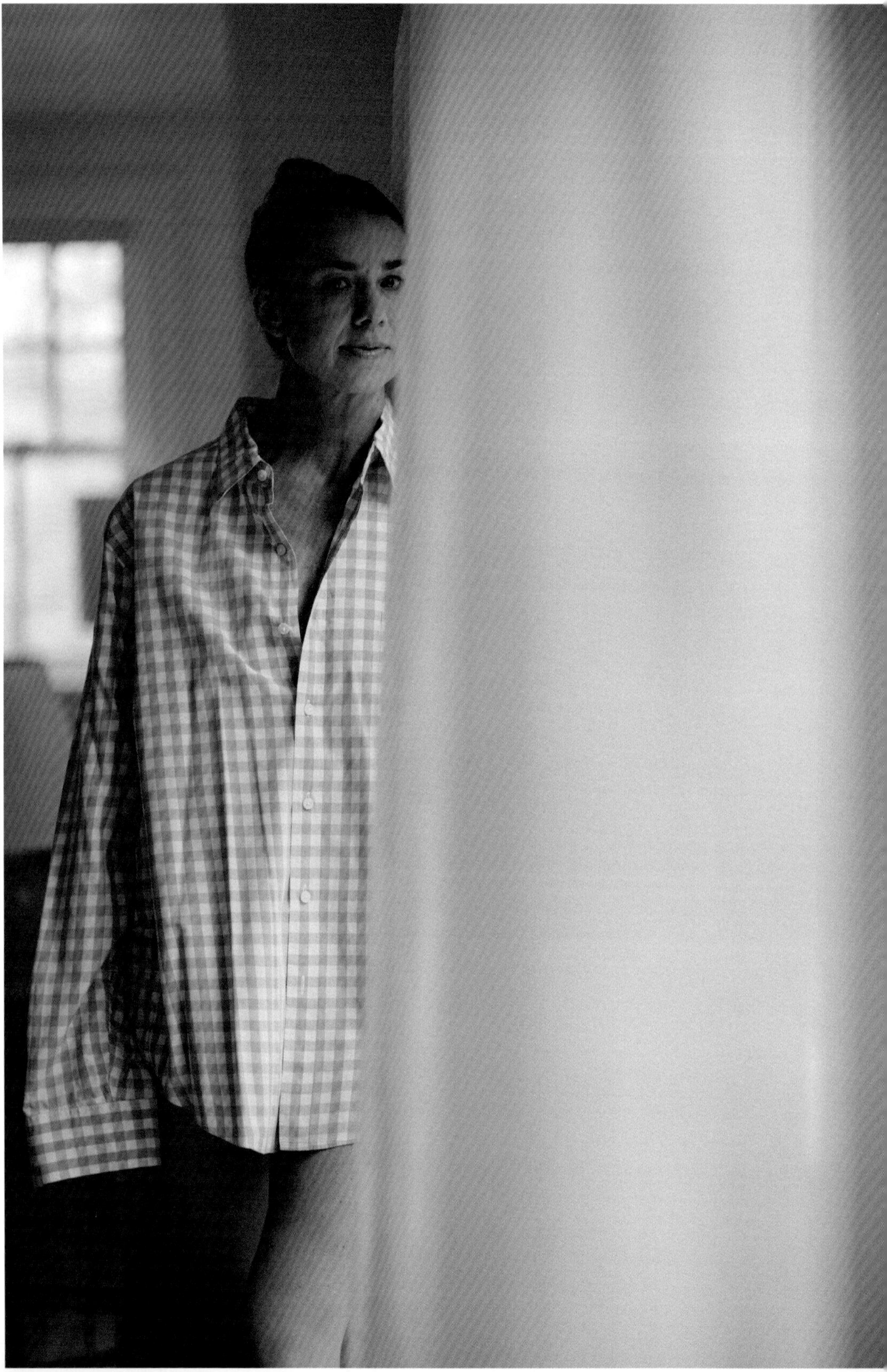

I'm Right Here with You

Katie and Tommy were the noticeably gorgeous couple who started coming to my early morning classes in 2016. Consistently five minutes late but always courteous, they tiptoed to the back of the room so they wouldn't disturb anyone.

Katie is a tall and sinewy beauty, each limb exactly one mile long, with a yoga practice that made it obvious she was a professional dancer for at least some portion of her life. Tommy was so handsome it was cliché. A collegiate football player and now a surfer/yogi/real estate developer, he was tall and strong and kind and in love with his fiancée, Katie. She was in her late 40s and had three beautiful daughters, he was in his mid-50s with three handsome sons. Both divorced and living in Wellesley, MA, they were set up by a mutual friend, and as the story goes, they took one look at each other and fell in love.

More than once—but always during tree pose—I saw Tommy step off his mat to stand behind Katie on hers. He'd put his hands on her waist, then move them up her torso until they were holding hands with their arms stretched above them. Her eyes were closed, she was leaning back on him, and her smile looked like a smile of someone madly in love. This sort of thing in the middle of a yoga class is distracting, but they were in the back of the room, and no one saw them but me. I loved it.

Katie and Tommy soon started to linger after class, and though their sheer confidence and intelligence rightfully intimidated me, they were also kind and gentle. We were becoming friends.

A year into them being my students, in March 2017, they lingered after class as usual, but this time it was obvious they had something serious to discuss. "As you know we're getting married in July," Katie began.

"Yup. So cool. In your parent's yard," I confirmed, nervous for no reason.

"Well, we've been talking, and both Tommy and I would love it if you officiated our wedding."

I wanted to tell her that I was not good enough or smart enough to do that, but I let her continue. "There's no one else. You're our High Priestess."

I accepted the honor, and they left the studio. How could I possibly be up to the task of marrying these two? I needed a stunt double.

Studio records show that Tommy attended my class more than a hundred times, and one of those times, on May 17, 2017, Katie and Tommy were characteristically five minutes late to my 5:45 a.m. class. The class was packed, and the back row was full, but there was space at the very front of the room so there they went—their affection on display for all to see.

The class ended, and everyone left except for Katie and Tommy. I mopped the studio floor while Tommy did pushups, and Katie and I discussed the changes they were making to the ceremony. Tommy finished his pushups, I teased him about it, and he walked into the lobby with his mat under his arm. Katie and I lingered in the studio to finish our conversation and walked out five minutes later. When we walked into the lobby Tommy was lying down on a bench, pale white and sweating. He said he couldn't feel his tongue.

I picked up the studio phone and called 911. Katie knelt by his side and held his hands. The 911 operator peppered me with the standard questions, and I relayed the conversation between Tommy and the operator.

How old is he?

56

Has this ever happened before?

Yes. About three years ago.

I told them he couldn't feel his tongue. I begged them to come quickly, and they arrived within minutes.

Tommy lost consciousness on the lobby floor. The paramedics used the defibrillator paddles to resuscitate him. He came back to consciousness and yelled out, "Katie!?"

Already kneeling beside him, she held both of his hands in hers, put her nose to his, looked right in his eyes, and reassured him, "I'm right here with you."

Those were the last words Tommy heard. Her name was the last word he said. He was brought to a local hospital, but it was too late. He was gone.

By the time I arrived at the hospital I could hear Tommy's sons crying from halfway down the hall. I almost fainted. The hours that made up the rest of that day are a nightmare. I called the owners of the studio, I called people who were in the class that morning, and by mid-morning most of our community had heard the news.

People were shocked. They also knew me well enough to guess how I might be feeling. Many of my students and friends made sure the first words out of their mouths to me were, "This is not your fault," and I desperately wanted to believe them.

Soon my boss called to tell me that a fellow teacher, a 21-year-old woman, had just quit after hearing the news about Tommy. I considered her a friend, so I called her. "You quit today?" I asked. "Does this have something to do with Tommy? Do you think this is my fault?"

She paused. "Tara, your class is too hard," she answered. "All people will see is that Tommy walked into your class healthy and then walked out and died." She continued, "I gotta go," and we hung up.

As I digested her words, I put my hands on my kitchen wall so I wouldn't collapse. Within minutes of that phone call dozens of students were texting, "We love you" and "Tommy loves you" and "It's not your fault." Soon, a student called to let me know what was playing out on social media while family members of a great man were getting the worst news of their lives.

A former teacher at the studio, who had recently opened her own yoga studio, posted on Facebook as soon as she heard about Tommy's death. Many of my students screenshot her post because they were so blown away by her cruelty and wanted to make sure I saw it. The post went something like this: *Any studio owner who lets their teacher teach a break-neck fast yoga flow in 106 degrees is negligent. You can rest assured at (her new studio's name) your safety is our first priority.*

That was this woman's gut reaction. She heard that a good man died, and she posted—*on Facebook*—insinuating that it was our fault while plugging her own studio. The wretched and unforgivable cruelty of that woman will take care of itself in time, but oh, my god, did that take me down.

Because *of course* I blamed myself. Wouldn't you? Or is it just too scary to hold something so enormously heavy? Of course I blamed myself. Of course I wished it was me. Of course I did. But normal people reached out to me. Because normal people have empathy. Students who were also cardiologists called me, took my class, and wrote me letters explaining how heart attacks happen. This is life. Accidents happen. Tragedies happen. Nature is a brutal, unfair, unrelenting force, and we are all subject to it.

A few days later, at Tommy's wake, Katie told a fellow teacher, Jordan, that she had practiced yoga that morning.

With kindness and compassion, Jordan reassured her, "'This is what we practice for."

****

Huge love to Katie Swenson, who is a downright soulmate of mine. I love you. In her grief Katie wrote a book, In Bohemia, and I highly recommend it.

And huge love to Debra Goodman, Dennis Ozer, and all my students at HYP who carried me through those days.

And forever love to Tommy Niles and his family.

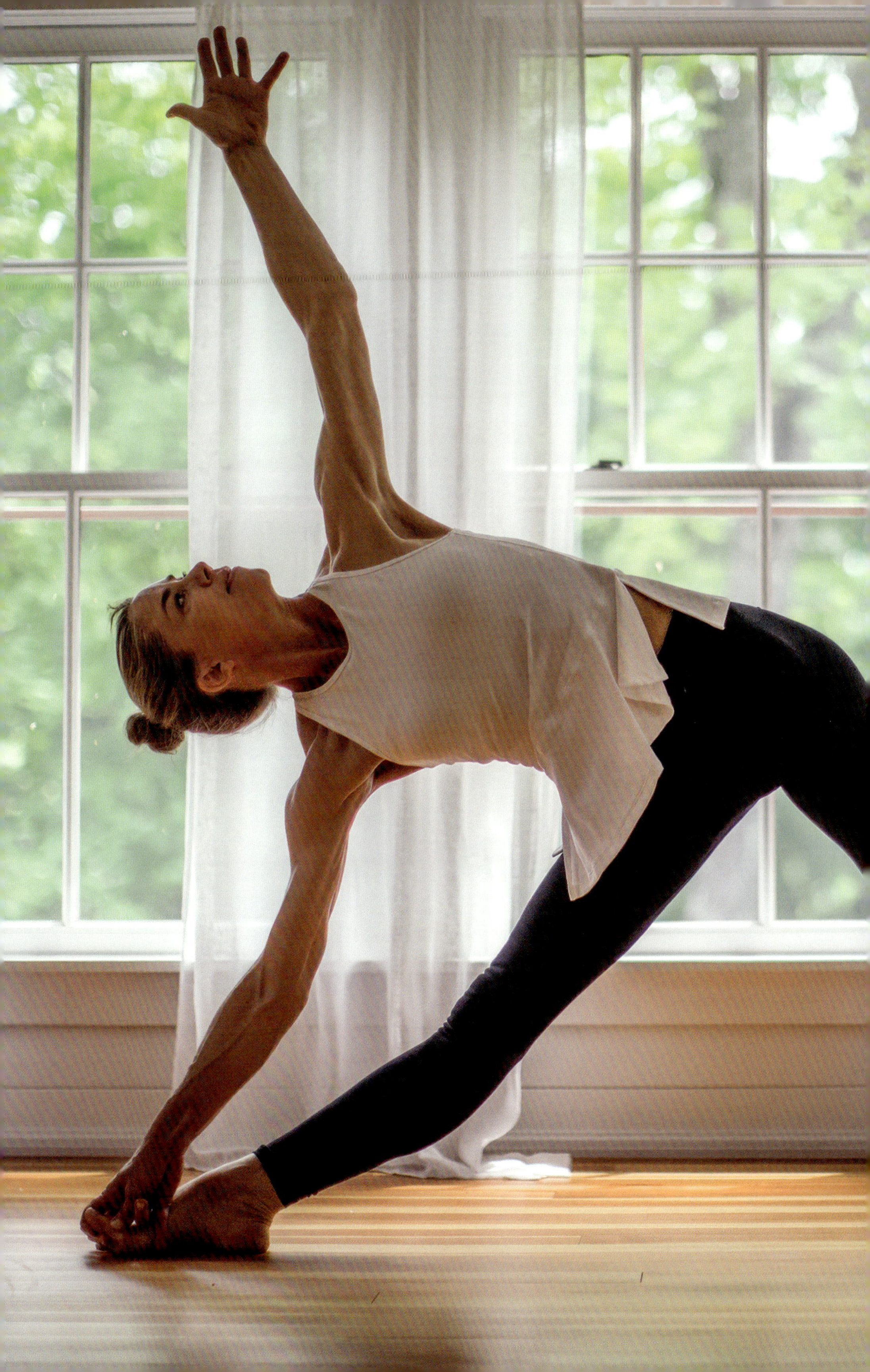

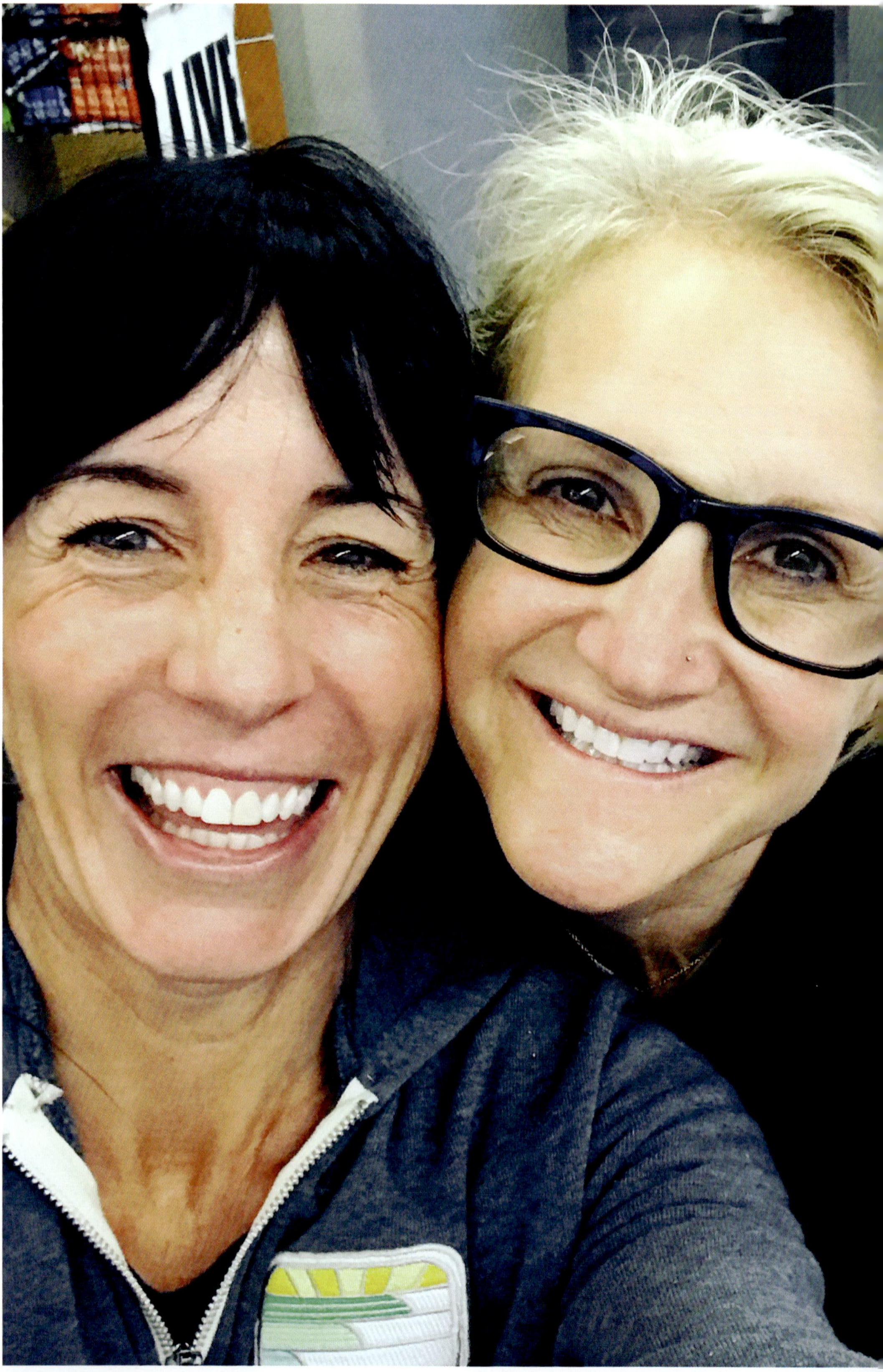

Mel Robbins

When someone follows me on Instagram they almost immediately notice that Mel Robbins, the world-famous podcaster, bestselling author, and motivational speaker, also follows me on Instagram. Everyone wants to know how and why. Here's the story of how Mel and I met and became friends.

It was early spring of 2017 and a beautiful and ultra-confident woman started taking my 5:45 a.m. yoga classes in Wellesley, MA. She got my attention the moment she walked into the studio because she's an actual superstar and impossible not to notice. She was warm, friendly, and inquisitive, and I liked her immediately. She told me that she and her family lived in a neighboring town and when she wasn't traveling for work, she practiced yoga as much as she could.

I mostly teach with my eyes closed, but one morning I noticed her standing up straight in the back row, smiling at me while everyone else was folded forward. I smiled back. After class she poked her head in the back office, thanked me for class, we chatted a bit, and then she asked, "Hey, you don't know who I am, do you?"

Mel has a quality famous people have, and I knew I should have known her, but I didn't. A few weeks earlier I had overheard her talking to another student about Donald Trump and something about CNN, so I guessed, "Are you a CNN correspondent?"

She laughed her famous laugh and answered in an elevator pitch every human should have on hand for themselves, "I'm the number one most booked female motivational speaker in the world," she answered. "I just wrote a bestselling book called *The Five Second Rule*."

Immediately impressed, I asked her an endless number of fan-girl questions, but mostly Mel made sure I knew how much she valued my class. "I use some of the things you say in class when I'm on stage, and I want to help you. What do you need? How can I help you?" she asked.

Sensing a true no-bullshit honesty from her, I answered in kind, "I need you to hire me to photograph you. Behind the scenes, day-in-the-life style."

"Easy," she said, and we exchanged phone numbers. I remember thinking, damn, that chick is cool as fuck.

Weeks later, I spent a full day photographing Mel's team in her busy home office. There must have been eight staff members scattered throughout every room—posting, engaging, filming, planning—a small but mighty army running at full speed. Then her kids came home from school—also gorgeous superstars, just younger ones—and her saintly husband, Chris, jumped into the mix. The whole place felt like a pep rally.

A year later, I photographed her and her team at their new Boston office, hard at work creating new ways to help their growing audience. In the meantime she continued to take my class as regularly as she could, and we became friends. Every time she would take a yoga class from me, she would immediately post on social media gushing about it. Within minutes I'd have hundreds of new followers.

In July 2019 Mel hired me to photograph her on a cross-country trip as she gave her trademark motivational speeches. We started out in Nashville, where she brought the house down, then walked right onto a flight to Las Vegas. I followed this woman around Vegas as she promoted her upcoming TV show—hosting parties, leading meetings of TV execs, and being a guest on someone else's talk show. Fueled on pure adrenaline, she then sat for hair and makeup before walking out on stage at the MGM Grand Theater to 17,000 adoring fans. Watching Mel and the crowd from behind my camera, I could tell that every single person in that arena walked out of that place knowing they were unstoppable. Mel Robbins's stage performance is phenomenal, and as an entrepreneur she is a machine. I have never seen anyone work so hard in my life.

Our last shoot together was in late February 2020 in Manhattan when she asked me to photograph behind the scenes at the *Mel Robbins Show*. There she was: walking out on set waving to her live audience as they stood in ovation. The show wasn't picked up for a second season, which allowed her to reinvent herself yet again. In September 2022 we spent a weekend together at a mutual friend's house on Martha's Vineyard. As we were leaving, I asked her, "So, what's next for you, Mel?"

She looked up from the suitcase she was packing, and with her trademark confidence, said, "I'm gonna start a podcast. We're gonna be number one." The rest is podcast history.

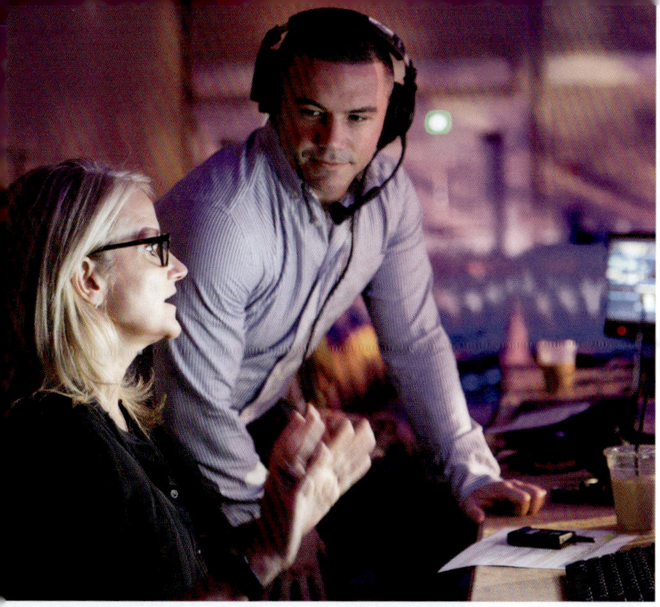

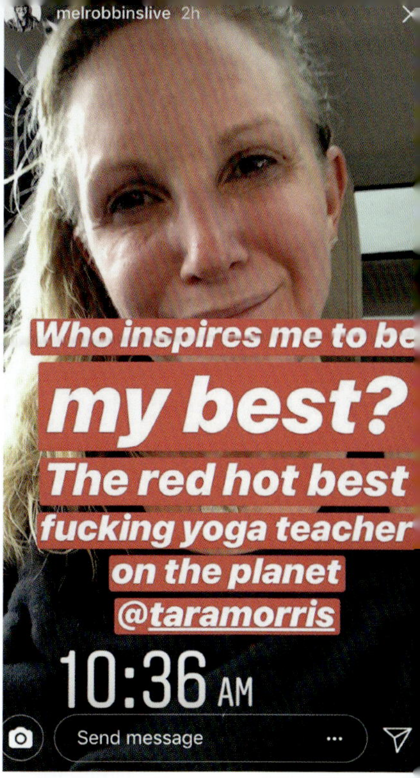

melrobbinslive 2h
Who inspires me to be
my best?
The red hot best
fucking yoga teacher
on the planet
@taramorris
10:36 AM
Send message

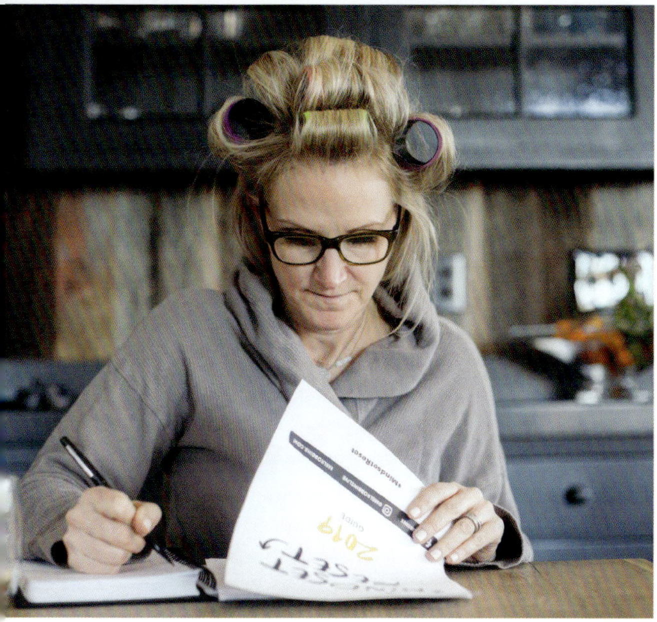

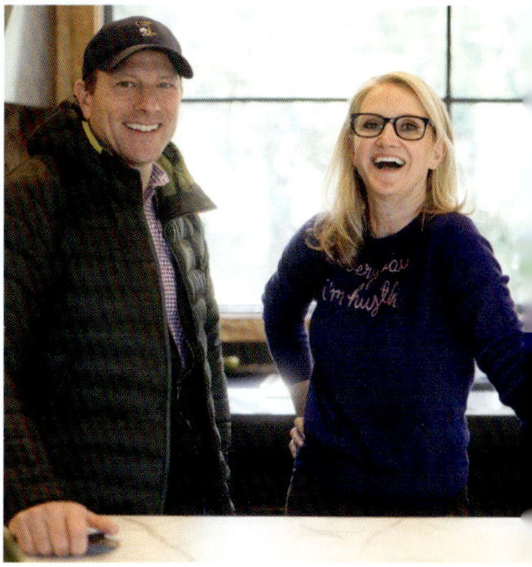

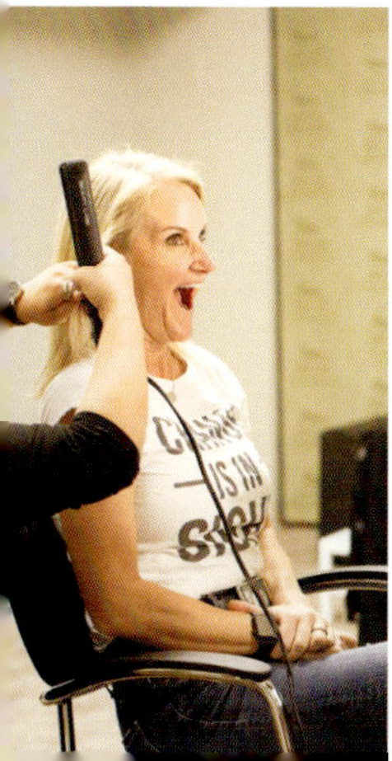

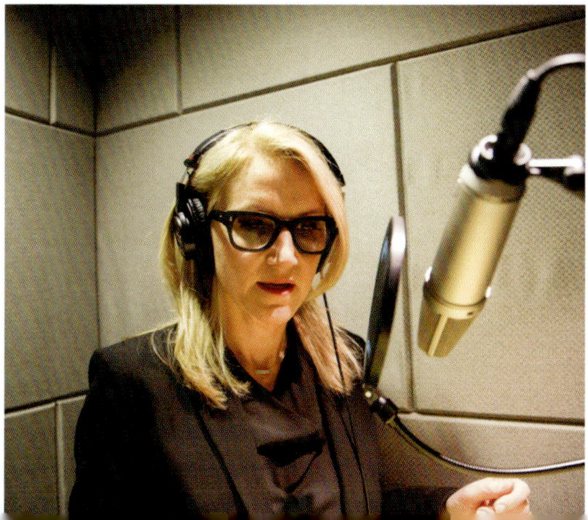

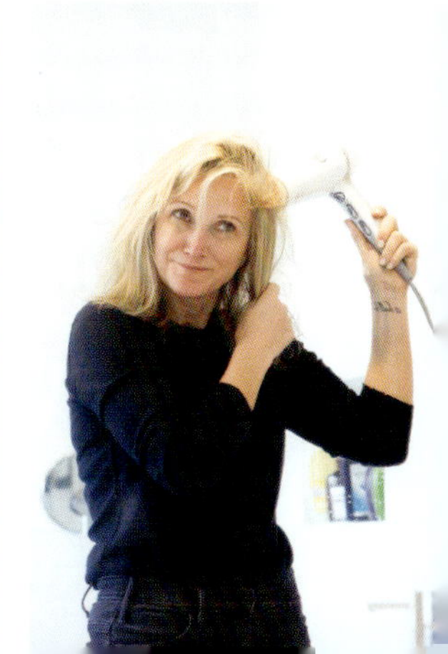

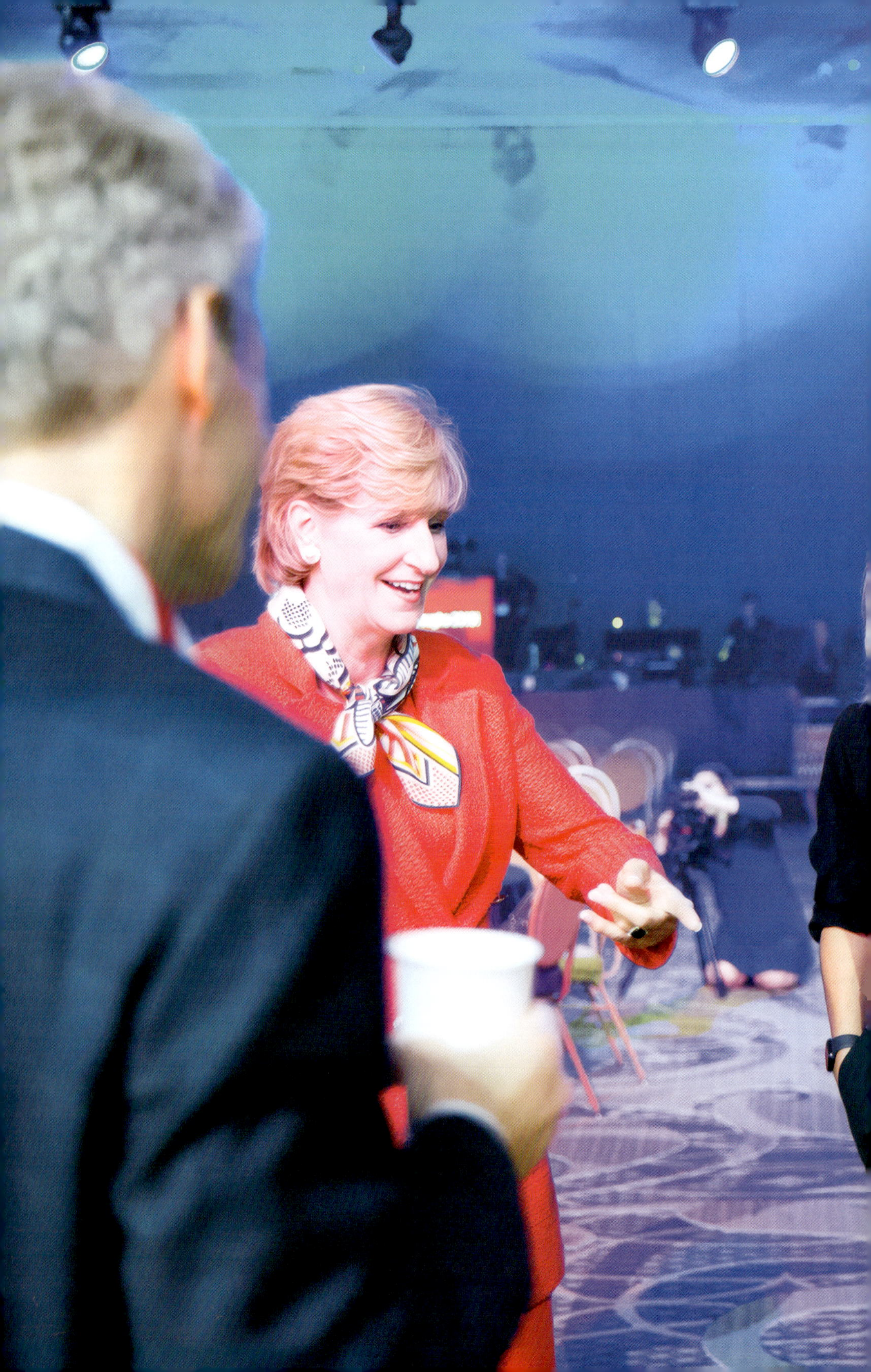

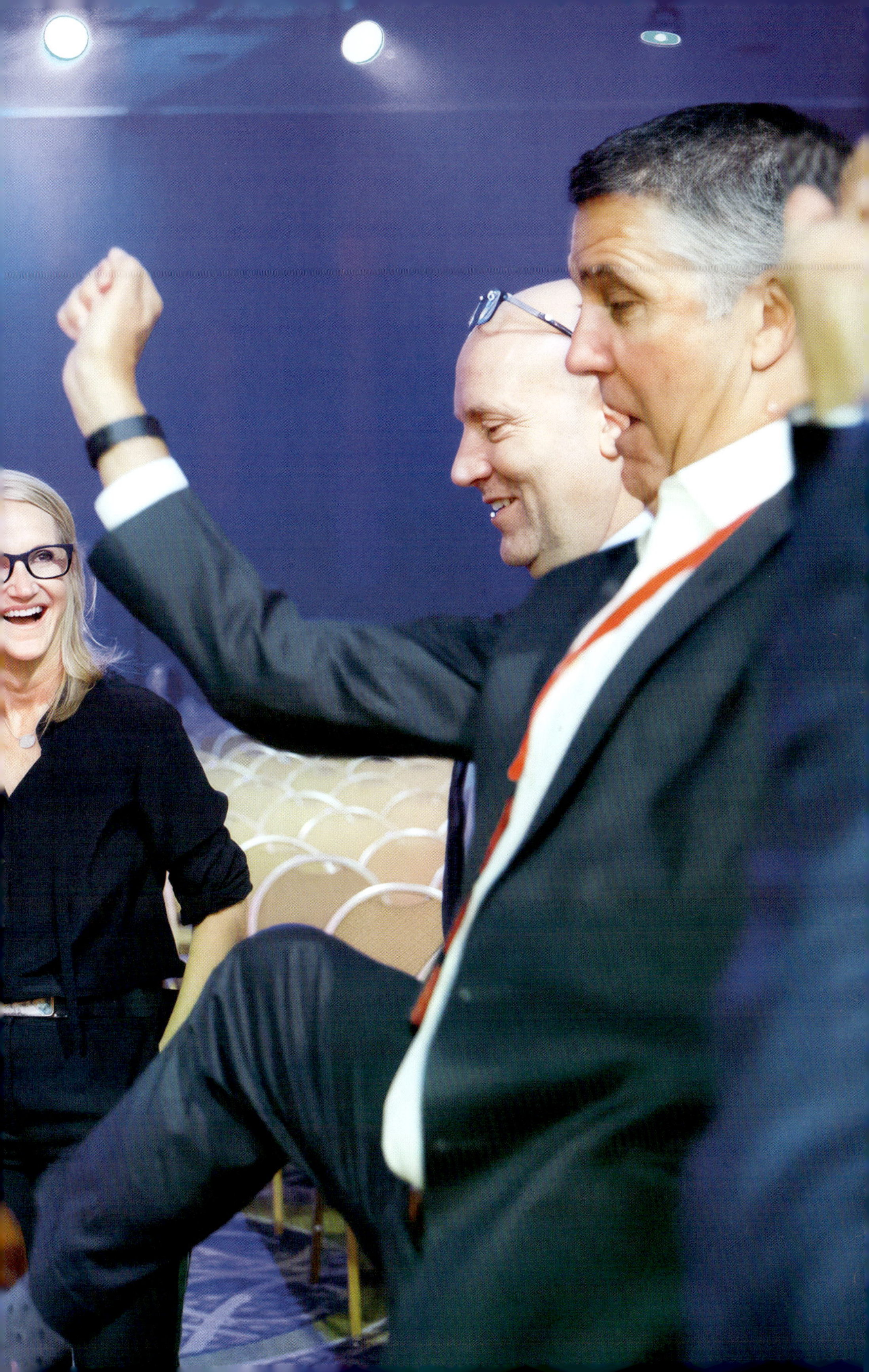

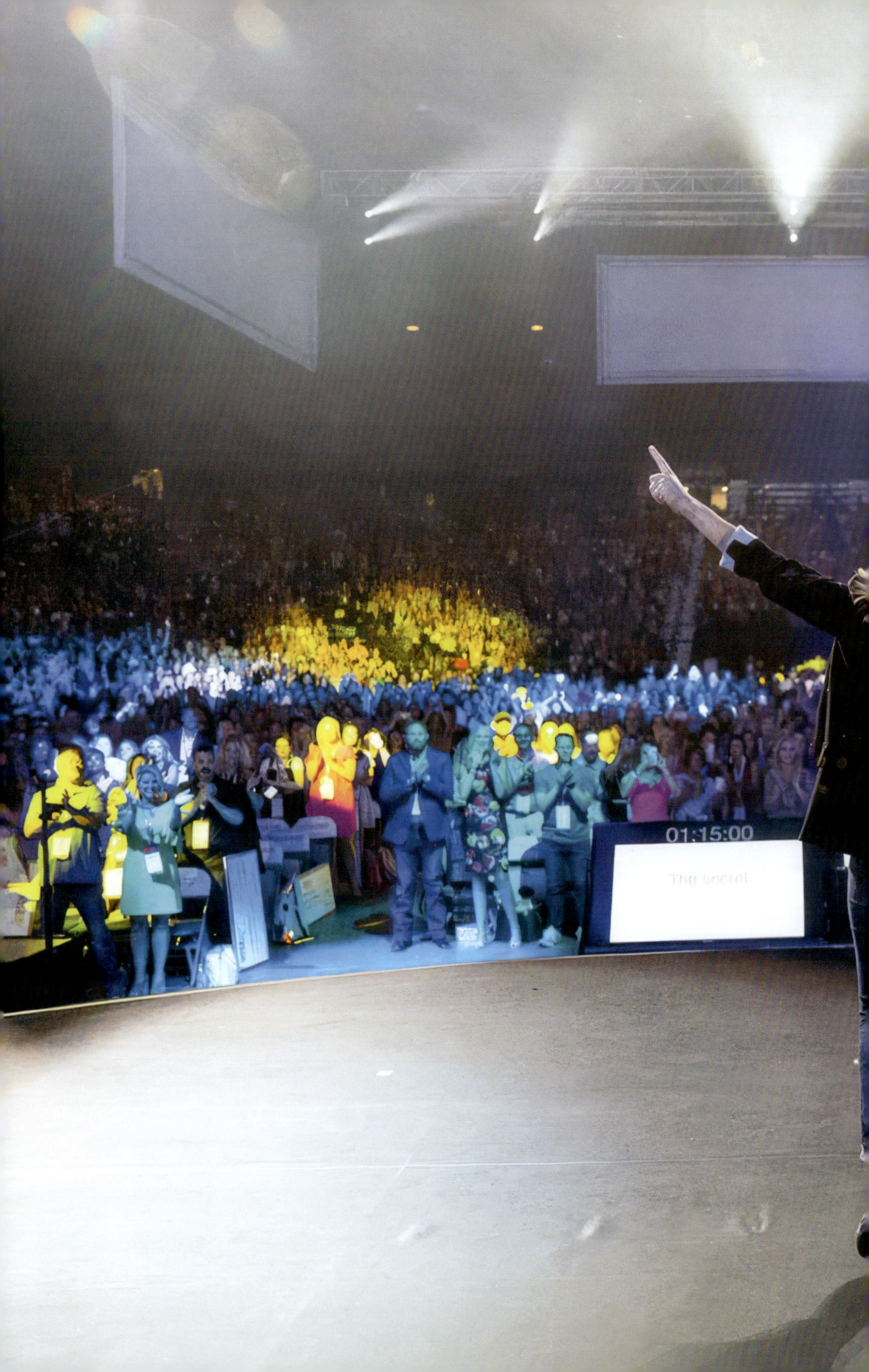
01:15:00

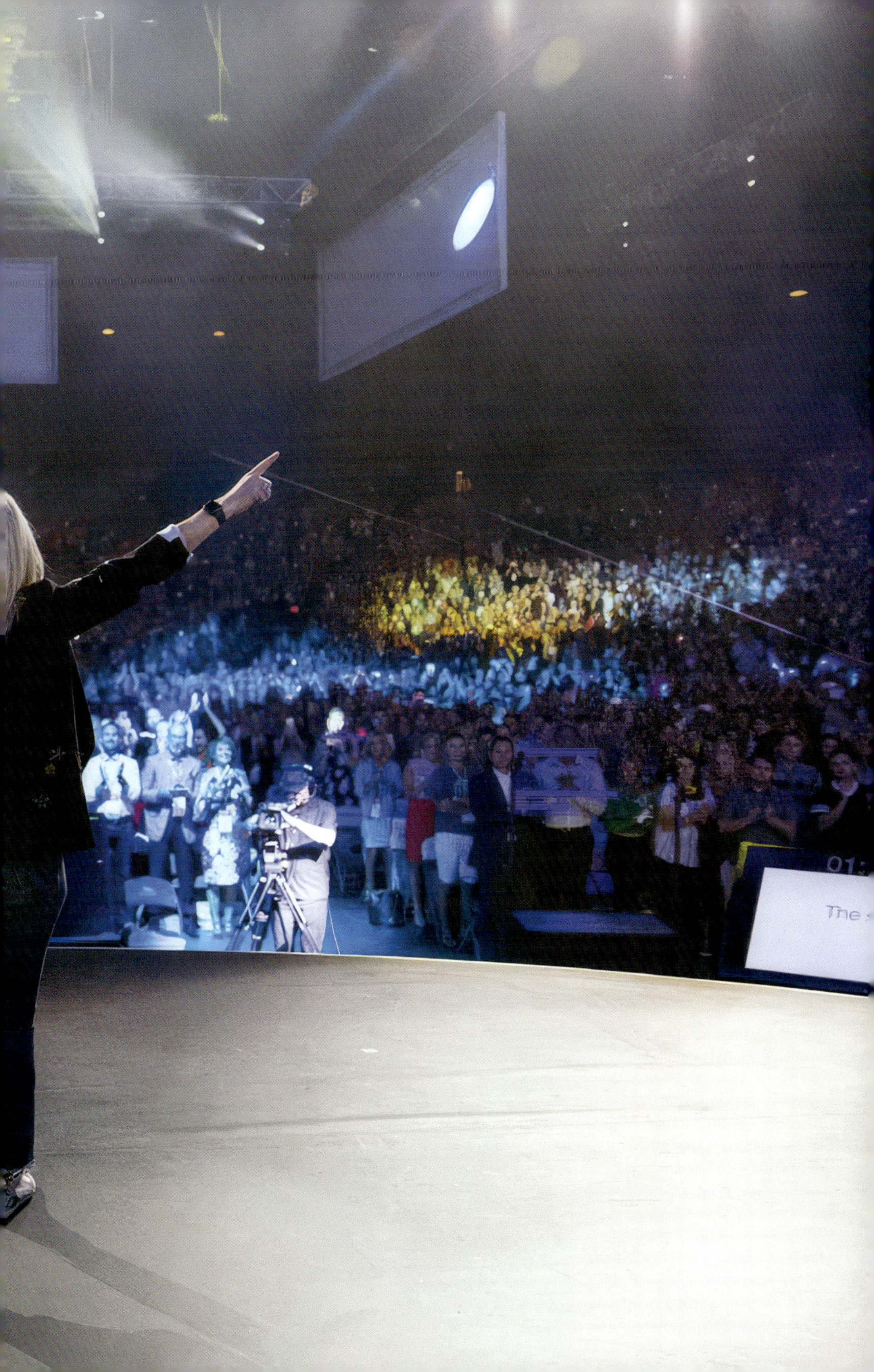
The

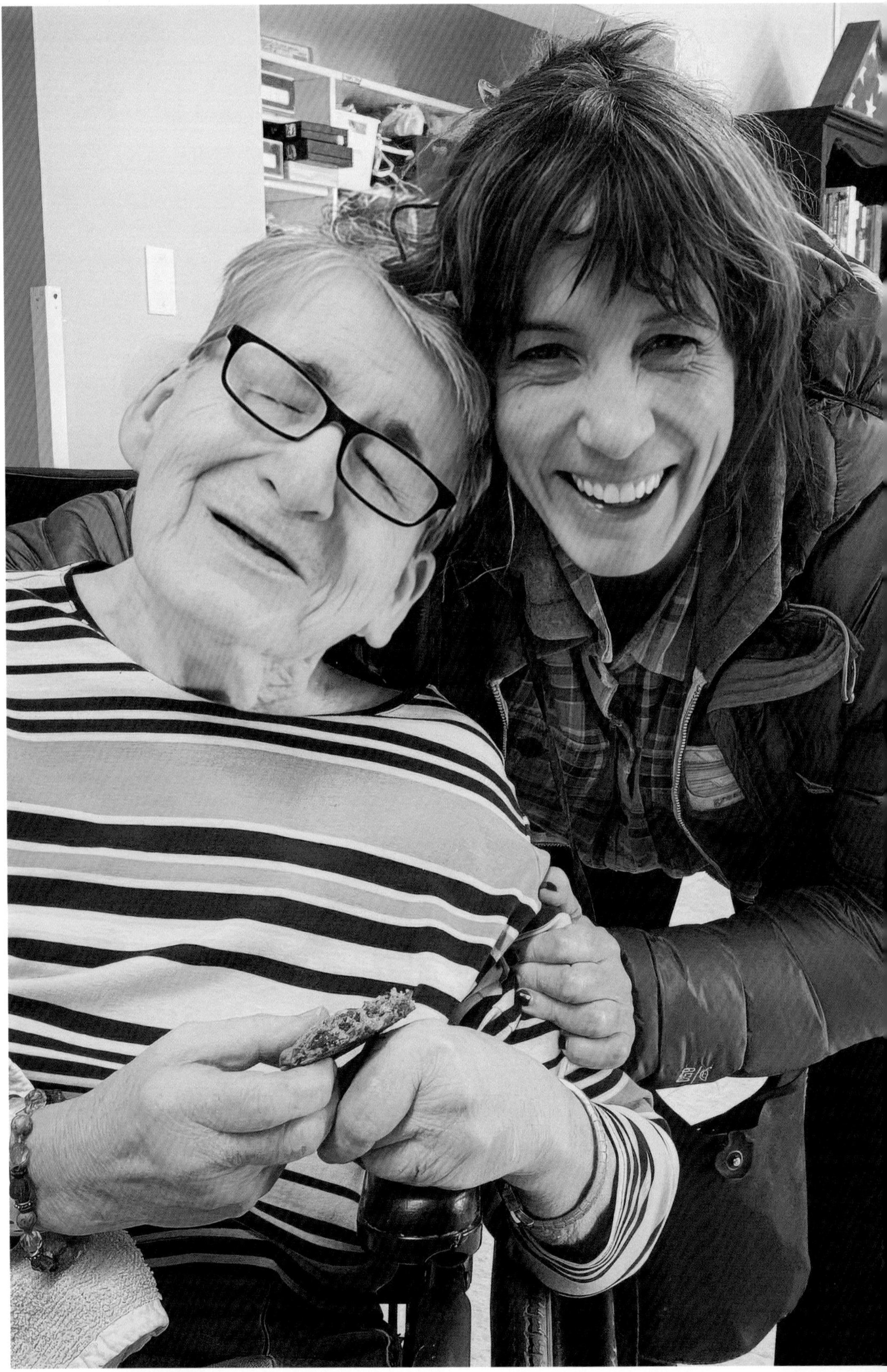

Last Little Bird

On September 20, 2020, in a rare moment of ease, our mom's heart simply stopped beating during a Sunday afternoon nap at Bay Path Nursing Home in Duxbury, MA. Just like that our mother's twenty-seven-year battle with Parkinson's disease was over, and our mom was free. The nurses tell us that on Saturday night she had two dinners as well as ice cream and donuts for dessert—her dream last supper.

As too many of us know, losing someone after a very long disease brings a baffling mix of emotions. The initial relief and happiness for her freedom gave way to bewildering sadness, profound admiration, and deep gratitude as I reflected on her life.

There are all kinds of mother-daughter relationships, and my mom and I were a team. We hosted parties, ran student council campaigns, and choreographed talent show routines. She spoiled us rotten, giving us piles of gifts not just for the regular holidays but for shit like St. Paddy's and Valentine's Day. And when I was 18 years old she got her first signs of Parkinson's Disease as her last little bird left the nest she spent the best years of her life building. As my adult life was beginning, hers was closing in on her in equal measure.

My mother's life was the very definition of resilience. I don't know anyone who endured so much physical pain, existential fear, and crippling loss without a single utterance of self-pity. Like all the misfortune she was dealt, Parkinson's gave my mother a formidable enemy to face every morning, a mountain to climb every day. I've said this many times, but my mom did not—not one single time—make Shannon or I feel responsible for her care or burdened by her disease. I will forever be inspired by the way she held that burden from us. It is the very definition of love.

My mom's disease eventually propelled me toward a life that feels limitless and free. Everything I've done, seen, and accomplished has been a response to watching my favorite person in the world face her fate. In yoga I share the lessons I have learned from my mom about suffering. I hope that her struggle helps my students realize how lucky they are. For my photography clients, I hope to offer a record of the good days. Everything is temporary. Even us.

And now she is gone. The 1958 Bennington High School Best Dancer, the ceramic artist, the funny friend, the doting mother, is back in a body that is free. Here's my wish for you, Mom: Cosmic cartwheels and backflips through the universe and an uncontrollable giddy laugh as you feel your body beneath you again in freedom, grace, and strength. I love you.

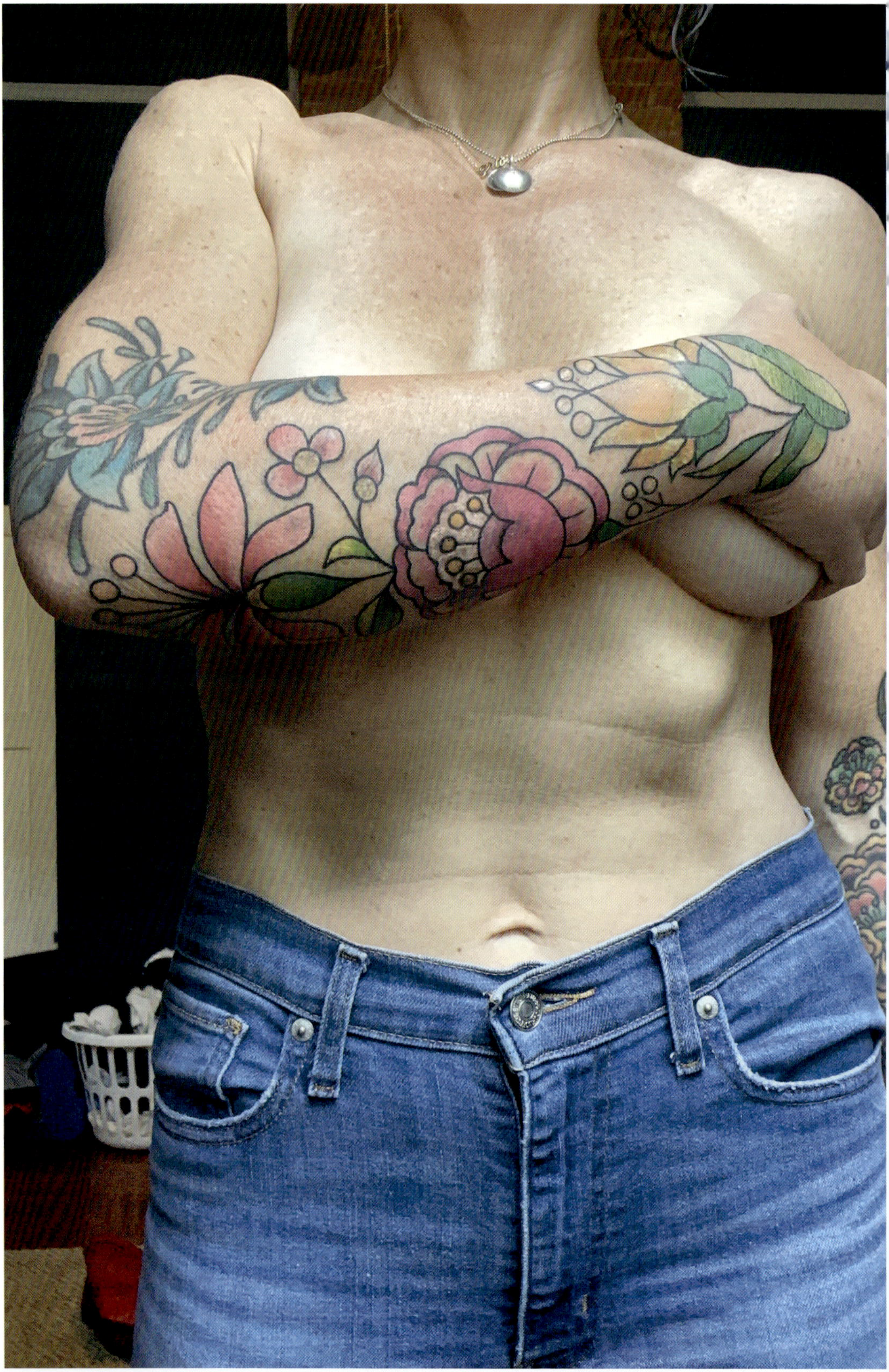

Feels Like Freedom

There are a bunch of ways to get burned out and begin questioning your entire life. The way I did it was by commuting from Providence to Boston every day at 4 a.m. to yoga studios I didn't own, to bleed out emotionally every time I taught—for six years.

And then the pandemic hit. During the lockdown I was trying creative ways to cheer myself up. Once, I took too many mushrooms before I taught a yoga class to the death void of Zoom. When I was trying to describe how good it felt to do a twisting lunge, I made an air horn sound like a club DJ to illustrate my joy. I was so high on mushrooms and laughing so hard at myself that I fell over in the middle of class and had to lie down on my mat in silent laughter. So, I guess there was that one highlight of the pandemic.

The isolation and sadness of the pandemic almost killed me as it did so many other people. I'm not stating an opinion on how the CDC handled the thing. I'm talking about how I handled the thing. I dated—I mean, where would we go? I guess I hunkered down with—a guy during the lockdown. We split up on a Friday in September 2020. I remember it was a Friday because my mother died two days later that Sunday. I was having friends over on Monday for a (ugh) socially distant dinner party in my yard, so I was chopping vegetables on Sunday afternoon when the phone rang. It was my mother's nursing home.

"Hi, Tara, this is Jen, one of your mom's nurses."

"Hey, Jen, what's up?" I answered halfheartedly.

"Your mom has passed. I just went into her room to give her the five o'clock meds, and she's gone."

I sat down on the floor.

"I need to call the coroner. Do you want to see the body?" she asked.

"Yes," I said, and hung up. I called Shannon from the floor.

This combination—the end-of-days feeling of the pandemic, the loss of a relationship, and my mom dying, all on the same weekend—absolutely gutted me. All that loss at once made me feel like all the adventures, the careers, and the confidence of my life were a lie, like it had all been a frantic attempt to outrun vulnerability.

What I *really* wanted, I decided, was a family, but instead I spent my whole life overdoing my fierce independence to protect my heart from rejection. I was 45 years old, utterly alone, and grasping for reasons to live. In my sadness I felt trapped in an obsessive thought loop: the reason I wasn't a mother was because I was unlovable, and I was unlovable because of my appearance. I was possessed with the thought of my own ugliness. In the middle of conversations, driving down the road, or teaching yoga, I would be fine one moment and soaked in sweat in a panic attack the next. I lost fifteen pounds without changing anything and noticed people who I hadn't seen in a while gasp when they saw me. A doctor later told me that I was experiencing "failure to thrive" brought on by emotional stress. In plain sight I was dying.

I needed something to create, something to focus my thoughts on, a reason to keep going. So I planned an eight-week road trip with my dogs to Texas and back. To pay for the trip I rented out my home on Airbnb and pre-sold family photography sessions and spots in my 2021 retreats. My friend Ann got me a paid sponsorship with a cannabis tincture company, which meant I got paid to get stoned then teach yoga on Zoom and talk about it. I hope for your sake you have a friend like Ann.

When I pulled out of my driveway on December 14, 2020, I drove in complete silence for several hours, feeling like a freed prisoner. Every passing minute, every passing state, brought with it a settling back into my own skin. It's a tricky balance between loneliness and freedom; they look a lot alike from the outside. The decisions I have made in my life, over and over, professionally and personally, have been attempts to tip toward the right side of that balance, and they don't work when I'm stuck in my house. Sitting in the house in a pandemic with both my parents dead and no kids and no partner, I became desperate. I didn't carve out this life to be alone, I carved it out to be free.

My father was a traveling salesman, and I could tell he felt free in his car: to sing at the top of his lungs, to go wherever he wanted, to answer to no one. I felt his spirit more than I ever had on that trip, not from the view of his disappointed daughter but from a long-fought understanding of who he was and who I am in turn. He loved his friends like I love my friends. On that trip I remembered I love having the time and energy to have so many deep friendships with so many incredible people. I love photographing families to show people how beautiful they are, and I love being able to help so many people in the way I teach yoga. Slowly but surely, I was remembering who I was, and mile after mile I saved my own life.

I got tattooed in every city I visited until I had two full sleeves of pink floral tattoos in honor of my mom. I found a lost dog named PopTart between two parked cars in New Orleans who escaped his new home while his mom was on a first date. A guy named Alex fixed my car on the side of the road in

Venice, Louisiana, where the Mississippi dumps into the Gulf of Mexico. I gave him $300 for his help, and he collapsed crying in my arms, squeaking out that I had just changed his life. One morning I overheard three women who were working at a gas station in rural Texas. They were trying to calm a coworker who was angry about how their boss recently acted. One woman said to the other, "Girl, you know you don't have to react to everything that happens to you, right?" I spun on my heels, walked back in, and put those bitches into chair pose. I didn't really, but I did turn around and ask them if they had ever tried yoga and we talked for a while about the concept of non-reaction. I accidentally hosted a party in Miami for mostly strangers where I was one of two people not doing cocaine. It was New Year's Eve, and I was alone in my room by 10:30, listening to people gag in my bathroom all night. That was a low point. I did yoga in every city I visited, and my favorite yoga teacher on that trip had an anxiety attack in class, so I held her in the locker room until she cried so hard we started laughing. That was a high point. I missed my mom so badly when I walked onto the campus of University of Alabama that I burst into tears before I acknowledged I was sad. This time I could actually drive away from that fucking place, but this time I couldn't call my mom to tell her how much I missed her. I was in an old house on the Outer Banks of North Carolina for a five-day Nor'easter. The ocean, wind, and rain were so relentless I felt like I was sitting on trial for every bad decision I had ever made. I've had easier nights on ayahuasca.

I was also seeing visions of yoga studios that were small and homey, beautifully decorated and warm. I met so many studio owners and got a glimpse into great local communities. I began to believe that a lifelong dream of mine was within my reach: to own a studio of my own. For months I had thought everything I lived for was either a lie or behind me, but on this trip I began to remember who I was and what I could do. I could build the community I had always wanted to. I could build the studio I had been dreaming about since college. I could build a reason to live again.

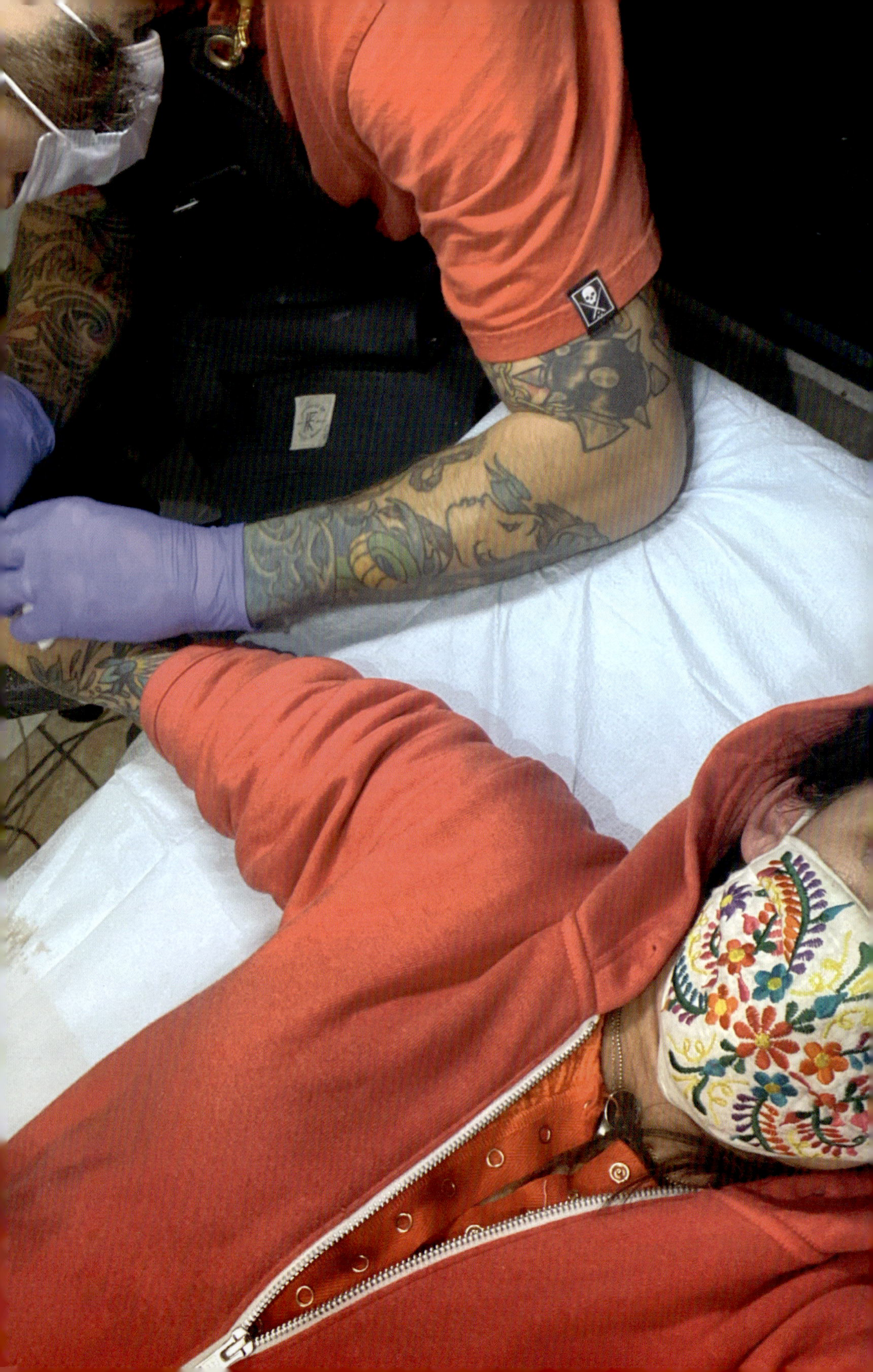

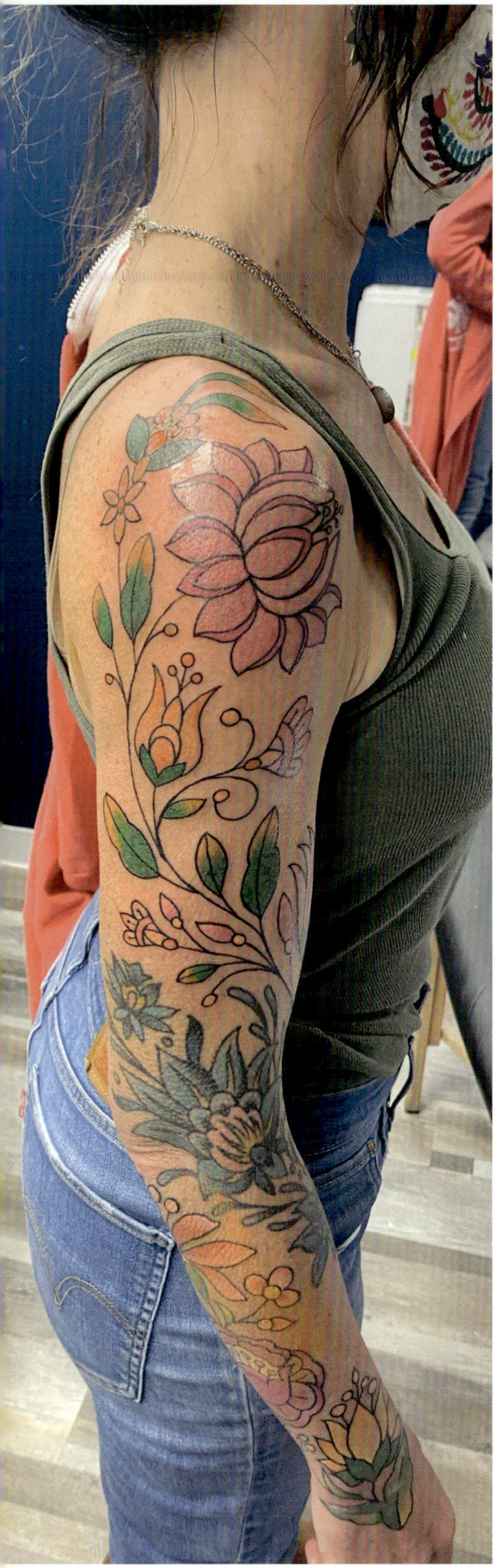
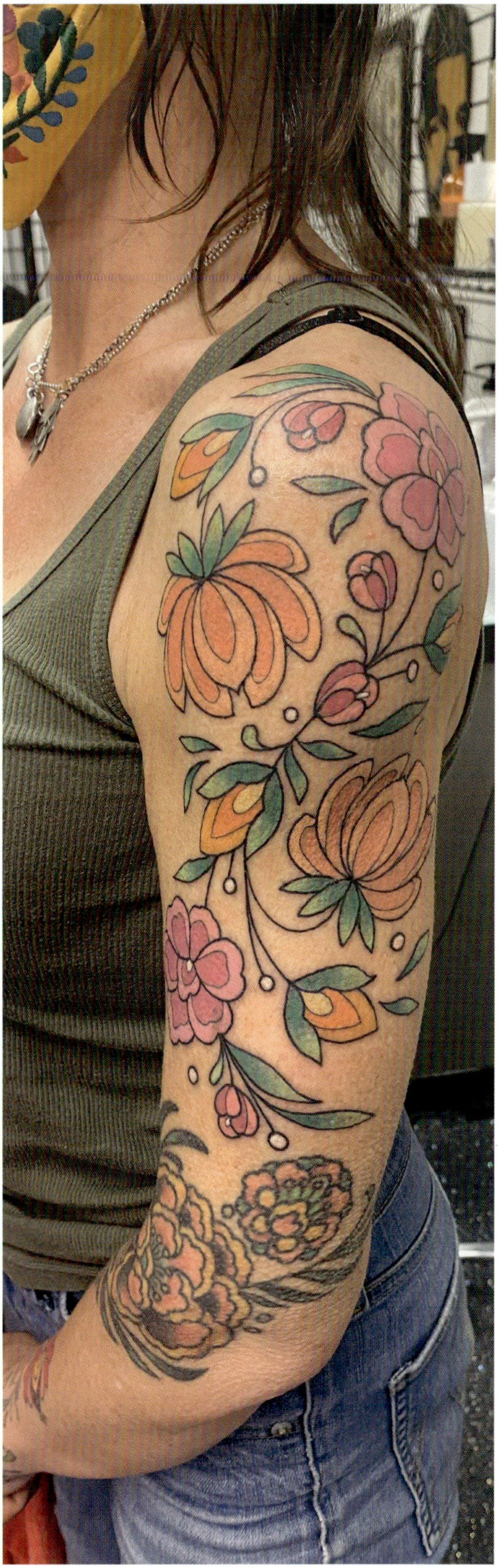

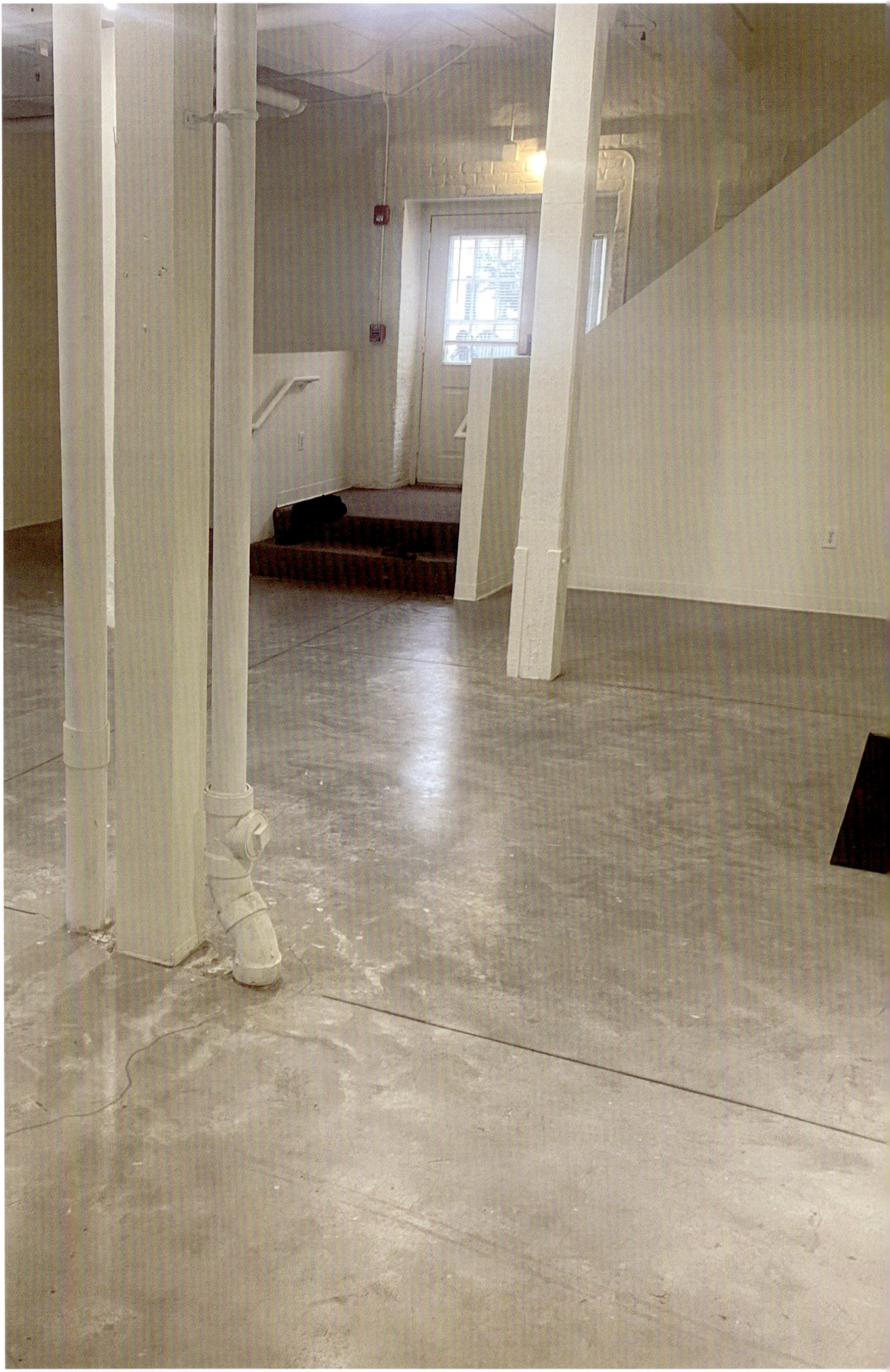

The Love Offensive

After my big road trip where I vowed everything would change, nothing changed. I was still commuting at 4 a.m. to teach yoga, having panic attacks, pissing people off, and having unexplained weight loss.

One of my favorite yoga teachers of all time tells us in class, "Help is not on the way." This is a reminder that no one can save our lives but ourselves. The time to save my life had arrived.

In September 2021 I sat down at my computer and searched for commercial spaces in Providence and saw one for rent in a gorgeous live/work building just around the corner from my house. Without even calling the realtor I went down to peek through the windows, and when I got there the door was unlocked.

"Hello?" I opened the door slowly. The place was empty. One step inside and I knew I had found my studio. It had concrete floors and walls and a loft space upstairs, and it overlooked an absolutely gorgeous courtyard. The space was small, it wasn't perfect, but it could work.

I called the realtor to ask if I could officially see the space, then called Laura and Nina and asked if they'd join me—along with my friend Albee, who was visiting—for the first official walkthrough. When Nina arrived at my door she told me she had just signed the lease on a space that would become her hair salon. Both Laura and Nina would be living and working in Providence. That was all I needed to know.

"Ya, I'll take it," I said to the realtor as the four of us stood in the middle of what would soon be the studio floor. I was in a lease by 3 p.m. I wrote an email to the Boston studio and quit, effectively immediately. I ripped the safety net out from under me and forced myself to jump.

"When you're ready to build an empire, let me know," a yoga student once told me. Over the years, many of my students had encouraged me to open my own place, and now was the time to ask for their help to do just that. An hour after I signed the lease, with the help of my friend Lily, I opened a GoFundMe campaign asking for $50K. I made a post on Instagram, I wrote a newsletter, and I held my breath.

Over the next two weeks I raised $85,000. Friends, students, and clients from my entire life pitched in. Every morning I would check my GoFundMe page and blink in disbelief as I read the names of the people who donated.

My friend Lyn gave me an amount so large that I thought it was a mistake, so I texted her to make sure she hadn't accidentally added three zeros. She told me that she wanted to invest in female business owners who were making a real difference. I looked around the room for whoever that could be. Then two of my best friends, Felicia and Evan, gave me a very large sum of money because they are insanely generous people who knew I could do it if I just had the support.

By late September I had the money I needed. In utter disbelief at my own audacity, and now trapped in my own choices, I began building my studio like I said I wanted to. I was still so sick and fragile that the enormity of the task terrified me, but I knew I had to make it happen. I couldn't quit.

My friend Shawna drove to Providence to help me imagine the space as a yoga studio. She called her contractor friend, Sean Kiley, and asked him for a favor: Would he drive to Providence and build out my entire studio? Like, right now? On October 14 Sean and his two sons began working. They laid the floors and the walls of the place in two days.

Aaron Santos, an incredible photographer and friend, taught himself how to paint during Covid, so I asked if he would create a mural for the studio walls. With lingering travel bans limiting his commercial photography business, he had the free time and was excited for the challenge. Aaron arrived in mid-October and, mostly with a one-inch brush, painted for twelve hours a day for the next sixteen days. On November 4, he returned to Brooklyn, leaving behind a four-walled masterpiece.

Ben Wight, who is always there for me when I need him, built out the upstairs in his signature urban-cottage aesthetic. My plan was to live above the studio and rent out my home on Airbnb while I got the studio off the ground.

Laura Ganci painted gorgeous birds in flight up the staircase, which made the entire studio one huge art piece. Mike Habib insisted that if I planned to really stand out amongst the rest, I needed interesting lighting and a killer sound system. Though he was a new father and a busy professional he came to Providence three times to transform the space with lighting and sound.

Sean Kiley and his sons returned in early November to hang the ten infrared heaters as well as an endless number of fans and lights and everything else I needed. Sean worked around the clock and even slept on the studio floor one night to get everything done in time. If there was an angel in this endeavor, it was Sean Kiley.

My best friend, Kristen, flew from Wisconsin for opening weekend just to support me, knowing how huge this was for me.

And Lily worked as my manager, marketer, therapist, confidant, web designer, and moral support.

And then, on November 13, 2021, eight weeks after I signed the lease, I opened the Love Offensive Hot Power Yoga. The room was filled with my best friends and favorite students from Boston and beyond. I did it. I fucking did it. I did it together with my best friends and students. My hardest days were behind me.

And then … the heaters didn't work. And the humidifier didn't work. And the place flooded on day three. And I forgot to put a front desk in the place. And I didn't know how to work the software. Then the omicron variant of Covid hit. Living at the studio was a nightmare; it was dark and lonely, and I listened to a guy have sex every night at like 2 a.m. directly over my head. Classes were practically empty, and the new people who tried my class hated it: way too hard, way too hot, way too emotional, way too intense. People would roll up their mats right in front of my face and walk out the door. One girl told me that she "didn't appreciate having a spell cast on her during yoga class." I told her if I could cast spells I wouldn't be living in Providence.

With quitting not an option, I emptied my 401(k), took out a home equity line, and did everything I could to keep this thing above water that first year. I knocked on the door of every business in town to tell people about my studio, I hung flyers at every shop, I gave classes away for free. I tried everything.

That first year of the studio feels like a nightmare. Nothing could possibly go that badly in real life. I made the wrong decisions and said the wrong things to the wrong people at the wrong time. I thought I was going to be the success I was in Boston, but it was the opposite. And the people who got mad at me or didn't like me? I wasn't just not liked, I was hated.

Desperate, sensing that my life was on the line, I remembered what I knew. I returned to the ways I had healed myself in the past: daily journaling, meditating, visualization, affirmations, counting backward, all of it. I listened exclusively to self-help podcasts and audio books. The only voices I let myself listen to had to be hopeful and encouraging. I was obsessed with healing myself and staying alive. I wrote this sentence hundreds of times in my journal, believing that my thoughts would become things: "This is a thriving and diverse community where people make friends, feel grateful, and heal themselves."

And then slowly, like a dripping faucet, students came. People who had been looking for classic hot power yoga found us. Those people told their friends. The room filled, and the ways I was healing myself now became my teachings.

Building the Love Offensive in the darkest days of my life reminded me that, no matter what, we always figure it out, whatever *it* is. Thoughts really do become things. Where we think is where we go. Think up! Go up! I reminded myself of this—out loud—in class.

I encouraged all of us to keep track of our wins, not just our losses. Noticing the good is both evidence of and fuel for resilience. It helps us build true confidence in who we are.

Exaggeration and enthusiasm can turn your whole life around. It's okay to try.

Hot power yoga is not easy, but it's the furthest thing from suffering. Revel in the difference.

We only have one voice. How we talk to ourselves is just how we talk. Be nice.

Just a reminder: Help is not on the way. No one can take a deep breath for you. You're the one calling the helpline, but you're also the one answering the phone. Trust yourself.

I remind myself of my mortality. I am alive today, but one day I will not be. All that matters is love. Whatever else there is, let it go.

I constantly try and try again to hone the skills that are most elusive to me—patience, non-reaction, and letting go, among many others. I always come up short, but I will never stop trying.

Concentrating on my own inhale and exhale are momentary distractions from my time-traveling mind. One breath at a time, I separate from my thoughts, and I am free.

Gratitude is our endless well of energy and our pathway out of suffering. We are living inside our wildest dreams. Notice it.

I remind myself that I am perfectly suited for the life I'm living, and I'm never alone. The students of the Love Offensive reflect that. They are an incredible group of human beings who saved my life. They are strong not just in their bodies but in their minds. They are beautiful not just physically but in their hearts. The studio is not only thriving, it's an utter love fest. It is truly beyond any hope I ever had. I love these people. The community of the Love Offensive is my wildest dream coming true.

And with my mom's life as an example that our health is our only true wealth, I begin and end every class reminding us to be grateful for:

one more day on this beautiful planet
(where the moon breathes the ocean)

in this beautiful body
(that can move in a genuine expression of how we feel)

with all these beautiful people
(who make this whole life worth living).

Forever and always, I'm just talking to myself.

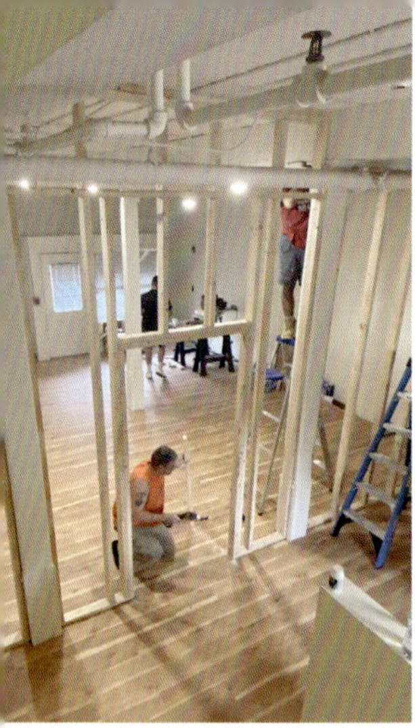
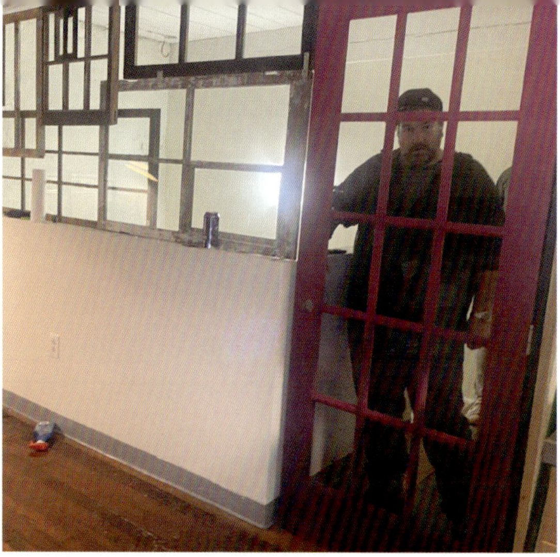
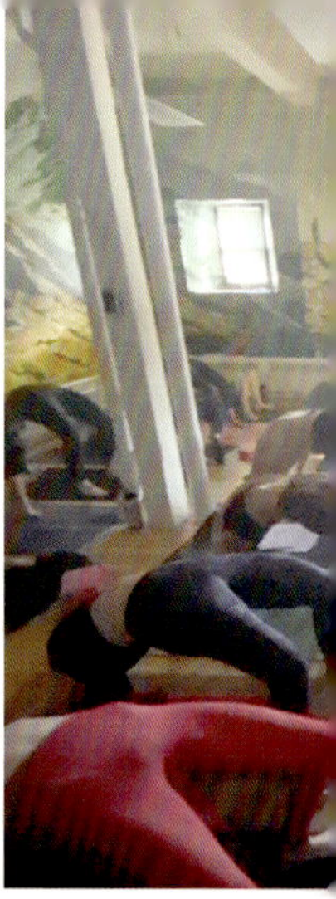
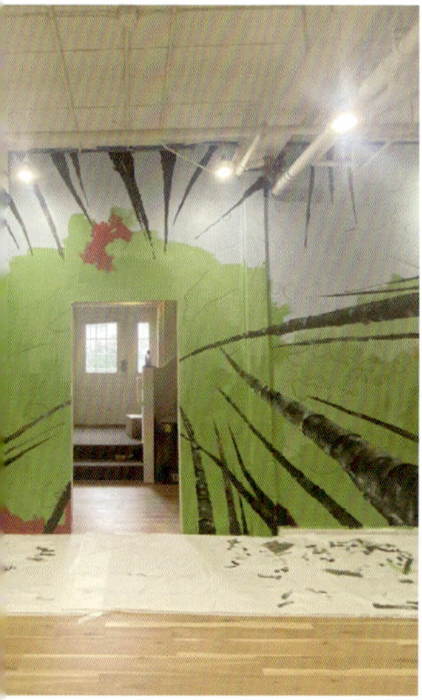
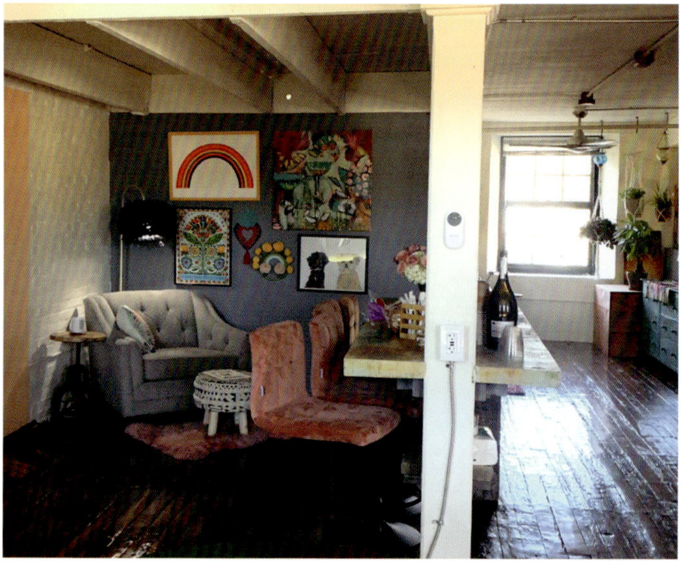

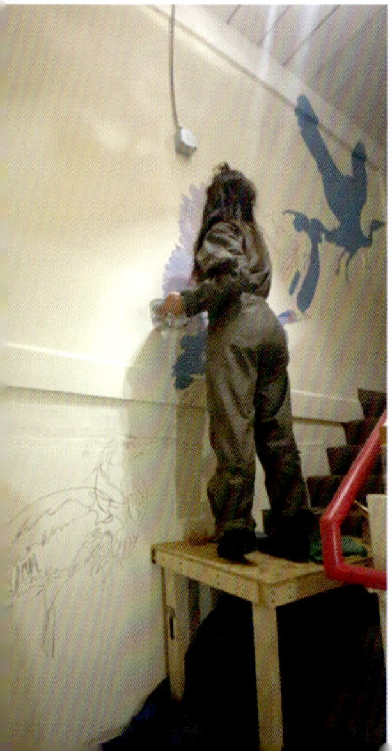
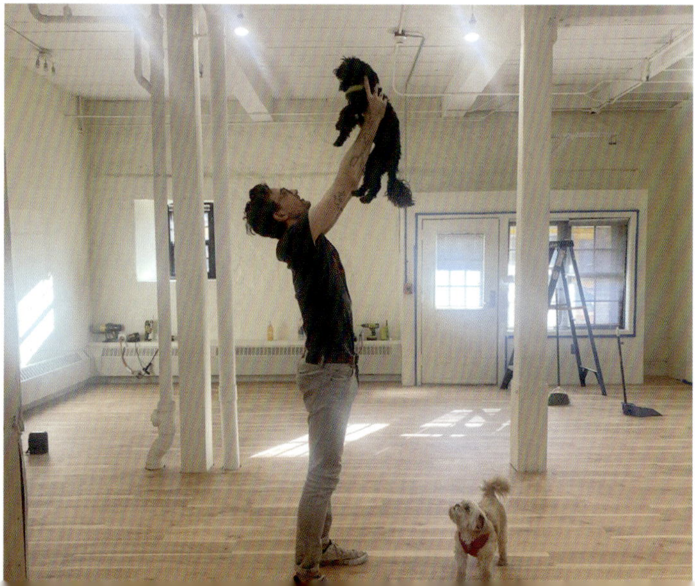
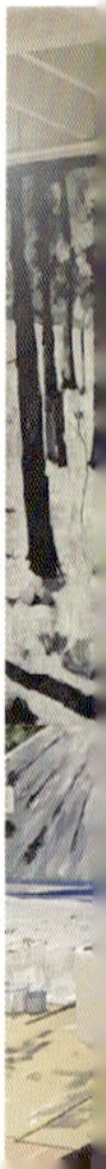

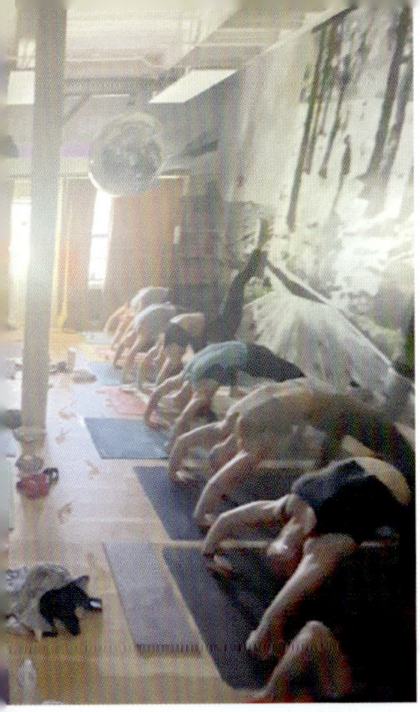
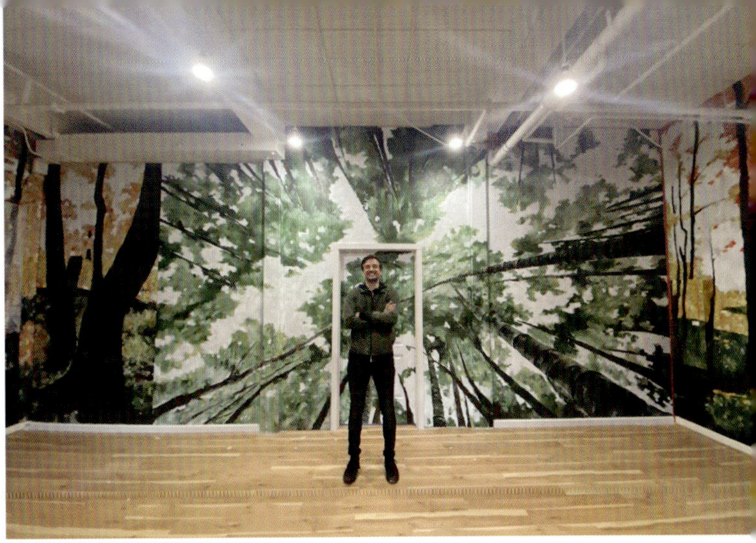
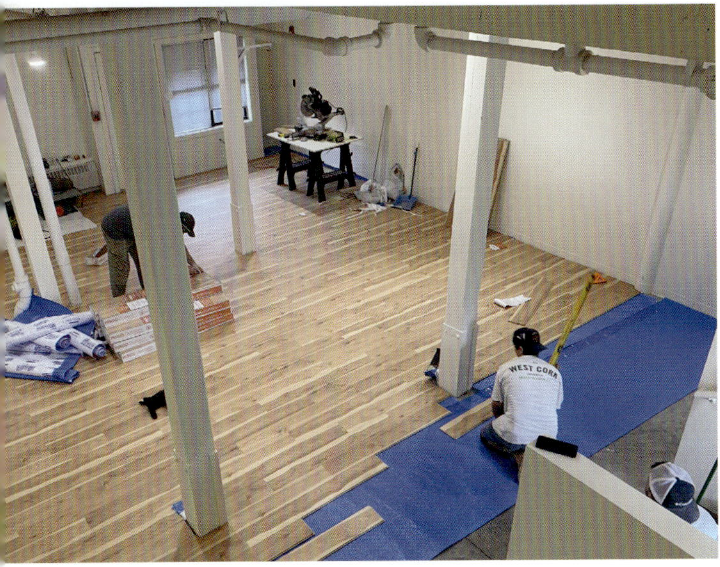
WEST CORK
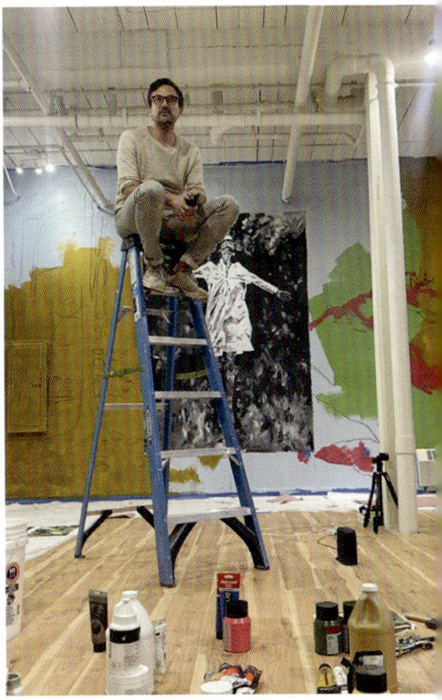
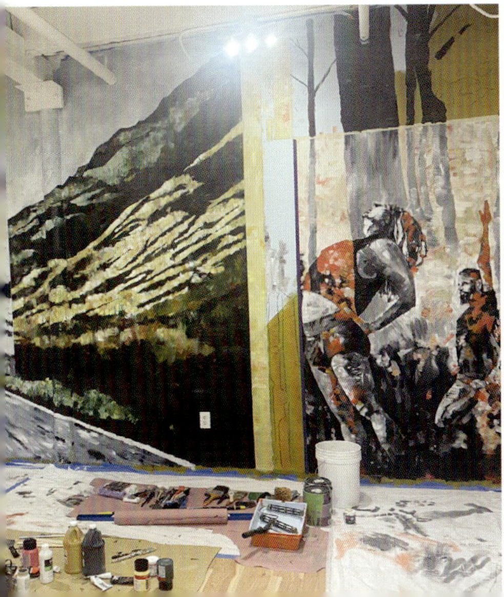
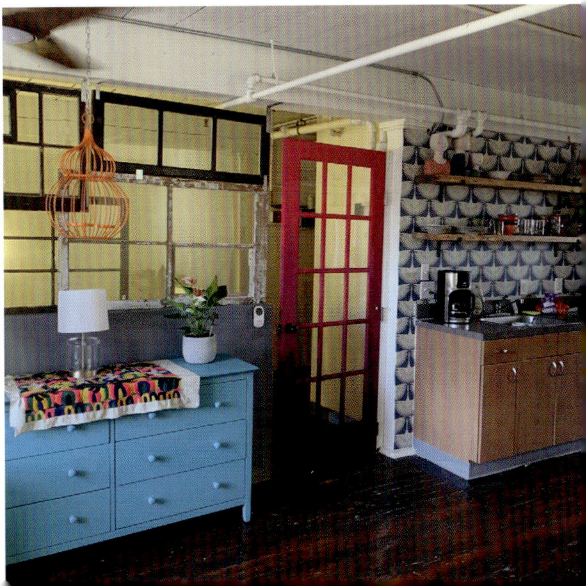

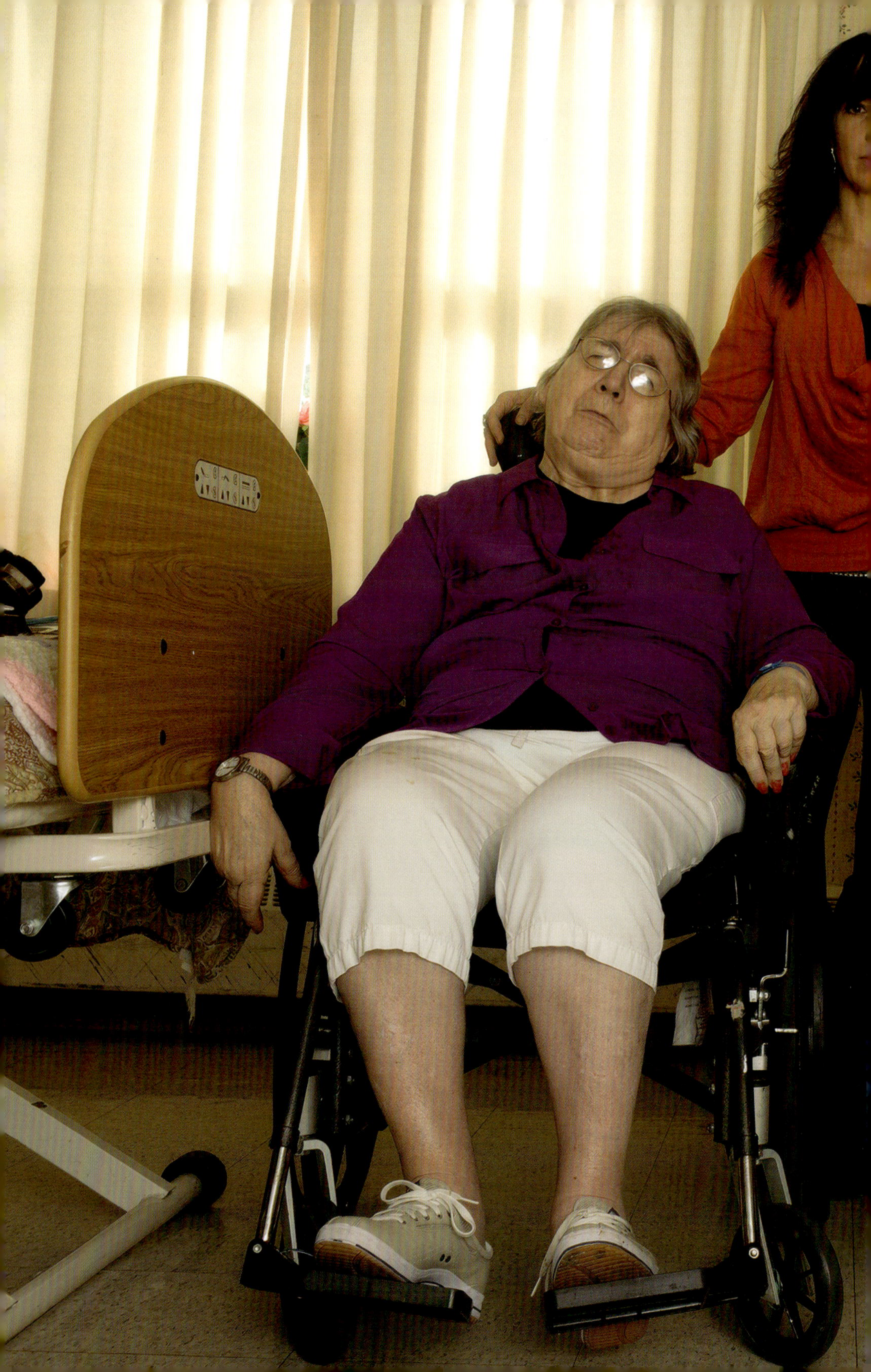

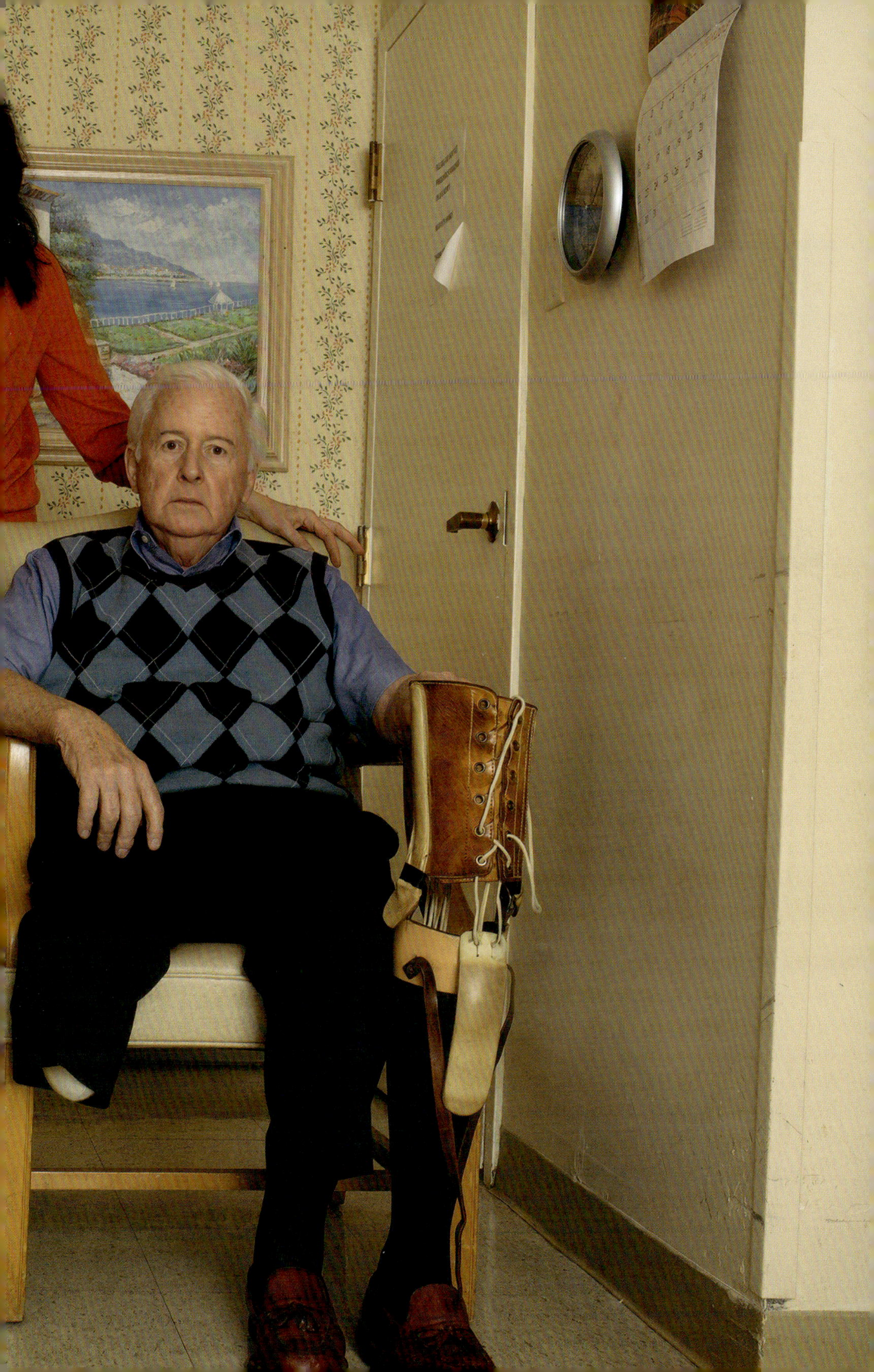

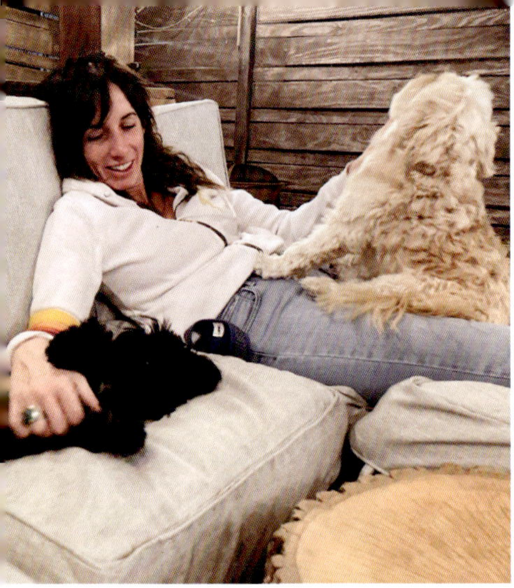

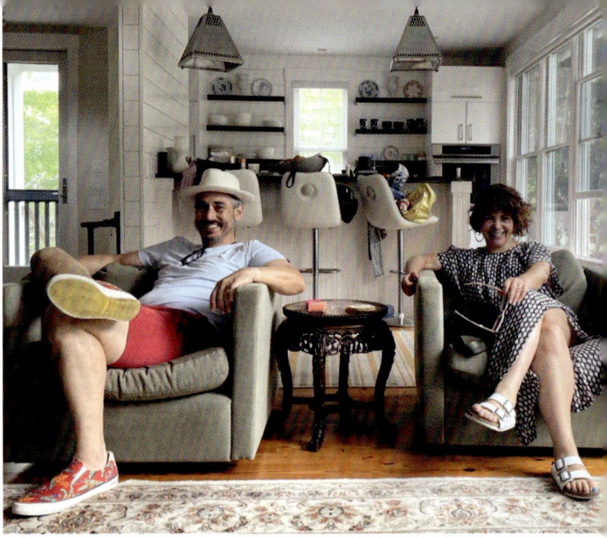

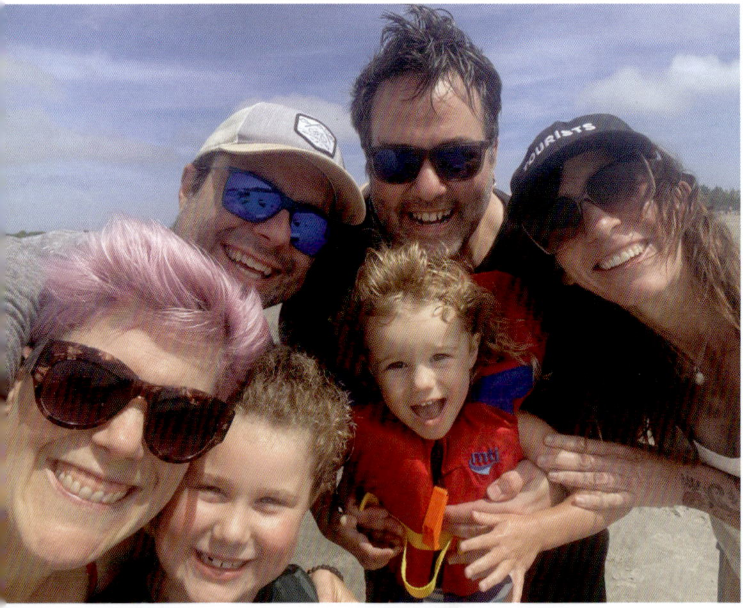
TOURISTS

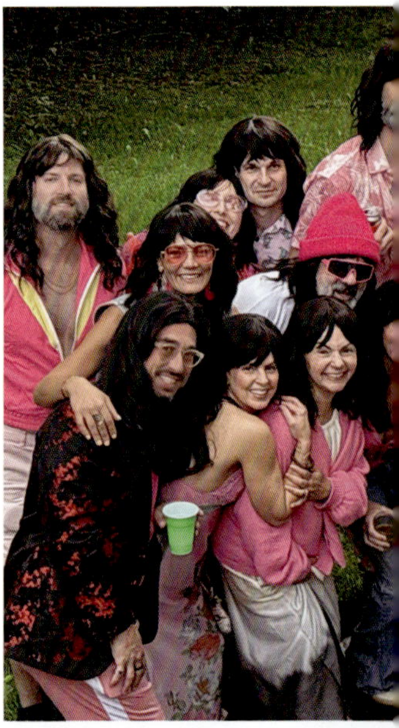

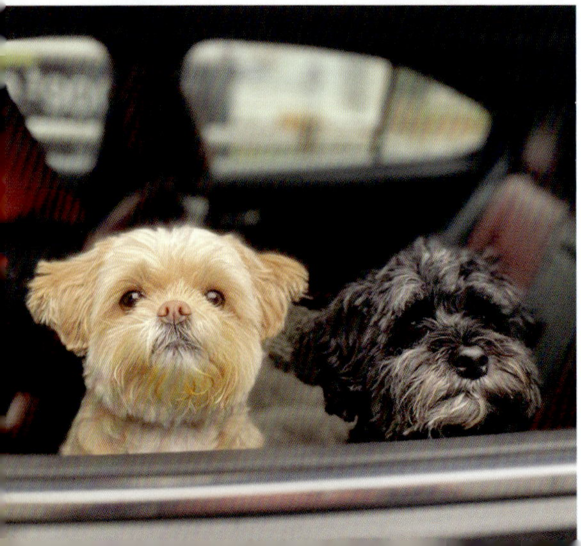

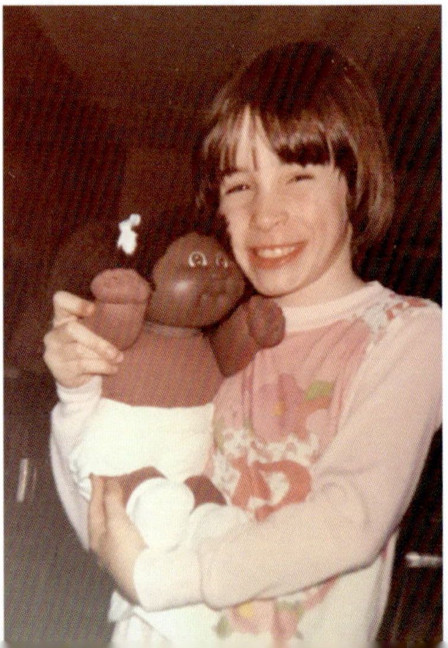

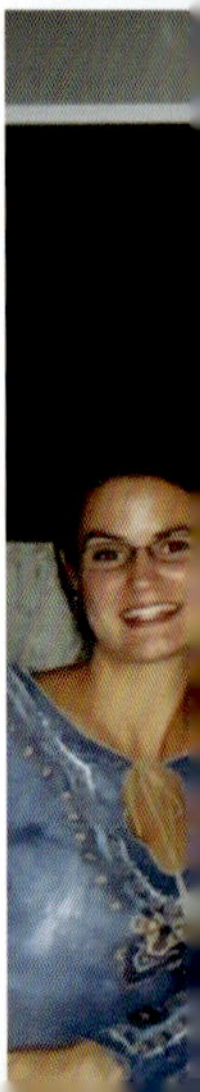

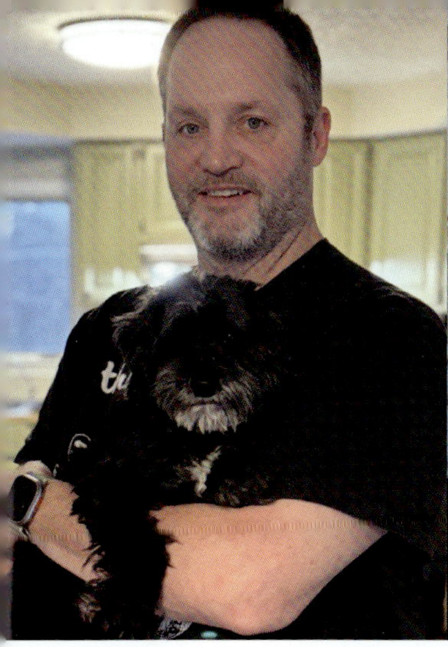
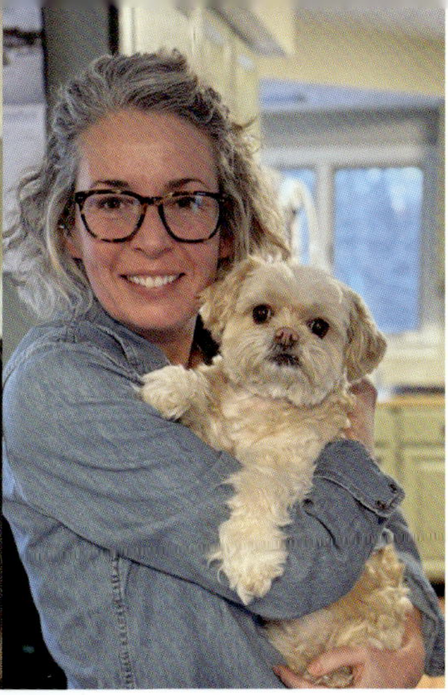
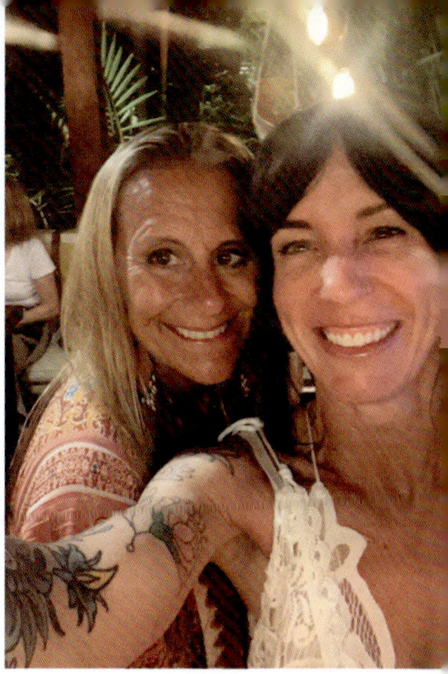
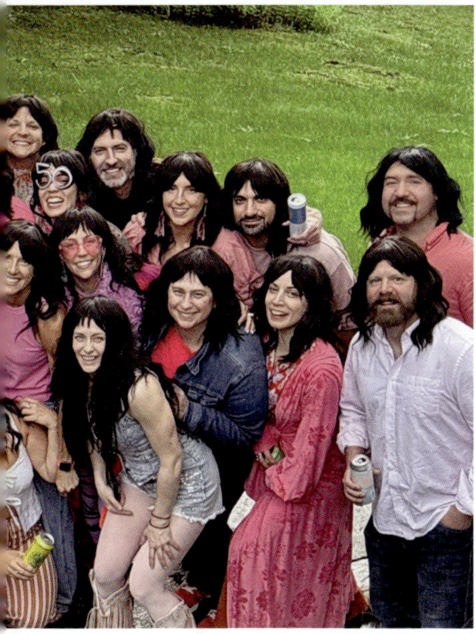
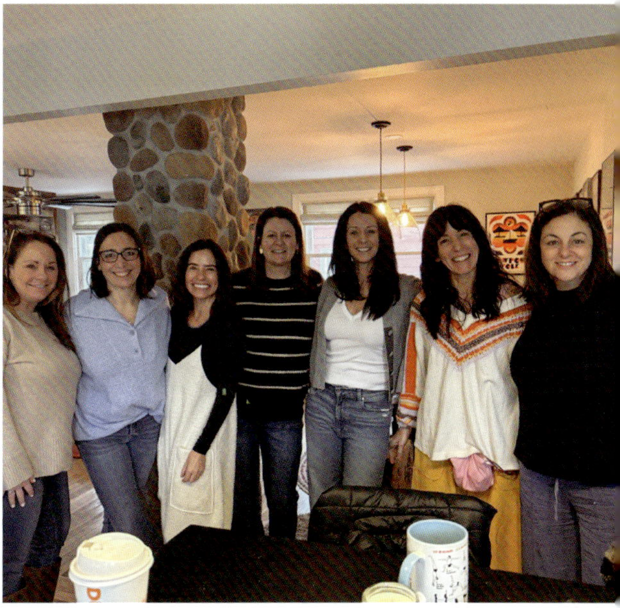
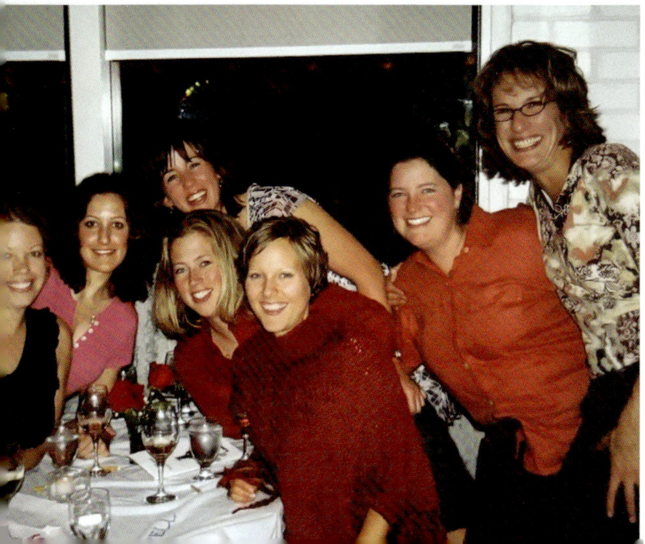
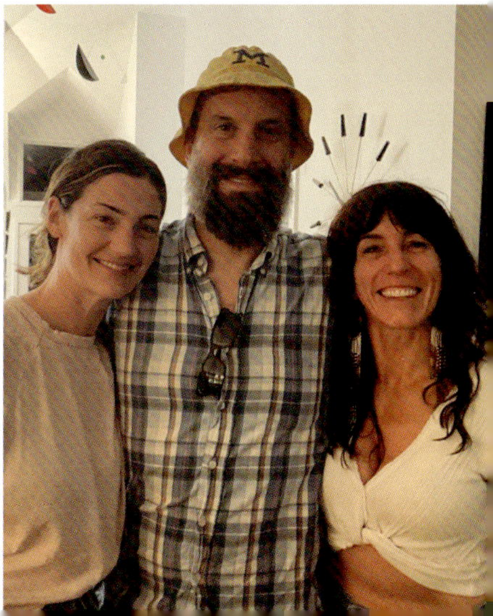

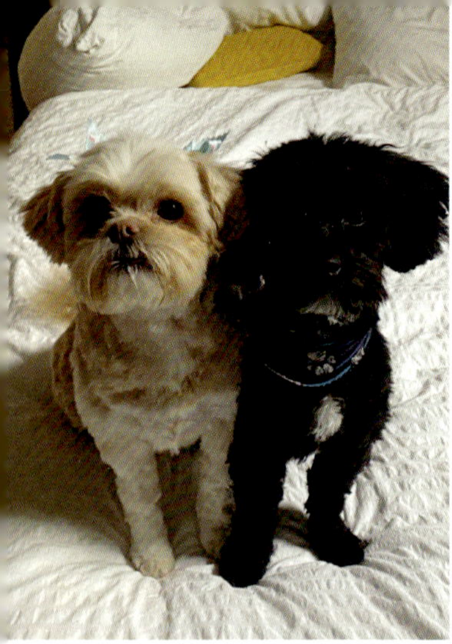

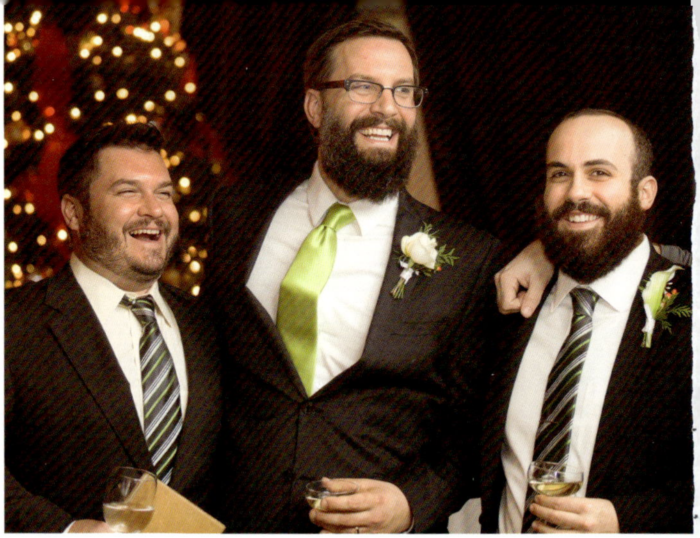

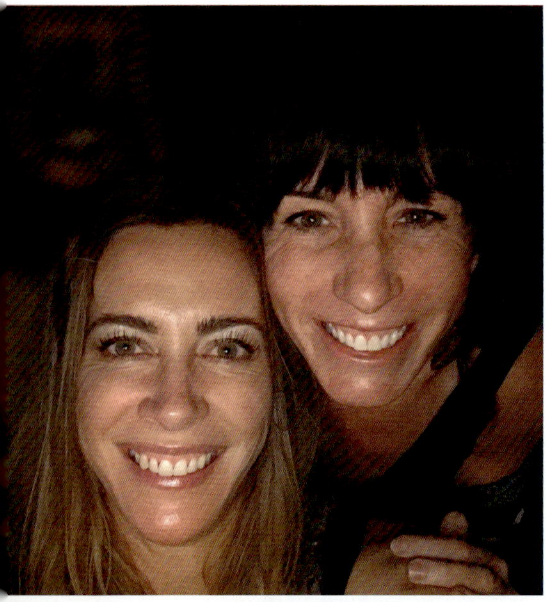

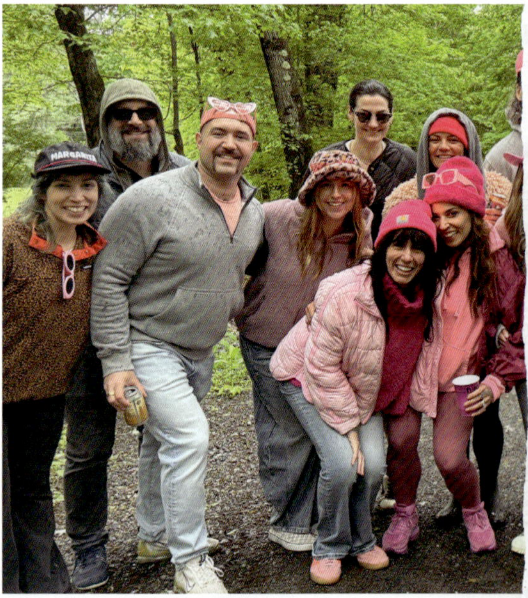
MARGARITA

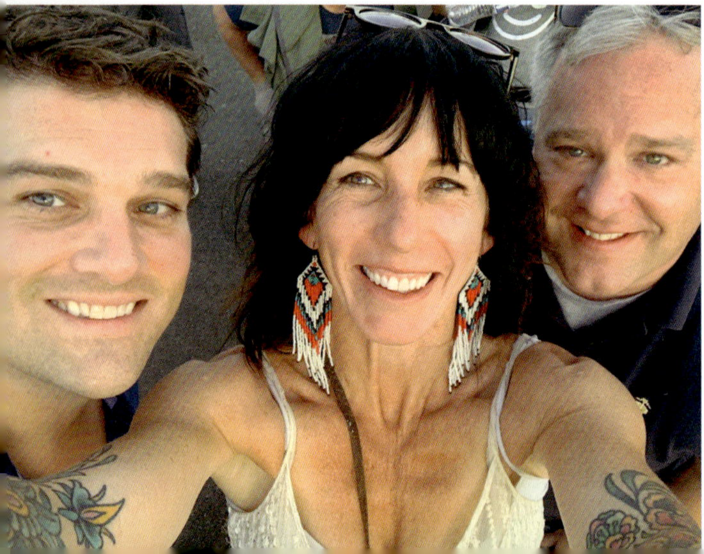

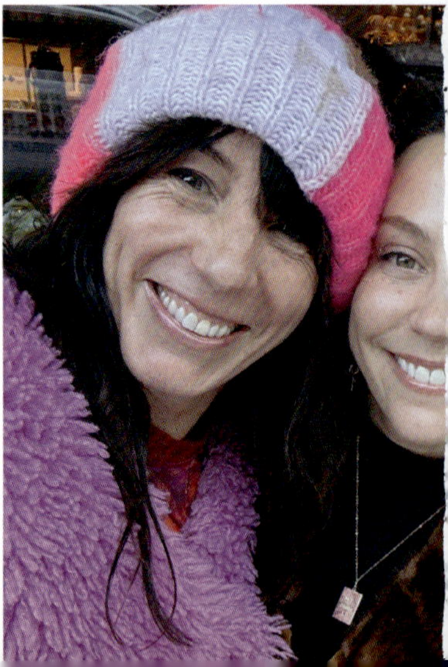

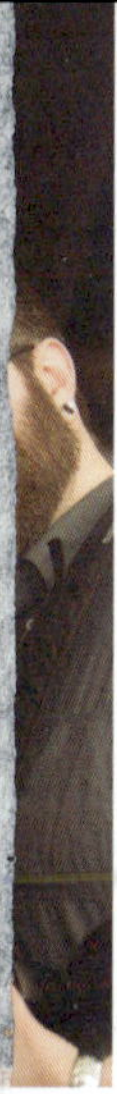

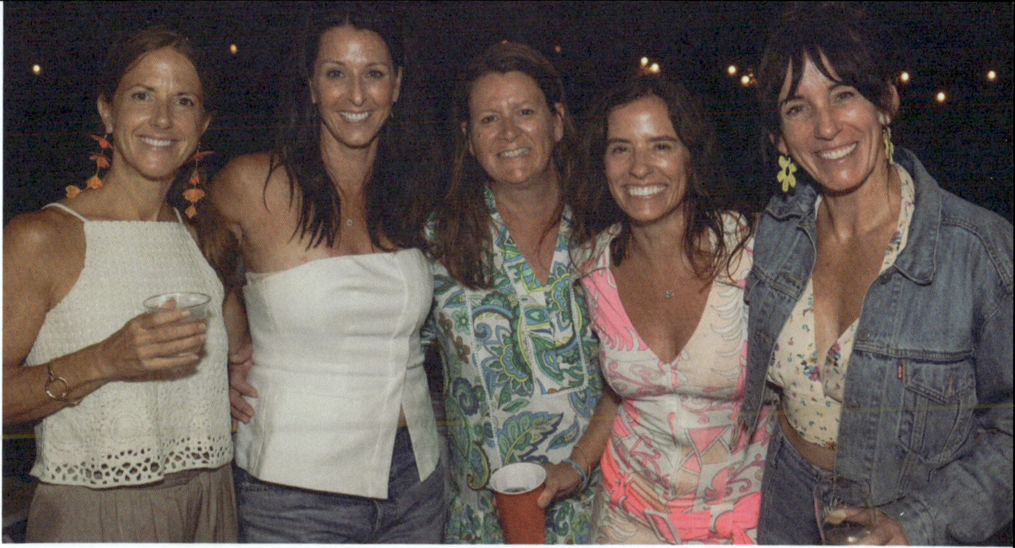

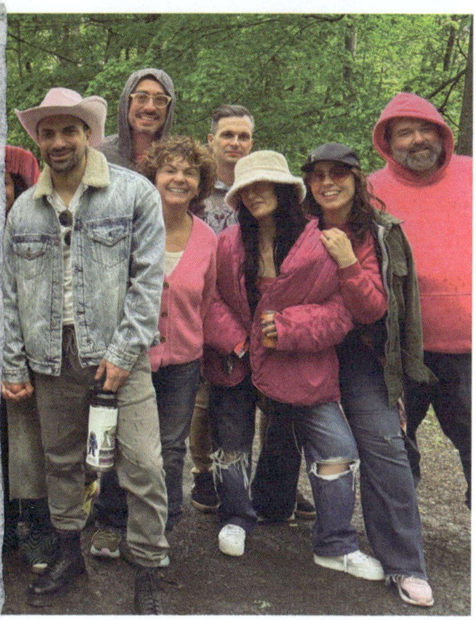

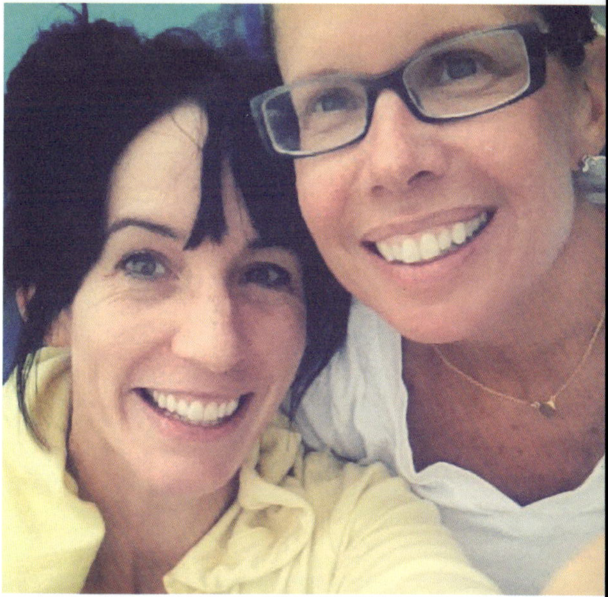

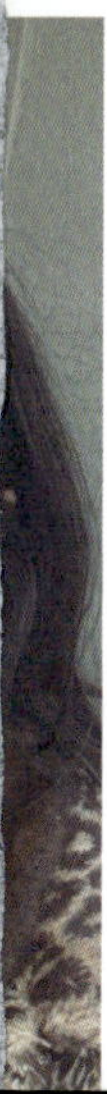

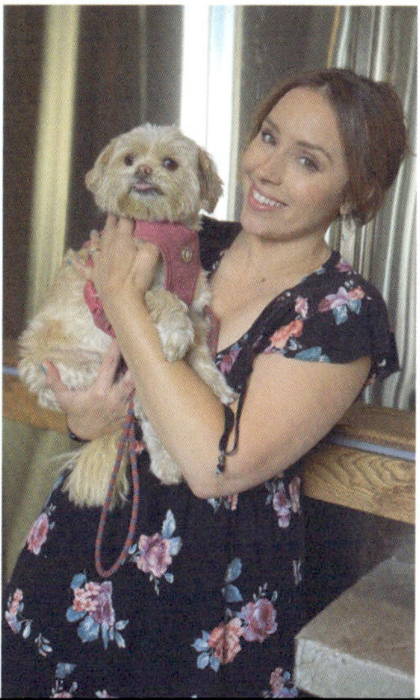

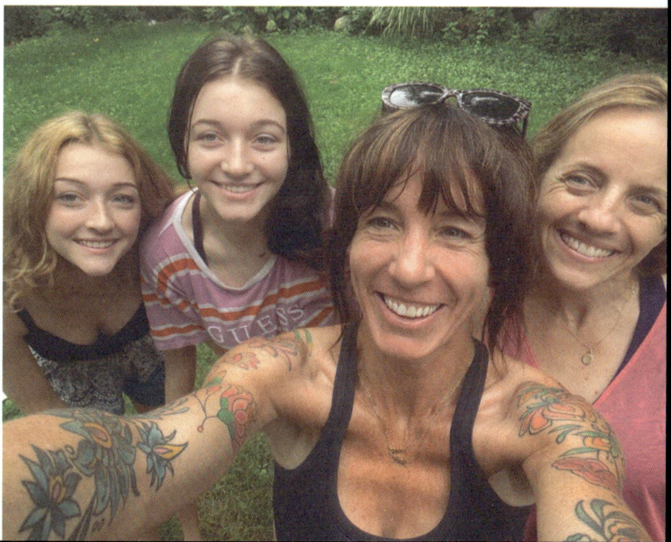
GUESS

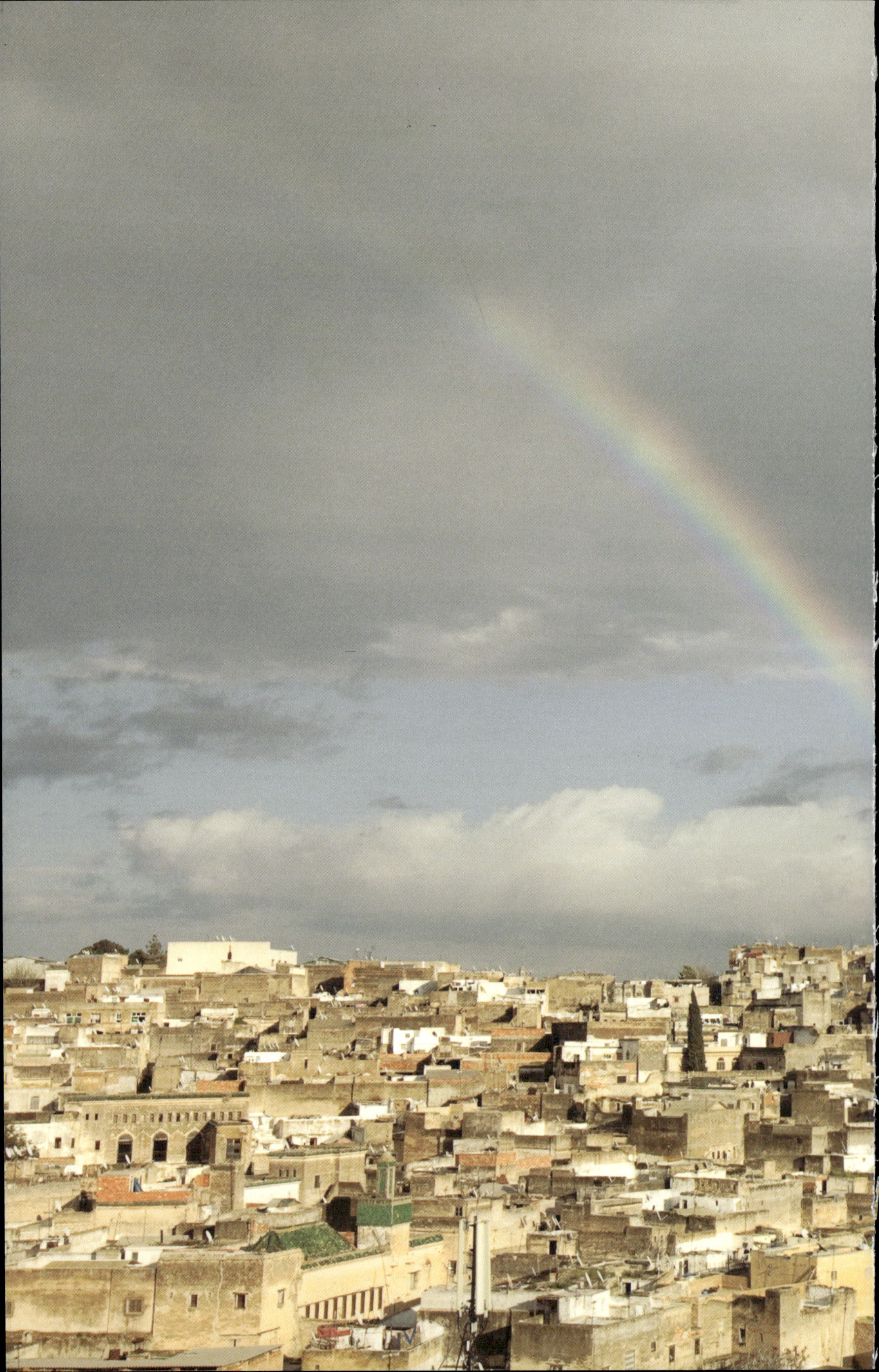

POLITICAL GEOGRAPHY

A New Introduction

Richard Muir

John Wiley & Sons, Inc.
New York. Toronto

First published in Great Britain in 1997 by
Macmillan Press Ltd, Basingstoke and London

Published in the United States and Canada 1997 by
JOHN WILEY & SONS, INC.
605 Third Avenue
New York, NY 10158-0012
USA

ISBN 0–470–23744–9

This book is printed on paper suitable for recycling and made from fully managed and sustained forest sources.

Printed in Hong Kong

Library of Congress Cataloging-in-Publication Data
available upon request
John Wiley & Sons ISBN 0–470–23744–9

For little **Kieran**, without whom this book would have been finished much sooner

Contents

List of Boxes, Maps and Tables

Boxes

Maps

Tables

Acknowledgements

The author and publishers acknowledge with thanks permission from the following to reproduce copyright material:

Lynne Rienner Publishers, for the quotation from R. B. J. Walker, *One World, Many Worlds* (1988) in Chapter 6.

The Guardian, for the quotation from Clare Travena, © *The Guardian* (1995) in Chapter 5.

Macmillan, for the quotation from Thomas Hardy, 'Departure' (1899), in *The Complete Poems*, in the Introduction.

Chatto & Windus, for the quotation from Aldous Huxley, *Themes and Variations* (1950) in Chapter 2.

Alternatives, for the quotation from R. B.J. Walker, 'Security, Sovereignty and the Challenge of World Politics' (1990) in Chapter 3.

Archives Européennes de Sociologie, for the quotation from M. Mann, 'The Autonomous Power of the State: Its Origins, Mechanisms and Results' (1984) in Chapter 4.

Clarendon Press, for the quotation from A. J. P. Taylor, *The Struggle for Mastery in Europe, 1848–1918* (1954) in Chapter 7.

Review of African Political Economy, for the quotation from B. Davidson, 'The Crisis of the Nation-States of Africa' (1990) in Chapter 7.

Newsweek, for the quotation from Frank Borman (1968) in Chapter 8.

Every effort has been made to contact all the copyright-holders, but if any have been inadvertently omitted the publishers will be pleased to make the necessary arrangement at the earliest opportunity.

Introduction

Letting a hundred flowers blossom and a hundred schools of thought contend is the policy for promoting the progress of the arts and the sciences.

Mao Tse-Tung, speech 'On the Correct Handling of Contradictions' (1957)

When shall the saner softer polities/Whereof we dream, have sway in each proud land . . . ?

Thomas Hardy (1840–1928) 'Departure' (1899)

It is now some twenty years since I published *Modern Political Geography*. When this book first appeared, in 1975, the rehabilitation of political geography had scarcely begun (Muir 1976), though during the 1980s the subject reclaimed a position near the centre of the geographical stage, and its prominence has been consolidated during the 1990s. The two decades which span the publication of *Modern Political Geography* and that of *Political Geography: A New Introduction* cover a most formative period in the development of the subject and provide interesting bases for comparison.

Twenty years ago the 'Quantitative Revolution', which wrought such havoc and alienated so many gifted scholars, was still a considerable force in geography. As a young and relatively inexperienced lecturer, I felt obliged to represent a spectrum of quantitative techniques in my text – even though many seemed only to describe the obvious or to have been adopted in research as ends rather than means. Now, however, and in keeping with most current practice, I have felt no obligation to impose a quantitative dimension: this book is very largely a positivist desert; an equation-free zone. Yet at least 'spatial science' produced some useful counter-actions: behavioural geography expanded and reminded us again that people are human, while: 'A movement toward or, more properly, a reawakened awareness of humanist principles and aims over and against a preoccupation with the techniques of scientific rationality began to emerge. Humanism, as it were, was rediscovered as the central concern for a geography of man' (Ley and Samuels 1978, p. 1).

In the book of 1975, and more particularly in the revised edition of 1981 and in my work with Ronan Paddison, also of that year, I stressed the importance of developing a more politically erudite political geography by establishing closer links with political science and International Relations, and of developing behavioural approaches as a means to understanding the processes of political perception and decision-making which serve to determine the nature of change effected upon the environment. These concerns are, to my mind, still central to political geography, and if interest in behavioural geography has, to some extent, gone off the boil, the post-modern fascination with deconstruction and discourse has definite links to the tradition.

Such ideas, however, are a matter of personal opinion. One happy and liberating aspect of the political geography of today (rather than that of a generation ago) is that there is now much more scope for individual judgement, sensibility and intuition. Long gone are the days when geography was expected to masquerade as an objective, dehumanised science. Those were the times when one might have imagined that the subject had a single, objective existence, one which could be divined by the initiates and imposed upon their disciples: the times when a mega-guru, such as Richard Hartshorne, could define a depoliticised political geography and then arbitrate on what the subject was, and was not, could or could not be. If we have not yet reached a point when all can simply accept that 'political geography is what political geographers do' at least there is a far broader toleration of diversity. And this, surely, is a mark of the greater maturity and confidence abroad within the subject. It is certainly true that neo-Marxists or structuralists will argue for one emphasis within the study of political geography and humanists for another, while pluralists will have their viewpoints and positivists will always be able to discover aspects that genuinely merit quantitative analysis. The important factor is that the prescriptive aspect has largely vanished from the rhetoric: the subject is much more inclusive than it was.

Today, at least in the UK, the teaching of political geography is dominated by structuralist perspectives, reflecting the fact that the two most prominent practitioners have, in their different ways, adopted Marxist- or neo-Marxist-based approaches, R. J. Johnston advocating a political economy perspective and P. J. Taylor having developed world-systems analysis in a geographical context. Despite their prominence, they have not escaped criticism, and several authoritative writers have criticised the reductionism inherent in Taylor's world-systems approach and faulted Johnston's interpretation of Marxism/structuration theory (Smith 1994 and Painter 1995).

Different approaches have their different merits, and while not seeking to suggest that one perspective on political geography is better than another, here I have developed and employed – though not slavishly – a humanistic approach. Within geography generally there has been a cultural turn towards a greater toleration of diversity and the unpredictable, and a recognition that subjects as elusive as the spirit of place can still be of crucial importance. Writing in 1987, Brunn and Yanarella thought that 'the contributions of humanistic geography and humanistic political geographers are only beginning to emerge in contemporary thought and research' (ibid., p. 4). Indeed, so limited was the development of a humanistic approach to political geography at this stage that they were obliged to create their own definition, according to which HPG 'is concerned with uncovering the dynamic social processes whereby the spatial dimensions of the natural and social world are organized and reorganized into geographically delimited and symbolically meaningful provinces by national and transnational groups' (ibid., p. 8). Thus far, the definition seems quite conventional, but Brunn and Yanarella continue: 'Among its most important issues and themes would be the role of the state in creating landscapes that yield attachment to places (including symbols, images, etc.) and the place of different groupings in the recognition of meaning of territory in nation building and state formation' (ibid., p. 9). What emerges from this exploration is a very exciting, new, and vital political geography which embraces human consciousness, experiences and perceptions of place and politics, landscape, the elusive sense of place, territoriality and identification with politically organised spaces and groupings.

Active discussion about the place of political geography within the social sciences will continue. Some will argue that there is no independent political geography and that it simply exists to enhance our understanding of the much broader world of the social sciences. Others will prefer to regard the subject as a systematic branch of geography, comparable to the social, historical or economic branches. Most of the time such differences of outlook will not matter a jot. Meanwhile, the rising status of the subject is reflected in the publication of papers by workers in disciplines like political science and International Relations in geographical journals and by the invitations to geographers to contribute to political journals and collections.

Gone then are the days when it was assumed if unstated that geographical writing should be politically neutral and preferably apolitical – the discipline's (largely conservative) establishment being hostile to any potentially disruptive or controversial expression of political outlooks or moral beliefs: human sentiment should not intrude upon the study of humanity. During the last two or three decades these unrealistic constraints have largely been abandoned. This is much to be welcomed, for in a world riven by cultural conflicts and rivalries and threatened by ecological disruption geographers must be able to contribute fully and freely towards the salvation of the planet:

> Geographers have much to offer by way of more cross-cultural and historical evidence from mankind's experiences in sociality and ecology. Attuned to the emancipatory role which humanist thought has played historically, too, they could reiterate at least the essential message that human reason cannot function without hope. Gaia's human envelope, the *anthroposphere*, needs to be understood as a drama more complex than simply as battleground of ecological versus economic rationality, but rather as **oecumene**, potential home for mankind, a species which urgently needs to discover the art of dwelling. (Buttimer 1990, pp. 27–8)

Political geography has become much more perceptive and erudite in its treatment of the subtleties of local political attachments – the politics of place – and it has become more concerned with the politics of identity, notably citizenship, gender issues and the politics of race. In the past, a preoccupation with state and nation may have obscured the close relationships between people, groups and territories which existed within, and occasionally even across, the sovereign boundaries. Fundamental questions concerning the (possible) biological basis of human territoriality are still routinely side-stepped by political geographers, though there is recent interest in territoriality as a form of social and political control.

The political geography of the mid-1990s is far better than that of the mid-1970s in respect of all aspects but one: communication. When Mackinder expounded his ideas at the start of this century, every educated man or woman in the English speaking world could understand and evaluate what he was saying. A generation ago, it would just about have been possible for a diligent geography graduate with a few years to spare to have read and understood everything ever written on political geography in the English language. Today the literature is far vaster – and this is good. Unfortunately, however, much of it is written in language that is overspecialised, ambiguous, jargon-laden, tortuous and, indeed, deliberately made difficult. Since the most influential political geographers of today – like Johnston, Taylor and O'Loughlin – manage to publish their work in language that is crisp and lucid, there can be no credible reason why others should not do the same. Perhaps editors should be more persistent in their reminders that the purpose of publication is the communication of knowledge?

Finally, I am indebted to Graham Smith of the University of Cambridge for his comments upon my text; various of his suggestions were incorporated, and where I have failed to follow his advice I have only myself to blame.

Chapter 1

The Politics of Territory and Place

I have heard by antient persons that at first there was onely three rows of Seates in Myddle Church, and that the space beetweene the South Isle and the South wall was voyd Ground, onely there was a bench all along the South wall. And that afterward Bayliffe Downton built for himselfe a large wainscott peiw att the upper end of this voyd ground, and Thomas Niclas of Balderton Hall built another nexte to him, and after, all the rest was furnished with formes.

Richard Gough, *The History of Myddle* (c.1700)

Political geography is involved in studying human claims and conflicts concerning the use, partitioning and ownership of the land and its resources. Such disputes can occur at many different levels. They can involve neighbours squabbling over the proper positioning of posts holding up a garden fence; territorial claims between rival tribes or different national groups living within a single state; territorial disputes between adjacent states, or competitions for global influence between great power blocs. They can occur within as well as between societies – as when environmental and neighbourhood groups oppose tree-felling or road-building operations.

As the study of geography has evolved, we have grown to recognise that territory amounts to much more than a resource containing farmland, minerals or real estate, while place is more than a location on a map. The words 'setting', 'locality', 'locale', 'territory' and 'place' have been interpreted in different ways by geographers, but invariably there is a psychological and emotional relationship between people and the spaces within which they follow their day-to-day lives. Perhaps the most fundamental questions in geography are about place, while the most basic aspects of political geography concern the politics of place. As is often the case, however, it is the most basic question that is the hardest to answer. Geography, having taken place for granted for almost the first century of its academic existence, has recently struggled to develop a doctrine of place. Frequently, lucidity has been an early casualty in this encounter, but gradually an understanding of places and their political associations is beginning to emerge.

The rediscovery of place is closely linked to the decline of spatial analysis (which so often condemned geographers to engage in sterile attempts at 'scientific' enquiry) and to the emergence of a new, humanistic geography, which delights in exploring the unquantifiable – like the nature, origins and effects of the human sense of place. Currently, human geography may be divided into three groups of activity and outlook: the positivist, the humanistic and the structuralist (Johnston 1990, p. 447). Positivists are interested in 'scientific' laws and quantification and will have little time for things like the emotional associations of place. Humanistic geographers regard the interaction between places and the human spirit as central to geographical enquiry. Structuralists, who include the supporters of Marx and World-systems theory, are interested in the way that a consciousness of places, like working-class neighbourhoods, may emerge in the course of struggles between workers and capitalism or in the ways in which places, like streets of industrial housing, may be products of a capitalist system.

■ Human territoriality

The most fundamental question that we can ask about conflicts involving the ownership and control of space concerns the biological basis of human territoriality. We all know that territorial behaviour is common in the animal world, and are familiar with images like those of howler monkeys howling at strategic points around the borders of their troop territories or the cock robin singing loudly from twigs spaced at intervals around the limits of his nesting territory. Such behaviour amounts to much more than ritual or self-expression; it broadcasts the claim of exclusive territorial rights to potential competitors from the same species.

The ethologist, Eibl-Eibesfeldt (1979, p. 41), described territoriality as 'space-related intolerance', while to Kummer (1971, p. 223) it was 'a field of repulsion . . . fixed in space'. The former explained the geographical justification of territoriality: 'If an animal population is to prosper, it must be spaced out in a way that avoids overpopulation of any particular area. By their aggressive behavior, animals exert a certain pressure on their conspecifics, enforcing their distribution over a wider area' (Eibl-Eibesfeldt 1979, p. 40). Territorial conflicts are often stylised in ways that prevent serious injury to the contestants, while in some cases rituals substitute for physical contests of strength: 'Sea lions mark out a territory by making themselves as tall as possible on their boundaries and barking across to their neighbor. The latter responds in the same way. Neighbors generally respect each other's territory, and fighting is rare' (ibid., p. 41).

But are human beings territorial in any comparable ways? In other words, is there an instinctive urge to acquire territory and then to operate an exclusive control over it? And to what extent are our urges to control space based in biological drives rather than the practical, economic necessities of survival? The topic of territoriality has been studied in some depth by political geographers, notably by Jean Gottmann (1973). Subsequently, Robert Sack (1980) produced a more intricate treatment, yet side-stepped a quite fundamental question when deciding that: 'I shall skirt the issue of whether human territoriality is a biological drive or instinct' (Sack 1983, p. 55).

In the animal kingdom, territorial behaviour offers certain distinct advantages. It helps, for example, to adjust the breeding population of a species to the available food resources or 'carrying capacity' by ensuring that only those pairs which have established control over territory will reproduce. Also, where breeding territories are held by pairs rather than by groups of animals, mates are only attracted to males who have demonstrated an ability to establish and retain a breeding territory. This helps to ensure that only the more vigorous and dominant males are able to contribute to the gene pool. Here, though, we can note that extreme sexual dimorphism (differences in size between males and females) amongst our ancestors seems to have come to an end as our distant australopithecine ancestors gave way to our human forbears:

> Extensive body-size dimorphism, like that in baboons, is usually associated with intense competition among the males for access to females, and the males in the troop are usually genetically unrelated to one another. A reduction in body-size dimorphism . . . is usually associated with reduced competition among males for access to females, and the males are often genetically related. (Leakey and Lewin 1992, p. 163)

Opinions differ about the nature of human territorial behaviour. In 1967, the right-wing author, Robert Ardrey, published a popular book in which he argued that humankind was essentially aggressive and dominated by the urge to exert an exclusive control over space. In reality, his identification of human descent from a cannibalistic meat-eating ape, which was invoked to underpin his interpretation of human territoriality, has been shown to be flawed. The cave assemblages of bones and associated South African australopithecine remains have been found to bear indentations which correspond to the spacing of the

Box 1.1 *Human nature*

Human nature is not something that can be extracted and analysed by scientific methods. It is of fundamental importance to our understanding of the social sciences – and much more besides – and yet it cannot exactly be defined. Therefore, human nature has been the subject of much argument. One of the most basic topics for discussion concerns the 'nature versus nurture' debate, over whether human behaviour is determined by our innate genetic characteristics, or whether, instead, it is moulded by the processes of nurture and socialisation? Both must contribute, and today the serious debates are about their relative importance. There is no doubt that we are the genetic products of millions of years of evolution, and ethologists, such as Konrad Lorenz, can argue convincingly that aggression is programmed into the biological make-up of the human animal (Lorenz 1966). In the animal kingdom aggression is extremely common and is thought to evolve whenever a species needs a form of deterrent behaviour to secure access to a resource – such as territory, food, females or a nesting place – which is in short supply. It may often be used against members of the same species to establish a hierarchy of dominance giving precedence in access to such resources. Recently, developments in sociobiology have shown that there is a continuity from animal to human behaviour, and though our psychological make-up and social behaviour are extremely complex, aggression, often in subtle verbal forms, does play a significant part in our efforts to secure access to scarce facilities – like promotion or the best seat in a crowded space.

More extreme ideas have been advanced by sociobiologists, who have reinterpreted Darwin's ideas about natural selection at the level of the gene and have attempted to present all human behaviour, whether high-minded or selfish, as attempts to pass on the individual's genes to a new generation. The perpetuation of the 'selfish gene' is said to be more likely if it can be housed in a body that is well equipped for survival and in an individual that is selfish in his or her behaviour (Dawkins 1976). On the whole, the advocates of right-wing political philosophies seem to expect to gain support for their advocacy of authoritarian controls if they can present human nature as being brutal, devoid of virtue and rooted in dark, biological drives, while socialists favour more optimistic interpretations which emphasise the plasticity of human nature. In this way, left-wingers tend to think that improvements to society will produce reciprocal improvements in its members. A different view again was expressed by the philosopher Jean-Paul Sartre (1905–80), who believed that each member of humanity enjoys the freedom of self-definition through his or her actions. In this way our day-to-day actions and decisions make up our identity; we exist first and define ourselves afterwards. Therefore, any claims that an inbuilt human nature exists would amount to an assault on that freedom.

canine teeth of leopards rather than scars caused by a (sub)human agency. Thus, the explanation for Ardrey's ideas may be found more in his political inclinations than in his evidence. More recent interpretations of the lifestyles of some hominids of the African plains suggest a phase of existence as opportunistic scavengers who picked over prey which had been killed and abandoned by large carnivores.

It is difficult to resist the belief that our biological make-up has a significant part to play in our attitudes towards personal space, property and homeland. At the same time, it would be wrong to draw simple analogies from the animal kingdom: the causes of our behaviour can not be related directly to the gannet which stabs its bill at other members of the colony which encroach on its nesting ledge or with the stags locking antlers in the glen. Our territoriality is heavily conditioned by cultural norms and by other factors of scale and place which make it unrealistic to generalise without reference to society and space. For example, most members of western societies seem to cherish bubbles of personal space, while in many Third World societies travellers on public transport seem to jostle together without regard for such cares. If this is the case, the difference cannot be attributed to biological causes and must be due either to cultural factors or to practicalities. Territoriality operating at different levels will be reflected in the street gang which leaves aerosol signals of territorial control on strategic landmarks and border markers around the urban landscape; in the people who campaign for the resurrection of the English county of Rutland or any other regional object of affection, or in national(ist) campaigns to resist the advance of some supranational authority.

To some commentators, territoriality belongs more in the realm of practicality than psychology. According to David M. Smith (1990, p. 3), for example: 'Territoriality is . . . not some innate human trait but a social construct . . . Territoriality and its various expressions must be recognised as means to some end, such as material survival, political control or xenophobia.' He believes that territoriality is more subtle than the assertion of a 'territorial imperative' analagous to those of the animal kingdom. He thinks that humans establish an identity with pieces of geographical space and acquire senses of place which are comparable with the deepest emotional ties and feelings and which operate on different scales – from that of the home and garden through that of the town football ground or significant scenic feature to that of the much-loved region or nation. But he points out that while territory is a source of human identity it is also a source of material existence over which exclusive claims are made. (I imagine, therefore, that to a white in the Old South of the USA the territorial associations of 'Dixie' were geographical; linked to a particular culture period and folk heritage; associated with a particular economy which sustained the social order, and also bound to an ideology of ownership embracing slavery and institutionalised inequality.)

A given place will not inspire the same emotions in different people; the Old South that was loved by the property-owning white was held in a different regard by his slaves, and probably by the poor whites as well. A measure of gentrification may cause a district that had been regarded as a 'bad address' to become 'desirable' in some estimations – and the more that the middle classes colonise it as a consequence then the more that middle class people will regard it as desirable. Thus the perceptions of place can be transformed while the place, in its physical essentials, remains the same. Also,

> there is much that is negative as well as positive here. The denigration of others' places provides a way to assert the viability and incipient power of one's own place. The fierce contest over images and counter-images of places is an arena in which the cultural politics of places, the political economy of their development, and the accumulation of a sense of social power in place frequently fuse in indistinguishable ways. (Harvey 1993, p. 23)

The denigration of others rather than of their places can play a very important part in development of political life, as reflected in Agnew's (1995, p. 169) study of the Italian Northern League and the rhetoric of regionalism: 'two populist ("common sense from ordinary folk") themes serve to anchor the League's localist support in the North (i) opposition to foreign immigration and (ii) the association of the South and southerners with *partitocrazia* [party-based political economy] and organized criminality.'

The combination of 'Us and Them' perspectives and territoriality can have violent consequences:

> In a context where the control of space is of crucial importance for the security it offers and the opportunities it provides, violence becomes a deliberate tool of social engineering. It is used, as in the case of North Belfast, both to defend space against invasion and to gain new territory; it is a means of ensuring social homogeneity. There have been examples in Belfast of orchestrated cycles of territorial violence which begin with group *A* forcing members of group *B* out of one area. These in turn made room for their co-religionists forcing members of group *A* out of another area; this cycle, in one form or another, has persisted for years. (Murray and Boal 1979)

Peter Slowe (1990, p. 17) reviewed the psychological and philosophical background to human assertion and aggression, but concluded that:

'All this was to ignore the fact that the causes of aggression were not so much to be found within individuals as within groups, especially when any of those groups considered itself to be a nation, a race or a state.' Turning to territory, he rejected questions of the biological basis of territoriality as being sterile, and pointed out that the analogy between animal territories and human property was unhelpful: animal territories were not associated with abstract rights of possession, sale and exchange or of ownership without occupation (but see pages 182–3). There was, too, another very important reason why the biological analogy could never work: the (hu)man–land relationship was a two-way process with people not only feeling that they owned some piece of land, but also that they belong to the land:

> They feel a sense of attachment which goes beyond the one-way idea of ownership . . . It is this sense of attachment which motivates otherwise tranquil people to fight to defend or to recover land either which they consider their own or to which they feel they belong; they will fight for land and covet it, they will yearn for land and die for it. (ibid., p. 53)

He thought that a better understanding of the strength of the human attachment to land might be gained by studying the theories of Jean Piaget on the intellectual development of children (Piaget and Inhelder 1956). Piaget emphasised the child's need to feel secure within its setting. He thought that the powerful mental links between the individual and the familiar environment persisted throughout life, with the strong emotional overtones in environmental perception always remaining. During the first two years of life, the objective and subjective worlds are mixed up, so that the child projects its emotions on to its surroundings: places and objects may accordingly be judged to be friendly or threatening. Thinking of all the things in the setting only in terms of their relationship to him/her, the child develops strong feelings about his/her surroundings in terms of territorial safety and territorial threats, closeness and separation. And so at an early stage in life we develop powerful emotions about our environments, even though the character of these feelings may originate in ourselves rather than in the setting. There are grounds for thinking that questions of security still play a fundamental role in our appraisals of place: a nationwide survey carried out in the UK in 1995 found that seven in ten people throughout the country considered that living in a safe neighbourhood was the main priority for quality of life (Mintel).

All attempts to relate human behaviour to biological drives must aim to be specific. As we have seen, there is not only disagreement concerning whether or not human beings share some kind of 'territorial imperative' with certain members of the animal kingdom, but also confusion concerning the nature of such drives. For example, the householder who behaves implacably in pursuing some petty territorial boundary dispute with a neighbour is unlikely to be governed by quite the same 'instinctive urges' as those which may underlie the ghastly scenes of genocide and 'ethnic cleansing' which currently disfigure Bosnia. In developing an understanding of feelings and behaviour of this intensity, perhaps more attention should be paid to the significance of mutual fear rather than to those of other biological drives, such as territoriality?

Probably the most widely used definition of human territoriality in circulation today is that provided by Sack (1986, p. 19), who identified it as being an 'attempt by an individual or group to affect, influence or control people, phenomena and relationships by delimiting and asserting control over a geographical area'. This definition recognises the importance of establishing control over the territory, although it fails directly to mention the importance that human societies attach to claims which serve to legitimise this control. Such claims may be based on tradition or on international law but they have existed since long before the codification of law. In the UK, for example, the collective tombs of the Neolithic era were frequently placed not on the highest ground of all or on the real topographical crest-lines or watersheds, but where they would be seen silhouetted darkly against the skyline by travellers walking the tracks below. Quite probably they establish claims to land by demonstrating that generations of ancestors have lived, died and been interred in the collective territory, and perhaps too by implying that the spirits of the dead were watching over their homeland (Taylor and Muir 1983, p. 99).

Clearly, the establishment of control over a geographical area offers distinct practical advantages, and may mean a difference between survival and starvation or independence and slavery. But it is no less plain that the human association with land involves much more than economic and political considerations. It has powerful *emotional* and *psychological* associations. When, as during the 1914–18 War, men march off to face the likelihood of extreme suffering and death they are not motivated by simple economic self-interests: much deeper currents of the mind are guiding them. Land may offer livelihood, but it also embodies emotive and less tangible factors, like a sense of place. Writers such as Cosgrove and Daniels (1988) and others such as Duncan and Duncan (1988) have developed landscape studies in the context of contemporary humanistic geography, exploring the symbolism or 'iconography' associated with landscape and revealing landscape and its associated sense of place as important components in the cultural, social and political systems of the countries concerned.

Territorial identification can also be an important strand in the process whereby people develop their sense of self. It enhances the perception of self by contributing to an awareness of one's own individuality, to some extent achieving this by imparting a sense of 'having roots'. In many a tired, drab and seemingly anonymous industrial town in the UK support for the town's football team, being a 'regular' at one of its pubs, and following the familiar route from home to workplace and back again furnish an awareness of belonging which may be territorial in its intensity. Particularly important is the football team, since support for the town's team provides a powerful sense of 'us-ness' which would scarcely exist could it not be counterposed to the 'thems' constituted by the rival teams and their fans. As Featherstone (1993) explains:

> the 'we-images' and 'they-images', which are generated within local struggles to form an identity and exclude outsiders, cannot be detached from the density of the web of interdependencies between people. Such struggles between established and outsider groups . . . will therefore become more common with the extent of contact with others, which bring groups of outsiders more frequently into the province of local establishments.

Returning more specifically to football, it is worth noting that support for a major team can be particularly effective in the process of bonding to place for it satisfies any cravings for ritual and symbols; each community of supporters has its own tribal anthology of chants and each team has its own colours and livery – even if now these change with an unbecoming frequency according to the dictates of the marketing interests. These identifications with place may be of increasing psychological value when seen in the context of one kind of developing global culture which may seem increasingly transient, standardised, footloose, insecure, depersonalised and insubstantial.

Territorial identification need not be an exclusive phenomenon. There will, for example, be many who regard themselves as being simultaneously Dalesmen or Daleswomen, Yorkshire folk and English and/or British. Similarly, there are loyal and committed Bavarians who have a well-developed sense of belonging to Germany, while other Bavarians might feel a stronger identification as Europeans. Taylor found a strange type of ambiguity associated with the English identity and he described the two 'territories' of Upper England and Greater England which represent a single, Anglo-British identity which should be regarded as a 'fused territoriality operating at two geographical scales' (Taylor 1991, p. 150). Upper England represents the cluster of counties around the capital known as the Home Counties: 'Other countries have "homelands" or "fatherlands" that encompass their whole territory. For the Anglo-British "Home" denotes only a few counties in one corner of the country' (ibid.). 'Greater England' has a much more expansive orientation: 'a military dimension represented by empire and an economic one represented by hegemony. Both have been promoted by the government in the 1980s as part of its anti-decline movement . . . Deindustrialisation has continued apace and the government has been re-elected twice. Such is deformed nationalism' (ibid., p. 156).

Sometimes, territorial identification may act like fibres running through the national community to strengthen its qualities of coherence, and as Fawcett (1919, p. 151) wrote: 'the man or woman who has no love for and pride in his or her home region is not thereby qualified for wider views of life. Provincialism is in itself a good thing, and a necessary factor in the well being of humanity'. In other cases, however, strongly developed territorial identifications with a particular homeland may threaten the integrity of the state, as with provincial loyalties in Spain. The state is not threatened when it is obliged to *share* loyalties with a province or cultural area, but it is endangered when the loyalties of an incorporated cultural community are *monopolised* by such a province. The violent Russian invasion of Chechenia in 1994–5 followed an attempted secession by Chechen people who apparently felt no bonds of friendship or identification with the Russian state. Nor is it unusual for members of a disaffected minority nation to become involved in criminal activities, notably drugs trafficking, which endanger members of the majority and other nations. Members of the Chechens, Kurds, Tamils and Ibos of Nigeria have all displayed a disproportional involvement in international crime.

The relationship between territoriality and national identity is important and multifaceted, for the emergence of a sense of nationhood has had great effects upon the perception of territory. Under the feudal state, land could be exchanged between states as a consequence of war or marriage. But when the state territory became the national homeland the bond between land and community became indissoluble: 'We can see this changing meaning of territory in the 1793 French constitution which debarred the state from ever making peace with a foreign power that occupied any part of French territory . . . In short it became the state's duty to defend the national homeland' (Taylor 1994, p. 155).

Whether operating at the local, the provincial or the national level, territorial identification is associated with unique assemblages of symbols which exert an almost mystical influence over their devotees. The red football shirts of Liverpool or Arsenal football clubs express a form of tribalism operating at a local or regional level; the azure of Italy or the dark blue shirts of Scotland reflect tribe-like associations at the national level. Similarly, emblems, anthems, folk songs and group mythology can be just as potent as components of the process of bonding with place and space as can national topographical symbols, such as Mount Rushmore, the white cliffs of Dover or Mount Fuji. The symbolic associations of place can be many, varied and potent, but the power of place is vested in places by humans and to think otherwise would be 'to engage in the grossest of fetishisms' (Harvey 1993, p. 21). Harvey points out how the creation of symbolic places is not given in the stars but is something that is

> painstakingly nurtured and fought over, precisely because of the hold that place can have over the imagination . . . The places where martyrs fell . . . have long gripped the imagination of working-class movements. Yet no amount of formal monument construction (the extraordinary monumental palace that Ceausescu had constructed in Bucharest, for example) can make a hated dictator beloved. (ibid., p. 23)

Rokkan and Urwin (1983) have explored the links between identity or self-awareness and what they term the 'lore of the land'. They claim that identity can be broken down into at least four component parts. These are:

1. **myth**, comprising a set of beliefs, of which the most notable are religion and nationalism;
2. **symbol**, representing the enduring expressive aspect of culture which is handed down from generation to generation, with language as the supreme expressive component of identity;
3. **history**, which in this context need not be factually accurate, but which involves a lore of the land incorporating the key emotive events in the past of the culture concerned;
4. **institutional factors**, involving those agencies, like the Académie Française or many educational institutions, which help to advance aspects of language and culture and therefore serve to strengthen the sense of identity.

Lore of the land is presented as focusing upon objects of interest which can range from the commemoration of fateful and symbolic past events – like the storming of the Bastille or the Battle of the Boyne – through ceremonial events, such as national saints' days or the

Box 1.2 *Gottmann's theories of territoriality*

'When he was a six-year-old orphan in exile in Paris from the Russian Revolution, Jean Gottman travelled with his Jewish grandfather to the Crimea as guest of the Muslim Khan of the Tartars. Later, he recalled this experience of cross-religious, cross-ethnic ties with joy. It must have been a factor in his emergence as a leading academic in political geography' (Mojtahed-Zadeh 1994). In his studies of territoriality, Gottmann described how human communities are simultaneously involved in the sharing and the partitioning of territory (Gottmann 1973). Cultural communities are obliged to make decisions about the proper extent of their communal territories, and about which sub-groups qualify for inclusion and which must be excluded. Occasionally, contests for the control of territory which may seem to be at worst quiescent and at best redundant may quite suddenly erupt into violent confrontation – as exemplified by the recent war between the Serbs, Croats and Muslims of Bosnia.

Gottmann also explored the significance of symbols, such as history, legend, literature and social habits to the construction and destruction of states. These historical beliefs, attitudes and ways of doing things which are embedded in the 'spirit' of a nation combine to form an 'iconography' of symbols and constitute a conservative system of attitudes which are resistant to change. A counter force is represented by what Gottmann termed 'circulation', which embodies movements and contacts between groups and across space, leading to the exchange and diffusion of ideas. Rather than revering the past, circulation exalts in change and continually threatens to destabilise established relationships (Gottmann 1952). He believed that there was some form of iconography which provided a foundation for regionalism, which de Blij (1967, p. 140) interpreted in the following way: 'Each political region cherishes some symbol, certain values. In no two of the many political compartments of the earth are these symbols and values exactly the same, and everywhere they are complex in nature, made of many interwoven patterns. It is the political geographer's task to identify as many of the strands and patterns as possible.' Earlier, in a manner which recalled the organicism of the primitive studies in political geography, Gottmann (1951) had mused on the distinctive spirits which each nation was supposed to embody – spirits composed of both environmental and historical components – while, 'boundaries exist because each country feels it is different from the other'.

Declaration of Independence, to aspects of socialisation, like the learning of history from official history books or participation in folk singing/dancing and the wearing of national costume.

In situations such as those explored by Rokkan and Urwin, the lore of the land has strong political associations concerning the process of bonding between distinctive cultural groups and their geographical and historical settings. But sense of place can be a powerful influence even when divorced from factors of culture and nationality. In the United

Kingdom, the county of Rutland was abolished in the 1970s; it seemed to be an anachronism which represented all that was worst in an outmoded system of administrative areas which were too small efficiently to perform the tasks of modern local government. Yet Rutland had somehow imbued its people with a strong sense of place, and this underpinned a dogged campaign to resurrect the old county. In 1994, two decades after its demise, Rutland was recreated.

■ Politics and place

Just as 'place' has recently commanded a great deal of attention in the geographical world in general, so the 'politics of place' are central to advancement in political geography. Nevertheless, the geographical literature on place is often impenetrable, ambiguous and confusing. The reasons for the geographical fascination with place are obvious – but it is often the obvious which is the hardest to convey. A part of the problem derives from the fact that geographers are attempting to ascribe precise technical meanings to place-related terms that are in simultaneously in common usage. As Harvey (1993, p. 4) explains:

> There are all sorts of words such as milieu, locality, location, locale, neighbourhood, region, territory and the like, which refer to the generic qualities of place. There are other terms such as city, village, town, megalopolis and state, which designate particular kinds of places. There are still others, such as home, hearth, 'turf', community, nation and landscape, which have such strong connotations of place that it would be hard to talk about one without the other.

One of the most incisive explanations of the significance of place was provided by the book reviewer for *Sociology* who pointed out that three distinct but not exclusive claims seem to be involved:

> firstly, that it matters that places are different from each other, i.e. social processes will be significantly different in different places; secondly, that it matters that social life takes place in relatively circumscribed spatial contexts and that distance imposes costs; thirdly, that people have ideas about place which have significant social consequences. (Buck 1990, p. 555)

Though written for a sociological audience, these statements should be quite acceptable to most geographers – and the fact that they are symbolises a shift in geographical thinking. This is a shift away from the quest to understand places in themselves and towards the desire to understand the way that they are moulded by social forces and in turn shape human culture. The change in emphasis reflects the fact that place has been the major focus of attention of humanistic geography in recent years.

The point about place being a product of human agency can be illustrated with regard to the brutish ritual of fox hunting and its effects on landscapes in the East Midlands of England (Williamson and Bellamy 1987). The ritual developed during the eighteenth century, yet if the pattern of property ownership in England had resembled that of France, with the countryside being divided between a multitude of freeholders, then it could never have flourished. In England, however, there were plenty of large, aristocratic estates, often standing side-by-side and almost invariably owned by people with ideologies sympathetic to upper-class hunting rituals. This allowed the fox to be hunted from estate to estate across extensive areas of rural land.

Box 1.3 *Culture*

Culture can be regarded as the 'social heritage' of a community. This heritage would embrace not only all the community's material goods and creations, but also its mental and spiritual artefacts, like ideas, values, beliefs and preferences. Culture is not innate, but is acquired as the individual develops within the cultural community. Therefore, it represents the influence of nurture over nature. The concept of culture not only has different emphases in the worlds of anthropology, archaeology and sociology, but can be controversial within a field of study.

In geography, the concept of the culture area – an area occupied by a single or similar cultures – was developed at the end of the nineteenth century by the German geographer, Friedrich Ratzel, who believed that every nation evolved as a symbiotic association of people and land. Ratzel's notion of the *Kulturprovinz* was developed to highlight the political claim that the German cultural area extended far beyond the boundaries of the German state. These ideas were then explored by the anthropologist, A. L. Kroeber, who demonstrated that the Great Plains formed a coherent geographical region characterised by the material, social and economic culture of the Plains Indians. Kroeber's work in turn influenced the great American cultural geographer, Carl O. Sauer, whose ecological approach to culture stressed the influences of environment and history on culture (Sauer 1952).

Recently, traditional geographical ideas about culture have been criticised on the grounds that by emphasising the uniformity of culture we are complying in the process whereby a culturally dominant group may impose its influence on sub-groups within that society. Emphasis is being placed upon cultural politics, involving the ways in which different cultural strands compete for recognition and influence. There is also a growing interest in the aspects of culture which help to provide a nation with its national identity.

Subsequently, jumping became a more important part of the ritual when Parliamentary Enclosure introduced networks of hedgerows into areas of previously open countryside. In due course fox hunting imposed changes on places, and in the nineteenth century countless small patches of trees and gorse (thorn) were planted to provide cover for foxes; later these fox covers were colonised by rabbits so that they furnished cheap protein for the poor rather than 'sport' for the wealthy. This example shows that, rather than the environment determining patterns of human behaviour, the evolution of place involves complicated processes of human agency, social development and historical accident.

Among the prominent geographers of recent times, both R. J. Johnston (1991) and J. A. Agnew (1987) have advocated the study of place, which they regard as being fundamental to any understanding of political geography, and Johnston recommends a refocusing of human geography upon place. However, place, as it is explored in modern geography, is much more emotive, complex and elusive than a simple intersection of coordinates on the map. As interpreted by Agnew, it has three major elements. These are:

1. **Locale**, which encompasses the settings within which social relations take place.
2. **Location**, which he interprets as being the geographical area which encompasses the settings within which the broader interactions between members of society take place.
3. **Sense of place**, which concerns the local structure of feeling and which involves nodes, like home, work, school and church, around which human activities circulate. The associations so formed combine to create the sense of place, which embodies both geographical and social dimensions.

In Agnew's formulation, place 'refers to discrete if "elastic" areas in which settings for the constitution of social relations are located and with which people can identify' (Agnew 1987, p. 28). He thought that the sense of place need not be confined to the scale of the locality, but could be projected on to the region or the nation to give rise to regionalism or nationalism. These ideas he summarised as follows: 'locale is the core geosociological element in place, but it is structured by the pressures of location and gives rise to its own sense of place that may in certain circumstances extend beyond the locality' (ibid.).

Although ambiguity about the terminology of place persists, more accessible definitions have been offered; Dickens (1990, p. 3) decided that the concept of locality was linking 'the ways in which people interact with one another, with the physical environment and how they articulate their experiences'. Giddens (1984, p. 375) conceived a 'locale' as a geographical area having 'definite boundaries which help to concentrate interactions in one way or another'. According to Berner and Korff (1995, p. 214) a locality is: 'the focus of everyday life; it is not merely the place where people reside but where they spend much of their life, their *Lebenswelt* (life-world)'. They also point out that evidence from their studies of Manila slums show that locality and community cannot be regarded as being one and the same: people felt loyal to their relatives and townsfolk from the home province rather than to their neighbours. Murdoch and Marsden (1995, p. 377) studied the spatialisation of politics and, like Dickens and like Giddens, they conceived localities in terms of networks and contacts: 'Drawing upon the localities literature, we adopted a view of the locality as a space which is constituted by a variety of different associations or networks of relations operating across varied scales and distances.' In exploring episodes of local environmental conflict they studied how actors are drawn into associations imposed from afar – for example, by government policies – and how the analysis of power becomes the study of associations: 'Society, structure and power are outcomes as actors are associated. Those who are powerful are not those who "hold" power but those who are able to enrol, convince and enlist others into associations on terms which allow these initial actors to "represent" all the others' (ibid., p. 372).

Agnew (1987) claims that Western thinking has been dominated by a 'modernisation' theory of social change. He believes that this has resulted in attitudes which regard place as being significant in traditional societies while holding that the process of becoming modern involves outgrowing the old associations with place and adopting an achievement-orientated and class-conscious self that is place-less. He also identifies a tendency to regard the modern nation-state as being 'natural', and believes that this is expressed in a 'state-centered' bias in the social sciences. He goes on to underline the importance of place and geography in the political arena and to point out the weakness of modernisation concepts and state-centred outlooks. It had been assumed that modernisation involved a 'nationalisation' process, whereby, as the state experiences industrialisation and urbanisation, so citizens are mobilised into a national political community, with the nation state commanding more and more attention and becoming ever more closely integrated, while the attachments to place, home and region are progressively diluted.

Since the late 1960s, the tendency to perceive a nationalisation of political life has been progressively undermined by events, as described in the chapters which follow. Regionalist and separatist movements and parties have arisen in many parts of Western Europe and in Canada, while election results have revealed the strong influence of place-specific influences. Thus, while interest in national political institutions may have become moribund or tainted by disillusionment, there has been a reinvigoration of the politics of place. Meanwhile, the great majority of people have continued to act out their lives within a familiar locality and to be profoundly affected by its geographical and social characteristics.

In these familiar localities, and over the course of time, people may develop a sense of identity; they will establish networks of friends and will acquire those aspects of culture which enable them to form opinions and judgements about other people and places beyond the locality. In the (post)modern world, in which the national and global media bombard us with a collage of images (in the way that TV news programmes present a rapidly changing pastiche of stories from different parts of the world), our identities tend to be constructed from experiences both of local events encountered in the course of day-to-day life and distant events intruded into our consciousnesses by the mass media (Giddens 1991).

To the sociologists Cuba and Hummon (1993, p. 112), place identity is an interpretation of self that employs environmental meaning to symbolise or situate identity:

> Like other forms of identity, place identity answers the question – Who am I? – by countering – Where am I? or Where do I belong? From a social psychological perspective, place identities are thought to arise because places, as bounded locales imbued with personal, social, and cultural meanings, provide a significant framework in which identity is constructed, maintained and transformed.

It is plain that place and space have important cultural connections, while places also have their political associations, as witnessed by the multitude of local conflicts concerning communities divided between members who wish to preserve particular places and those who seek or support changes to the geographical status quo. Arguing in favour of a symbolic notion of space, Aase (1994) invokes the case of the Gulf War of 1991. Westerners found it hard to understand the distress and anger in the Muslim world which was caused by the US and European attacks on Iraq following the expiration of the deadline for the withdrawal of Iraqi forces from Kuwait. After all, Iraq had been the aggressor and Saddam Hussein had already been implicated in a campaign of genocide against his own Kurdish subjects. However, as well as sharing

Box 1.4 *David Harvey and time–space compression*

According to Harvey (1989), the dimensions of time and space are not fixed. Capitalism has been characterised by a great speeding-up in the pace of life, while at the same time global barriers to communication are progressively broken down so that the world may seem to be collapsing in on one. As familiar patterns and places are transformed by the process of time–space compression, individuals may begin to perceive the world as a threatening, turbulent place. Elsewhere (pp. 9–10) he quotes the philosopher, Heidegger, to emphasise the sense of terror that the elimination of spatial barriers can cause: 'All distances in time and space are shrinking . . . Yet the frantic abolition of all distances brings no nearness; for nearness does not consist in shortness of distance . . . Everything gets lumped together into uniform distancelessness . . . What is it that unsettles and thus terrifies? It shows itself and hides itself in the way in which everything presences, namely, in the fact that despite all conquest of distances the nearness of things remains absent' (Heidegger 1971, p. 165).

The interpretations of place developed by Heidegger and Harvey are not universally accepted. Massey (1993, p. 63) points out that: 'Those writers who interpret the current phase of time–space compression as primarily generating insecurity also frequently go on to argue that, in the middle of all this flux, one desperately needs a bit of peace and quiet: and "place" is posed as a source of stability and an unproblematic identity.' She argues that such an interpretation could lead to a characterisation of place and the spatially local as being reactionary and she advocates a progressive sense of place that would link a place to other places beyond it: 'It is a sense of place, an understanding of "its character", which can only be constructed by linking that place to places beyond' (ibid., p. 68). She also muses as to whether the current characterisation of time–space compression represents a Western coloniser's view: 'The sense of dislocation which so many writers on the subject apparently feel at the sight of a once well-known local street now lined with a succession of cultural imports – the pizzeria, the kebab house, the branch of a Middle-Eastern bank – must have been felt for centuries, though from a very different point of view, by colonized peoples all over the world as they watched the importation of . . . the products of, first European colonization . . . later US products' (ibid., p. 59). Time–space compression is not an entirely new phenomenon, it must have been encountered as railways were introduced in Europe and the USA, but Harvey argues that today's postmodernism is a product of the heightened intensity of a new round of time–space compression.

The British sociologist, Anthony Giddens (1990), takes a more optimistic view of change as it is represented by the new information technology. He believes that telecommunications can transform time and space relationships in a way that will not lead to the demoralisation of people. Rather than being rendered powerless, they are able to exploit new possibilities, like participation in a form of politics which is not constrained by ethnic or national identities. Social relationships can be reorganised in large-space and short-time dimensions: the 'disembedding' of the local. He believes that we are not yet in a postmodern world, but in transition from the world which contains the information technology means of transformation to one in which we have the language, political institutions and objectives which are necessary for us to realise the potential of the technology.

the Western perception that the borders of nation states should be respected, people in the Middle East also construct space according to other principles. Important amongst these is the notion of *al-Ummah*: the Muslim community. The *Ummah* or place where Muslims live runs from Morocco and Mauretania to Malaysia and Indonesia. In violating the *Ummah* border, the combined American–European operation had, to some Muslims, caused greater offence than Saddam's invasion of Kuwait. Another discrepancy in symbolic space between the West and the Muslim world is represented by the Salman Rushdie affair, this author of the *Satanic Verses* having, in some Muslim eyes, committed a treason against the *Ummah* in the sense that by disclosing unaccepted topics Rushdie had betrayed the *Ummah* to its enemies.

The sense of place spans psychology, geography, sociology and human territoriality. It is not easily disected or defined, but it can exert powerful influences over human behaviour. Many of those who have marched away to lose their lives on the battlefield have been driven by a compelling infatuation with places and with the symbols associated with place. Such infatuations cannot simply be identified with a patriotic love of country. Some of those who marched will have despised the establishment and institutions of their country, yet loved their provinces, intimate homelands or personal settings.

Places exist at different scales and at the macro scale in the politics of place we encounter the political region. Political regions may be formally defined areas, like nation-states or administrative districts, or they may exist on the basis of cultural, historical or functional associations. In all cases, it is important to see them not only as 'handy containers that frame social interactions, but as sources of cultural identity and thus as part of the real world of social actors' (Entrikin 1994, p. 229) The political region must have some unifying political characteristic(s) to impart a political identity, in the way that the distribution of largely Muslim populations defines the *Ummah*. It might be the homeland of a dissident minority, in which case its identity should be sharply defined. Or its recognition could depend upon the application of expertise of an intuitive or positivist kind, like the political regions proposed by Cohen (1990) and by Russett (1967). While political issues and activities can 'fill' areas of different sizes and while the terms 'locality', 'region' and 'state' imply territorial units of ascending magnitude, it is often better to think in terms of spillovers between areas existing at different scales than in terms of barrier-like boundaries. Thus, in his study of the Northern League in Italian politics Agnew (1995) found that the movement shifted its rhetoric from regional separatism to national populism as its strength in the north increased while the established parties of government collapsed and as the League became involved in national politics and developed national ambitions.

The work on the politics of place overlaps with case studies in environmental politics and investigations of decision-making in a number of recent studies of local conflicts, many involving neighbourhoods which are mobilised and politicised in opposition to developers. In some of these, investigators, adopting Marxist or neo-Marxist stances, believe that place emerges through social struggle, as when a local community of workers struggles with capital (perhaps represented by a development initiative) to control the destiny of a neighbourhood. Merrifield (1993) explored such a struggle involving the working-class residents of a neighbourhood on the Baltimore waterfront, some land developers and the city government over the future of a derelict can manufacturing site. He found that neighbourhood identifications were deepened as residents became politically involved in the contest to dominate territory. Place-related political studies are not confined to the Western industrial world and Armitage (1992) investigated how the indigenous Innu people of eastern Quebec and Labrador campaigned with some success to block a military flight programme in the airspace above their homeland.

In one of the most imaginitive and lucid of the place-based studies, Berner and Korff (1995) explored how globalisation, which homogenises portions of global cities, also fosters the development of individual localities. As space is created for the affluent, high income groups in global society there is a much more differentiated use of urban land, with extensive speculation and sky-rocketing prices. The restructuring of the city leads to great movements of population; as their neighbourhoods are demolished and employment opportunities are relocated, people are forced to become more mobile. The city becomes increasingly polarised between the consumers and providers of low-cost services, while fewer and fewer citizens are able to meet the rising costs of land. Slums become an integral part of the metropolis. The city becomes less and less like a cultural melting pot as populations react to the polarisation of urban life by turning more and more to religious fundamentalism, ethnicity, nationalism and other particularist orientations. As the authors explain:

> Our basic hypothesis is, then, that present metropolises are characterized by conflicts between globalization and localization. Localization is the search for a local identity and the creation of localities as foci of everyday life. Although apparently contradictory processes, localization and globalization are closely connected: through globalization itself local diversity is created. (Berner and Korff 1995, pp. 211–12)

In the great cities of the world, globalisation can lead to a monotonous standardisation: 'Through globalization, urban traditions and symbols have been reduced to mere decor, and the economic production of urban space has given rise to uniform centres and dreary residential quarters' (ibid., p. 220). Meanwhile, however, the closely knit social networks developing in the slums form the bases of local organisations which can articulate and pursue the demands of their members. Consequently, the defence and preservation of localities allow difference and diversity to flourish in the city and to counteract the pressures to conform to the global norm. This work recalls Gottmann's concepts of iconography and circulation, but one cannot equate globalisation directly with circulation or iconography with locality, for Gottmann's circulation had overtones of extrovert progress, while the localities which Berner and Korff describe are dynamic and evolving rather than being conservative in the manner of iconography. Even so, the analogy is too interesting to resist.

■ *Chapter 2* ■

Society and Space, Nation and State

With equal pleasure I have as often taken notice, that Providence has been pleased to give this one connected country to one united people – *a people descended from the same ancestors, speaking the same language, professing the same religion*, attached to the same principles of government, very similar in their manners and customs . . .

This country and this people seem to have been made for each other, *and it appears as if it was the design of Providence, that an inheritance so proper and convenient for a band of brethren, united to each other by the strongest ties*, should never be split into a number of unsocial jealous, and alien sovereignties.

John Jay, appealing for popular support for the union of American states, *Federalist Papers*, no. 2, 1787

Within five years of achieving its liberty, every oppressed nationality takes to militarism and within two or three generations, and sometimes within a single generation, it becomes – if circumstances are propitious – an imperialist aggressor eager to inflict upon its neighbours the oppression which it was itself so recently a victim.

Aldous Huxley, *Themes and Variations*, 1950

It has been argued that the course of political evolution is to some degree pre-ordained. Such an assumption underlay the former practice in political anthropology of making a fundamental distinction between centralised or 'state' societies, loosely regarded as being modern, and uncentralised or 'stateless' societies, which appeared to be 'primitive'. Subsequently, such a distinction came to be regarded as unhelpful to an understanding of the dynamic and varied nature of political life. So during the 1950s, attention was focused more on the operation of power within societies and on the ways in which individuals and groups employed various strategies in order to gain power. While not seeking to enter into the debate, it is plain that distinctions can be made between small-scale traditional societies, such as survive in some of the less accessible and less developed (or exploited) parts of the world, and those modernised societies which occupy the nation-states of the Western world. Whether or not there is an inevitability about political evolution from small-scale society to nation-state society, one can say that while some societies have evolved to nation-statehood and others have consciously striven to achieve it, others still have had statehood thrust upon them as a consequence of colonial intervention and enforced contacts with the wider world. In this chapter we explore the complex and controversial ways in which broadening political outlooks and expanding territorial control can be interrelated parts of the broad pattern of social evolution.

■ Territoriality and social evolution

The nature of human territorial behaviour and the emotional reaction to place have plainly evolved over time. The human relationship with territory is not one that is fixed; instead, it changes as society progresses from one level of organisation to the next. Robert Sack has described the ways that different societies have different conceptions of space. He points out that social organisations are often territorial, and he describes their territoriality as 'the assertion by an organisation, or an individual in the name of the organisation, that an area of geographic space is under its influence or control' (Sack 1980, p. 167). He believes that there are two fundamental ways in which the conception of space by 'primitive' societies differs from that of civilised societies (Sack rightly uses 'primitive' in a non-pejorative sense). The first difference concerns the way that people regard the relationship between their society and its geographical place, and the second concerns the knowledge and attitudes that people hold regarding other people and places.

Within primitive societies, individualism has a low profile, and the individual is largely perceived in terms of his or her membership of a family, clan or tribal group. The organic relationship between the individual and society is paralleled by the relationship between society and its setting. Society is intimately linked to territory: 'The place and the people are conceptually fused. The society derives meaning from place, the place is defined in terms of social relationships, and the individuals in the society are not alienated from the land' (ibid., p. 177).

The Algonquinian and Iroquoian tribespeople of North America were amongst the most advanced of the indigenous peoples of North America, and they shared the view that man was a part of Nature, not outside it. In their view, natural resources could neither be owned nor exploited.

> Thus a man is born and for a time becomes a cannibal, eating and taking energy from his fellow creatures; when his soul and shadow leave his body, Earth Mother takes it back to nourish the plants which in turn feed both animal and men. His debts are repayed, his spirit freed, and the cycle of life complete. (Cleland 1973, p. xiii)

The intimacy of the bonding between 'primitive' societies and their geographical settings is vividly described in the reply given by the native American chief, Smohalla, when it was suggested that his people should use their land for mining and farming: 'Shall I dig under her skin for bones? Then when I die I cannot enter her body to be born again. You ask me to cut grass and make hay and sell it and be rich like white men. But how dare I cut off my mother's hair?' (Mooney 1973).

Among 'primitive' societies, the bonding between people and place is strongly coloured by the belief that the setting is permeated by mystical presences:

> Belief in the inhabitation of the land by spirits of ancestors and in the mythical bestowal of land to the people have occasioned a powerful communal sense of ownership and use. To have access to the land one must be a member of the society, which means partaking in the spiritual history of the group. (Sack 1980, p. 179)

Sack also notes that landscape features which are arresting in their morphology may be incorporated into myths and serve to anchor societies in space. Ayers Rock had a prominent place in the iconography of the indigenous people of central Australia, the natural arch of Window Rock in Arizona is believed by the Navajo to have sacred powers, while the Black Hills of Dakota contained tribal burial grounds and were crucial to the religious and ideological life of the Sioux Indians of the Great Plains – so crucial that the Sioux were prepared to risk conquest and all that this might entail in order to keep white prospectors out of this ancestral domain. Recent work on the North York Moors in northern England may exemplify such associations. Here, linear bank and ditch earthworks which cut across the ends of prominent upland spurs and promontories and are known as 'cross-ridge boundaries' appear to have defined pieces of territory used for ritual purposes in the Bronze Age. It is also suggested that: 'In making boundaries, the concern was to confirm the definition of small areas, the boundaries of which were already at least partly visible in the contours of the land, the courses of streams, low-lying and perhaps marshy areas' (Vyner 1994, p. 36). Mystical associations between people and symbols are by no means confined to 'primitive societies', and as we have seen, the modern state will possess a potent array of symbols: 'The United States has a "heartland", it has national monuments, shrines and "holy" places such as the Capitol, the Lincoln Memorial, Grant's Tomb; it has a mythologised past in the rugged frontiersmen and the "noble savage"' (Sack 1980, p. 193).

Stateless societies may be so closely bonded to their geographical settings that people and place become conceptually fused and society derives its very meaning from place. Sack writes that:

> Belief in the inhabitation of the land by the spirits of ancestors and in the mythical bestowal of the land to the people have occasioned a powerful communal sense of ownership and use. To have access to the land one must be a member of the society, which means partaking in the spiritual history of the group. (Sack 1980, p. 176)

He adds that: 'Society and place were so closely interrelated that for the primitive to indulge in speculation about society elsewhere or about society having a different spatial configuration, would be like severing the roots from a plant. It could be of no value' (ibid.).

Despite the intimacy of the bond between people and place, chiefdoms tended to be transient, with overcrowding of the setting, disputes about rights of succession or outright warfare frequently leading to the break-up and recombination of societies. Usually, such reorganisations took place within a reasonably confined area, but in a few cases, profound changes in setting and even culture could be involved. For example, when encountered by the explorer, La Salle, in 1680, the Cheyenne were living in Minnesota. They then migrated to North Dakota, where they abandoned their agricultural way of life and adopted the culture of the buffalo hunting Plains tribes which they encountered in the West. When Lewis and Clark met the Cheyenne in 1804 they had been evicted from the plains by the Sioux and were occupying territory in the Black Hills of South Dakota. By 1835, some Cheyenne and Arapaho tribespeople had moved together into eastern Colorado, while northern elements of the two tribes occupied parts of Wyoming and Montana. The Arapaho had a tradition of friendly relations with the Cheyenne, though they tended to be less warlike and had an economy based both on hunting the buffalo and trade. Like their comrades the Cheyenne, the Arapaho had also abandoned the cultivation of corn in favour of a Plains buffalo hunting culture, and legends placed their origins around the headwaters of the Mississippi, near Lake Superior. In 1851, a section of the Cheyenne migrated southward into the Arkansas River area and became closely associated with the Arapaho living there. Though split into groups separated by great geographical distances and divided socially into ten bands, the Cheyenne maintained their ethnic identity throughout their travels.

Not all the information recorded concerning the territorial aspects of clan and tribal life is reliable. Some anthropologists were so anxious to establish the virtuous nature of 'primitive' life that they ignored the evidence of territoriality and conflict which confronted them (Eibl-Eibesfeldt 1979, pp. 136–9). To demonstrate the existence of such factors in the lives of supposedly pacific peoples Eibl-Eibesfeldt quotes Schebesta on the Bambuti pygmies of the Ituri forest:

> The roving and hunting territory of the Bambuti group, which is marked off by precisely known boundaries, belongs to a definite group of related families who alone have a claim to it. They alone, to the exclusion of all other groups, are allowed regularly to seek their food within this territory . . . the intrusion of strangers for the purpose of hunting or gathering food is not permitted and leads to quarrels and wars. (Schebesta 1941, p. 126)

Kohl-Larsen (1958, p. 101) studied the three hordes of the Hadza of Tanzania, and found that each had its own distinct territory:

> I never saw the Matete horde hunt in the hunting area of another horde . . . in times of famine the boundaries of the individual hordes are lifted, so that they are allowed to hunt in areas allotted to other hordes . . . it seems to be the usual hunting practice that each horde respects its neighbour's hunting boundaries.

There is a general agreement that stateless societies will tend to evolve from the less complex forms towards more complicated and hierarchical organisations. Chiefdoms are regarded as occupying a middle stage in this progression: 'Chiefdoms are intermediate societies, neither states nor egalitarian societies' (Earle 1991, p. xi) and 'A chiefdom was rather loosely defined as a polity that organizes centrally a regional population in the thousands . . . Some degree of heritable social ranking and economic stratification is characteristically associated' (ibid., p. 1). In seeking to explain the emergence of chiefdoms, sociologists and anthropologists have tended to see the adoption of central leadership as a social solution to particular problems of an economic or an ecological nature which have been encountered. In other words, leadership would come into being when a society needed centralised management of its affairs in order to resolve a particular challenge. Now, however, such a simple explanation finds much less favour. As Earle (1991, p. 14) explains:

> The basis for the emerging concensus is that chiefdoms must be understood as political systems. To do this, attention must focus on political power and how it is generated and itself controlled. Especially important in this regard is how the subsistence economy becomes redirected to finance the emerging regional institutions of the chiefdoms.

It emerges that a combination of economic control, military power and ceremonial legitimacy is very frequently associated with the emergence of chiefdoms. Military and ideological leaders may combine to control the economy of the society concerned, with the surplus production being used to support the conquest of new lands, to finance ceremonial activities which establish the legitimacy of the ruling caste and to develop the economic base.

So as societies become more 'advanced', their organisation tends to be come more elaborate, as exemplified by the social complexity of the tribal confederation of the Iroquois of north-east USA. Whatever its actual evolutionary history may have been, the social structure was interpreted in Iroquois mythology according to the legend that the divine leader, Deganawida, and his disciple, Hiawatha, sought to bring an end to intertribal wars by forming an alliance between the Cayuga, Mohawk, Oneida, Ononodaga and Senaca peoples. Iroquois social organisation provided a common denominator linking these tribes. Its fundamental unit was the 'fireside', consisting of a mother and her children. Several firesides united to form a 'ohwachira', a group of related families, each tracing its lineage through its mother. Two or more ohwachiras formed a clan and several clans combined to form a tribe or nation. This was a matriarchal society; the heads of ohwachiras were always women, and the women chose the male delegates to clan or tribal councils.

However, studies of native American tribal groupings reveal a remarkable diversity of forms of political organisation. At one extreme was the League of the Iroquois, in which a measure of political organisation united distinct tribal groups, or the Cheyenne, where a council of 44 peace chiefs united 10 major bands. At the other extreme were groups which were united in language and culture but which lacked any political integration beyond the extended family or the temporary village.

> Much more common were groups in which political power, such as it was, was concentrated in the village, band, or kinship group. These might join together in occasional or seasonal enterprises, but in general, while they shared language, culture, and to some extent territory, they were autonomous, lacking political integration at the tribal level . . . Prominent examples include the Comanches, Navajos, the Apache groups, and many others. (Cornell 1988, p. 29)

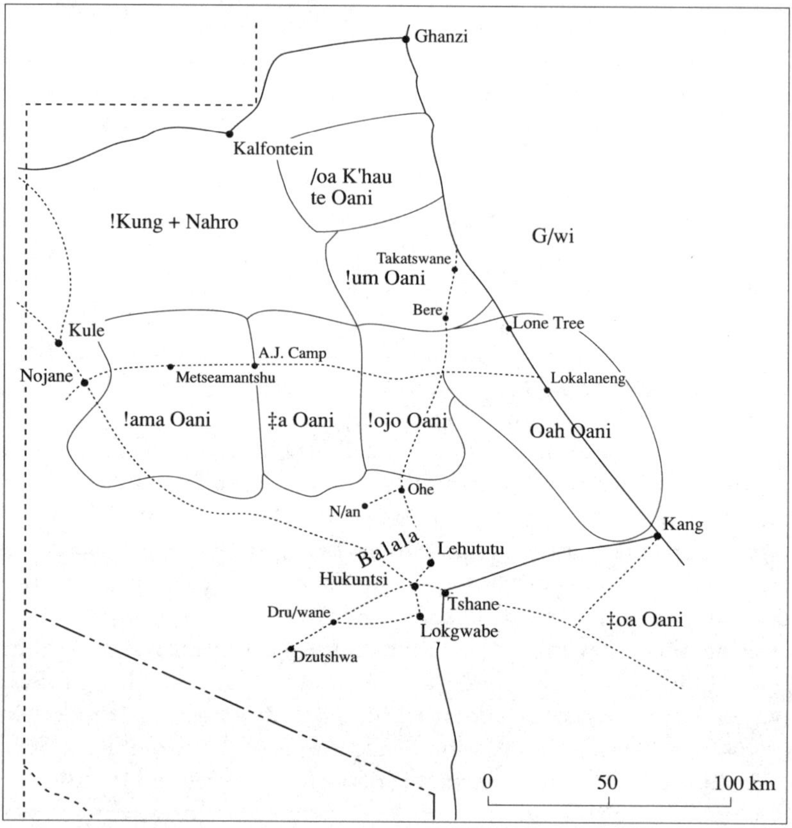

Map 1 Territories of the !Ko bushmen
Sources: Developed from H.- J. Heinz, 'The Social Organisation of the !Ko Bushmen', Master's thesis, University of South Africa, Johannesburg (1966); and Eibl-Eibesfeldt (1979).

Great variation was also apparent among the tribal societies of Africa. The Tiv of what is now east-central Nigeria had no king, central government or officials, but all members of the tribal community were united in their belief in being descendants of a single ancestor, called Tiv. Within this community, individuals enjoyed equality but belonged to different lineages, each lineage consisting of people who traced their descent through the male line to a forbear living a few generations previously. There was no system of authority, but when lineages came into conflict, a council of elders would be convened to listen to the arguments and provide a forum in which a ritualised reconciliation could be enacted. While lineages subdivided the society of the Tiv, that of the Karimojong of Uganda was, like many others, divided into 'age-sets', with men of different ages belonging to different sets which performed different tasks within the tribal economy. The more 'advanced' society of the Hausa people, who lived to the north of the Tiv, had a more complex social organisation, though prior to its convertion to Islam their society had been stateless and relatively egalitarian. During the European Middle Ages, the Hausa territory existed as a confederation of city statelets, each city constituting a defensive nucleus for the peasants of the surrounding countryside. Though each city had its own ruler, nobility, warriors and taxation system, there was no centralised government for the Hausa territory, although ad hoc alliances of cities would form to resist external aggressors.

While political anthropologists now focus on the distribution of power within society, the case of the North American Indian societies demonstrates how external circumstances – in the form of the arrival of European settlers – could contrive to impose political consolidation:

> In their dealings with native peoples Europeans searched for political structures similar to their own: individuals or councils with authority to act on behalf of the nations or peoples they encountered. Where such comprehensive structures were absent, they encouraged their development, trying to reproduce the processes of interstate politics by which their own external relations were governed. (Cornell 1988, p. 31)

There was a variation in the territoriality of the tribes of North America; some had very clear perceptions of the extent of the tribal lands, while others only established claims to a tribal territory when put under pressure during negotiations with land-hungry whites (Sutton 1975).

Some anthropologists and archaeologists have regarded the vestigial state as playing a vital redistributive role within society (Renfrew 1972). Such an interpretation could be advanced in the case of the larger hillforts of Late Bronze Age and Iron Age Britain. On excavation, several of these heavily fortified hilltop settlements have been found to have contained disciplined rows of raised buildings which have been interpreted as granaries. Perhaps the harvest from the surrounding tributary area was hauled up to the hillfort as tribute to the local ruler and was stored there, later being traded for exotic products or redistributed to the families of the tributary area as largesse?

With the arrival of civilisation, the relationships between society and its setting are changed. The homogeneous, classless society is replaced by a much more complex and hierarchical class society, and at this

Box 2.1 *Indigenous peoples and their plight*

Indigenous peoples are descended from the populations which existed in state territory prior to its conquest, occupation and colonisation. Normally they existed as cultivators, herders or hunter-gatherers, though frequently their traditional lifestyle – and consequently their culture – has been undermined by contact with more 'advanced' and politically dominant cultures. Disease, demoralisation and social disintegration were commonly the results of exposure to Western influences. In some parts of the world, there is continuing hostility between indigenous peoples and the non-European inheritors of a state-based political culture, as with the natives of East Timor and the Indonesian authorities, the Cordillerans and the government forces of the Philippines or the Karen and Shan people and the state of Burma, while in states like Canada, the USA, Australia and New Zealand, Europeans still control the destiny of their territorial predecessors. In the 1980s the government-sponsored settlement of Bengalis in the Chittagong Hill Tracts of Bangladesh resulted in guerilla warfare and the displacement of more than 50 000 indigenous Buddhist tribals to Tripura in India. Subsequently the Bangladesh government admitted that the state-engineered influx of settlers was a mistake, but refused to remove them. In 1995 the Namibian government contracted the construction of a hydroelectric dam at Epupa on the Cunene River which will result in the inundation of 100 square miles of territory occupied by the cattle-herding Himba people. Meanwhile, in southern New Mexico, the families of the great nineteenth-century Apache chiefs, Cochise and Geronimo, have become divided in a feud which has split the surviving members of the tribe since Silas Cochise and residents of the Mescalero reservation agreed to store 2000 tons of radioactive waste in their sacred mountain, Sierra Blanca (Vulliamy 1995).

Gradually, however, the prospects for indigenous peoples may be becoming a little brighter as they begin to assert their rights. In 1867 the Maori of New Zealand recovered control of some traditional lands and obtained representation in the English settlers' parliament, while 'the Miskito Indians of Nicaragua were recognised as constituting an autonomous state from 1860 to 1894. And the Kuna Indians of Panama gained local autonomy as the result of a rebellion in 1920' (Gurr and Harff 1994, p. 21). Following the formation of the League of Nations in 1919, the Maori and several North American tribes petitioned the organisation, but most of the progress gained has been won during the last quarter of a century. The World Council of Indigenous Peoples was founded in 1975 as a non-governmental body which publicises the plight of indigenous peoples and promotes their interests. The UN has a Working Group on Indigenous Populations which assembles the representatives of 200 such groups for annual meetings in Geneva and which has issued a draft declaration on indigenous rights which may be integrated into international law. In 1992 an Earth Parliament was held in Rio, involving representatives of indigenous peoples affected by environmental degradation who issued a series of cultural and ecological demands in advance of the Earth Summit conference. And yet, 'In 1991, while environmental bureaucrats pored over their documents in Geneva and New York, the Catholic Land Commission in Brazil reported that some 242,196 people were involved in land struggles over rights to more than 17 million acres, a number that does not include the 15 million acre Yanomani struggle. Some 54 peasant organizers and rural workers were killed. Brazil's native population was reduced by 27 murders, 21 suicides as a result of cultural dislocation, and 206 deaths from epidemics' (Hecht and Cockburn 1993, p. 100).

stage, it has often been argued, the state is needed to reconcile the differences between members of the stratified society. Here, Sack quotes from Engels (1972): 'in order that these antagonisms, classes with conflicting interests, shall not consume themselves and society in fruitless struggle, a power, apparently standing above society, has become necessary to moderate the conflict and keep it within the bounds of "order"'. The identification of the state as a neutral umpire presiding even-handedly over the affairs of a heterogenous modern population is, of course, open to criticism, not least in the cases of the numerous countries in which the state is the instrument of its majority nation and serves to perpetuate inequalities within its society.

There seems to have been nothing simplistic or predictable about the emergence of particular states. Ferguson (1991) studied the transition from chiefdoms to city states in Greece around the eighth century BC and described a process that was complex, variable, layered and involved continuity as well as change. The city state or polis was not a state in the modern sense; the cities were straggling agricultural settlements where citizens clustered around a citadel and the territories that they controlled covered only a few hundred or a few thousand square kilometers; populations ranged from about 40 000 to only 2000. Nevertheless, the city states were different from the chiefdoms which preceded them and the change was due, in part, to a phenomenal increase in agricultural surpluses and population. At the same time, there was a desire to regularise the worship of cult gods at a centralised sanctuary, and meanwhile the Phoenicians, who were literate traders and the founders of coastal cities, were influencing Greek society. Such influences from other state societies combined with enduring memories of the former Heroic Age of states provided concepts and models for city state formation, though the quite rapid emergence of states did not immediately involve the substitution of an identification with the territorial community for the old ties of kinship. 'Factors apparently influencing the emergence of the city-state were the need for centers for cult worship, a population explosion, transition from pastoralism to agriculture, and the relative independence of Dark Age peasants' (ibid., p. 192). As an example of the continuity factor, under the city state as under the preceding chiefdom, war was regarded as a means of augmenting personal, family and communal wealth, while death in battle was considered heroic. What changed was the way in which battle was waged and the community for which men fought. Here, the emergence of states appears to have involved some factors which were unique and some derived from the preceding chiefdom societies.

Taking the case of Athens, in the Heroic Age the Athenians consisted of four tribes occupying distinct territories and were governed by a tribal council. With the progression towards civilisation, society became more mixed and more stratified into classes, with power becoming concentrated within the social elite. Meanwhile, people came to be divided and united not along ethnic lines, but in terms of territory. Thus the old tribal alignments were undermined when a new system of districts (*Naukrariai*) was introduced, each district being responsible for providing the city with a ship and a body of cavalry. People were grouped into these districts not by kinship but by places of residence. Gradually, Athenians developed territorial systems of organisation and loyalty to replace the older tribal and kinship systems (Sack 1980, pp. 180–1).

The emergence of the state marks a significant development in the relationship between society and territory. The state is essentially a territorial institution: its authority extends unambiguously across its territory. Any attack on territory is a challenge to the state's order and authority. This territoriality is important for many reasons, not the least being that it amounts to a very visible statement of state power: 'By expressing power territorially there does not need to be a complete specification of the objects, events and relationships, which are subject to the authority of the state. Anything, both known and unknown, can fall under its authority if located within its territory' (ibid., pp. 40–1). The importance of territoriality in the profile of the state has been emphasised by Mann (1984, p. 198), who wrote:

> Only the state is inherently centralised over a delimited territory over which it has authoritative power. Unlike economic, ideological or military groups in civil society, the state elite's resources radiate authoritatively outwards from a centre but stop at defined territorial boundaries. The state is indeed a place – both a central place and a unified territorial reach.

There were fundamental differences between the states of the ancient world, the state as it existed under feudal society and the modern state. In the European feudal state, all land was considered to be the property of the monarch. Under the institution of vassalage, which governed social relationships within the social elite, a subordinate vassal held an estate or 'fief' either directly or indirectly from the crown. In return, that vassal was obliged to perform military services at the monarch's command. Land could be sublet or subinfeudated by the monarch's tenants in chief, with the lesser lords being linked to the greater by a hierarchy of obligations. The basic territorial unit within each state was the manor, and on each manor the lord or lady was empowered to demand allegiance, labour services and money rents from his or her servile peasant tenants, notionally providing them with protection in return. The peasants, meanwhile, being prevented from working elsewhere, were effectively the prisoners of the manor.

Standing somewhat apart from these plainly defined, stable and hierarchical relationships were the city and the Church. The Church was a supra-national organisation in which the papacy extended its influence across many feudal states. In the spiritual sense, it was more than supra-national, because it embraced heaven and earth, present, past and future. Then the city became a powerful symbol of the fact that feudal bondage was not an inevitable condition of life. Cities were centres of commerce, and for commerce to flourish it was essential that manufacturers and merchants should have freedom of movement and initiative. The entrepreneurial communities established in cities developed their own arrangements for self-government, while craft guilds regulated affairs within each branch of manufacturing. Any peasant who succeeded in escaping from the manor and surviving in a city for a year and a day was entitled to enjoy the freedom endowed by the urban setting.

According to Mann (ibid., pp. 188–9), state power has two dimensions: despotic power and infrastructural power. The despotic power of the state elite embraces the range of actions which the elite is empowered to undertake without routine, institutionalised negotiation with civil society groups – as when the Chinese Emperor, as the Son of Heaven, had total power over everybody within his domain. Infrastructural power concerns the capacity of the state actually to penetrate civil society, and to implement logistically political decisions throughout the realm – as when the state taxes our income at source. Mann believed that the feudal state was weak because it had low despotic power and low infrastructural power: rulers governed largely by indirect means, depending on infrastructures controlled by feudal magnates, churchmen or cities.

As the feudal state was gradually transformed into the capitalist state, the relationship between people and place was changed. The better communications, which were needed to assemble materials at the factory and distribute manufactured goods, provided the infrastructure necessary for a more mobile society. Labour was trained, worked for wages, travelled to work, and had to be ready to migrate to the places where expanding production created rising demands for labour. People whose horizons, social acquaintances and ties to place may have extended no further than the manor, parish, congregation and locality now developed broader associations, embracing the city, region, province and then the state.

Nations, nationality and citizenship

We cannot simply explain the bonding between a civilised people and a territory by a reference to the functioning of the state: this functioning concerning the way that it broke the bonds of parochialism and expanded the social and political horizons of its subjects. Any awareness, for example, of contemporary Europe will emphasise the fact that people and state are often in conflict, with the territorial bonding of the nation threatening the territorial integrity of the state. State and nation are often rivals, and as Connor observed in 1978 (p. 377):

> Rather than witnessing an evolution of stable state- or suprastate – communities, the observer of global politics has viewed a succession of situations involving competing allegiances in which people have illustrated that an intuitive bond felt toward an informal an unstructured subdivision of mankind is far more profound and potent than are the ties that bind them to the formal and legalistic state structure in which they find themselves.

The story of modern Europe – and to a considerable degree of the post-colonial world too – is one in which nationalism demands pride of place.

The relationship between chiefdom societies and territory is transformed by the progress into civilisation; any understanding of the relationship between 'advanced' societies and territory in the modern era must involve nationalism. During the last two centuries, the nation-state has come to be regarded in most quarters as the most fitting form of political organisation and control. Indeed, to many it is seen as the only legitimate vehicle of political rule, any other arrangement being denounced as an affront to national integrity. And during these centuries too, nationalism has torn apart the multinational dynastic states and empires and reconstructed the political map of the world using the nation as the building block. Today, even at a time when the nation-state has begun to seem passé, inadequate and doomed to the more sophisticated commentators, new generations of national struggles have set the world ablaze.

Before looking at the nation-state as the political geographical expression of the nation, it is necessary to look more closely at the nation, and particularly at its antiquity. The origins of the nation have recently become highly controversial – the controversy extends to a questioning of the very reality of nationhood. In part the dispute concerns whether nations are deeply rooted and 'viable' or, instead, relatively recent, synthetic creations. Anthony Smith, supporting the former view, has criticised what he terms the 'myth of the modern nation' and the 'instrumentalism' associated with the view that cultural characteristics and cleavages are 'infinitely malleable and subject to manipulation by elites and vested interests' (Smith 1988, p. 2). He characterises the notions associated with the myth as follows:

> The nation, it holds, is neither natural nor immemorial, much less self-generative. On the contrary, it is a relatively modern phenomenon arising out of specific modern conditions and ideally suited to those conditions. It is also a construct. Human beings, specifically nationalists, invent nations, though they may not do so wholly of their own volition. (ibid., p. 3)

To Smith, modern nations have emerged from what he terms 'ethnies', a name coined from the French equivalent of the ancient Greek *ethnos* (Smith 1986). These cultural groups existed well before the emergence of nationalism as a political force, but with the dawning of the age of nationalism, the new drive to achieve national sovereignty could be wedded to the long-established culture, iconography and folk myths of the ethnies to produce nations.

According to Smith (1988, p. 9): 'An ethnic community, or *ethnie*, may, in fact, be defined as a named human population possessing a myth of common descent, common historical memories, elements of shared culture, an association with a particular territory, and a sense of solidarity.' Ethnies with these defining characteristics can, Smith believes, be traced back into pre-modern history and existed in many parts of the world in ancient and medieval times. (Smith 1989). He believes that two types of ethnies existed; territorial 'civic' nations, like England, France and Spain, tended to develop from aristocratic 'lateral' ethnies through a process of 'bureaucratic incorporation', whereby the outlying regions and the lower classes were incorporated into the ethnies established by the upper classes. In such cases, the influence of the state and its bureaucracy are paramount and the state purveys down the social scale the culture of the aristocratic ethnie, displacing or incorporating the influences of the church and local nobility. In the case of England, according to Smith, this involved a lateral ethnie of Norman origin incorporating the Anglo-Saxon population. By the late fourteenth century linguistic fusion had been achieved and a common myth of British descent had taken root. More numerous, however, are the 'ethnic' nations which have emerged from demotic 'vertical' ethnies through processes of cultural mobilisation which convert passive communities which were often defined in religious terms, into active, politicised nations. In these cases the ethnie may be subject to an alien state or empire and it is the middle-class intelligentsia rather than the state which fosters national identity, deliberately creating and

Box 2.2 *The nation*

A nation is a body of people bound together by a common cultural heritage. These words will not, however, serve as a definition, for they might equally be employed to describe a tribe or a clan. To constitute a nation, the group needs to be quite numerous and to have achieved a certain level of political maturity. Normally, the unifying cultural factors include language, religion, historical heritage and tradition – but these objective factors do not always need to be present: the German nation does not share a single religion, the Swiss nation embraces several linguistic groups, and so on. Much more important are the subjective factors, involving an awareness among members that they belong to the nation and wish to be governed by themselves, and nobody else. Thus, in framing a working definition of the nation, Emerson (1960, p. 95) described 'a community of people who feel that they belong together in the double sense that they share deeply significant elements of common heritage and that they have a common destiny for the future'. According to another working definition of the nation, provided by A. D. Smith (1989, p. 342), 'A nation is a named community of history and culture, possessing a unified territory, economy, mass education system and common legal rights.' Some of the elements in this definition imply that the nation defined already possesses its nation-state, but alternative definitions emphasise the psychological associations of belonging to a nation.

Authorities are divided concerning the relationship between nationhood and nationalism. To some, the struggle to achieve national goals – notably national unification and national independence – are the essence of nationhood, while to others, the quest for nation statehood is but one amongst several expressions of national sentiment. Ernest Gellner (1983) considered that the urge for self-government was central, and wrote that: 'Nationalism is primarily a political principle which holds that the political and national unit should be congruent. Nationalism as a sentiment, or as a movement, can best be defined in terms of this principle. Nationalist sentiment is the feeling of anger aroused by the violation of the principle, or the feeling of satisfaction aroused by its fulfilment. A nationalist movement is one actuated by a sentiment of this kind.'

The distinction between the objective and the subjective aspects of nationhood can be reflected in a distinction between cultural and political forms of nationalism. Whereas political nationalism focuses activity on the overriding goal of achieving national independence, cultural nationalism is concerned with protecting and advancing the cultural identity of the group concerned. Thus, Kurdish nationalism would be of the political type and Welsh nationalism of the cultural kind. But these identifications are not fixed; for example, in the course of recent decades the nationalism of the French Canadians of Quebec has drifted from the cultural category to the political. A degree of looseness attaches to all identifications of the nation. There may be some strong grounds for believing in the existence of an American nation, and others for emphasising the diversity and cultural disunity of the people of the USA. But if there is an American nation, then it is a nation of a kind which cannot be equated with nations of the European kind; a nation of recent immigrants differs markedly from an historical nation: 'It is difficult for an American to appreciate what it means for a German to be German or for a

Box 2.2 *continued*

Frenchman to be French, because the psychological effect of being American is not precisely equatable. Some of the associations are missing and others may be quite different' (Connor 1978, p. 381). Again, people sometimes speak of a Red Indian nation, yet the only common denominators among the native Americans are provided by their long tenancy of North American lands and the disgraceful treatment meted out to them by white settlers and governments. In view of the circumstances of the American Civil War, a strong case could be made for the existence of a Southern or Confederate nation – but if such a nation existed, where is it now? Even the mention of the nation can be a political act, since to recognise the existence of a nation is, in an age of nationalism, virtually to recognise its right to independence.

The study of nations and nationalism presents problems of comparison and generalisation, for it is not always clear whether we are encountering differences of degree or of kind; as Williams explains: 'In the past we have been encouraged to conceive of the nation as an objectively defined social entity, capable of being identified precisely in many diverse territorial and cultural contexts. Is this an appropriate assumption? Is the Jewish "nation" of Old Testament times sufficiently similar to the current Nigerian "nation" to warrant comparison within the same conceptual framework?' (Williams, 1988, p. 331). According to Smith (1988, pp. 8–9), the modern world contains two overlapping concepts of the nation, the civic or territorial and the ethnic or genealogical. The civic concept regards nations as groups which inhabit a distinct territory, share a common economy, have common laws and a public education system – in other words, according to this conception, which is founded on Western modernity, territory, economy, law and education constitute the four spheres through which nations are formed. But the ethnic conception regards nations as named human populations which claim common ancestry, history, customs, vernaculars and solidarity. Here, in a view of the nation which has found favour mainly outside the West, genealogy, demography, traditional culture and history furnish the main resources for the formation of nations.

developing an emotional attachment to landscape, folklore and mythology in the rediscovery and reconstruction of the communal past. Ireland, Finland and Switzerland are given as examples.

There seem to be almost as many theories about the origins of nations as there are theoreticians. Beginning with the writers which Smith categorised as instrumentalists, for Ernest Gellner (1983), nationalism was produced by the transition from immobile peasant societies to industrialism. When the traditional, stable agrarian societies held sway there was a cultural stratification which kept the illiterate farming communities and the literate urban elites apart, preventing the growth of homogeneous nations. The process of industrialisation caused mobile, culturally homogeneous societies to form as the old class system was broken down and replaced by urban industrial communities.

People in these new communities needed to learn new skills and the use of a standardised language, and once the state had provided such training and education, strangers were able to communicate in a meaningful manner. In the course of industrialisation and modernisation, intelligentsias emerge who are inspired by a sense of nationalism and call for the creation of mass, culturally homogeneous nations. In this way the drive for modernism serves to create the nation: 'Nationalism is not the awakening of nations to self-consciousness: it *invents* nations where they do not exist' (Gellner 1964, p. 169). Thus, according to Gellner, the flourishing capitalist economies of the late eighteenth and nineteenth centuries produced social mobility and universal systems of education. These led to the disintegration of old outlooks, class structures and localised or parochial outlooks and created conditions in which nationalism could take root in the broadened, more homogeneous, industrialised community.

Karl Deutsch (1961) thought that nation-building resulted from the processes of communication and social mobilisation which become activated during the process of modernisation. He described a progression from society to community to people to nationality to nation which took place in relation to parallel increases in urbanisation and commerce; the growth of communication networks; the adoption of group symbols and traditions, and increases in the efficiency with which members of the group were able to communicate with each other ('communicative efficiency'). Deutsch defined nationalism as 'The preference for the competitive interests of this nation and its members over those of all outsiders' (Deutsch 1953, p. 169) and thought that the growth of nations involved an intensification of the effectiveness of communication and an expansion of the area in which this communication took place; members of the nation were deemed to be able to communicate more effectively, and over a wider range of topics, with each other than with outsiders (Deutsch 1966).

For the supporters of Marx and Lenin, the real divisions in society are the vertical ones which divide us into classes; therefore the horizontal divisions into nations must in some way be false, illusory and the product of some conspiracy concocted by the ruling classes. To various Marxist and radical geographers, such as Blaut, nationalism is a form of class struggle in which a colonial power is opposed by an indigenous ruling class. This ruling class seeks to assume for itself the role of exploiting the masses as practised at the time by the colonial power. Meanwhile, the masses too wish to assume control, and may combine in an alliance with their ruling class to oppose colonialism under a nationalist banner. Nationalism pervades the competing parties, with imperialism and the institutionalised racism which it embodies being regarded as an extension beyond its boundaries of the national struggle of the great imperial power (Blaut 1986, pp. 5–10). To the Marxist, Hobsbawm (1968; 1984), the nation is a modern creation, resulting from the need of capitalism to remove outmoded class structures and values and to create large, centralised states to answer its need for markets. In his view, nations are the inventions of the capitalist system, resulting from a selective stitching together of historical and cultural aspects from the past. Nairn (1977) believed that while ethnic groups existed prior to the nineteenth century, they were politically dormant. As capitalism gradually and erratically expanded across the globe from its homelands in England and France, it incited the emergence of nationalism in the colonised areas as the elites in the countries affected developed national movements which were created to mobilise mass opposition to the changes.

Benedict Anderson questions the reality of the nation, which he regards as an 'imagined community' whose existence was made possible by the emergence of 'print capitalism', the newspaper and novel, during the eighteenth century as new printing technology and capitalist methods of book production made possible the mass production of popular literature. This had been preceded by the development, after the fifteenth century, of a 'print culture' and the decline of Latin, the universal sacred language: 'In a word, the fall of Latin exemplified a larger process in which the sacred communities integrated by old sacred languages were gradually fragmented, pluralized, and territorialized' (Anderson 1991, pp. 18–19). While the influence of religion on society was declining and the belief in the afterlife receded, science and modernity were advancing so that the nation filled the vacuum caused by the retreat of faith. Meanwhile, the new capabilities for communication across broad territories in the national languages made it possible for individuals in each territory to imagine that they all belonged to the same national entity. And so: 'The lexicographic revolution in Europe . . . created, and gradually spread, the conviction that languages (in Europe at least) were, so to speak, the personal property of quite specific groups – their daily speakers and readers – and moreover that these groups, imagined as communities, were entitled to their autonomous place in a fraternity of equals' (ibid., p. 84).

A different approach has been followed by Williams (1982), who regards discontent among national or regional communities as a response to slights to their status, cultural identity and special interests effected by insensitive, centralised governments. These slights or offences reopen old sores and bring long established grievances back into the forefront of debate and so help to politicise the populations concerned.

Different yet again is the interpretation of the nation provided by Connor, who stresses the importance of the belief in common descent and the sense of consanguinity: 'Our answer, then, to that often asked question, "What is a nation?" is that it is a group of people who feel that they are ancestrally related. It is the largest group that can command a person's loyalty because of felt kinship ties; it is from this perspective, the fully extended family' (Connor 1993, p. 382). He adds that the fact that all nations are blends of numerous ethnic strains does not really matter: 'All that is irreducibly required for the existence of the nation is that members share an intuitive conviction of the group's separate origin and evolution' (ibid.). Referring to the certainty with which national leaders, tyrants and demagogues have been able to manipulate the belief in consanguinity, Connor (ibid.) quotes Bismarck's exhortation to Germans to unite in a single state: 'Germans, think with your blood!' and Hitler's rant in Konigsburg (Kaliningrad) in 1942: 'Man today refuses any longer to be separated from the life of his national group; to that he clings with a resolute affection. He will bear extreme distress and misery, but he desires to remain with his national group . . . Blood binds more firmly than business.'

This amounts to no more than a sample of the different interpretations of national origins that are available. Most of them offer some interesting perspective on the highly complicated topic. No consensus is to be found, but there are good grounds for supposing that in late eighteenth- and nineteenth-century times, special conditions came into existence which allowed the sparks of nationalism to ignite into political life communities who had been politically inactive though partially unified by cultural factors such as language, folklore and religion. The process of political activation must have been assisted by all those modernising factors which made it increasingly easy for members of the developing nation to communicate with each other and expand their horizons beyond their immediate localities. Changing patterns of work, transport, publication and distribution must all have played their part. Even so the very antiquity of the nation remains disputed. As John Hutchinson (1994, p. 2) points out, such questions 'are still the subject of lively debates between those we might characterize as modernists and ethnicists. These controversies are of great interest, for they raise important questions about the nature of social identities, of modernity, and our relationship to the past.'

Ethnicists, such as Smith and Connor, whose ideas we have met, argue that nations existed for centuries before the age of nationalism, with ethnic identities being forged by, or during the Middle Ages, and with national sentiments 'bubbling under' during the era of feudalism, the universal church and the dynastic empire. Modernists,

Box 2.3 *National character*

If national character exists then, as a phenomenon subject to spatial variation of a kind which displays a territorial congruence with important cultural characteristics, it should be of considerable interest to political geographers. There are two dimensions to national character: the objective (if it exists) and the subjective. The latter can be of great importance in forming policies, though these policies will be flawed if false assumptions about national character are incorporated into the policy-making process. At the time of the Falklands War, British military leaders were heard to express the hope that the Argentinians would fight like Italians rather than Spaniards (both Italy and Spain having contributed large numbers of settlers to Argentina). Doubtless this attitude was coloured by memories of the fierceness of combat during the Spanish Civil War and of the mass surrender of Italian troops to the British during the North African campaign. Yet such perceptions were unreliable; the fighting in Spain reflected the intense passions of the ideological struggle between socialists and Phalangists, while the Italian performance during the 1939–45 war echoed the superficial nature of Mussolini's efforts at state- and nation-building in the face of the fact that at the start of this century Italians, particularly southerners, still identified themselves primarily with provinces and localities rather than with the Italian nation.

There is good evidence to believe that national character does have an objective existence, though the subject has received less attention from geographers than it deserves. In one recent study Kamann (1994) explored the communication problems which are encountered and the cultural differences found between EU member states and discovered that managers from different national backgrounds have different ways of doing things. For example, in a comparison between France and the Netherlands it emerged that in terms of leadership the French appreciate intense supervision and obey authority, while the Dutch prefer a more participatory style and resist authority. Thus, in decision-taking situations the French favour autocratic, paternalistic and independent forms, while the Dutch prefer consultative group decision-taking.

The founding fathers of both political and cultural geography were keen to explore how ethnic groups left their distinctive imprint on the landscape. Plainly, in the countries of the Third World the European colonial cultural legacy is often expressed in the retention of the colonial language as a lingua franca or in the adoption of a political constitution modelled on that of the former imperial power. National character and preferences can also leave more subtle expressions in the distinctive quality of place. Swakopmund in Namibia was founded by German colonialists in 1892, and the German domination lasted only until 1915, when South African forces landed and took over the territory. Yet 80 years later one not only finds Bavarian architecture enduring in Swakopmund, but can also buy apple strudel, locally brewed German-style beer and sauerbraten. The roughly 2000 Germans remaining form only about a third of the white component of the town's population and are a minute fragment of the state population of 1 574 000, but there is still a Kaiser Wilhelm Street and a vigorous German presence in the urban landscape of Swakopmund (Daley 1995). In any study of national character it is important to remember that cultural characteristics are not

Box 2.3 *continued*

innate, but are moulded by evolving environmental circumstances. Thus they may change quite dramatically over time: 'In the seventeenth century the English were regarded to be the most turbulent nation in Europe and in the eighteenth the Germans the most romantic and peaceful' (Frankel 1964, p. 117). (Now we must wonder whether English and German national characters have reverted to their seventeenth- and eighteenth-century stereotypes since Frankel wrote these words more than 30 years ago.)

There are distinct differences in the manner in which members of different nations regard the world. In a four-nation poll conducted in 1994 it emerged that the British thought that war was the most serious problem facing the world. This view was held far more emphatically by Germans, though the Japanese were most concerned about ethnic strife, and the Americans most fearful of crime. In all the countries the majorities of those who detected changes felt that the world had become more rather than less dangerous since the ending of the Cold War, though the proportions varied greatly (Japan 37 per cent, Germany 50 per cent, UK 51 per cent and US 67 per cent) (Hutton and Linton 1994).

on the other hand, see the nation as a modern institution and as something that was part and parcel of the industrial, democratic and rationalist revolutions which were associated with the rise to modernity during the last two centuries. Certainly, there are important aspects of nations which seem distinctly modern. Some of those which Hutchinson identifies include the existence of the nation-state as the nationalist goal. Such an objective embodies a reverence for the will of the people and implies the enfranchisement of the masses – both of which belong to the Age of Enlightenment and were quite alien to the norms of the previous age, when the monarch was thought to rule as God's representative on earth (Hutchinson 1994, p. 4).

Secondly, national integration depended upon the formation of associations which were broader than the regional and local contacts of pre-modern times. The rise of modern market economies made it possible for wider networks of interaction to develop. Also, the middle classes were generally the driving force behind movements of national self-discovery and politicisation – but in pre-modern agrarian societies the middle class was poorly represented and society was characterised by the canyon-like cleavage between lords and tenants. In the modern era, however, the emergence of integrated industrial societies, which were literate and served by a press publishing news and literature in the national language, helped to create the conditions in which nationalism could emerge and flourish.

Yet ethnicists see the roots of the nation as extending far deeper in time than the French Revolution, that landmark event which overturned the old dynastic order and converted passive, subservient subjects into citizens endowed with rights and freedoms.

Anthony Smith has provided one of the most recent interpretations of the ethnicist case, arguing, as we have seen, that the foundations of nations and nationalism were laid well before the modern age. Settling in a territory following a period of migrations, members of an ethnie developed a bonding with place, while in the course of wars with neighbouring populations the people gained an awareness of themselves as being distinct from outsiders and of the location of the boundaries of their territory. Resulting from these shared experiences was a body of myth and legend which expressed the historical identity and heritage of the nation as a heroic community of 'special' people united by a tradition of valour in resisting pressures from 'outsiders' (Smith 1981).

A crucial element in this long-standing debate about nationhood concerns the matter of self-awareness. For while scholars might argue interminably about the nature of the nation and its origins, the discussion would be of no more than academic interest if members of the mass of the population had no perceptions of themselves as belonging to particular nations, and no strong emotions associated with this identification. Without the development of a perception of a distinctive group identity there could be no nationalist movement. Most of the evidence shows that until quite recent times ordinary people did not regard themselves primarily as members of nations, but as belonging to families, villages, localities and provinces. National consciousness arose as a romantic movement among the European middle classes. But having said this, when it did arise, there already existed amongst the various peasant societies a long-established heritage of national folklore, costume, dance and mythology to sustain it. There was also a powerful territorial component – the national territory – which gave issues of nationalism the potential to reshape the world.

■ State and nation, nation and territory

Earlier in this century it may have seemed that the nation-state represented the culmination of political geographical evolution. Indeed, the term 'nation-state' has enjoyed such widespread use that it is frequently used as a synonym for 'state'. Consequently it may be as well to begin this section with a reminder that nation-states are far from being universal in the modern world. Writing in 1978, Connor (1978, p. 382) showed that of 132 entities generally regarded as being states in 1971, only 12 or 9.1 per cent were in fact states whose borders coincided or nearly coincided with the territorial distribution of a single national group. There were a further 25 cases in which members of a single nation accounted for more than 90 per cent of the state's total population, but which also contained an important minority, while in another 25 cases a national group amounted to 75 per cent to 89 per cent of the population, but in 39 cases the largest nation or potential nation accounted for less than half of the population. Later, in 1993, he calculated that:

> Of some 180 contemporary states, probably not more than fifteen could qualify as nation-states: Japan, Iceland, the two Koreas, Portugal and a few others. The *multinational state* is therefore easily the most common form of country. It contains at least two statistically and/or politically significant groups. In 40 per cent of all states there are five or more such groups . . . Perhaps the most startling statistic is that in nearly one-third of all states (31 per cent) the largest national group is not even a majority. (Connor 1993, pp. 374–5)

As a further reminder of the heterogeneity and instability of the so-called nation-state system, Falk (1992, p. 202) writes that:

> By 1990 there were more than 800 nationalist movements in the world but less than 200 states. Many among these 800 claimants are small, weak, dispersed, nonviable, but not necessarily resigned to their fate. There is no prospect that all these nationalisms can be accommodated by grants of statehood. In fact, territorial claims are often layered in such a way that the vindication of one national destiny would displace another.

The nation-state arose from the territorial and political merging of state and nation; nations, their complexity and contradictions we have already reviewed, but the state is still to be explored. Oppenheim (1952) provided a concise definition of the state which will still serve as well as any when he wrote that: a state 'is in existence when a people is settled in a territory under its own sovereign government'. Of the four characteristics he gives, the one which differentiates the state from other units of organised space, like tribal territories or administrative counties, is that of sovereignty. One may debate as to whether sovereignty is vested in the lawful government, the constitution, the people or the monarch (in the UK, which lacks a constitution, the situation is even more confused; sovereignty is said to be associated

Box 2.4 *Citizenship*

Most authorities will agree with Brubaker that the first conception of a modern, state-centred national citizenship was a creation of the French Revolution: 'The formal delimitation of the citizenry; the establishment of civil equality, entailing shared rights and shared obligations; the institutionalisation of political rights; the legal rationalisiation and ideological accentuation of the distinction between citizens and foreigners; the articulation of the doctrine of national sovereignty and of the link between citizenship and nationhood; the substitution of immediate, direct relations between the citizen and the state for the mediated, indirect relations characteristic of the ancient regime – the Revolution brought all these developments together on a national level for the first time' (Brubaker 1992, p. 35).

Citizenship concerns the relationship between the individual and the state within which he or she lives. As a member of the state community, the citizen has certain duties or obligations, but also expects to enjoy certain rights and benefits. In its legal aspect, citizenship is a formal status which carries certain entitlements – like the right to live and work in the state. But citizenship also incorporates an emotional dimension, which is associated with the sense of belonging to a particular state or national community. The possession of legal citizenship does not automatically determine the nature or intensity of the emotional aspect: it is perfectly possible to enjoy all the benefits provided under legal citizenship, and yet feel alienated from the state and the cultural mainstreams of its population. For example, many coloured people living in Britain enjoy exactly the same legal rights as do white citizens, and yet their sense of belonging to a British national community is undermined and negated by factors like racial abuse, discrimination at work and in housing and by police harassment.

The discussion on citizenship still refers frequently to the work of T. H. Marshall (1950). Marshall believed that citizenship rights were of three kinds: civil rights, concerned with individual freedom and including freedom of speech, equality before the law and freedoms of movement, assembly and conscience; political rights, concerning rights to vote, hold office and engage in political activity, and social rights, involving rights to social security, economic welfare and a standard of living compatible with a civilised society. Since 1950, the development of supra-national organisations, notably the EU, have added an extra dimension of complexity by assuming responsibility for additional rights of citizenship, such as the right to move freely and obtain work within the territory of the community. Meanwhile, the spokespersons of the New Right have attacked the notion that the citizen should be entitled to enjoy social rights and they have promoted the free market as the best instrument for distributing resources. Writers on the Left have introduced the geographical concept of locality into this debate. Marquand (1988, p. 239) has argued that a nationally flourishing political community would be 'a mosaic of smaller collectives, which act as nurseries for the feelings of mutual loyalty and trust which hold the wider community together, and where the skills of self-government may be learned and practised', and S. J. Smith (1989) has also advocated a strengthening and broadening of citizenship rights through decentralisation, the exercise of local initiatives and the reconstitution of 'locality'.

Box 2.4 *continued*

Citizenship is of interest to political geographers not least because it varies in intensity and character from place to place. The British educationalist, Nicholas Tate (1995), writes: 'Citizenship is not a concept that comes easily to the English. It is something we traditionally associate with foreigners: with the French (A Tale of Two Cities), the US (Citizen Kane), and ancient Greece (the citizens of Athens and Sparta). We have always seen ourselves as "subjects". We are most conscious of citizenship as something acquired – or denied – rather than inherited.' Brubaker (1989) argues that different traditions of nationhood have shaped the politics of citizenship. In France, citizenship reflects the fact that the nation was conceived in terms of the institutional and territorial framework of the state, with the emphasis being placed upon political unity rather than shared culture. Thus the indigenous population of the far-flung French colonies were regarded as French citizens who could be assimilated by French institutions and the machinery of state. In Germany, by contrast, the idea of a German nation existed long before the formation of a German state and over time this produced a policy of citizenship which focused on exclusion of non-Germans rather than inclusion of all living within the German state. But in Britain a clear conception of nationhood was lacking and: 'The concept of citizenship as membership of a legal and political community was foreign to British thinking. Legal and political status were conceived instead in terms of allegiance – in terms of the vertical ties between individual subjects and the king. The ties of allegiance knit together the British empire, not the British nation' (ibid., p. 10). Citizenship was born along with the modern nation-state system, but state-based citizenship cannot provide expressions for feelings of regional, international or global citizenship – all of which may intensify in the years to come.

with the Crown in Parliament – a situation unlikely to be understood by one British subject in a hundred), but the essence of sovereignty lies in the refusal to accept the existence of any superior authority. Thus, sovereignty is the 'supreme authority which recognises no superior and beyond which there is no legal appeal' (Frankel 1964, p. 13) As a result, states claim to monopolise legitimate authority within their particular territories and:

> Much of the history of the last half millennium can be written as an account of the energy and violence required to ensure that the monopolistic claims of states be respected. Whether through appeals to the nation, the flag, or the national interest, states continue to deploy immense resources on an everyday basis to ensure that this monopoly is maintained. (Walker 1990, p. 6)

Under the umbrella of its sovereignty the state exists as a continuing relationship or dialogue between people, government and territory.

Echoing Mann, Driver (1991, p. 273) notes that: 'it is the territorial organization of the state which gives rise to the distinctive form of its power. In contrast to other power groupings within civil society, the state is centralized over a delimited territory over which it exerts or attempts to exert authority. Thus the issue of territoriality lies at the very heart of state theory.' The fact of state sovereignty encourages people to think in terms of a world that is fragmented into sovereign territories rather than to consider humanity as a whole. Meanwhile, by seeking, as it often does, to integrate all those diverse cultures living within its boundaries into a single coherent state community and at the same time controlling or preventing contacts with groups living outside its borders, the state sets a scale for our perceptions of territorial communities. It also encourages people to visualise the world in terms of inclusion and exclusion or 'us' and 'them' relationships: 'If the world is in fact organized as a series of sharp divisions between inclusion and exclusion, community and anarchy, civilization and barbarism, then the maxim that preparations for war are the only guarantee of peace does make some sense' (Walker 1990, p. 21).

We have noted the common lack of spatial congruence between state and nation, so while the sovereign state must have a population, this population could be culturally completely heterogenous. The nation, in contrast, consists of a people united by various cultural, political and historical characteristics like a common language or religion, but more important are the factors of a shared experience, shared aspirations and the physical and/or emotional links to a particular territory. The factors of nationhood and territoriality have combined in different ways. The Jews, for example, were physically dispersed, partially divided by language, marginally divided by religion, but linked by the common aspiration of recovering Israel, a precisely located territory. The English and French nations were incubated within the territorial shells of pre-existing states, so that the nations post-dated their states, while for nations like the Kurds of the borderlands between Turkey, Iran and Iraq or the Basques of Spain, the nation-state is still an aspiration. Each national group has its own particular association with territory.

English territoriality has been investigated by Taylor (1991b). While adopting rather scornful attitudes towards nationalism, the Anglo-British are in fact extremely nationalistic in their way – a fact borne out by their devotion to pageantry and national spectacles. The Anglo-British attempt to substitute patriotism for nationalism, and as a result 'There is a sense of something missing in English nationalism: the people . . . We can interpret Anglo-British identity, therefore, a particular deformed nationalism hiding behind its self-ascribed patriotism'

Box 2.5 *Sovereignty*

The concept of state sovereignty was developed in sixteenth- and seventeenth-century Europe and arose as the feudal institutions decayed. Previously, loyalty had been owed to dynasties rather than to territorial states, while the primacy of God and the Church had demonstrated the existence of authorities higher than the king or emperor. Towards the end of the Middle Ages, the rise of the Tudor dynasty in England marked the emergence of secular rulers who were able to exercise absolute power. While Henry VII concentrated military power in the monarchy so that it was no longer feasible for the barons to resist the royal will, Henry VIII broke the ties with the universal Church of Rome to underline the supremacy of the throne. A major landmark in the development of a legal concept of sovereignty was reached at the end of the Thirty Years War with the signing of the Treaty of Westphalia in 1648, whereby members of the international community of states accepted the principle of non-interference in each other's internal affairs. Mutual recognition among states had important consequences; firstly, it marked the triumph of the interstate system over long-established concepts of a universal political system, represented by the Roman Catholic church or the Holy Roman Empire. Secondly, it enabled the sovereign states to determine which political territories were sovereign and which were not, for while a power might be able to impose its will internally, recognition by other sovereign states was essential for external sovereignty to be established.

States claim both internal and external sovereignty. Internal sovereignty concerns the absolute and ultimate authority of the state over all individuals, groups, organisations and institutions within its boundaries. Even so, there is considerable – if largely academic – debate about where this sovereignty is actually vested – in the monarch, according to some; in the general will of the people, according to the eighteenth-century philosopher, Jean-Jacques Rousseau; in the laws of the state, say some, and in the constitution, say others. External sovereignty concerns the relationship between the state concerned and other states. It involves the right to self-government free from interference by outside parties and the demand for equality of status in any international dealings with other sovereign states. One's conception of the sovereign state will depend on one's vantage point: stand within the state and one is aware of the ways that it concentrates and centralises decision-taking; adopt a more global stance and one realises that state sovereignty is a force for division in the world. Walker (1990, pp. 9–10) expressed these notions as follows: 'Theorists of international relations refer to state sovereignty in terms of fragmentation, whereas theorists of political life within states refer to the centralization of power/authority . . . State sovereignty is in effect an exceptionally elegant resolution of the apparent contradiction between centralization and fragmentation, or, phrased in more philosophical language, between universality and particularity.' In the age of the nation-state, the presumed right to national sovereignty has come to be regarded as a prerequisite of freedom. Yet although sovereign rights are still jealously guarded, the condition of the sovereign territorial state seems increasingly threatened. Territorial boundaries were formerly defended by frontierworks, batteries and armies, but such frontier defences are less than paper-thin in the age of the intercontinental ballistic missile. No government can sensibly

Box 2.5 *continued*

contemplate making financial policies or launching costly social programmes without the approval of the international banking system, while transnational corporations can make or break the industrial output of an economy by opening or abandoning industrial operations. Short (1993, pp. 169–70) writes that: 'The state in the modern world is caught in the pincers of irrelevancy . . . there seem to be two trends . . . the increasing perception that the major problems and issues which face us are global . . . [and] a concern with the local, an awareness of the importance of place, an identity with community.' As the member states of the EU contemplate the presumed surrenders of sovereignty required to establish a common currency, common foreign policy or Federal Europe, the issue of sovereignty assumes a crucial importance. In the UK, in particular, it divides the party of government and splits generations between the pro-European young and anti-European old.

(ibid., p. 148). According to Taylor, 'Anglo-British identity encompasses a dual territoriality that is simultaneously more and less than England' (ibid., p. 150). As described in Chapter 1, he termed these two territories Upper England and Greater England. The former equates with the group of counties around the capital in South-East England known as the 'Home Counties' and is the heartland of a particularly conservative form of nationalism and associated with romantic visions of (southern) England. This has been noted in other contexts by a variety of geographers, including Agnew (1987, p. 85), who identified the Conservatives as the party of the core: 'The south of England has always been a conservative heartland . . . Moreover, the Conservative vote has tended to decline with increasing distance from the south-eastern core. This is particularly true with respect to Wales and Scotland.' The latter is the British face of English identity, and is outward-looking and expansionist, associated with a yearning for greatness in the face of an economic and political decline that has continued since about 1870 and which has left the financial institutions of the City of London as the sole surviving aspect of greatness.

A strange feature of the territorial aspect of English nationalism is the apparent lack of concern with territorial issues, reflected in the indifference associated with the return of Monmouthshire to Wales in 1974 and the apparent readiness of many English people to see Berwick transferred to Scotland or Northern Ireland merged with the Republic of Ireland. Taylor ends by noting that the recent intensification of inequalities associated with Thatcherism and de-industrialisation have reduced the importance of the old national divisions and produced a situation in which 'a more accurate depiction contrasts south-east

England against the rest' (Taylor 1991b, p. 158). Here he echoes Johnston (1985, pp. 234–5), whom he quotes as follows:

> It makes sense to view British society as a series of concentric circles which are both social and geographical in their nature. To be at the epicentre – in the royal enclosure at Ascot or on the boards of the great merchant banks – is not just a matter of being socially and economically more upper class, but also, in a sense, more English. The real outer groups are not just the poor, the black or the working class, but those furthest from the geographical epicentre of the South-East.

Nationalism is not a condition that is fixed for all time; it can lie dormant and it can be fostered and moulded by particular circumstances. Culture, territory and history all have their parts to play in the formation of national identities. One of the earliest and most influential accounts of the process whereby the qualities of territory could shape culture was provided by F. J. Turner in 1893. Writing just as the great moving frontier of settlement in the USA had ceased to exist, he claimed that American nationhood and identity had been forged at the frontier as it advanced westwards across the country. Pioneers and colonists who had carried a European cultural package of habits, outlooks and beliefs with them from the east were Americanised in the course of their interaction with the wilderness. When this happened, European institutions were discarded and new, democratic, American ones were adopted. The frontier created an American national character, a resourceful individualism born of the dialogue with the wilderness. He wrote of the frontiersman:

> Little by little he transforms the wilderness, but the outcome is not the old Europe . . . The fact is, that here is a new product that is American. At first, the frontier was the Atlantic coast. It was the frontier of Europe in a very real sense. Moving westward, the frontier became more and more American . . . Thus the advance of the frontier has meant a steady movement away from the influence of Europe, a steady growth of independence on American lines. (Turner 1893, p. 203)

Turner's frontier hypothesis has been re-evaluated many times. It was, of course, very much a part of the philosophical mainstream of its day. It embodied the organismic concept of society as a social organism, a concept developed in the political geographical context by Friedrich Ratzel (1897) and it also embodied a strong dose of environmental determinism. One of the most penetrating analyses of Turner's ideas was provided by Berkhofer (1964). He pointed out that Turner was an American patriot who was keen to devalue the current orthodoxy, which highlighted the European origins of things American. If Turner had referred either to the culture or history of his settlers then he would have been forced to confront their European origins. But by giving the formative role to the American environment he has able to argue for a home-grown American nation. In any event, Turner described the Americans as home-grown, resourceful, independent, self-sufficient frontiersfolk – and the Americans loved him for it.

All nationalisms are to some degree bound to territory and to the goal of obtaining/preserving the unadulterated control of the national homeland. Nationalism involves the horizontal division of territory between nations, but nations are not homogeneous; they do not form horizontal patterns in which each national component is as distinctive and homogeneous as the patches in a patchwork rug. They are divided by conflicts of interest which are frequently rooted in class issues which produce a vertical fragmentation of society. If the division between the exploiters and the exploited coincides with a cleavage on national lines – as between the dominant Germans and Hungarians and the subordinate Slavs in the Austro-Hungarian Empire – then the nationalist sentiments will be reinforced. If, on the other hand, there is a high level of exploitation within the nation then its coherence may be undermined: Connor (1990, p. 101) has quoted the case of the Croat aristocrat who would rather have regarded his horse as a member of the Croat nation than any of his peasants.

To some extent national characteristics and tradition are portable and can be transported across the globe to influence the nature of new territories. The Irish who flocked to the US in the years after 1845 to flee the hardships caused by the potato famine were an extremely homogeneous community, united by their religion and by their history of exploitation, and they had already developed underground political organisations and habits of cooperation in their struggles with the British establishment in Ireland. And so when large numbers of Italians, Jews and Slavs began to arrive, about half a century later, they discovered that the large cities of the eastern seaboard were well and truly dominated by Irish political machines. In contrast to the Irish, the Italians were disunited. They were loyal, above all, to the family, then in smaller measures to their locality, village or town, then to their province, but scarcely at all to the concept of an Italian nation. Thus the Italians generally failed to create effective urban political machines, while in many wards where Italians greatly outnumbered the Irish, defections by Italian voters would often secure the election of the Irish candidate (Sowell 1981). But this pattern of ethnic life in the US during the nineteenth century could not simply be interpreted in terms of Irish solidarity. When the famine Irish arrived in their hundreds of thousands in the middle of the century, much smaller Irish communities were already well established and well integrated into American society in 'respectable' occupations. These assimilated Irish-Americans did not tend to welcome their suffering fellow countrymen. Instead, they often argued for a restriction on Irish immigration, fearing that the arrival of hordes of destitute, semi-literate Irish peasants would fuel an American backlash against the whole Irish community. True to the contradictory character of the nation and nationalism, this example serves both to demonstrate the strength and the frailties of national ties.

The bonding between a nation and the national territory can have various dimensions. In some cases the occupation of the territory may be no more than a 'folk memory', in the way that the aspiration to recover Israel united Jews for many centuries. There may be cases where the territorial aspect is not the strongest component in the national identity. But there are other cases where territory and location have governed the formation of nations, as with the several South Slav nations, the subjects of this extended example. Well back in prehistoric times, people who spoke an ancestral Slavonic language emerged in the regions of Belorussia and the northern Ukraine. Subsequently, waves of Slavonic migration took place in different directions. One large group formed the West Slavs, who gave rise to the forbears of the Poles, Czechs and Slovaks. Other ancestral Slavs stayed where they were or moved northwards or eastwards and became the forerunners of the East Slav group, which divided into the Belorussians, Ukrainians and Great Russians. Others still drifted southwards into the Balkans and became the South Slavs.

At this time, it is probable that the South Slavs were a culturally homogeneous people. But as they dispersed into the strongly compartmentalised terrain of mountain and valley and became separated, differences began to develop. The terrain conspired to ferment contrasts as a consequence of separation, but other locational factors also played a crucial part as different groups fell under the control of different alien dynasties. In the north, the Slovenes fell under Roman Catholic domination and their territory was annexed by Austria. Further south, the Croat lands fell under Hungarian control. The Croats took their spiritual lead from Rome, and in due course the Habsburg Empire embraced both Austria and Hungary. But further to the south and east, the Serbs were converted to Christianity by Byzantine influences. Consequently, as well as adopting the Orthodox faith, they also adopted the Cyrillic script.

Despite the political divergence that had occurred, the Serb and Croat languages remained close, but as a result of the contrasting cultural influences, Croat is written in the Latin alphabet and the Serb language in Cyrillic characters. Around a thousand years ago, the Slovene language, described as the most beautiful of the Slav languages, had begun to diverge from the other South Slav tongues. After the battle of Kosovo in 1389, the Serb territories fell under Turkish control, and they remained under Turkish domination until the nineteenth century. Economic factors were now added to those of geography, politics and culture which progressively diversified the South Slav people. The Turks practised a severe and exploitive rule and their territories experienced less industrial, agricultural and educational development than did the territories under Austrian and Hungarian control. Meanwhile, the Serbs themselves became culturally divided. The Orthodox nation was subordinated to a Muslim ruling caste dominated by soldiers, the Janisaries, who were largely recruited from Orthodox Christian boys who had been taken from their parents, converted to the Muslim faith and subjected to an intensive military training. Some Orthodox Serbs managed to escape the harshest features of Turkish rule by migrating northwards or moving into the mountains, with their church organising the secret migrations (Mellor 1975). Other Serbs remained where they were, and many found an advantage in converting to the faith of their conquerors. In this way, a large Muslim component developed within the Serb population of Bosnia.

Different components of the South Slav peoples gained independence at different times, and often the liberation experience became a divisive rather than a unifying factor. Serb revolts against Turkish control began in earnest in 1804, but full independence was not gained until 1878. Serbian nationalism could be used as a tool to further Russian interests, and both Serbian and Tsarist politicians exploited panslavism – an otherwise idealistic movement seeking to reunite the fragmented and exploited Slav peoples. By fostering Slav nationalism in subject nations, the Russians connived to undermine Turkish control in the Balkans and to weaken the other multinational empires of Europe.

If the causes of the Great War are even now too complex to comprehend, we know that the starting gun was fired when an Austrian archduke was assassinated in Sarajevo in Bosnia. The Austro-Hungarian Empire then declared war on Serbia, Russia mobilised on the Serb side; Germany mobilised in support of Austria-Hungary, and France intervened in support of Russia. The events of the 1914–18 war served to widen the rifts among the South Slav nations. The two independent states of Serbia and Montenegro fought against the Austro-Hungarian Empire, while Croats and Slovenes were recruited into the Habsburg armies; the Serbs suffered terribly in this war, almost one-third of the nation being killed on the battlefield or perishing through other consequences of the bitter fighting.

After the defeat of the Central Powers, Britain and France sought to punish their enemies and destroy their capabilities of going to war again. The US adopted a more idealistic stance and supported a policy of national self-determination. This was the perfect opportunity to implement such a policy: Tsarist Russia was in the throes of revolution, while the Austro-Hungarian, Turkish and Prussian Empires had all been defeated. Now the map of Europe could be redrawn in a way that would release the pent-up aspirations of Europe's subject nations. And so the victors proceeded to provide sovereign states for the main national groupings, while at the same time seeking to create a tier of strong buffer states between Germany and Russia.

The representatives of the Slovenes, Croats and Serbs pre-empted any solution which the allies might impose by meeting in Corfu before the end of the war and agreeing to form a united South Slav state after the Central Powers had been defeated. Their plan won strong American backing. While motivated partly by a desire to recreate the long-lost unity of the South Slavs, the delegates were also fearful that Italy might advance along the Adriatic and into the Balkans to seize territory from the wreckage of the Austro-Hungarian and Turkish Empires. However, time and distance had created differences between the South Slav peoples. The Serbs provided the political leadership and enthusiasm, but in the eyes of the Slovenes and Croats, whose Roman Catholic culture had developed under the Austro-Hungarian Empire, the Serbs were an uncouth and backward people. Also, they feared that the South Slav state might prove in effect to be a Greater Serbia, to the disadvantage of the non-Serb minorities. Meanwhile, the Serbs were themselves divided between Orthodox Christians and Muslims, the latter being dismissed as 'tribesmen' by the former. The different nations entered the new state with different goals and expectations. To many members of the Serb ruling elite Yugoslavia was a reward for the sacrifices and suffering inflicted on their nation by the war, but to large sections of the Croat and Slovene leaderships, Yugoslavia was just a transitional stage in the progress towards national independence; meanwhile, to many of the more backward, oppressed and exploited communities, any state was to be regarded as a hostile power (Licht 1993, p. 485).

The Yugoslavia that was born in the December of 1918 began life as a centralised monarchy under the crown of Serbia. At this time, it was a state without boundaries, these being settled piecemeal by negotiation. During this boundary-making process, Yugoslavia acquired various non-Slav minorities, which added extra dimensions of tension, with the potential for irridentism or invasion by conationals living outside Yugoslavia. The new boundary with Hungary gave Yugoslavia territory containing large Hungarian and German populations; in the South the boundary included many Muslim Albanians, while Slav territory was lost to Italy along the Adriatic. From the outset, the lack of cohesion between the constituent South Slav nations was apparent, for when a plebiscite was organised by an Inter-Allied Commission in the area of the town of Klagenfurt, it revealed the embarrassing result that Slovenes there preferred to retain their Austrian links – and so the plebiscite was abandoned.

In the new state the Serbs had a numerically and politically dominant position. The Christian South Slav population consisted of around 6 million Serbs; 2.6 million Croats; 1.1 million Slovenes, and ½ million Macedonian Slavs. In addition, Yugoslavia included about 600 000 Muslim Serbs and various non-Slav peoples. These included 450 000 Magyars; 400 000 Germans; 250 000 Albanians; 150 000 Rumanians; and about 175 000 people of other nationalities.

During the interwar period, the *raison d'être* of Yugoslavia was largely based on South Slav fears of invasion by Italy, Bulgaria, Hungary or Germany and by suspicions that an alliance might be formed between Italy and Albania to sever Yugoslavia from its sea routes. The Serbs dominated the army and the administration of the new state, confirming Croat and Slovene fears of a Serb ascendancy, while the compartmentalisation of the country by mountains made it difficult to integrate the economy and transport system. When the threat of invasion by Nazi Germany loomed larger in the 1930s, an attempt was made to adopt a more devolved form of government, in the hope that this would ease internal tensions and foster unity. A federal constitution was adopted and Croatia was given a measure of home rule.

Following the German invasion in 1941, Yugoslavia was dismembered, with Slovenia being divided between Germany and Italy; Croatia being set up as a fascist client kingdom and gaining Bosnia, while Serbia functioned as a heavily occupied German puppet state. In the course of the occupation, the most horrific attrocities were committed by Croat fascists against Serb nationalists and vice versa, adding to the legacy of ethnic hatred; Western estimates of the number of Serbs who were murdered by the Ustashe of the so-called Independent Croat State range from 600 000 to 1 million.

Even so, Yugoslavia and Albania were the only countries to free themselves from Nazi control without strong Allied intervention, though the struggle to liberate territory from German, Italian, Bulgarian and Hungarian occupation forces was accompanied by civil war which pitted Yugoslavian nations and political ideologies against each other in a multifaceted contest. Substantial numbers of South Slavs discovered unity in their support for Tito, the communist partisan leader whose forces had fought bravely and effectively against the invaders and who obtained a landslide victory in the elections in the recreated Yugoslavia. During Tito's lifetime, the combination of his personal magnetism, firm government and the fear of external forces bound Yugoslavia together. In 1946, a new federal constitution was adopted which divided the country between the republics of Bosnia and Herzegovina, Croatia, Macedonia, Montenegro, Serbia and Slovenia, created the autonomous provinces in Serbia of Vojvodina and Kosovo and recognised the separate national status of the Muslims, while in 1948 Tito refused to toe the Moscow line and Yugoslavia was excluded from the Communist bloc. During the 1950s and 1960s, economic expansion and rising prosperity helped to divert attention from internal divisions, and this was reinforced by the federal concessions to minorities and the need to maintain a delicate political balance in relations with the Eastern and Western power blocs. Nevertheless, the state apparatus suppressed any attempts to air ethnic differences so that Yugoslavian unity was imposed from above rather than growing from the grass roots of community – and meanwhile the federal political structures provided media in which crypto-nationalist politicians could develop their careers, particularly after decentralisation policies introduced in the 1970s.

However, it was plain to many observers that South Slav unity would not survive the death of Tito for very long. In the Balkans region, which has long existed as a geopolitical hotbed of nationalism, Yugoslavia, as a multinational state, had an anomalous existence. In May 1980, Tito died, and gradually the centrifugal forces which had lain semi-dormant in the country began to strengthen. To the surprise and consternation both of political leaders who genuinely believed in the multi-ethnic state and the grey apparatchiks who had assiduously ascended the ladder of the communist power structure, rabidly nationalistic politicians, like the Serb Slobodan Milosevic, began to emerge from within the upper strata of government. Serbs began to express their anger at what they regarded as overgenerous concessions to the non-Serb minorities, fuelling fears of a Serb hegemony. In November 1988, 1 million Serbs demonstrated in Belgrade in a synthetic and carefully orchestrated campaign against alleged attacks on the Serb community in Kosovo province by Albanians: although the area had a large Albanian population, it was also regarded as the home of Serb culture.

Serb resentment was to some degree a response to economic difficulties, reflected in strikes, a wage freeze and an inflation rate of 200 per cent. By the middle of 1991, civil war had erupted, with bids for independence in Croatia and Slovenia. These two territories had much higher standards of living than those experienced in the other four republics, but had only 20 per cent and 8 per cent respectively of the population of Yugoslavia, with Croats and Slovenes becoming increasingly distrustful of the Serbs, who constituted 36 per cent of the population and who dominated the army. Slovenia achieved independence with relative ease, Croatia after a bloody war, but the worst fighting took place between Serbs, Muslims and Croats in the ethnically diverse state of Bosnia. This fighting added new chapters to the mythology of national hatred and the obscenity of the 'ethnic cleansing' of captured territory has served as a reminder of the dark forces that nationalism can unleash.

In November 1995, representatives of the Serbs, Croats and Muslims signed a peace deal agreed in Dayton, Ohio. Under the Dayton agreement, Bosnia is effectively divided into two mini-states, the Bosnian Serb republic and the Muslim-Croat federation, the Serb territory being virtually divided into two parts by that of Bosnia, with the Posavina corridor providing a link between the two components in the extreme north of the country. Following a long phase of Serb victories and expansion, the agreement was achieved following a phase of rapid Croat and Muslim advances. The only group to benefit from the settlement were the Croats, who gained positions of influence and bargaining power while the Serbs of Sarajevo and Pale and the Muslims of eastern Bosnia and Banja Luka lost territory. As a result of the war, half of Bosnia's population became refugees and around 200 000 people were killed. When the Croat forces retired from territory exchanged under the Dayton agreement they set fire to the villages as they left.

The problems associated with the eruption of the 'new tribalism' in what was Yugoslavia are every bit as much geographical as they are political. It was geography as expressed in terrain and relative location which resulted in the fragmentation of the South Slavs in the Balkans and in the exposure of these fragments to different culture-forming influences. When the fighting between the ethnic–federal components ignited in the 1990s, geography also played a major role. Slovenia, where independence was declared in 1991, obtained self-rule relatively easily, partly because of its distance from Serbia, but mainly because it did not have a large Serbian minority, Slovenes forming 91 per cent of the population of almost 2 million. In Croatia, where independence was claimed at the same time, fighting was fierce and prolonged because 12 per cent of the population was Serbian and 30 per cent of the territory of the former republic was controlled by the indigenous Serb separatist population. In 1995, a major Croat offensive recovered the Krajina

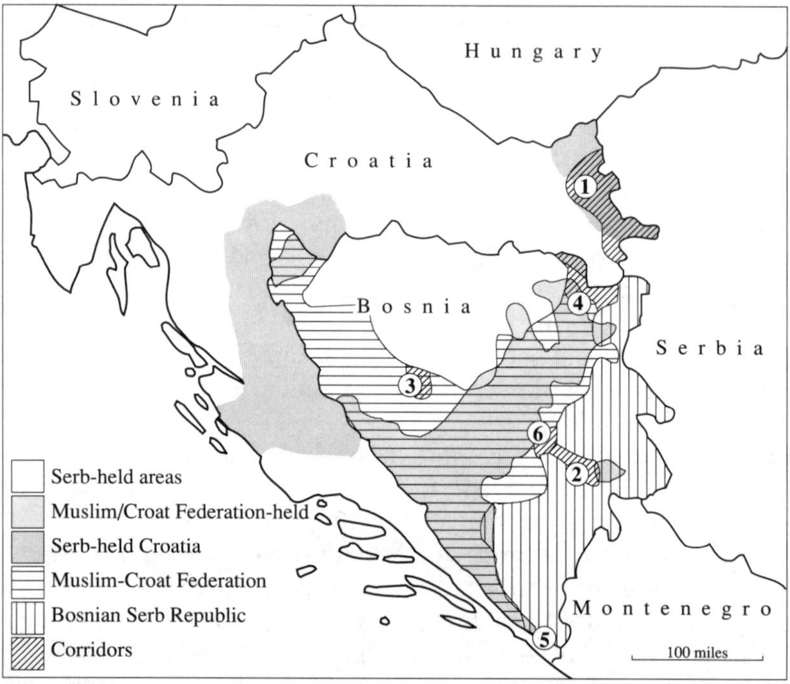

Map 2 Yugoslavia: ethnic divisions and territories as they existed late in 1995

territory in the south-east of the country, evicting the Serb population. But it was in Bosnia that both the slaughter, much of it cold and calculated, and the interdigitation of the ethnic elements have been greatest. Here Serbs, Muslims and, sometimes, Croats have struggled not only to maximise their territorial gains, but also to acquire, by war or negotiation, lands in a geographical form necessary for the creation of a viable state. Thus the Bosnian Serbs have pressed towards the Croat port of Dubrovnik in attempting to gain access to the sea, while also seeking to maintain all road connections with their patrons in Serbia. (Similarly, the Croats needed to regain control of their route-ways to the Adriatic ports which were cut by members of the Serbian minority as they entered the Krajina province.) In the early stages of the Bosnian war in 1992, Serb forces seized more than two-thirds of Bosnia, with Muslim populations being slaughtered, driven from captured towns and villages or stranded in besieged urban enclaves, like the ill-fated Srebrnica and Gorazde and Sarajevo. In the course of the fighting the ethnic patterns have been rewritten; Serb onslaughts removed most of the Muslim population from the east of Bosnia, with the populations of the towns of Srebrnica and Zepa being evicted or exterminated when these towns fell in July 1995, though in 1992 Muslims had formed a majority in the towns of eastern Bosnia. In August 1995 the long-established Serb population was evicted from the Krajina province by a major Croat offensive, and a subsequent Croat offensive drove Serbs from the area of western Bosnia to the south of the towns of Drvar and Jalce. But then, having depopulated and captured territory, the Serb, Croat and Muslim victors have found that they lack the reserves of population needed to repopulate it.

The political geographical problems also found expression at the macro scale as historical, partisan and clientelist attitudes coloured the international approaches to the problem. When Germany recognised Croatia with untimely haste, recollections of the Nazi puppet state and the atrocities committed by the Ustashe were evoked. And when, after months of vacillation by the UN, NATO aircraft intervened to prevent the shelling of Sarajevo by surrounding Bosnian Serb artillery and to demonstrate an intent to protect civilian lives in other besieged urban safe areas, Russian nationalists and officials threatened to reactivate the Cold War as part of a policy reflecting the long-standing tradition of Russian support for Serbia (usually as a pawn in Russian geopolitical strategies). Prior to the overdue NATO action, the Muslim world observed with disgust the murder and 'ethnic cleansing' of Muslim populations in Bosnia which was taking place so recently after the massive NATO action to liberate Kuwait. The conclusion that Western politicians cared more about cheap oil supplies than they did about Muslim lives was hard to avoid.

There were political geographical consequences too at the macro regional level. Most of the states in south-east Europe contain substantial ethnic minorities, and many are plagued by a legacy of border disputes. All must fear the spread of the 'Yugoslav virus'. Thus:

> Hungarians are already scared to enter Slovakia with cars with Hungarian license plates, although only a few months ago almost everybody was sure, in both Bratislava and Budapest, that there would be an open, or at least soft, border between Slovakia and Hungary. The Romanian, Hungarian, and Slovak nationalists are talking more and more about mutual territorial claims based, of course, on 'historical' rights. (Licht 1993, p. 490)

Relations between nation, territory and environment have been explored on a much broader scale by Armstrong (1982). He describes how two different forms of relationship between the ethnic community and their territorial context developed in Europe and in the Middle East. In Europe, sedentary agriculture helped to establish a bond between the people and the territory where they lived and farmed, while cities subsequently emerged as the hubs of civilised social life. In the Middle East, in contrast, the environmental conditions were such that the ethnic groups led nomadic existences. Thus, instead of there developing a strong bonding between these groups and particular territories, identities were established in terms of family and ancestry. Later, as the nomadic lifestyle withered, emotional attachments were associated not with specific places, but with the disappearing world of desert nomadism.

National territories have varied considerably in size. Some, like those of the Bretons and Slovenes, were quite small, while others, like those of the French, Germans and English, were much larger. The size of the national territory was a considerable factor when each experienced its industrial revolution. In a state such as Germany, the nation-state provided an infinitely superior milieu for the operations of industrial capitalism than had the earlier political patchwork of small principalities, cities and ecclesiastical territories. In the USA, meanwhile, the vast territory of the state may not have existed as an ethnic melting pot, but it did provide sufficient space comfortably to accommodate immigrants of a diversity of backgrounds as well as supplying an exceptionally fine spatial basis for manufacturing.

But economic consequences were not always in the forefront of the minds of those who argued the national case. New and reconstituted states like Slovenia, Croatia, Estonia and Slovakia may prove too small to flourish without very substantial sacrifices of the same, hard-won national sovereignty which has constituted their *raisons d'être*. The spatial distribution of nations has often affronted geographical realities: the modern history of Franco-German relations would surely have been less ghastly had the boundary between the nations precisely followed the Rhine. In some cases, national distributions have defied the realities of economic geography. Thus, in the former Soviet Union the geographical and economic unity of the Fergana valley was sundered by the superimposition of a boundary marking the ethnic division between the republics created for the Tadzhik and Kyrgyz nations.

This section has explored the associations between nation, state and territory, but while nations are variable and difficult to embrace within a single definition, the terminology in common use is also confusing (Connor 1978, pp. 386–94). Ethnicity, relating to the identification with one's ethnic group, is associated with a variety of groups in common parlance, but Connor suggests that it should be confined to those that are not yet self-aware; when the ethnic group becomes self-aware it then becomes a nation and as such it will be responsive to the appeals of nationalism and the desire to control the national territory. Primordialism and tribalism are both words sometimes applied to nationalism, sometimes in a patronising manner by those who wish to highlight its apparently primitive aspects and to assert that as modernisation proceeds, so these primitive characteristics will wither away. Pluralism is a word originally coined to describe colonial societies in which indigenous peoples, colonials and peoples imported by the colonials lived side by side yet apart, though later it was adopted to describe a form of political decision-taking in which power and influence were dispersed among different groupings (see Box 9.2). The tribe is also a term fraught with confusion, for most of the distinctive ethnic groups of non-Arab Africa which are described as tribes are confederations organised on a multitribal basis. It could also be regarded as a patronising Western term which assumes that the 'tribes' of Africa are somehow more primitive than the 'nations' identified elsewhere, even though good cases might be found for describing groups like the Ashanti, Ibo or Zulu as nations. Regionalism is no less confusing a term, for it is used to describe supposedly distinctive subdivisions of the state but also regional groupings of several states. Having reviewed the ambiguities in the terminology relating to nation and territory, Connor (1978, p. 395) remarks:

> In this Alice-in-Wonderland world in which nation usually means state, in which nation-state usually means multi-nation-state, in which nationalism usually means loyalty to the state, and in which ethnicity, primordialism, pluralism, tribalism, regionalism, communalism, parochialism and subnationalism usually mean loyalty to the nation, it should come as no surprise that the nature of nationalism remains essentially unprobed.

The psychological association between people and territory has evolved, and it will continue to evolve. What remains to be seen is whether it will evolve sufficiently quickly and with the requisite capacity for responsive adaptation. The global economic and technological patterns are evolving rapidly, so that a large portion of humanity may find itself emotionally attached to small pools in circumstances which are oceanic in their demands.

■ *Chapter 3* ■

The Growth of the State

Much of the history of the last half millennium can be written as an account of the energy and violence required to ensure that the monopolistic claims of states be respected. Whether through appeals to the nation, the flag, or the national interest, states continue to deploy immense resources on an everyday basis to ensure that this monopoly is maintained.

R. B. J. Walker (1990)

During modern times, the profile of the state has steadily risen as governments have discovered – or people have demanded – new functions for the state to perform and new services for it to supply. Ever-growing proportions of the population have been recruited into employment in the ever-increasing agencies of the state, while more and more aspects of life and society have been deemed to be proper subjects for state scrutiny, intervention and regulation. The modern state is an awesomely effective device for integrating, homogenising and controlling people and territory. With its national communications media and its governmental information services it has an impressive capability to mould the opinions and aspirations of its population. The modern conception of the state is embodied in Mellor's (1989, p. 32) definition: 'The state is a legal entity, internationally recognized, whose responsibility is to organise and guarantee the welfare and security of its citizens within its territory, where it is the supreme authority, tolerating no competitor or challenge to its sovereignty and demanding obedience from its inhabitants.' However, this image of the state is far removed from the state as it existed in feudal times or during the seventeenth or eighteenth centuries. Gradually, the state has changed and changed again, with the emphasis during each metamorphosis being on the acquisition of new roles and responsibilities. Nevertheless, in recent times more and more chinks have been discovered in the armour of statehood, and paradoxically the centralisation of functions in each state apparatus has been paralleled by a broadening awareness of the inadequacy of the state. The modern state often displays a schizoid nature; on the one hand it impresses us with the breadth and depth of its powers, while on the other it appears vulnerable to forces, both internal and external, which it is unable to control.

■ The state, armed and evolving

As Europe emerged from the Middle Ages and the narrowly circumscribed world of the feudal state was left behind, the changing interpretations of the state, its role and relationship to society were reflected in the development of contract theory, which explored the concept of there being a social contract between the individual and the state. This contract involved the citizen in accepting certain sacrifices of freedom, resulting from recognising the authority of the state, in return for receiving the benefits which sovereign power could provide. Hobbes, in his *Leviathan* of 1651; Locke in the *Second Treatise of Civil Government* of 1690, and Rousseau in his *Social Contract* of 1762 took rather different views of the relationship. The question had an important spatial dimension, and Hobbes and Locke realised that problems would result when large numbers of individuals, each one with his or her own particular interests and attitudes, were obliged to inhabit a territory of limited extent. They decided that the state derived from a general agreement that these problems might best be resolved by the creation of the state as a supreme authority. In this way, while government and law were not part of the natural order of things, people recognised an advantage in agreeing to have their selfish instincts constrained and regulated. Hobbes used this concept of a social contract to demonstrate the necessity for an absolute sovereign entity whose command was law but whose supreme position resulted not from Divine Right but from common consent. He had a pessimistic view of human nature, believing us to be motivated by the lust for power and the fear of death: it was this fear of death which terrified people living in a 'natural' world and motivated them to create a government for their own safety.

While Hobbes had argued that the power of the ruler must be absolute, Locke rejected the authoritarian stance and believed that since society had assigned powers to the ruler, it could equally take them away if the contract was broken, and that as beings possessed of rationality, people could be trusted to pursue sensible principles of conduct. Rousseau claimed that in the natural state, humanity was essentially good, but had been corrupted by civilisation and the spread of the urban culture. He believed that sovereignty must remain with the citizen and that the whole of society should be involved in decisions concerning the laws that bound it (he favoured a political system of mini-states in which each unit was governed by majority rule, but was not entirely convincing in arguing the case that the minority should be bound by the will of the majority).

In reality, of course, people are not consulted about whether they choose to be parties to a social contract, but the emergence of these philosophies reflects important changes in attitudes towards the state, its nature and function. Geography has a significant part to play in discussions concerning the social contract because: 'The geographical or territorial extension of the state is important in that it sets the boundaries within which the contract is binding . . . The spatial qualities of the state, understood as a geometric entity with precisely demarcated boundaries, is integral to the notion of sovereignty and to international relations theory' (Camilleri and Falk 1992, p. 238).

State formation often seems to have happened in conditions of population pressure on communal land resources. In this situation, the bureaucratic and warrior classes could organise the acquisition of new territory and become involved in the pacification and administration of conquered lands. Whatever the situation concerning the initial formation of a state may have been, in the course of its evolution warfare seems frequently to have played an important role in moulding the state. It did this not only by the process of carving out political territories by force of arms, but also by encouraging the development of centralised government through the need to establish the authoritative hierarchical command structures needed to muster and marshal an army and secure and administer captured territory. Warfare could also help to endow a vestigial nation-state with a sense of collective heritage. In Kyrgyzstan, for example, the government of the newly independent republic is currently heavily promoting the tales of Manas, said to be the world's longest epic poem, which tells the story of a mythical Kyrgyz warrior who fought to unite the scattered and disparate Kyrgyz clans against their Mongol conquerors. The epic was passed down by word of mouth for almost a thousand years before being preserved in the newly created Kyrgyz written language in the 1920s: 'Manas is a metaphor for the sense of self-preservation the 3 million ethnic Kyrgyz are seeking. And the power of The Manas – as the epic is known – to bind the Kyrgyz is not lost on political leaders' (Germani 1995). In considering its military role one may choose to stress the essential defensive function of the state as the guardian of its population, though some influential early geographers took a somewhat different view and saw the state as possessing the sort of raw, animal instincts that Hobbes had tended to attribute to humanity.

The association between the state and organised warfare can be traced back to the dawn of civilisation; the paintings, reliefs and

Box 3.1 *Stephen B. Jones and the 'unified field theory' of state creation*

One of the classic political geographical accounts of state formation was published by Stephen B. Jones of Yale University in 1954. The strange term 'unified field' expressed his attempt to bridge the fields of geography and politics and unite the ideas of three leading geographers, Derwent Whittlesey, Richard Hartshorne and Jean Gottman. According to this theory, 'Idea' and 'State' represented respectively the beginning and end of a chain, with the intermediate links being signified by what were termed 'Decision', 'Movement' and 'Field'. In summary, the dawning of an important idea would be followed by the formulation of a decision which was developed in respect of this idea. The decision would precipitate movement within a particular activity area or field, and as a culmination of these processes, a new political area, normally a state, would materialise. As developed by Jones, the theory was more complicated than this sketch suggests, and, for example, the progression could take place in the reverse direction. But the more that he tried to incorporate flexibility, the less convincing his idea tended to become.

Jones provided various illustrations of his theory at work, and I could suggest others. For example, in the middle of the last century, the idea that the newly elected President, Abraham Lincoln, might impose abolitionist policies upon the American South resulted in the decision of those southern states seeking to preserve the institution of slavery to secede from the Union and form a looser confederation. This, and confederate attacks on a Union garrison, resulted in the outbreak of the American Civil War, with Jones's 'movement' stage presumably being represented by the movement of armies and the Confederate thrust upon Washington. Had such advances proved more successful, a new state, the Confederate States of America, would certainly have resulted.

Jones did not believe that his idea should provide an excuse for over-simplification: 'The theory provides a path between geographical and political study, but not necessarily a short-cut. It does not reduce political geography to five easy steps. It does not permit world politics to be shown on a chart in five columns headed "idea", "decision", and so forth. It may, however, provide some intellectual clarification and it may prove a handy way of working back and forth among historical, political, and geographical ideas and data' (Jones 1954, p. 18). In assessing the utility of his theory, Jones wrote: 'It is as a tool for better work that I have the most hopes for this mental gadget. The chain of words in which the theory is expressed constitutes a sort of check-list ("check-system" might be better), by means of which one can orient oneself and tell where one should explore further' (ibid., p. 22). This is a fair appraisal. The unified field theory did not offer any penetrating new insights into political geography, but it did help to focus attention on the way that human ideas and choices could have political geographical consequences. It might usefully be adopted in the study of how a political area, such as a state, has come into being, though alternative approaches could prove equally successful. Though at worst innocuous, the theory was of a type destined to upset geographers of a certain radical persuasion. Thus, to Abdel-Malek (1977, p. 33) it was 'clearly heavily loaded with behaviorist assumptions and an even heavier neglect of the fundamental role of economic infrastructure'.

historical literature recovered from inscriptions and clay tablets of ancient Egypt testify to the importance of the association between the pharaohs and the waging of war, involving the destruction of foreign cities, the execution of prisoners and the taking of hostages. To fight wars of conquest or to resist the onslaughts of others, a military war machine was necessary – and the existence of such a machine greatly enhanced the power of the leaders over the subjects. At the same time, to endure a dynasty needed legitimacy. This could be provided by religion, mythology and organised ritual, which could be orchestrated so as to present the controlling dynasty as the god-given rulers of their people and territory. Normally, the bridge between the ruler and the masses would be provided by a caste of priests, who would formulate, broadcast and protect the doctrines used to legitimise the power of the governing class. Along with influences from other societies engaged in the transition to statehood, war; conquest; population pressure; the production of a surplus; and ideology are the factors which Claessen and Skalnik (1978) have identified as being crucial in the progress to statehood.

The functions performed by the early states were limited and tended to focus on the use of coercion to secure conformity in loyalty and belief, the imposition of a system of laws and the extraction of taxes from the populace. In return, the state offered protection from external aggression, though there was no suggestion that it had any obligations regarding welfare, universal education, health or housing. According to Johnston (1982, p. 41):

> Organisation of the territory was not usually strong, however, especially in larger states, because of the difficulties of maintaining contact and control. Each early state tended to have a single major core, which was the focus of state power and the home of the sovereign. Beyond the core, the territory was organised in a series of sub-states, comprising the land owned by individuals who owed fealty and tribute to the sovereign but were, in certain respects, independent. The stability of the state depended on the core maintaining its hold on this periphery.

Since the feudal states which developed in Western Europe in the aftermath of Roman rule were characterised by a hierarchical society defined by a clear-cut system of obligations, and defined too by a rigid social system which was resistant to change, one might suppose that prolonged political stability would have resulted. In fact, however, the early feudal states faced challenges both from above and below. Feudal society was, by definition, a military society. The propensity of the knights and barons frequently to wage war, coupled with the periodic

Box 3.2 *Friedrich Ratzel and the state as an organism*

The German geographer, Friedrich Ratzel (1844–1904), was the most influential thinker in the early history of political geography. He was very much a man of his time and place, and he applied the 'big ideas' of his day to the geographical context. After graduating from Heidelberg in zoology, geology and comparative anatomy in 1868, he joined the Prussian army and was twice wounded in the Franco-Prussian war. When Germany was unified in 1871 his burning nationalism led him to study expatriate German communities in eastern Europe and in North America, although his urge to explore was always constrained by his lack of a personal fortune.

Ratzel was strongly influenced by Darwin's ideas about evolution and natural selection, and by the social Darwinism of Herbert Spencer and Oskar Hertwig, which was associated with the concept of the survival of the fittest. Social Darwinism drew analogies between animal organisms and human societies, and Ratzel developed such notions in a political geographical context, presenting the state as an organism which was attached to the land (Ratzel 1897). He looked at the biological world and decided that every living organism demanded a measure of territory – a *Lebensraum* or living space which would provide it with sustenance and within which it could breed (Ratzel 1901). Plainly, the state was not directly analagous to a privet bush or a panda, but Ratzel also talked of aggregate-organisms, like forests, herds and flocks, which had collective needs for *Lebensraum*. Social Darwinists like Albert Schaffle, Albert von Krieken and Oskar Hertwig had already identified the state as one form of aggregate organism and Ratzel proceeded to suggest that if the state was confined then there would be a 'flowing over' of excess population beyond its legal boundaries (Bassin 1987a). Also, during his studies of the German communities in North America, Ratzel had become aware of the consequences of the impact of dynamic and aggressive immigrant communities upon native American society, and he believed that strong polities had the right to grow at the expense of their weaker neighbours. He wrote: 'over the entire earth, life struggles with life unceasingly for space. The much misused, and even more misunderstood expression "the struggle for existence" really means first of all a struggle for space. For space is the very first condition of life in terms of which all other conditions are measured, above all sustenance' (Ratzel 1901, p. 153).

As Bassin (1987a, p. 473) points out, Ratzel's ideas were associated with a new, expansionist imperialism which represented a radical departure from the nation-state concept which had exerted so much influence on political thinking during the nineteenth century: 'As an ideal for social and political organization, the nation-state concept had inspired virtually the entire spectrum of European civic life since the French Revolution, and did not cease to do so even after the 1870s. Yet . . . the openended political and territorial expansion of the developed world across the globe . . . was irreconcilable, both logically as well as practically, with the territorially limited and socially homogeneous unit implied by the nation-state.' Even so, Ratzel considered that Germany was obliged to acquire colonies if it was to survive, though most of the land suited to European colonisation had already been seized: Germany must make the best of what remained.

Box 3.2 *continued*

In reality, any resemblances between states and organisms are superficial and misleading. States are man-made territories within which complex associations of interests compete in a manner in which the cells or organs in a body do not. All decisions are taken by human beings, either individually or collectively; the state itself is an inanimate territorial package or container existing at a certain stage in history, partly as a consequence of historical accidents. It is utterly incapable of feeling, caring, responding or deciding and its pattern of growth will be determined by chance and the complexities of history rather than being genetically programmed and entirely predictable, as with an organism. Any decisions made in its name are made by humans – who must then bear any guilt that accrues. The ethical objection to Ratzel's theory of the state – formed at a time when organismic theories were very much in vogue – is that it could quite easily be applied to justify conquest, war and ethnic cleansing in quests for *Lebensraum*. And to argue that the conquest of territory is a natural and essential condition for the survival of a state is to sidestep the question of human responsibility. Ratzel was highly perceptive and recognised the weaknesses in his own analysis, but he liked to paint on the broad canvas and was probably unaware of the dangerous directions in which his work would be developed.

In due course the dangerous potential of his organismic concepts was realised; the supposed need for *Lebensraum* was regularly aired in Hitler's speeches – despite the embarrassing lack of population pressure in the eastern regions of Nazi Germany. In *Mein Kampf* Hitler (1940, p. 595) wrote: 'We [are] able to imagine a State only to be the living organism of a nation.' However, despite the fact that Ratzel's ideas about the state were embraced and developed by the odious Nazi regime, recent reappraisals of the man and his work have shown that there was no general alignment of thinking between Ratzel and the extreme Right. Most notably, Ratzel was not a racist, even though living at a time when and in a continent where racism was conventional; though a patriot and an apostle of imperialism he believed that biological science demonstrated the essential unity of the human race (Bassin 1987b).

local peasant uprisings against the perceived injustices of manorial life, frequently threatened to fragment the kingdoms into their provincial or regional components.

Then as now, universalism and localism or particularism tugged society in different directions and there was, for a brief period at least, the existence of a distinct possibility that the early states could yield to a superstate of an unprecedented kind. This would have been a theological superstate created by militant Christianity. Although the Church of Rome had its universal qualities, in practice churches tended to be provided and controlled by the local feudal warlords. During the eleventh century, however, a movement developed amongst the religious community at the great ecclesiastical focus at Cluny, in France, which resulted, in 1073, in a radical extremist being elevated to the papacy as Pope Gregory VII. Pope Gregory then proceeded to challenge the existing political order, in a bid to establish Christendom as the supreme authority and to advance its boundaries so that it could truly become the universal church. In the pursuit of this goal, both the King of Germany and the Patriach of Constantinople were usurped and progress was made in obtaining the loyalty of the warrior caste in the role of defenders of the papacy. Later, when Pope Urban received a letter from the Byzantine emperor, Alexis, requesting military assistance to repulse the Muslim Turks, Urban seized upon this opportunity to expand the empire of Christendom eastwards, and the gruesome First Crusade was launched.

Eventually, both particularism and universalism failed, leaving the state supreme. The peasants were generally unable to coordinate local opposition to the feudal system in the manner necessary to produce a state-wide uprising, while the West European monarchies were able, eventually, to marshal sufficient combinations of royal fortifications and mercenary armies to suppress any baronial opposition. Meanwhile, faced with the problems of expensive and ill-fated Crusades, internal divisions and then Protestant defections, the papacy pursued the role of arbitration between monarchs and hopes of global hegemony were abandoned.

According to Tilly (1975): 'War made the state and the state made war.' War certainly played a significant role in influencing the development of the modern state, though we must be careful to avoid the crude, militaristic social Darwinism associated with the Germanic writers of a century ago, like Ratzenhofer, who regarded the armed and aggressive state as the supreme force in human society. War was almost a defining characteristic of the feudal state, and feudal society has been described as a society organised for war, with the manor often being regarded as a territorial unit yielding sufficient wealth to arm and mount a knight, and with military service being owed by the lesser knights to the greater nobles in a hierarchy of martial obligations. War was the profession of the nobility, and the acquisition of land was often its objective:

> The categorical object of noble rule was territory, regardless of the community inhabiting it. Land as such, not language, defined the natural perimeters of its power . . . A given barony or dynasty could thus typically transfer its residence from one end of the continent to the other without dislocation. Angevin lineages could rule indifferently in Hungary, England or Naples; Norman in Antioch, Sicily or England; Burgundian in Portugal or Zeeland. (Anderson 1983, p. 143)

Moreover, 'No common language had to be shared between lords and peasants in these varied lands. For public territories formed a continuum with private estates, and their classical means of acquisition was force, invariably decked out in claims of religious or genealogical legitimacy' (ibid.).

The absolutist state which followed was also, in Anderson's words, 'built for the battlefield', but its armies tended to be much larger and far more professional and skilled. Feudal lords had always been reluctant to arm their servile peasants, who were ever likely to revolt. As the tenancy of land by feudal military service was replaced by money rents, kings and warlords came increasingly to rely upon foreign mercenaries. Such troops were not only valued for their ruthless professionalism, but also because, as foreigners, they could be impervious to the pleadings of any peasant community that they were commanded to oppress, rob or slaughter.

Mercenary armies played important parts in the transition to the absolutist state. It has been claimed that the 'gunpowder revolution' played a decisive role in smashing the power of the feudal aristocracy and allowing absolute power to be concentrated in the person of the monarch (see Box 3.3 Defending the Territorial State). In England, the first absolutist monarch was Henry VII, though gunpowder had been known there since the thirteenth century. So far as artillery was concerned, 'one of the most cogent arguments for believing that artillery played a very small part in the abandonment of the castle in this country is the almost total absence of any serious effort to combat it' (Thompson 1987, p. 35). Also, artillery could be, and was, used to advantage by the defenders of castles:

> In fact, the invention of the gun was of the utmost advantage in the first place to the defence; one can tell as much from the eagerness with which castle-builders everywhere found place for the new weapons. The whole mass of offensive siege-apparatus up to this time had been carpenter's work: pavises, cats or sows, rolling belfries, slinging engines; and all were now exposed to new and more penetrating missiles on the part of the defence. (Cathcart King 1988, p. 168)

In political geographical terms, the typical medieval European landscape could be conceptualised as a cellular structure containing (defensive) nuclei – the castles – and the surrounding territory which each castle dominated, each cell being differentiated according to whether it was royal and controlled by the state or baronial. The main reason for the eclipse of the baronial castle and the semi-autonomous feudal fiefdom was the centralisation of power under the monarchy. The last practical defence of a baronial castle in England ended in failure at Alnwick, in Northumberland, in 1462. Private armies were banned and the mercenary armies of the monarchy became simply too large to be resisted, allowing the absolutist kings of the Tudor dynasty to govern with a confidence unknown to their predecessors. As they did so, the effective political territory ceased to be composed of fragmented, castle-guarded feudal domains and became the kingdom. The defensive perimeter moved out from the curtain walls of the bailey to the frontier or shoreline. This was plainly demonstrated by the way that Henry VIII was not, like his predecessors, preoccupied with countering or destroying private castles in England and Wales, but with establishing an extensive network of anti-invasion artillery forts along the Channel shores. Internally, his realm was pacified and obedient; beyond there were enemies a-plenty.

The relationship between war and political geography has been described by Mann, who explained how, from the thirteenth century onward, the principal social processes favoured a greater degree of territorial centralisation in Europe:

> First, warfare gradually favoured army command structures capable of routine, complex co-ordination of specialised infantry, cavalry and artillery. Gradually, the looser feudal levy of knights, retainers and a few mercenaries became obsolete. In turn this presupposed a routine 'extraction–coercion cycle' to deliver men, monies and supplies to the forces . . . Eventually, only territorially-centred states were able to provide such resources and the Grand Duchies, the Prince-Bishops and the Leagues of Towns lost power to the emerging 'national' states. (Mann 1984, p. 208)

The costs of defending the state continued to escalate. The need to finance ever-growing armies to defend its territory required the establishment of a taxation system and a bureaucracy to run it, and this stimulated the progress towards the modern state. The army of Louis XIV numbered 300 000 men; in the late eighteenth century two-thirds of French state expenditure was consumed by the military, while: 'By the mid-seventeenth century, the annual outlays of continental principalities from Sweden to Piedmont were everywhere predominantly and monotonously devoted to the preparation or conduct of war, now immensely more costly than in the Renaissance' (Anderson 1983, pp. 143–4).

In Western Europe the transition from the feudal state to the capitalist state had been marked by the emergence of the absolutist states in the sixteenth century. These states, in which all power and legitimacy focused on the monarch, displayed a blend of feudal and modern features. The centralised monarchies of England, France and Spain had professional standing armies; state bureaucracies, taxation and legal systems; diplomats, and trading policies. But they were also archaic, for the traditional feudal aristocracy still maintained a position of privilege: 'Throughout the early modern epoch, the dominant class – economically and politically – was thus the same as in the medieval epoch itself: the feudal aristocracy' (ibid., p. 138).

In Anderson's view, the decay of the institutions which had oppressed the feudal peasants at the local level was compensated by the growth of the powers of oppression as the state level, so that 'The royal states of the Renaissance were first and foremost modernized instruments for the maintenance of noble domination over the rural masses' (ibid., p. 139). (Here, perhaps, we should recall Driver's (1991, p. 270) warning against essentialism: 'Essentialism is defined here as the reduction of complex social phenomena, diverse in their appearance, to simple, innate essences of form or function. Examples would include the identification of the policy of states (in general) with the will of the people, or the claim that capitalist states (in general) are merely committees for managing the affairs of the bourgeoisie.')

Meanwhile, the aristocracy was challenged by the rise of the mercantile classes which had begun to flourish in the towns. But as the absolutist state engaged in its programmes of centralising and standardising, it disposed of internal barriers to trade; promoted economic policies which discriminated against competitors from overseas; sponsored colonial trading ventures, and provided employment for bureaucrats in the state apparatus. In these and other ways, the absolutist state helped to pave the way towards the capitalist state: 'For the apparent paradox of absolutism in Western Europe was that it fundamentally represented an apparatus for the protection of aristocratic property and privileges, yet at the same time the means whereby this protection was promoted could *simultaneously* ensure the basic interests of the nascent mercantile and manufacturing classes' (Anderson 1983, p. 147).

The nature of the seventeenth-century state came to be established according to a new doctrine of international law. As noted in Chapter 2, the Treaty of Westphalia of 1648, which signified the end of the Thirty Years War, marked an important change in the notion of sovereignty. For now sovereignty was deemed somehow not to reside exclusively in the person of the monarch, but also in the territory of the state. Basic principles which still guide international relations concerning the integrity of territory, the inviolable nature of state boundaries and the supremacy of the sovereign state (rather than of the Church)

Box 3.3 *Defending the territorial state*

In 1957, John Herz wrote what would prove to be an influential and much-discussed paper on the past and future of the state. He argued that the political situation then prevailing could be compared to that which existed in Europe during the sixteenth and seventeenth centuries. At both times, technological advances in warfare had undermined the current political territories. During the Middle Ages, the 'perimeter of security' had been marked by the walls of the feudal castle, but according to Hertz, the introduction of gunpowder and large mercenary armies had rendered the baronial fortress obsolete. As a result, the perimeter of security had expanded from the walls of the local strongholds to the limits of the developing territorial state.

Under the terms of the Treaty of Westphalia, the boundaries of the territorial state became sacrosanct according to the new interpretation of the doctrine of state sovereignty, while the concept of legitimacy, involving mutual recognition by the various European dynasties, helped to reinforce and stabilise the political system: 'Sovereignty, after all, was a concept elaborated in the specific circumstances of sixteenth and seventeenth-century Europe to explain and legitimize the rise of the centralized and absolutist state' (Camilleri and Falk 1992, p. 239). Each state was internally pacified, and each was protected by a hard outer shell of frontier defences, so that the state boundaries were legally guaranteed by the doctrines of state sovereignty and legitimacy and physically guarded by massed armaments and frontierworks.

However, during the twentieth century, changes in the technological basis of warfare undermined the hard-shelled defences of the territorial state. During the 1914–18 War, long-range artillery, zeppelins and bomber aircraft all demonstrated the possibility of bypassing the armoured perimeter of security to attack civilian populations in the 'soft' interior. During the 1939–45 War, the bombing of civilians became a strategic objective, while the dropping of leaflets and the use of the airwaves allowed propaganda to be transmitted in attempts to undermine civilian resolve. Also, having industrialised, the territorial state was likely to have acquired a dangerous dependency on foreign sources of supply. Blockades were employed effectively during the Napoleonic wars; in both World Wars the United Kingdom was brought close to defeat by submarine attacks on shipping using its supply lanes, while in the 1939–45 War Germany had an unhealthy dependence on Romanian oil.

Finally, in the post-war period, the development of the H-bomb and delivery vehicles represented by the jet-powered long-range bomber, the intercontinental ballistic missile and the Polaris-type missile tended to negate the state's ability to defend its population. President Reagan's now largely aborted 'Star Wars' programme, which was announced in 1983 as an initiative which could 'change the course of human history', may represent government's final attempt to suggest that the state can guarantee the safety of its population against external attack.

Herz's ideas are still discussed, but events since 1957 suggest that the viability of the state was not so strongly rooted in its ability to protect and defend its population as he imagined. Had he been correct, then states, no longer being able to enforce the impenetrability of their territory, should have

Box 3.3 *continued*

collapsed when this, the very basis of their sovereign existences, crumbled. As Taylor remarked (1995, p. 11), 'The late 1950s were a bad time to predict the end of the state', for it was at this time that decolonisation was giving rise to a multitude of new states. The territorial state is challenged today and the possibility of its ultimate demise cannot be ruled out. But the main threats in this, the age of globalisation and the 'new tribalism', do not involve the issue of national defence so much as economic questions concerning the need for larger and more tightly integrated trading arenas, and internal political challenges from cultural minorities. Even so, Taylor warns against confusing the demise of the state with its adaptation for survival in a rapidly changing world. As a counter-balance to Taylor's critique, we may note Walker's remarks about the association between the state and defence and the remarkable psychological consequences that this prolonged relationship has wrought: 'The security of states dominates our understanding of what security can be, and who it can be for, not because conflict between states is inevitable, but because other forms of political community have been rendered almost unthinkable. The claims of states to a monopoly of legitimate authority in a particular territory have succeeded in marginalizing and even erasing other expressions of political identity' (Walker 1990, p. 6).

were codified. But although the new legal order transferred some of the powers of the monarch to the state, it also produced a more orderly international system and rewarded monarchs with a safer and more stable environment in which to rule.

After the absolutist state

Interpretations of the evolution from the feudal state (via the absolutist state) to the capitalist state tend very much to depend upon the broader political sympathies of their authors. It certainly involved the replacement of personal sovereignty, according to which loyalty was owed to a particular monarch, by national sovereignty, whereby people focused their allegience on the territorial state. At the same time, the governmental powers which had been institutionalised in the landowning aristocracy were eroded and a parliamentary government of elected representatives emerged. The transition also involved a restructuring of the class system, with societies that were essentially divided between feudal landlords and their peasant tenants being superseded by societies containing entrepreneurial employers, their increasingly urbanised industrial workforces and the merchants who obtained raw materials and dispersed the finished products of manufacturing. Involved, too, was the appearance of mass production for members of the mass culture of nationalism.

To writers of a Marxist inclination, the state is regarded as an instrument of the ruling class, and in the transition to capitalism the state was needed to enforce the conditions of stability which were essential for the conduct of trade and investment. It legitimised the position and activities of the capitalist class and provided the legal system that was needed to regulate trade. If the domestic role of the state concerned the provision of a harmonious social environment within which the members of the bourgeoisie could maximise their economic activities and advantages, its external role involved supporting their enterprises in foreign places. Often, this would require the use of the military resources of the state to invade, pacify and annex colonial territory, to frustrate the colonial ambitions of other states and to control trade routes. But it can also be argued that the mercantilism of the seventeenth and eighteenth centuries was mainly concerned with enhancing the power of the absolutist state. For while this system of trading helped to break down the internal barriers to trade and open up a single domestic market, it served the sovereign rather than society. According to the crude economic doctrine of the times, success was to be measured in the degree to which the value of exports exceeded that of imports.

> The aim of mercantilism, both in its domestic and in its external policies, was not to promote the welfare of the community and its members, but to augment the power of the state, of which the sovereign was its embodiment. Trade was stimulated because it brought wealth to the coffers of the state; and wealth was the source of power, or more specifically of fitness for war. (Carr 1945, p. 4)

War and trade were regarded as partners, for the wealth of the state could be increased by increasing exports, while export trade could be enhanced by capturing or conquering the markets of competitors.

Of the various factors which influenced the transition to the capitalist state, the most geographical was land itself. Arguing a form of Marxist case, Johnston (1982, p. 52) states that in agriculture the shift to a capitalist mode of production required that peasants be deprived of their traditional rights to use the land. The landlords either drove out these rustic tenants, converting them into wage-earning farm labourers; leased or rented the land to them under a new, capitalistic arrangement; or sold them the land in such a way as to create a new class of landowning petty capitalists.

Box 3.4 *Parliamentary Enclosure*

Given that Parliamentary Enclosure in England and Wales was a profoundly important movement which involved many of the essential ingredients of political geography – such as class, conflict, the state, property and land – it is surprising that political geographers have largely ignored it. Parliamentary Enclosure was a great, state-sponsored privatisation campaign, whereby the communal farmland comprising open field ploughlands, common moors, pastures and hay meadows, and even many village greens, were transferred from the community into private ownership.

This was accomplished on a parish-by-parish basis. When the leading landowners within each parish expected that they could benefit from the partitioning of common land resources they would petition Parliament to produce the necessary Act. This done, commissioners would be officially ratified to produce the new allocation of land. These commissioners were normally three in number and almost invariably males drawn from the local establishment classes: the nobility, landowners and the clergy. Even so, it would be wrong to imagine that Parliamentary Enclosure, which ultimately proved so very effective at removing the peasant classes from the land, was a carefully calculated conspiracy by the property-owning classes. The first Act occurred in 1604, affecting Radipole in Dorset, but attracting little attention. A trickle of Acts followed, but more than a century passed before the real potential of Parliamentary Enclosure was recognised, with 200 parishes being affected in the reign of George II (1727–60) though the great spate of enclosures did not occur until the century 1750–1850. Although the General Act of 1836 made it possible for enclosure to be accomplished without special application to Parliament if the consent of two-thirds of the interests concerned was achieved, by this time the movement had passed its peak. By the time of the last Act, in 1914, an area equivalent to the four largest plus the four smallest of the old English counties, or about one fifth of England, had been affected.

If Parliamentary Enclosure did not originate as a ruling class conspiracy, it certainly did stamp the interests of the property-owning classes on the landscape in a most striking and distinctive manner. In each parish concerned, the commissioners appointed a surveyor and a valuer, and the resources of common land were then partitioned in a manner which notionally provided landowners and tenants with compact holdings equivalent in value to their earlier, dispersed holdings. In reality the changes benefitted the wealthier landholding classes but sentenced the traditional peasant class to extinction. Many small tenants found that they could not meet the costs of the obligatory hedging or walling and sold out to richer neighbours. But the greatest crisis concerned the partitioning of the vast commons, where the resources of grazing, bedding and fuel had permitted the poorest of the rural classes to achieve a basic subsistence. Broken peasants flooded from the countryside, some destined for the expanding industrial towns, some seeking a passage to the New World, while most of those who remained in the village now did so as hired labourers rather than as small tenants. Enclosure transformed the patterns of population and class in rural England, while the angular surveyor's geometry of its allocations still provide the essential outlines in the landscapes of thousands of parishes.

The first economy to develop into industrial capitalism was that of England, and Horsman and Marshall (1994, pp. 7–8) believe that the transformation of agriculture was perhaps the most important factor involved:

> By removing land from the community through widespread enclosure of fields and commons formerly held collectively, England created a rural population indentured to the landowning class. That led to the production of food for the market, not just for the subsistence of agricultural labourers, as surpluses were channelled toward the non-rural population, with the profits accruing to the landowner.

Industrialisation played a complementary role in paving the way towards the modern state in Western Europe, though as with Parliamentary Enclosure it would be wrong to regard it as part of a great conspiracy formulated by the ruling classes. Indeed, in Britain (though not elsewhere) industrial society emerged during a period when the state was pursuing a *laissez-faire* or 'hands-off' economic policy. Even so, the state could and did do much to create the sort of environment in which industrialisation could flourish. It promoted law and order, which created a stable environment for manufacturing and trade; facilitated the enclosure of peasant land; promoted the removal of barriers to trade; produced legislation to make the financial markets more efficient, and generally helped to create commercial conditions in which labour, enterprise, goods and capital could flow freely. Britain was also unusual in that the state was not heavily involved in stimulating industrialisation and national integration by helping to create a rail network. For 'in Britain, the railways *followed* the Industrial Revolution: they came to a powerful and wealthy society which did not need the help of the government to mobilize financial resource' (Supple 1983, p. 176).

The speculators financing the rail network that was so vital to the expansion of manufacturing and commerce were helped by the geographical unity of Britain. In Germany the situation was less advantageous, for the national area was still divided into a patchwork of different political entities at the time that industrialisation was developing. And so, in the 1830s and 1840s, when railways began to be built in the various statelets within German territory there was no effort to build a national network, though such a network could have played a crucial role in furthering national integration and economic development. The establishment, in 1834, of a customs union, the *Zollverein*, embracing around 33 million German people was a vital step in the unification of Germany under Prussian leadership. In the middle years of the century, the Prussian government recognised the economic, political and military importance of the communication system and increased its control over the expanding rail system (ibid., p. 177).

The period of transition to the capitalist state was also the period of nationalism, nation-building and of the dawning of an age of masses. In industry the individual entrepreneurs and family firms whose fairly small-scale operations had pioneered the Industrial Revolution were being overtaken by the joint-stock company and the enterprise engaged in mass production. In politics the gradual progress towards democracy was beginning to give the masses some voice in their future, while the spread of mass education, which was essential to industrial and commercial expansion, would help to mould the form of mass attitudes and aspirations. Education imparted a sense of responsibility to the mass state community and a fluency in the mass language of the state; it also assisted the evolution of the state community into the nation by introducing the masses to a selective and nationalistic version of the national history and culture. The development of the ability to communicate within the state territory was vital to the process of nation-building:

> one of the strongest glues of the nation-state, as found in the European model of the eighteenth and nineteenth centuries, was undoubtedly the emergence of a common, national language. Language reflects the public sphere of government above all. The tentacles of the state – tax collection, postal service, a host of regulations and permits – required a common administrative medium, regardless of what people spoke at home. But economic growth, and the concomitant expansion of the activities of the modern state, particularly by the nineteenth century, meant that more and more people were required to operate fluently in their public language. (Horsman and Marshall 1994, p. 11)

■ The nature of the state

From feudal to modern times, more and more functions have been found for the state to perform. Again, the way in which this progress of events is viewed will depend very much on the broader political orientation of the observer, and where some see a haphazard process at work, others will see the instruments of class domination and exploitation. There are also conflicting perceptions of the state which are rooted in academic outlooks rather than political philosophies. Camilleri and Falk have identified some of the problems associated with the characterisation and conceptualisation of the state; firstly they ask: 'Is the state at the end of the twentieth century the same political entity which emerged in sixteenth-century Europe? Is it a generic term referring to the formal institutions of government? Or does it denote the individuals and organisations canvassed by decision-making theory or foreign policy-making analysis?' Then they ask: 'Alternatively, is the true meaning of the state the more abstract "national territorial totality" conveyed by political geography, with territory, government, population and society conflated into one entity and international relations reduced to the interaction of billiard balls?' Finally, they argue that: 'Analytically more rewarding definitions of the state emphasize its relationship to the ordering and reproduction of social relations at a given historical moment' (Camilleri and Falk 1992, p. 239). Later, they criticise the tendency 'to view the state as a frozen geopolitical entity instead of an evolving phenomenon situated in time and place' and suggest that: 'the principle of sovereignty as the defining category of international political theory, tends to overlook or understate the instrumental role of the nation-state, that is its historical function in the formation of national societies and national markets' (ibid., p. 241).

To liberal democratic thinkers, the state is the product of a voluntary contract, freely entered into by its population, to establish a sovereign power which would offer them protection from violence and disorder and which would also serve as a neutral umpire and arbiter, presiding over disputes and supporting the common good. According to this view, the state has no point of view, but acts as an impartial umpire to ensure that the competition between the different interests which it contains is carried out in a fair and lawful manner.

To traditional Marxists, however, the state is something quite different, and according to Marx writing in 1848, 'the executive of the modern state is but a committee for managing the common affairs of the whole bourgeoisie' (Marx and Engels 1976, p. 82). Thus, the state is characterised as an instrument of the ruling class – a view echoed by Lenin when he described the state as being a machine for the suppression of one class by another. (However, the development of the welfare state during the twentieth century has made it rather difficult to explain why the instrument of oppression should be providing old age pensions or using taxation policy to redistribute incomes?) Traditional Marxists believed that in the course of the inevitable socialist revolution the proletariat would take over the state apparatus and use it as a weapon against their former exploiters during a transitional phase known as the dictatorship of the proletariat. Then, as the socialist period gave way to the age of communism and the contradictions in society were removed, the state, as a now redundant instrument of coercion, would simply wither away and cease to exist.

Subsequently, various other Marxist interpretations have been produced. To Antonio Gramsci (1971), the state was not an instrument of a particular class, although it does shape society under the authority of a broader ruling power bloc. In this capacity, it is involved in achieving consensus and conformity within society and forming alliances and compromises between conflicting elements. When it is successful, it not only preserves the authority of the dominant social forces, but also enjoys the consent and support of those who are dominated. Another neo-Marxist, Nicos Poulantzas (1968), thought that the state could play a unifying role within society, for example by making welfare benefits available to the most needy and thereby reducing class tension. But though the state could arbitrate against injustice, he thought that on the broader scale the state functions to serve the needs of capitalism and therefore to preserve the existence of inequality and exploitation within society.

To appreciate the Marxist interpretation of the state one must explore the useful concept of superstructure. Marx and Engels considered that the structure or the real foundation of society was composed of its economic system, productive forces and socio-economic classes. Upon this foundation a superstructure of law, politics and belief arises. Thus in his *Contribution to a Critique of Political Economy* of 1859 Marx wrote that: 'The mode of production of material life conditions the social, political and intellectual life process in general. It is not the consciousness of men that determines their being, but, on the contrary, their social being that determines their consciousness' (Marx 1968). Marx considered that the superstructure had, as it were, two layers: firstly the state and its institutions of law and government, and secondly the ideology of the system, comprising the beliefs, philosophies and ethics which serve to confirm and validate the prevailing arrangements of society concerning fundamental matters like the ownership of property and the distribution of profits. The essence of his argument was that the nature of the superstructure was determined by the economic base or structure of society, so that we will change our political institutions, religious beliefs and social attitudes in accordance with the development of productive forces rather than as a consequence of the independent creation of new political, religious or moral doctrines. Thus to the Marxist the state does not play an independent role in directing the course of economic, social and political change, but rather, as part of the superstructure, they are the prisoners of the economic forces which determine their character and policies. Consequently, the function of the capitalist state is that of maintaining the conditions of capital accumulation. This is an approach based on 'economism' or the belief that some sort of priority attaches to economic processes, allowing them to determine the nature and outcome of other processes.

In British political geography one of the most influential observers of the state, R. J. Johnston, has espoused a Marxist political economy perspective, while in the discipline in general, 'such is the dominance of political economic ideas, particularly in British political geography, that reactions against them (e.g. Nientied 1985) can sound like crank telephone calls' (Peet 1989, p. 262). Given this dominance it is not surprising that critiques of Marxist analysis have tended to be few, while non-Marxists seldom recognise a need to develop the understanding of Marxist theory which is necessary to confront the Marxists on their own ground. Driver, however, has provided a critique and has noted a contradiction in the identification of the function of the state: 'In Marxist state theory, state policies are frequently interpreted as functional either for a particular class (the instrumentalist view) or for the mode of production (the structuralist view)'. He points out that: 'In the former case, the state is a tool in the hands of the dominant class and its policy is directed to the interests of that class; in the latter the state acts independently of any single class and its function is to maintain the balance of forces between groups and classes, to defuse economic conflict by political means, and so ensure the reproduction of the mode of production as a whole' (Driver 1991, p. 271).

Plenty of other interpretations of the fundamental nature of the state are available, and those quoted do not even represent the extremes, for to anarchists the state is intrinsically evil and an instrument for the oppression of the masses. At the same time, there is a world of difference between libertarian anarchists, some with views similar to those of the far Right in the USA, who denounce any attempt by the state to interfere with the individual's ownership of self and property, and anarchists of the more traditional kind who were/are generally hostile to the concept of private property and occupied political positions to the Left of the socialist parties. Every political philosophy or creed must have its own particular interpretation of the origin, role and social function of the state, so that analyses of the state are almost invariably rooted in much broader packages of belief.

Box 3.5 *Capital accumulation*

This, in Marxist terms, is the process by which capital is reproduced at an ever-accelerating rate through the continuing reinvestment of surplus value or profit, and it constitutes the driving force in capitalist society. Marx regarded capitalist society as being divided between the capitalists who own the means of production, and their workers. With the rise of capitalism, the status of labour was changed as rural families lost control over their tools and land (as with Parliamentary Enclosure). The displaced countryfolk were therefore obliged to sell their labour to the emergent capitalists who owned the new means of production. Here, Marxist theory departs from conventional economics; Marx decided that a distinction could be made between the exchange value of a commodity, which was the value at which it could be exchanged for other commodities, and use value, which represented the use of a commodity to its owner. Capitalists sold their products for a price greater than the cost of the wages paid to the workers that had produced them, so that the use value of labour to the capitalist is greater than its exchange value. The difference between the two was surplus value, which constituted the capitalist's profit, while the failure to reward the workers in full for their toil formed the basis of their exploitation. Herein, however, lay the downfall of capitalism. Wealth accrues to the capitalist class while conditions for the workers remain poor; capitalists could return surplus value to the workers by paying higher wages; they might consume their profits by spending on luxury goods, or they can reinvest it in the productive system. But as more goods are produced, so more must be sold, and if the workers are impoverished they cannot afford to buy the extra production. On the other hand, if they are paid more wages then the capitalist's production costs will rise, making his products less competitive in the market place. And if the profits are invested in labour-saving machinery then unemployment and impoverishment will be intensified. However, competition between different capitalists leads to wage cuts and investment in machinery, and in the course of this competition, many firms fail, though those that survive become powerful monopolies. Ultimately, the intensifying exploitation forces the workers to rise up and overthrow the capitalist system.

According to Harvey (1975, p. 10): 'Economic growth under capitalism is, as Marx usually dubs it, a process of internal contradictions which frequently erupt in crises . . . Marx's analyses of this system of commodity production led him to the view that there were innumerable possibilities for crises to occur as well as certain tendencies inherent within capitalism which were bound to produce serious stresses within the accumulation process.' Crises of over-accumulation are associated with the simultaneous existence of three over-accumulations or surpluses. Firstly, there is a labour surplus produced by the unemployment that occurs as businesses collapse and workers are put on short time or made redundant. Secondly, there is a surplus of productive capacity as machines and factories are underused or stand idle. And thirdly, there is a surplus of capital, because in the depressed economic condition investors are starved of attractive opportunities to profit by investing their capital.

Events appear not to have followed quite the direction which Marx envisaged, and Gramsci (1971) and his followers have sought to develop Marxism through the identification of different regimes of accumulation.

Box 3.5 *continued*

These are Fordism, named after Henry Ford, the American industrialist, which has been typified by mass production and mass consumption associated with enormous capitalist corporations operating production lines under conditions which were closely regulated by the state, and post-Fordism, which has displaced Fordism in recent years and which involves down-sizing and the introduction of flexible methods of production and employment with diminishing levels of state involvement.

■ *Chapter 4* ■

The Modern State

> **The state penetrates everyday life more than did any historical state. Its infrastructural power has increased enormously. If there were a Red Queen, we would all quail at her words – from Alaska to Florida, from the Shetlands to Cornwall there is no hiding place from the infrastructural reach of the modern state.**
>
> M. Mann (1984)

■ The modern Leviathan

When Thomas Hobbes produced his celebrated analysis of the state in 1651, he titled the book *Leviathan.* A leviathan is a gigantic monster or a person of enormous power, but the state as it existed in Hobbes's day was puny in comparison to the modern version. During the last century or so, states – and particularly the states of the Western developed world – have acquired remarkable assemblages of functions and responsibilities. In the course of this process, peoples' perceptions of what the state is for have changed profoundly. A seventeenth-century contemporary of Hobbes might have considered that the state had some sort of obligation to defend its people as well as its territory, to protect property and to enforce a measure of law and order – even if it was not always capable of doing all these things very well. But such a person would never have imagined that the state could become involved in providing a health service, subsidising development in depressed regions or disbursing overseas aid. Subsequently, perceptions of the realms of state responsibility have changed profoundly.

In the course of the twentieth century, the profile of the state rose and rose until about the 1980s. Then, in the context of an assault on the concept of 'big government' by the thinkers (and non-thinkers) of the New Right, it stabilised in some countries, and in a few may even have declined. Surprisingly, however, the rise of the state took place in a period when its future was increasingly coming into question. In one major area after another, the ability of the state to endure has been called into question, while layers of state influence and control have been stripped away to be assumed by non-state authorities like multinational corporations and international organisations.

The acquisition of new state functions has been interpreted as the transformation of the 'nightwatchman state' into the 'welfare-corporate state' (Esping-Andersen 1990, p. 1). For instead of merely providing its citizens with a measure of protection against foreign aggressors or home-grown miscreants, the modern state has assumed responsibility for the medical and economic well-being of its population, their education, their rights as consumers, their equality of opportunity in various areas of life, and a host of other responsibilities.

The functions of the modern state have been summarised by Johnston (1982, pp. 11–15). Firstly, the state performs a range of functions in its capacity as a **protector**. These include the well-established nightwatchman functions of protecting citizens from outsiders and from each other. In many respects this nightwatchman role could be interpreted as the protection of privilege and the status quo, for the state may 'protect the majority from arbitrary usurpations by socially and economically powerful groups, other than those allied to the state. But probably the main benefit is to protect existing property relations from the mass of the property-less' (Mann 1984, p. 196). In the modern age the greatest threat to the security of a population may derive from the state itself:

> 'National security' in the nuclear age has produced the persisting possibility of 'nuclear winter' not to mention environmental degradation on a global scale. It may have rendered the geopolitical order of the cold war relatively stable and done much to constitute the political identity of modernity, but it has not rendered women, the poor or the politically marginalized 'secure'. (Dalby 1992a, p. 517)

Yet it could also be argued that the protective role has been expanded to create the welfare state in which protection is given to the unemployed in terms of benefits, to the sick in the form of medical services and sickness payments, and to the family in the shape of benefits and allowances available to parents.

Secondly, the state performs a role as an **arbitrator** in disputes between its citizens, enterprises, interests and so on. Not only does the state produce a body of law to govern relationships, it also provides the judiciary needed to apply and interpret the law. In addition, the state may provide a variety of arbitration services which are less closely associated with the law, like marriage counselling or arbitration on levels of pay.

Thirdly, as we shall see in Chapter 5, the state functions as a **cohesive force**, and in this role the institutions of the state seek to integrate conflicting elements of the national community and to bind them together into a coherent whole. Here the existence of state-owned or state-controlled media and information services is a great advantage, while the presence of state symbols, ranging from the national football team to the parliamentary buildings, also assist. In performing this role, the state resists any separatist tendencies which might divide its territory and seeks to prevent the eruption of social or political divisions which could disrupt the economic life of the community.

Fourthly, the state acts as a **facilitator**. This is to say that it helps to stimulate or catalyse social and economic interaction by engaging in activities like subsidising transport, providing and repairing roads or becoming involved in the generation and transmission of electricity.

Fifthly, the state has an important role as an **investor**. It works to improve the performance of the economy by making investment available to firms in the form of various kinds of development grants and subsidies. It also invests in research which can be commercially exploited and it invests in the education system which determines many of the qualities and capabilities of the workforce.

Finally, the state performs a **bureaucratic** role. Bearing in mind all the other tasks which the state performs, it is inevitable that it must support its own gigantic workforce – and the elements within this powerful workforce discover and further their own vested interests. In this way, the state does not exist solely to carry out the functions listed above, but develops a life of its own with an interest in protecting the functions it already operates, while at the same time seeking for opportunities to extend its operations. In addition to these broad categories of activity which Johnston has outlined there are other arenas in which the state is active, such as immigration control, the standardisation of measures and quality control, support for the arts, and so on. Fittingly, he begins his analysis of the place of the state in political geography by pointing out that geographical analysis has been considerably devalued by the neglect of the importance of the state (ibid., 1982, p. 1), and he then presents the following telling quotation from Teitz (1968a, p. 36):

> Modern urban man is born in a publicly financed hospital, receives his education in a publicly supported school and university, spends a good part of his life travelling on publicly built transportation facilities, communicates through the post office or the quasi-public telephone system, drinks his public water, disposes of his garbage through the public removal system, reads his public library books, picnics in his public parks, is protected by his

public police, fire and health systems; eventually he dies, again in a hospital, and may even be buried in a public cemetery.

The functions of the state can be classified in different ways and Mann (1984, pp. 196–8), while pointing out that many types of activities tend to be functional for different constituencies in society, believes that the most persistent types of state activities can be grouped under the headings of the maintenance of internal order; military defence/aggression; the maintenance of communications infrastructures, and economic redistribution. Given the enormous burden of responsibilities which the state has undertaken, it is not surprising that it exists as by far the greatest employer, spender and debtor within its territory. In Canada government has a lower profile than it does in many other Western developed countries, but in 1991 the state employed a quarter of the Canadian labour force, state activity accounted for 47 per cent of GDP and state debt amounted to 90 per cent of GDP (Gross Domestic Product is a monetary measure of the value at market prices of goods and services produced within a national economy over a given period of time). The Canadian levels of state involvement are modest compared with some other examples; in Sweden in 1985 the state collected just over half of the entire GDP in taxation (Johnston 1993, p. 117) and in that country the state employs about half the labour force.

In 1988, governmental spending amounted to 30 per cent of world income, a sum equivalent to US$ 6 million. In Norway in the same year, the government spent US$ 9952 per head of population, while in Sweden, the Netherlands and Denmark the figures in US$ were 8621, 8544, and 8731 respectively. In the same year, central government spending amounted to more than 40 per cent of Gross National Product in some 28 or the world's states. These included most of the developed states of Western Europe: France, Ireland, Netherlands, Austria, Italy, Denmark, Norway and Sweden (Kidron and Segal 1991, pp. 58–9); (Gross National Product equals GDP plus net income from abroad).

The amount of state spending depends partly upon the wealth of the state concerned, but also upon its levels of borrowing and its taxation policy. In the USA in 1988, government spending amounted to 19.8 per cent of spending by all the world's governments, though government spending in the USA was relatively modest as a percentage of GNP. In 1989 the GNP of the USA in US$ was 5238 billion, and in 1988 central government spending was 22.9 per cent of GNP. As examples of the geographical variation which exists in state taxation policy, Japanese citizens are taxed at only half the world average level, American citizens at slightly less than that level and Germans at about that level (ibid., p. 137). In Japan, government spending in 1988 amounted to only 16.8 per cent of GNP, while in Qatar it registered a massive 82.5 per cent; in Qatar there is a population estimated at numbering only 484 000 in 1992 but a national budget in 1991 of some US$ 3.2 billion expenditures, with oil revenues giving the state one of the highest per capita incomes in the world. In most of the West European nation states, government spending amounted to around one-third to one-half of GNP: 44.4 per cent in the case of France, 53.8 per cent in that of Italy and 34.9 per cent in that of the United Kingdom (ibid., pp. 110–18).

In Germany and Austria, trade union representatives and employers' organisations are involved in governmental decision-making on a routine basis. In France and Germany, where the corporatist tradition is strong, workers are better protected than in post-Thatcherite Britain or the USA and cannot be made redundant without consultation. Employers there tend to shorten the working week rather than shed workers in times of difficulty, and therefore they tend to develop better long-term relationships with their workforces. The median period for employment with the same company is only 3 years in the USA and 4.4 years in the UK, but 7.7 years in both France and Germany – and 8.2 years in Japan, which has its own strong corporatist tradition which focuses on the strongly developed relationship between the firm and its employees. The more that a company feels free to lay off its workers, the shorter will be the period of employment with that company, and therefore the less likely it is that the company will invest in training its employees. In France the average period of tenure of a job is 10 years and over 30 per cent of employees are given training; in the USA the average tenure is under 7 years and only 17 per cent of workers are given training.

The corporate state was generally also the welfare state, and issues of social justice came to the fore in Europe in response to the hardships which resulted from the Great Depression of the 1930s. Welfare policies have operated through taxation, the redistribution of wealth, and investment in an infrastructure of public services. Yet while the extremes of deprivation in terms of poverty, lack of opportunity, health care and homelessness have often been alleviated, governments have also experienced problems of targeting investment. Welfare benefits do not only reach the deprived sections of the community, but can also be enjoyed by the privileged, as evidenced by the strong middle-class bias in university recruitment in the UK during the time in the 1960s and 1970s when there was a cross-party consensus on the value of the welfare state.

The corporate welfare state exists in as many different forms as there are governments sympathetic to its essential aims, and spatial variations

Box 4.1 *The corporate state*

The corporate state has been defined as: 'A state in which government represents and is answerable, not to the individual citizen, but to the various corporations of which the individual is a functional part' (Scruton 1983, p. 98). During the first quarter of this century, governments considered that the management of the economy should be left to market forces. The state, it was assumed, had a useful role to play in ensuring that trade unions and militant workers were not allowed to disrupt the market by launching damaging strikes or by obtaining unacceptably high pay rises. However, with the emergence of governments of the centre and left which were pledged to social and economic reform, the ideas of the economist John Maynard Keynes influenced policies in several states. Such policies, designed to cut unemployment and encourage growth, involved much higher levels of government involvement and intervention in the economic affairs of the state, with the government borrowing, spending, investing in public works and becoming the most influential of all the actors on the economic stage. Although one form of corporatism has been developed by post-war European governments of the centre and left, the theory of the corporate state was developed in fascist Italy. There it was argued that since individuals were politically ineffectual their interests should be articulated by institutions which were directly tied to their occupations as workers, professionals and employers – though in practice this system of associations or 'syndicates' was entirely permeated and controlled by agents of the fascist state.

As the corporate state developed in the Western democracies, its various agencies were broadening and deepening their relationships with employers' groups and with organised labour. The state and the non-state interests became enmeshed in complex patterns of influence consultations and decision-making. The representatives of the employers and labour not only helped to influence and shape state policy, they could also assist in implementing it. The progress towards corporatism was easier in states where policies of nationalisation had created 'mixed economies', as in the UK, where the nationalisation of coal, the health service, the railways and various utilities created the mixed economy in the early post-war period. As well as fulfilling social and political aims, nationalisation helped to undermine the power of big business and added an extra facet to the corporate relationship between government, labour and economic management.

The success and extent of the corporate state has varied from state to state. Under the Labour administrations in the UK during the 1960s and 1970s the government sought to achieve a high level of welfare provision married to full employment. This required that the economy should perform in a competitive manner, which drew government further and further into economic planning, modernisation and management. Meanwhile, as standards of living rose there were mounting pressures for ever higher wage settlements from the most powerful trade unions. In attempting to tackle the destructive threat of inflation through corporatist methods, government became wedded to policies of pay restraint and attempts to link prices to wages – but these attempts did not succeed because they failed to secure and maintain the undivided support of organised labour. Thatcherism, armed with the anti-corporatist policies of the New Right, was waiting in the wings. In a few other states, like Austria, cooperative incomes policies were introduced successfully, and in Sweden, the Netherlands and Germany strong traditions of consultation and agreement between government, employers and labour have been established.

in its nature provide a significant dimension of political geographical interest. These differences have been condensed into three broad types by Esping-Andersen (1990, pp. 26–32). The **liberal welfare state** provides a minimal level of support, a safety net for those members of society who are otherwise unable to survive. This model is associated particularly with Anglo-Saxon countries of the New World, like the USA, Canada and Australia, where corporatism has made only modest headway and where popular culture favours the work ethic and is suspicious of state dependency. The **conservative and strongly corporatist welfare state** is associated with a higher level of provision, but benefits are closely linked to jobs and to the principle of 'paying in' for support which may be claimed at some future date. There is a strong emphasis upon family values rather than a reverence for the market mechanism, and the state may only intervene to assist when the family itself is unable to support its members. In these states, of which France, Italy and Germany are said to be examples, social stratification is not regarded as an evil, and policies designed to transfer wealth from the richer to the poorer classes are not prominent. In the **social-democratic welfare state** a different perspective prevails, for here equality is regarded as a primary ethical objective and there is a desire to provide a high quality and broad range of public services, with these services being supported and enjoyed by all rather than reserved for a deprived minority. The maintenance of full employment and the provision of universal benefits are regarded as important responsibilities of the state. The Netherlands and the Scandinavian countries have inclined towards this ideal, although under the Conservative governments of the 1980s and 1990s, the UK retreated from it.

A different form of corporatism prevailed in the 'communist' world. In the former Soviet Union under the firm leadership of Leonid Brezhnev (1964–82), tensions between the (effectively) centralised communist state and its numerous component nationalities were limited under a policy by which the state and the leading minority interests explored the areas of consensus and cooperation. Government figures ceased to argue that differences between the different national groups would cease to exist as the socialist state developed, and instead they spoke in terms of taking account of the ethnic and cultural differences between peoples while at the same time developing the spirit of 'proletarian internationalism' (G. Smith 1990). Bureaucrats in the various national republics were given security of status, more career opportunities and a measure of autonomy, while in return the native political leaderships helped to cultivate stability within their republics. Thus the Soviet state and its component national republics developed cosy, corporatist relationships.

Box 4.2 *The state and welfare*

During the second third of the twentieth century a consensus developed in most advanced countries around the notion that the government had a responsibility to promote the general well-being of its citizens. However, there was little consensus concerning the extent of this responsibility or the means by which it should be achieved. Even so, very few states in the modern world still aim to perform only the minimalist or 'nightwatchman' roles of maintaining security and law and order which were characteristic of even the most advanced states in the nineteenth century. In capitalist states, the welfare state operates to provide services which the market cannot or will not deliver. It is not possible to draw a clear line between those services which are provided for charitable or ethical reasons as opposed to those which have an economic rationale. For example, by providing a free state health service workers may be returned fit to their employers, while a free and advanced education service will provide private industry with a stream of well-qualified recruits.

The most comprehensive welfare state emerged in the UK following the 1939–45 War, and was formed according to the guidelines of the Beveridge Report of 1942. As other states of Western Europe gradually recovered from the wreckage of war, the British model of the welfare state was widely adopted and adapted. But concerns with social welfare were not invented by the European politicians, and state welfare programmes have a long history in the USA, a country generally associated with individualist rather than collectivist principles. In 1933, when explaining his plans for the New Deal, which included a massive programme of state-financed public works, President Roosevelt broadcast in highly collectivist terms: 'Let us unite in banishing fear . . . It is your problem no less than it is mine. Together we cannot fail.' In the following year, US$ 950 million was fed into the Civil Works Administration, which employed more than 4 million people in projects like building roads, schools, airfields, parks and playgrounds. In the following year a Social Security Act was passed to provide pensions to Americans over the age of 65 and assistance to the blind and disabled, while in 1938 the Roosevelt administration set a minimum wage of 25 cents an hour and mandated a 44-hour working week.

The welfare state can take a variety of forms. Some believe that all allocations should be left to the market; some that the welfare provisions should amount to no more than a safety net to provide minimal standards of subsistence to the most helpless and deprived elements in society, while others believe that the state should actively pursue equality of opportunity and that the taxation system should be employed to redistribute wealth. The situation is complicated further by the fact that deprivation is relative and different societies have different perceptions of what constitutes poverty. Some western European social workers have been known to argue that video recorders are basic necessities of modern life, while in the developing world there are members of the more privileged classes who live in homes which lack electricity.

Under the Gorbachev leadership, however, the established corporate relationship between the Soviet state and the nationalities broke down. On the one hand, the need to expand and modernise the economy created a need for the state to increase its control over the national territories. But at the same time, the leadership was seeking to promote reform and encourage the multinational Soviet society to participate in the programmes for reform, 'openness' and democratisation. As corrupt or intransigent republican *apparatchiki* (loyal, professional communists) were removed, the snug relationship between Moscow and the national republics was breaking down, with the political reforms creating climates in which nationalism could threaten the stability of the state. Inadvertently, by promoting change and inviting citizens to evaluate the Soviet state, the Gorbachev reforms led to the reawakening of national separatist sentiments. In Kazakhstan, Russian immigrants had come to outnumber the indigenous Kazakhs by 41 to 36 per cent, creating a highly sensitive political situation. In 1986, Moscow criticised the poor economic performance and mismanagement of the Kazakh republican government and the First Party Secretary, by established custom a Kazakh, was replaced by a Russian outsider. This perceived affront to Kazakh interests resulted in the first major eruption of ethnic riots in Alma Ata in modern times.

Although the corporate welfare state has not always declined in the Western developed countries, its advance can frequently be seen to have halted. Since the 1970s the ideas of the New Right have been increasingly influential. There has always been debate about the extent to which the state should be entitled to intervene in the affairs of its citizens, but the ideology of the New Right has bypassed established consensus about rights to basic services like education and health care. New Right ideology is hostile to the corporate welfare state, while sometimes reservations even about democracy are voiced by its ideologues, who argue that the existence of elections encourages politicians to buy votes by offering extra state benefits. The state itself is seen as a rapacious monster and a pervasive parasite which preys upon individual liberty. Corporate links with business, labour and other major interest groups are also frowned upon, since it is thought that such contacts only serve to raise the pressure for pay rises, government sponsored pay or income policies, state subsidies, and other such things which are anathema to New Right philosophy.

According to the New Right, the only justifiable mechanism for allocating resources is not the state but the market. The plain implication of this is that such allocations will be driven by demand rather than need. Thus, while one might desperately need hip replacement surgery, somewhere to live or a job qualification, these things would be allocated according to demand as represented by the ability to pay. According to this logic, a starving but penniless person who staggered into a restaurant should not be fed because he lacked the capability to convert his intense need into demand. The political philosophy of the New Right attempts to marry both liberal and conservative beliefs, the radicalism of the former clashing with the desire to preserve the 'safe' and familiar which is associated with the latter. In fact, the doctrines, as developed during the 1980s in the USA under Reagan and in the UK under Thatcher, are seen to be contradictory in other respects. On the one hand, there is the neo-liberal drive to roll back the frontiers of the state and to promote an extreme form of individualism: a form of social Darwinism in which individuals strive to succeed without the support or safety nets provided by public services and social welfare. Yet at the same time there is the urge to create a powerful, authoritarian state, bristling with armaments and furnished with all that might be needed to impose public order, crack down on dissidents, punish those who do not conform and oppose permissive values. And so the New Right objectives are a strange blending of neo-liberal individualism and authoritarian social conservatism. Other contradictions emerge – as they must in a forced marriage of dogmas which trumpet the virtues of the nation and national territory in the most jingoistic of fashions yet simultaneously relish the destruction of those very provisions which gave the nation its health, skills and dignity; dogmas which rejoice in the existence of distinctive, unspoiled regional countrysides and architecture while eagerly discarding all those planning restrictions and development controls which have allowed them to survive.

In the UK, while the New Right Thatcherite doctrines led to a drastic pruning of the welfare state and the adoption of inappropriate but costly managerial techniques in the provision of its services, the profile of the leviathan was scarcely diminished. The state did not become smaller, only less responsible. In seeking to emasculate and marginalise Leftist local councils, the government stripped local government of many of its powers, assumed these powers for itself and created a much more centralised state. Meanwhile, scores of other functions were handed over to newly created quangos (quasi-non-governmental organisations) which were not directly accountable to the public and which were frequently staffed by influential supporters of the government: 'The result of this has been the most centralised British state in its peacetime history, with unfettered market institutions protected by authoritarian, unaccountable, quasi-governmental apparatus. It is this leviathan, constructed to serve Tory objectives and manned by a new class of *nomenklatura* [state appointees] – that Labour would inherit' (Gray 1994). In France, where the welfare state survived more strongly, attempts under the new President to prune public pensions, employment and benefits in order to meet economic convergence targets associated with the adoption of a single 'Euro' currency resulted in devastating strikes and a tactical withdrawal by the government at the close of 1995.

■ The decline of the state?

Nothing is forever, and the days remaining for the nation-state system may be fewer than many people suppose. Writing as long ago as 1981, Karl Deutsch described how the state was an instrument that was indispensable to the tasks of 'getting things done', and yet was inadequate in its ability to cope with the increasing number of problems facing its population.

> No state today can protect the lives of its citizens in the case of thermonuclear war against it, nor against the poisonous fall-out from thermonuclear war outside its borders. No national state can protect the world's ecology, the oceans and the atmosphere, nor can any one state solve the problems of worldwide population growth or lack of raw materials, energy or food. In all these respects, the first and basic promise of government – to protect the lives of its citizens – has become illusory. (Deutsch 1981, p. 331)

From the French Revolution, which embodied the belief in the sovereignty of the people, up until the contraction of Europe's overseas empires, the nation-state existed either as a hard-won reality or as a fiercely pursued aspiration. Throughout the twentieth century, the world's leaders struggled to shift and fine tune international boundaries in order to achieve the best possible geographical match between nation and state. Yet even before the last territorial dispute has been settled or the last line redrawn on the political map, the state itself is confronted by redundancy. Hutchinson made the point that as the Soviet empire collapsed and fragmented at the end of the 1980s, its ethnic components adopted as their political model the classical norms of the nation-state, but he added:

> How ironic then that this shift to nation-statism in the East should be occurring at a time when it has recently been argued that the assumptions on which this model is based are no longer valid, and that even in its own European heartland the nation-state is increasingly anachronistic as a result of the processes of internationalization. (Hutchinson 1994, p. 134)

For a while, the full extent of the challenge to the nation-state had been masked. This was because the division of the world into the respective spheres of two great ideological heartlands, the USA and USSR, imposed powerful pressures for stability and conformity. The watershed was reached in 1989 when the Berlin Wall was beaten down and the crumbling of Soviet power signalled the end of the bipolar superpower system. At the time, the joyful reunification of Germans after decades of separation might seem to have reaffirmed any beliefs in the majesty and magnetism of the sovereign nation-state. But in other ways it marked the arrival of a new fluidity in political thinking as alternatives to the conformity imposed by membership of one or other bloc in the disintegrating bipolar power system were explored. As the new, multipolar system took shape there was a loosening up of international boundaries and the emergence of a an era of change and uncertainty.

In the context of Western Europe, Hutchinson (ibid., pp. 135–7) described three different but increasingly interrelated challenges to the nation-states which have emerged in the post-war period. The first comes from supranational organisations, notably the EU, which give institutional form to the movement to integrate national economies and political systems. The second comes from the local or regional level and is represented by ethnic-based movements campaigning for cultural or political autonomy – a movement referred to elsewhere as the 'New Tribalism' – while the third challenge derives from the increasingly polyethnic character of the European states, resulting from declining birth rates and labour shortages in Western Europe which encouraged large-scale immigration from Mediterranean and Third World countries. This has produced tensions between the indigenous and immigrant communities, inequalities in the provision of full rights of citizenship and drives to change the constitutional and institutional character of the state in accordance with its new, multicultural character.

Sovereignty still remains vested in the state, but while once sovereignty was – by definition – indivisible, today it is being eroded and compromised, often as part of the state's own strategy for survival. The decisions that really matter are no longer reserved for members of the state political and governmental elites: of the 100 largest economies in the modern world, 47 are not state economies but those of transnational corporations (TNCs) (Horsman and Marshall 1994, p. 201). Horsman and Marshall (ibid.) also point out that if General Motors were a country it would have the world's twentieth largest economy, with Ford coming in just behind Denmark and IBM behind Thailand. Actors of a different type are now beginning to command the economic

Box 4.3 *Peter J. Taylor and the state as a container*

In a landmark paper written in 1994 the influential British political geographer, Peter J. Taylor, likened the modern state to a container and argued that the awesome dominance of the state was premised upon the highly geographical fact of territoriality. The state had previously been described as a 'power container' by Giddens (1985). Taylor traced the development of the state as a 'wealth container' as states competed, under mercantilism and capitalism, to maximise their shares of the world's wealth; as a 'cultural container' which rose in importance during the age of nationalism when the state became the guardian of the national homeland, and as a 'social container' as the state discovered a moral obligation to look after its people. Territoriality was defined as 'a form of behaviour that uses a bounded space, a territory, as the instrument for securing a particular outcome', while: 'By controlling access to a territory through boundary restrictions, the content of a territory can be manipulated and its character designed' (ibid., p. 151). Territoriality can find expressions at many levels, but all others 'pale in significance when compared to the territoriality that underpins the interstate system. Across the whole of our modern world, territory is directly linked to sovereignty to mould politics into a fundamentally state-centric social process . . . so much so that conflicts not involving the state are often seen as outside politics as generally conceived' (ibid.). The might of the state derives from the territorial link between state and nation: both states and nations have, in the sovereign territory and the national homeland, a community based on place which enables them to be linked together as nation-state. 'The dominance of political practice in the world by territoriality is a consequence of this territorial link between sovereign territory and national homeland' (ibid.).

Taylor then turned to the question of whether the container had begun to leak? He reviewed arguments, like those of Herz described earlier, which claimed that the military demise of the state is at hand, but found them wanting: 'the contemporary states are more secure and stable than at any time in the history of the modern world-system. By this I mean that the international regime since 1945 has effectively protected states by guaranteeing their international existence. Hence despite the many political upheavals since 1945, the physical boundaries on the political map have changed little. Neighbours respect neighbours' (ibid., p. 158). Next he looked at the impact of factors like globalisation upon the economic independence of the state, and found that states were responding to the challenges by forming international economic organisations in their attempts to create wealth containers on a scale larger than that of the individual state. Turning to the fragmentation of territory in the face of pressures which are explored in chapter 5, Taylor described a 'triple layering of territoriality': 'the state as power container tends to preserve existing boundaries; the state as wealth container tends towards larger territories; and the state as cultural container tends towards smaller territories' (ibid., p. 160). Although the state was a leaking container it could not yet be disregarded in world politics, though Taylor predicted a new centre politics built upon an alliance of state elites and the people which would confront the anti-territoriality of the New Right offshore economy and New Left globalism. Ultimately, however, the state was doomed since 'the whole structure of the world system is predicated on economic expansion which is

Box 4.3 *continued*

ultimately unsustainable. And the states are directly implicated as "growth machines" – it is unimaginable that a politician could win control of a state on a no-growth policy. The people expect more, that is the essence of progress. But progress cannot be for ever if the Earth is too small for ever-expanding capitalism' (ibid., p. 161). In this way Taylor predicts the end of our familiar world; his conclusions seem chillingly probable.

stage: each of the ten largest TNCs produces more than 87 of the world's nation-states (Healey 1995). Yet this is not to say that the TNC could appropriate the functions of the state: 'General Motors and the capitalist class in general, or the Catholic Church, or the feudal lords and knights, or the US military, are or were quite capable of keeping watch on states they have propped up. Yet they could not do the states' jobs themselves unless they changed their own socio-spatial and organizational structure' (Mann 1984, pp. 200–1).

The question of the size of states has always been of great interest to political geographers, and the recent developments have stimulated fresh debate. While globalisation scorns the state for its smallness, the New Tribalism, that other great movement of the dying years of the twentieth century, is undermining many of the states containing minority nations. There may never have been an identifiable 'right' size for a state, but in the modern world the internationalisation of the human capacity for environmental destruction has made the state too small a vehicle for the operation of effective conservational policies. Even where states have the resolve necessary to tackle these problems, it is increasingly the case that the extent of the problem or the spread of its consequences far exceed the sovereign territory of the state. As a result, the state may appear as a misfit: 'too big for the task of devising viable strategies of sustainable development which can only be developed from the bottom up; and too small for the effective management of global problems . . . which by their nature demand increasingly wide-ranging forms of international cooperation' (Hurrell 1994). Therefore, the state which is far too small to tackle environmental problems may yet be too large to accommodate an ethnically diverse population with comfort, especially if we follow Deutsch (1981, p. 342) and consider the 'psychological distance' between ruler and ruled. Concerning the state's neglect of the affairs of populations or territories which are regarded as marginal in the political, economic or geographical senses he writes: 'It is this declining attention and the consequent decline in governmental performance and services for these marginal regions and populations that in turn tends to bring about declining loyalties and growing resistance, and thus to limit the size of states' (ibid., p. 343).

The citizens of the corporate welfare state have become accustomed to regarding their elected government as being responsible and accountable, but now they find that their lives may be transformed by decisions taken by TNC executives who wield authority without being answerable to most of those affected by their decisions. As Healey (1995) explains:

> Up to 1,000 billion dollars a day are moved across the exchanges by a mafia of young lemmings in the dealing rooms of business and financial institutions. These movements determine a country's exchange rates, interest rates, balance of payments, investment and output, irrespective of the will of its national government . . . And all firms now put new factories wherever the relevant labour is cheapest and their ultimate market is nearest – whatever their government may say.

The transfer of power from the known and accountable national politician or official to the faceless TNC executive not only poses a challenge to democracy, it may also threaten to undermine the economic basis of the state. Where once the scoreline in the competition between states could be measured in terms of battalions recruited, battleships built and squadrons formed, later it came to be measured in balance of trade statistics, GNP and other indicators of economic strength. Automobile industries, electrical manufacturers and engineering concerns became the flagships of state, with brand names like Fiat, Simca or Austin symbolising the strength or weakness of the national economy. But with the emergence of the global economy, strategic industries can vanish in an instant as TNCs relocate their computer industries, pull out of electronics or transfer their truck-building operations. Such changes could undermine vital national defence industries or remove cornerstones of national production – but this is not a concern for the TNCs or the global market (Moran 1990).

Similarly, the erosion of the authority of the state is affected by the globalisation of financial markets. The withering away of the state was regarded by Marxists as a process that would take place in the transition from socialism to communism, but recently Giddens was persuaded to pose the question: 'Is capitalism causing the withering of the state?' (Giddens 1995). The moods and reactions of the currency traders have always been considered in the course of government decision-making. What is different today is the scale and speed of the transactions: 'With the volume of daily currency exchanges well in

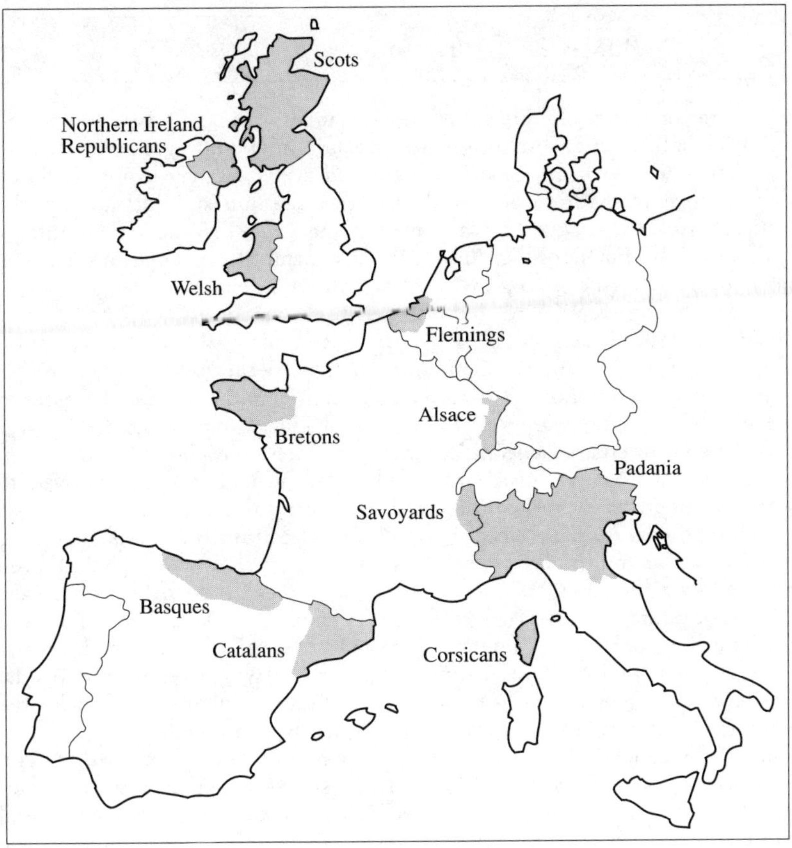

Map 3 Minority nationalism in Western Europe

excess of the GNPs of many countries, individual governments and finance ministers have much less command over the system than they had a quarter century ago. Simply the awareness of the market's disapproval of certain measures (like raising taxes) can deter so-called sovereign governments from implementing them' (Kennedy 1993, p. 129). There must be many cases where government choices to improve welfare provisions have been shelved in anticipation of a hostile reaction from the international financial community, while, for example, any British decision to opt out of the EU would undoubtedly propel the pound into freefall. Thus: 'Corporations treat the world like a global chessboard bidding down wages and taxes, avoiding environmental regulation and pillaging natural resources. Their right to do this is no longer considered controversial. They are courted by politicians of all political stripes' (Swift 1994, p. 5).

Box 4.4 *Supra-national regionalism*

While transnational organisations merely happen to operate between states, international organisations originate from multinational agreements set up between states. Such organisations have had a role to play in international affairs since the Congress of Vienna; they became significant with the institution of the League of Nations after the 1914–18 War and important with the establishment of the United Nations, formed by negotiations between the Allied Powers beginning in 1942. Regional political alignments of states had existed for some time, but the process of association gained a new dimension with the signing of the Treaty of Rome in 1957 and the institution of the European Economic Community in 1958, because these moves represented a stage in the transfer of sovereign power from the constituent states to the international organisation. A number of factors operating in post-war Western Europe created a political climate in which supranational regionalism could flourish. Many Europeans on the Continent had been involved in wartime underground resistance movements, and these had fostered a desire for closer integration between states. More significantly, it was becoming plain that the multipolar power system of the pre-war world had been replaced by a bipolar system, so that the partition of the world between the spheres of influence of the two superpowers appeared to be at hand. To avoid this fate, European states might be obliged to form a new power bloc and economic grouping of their own. Thirdly, there was a realisation by the French economic strategist, Jean Monet, that France could no longer delay the economic recovery of Germany. Consequently, he sought to develop a mutually beneficial association with Germany, and his collaboration with his German counterpart, Robert Schuman, resulted in a plan for the cooperative development of their coal and steel resources, then regarded as essential strategic resources to the waging of war. These were to be removed from national control and placed under an independent authority. The European Coal and Steel Community which resulted in 1952, and involved France, Germany, Italy, Belgium, the Netherlands and Luxembourg, represented the most purposeful step towards European integration.

The ECSC was regarded as a success and the French were encouraged to press for the creation of a European army. When these moves were blocked by the French opposition parties, Monet sought to advance integration in the economic direction and the EEC was formed with a mission to establish a common European market with the elimination of internal barriers to trade and the establishment of a common external tariff. In 1967 the ECSC, EEC and the European Atomic Energy Community formally amalgamated into the European Community. The following year a customs union with a common external tariff was established. The internal market was completed with the Single European Act in 1993. The first direct elections to the European Parliament were held in 1979. The Maastricht conference of 1991 established the European Union and plans for an economic and monetary union by 1999 were drafted. The Maastricht Treaty with its intent to create an ever closer union among the peoples of Europe represented a crucial move in the further integration of the organisation.

No other voluntary association of states has moved so far in the direction of association and, not surprisingly, tensions between and within the member

Box 4.4 *continued*

states have resulted from different perceptions and priorities associated with the issues of national identity versus internationalism. Having failed in attempts to sabotage the organisation, the British applied for EEC membership in 1961, suffered a veto by the French, but then joined along with Ireland and Denmark in 1973. Subsequently British policy, particularly in the 1980s and 1990s, has sought to limit the organisation to the operation of a European free trade area and to resist efforts associated with regulation, workers' rights, consumer protection and political integration. While the British role has been consistently obstructive, public opinion within the continental member countries is divided; referenda associated with the ratification of the Maastrict Treaty in France and Denmark revealed that sentiments for and against further integration were almost equally divided, while though Austria, Finland and Sweden acceded to EU membership in 1995, the Norwegian referendum on membership produced a negative result. Currently, the greatest challenge facing the EU is that of incorporating Cyprus, Malta and the former communist states of Eastern Europe, which might result in a rise of membership from 15 to 27. The broadened membership could result in a greater diversity of opinions and a resultant dilution of policy objectives, urging the abandonment of the right of individual states to operate a policy veto. Even so, opinion surveys conducted on the eve of the 1996–7 intergovernmental conference reveal high levels of public support in the EU for the establishment of a common foreign policy and defence policy. Other developments in international regionalism were less ambitious than those undertaken by members of the EC/EU and they have tended to focus on the economic rather than the political arena. However, tensions have often resulted when different perceptions of the state destiny have been in conflict: 'the debate in the United States and especially in Congress leading up to the passage of the NAFTA [North American Free Trade Area] legislation in November, 1993, was heated. U.S. labour and environmental groups, and many in Congress, like their counterparts in Canada, were worried that business would close and relocate in Mexico to take advantage of lower labour costs and environmental standards . . . Americans had to decide between protectionist and internationalist visions of the future of the U.S. economy and its relationship to the North American economic region' (Leyton-Brown 1994, p. 363).

The globalisation of the economy has created a variety of problems for national governments. At the socio-political level it can be argued that the takeover of national brands by TNCs marketing 'global' brands, like Coca-Cola, can weaken the national identity. Meanwhile, brands which are assumed to be national and are bought on this basis in their countries of origin may later be found to have been taken over by a TNC and could be manufactured on the other side of the globe. Also, members of the national community who become TNC employees may develop global perspectives and feel less identification with the national state. Another, quite different, aspect of the globalisation of economic activity is reflected in the increasing likelihood of hazards combined with increasing difficulties of establishing responsibility for any accidents which may occur. Potentially dangerous forms of manufacturing may be located in Third World countries, where the safety legislation or inspection of plant may be less stringent, while the global economy links different parts of the world in systems of exchange which often involve dangerous cargoes. At the same time, the production of hazardous chemical by-products can lead to a search for toxic waste dumping sites in the less carefully regulated Third World countries.

The role of the TNC in modern society is likely to cause concern to all but the most fanatical advocates of *laissez-faire* capitalism. It can

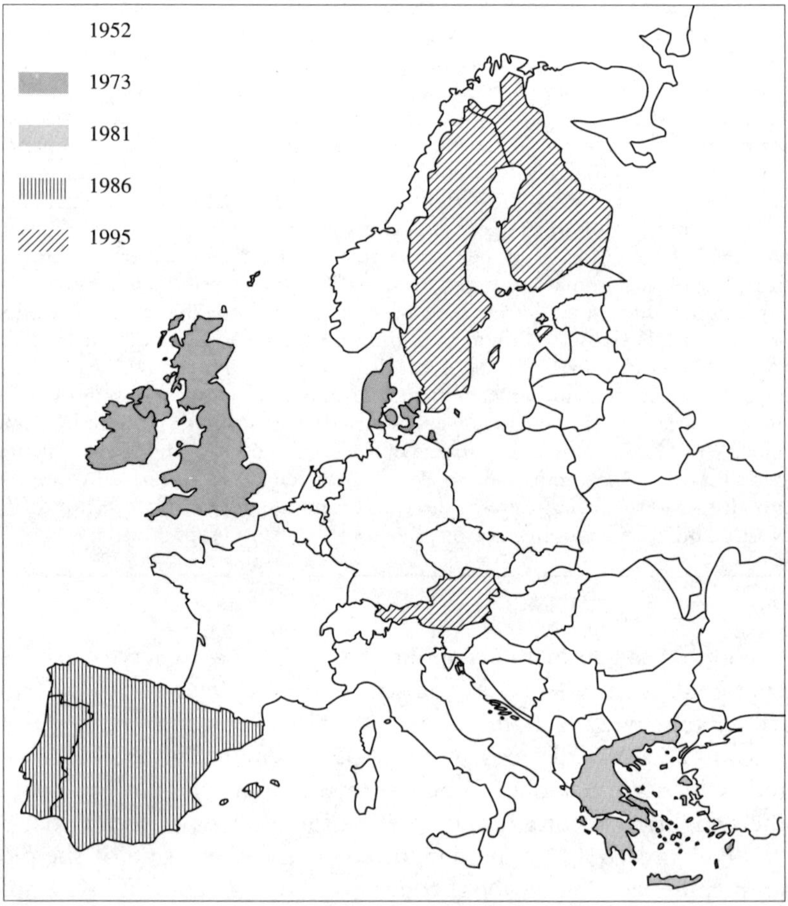

Map 4 Growth of EU membership of the EEC/EC/EU

exert a profound effect upon the social life and economic well-being of a community while being responsible only to its own directors and shareholders. The relationship between the TNC and its host is a dependent one, in that it depends upon the labour resources of that state and is supposed to abide by its laws. But the dependence carries no enduring obligations, and the TNC will depart whenever the opportunities elsewhere seem more inviting. The rise of the TNC has introduced a measure of anarchy into the international system, giving rise to power without accountability and displacing order: 'In the mix of globalism, regionalism and localism, where is authority to be located? Who has power? To whom are the TNC, the state, indeed the market, accountable?' (Horsman and Marshall 1994, p. 215).

A facet of the relationship between the state and the TNC is provided by the new technologies, and it has been argued that they have helped to shift power away from the state towards a diversity of lesser interests:

> By sapping the authority of the centralized state, the new technologies have shifted the locus of decisive action to the more modest concentrations of intellect and will. These smaller organisms can be defined as the transnational corporation, as the merchant city-state (Singapore, Taiwan, Hong Kong), as militant causes (the PLO or the IRA), even as individuals as intransigent as Manuel Noriega or Muammar Qaddafi. (Lapham 1988, pp. 8–9)

A tangled complexity of allegiances is developing, with some people being more dependent upon the company that pays their wages, pensions and insurance bills and rewards their loyalty with status and identity, while criminals and terrorists all defy the state-based rule of law. Referring to the geographical expression of the new order, Lapham wrote: 'As yet nobody has drawn a map that reflects the new order, but if somebody were to do so, I suspect that it would look more like medieval France than nineteenth-century Europe' (ibid., p. 9).

The nation-state is also being weakened in terms of its military role. We have seen how warfare played a vital role in the formation of many states, while fundamental obligations of the state involved the protection of its citizens against violence from their fellow citizens and against attacks from other states. In the modern world, however, states experience mounting difficulties in attempting to preserve credibility in the traditional role of the protector. Firstly, the globalisation of the world economy and communications systems have the effect of allowing conflicts to rebound rapidly around the international system. Thus, an upwelling of militant Muslim separatism in one republic of the CIS is likely to promote a reaction within hours in other Muslim republics. At the same time, war becomes increasingly destructive as the technological basis of slaughter is refined. Had Soviet troops invaded Chechenia a generation ago they would have arrived with automatic rifles, tanks and aircraft armed with high explosive bombs and canon, but when they attacked in 1994, cluster bombs, which kill and maim profligately and indiscriminately, were an important part of their armoury.

One sort of weapon above all has undermined the status of the nation state:

> Of all twentieth-century developments, it is the discovery of the atom bomb that has most clearly rendered the exclusive sovereignty of the nation state anachronistic . . . There is simply no defence against nuclear weapons, and the threat of mutual destruction which acts as a substitute for defence, depends entirely on the actions and mental processes of potential enemies, which are by definition outside the control of the individual nation state. (Beetham 1984, p. 215)

Although it was the change in technology associated with weapons and their delivery that signalled the demise of the territorial state to Herz back in 1957, now the nuclear problem is seen as but one among the many issues which conspire against the sovereign nation-state:

> What nation can defend its borders against disease, ballistic missiles, the drug trade, or the transmission of subversive images? What nation can hold harmless its air or its water against the acid rain drifting east across Canada or the radioactive cloud blowing west from Chernobyl? What nation can protect its currency against predatory speculations on the world money markets? (Lapham 1988, p. 9)

It is perhaps amongst the newest recruits to the doctrine of the sovereign nation-state that the disillusionment has been greatest. In Africa, where each Independence Day witnessed the metamorphosis of one more arbitrarily defined European colony into a hopeful nation-state, several of these synthetic state creations have collapsed in turmoil. While their boundaries may still define the state in *de jure* terms, they delimit a hollow shell which central authority is unable to fill. In Liberia (a unique state created by the American Colonisation Society in 1822 as a homeland for liberated slaves), around 150 000 lives have been lost in recent wars between rival warlords. In 1995, the territory of the state was divided between seven rival factions and central government was almost powerless. On the other side of the

Box 4.5 *The transnational corporation*

Businesses controlling assets in more than one state have existed for centuries; the Dutch East India Company was chartered in 1602 and granted quasi-sovereign powers, including the rights to make war and coin money, while Hastedt and Knickrehm (1991) point out that Singer Sewing Machines had a Scottish assembly line operating in 1878 and Ford opened its first European plant in 1911. The growth of the TNC became rapid in the post-war world, with the number of US-based TNC affiliates increasing from 7000 to 23 000 between 1950 and 1963 (ibid., p. 403). Transnational corporations appear to be emerging as the victors in a contest between national authorities and international corporations which has continued for some decades. This contest became visible in the 1950s and 1960s, when American multinational corporations became involved in the exploitation of primary products, such as oil, minerals, fruit and other foodstuffs in developing countries. Sometimes the American involvement was regarded by the host country as a colonial intervention, and there were numerous cases of hostile reactions to foreign investment and even the nationalisation of foreign assets, as when Chile and Zambia nationalised copper industries or when Mexico nationalised foreign banks. However, while the states of the Third World controlled territory and resources, the multinationals had wealth, expertise, technology and access to markets. So as Third World countries sank deeply into debt during the 1980s it became progressively harder to shun the tax income and other revenues that involvement with the TNCs could offer. Meanwhile, the US-based multinational had given way to the global TNC, which was just as likely to be involved in operations within the economies of the developed world as in the exploitation of Third World resources. In 1985, 46 per cent of TNCs had their headquarters in the USA, but by 1989 this figure had fallen to 33 per cent, while during the same period the proportion of TNCs with headquarters in Japan rose from 16 per cent to 22 per cent (Kidron and Segal 1991, p. 81).

By the end of the 1980s, 600 TNCs were generating half of the world's industrial output, with economic power being concentrated in the control of a diminishing number of top executives. But the individual TNC is a shadowy and transient force in world affairs. Information on its activities is likely to be very difficult to obtain, while TNCs themselves are frequently transformed by mergers, takeovers, asset stripping and failure. The volatility of the TNC is evident in the way that corporations may rapidly shoot up or tumble down the ratings tables; in 1989 the TNC rated highest on the basis of wealth was General Motors, whose wealth of $121.1 billion was exceeded by just 22 states, while General Electric ranked 47th on the listing of states and TNCs (Hastedt and Knickrehm 1991, p. 405). Within five years, however, General Electric was the largest US-based company, with its assets of $251 billion exceeding those of all but ten nation-states.

Although TNCs can cause enormous social and economic disruption by transferring their operations from one country to another, their plans, finances and profits are usually closely guarded secrets and host governments may know very little about the affairs of the TNCs which operate within their territories. Because of the global nature of their operations and the globalisation of world trade, the TNCs can exert enormous leverage: they are not obliged to establish plants in any particular host country, and having done so

Box 4.5 *continued*

they can always threaten to relocate in any other country that offers better cost advantages. TNC status confers enormous advantages upon the corporation; with careful planning it can have host governments competing to subsidise its operations, while organised labour becomes powerless when faced by the threat to transfer operations to a different country: the German car firm, BMW, recently sought to relocate in South Carolina to avoid the statutory trade union involvement associated with manufacturing in Germany. TNC involvement is not always welcomed, and the fact that Japanese car manufacturers have established in the UK in order to obtain access to the EU market may not reflect British competitive advantage so much as a reluctance to host Japanese motor industries by other EU member states with domestic vehicle industries.

continent, the state of Somalia is no more than a territory within which clans and their respective warlords pursue their sectarian aims through war and banditry. Rwanda has been torn apart in a genocidal political power struggle with strong ethnic dimensions; Liberia's ills have infected neighbouring Sierra Leone; in Zaire central authority has contracted and exerts little control over much of the country, while even Nigeria is threatened by ethnic tensions (McGreal 1995).

Traumas such as these undermine the nation-state's claim to be the guardian of the national culture. In a great many states there is not just one national culture, but a dominant culture and several other cultures whose members fear the centralising and assimilationist policies of the state. In Europe, Hechter (1975) identified institutionalised patterns of discrimination in the allocation of resources. He claimed that states there have formed by a process of 'internal colonialism' whereby one ethnic group has established an imperialist domination over neighbouring cultures, so that when industrialisation took place positions of privilege were reserved for members of the dominant elite while development of the peripheries was subordinated to the interests of the centre. In Africa comparable tensions may be expressed in intertribal conflicts or in challenges to the state from clans and warlords.

One might have assumed that the globalisation of the world economy would encourage people to assume international identities and to regard themselves as citizens of the world. But there is an alternative scenario, which Beetham (1984, p. 219) describes:

> The way in which the operation of the international economy reinforces regional disparities within countries, again leads to the re-emergence of regional nationalisms that have previously accommodated themselves to the

larger nation state, and whose demands for greater political or cultural autonomy cannot be ignored or suppressed without increasingly bitter conflict.

Thus, globalisation can be paralleled by the rise of regional nationalisms.

Similar ideas can be linked to the revolution in information technology. Today the great cities of the world are constantly engaged in a multifaceted dialogue which is largely beyond the control of national governments. In information terms the gap in wealth between the city and its rural setting is ever widening, perhaps leading to the decay of the city-region as a functional and social entity. And certainly, the attention of world cities, like London, is being diverted away from the national context and towards the specialised arena of world financial centres. When regarded from this perspective, globalisation is not really a global phenomenon: it has little impact on most parts of the world and is really concerned with a global network of cities, financial and manufacturing centres. If society becomes divided between an elite, composed of well-educated and affluent members who are conversant with information technology and employed in hi-tech services, and a deprived majority, who are not, then one can imagine a segregation and disaggregation of society as the elite cluster together behind the security fences hedging their exclusive neighbourhoods.

Many of the political implications of the revolution in information technology are as yet scarcely understood. At a meeting of the Group of Seven industrialised nations in 1995, fears were expressed that the information superhighway could become a pipeline for American interests and culture which would destroy the cultural distinctiveness of nations sharing the superhighway. It was also confirmed that the revolution could create a divide between the information haves and have nots. Thabo Mbeki, the deputy president of South Africa, reminded delegates that half of humanity had never made a telephone call and that there were more telephone lines in Manhattan than in the whole of sub-Saharan Africa (Bell 1995).

At present, the scenarios suggested above may seem fanciful, but many of their elements already exist in Western society. Technological change has already destroyed countless low-skilled manufacturing jobs, which have either been lost forever or else replaced by even less-skilled and poorer paid jobs in service industries. Meanwhile, the gap between rich and poor is widening and the world's 257 billionaires earn as much as all the people of China and Indonesia combined (Kidron and Segal 1991, p. 37). In the UK, the bottom 50 per cent of the population owns just 8 per cent of the nation's wealth, while the top 10 per cent have 27 per cent of total income and 49 per cent of total wealth. Between 1978 and 1994 the numbers living on less than half average income tripled, and around 30 per cent of society did not share in the gains in economic growth made since 1979 (Rowntree Foundation 1995). All forces which widen the economic divisions between social classes are likely to encourage members of society to regard the world in class-based terms rather than to consider themselves to be part of a homogeneous national community.

Plainly, the state is under threat, but throughout most of the world it is still far from dead. Rather than being the passive victims of circumstances, states have explored the ways in which they may survive within an increasingly difficult world. In so doing, they have discovered that the preservation of state sovereignty may be achieved through the partial surrender of sovereignty. Defensive military alliances have existed for centuries, and these offer enhanced security at the cost of a measure of independence. (Occasionally, the sacrifice may become an embarrassment, as exemplified by the public outcry in the UK after US bombers flying from UK bases killed a number of Libyan civilians in 1986.) Membership of economic trading organisations may require a larger sacrifice of sovereignty, though the alternatives may seem ever more unattractive as domestic markets become increasingly unable to satisfy the economies of scale demanded by modern production techniques. The EU is currently riven by disagreements about the degree to which economic integration should be paralleled by a shift to federal institutions, while the British government strives to prevent or delay the adoption of a single European currency.

If the state is to survive, it can only do so by adapting to the changes in its international milieu. In many places, human society is not yet ready for the psychological adjustments necessary for the abandonment of the nation-state in favour of some economically superior supra-national organisation. Yet the loyalty of a large part of its population alone will not sustain a state through conditions of severe hardship. Survival requires that the state should surrender some of its sovereignty to international organisations, but it may also demand that sacrifices are made at the domestic or internal level, with measures of self-government being offered to regional minorities who feel economically or ethnically disadvantaged.

During the 1990s, political commentators have recognised that the state is much more exposed and vulnerable to change than had been imagined during the preceding decades of the century. The amount of vitality left in the nation-state was evident during the July of 1994, when domestic lives and day-to-day routines throughout the world were transformed as ordinary people found their attention riveted on the performances of their national-state teams in the football World Cup. Anyone who doubted the potency of the emotional forces underpinning the nation-state had only to study the expressions on the faces of the respective fans as they swiftly ranged from agony to ecstasy and back again. In the words of Beetham (1984, p. 220):

> Daily we are invited to regard the achievements of our own nation, whether in sport, industry or whatever, as especially noteworthy and meritorious, and to count the lives of our fellow nationals as of higher worth than the rest of humanity. It is the continuous reinforcement of such assumptions that provides the basis for the oft-asserted claim that the nation state 'has a lot of life in it yet'.

If the state can achieve a harmonious redistribution of its powers then it might expect and deserve to survive, for a number of valuable roles will remain. It will be needed to serve as an umpire in disputes between its social and regional components, to protect the more vulnerable elements in society by controlling the worst excesses of capitalism and to harmonise the development of its territory. And until a new form of tribalism which is more potent than nationalism can come into being, then the well-established nation-state is likely to retain a grip on the human psyche which is stronger than any supra-national, commercial or city-state-based sense of identification.

■ *Chapter 5* ■

The State from Within

'English people think of Quebeckers as inferior,' says France. 'They perceive us as a people who are losing our identity, losing our way – a people without a future.' She grew up in an exclusively Francophone village, but adds: 'When I came to Montreal, it was difficult for me to get respect.'

Clare Travena, *The Guardian* (28 October 1995)

The work we are going about is this, to dig up George's Hill and the wasteland thereabouts, and to sow corn and to eat our bread together by the sweat of our brows, and lay the foundations of making the earth a common treasury for all.

Gerrard Winstanley, *The Diggers Movement* (1649)

The simplest measure of the success of a state must be its ability to survive. In turn, this ability to survive will, to a considerable extent, reflect the ability of the state to reconcile the conflicting ambitions of the various groups living within its borders. We have seen that the sovereign nation-state is threatened from 'above' by the development of international organisations and the globalisation of communications and markets. Many states are also threatened from within, by minority nations or regional groupings which aspire to gain autonomy or independence or to form new associations with different states. Thus: 'The assertive upsurge of national, regional and ethnic identities has upset the received wisdom of classical–liberal and Marxist thought, which held that, in the context of the shrinking, interdependent and homogenizing world of economics and communications, such bourgeois anachronisms as nationalism would inevitably melt away' (Hooson 1994, p. ix).

A number of political geographical concepts can be applied to a study of the state and its relationship with its parts; some are quite old, some new, some well established and others, less familiar. All emphasise the fact that the interior of the state is not uniform. There will be differences from place to place in the level and nature of economic development and opportunity; contrasts of a cultural and historical nature; variations in the political preferences and aspirations of the population and their attitudes towards the state, and also inequalities in the extent to which government can impose its will upon the subject territory. These patterns are not fixed in time, and the relationships between people, place and government are ever in a state of flux. The dynamic nature of these interactions was described almost half a century ago by Richard Hartshorne (1899–1992) in his 'functional approach' to political geography (Hartshorne 1950).

Government and territory

The state seeks to impose a measure of uniformity and control upon its territory, and the extent of its success plainly varies from case to case and from time to time. One geographical concept of long-standing which could usefully be employed to explore this process is that of 'effective national territory'. Sadly, however, it seems to have vanished completely from modern geographical thought, and does not even rate an entry in the otherwise excellent *Dictionary of Human Geography* (Johnston *et al.* 1994).

This concept of effective national territory relates to the fact that there can be a lack of correspondence between the total (legal or *de jure*) territory of a sovereign state and the area which is effectively controlled by its government (the *de facto* territory). Originally, the concept was applied largely in terms of economic development. It was proposed by the American geographer, Preston E. James (1959, p. 11), in relation to Latin America, where several states had vast interior expanses which were not effectively governed. He identified the effective national territory of the state as being that part of its territory which actually contributed to the economic support of the citizens of the country.

James was influenced by the ideas of another notable American geographer, Derwent Whittlesey (1935, pp. 453–4), who had formulated a notion of an 'ecumene'. The ecumene was the portion of the state that had the most concentrated population and the densest network of communications. Within the ecumene, the success of the government in stamping the landscape with visible symbols of state control, such as post offices or state sponsored developments, would be at its most obvious. Much later, Zaidi (1966) employed the term 'effective state area' in a study of Pakistan. He defined this effective state area or ecumene as being that part of the total state territory which had a population density of at least 25 people per square mile and which lay within 10 miles of a railway station or a road which was passable by motor traffic, while outside it was the 'extra-ecumenical'

Box 5.1 *Hartshorne and the 'state idea'*

In his paper of 1950, Hartshorne remarked that the state could be studied in terms of its evolution through time: an historical approach, or with regard to its shape or structure: a morphological approach. He then advocated a more dynamic approach which would focus on the functioning of the state. He recognised that the state was engaged in a constant struggle to impose its control over territory in the face of challenges or potential challenges from outside and within: 'Finally, and most importantly, because we live in a world in which the continued existence of every state-unit is subject to the threat of destruction by other states, every state must strive to secure the supreme loyalty of the people in all its regions, in competition with any local or provincial loyalties, and in definite opposition to loyalty to any outside state-unit' (ibid., p. 105).

He argued that at any point in time there existed inside the state a particular balance between what he termed 'centrifugal' and 'centripetal' forces. The centrifugal forces are those which make it difficult for the state to integrate its people and territory in a coherent and harmonious whole. Cultural, political or economic differences between populations or geographical barriers to contact between regions could all act as centrifugal forces. If left unchecked by any system of counter-balances, the centrifugal forces would cause a state to disintegrate. In contrast, the centripetal forces operate in the opposite direction and serve to bind the state together.

The most important of the centripetal forces was what Hartshorne termed the state's *raison d'être* or 'reason for being'. Here, he drew upon the work of Friedrich Ratzel (1897, pp. 2–6), who had written about the 'political idea' of the state. The *raison d'être* or 'state idea' involves certain crucial beliefs or aspirations that can unite the population of the greater part of the state. Thus, Zionism and the desire to secure the land of Israel for the Jewish people is at the core of the state idea of Israel, even though they are deeply resented in localities occupied by Palestinians. The state idea may flourish across the length and breadth of a state or it may not fill the state boundaries. The larger the portion of the population which does not subscribe to the state idea, the less secure the future of the state is likely to be.

Although the political geographer's conceptual armoury is far more heavily stocked than in Hartshorne's time, the concepts of *raison d'être* and centrifugal and centripetal forces are still useful and relevant. Even so, Hartshorne's contribution to political geography has recently been reassessed. O Tuathail has located it in the post-war American 'politics of growth' era, when eyes were fixed firmly on future prosperity and harmony and when awkward political questions were unwelcome and actively contained: 'Hartshorne's attempt to develop a functional approach in political geography in 1950 was an attempt to create a political geography without politics, a diligent, scientific, civic-minded knowledge that was uncontroversial and consensual' (O Tuathail 1994c, p. 325).

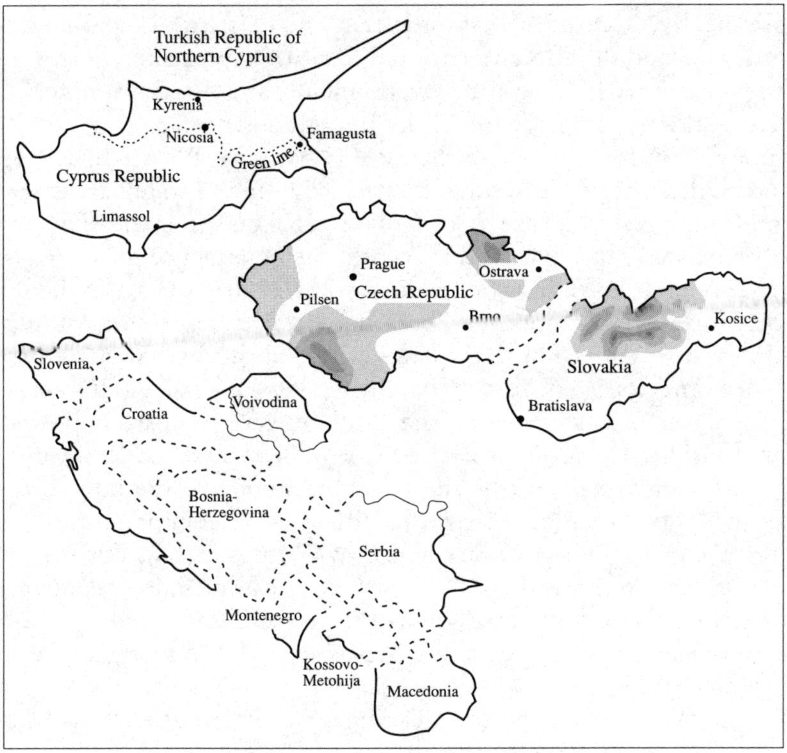

Map 5 Examples of states that have failed to overcome cultural divisions: Cyprus, Czechoslovakia and Yugoslavia

territory of the state. On the basis of increasing population and transport network densities, he divided the effective state area into a minimally effective area, intensively effective area, subcore and core area. Zaidi was concerned to explore the functional relationships developed between the political ideas and institutions, populations and regions of the state; he thought that: 'Mere description of size, shape, or preparation of an inventory of the contents, or even of resources, can hardly provide a meaningful approach to a proper understanding of the institutional–areal relationship' (ibid., pp. 52–3).

While all these concepts underline the discrepancies between state control in the *de jure* and *de facto* senses, they tend to focus on relative levels of economic development and on access to the state communications network. At the times when Whittlesey and James were writing, various states of the developing world contained interior expanses of territory which could be unexplored as well as unintegrated.

Consequently, it could be assumed that the existence of unintegrated territory beyond the effective national territory represented only a stage in the process of economic development, and that ultimately the effective state would grow to fill its boundaries.

Today, however, we find that even in many Western developed countries there are what we might term 'holes in the state': areas where normal state controls are not applied. Pockets of lawlessness have always existed, but particularly with the emergence of a massive international drugs industry and the associated drugs culture, the holes in the state are expanding. Sometimes the holes represent urban localities, districts or housing estates where authority has passed from the state and its agencies to anarchistic local mobs, 'godfathers' or organised crime. In some cases, the holes are very localised and exist at a particular vertical level (as in the Moscow students' hostel, where one floor has been taken over by the Russian 'mafia', or the international hotel in a city in China, where the top floor accommodates a disco operated independently of the owners by a drugs cartel). But the holes in the state are not always so localised: they can include sizeable areas of large cities, and in the cases of certain Andean states, like Colombia, it is arguable that the holes may have expanded and merged to engulf the whole state.

The threat posed to the state by organised crime is quite considerable. As Healey (1995) points out:

> Perhaps $1,500 billion of criminal profits are laundered worldwide every year – one third of them from the drug trade. The criminal mafias co-operate with one another far more closely than the governments which are supposed to suppress them. A few weeks ago the United Nations Conference on Crime in Naples was informed that the Sicilian mafia is forging dollars for sale to the Russian mafia.

While the current global levels of crime may not be unprecedented, the scope for serious, organised and highly dangerous crime is greater than ever before. During the first half of the 1990s the German authorities alone uncovered 46 cases of nuclear smuggling, probably only a small fraction of the total instances, while in 1994 a single operation resulted in the capture of 100 criminals involved in the importation of cocaine via fishing ports on the Spanish coast (Coughlin 1995). The cancer of lawlessness is spreading to states normally regarded as reasonably crime-free. Even in the Netherlands, which has Europe's most liberal drugs laws, drugs related crime takes up half of all police and prosecutors' time and costs the government an estimated £700 million a year. Here too there are 25 000–50 000 commercial growers of cannabis and the sale of their crop generates around £170 million a year (Healey 1995). In the USA official estimates recognise half a million heroin addicts and 3 million regular users of cocaine and crack. Unofficial estimates put levels of illicit drug use at three times these figures.

The modernist conviction that rationalism would rule the world is now being replaced by doubts as the state apparatus seems unable to check the expansion of underworld influences. The emergence of 'grey zones' and no-go areas, the places where state power does not operate and where the only forceful organisation is that which is imposed in the cause of criminal exploitation by the drugs cartels testifies to the weakness of the legal authority. Conditions in Chicago, Washington DC and Detroit are well known, but now districts of Birmingham, Manchester, Paris and large parts of Marseilles function as extra-ecumenical areas. When the concept of effective national territory was first advanced, it related to areas within the territory of Third World states which were remote from the organised centres of population and not integrated into national economy. Today, however, the areas or 'holes' lying outside the effective national territory are not peripheral or underdeveloped and can be located in the very heart of the Western state.

People who grew up during the threatening decades of the Cold War may soon be obliged to come to terms with a political situation in which the greatest and most numerous threats to life and stability derive not from the sudden ignition of superpower rivalries, but from the eruption of tensions within the states of the world. Perhaps those days have already arrived, for as Denis Healey, the former British defence secretary, noted, all but three of the 82 armed conflicts then being fought around the world took place inside the frontiers of nation states. He made this point in March 1995, and shortly afterwards the increasing severity and unpredictability of internal conflict was underlined when members of an obscure religious sect released poison gas in an attack on commuters using the Japanese subway system; a few weeks later, members of a right-wing extremist militia associated with the gun lobby in the USA killed around 200 civilians when they bombed a government building in Oklahoma City.

These incidents exemplify a tendency towards seemingly indiscriminate acts of terrorism which are often associated with obscure minority groups. But there are other internal conflicts still which seem to have no apparent political motives and involve disruption for its own sake – as in the turmoil currently engulfing some African states, where any initial reasons for strife have been overtaken by a descent into almost randomised violence. Meanwhile in China, one of the most authoritarian and tightly regulated societies in the world, a new generation of warlords appears to be emerging in the provinces. The classical period for warlordism in China was 1916–28, but it has been suggested that a study of this phenomenon may cast light on the traumas affecting some modern Third World states. According to Sheridan (1966, p. 1): 'A warlord exercised effective governmental control over a fairly well-defined region by means of a military organization that obeyed no higher authority than himself.' In China there were always strong centrifugal tendencies as well as a recurrent pattern involving the decay of central government power and the emergence of regional power centres. Wilbur (1968) argued that geographical factors greatly affected the ability of a warlord to secure control over a particular region. Access to the sea made it far easier for arms to be imported, while the presence of urban populations which could be taxed greatly enhanced the desirability of a territory. Revenues were vital; by 1928 there were about 2 million soldiers under arms in China, excluding others better regarded as bandits than the followers of warlords, and the leaders were obliged to extort crippling sums from the territories they controlled, causing the impoverishment of their subjects and the stifling of industry.

If the retreat of the Chinese state has been associated with periodical weaknesses in central control, in other cases still, the contraction of the effective state area results from the intervention of external forces. In the case of Mozambique, South African (and, in the earlier days, Rhodesian) strategy undermined the state and prevented it imposing its rule throughout its territory. Instead, its jurisdiction was confined to some towns and major routeways. As the state lost control of most of its territory and much of its transportation system it was often unable to feed or pay its troops, and as these forces scavenged for food or conscripted unwilling recruits the prestige of the state suffered further. 'Most significantly, though supporting the rebel movement of Renamo (Resistencia Nacional Mocambicana), the South African military have aimed to weaken the Mozambican state, undermining its ability to mobilize against South Africa and compelling Frelimo (Frente de Libertaco de Mocambique) into a more compliant regional and domestic posture' (Sidaway 1992, pp. 239–40).

Finally, Deutsch (1981) has related the concept of effective national territory – which he terms 'effective domain' – to the size of the state. He points out that for the state to endure, its commands (laws, decrees, regulations, etc.) must be seen to be binding on most people for most of the time: 'The limits of the effective domain of the state are thus the limits of its probability of finding popular obedience, both in regard to the territory where its writ runs with effect, and to the set of persons who are likely to obey it' (ibid., p. 342). The more 'distant' peoples are from the government, the less likely they are to obey its commands, with distance having cultural, social, economic and geographical as well as linear dimensions. Most important is the psychological distance between the bodies: 'This declining probability of obedience with increasing psychological distances . . . has limited the size of states ever since states have existed in proportion to the activities and capabilities of their populations' (ibid.).

One geographical solution to the problem of the lack of congruence between *de facto* and *de jure* territory might be the sovereignty bargain, whereby a state surrendered some measure of its notional control over part of its territory in order to increase the overall effectiveness of its sovereignty. Though almost unthinkable at present, at some future time the benefits of such arrangements may be recognised:

> The effectiveness of the government of Ethiopia, for example, is currently rather questionable, as significant parts of Ethiopia are in the control of various rebel fronts. Its effective sovereignty would probably increase if it struck a sovereignty bargain and agreed to relinquish some measure of control of certain portions of its territory. The same might be true in Brazil, where the Iquitos Declaration seems to make exactly this demand of the state government. (Byers 1991, p. 73)

■ Cores and peripheries

In the social sciences in general, and in political geography in particular, a fascination with centres or cores and their relationships with peripheries has grown in recent years. When interpreted at the global level, the core–periphery concept is central to world-systems analysis. It can also be developed at the supra-national level, as when Wallerstein (1974) divided Europe into an innovative and influential core in the north-west, a stagnating semi-periphery in the south, and a dependent agricultural periphery in the east. In addition, it is applied at the state level in studies of the tensions and inequalities which result from the state's internal geographical, cultural and economic diversity. Inherent in the concept are the factors of domination and exploitation in the core–periphery relationship. A core–periphery terminology 'implies that the core's capacity to acquire, rule and derive benefit from ruling the periphery reflects enduring factors; probably both inherent or natural advantages of geography, and those constructed by man and built into the political, cultural, economic and social fabric of the state' (Steed 1986, p. S98). Also, 'It implies that where the particular geographical and historical circumstances do give rise to such unevenness of advantage in a state, which is then maintained through political structures, the development of democratic politics will see the expression of territorial tensions' (ibid.).

One of the political manifestations of the core–periphery relationship is peripheral nationalism, 'defined as an emotive reaction of cultural defense against the diffusion of economic, political and cultural dominance from the core' (Wellhofer 1995, p. 505). For more than a decade after the end of the 1939–45 war it could be argued that nationalism was a spent and discredited force, while the minority national movements which existed within many European states could be dismissed as belonging to the realms of cranks and misfits. During the 1960s, and increasingly during the decades which followed, regionally based ethnic groups have gained prominence in the majority of European states.

Rokkan and Urwin (1982, p. 3) have remarked that most if not all states of Western Europe are multi-ethnic and house populations which have 'several layers of identity'. They believe that since 1945 the relationship between cores and peripheries in European states have been affected by a number of factors. These are:

1. A continuing internationalisation of the economic life and communications of the states, resulting in a reduction of the effectiveness of international boundaries as cultural and political barriers;
2. Increasing expectations of the welfare state and growing demands for it to intensify its assistance to the less productive sectors and regions;
3. Increasing efforts to mobilise the peripheries and regions of the state against its centre, accompanied by claims for cultural autonomy and the devolution of political powers from the centre.

As described by Rokkan and Urwin, peripheries tend to be dependent upon other portions of the state; they have little control over their destinies and few resources which they can use to defend their distinctive identities (ibid., p. 2). In geographical terms, they are outlying areas within the overall territory controlled by a centre. Sometimes, peripheries are composed of conquered territory and are administered by officials acting upon instructions from geographically remote centres. Peripheries also tend to have poorly developed economies which are vulnerable to external economic conditions. Finally, they tend to have 'marginal cultures' which are fragmented and parochial. These characteristics are not encountered in all peripheries, but the essential characteristic of the periphery concerns its dependence upon one or more centres. 'Centres, then, can be minimally defined as privileged locations within a territory' (ibid., p. 6). They are the meeting places of the most influential people; the locations of national ceremonies; the places where symbolic national monuments are erected, and they accommodate the main military, economic and cultural institutions of the state. Some states have all these features concentrated in a single centre, while in others several centres exist, each with their own particular elite groups (see also pp. 206ff on internal colonialism in the Third World).

Until recently the core–periphery concept was inadequately tested, but this defect is in the process of being remedied. Wellhofer (1995) explored the rise of peripheral nationalism in late-nineteenth-century Britain and early-twentieth-century Argentina and found that in both places it was the product of the economically and culturally marginal middle strata of society who were threatened by the expanding influence of the core. The research also suggested that at the periphery of the world economy in times of economic recession, the economically and culturally marginal lower classes may be mobilised into mass movements. He concluded that the research provided 'strong support for geographic context in political analysis in general and of core-periphery dimensions in particular. To the extent that peripheries constitute distinct contexts, they form units of analysis worthy of our attentions' (ibid., p. 519). Steed (1986) evaluated a range of different approaches used by political scientists to study territorial variation within Britain and found that the core–periphery concept was to be preferred. It articulated the enduring dichotomy between lowland and upland Britain and the core-based character of the English–British state, with its persistent claim to the whole of the periphery. He thought that:

> The confusion over what is England is part of how . . . the centre manages its territory or, in my terms, the core holds the periphery. Social scientists looking at territorial politics in Britain would do better to pay more attention to this persistent pattern rather than assuming that political differences are to be explained in terms of three component countries. (ibid., p. S102)

Finally, a study commissioned by the Council of Europe (1992) found that within the EU the most centralised states tended to contain the least developed frontier regions, suggesting but not proving that centralisation and peripheral economic backwardness are part of the same political package.

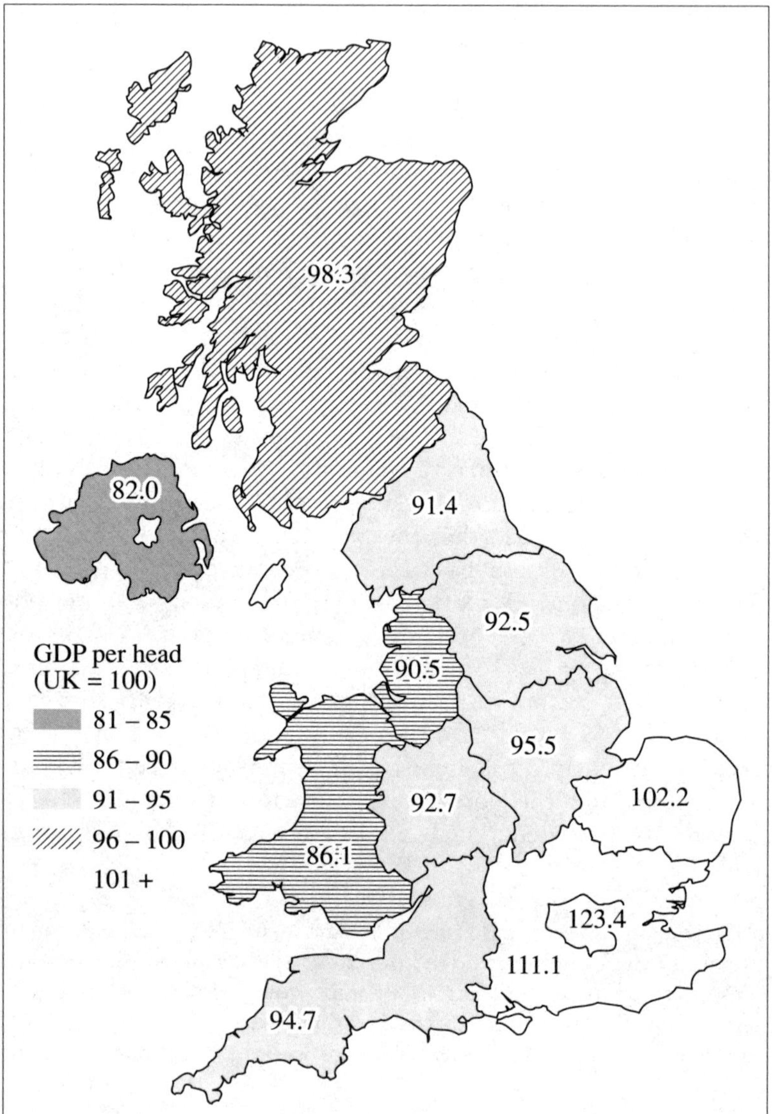

Map 6 Core and periphery: variations in *per capita* GDP between regions in the UK, October 1994

Migration and the state

According to Castles and Miller (1993, p. 260):

> Over the last five centuries mass migrations have played a major role in colonialism, industrialisation, the emergence of nation-states and the development of the capitalist world market. However international migration has never been as pervasive, nor as socioeconomically and politically significant as it is today. Never before have statesmen accorded such priority to migration concerns . . . The hallmark of the age of migration is the global character of international migration; the way it affects more and more countries and regions, and its linkages with complex processes affecting the entire world.

Migration can cause tensions at both the national and the international level; the movements and attempted movements of peoples across borders can produce not only international tensions, as when Cuba appeared to be encouraging the exodus of 'boat people' to the USA in 1994, but also internal tensions, as when the immigrants are regarded as depriving established populations of employment and benefits; in addition migration takes place within states, as when hundreds of thousands of Oklahomans and Kansans and folk from Arkansas quit the Dustbowl states in the depression years and headed across the Great Divide to California. Migration causes both internal and external problems, but the most powerful social consequences of migration are normally experienced within states, which is why the topic is covered here rather than in later chapters. Although the topic of migration has been somewhat neglected by political geographers, migration is nevertheless an issue of pressing importance in the modern world. Some of the political aspects are related to the broader political context. Frelick (1993) has related the diminishing levels of humanity evident in Western attitudes towards the plight of refugees to changes in the World Order. Previously,

> The notion of a well-founded fear of persecution based on deprivation of certain civil and political rights accorded easily with the Western view of Soviet-style communist repression of dissidents and minorities, accommodating the bona fide needs of those people, while at the same time enabling the West to score points in the Cold War's ideological battle by encouraging disaffected elements within the East bloc to 'vote with their feet'. (ibid., p. 163)

He notes that in 1991, 452 000 Kurdish refugees from Iraq were denied access to Turkey, in full view of the world's media; in this year

Box 5.2 *The core area concept*

The core area concept in political geography seemed to be destined for dereliction, but the current surge of interest in centre–periphery relationships has revitalised interest in the way that many states have grown from the accretion of territory around the nucleus of a core area. The concept was developed by the American geographer, Derwent Whittlesey (1939, p. 597), who defined the core as 'the area in which or about which a State originates'. Much more recently, Taylor (1991b, pp. 149–50) wrote that: 'Distinctive core-areas are found in most modern states. Typically they are the historical zone in which a state emerged and around which it accreted lands to occupy its contemporary territory.'

Normally, the core area would be the most populous part of the state, would have the richest endowment of natural resources and the closest mesh of communications, and would contain the capital city. The growth of the state concerned would be accomplished by the continuing expansion of the territory which was controlled and dominated by the core area. In this way, the typical state had, in Whittlesey's view (1939, p. 2), 'crystallized about a nuclear core that fostered integration'. Later, A. D. Smith highlighted the cultural associations of the core area, claiming that an ethnic foundation was needed to mobilise and integrate often diverse cultural and social elements. Thus 'by the fifteenth century, one could speak with some justification of a French or English ethnie which formed the core of the French and English kingdoms, and which had begun to expand into outlying territories inhabited by other, smaller ethnie' (Smith 1988, p. 11), and: 'The population at the centre was culturally relatively homogeneous; they were not riven by deep ethnic cleavages at the moment when expansion took place' (ibid.).

In 1964, Pounds and Ball published the results of their search for core areas in the European system of states. They studied 24 states and concluded that 15 of them had achieved their present limits by a process of accretion around a core area. These core areas were almost invariably the foci of trade routes and areas which had produced an agricultural surplus during the early periods of territorial expansion, this wealth being reflected in the medieval architecture of the region. A further four states were found to have grown from core areas that are peripheral to or even outside their present territories. Pounds and Ball also considered that those states which had grown by the crystallisation of territory around a core tended to have a higher degree of cohesion and political and social unity than those which lacked cores. France, the UK, Switzerland, Sweden and Denmark were given as examples of such unified and coherent states.

The best examples of the progressive expansion of core area domination are provided by Russia, which developed around a nucleus in the Moscow region, and France. France grew from a core area, the Isle de France, as successive French monarchs extended the area over which they were able to exert *de facto* as well as *de jure* control, a process which spanned the Middle Ages and was completed around the start of the seventeenth century, though most of France had been brought under the control of Paris by the middle of the fourteenth century.

Outside Europe, however, the core area concept has much less credibility. Many states of the developing world are not the products of 'organic' growth,

Box 5.2 *continued*

but rather the results of the arbitrary divisions of colonial territory amongst the European powers. This very artificiality has often created instability in states which contain an assemblage of unintegrated peoples. Frequently, however, a form of internal colonialism has become established, which echoes the unequal relationship between core and periphery in the West – though usually with a stronger ethnic dimension (Hechter and Levi 1979). The superiority of the organic state, implied by Pounds and Ball, should not be assumed. England, described by Taylor (1991b, p. 150) as being a place where a deformed nationalism has been constructed on a deformed territoriality, was cited by these writers as exemplifying cohesion and unity, while Germany was listed in a group of five states which lacked distinct core areas. With the removal of the Berlin Wall and the frontier between East and West, core-less Germany might be regarded by many as a more cohesive state than the UK, which is riven by widening gaps between rich and poor and threatened by unresolved issues of minority nationalism.

too, 17 000 Albanian asylum seekers were herded to a pier and shipped out of Bari in Italy without being given the opportunity to raise asylum claims; in 1992 the US summarily returned Haitian asylum seekers interdicted by the coast guards, and in the same year the US took no action when the Yemen refused to allow a boat laden with sick and dying Somali refugees to land. This was also the year when European countries introduced restrictive visas to exclude those fleeing from the carnage in the former state of Yugoslavia (ibid., pp. 162–70).

Widgren (1990, p. 749) has shown that the concern with levels of international migration were growing at the time of the changes in the World Order: 'In 1976 only 6.4 per cent of all states on earth considered their immigration levels too high; but in 1989 this proportion had risen to 20.6 per cent. In the same year, as many as 31.8 per cent of states hinted that they would like to put a brake on immigration so as to lessen pressures on national borders.' At the global level, one of the major components of the modern tension between the affluent North and the impoverished South is the attempt by the Northern states to stem the influx of immigrants from the South. While seeking to remove internal frontier controls, the EU is also seeking to strengthen its external frontiers as the disadvantaged beat at its doors; across the Atlantic, frontier patrols glare across the Rio Grande as more and more Mexicans gather to attempt a night time crossing.

In the North, fears of the rise of Muslim fundamentalism, economic recession with rising levels of unemployment and an awareness of growing immigration pressures from the Third World have created tensions which are ripe for exploitation by the populists of the far right. Meanwhile, in the South:

> Accelerated rural–urban migration is a major factor behind the rapid growth of overcrowded mega-cities, causing congestion and environmental damage. Sending the unemployed abroad brings back some $15 billion annually to the Third World in the form of workers' remittances (accounting in many countries for half the capital inflow), but the abrupt closure of first the European and then more recently the Gulf labour markets highlighted the vulnerability of the contract worker system. (ibid., p. 751)

However, emigration also drains the Third World countries of many of their most talented and well-qualified citizens and: 'The world's refugee burden is still carried overwhelmingly by the poorest states (the 20 countries with the highest ratio of refugees have an annual average per capita income of $700)' (ibid.).

In 1989, an annual world refugee survey put the total number of refugees at 15 million (US Department of State 1989). The countries hosting the most refugees were not the countries of the North which have recently been so vocal in expressing their concerns about asylum policy, but Pakistan, Iran, Jordan and Malawi – in fact every one of the 11 countries listed as being host to more than 2 per cent of the world's refugees belonged to the Third World (Black 1991, p. 282). Today, according to the United Nations High Commissioner for Refugees, about one person in every 130 people in the world has been forced to flee his or her home territory (UNHCR 1993). Some 24 million people are internally displaced within their states, while a further 18.2 million people have been forced out of their state of residence:

> To these numbers, we must now add the horrific experience of Rwanda where government-sponsored genocide left an estimated 500 000 dead and produced the single largest refugee crisis in modern times in a matter of weeks, as over 1.4 million fled the country in the wake of rebel army advances. Refugees are the continual products of ethnic cleansing in Bosnia and Bhutan, economic collapse in Cuba, civil war in the Caucasus, Somalia, Liberia and Togo, state repression in Guatemala, Turkey, Iran and Indonesia, and random xenophobic terrorism in many other states. (O Tuathail 1995, p. 260)

Changes in political geography can rapidly rewrite the geography of migration. For example the collapse of the 'Iron Curtain' resulted in a total of about 1.2 million people leaving the Warsaw Pact states during 1989. A torrent of emigrants was released on Austria, which occupies a key position in the heart of Europe and is embraced by formerly communist countries: the Czech republic, Slovakia, Hungary and Slovenia. Professional couriers help to direct the flow of illegal immigrants, with some 30 000 such people being arrested in Austria during the first half of the 1990s. Germany, with its proximity to Eastern Europe, its historical circumstances which result in immigration by ethnic Germans and ex-Soviet Jews, and also its political attitudes towards Croatian and Bosnian independence, which have resulted in the acceptance of thousands of refugees from former Yugoslavia, is now the main immigration country in Europe, receiving more than half of the European refugee total and ranking second only to the USA in terms of the numbers of immigrants received. In 1989 alone it was the destiny for about 700 000 German settlers returning from Eastern Europe.

The legal and illegal movements of people take place on scales which are becoming comparable to the great folk wanderings of the Dark Ages, and all the main states of the EU have major internal problems associated with these migrations. According to Widgren (1990, p. 754), 'Italy, Spain and Greece between them probably host over a million foreigners from non-Europe-bordering countries staying illegally.' He adds that 'Super-organised Switzerland estimates that there are 110 000 aliens unlawfully resident within its borders. And recently even Japan's impenetrable borders seem to have been conquered by an army of 50 000–100 000 illegal foreign workers from neighbouring countries, including the People's Republic of China' (ibid., pp. 754–5). Pointing out that East European countries, including Russia, were swamped by migrants from the Middle East and those who had arrived on old Warsaw Pact guest worker programmes, he concluded that practically any border had become penetrable apart from those of a few remaining terror-states (ibid.).

As a result of the large-scale patterns of migration resulting from the recruitment of foreign labour, by the latter part of the 1980s around 12 million foreigners were resident within Western industrialised states, about half of whom were 'denizens' enjoying limited rights of citizenship (Hammar 1990, pp. 19–23). The guestworker system arose in the late 1950s to provide cheap labour to assuage the labour shortage in Western Europe – labour which would be regulated in such a way that the workers would return to their countries of origin before they could take advantage of the state welfare systems. Fairly soon it was realised that expectations of the need for immigrant labour had been too great and that some guest workers had introduced their families. The energy crisis and recession of the early 1970s triggered a rethinking of immigration policies, which caused attempts to stem the entry of further workers and to repatriate some of the guest workers who were

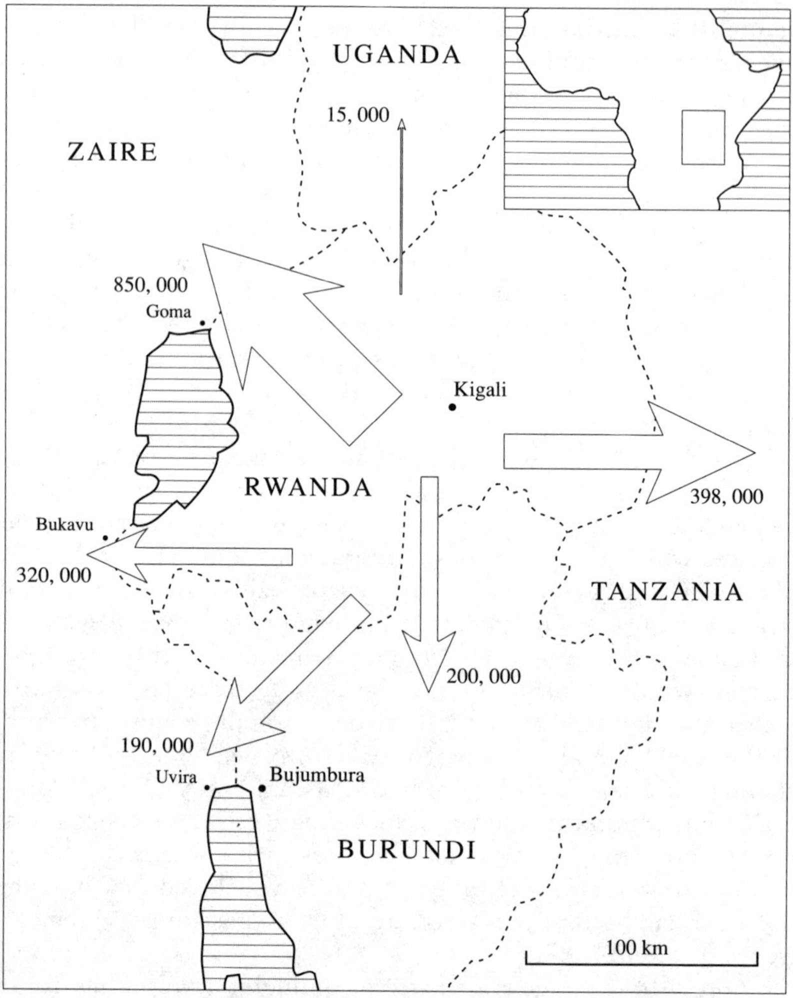

Map 7 The flight of refugees from Rwanda, 1994

unemployed by offering return bonuses. Then, having failed to control the presence of these workers, governments found that they and their families and children were in danger of becoming a deprived underclass of 'outsiders' whose plight could be manipulated to ferment racism and unrest, and so measures were taken to improve their social position and relationships with the domestic population. According to Leitner (1995, p. 264), the system 'is a clear example of the self-interested way in which nation-states deal with foreigners; and of how borders are made permeable for those types of foreigners needed on the domestic labour market, without any intention of admitting them as full members of the receiving society'. In Germany, the Turkish guest workers, who helped to keep the economy expanding during the growth years of the 1980s, have increasingly become the targets of racist attacks. Meanwhile, they can reflect with indignation upon the way that German citizenship is so readily granted to the white descendants of Germans who moved into Eastern Europe centuries ago, yet withheld from Turkish residents who helped to forge the modern German economic miracle. (Many of those who have returned to Germany since 1989, and who have qualified for immediate residence and citizenship under German Basic Law, have as their only connection with Germany a forged certificate bought on the Polish black market which purports that an ancestor served in the German wartime forces (ibid., p. 269).)

In Italy, frontiers are breached by large numbers of illegal immigrants arriving by sea from Albania and North Africa, while in France, racially motivated attacks on the large Algerian immigrant population are increasing. Amongst the most unfortunate victims of prejudice are the 'Harki', Algerians who supported France during the Algerian war of independence, but who are now victimised both by their countrymen and their hosts. In a world that is increasingly partitioned between 'haves' and 'have-nots', it seems that Europe is destined to become a fortress of privilege beset by the poverty-stricken masses of the Third World who are desperate to penetrate its defences and secure some small measure of privilege for themselves. In 1993 the internal borders between the 12 members of the EC/EU were removed to allow the unimpeded movement of people, goods, services and capital. At the same time, attempts had been made to strengthen the common external boundaries to make it more difficult for migrants to enter or for asylum seekers to remain (this is not to suggest that asylum was ever easily obtained; in 1991 Germany received 256 000 applications for asylum and accepted only 11 597). Leitner (ibid., pp. 275–6) believes that such policies are misguided:

> The recent actions taken by governments in the advanced industrialized world do not suggest that they have grasped or wish to grasp the fact that enhancing barriers around their territories and societies, by deporting asylum seekers, preventing refugees from reaching their borders, deterring illegal immigrants and continuing to exclude resident aliens from civil and political rights, do not constitute a long term solution. Rather they need to acknowledge that participation in a global political economy also requires rethinking conceptions of nationhood, accepting diversity within their territory, and being willing to protect and extend political and civil rights to resident foreign nationals.

Currently, in China, masses of peasants abandoning the vast expanses of land rendered infertile by soil erosion and bad farming practices are arriving in provincial cities where the employment opportunities are hopelessly outstripped by the scale of the exodus from the countryside. Here, migration is largely an internal problem, yet one which can still work to destabilise the state. A reluctantly footloose condition is affecting an ever-growing portion of humanity, as natural disasters, bad husbandry, excessive population growth and political repression seem to form an unholy alliance against the settled life: 'The exodus from the world's poorest and driest regions has already begun. In the past 15 years the number of refugees fleeing from political repression or economic hardship has risen from 5 to 20 million. And UN experts estimate another 10 million have fled environmental disasters such as floods and famines' (Ghazi 1994).

Meanwhile, across the Atlantic in the US, the plight of the 'illegals' has worsened. In 1986 some 3 to 5 million Hispanic people succeeded in crossing the porous border between Mexico and the USA. During the remainder of the decade, the number of illegal immigrants declined, but in the 1990s it has risen again. For decades the 'wetbacks' who had crossed the Rio Grande were welcomed by Californian fruit growers during the harvest season, even if many of the illegal immigrants were evicted once the fruit was picked. But in 1995, Californians voting in a state referendum adopted Proposition 187, decreeing that the illegals should be denied welfare, medical care except in emergencies and that their children should be removed from Californian schools.

Migration gives rise to important questions of citizenship, and Thranhardt (1995, p. 19) has described the way in which language has been used in Germany to underline the status of immigrants as outsiders: 'In keeping with the official idea of not being an immigration country, the term *Einwanderer* has never been adopted, as it has in France, Britain or Sweden, and in the traditional immigration countries. Instead, a variety of expressions have been used, always stressing the 'otherness' of foreign immigrants and the temporary character of the immigration.' The traditional term for working migrants, *Fremdarbeiter*, meaning foreign or alien workers, was dropped around 1960 because of its association with the forced labour of the Nazi era and the term *Gastarbeiter* or 'guest worker' was invented, while *auslandische Arbeitnehmer* was used in official communications. Both these terms drew attention to the 'otherness' of the workers, and in the early 1970s the label *auslandische Mitburger* or 'foreign co-citizens' was considered more considerate, though in the 1980s *Auslander* or 'foreigners' became almost universal.

Each episode of migration has its own particular characteristics and produces its own tensions and consequences, as the following examples show. American culture and what might be termed the 'national character' have been determined by the nature of the migration process. For most of the first century of the republic's existence, the patterns of immigration were influenced by those of maritime trade. The triangular trade network between Europe, Africa and the Americas introduced many of the earliest settlers to the US: the negroes. Trading links also brought emigrants from Europe, who crossed the Atlantic in the part-empty holds of cargo ships engaged in exporting bulky primary products from the US to the countries of Europe's Atlantic seaboard. During the days of sail, emigration to the US was dominated by the British, Germans and, to a lesser extent, Scandinavians. While the native Americans and negroes were, in their different ways, the victims of heartless exploitation and injustice, amongst the European settlers there was very little tension or discrimination.

The first mass migration to affect the US came with the arrival of the 'famine Irish' in 1845 and the years which followed. This migration produced the first urban ghettoes and the first stirrings of nativist sentiments amongst members of the Anglo-American, rural, Protestant cultural majority, who thought that the hordes of impoverished, urban, Roman Catholic Irish presented a threat to the established character and traditions of the republic. Although most of the immigrants had been peasants, they lacked the funds or the opportunities to break out of the great east coast ports of arrival, and as the refugees from the Irish potato famine poured into the central and waterfront districts of Boston, established Bostonians fled to the outer suburbs. Ghettoes formed as their large family homes were subdivided into tiny apartments and as cramped tenements erupted throughout the Irish districts.

During the second half of the century, changes in the transport patterns affected migration. Firstly the transition from sail-powered cargo ships to steam-powered passenger vessels made the Atlantic crossing a much swifter and safer undertaking. Also, as the railway network – which connected inland populations with the ports of embarkation, like Hamburg – was extended eastwards, so new communities were given the opportunity to emigrate. As industrialisation in Germany created new employment opportunities and stemmed the flow of migration from Germany, the newer railways were reaching into Eastern Europe and taking masses of Poles, Bohemians and the Jewish victims of Russian persecution to the seaports. Meanwhile, rural poverty and overpopulation in southern Italy unleashed a tide of emigrants from southern Europe on the east coast cities of the US.

By the close of the nineteenth century, the character of the American inner city as a patchwork of ethnic ghettoes had become established. Each cultural group had its own particular relationship with the dominant Anglo-Saxon Protestant group and its own particular relationship with other immigrant groups. For most of the century the negroes and the Irish Catholics experienced the worst discrimination, but later in the century the cruellest persecution was directed at the Chinese, who were not only coloured, but also not Christian. Nativist ideology tended to contrast solid, Anglo-American rural values which were underpinned by the Protestant work ethic with the squalor, violence and religious diversity of the 'immoral' city. That nobody in the country was working harder than those, like the Jewish garment-makers or Bohemian cigar-makers, who toiled in the tenement sweat shops of despised New York was a fact of little account to the self-styled patriots whose immigrant predecessors were a generation or two removed in time.

Gradually, the members of a particular minority could expect to have moved a few rungs up the ladder of opportunity, with the toughest, most poorly paid employment being taken over by members of the most recently arrived ethnic grouping. Differences between these groups affected their prospects within the US. When the famine Irish arrived their experiences of opposition to the British landlord class had already endowed them with skills of political organisation and a tradition of unity. The first step on the long road which has made Irish Americans slightly more prosperous than the American average involved the capture of the urban political machines in the cities where the Irish had settled in numbers. The machine could then be exploited to create municipal employment in fields like the police and fire services for members of the Irish community. The ability of Irish Americans to unite behind Irish candidates and the Democrat party contrasted with the political fragmentation of the Italians. For the Italians, who arrived in their millions in the decades around the turn of the century, identified with family, locality, village and town and had little sense of belonging to a far broader Italian community. So even in districts where Italians were easily in the majority, the Irish still succeeded in securing the election of Irish candidates.

With the growing acceptance of multicultural values, the inaccurate characterisation of the US as a 'melting pot' is being replaced by one based on a 'salad bowl', in which each ingredient retains its distinctiveness. Members of each immigrant nationality have developed their own patterns of identification, and within each group and within each family and generation there have been those who inclined more to the new and others who cherished the links with the old country. Perhaps the most successful transition has been made by the Irish Catholics, who managed to rejoice simultaneously in their Irishness and in their American citizenship. Marston (1989) applied social theory and discourse analysis to the study of Irish immigrants to Lowell in Massachusetts. She found that:

> The juxtaposition of Ireland's pitiable plight with the opportunities in America was a theme which appeared in speeches year after year. Political and moral condemnation of British imperialism was finely interwoven with optimism and support for the American republic . . . Routinely, St Patrick's Day dinner speeches were occasions for praising St Patrick, condemning British intervention in Ireland and commending America for all the opportunities it afforded the Irish. The American Revolution was seen as a glorious victory over British tyranny from which the Irish derived great satisfaction and the benefits of liberty and freedom. (ibid., pp. 441–2)

Most attention has been paid to international migration, but more localised movements of population can also be a source of considerable political tension. At the micro-scale, this has been studied in the case of the Isle of Man, a self-governing British Crown dependency (Prentice 1990). During the 1950s, the government of the island, which was experiencing net population loss, created a new tax regime intended to attract wealthy residents from the nearby UK. In the late 1980s, the island's booming 'offshore' financial sector and special tax arrangements proved particularly attractive, and an influx of affluent new residents pushed up the price of housing on the island. The new residents, consisting of former colonial administrators and settlers and business people, contrasted markedly with the indigenous Manx population and it became clear that the two populations were divided on important issues like the inflation of house prices on the island, rents, eviction and homelessness. Native islanders found that young Manx couples were encountering difficulties in being able to afford to buy houses on Man; most thought that immigration was threatening the island's character and undermining the 'Manxness' of Man and they felt that further immigration should be strongly regulated.

While migration is a source of anxiety and intercommunal tension in the Isle of Man, in the former constituents of the Soviet Union its consequences exist as serious threats of future war. The Soviet Union was the world's most multinational state and contained well over 100 different nationalities. Nevertheless, one nationality, the Great Russians, constituted an absolute majority within the USSR. Although most of the political difficulties which one associates with migration today concern the tensions between an indigenous majority and an intrusive, alien minority – as with the difficulties associated with

Pakistani immigrants in Britain or Algerians in France – in the USSR, the problem involved the expansion of members of the dominant majority into minority homelands. The state which fell to the Bolsheviks in 1917 was the world's largest terrestrial empire, the product of the expansion, over many centuries, of the territory controlled by the Moscow core area. Having espoused internationalist, anti-imperialist ideology, after the 'October' Revolution the Bolsheviks found themselves presiding over a multinational imperial territory, created largely by conquest, in which the Russians and their Slavonic cousins, the Ukrainians and Belorussians, existed as a colonial elite.

Rather than dismantling the empire according to the best anti-colonial traditions, the Bolsheviks sought to preserve the territorial integrity of the Tsarist state so far as they could, while still seeming to observe the principles of national self determination. A new constitution of an extremely federal complexion was adopted, according to which those large and most advanced national groupings which also had common boundaries with external states were awarded Union Republic (SSR) status. These SSRs enjoyed a great deal of nominal autonomy, including the right to secede from the union. However, since the Communist Party, which was the seat of all significant power, remained a centrally organised institution, the federal concessions were destined to be more cosmetic than real.

Even so, the possession of SSR status did have distinct advantages for a national minority, not only in preserving the national language and culture, but also in providing career opportunities within the republican apparatus. But in the course of the Stalin era, the accelerating industrialisation and the associated colonisation and development of minority territories resulted in high levels of internal migration by members of the relatively advanced Great Russian majority. Some arrived in minority republics as administrators, technicians and teachers, others as industrial workers or peasants. Fears that Russian immigration constituted a threat to republican privileges were confirmed in 1956, when the Karelo-Finnish SSR was demoted to the status of a mere Autonomous Soviet Socialist Republic (ASSR) after a mere 16 years of existence. The indigenous Karelians had numbered about 170 000. During and after the Second World War there had been intense Russian immigration associated with port and industrial developments and mining. As a result, the Karelians became a minority within their homeland, and by the 1960s, Russians formed about 70 per cent of the population in the former republic.

The main threat of immigration-inspired suppression then seemed to be directed at the Kazakh SSR. For a period during the 1960s and 1970s, Russian settlers actually outnumbered the Kazakhs, but then the

Kazakhs were restored as a majority because they retained a high birth-rate, contrasting with the 'developed' pattern of low birth-rates associated with the immigrants. In the census of 1989, the Kazakhs formed a slender majority of 39.7 per cent in their republic, with the Russian component amounting to 37.8 per cent and Ukrainians totalling 5.4 per cent.

With the partial disintegration of the USSR early in the 1990s, the problem of Russian emigration took on an entirely new dimension. The Russians were transformed into significant and politically sensitive minorities in the chain of newly independent states which now bordered Russia. In each case they posed the possibility that one day they might serve a re-invigorated and expansionist Russia in the way that the Sudeten Germans of Czechoslovakia had served Nazi Germany: as a pretext for an invasion masked as an attempt to rescue oppressed co-nationals. The Baltic republics of Latvia, Estonia and Lithuania emerged as sovereign entities after the First World War, but survived only until 1940, when they were annexed by the USSR. In 1991, after brief and largely bloodless but intense campaigns for independence, they re-emerged as sovereign states – though in the meantime they had acquired substantial Russian immigrant populations. In each Baltic republic a referendum on independence was held in 1991, and in every case there appeared to be a potentially sinister association between the 'No' vote and the size of the Russian minority (Table 5.1).

However, research has shown that a third of the Russians in each Baltic state voted in favour of Baltic independence, and without this qualification the table is misleading. Even so, the governments of Estonia and Latvia have denied the Russian elements in their populations the right to automatic citizenship (G. Smith 1994b). This was

> because (a) they were illegal immigrants that came in during the Soviet period (b) they threatened the national cultures and demographic balance in the Estonian or Latvian homelands and therefore had to be marginalised (c) they were disloyal (as wrongly claimed in terms of their non-commitment during the referendum on statehood). As a result, the 1992 citizenship law in Estonia and 1994 equivalent in Latvia have made it very difficult for them to become citizens. Over 1.2 million have in effect become an urban underclass, deprived of full citizen rights, which excludes them voting in national elections, owning property or forming political parties/movements. (G. Smith 1996)

In the January of 1991, massive price rises in Lithuania provided a cause or a pretext for angry demonstrations by ethnic Russians, and a few days later Russian troops fired on Lithuanian nationalist

Table 5.1 *Referenda in the Baltic Republics*

	Size of 1991 referendum 'Yes' vote for independence as a percentage of total	*Size of Russian minority as a percentage of total population*
Latvia	74	34
Lithuania	91	9
Estonia	78	30

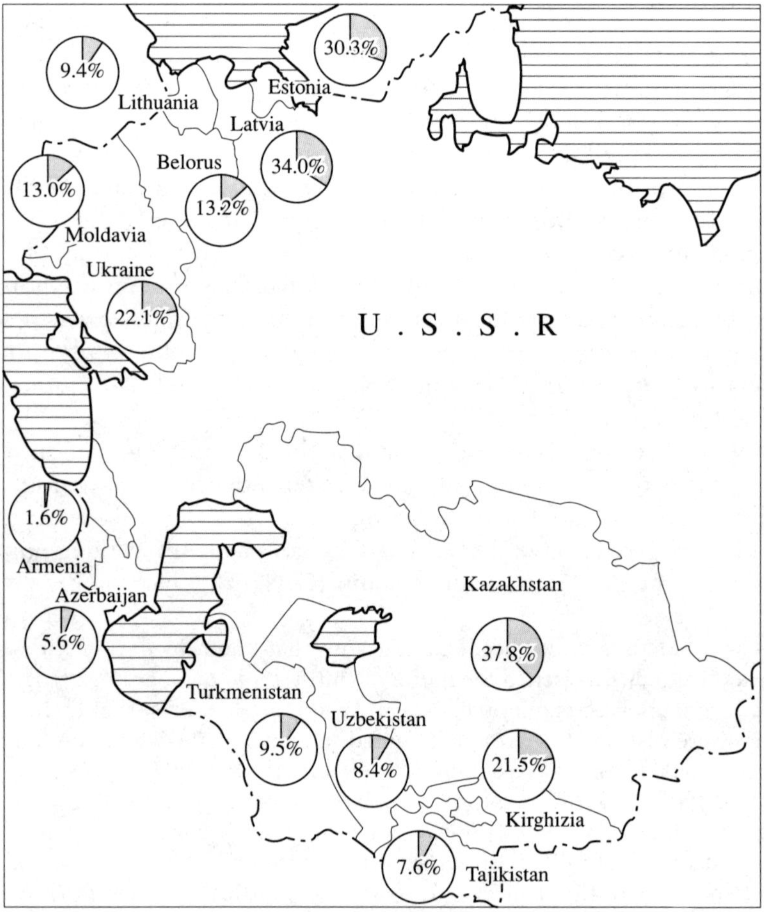

Map 8 Russian minorities living outside Russia; the shaded segment shows the Russian population as a proportion of the total population of each former Union Republic

demonstrators. If, in the post-independence era any of the Baltic economies perform poorly then pressures from Russian nationals for reintegration with Russia may be intense. Meanwhile, Russians in Latvia face an uncertain future, aware of the hostility of their hosts and doubtful of their own ability to obtain equality of citizenship.

The recent upswing in interest in citizenship amongst Western geographers has provided useful perspectives on immigration problems. Many of the divisive issues in the relationship between immigrants and indigenous groups concern questions of entitlement to state benefits and other privileges of nationality, while the divisions themselves concern problems of an 'us and them' nature and perceptions of factors involved in the condition of being a stranger. As expressed by Painter and Philo (1995, p. 100):

> The linkage of citizenship and space here becomes one in which citizenship is measured not only against 'them there' but also to some extent against what might be termed 'them here': and in this case the bounded space of citizenship becomes one that cannot be straightforwardly inclusionary because some of the people resident within the territorial limits are not properly regarded as being 'like us' who are fashioned out of the same historical, cultural, ethnic, linguistic and even religious materials (the soil of the nation-state).

They add that: 'social–cultural relations are intrinsic to the political relationship between citizenship and space, in that who gets defined as a "true" citizen within the city-state or the state-area depends in part on who carries with them what is deemed to be the correct baggage of history, culture, ethnicity, language and religion' (ibid.).

However, one can carry all the approved 'baggage of history' and yet still be a stranger in some parts of the world. In Africa the superimposition of colonial boundaries by the European imperial powers divided numerous tribal and ethnic entities, in the way that Somalis became fragmented between Ethiopia, Kenya and French, Italian and British Somaliland. In the post-colonial era, the old imperial boundaries tend to have hardened rather than loosened, so that members of the same tribal culture can become foreigners and strangers rather than compatriots. Equally, the colonial period tended to be a time when the divisions between different tribes and nationalities were diluted, so that the social systems became less exclusive and in the British East African colonies, for example, members of many indigenous tribes, Europeans and Indians could at least coexist if not enjoy equality. But, 'Political independence and the emergence of new African states brought about a rebirth of the "closed" system . . . Thus in several new African states, strangers who were formerly "accepted" . . . have been expelled or mandated for repatriation' (Shack 1978, pp. 44–5).

City, megacity, state and world

The city is both a part of its state and an island within it. Cities have their own particular political geographies of commercial centres, affluent suburbs, slums, ghettoes and no-go areas. In some ways they have more in common with each other than with the rural settings in which they stand. And as I have remarked, in a world increasingly dependent upon information technology, it is possible to imagine a future world in which the information-rich global cities engage together in intense dialogue, oblivious to the concerns of the information-poor deserts that surround each of them. Writing of the City of London, Nairn (1988, p. 240) considered that 'The City regards itself as separate from the country at large', while Taylor (1994, p. 156) believes that 'the City is a world city, not a national one . . . The City is not the financier of the British economy but something different altogether'.

While cities have problems and interests in common, they are also divided, every one having its own particular history of rivalry between its rich citizens and its slum dwellers and those with power and those without it. Short (1993, p. 149) notes that the building blocks of urban social movements are the citizens and that in the political arena of the city, citizens play a number of roles. They perform as *workers* employed by or within the city; as *tax-payers* funding city services, which involves them in seeking to maximise their benefits while minimising their payments and in developing opinions about how the city should be administered and how its employees should be paid; they perform as *users of city services*, which again gives rise to opinions about the way that their city is run, and they also perform as *residents*. They are residents in a double sense: they live in particular neighbourhoods which have their own cultural identities and they are also residents of general urban space, which Short describes as a 'changing externality surface' (ibid.). Some of these externalities are positive, like pleasant parks or useful transport links, while others are negative, like noisy thoroughfares or polluting factories. Residents, who are often property-owners and whose homes are usually by far their most valuable assets, are anxious to attract 'public goods' to their neighbourhoods and exclude 'public bads'. Citizens have important interests associated with their place of residence; it constitutes their living environment and often their main investment too. Consequently, they will mobilise to oppose any changes which might threaten their amenity and assets.

As individuals, citizens wield little power, but collectively they may exert considerable influence when organised in pressure groups (see p. 269 *et seq*.). Some pressure group activity may be directed towards changing the administrative and political structures of the city in order to create systems which are more responsive to the needs of the citizens. Most activity involves struggles launched to protect the status quo against some specific threat, which may involve the perceived social and economic deterioration of neighbourhoods or the challenge posed by commercial or transport developments. There are also struggles, not always linked to formal pressure groups, which are concerned with the cultural identity of places and fears of the colonisation of neighbourhoods by 'others' of a different colour, nationality or class. These conflicts do not always represent an opposition by the 'haves' against encroachments by the 'have nots' – such as culminated in the 'white flight' which took place as whites abandoned the inner cities of the US to disadvantaged coloured colonists and resettled in the suburbs. They can also involve resistance by deprived groups to infiltration and domination by more affluent and influential elements. Such a struggle occurred in London's Docklands when members of the indigenous working-class community struggled to resist efforts to redevelop the area by the London Docklands Development Corporation, an undemocratic body imposed upon the area by the government in 1981.

> Docklands has become a showcase for the display of post-industrial employment and the presentation of housing forms for the newly affluent . . . Two societal forces are meeting in the same social space. On the one hand there is *yuppification* involving the destruction of an existing community and its replacement by a new middle class, with consequent changes in the meaning and use of space. On the other hand, there is *local resistance*. (Short 1993, p. 159)

In the US some 32 000 communities exist within gated and guarded compounds, but the most intense struggles between opposed societal forces are threatened in the cities of the Third World, where affluent neighbourhoods and destitute but rapidly expanding shanty towns exist side by side. The urban issues of race are generally less well publicised than in the West, but they are important in many multiracial cities. In 1992 bus loads of youths from the impoverished North Zone of Rio de Janiero made 'sweeps' to terrorise beachgoers on the select beaches in the city's South Zone.

> The reaction to this event by South Zone residents revealed their prejudices and insecurities about the poor residents of the North Zone and from the highly visible, but socially distant, *favelas* of nearby hillsides. Furthermore,

> the fact that the youth from the North Zone were predominantly black or brown, that the South Zone residents were virtually all white, and that those involved were quite conscious of and even haunted by the colour differences, made this a racial as well as a class issue. (Telles 1995, p. 397)

Often the response to such stresses involves the middle classes in strengthening their defences and intensifying their isolation from the feared residents of the shanties and ghettoes. When this happens, their contacts with the poor are reduced and it becomes easier to regard the underprivileged as being outsiders; their 'otherness' increases and understanding and concern about their plight and needs is diminished.

On the basis of evidence drawn largely from Chicago and New York, Hernandez (1985) described five community types. *Firstly*, there was the ghetto or *barrio*, where one ethnic or racial group was dominant, but where the capacity to absorb new immigrants was limited. *Secondly*, there were also heterogenous new immigrant districts, in which the more recent arrivals of various ethnic origins compete with each other for employment, housing and services. *Thirdly*, there are areas which are being recolonised by middle-class whites. Immigrants renting property are displaced by property developers and speculators as 'back-to-the-city' movements become involved in the gentrification and refurbishment of properties. *Fourthly*, there is the movement of immigrant families and their descendants to middle-class districts in the older neighbourhoods of satellite cities, and *fifthly*, there are scattered suburban settlements containing a mix of affluent migrants and long established whites and blacks. This classification embodies integrationist and assimilationist assumptions, but:

> For blacks, race and place remain closely intertwined because of majority group prejudice and discrimination as well as the operation of the urban economy. For the members of groups based on religion and ethnic origin, ethnicity and place have become more or less dissociated, with associations being determined largely by ethnic desires rather than majority group pressures. (Eyles 1990, p. 62)

Eyles concludes that 'Blacks remain largely excluded while ethnic minorities may more successfully alter the boundary relations between themselves and the majority' (ibid., p. 63).

While the state may operate immigration policies designed to prevent the establishment and development of cultural rivals to the dominant state culture, similar policies may be found to operate at municipal levels. Minority groups may be confined within certain districts, their opportunities to advance being blunted and their ability to influence mainstream culture and attitudes greatly restricted:

> Thus, most public housing projects in American cities and some (usually inferior quality) council blocks in British cities may be occupied exclusively by blacks, despite supposedly 'colour-blind' housing allocation policies, the outcome being accepted within an ideology or commonsense understanding in which race is a relevant criterion in the differential treatment of people. Racism is thereby reproduced, in the spatial form of the city as well as in people's consciousness and social practice. (Smith 1990, pp. 10–11)

Berner and Korff believe that the metropolises of today are characterised by confrontations between the processes of localisation and globalisation. The former involves the search for a local identity and the creation of localities as the foci for everyday living. Despite the seeming contradictions, it is closely linked to globalisation, which creates local diversity.

> Instead of a mere differentiation between world regions, centre and periphery today indicate a differentiation between global society and segmented localities, both spatially anchored in world cities. Centre and periphery face each other within the metropolis and form the background of intensifying urban conflicts in London, Paris and Los Angeles as well as in Bangkok, Manila, Rio de Janeiro and Mexico City. (Berner and Korff 1995, p. 212)

In the megacities of the Third World the process of globalisation leads to intensifying struggles over the use of urban land. To the elites it offers increasing opportunities and incentives to expand the area of their activities, but for the other groups, the expansion of affluent residential and business districts produces pressures to displace them from their neighbourhoods and places of work. As the disadvantaged members of the urban community rally to defend their localities, closely knit local organisations are formed and the process of localisation is strengthened.

Whilst many Western countries have experienced a decline of the inner city areas and a drift of population to outer suburbs, satellites or the countryside, urban growth in most Third World countries has continued to accelerate: 'The sprawling shanty towns of the Third World city are the physical expression of this explosive growth. In the OICs [old industrialised countries], as we have seen, most industrial growth now occurs away from the major urban centres; in the Third World the reverse is the case. Virtually all industrial growth is in the big cities' (Dicken 1992, p. 447). Nevertheless, according to Friedmann's classification (1986, pp. 69–84), only two 'primary world cities', São Paulo and Singapore, lie in semi-peripheral countries, the remainder – London, Paris, Rotterdam, Frankfurt, Zurich, New York, Chicago and

Box 5.3 *Social justice*

The study of social justice concerns investigating and explaining the distribution of society's burdens and benefits. D. M. Smith (1994, p. 564) notes that it is *in*equality or *un*equal treatment that requires explanation and writes that: 'People's common humanity and capacity for pleasure and pain is a plausible starting point for equalitarianism, with such individual differences as strength, skill, intellect, family, race or place of birth being regarded as fortuitous and hence morally irrelevant to the way in which people should be treated.' The landmark early study of social justice and the city was accomplished by Harvey (1973), who placed issues of class and inequality in a geographical context by arguing that an equitable territorial distribution of income would be achieved when the needs of the people in each territory were satisfied, when the allocation of resources rewarded contributions to the national economic well-being, when extra resources were directed to overcoming special circumstances of difficulty deriving from social or physical factors and when the distribution maximised the opportunities of the least-advantaged territory.

Geographers have long recognised that individuals and communities occupying different places have different opportunities, with the social and political factors which vary from place to place being no less important as determinants of the life chances than factors of a physical nature. The nature of the political structures which develop can have profound effects upon the ways in which resources are redistributed: 'All states are constrained by external economic and political forces; all states develop bureaucratic structures to allocate resources and facilities necessary for social reproduction and all organizations have their internal logic of displacement of goals' (Pahl 1979, p. 39). Pahl goes on to note that: '. . . some decisions float at the top but many more sink. Those who deal with the sinking decisions are the managers and those working for managers face to face with recipients are gatekeepers . . . seen from the position of the applicant, client or recipient of urban services and facilities the gatekeeper is the source of power' (ibid.). (Subsequently, it has become common practice to regard *urban managers* as being bureaucrats employed in the public sector and *gatekeepers* as being employed in the private sector professions: people such as bank managers and estate agents.) Pahl (1975) and Rex (1968) demonstrated how managerial processes involving managers and gatekeepers could greatly affect the life chances of individuals or groups (as when West Indian immigrants were discriminated against by the functionaries in English local council housing departments), but as interest in radical geography grew, attention was directed away from managerialism towards Marxist perspectives, which regarded managers as being no more than the instruments of the capitalist elite and interpreted inequality within the broad framework of the class struggle and capitalist exploitation. To most conventional Marxists, concerns about morality and social justice are merely ideological constructions used by the ruling elite in order to legitimise their dominance of society.

Los Angeles – all lying in core countries. Within the Third World there is great variation in the pattern of urbanisation:

> some countries (the NICs and proto-NICs) are expanding the semiperiphery of the world economy, while some key cities in the NICs are becoming important continental and global financial centres in their own right (e.g. Singapore, Hong Kong and, to a lesser extent, Sao Paulo). On the other hand, with very few exceptions, the countries of sub-Saharan Africa seem destined to remain very largely in the new global periphery, suffering growing urbanization and poverty together with economic stagnation, marginalization, and environmental degradation. (Simon 1995, pp. 151–2)

The link between globalisation, urbanisation and political evolution is a very close one: 'With the advent of the global economy, nation building is becoming more and more synonymous with city building. Cities serve as the nexus of the global society' (Knight and Gappert 1989, p. 12).

The spectacular growth of cities such as Singapore and Hong Kong has led to suggestions that the city-state will provide a model for future development in political geography. With its rapidly expanding economy, authoritarian government, conformist population and carefully regulated immigration policy, Singapore seems to some to epitomise the pattern for the twenty-first century. The cities of Asia have their own remarkable dynamic:

> The new Asian cities owe nothing to the European ideal of picture-postcard Tuscan hill towns, or even the boulevards of Paris. They are dense, raw, chaotic, and they are vast. They have shopping malls and skyscrapers, airports and business parks. But all of these apparently familiar landmarks have been subverted into something very different from their western originals . . . Public spaces, grand plans, picturesque skylines are all but non-existent. (Sudjic 1995)

Hong Kong and Shenzhen seem destined to become the world's largest city. Shenzhen has grown as a special economic zone on a previously empty site on the Chinese side of the Hong Kong border in the years since 1970. Such was the haste with which it grew that the disruption of the local ecosystem resulted in severe floods that caused extensive damage and closed Shenzhen's main hotels in 1993. With the removal of the international boundary the as yet nameless city resulting from the amalgamation of Hong Kong, Shenzhen, the special economic zone of Zhuhai and the rapidly urbanising land along the Pearl River may surpass Mexico City and Tokyo-Osaka to become the world's largest city: 'Once a city's geography was determined by the endurance of its pedestrians. It expanded to accommodate rail and road commuters. But a city of 40 million people is a different kind of organism altogether. Its economic power is such that it makes the nation state redundant so long as it can retain the cohesion that cities need to be workable entities' (ibid.).

While there is no doubt that city-states such as Singapore can now be spectacularly successful, is there cause to suppose that they represent a more general political destiny? The Hong Kong conurbation will exist to serve the needs of China rather than itself, and there is no prospect that many cities will seek – or much less likely, achieve – political detachment from the states of which they are parts. There is, however, the probability that the effect of cities on their tributary areas will change and the differences in influence and affluence between city and country and between different districts of the city will intensify, while the globalisation of culture will find its strongest expression in the world cities. The peasant regards the city as a haven of opportunity where the chances for employment and for obtaining education and housing for his family are far better than in the village, while the more affluent citizens realise that the city offers unrivalled business opportunities, contacts with government, links with the outside world and access to labour (Garau 1989). However, all who doubt that a spectacular political destiny awaits the world cities should at least take account of the concluding words of Taylor's (1993b) highly influential study of political geography:

> Our whole analysis has been premised on the existence of a modern world-system wherein the inter-state system is integral. Every chapter of the book has provided material on the power of these states and their importance to understanding our world. But the capitalist world-economy is only an historical system; it will not and, at the rate it is using up the world's resources and polluting the world's life support system, it cannot endure forever. World cities taking functions away from territorial states, may be a key indicator that we are indeed at the beginning of a transition to a different world system with a fundamentally different politics.

■ Divide to rule

Only in the cases of the smallest of states would it be feasible to govern the state territory completely and directly from the capital without the adoption of one or more intermediate tiers of administration. But the choice of an internal system of subdivisions and an associated division of administrative functions is not simply a matter of administrative expedience: there are also important questions concerning the emotional and political links between peoples and places. Sometimes it is argued that the political integrity of the state may best be preserved by recognising ethnic and cultural diversity and providing a highly devolved system of administration which will allow them the maximum expression. Equally, recent examples can be cited to argue that such allowances will ultimately facilitate the disintegration of the state.

In categorising forms of government, it has been conventional for authorities to make a distinction between the unitary state and the federal state. Although federal states – which include giants like Canada, Australia, Brazil and the former Soviet Union – cover more than half of the land surface of the world, three-quarters of all states have unitary constitutions. The unitary state is rooted in the centralist tradition of French political philosophy and the belief that power should only be devolved for administrative convenience and that the territorial components of the state should, in all respects, be subordinate to the political centre (Kesselman and Rossenthal 1974). In contrast, 'In federations, one level of local state has a guaranteed existence within the political system . . . Thus the American Federal government cannot build highways, pay social security and unemployment benefits, and create a national health service, for example; since these tasks are not enumerated in the Constitution, they are reserved to the States' (Johnston 1982, p. 188). In reality, the distinction between unitary and federal states is often blurred, particularly in terms of the behaviour of the state.

> Part of the difficulty stems from differences between countries in the ways in which federalism operates. In general, a minimal definition will include recognition of two levels of government that constitutionally are considered equals; this being so a number of countries, notably those in the Third World and in the socialist bloc, with federal constitutions but that otherwise are autocratically governed are described as not 'truly federal'. By implication, democracy is a necessary condition for federalism to operate. (Paddison 1983, p. 98)

It is, in fact, one of the great ironies of comparative politics that the state with the most liberal of all federal constitutions, one which offered its constituent republics the right to secede, was Stalin's Soviet Union.

While federal constitutions have provided no guarantee of federal behaviour, unitary states are not debarred from the devolutionary processes. An oft-quoted case of unitary complexity is that of the UK, and here it can be seen that the degree to which a state satisfies the demand for devolution can vary sharply through time. Wales was incorporated into the English kingdom by conquest during the Middle

Ages, while the Crowns of England and Scotland were united in 1603 and the Parliaments were combined in 1707, when the Scottish parliament voted itself out of existence and Scottish representatives joined the Parliament in London. A nationalist uprising in Ireland was defeated in 1798 and the Irish parliament was abolished in 1801, when Ireland joined England and Scotland in a United Kingdom of Great Britain and Ireland. In 1921, Ireland was partitioned, with 26 of the 32 counties breaking away from the United Kingdom. The state which exists today is, in many respects, anachronistic, with aspects of the past being represented by factors like the independent Scottish legal and educational systems or the existence of English, Scottish, Welsh and Northern Irish national soccer teams. At the same time, the system fails to reflect the powerful cultural and political influences of the past on the present. Formerly, the anachronisms could be regarded as expressions of the highly regarded British identity and from the late Victorian era in the eventide of British hegemony through the shared hardships and sacrifices of two World Wars until the late 1950s the minority nationalist movements were irrelevant. In the general election of 1945, the Scottish Nationalist Party (SNP) polled a mere 1.3 per cent of the Scottish vote, and the Welsh nationalist party, Plaid Cymru, attracted only 1.1 per cent of the Welsh vote. 'Despite the incomplete unification of the UK, the upsurge of its nationalisms in the 1960s came as a surprise. Centre of an Empire being transformed into a Commonwealth, the UK, far from appearing vulnerable, had indeed seemed a particularly successful case of political integration' (Anderson 1989, p. 42).

Gradually, however, dissatisfaction in the Celtic periphery increased. In the 1994 elections to the European parliament, the SNP took more than a quarter of the vote in every single Scottish seat and polled 33 per cent of the Scottish vote (to Labour's 43 per cent). In Wales, Plaid Cymru won 17 per cent of the total vote and took more than a third of votes in the traditional Welsh cultural heartland around Snowdonia. One significant factor in the rise of Scottish separatism concerned the discovery of substantial oil reserves in waters off the Scottish coast. The oil gave rise to claims that the English were pirating a Scottish resource and also increased confidence in Scotland's ability to survive as an economically independent entity. The Labour party, whose ambitions depend upon the election to Westminster of substantial numbers of Scottish and Welsh Labour MPs, approached the rises in nationalist support with policies of appeasement. In 1969 a Commission on the Constitution was set up under Lord Kilbrandon; in 1973 its Majority Report favoured a devolution of powers from Westminster to Scotland and Wales, while the Minority Report advocated a devolution to English regions too. In 1974 the SNP obtained its best general election

Box 5.4 *Electoral geography*

Electoral geography concerns the geographical aspects of elections and referenda, their organisation and, particularly, their results (with the similar aspects of opinion polls often also being included within the scope of electoral geography). Interests in such topics can be traced back to the years immediately preceding the 1914–18 War (Siegfried 1913), but electoral geography seems to have commanded the greatest support in the years around 1970, when positivism was still a dominant force in geography and when election results provided masses of readily quantifiable data. At this time, electoral geography achieved an almost hegemonic status within political geography, but subsequently interest has declined and the subject has not achieved its (apparent) potential. In part this was probably due to a misplaced emphasis on searches for data to quantify rather than for problems to solve, giving rise to conclusions that were vacuous or banal. It is no more an achievement to prove that working-class districts tend to have socialist electorates than it is to demonstrate that voters for the Ulster Unionist parties tend to be Protestants. Taylor (1993b, pp. 253–4) has criticised the failure of electoral studies to integrate into the political geographical field and has proposed a revised model of political geography. He points out that firstly, parties organise the politics of the state and then they mobilise the population behind that politics – though a party cannot do this in isolation but depends upon the development of a competitive party system, which in turn depends upon opposition groups being perceived as alternative governments rather than enemies of the state. He believes that there are two electoral geographies: 'the familiar studies in the "geography of voting" . . . and which here becomes the geography of support. Second there is the much less familiar geography of power, of interest group funding and policy outcomes. With two electoral geographies to deal with we are now in a position to introduce a revised model' (ibid., p. 258). Attracted by the masses of data available, established electoral geography has focused on the geography of support, while the geography of power, which includes issues of party funding and covert deals, is much less accessible to the researcher. Here Taylor provides an electoral model which is more rewarding than the simplistic forms which Johnston (1986, p. 15) has criticised: '[The] consumer sovereignty model of politics, set in a geographical context, assumes that voters decide what they want and parties set out to satisfy them. Thus parties are relatively passive agents, conducting private polls, identifying the salient issues, and then producing a package of policies which will make them most attractive to a majority of voters in a majority of constituencies. But is this really so, any more than producers of goods for sale are passive responders to markets? . . . Reflection on the choices available showed that the menu is being drawn up not by me and my fellow-voters but by the parties'.

The most useful work in electoral geography will be that which combines relevance and originality with a strong spatial aspect. A good early example of this combination would be McCarty's (1960) investigation of the degree to which voting for Senator McCarthy in Wisconsin in the elections of 1952 was a function of the distance from the Senator's home town. Geographers can play useful roles by revealing the way that constituency boundaries are manipulated to generate electoral bias, the process of gerrymandering (which

Box 5.4 *continued*

derives its name from a Governor Gerry of Massachusetts who distorted boundaries to favour his party early in the nineteenth century). In the modern world arguably the most vital task awaiting geographers concerned with parties and voting involves the demonstration of the ways in which the *focused pursuit of party advantage* within the *temporal framework* provided by the electoral system has resulted in the failure of governments to tackle the gigantic environmental, demographic and egalitarian problems which confront the world and threaten the very survival of humanity.

result and polled 30.4 per cent of the Scottish vote. Government plans were set in motion for the installation of elected assemblies in Edinburgh and Cardiff, but firstly the measures would have to be approved by referenda to be held in 1979 in the two countries concerned. The results marked a new watershed in the constitutional saga; the Welsh assembly was crushingly rejected by 80 per cent of the people of Wales in a turn-out of only 58 per cent, and while the Scottish assembly won the support of 52 per cent of those who voted, it achieved the positive support of only 33 per cent of the total Scottish electorate, rather than the 40 per cent needed to succeed. A little later in 1979 the Labour minority government was defeated by the Conservatives under Margaret Thatcher, who made her antagonism towards further debate about devolution quite plain.

In the general election of 1983, support for the SNP crumbled to 11.3 per cent. Subsequently, there has been a revival of nationalist fortunes, largely due to the ineptitude with which Conservative governments have handled Scottish affairs and a widening gulf in the political cultures of Scotland, with its strong socialist sympathies, and Thatcherite (southern) England. Initially Labour reaped the benefits, and in the 1987 general election the Conservatives lost half their Scottish seats; Labour won 40 per cent of the votes, while the SNP won only 14 per cent. However, when the Conservative government imposed a grossly unjust new system of local taxation on Scotland prior to its introduction in England, the initiative returned to the SNP. Labour was cultivating an image of responsibility and was sensitive to charges of left-wing lawlessness, while the nationalists felt free to urge non-payment of the 'poll tax'. By the 1992 general election, however, the advantage had returned to Labour, which won 49 of the 72 Scottish parliamentary seats, while the SNP, with 21.5 per cent of the Scottish vote, won only 3. In 1995 the question of the devolution of power to Welsh and Scottish assemblies returned to the political agenda, with the Labour opposition promoting such changes and the Conservatives claiming that they would require income tax rises of 3 per cent in Scotland and Wales and would constitute a slippery slope leading to the break-up of the UK.

This example demonstrates the difficulty of tailoring political institutions to public opinion; institutions must be durable, while popular sentiments are volatile and not always very clearly defined. In 1979, 52 per cent of those Scots who voted in the referendum favoured devolved government as represented by the Scottish assembly; in 1988 an opinion poll showed that 35 per cent of Scots sought total independence, 42 per cent desired a devolved Scottish assembly, while 20 per cent favoured the status quo; but early in 1992 an opinion poll showed that 50 per cent of Scots agreed with the SNP policy of Scottish independence within a closely integrated European Community. Yet a few weeks later, the SNP won the support of scarcely more than one voter in five.

The experience of devolution in Spain is much more advanced. In 1978, after a long phase of centralised and autocratic government, the country obtained a new constitution which apparently makes it the country with the most devolved form of government in the EC/EU apart from federal Germany. At the time, the demands for devolution or separatism came from the 'historical nationalities' of the Basque country, Catalonia and Galicia. But instead of creating regional governments for just these territories, a universal regionalisation took place. The country was divided into 17 autonomous regions, each with its own president, cabinet and flag and each enjoying a measure of self-rule, but with the nature and scope of the powers devolved to the regions being uneven, so as to reflect the different conditions and requirements. On the whole, the devolution appears to have been successful. Despite the perpetual trials of strength which are inevitable given the vagueness of the 1978 constitution, rivalries between regions and between the regional and national levels of government have existed but have been contained within the constitutional structure and separatist violence has declined. The experience seems to show that the more autonomy a region enjoys, the better able it is to attract foreign investment, though central government has failed to shed bureaucrats at a rate consistent with the transfer of government functions to the regions (Hooper 1995). Here, devolution appears to have helped to perpetuate the state rather than to have undermined it. Some highly controversial interregional transfers of water were achieved during the drought summer of 1994 – though it is questionable whether those between Castilla-la Mancha, Valencia and Murcia would have been possible had not each region had a socialist government.

Elections in the March of 1996 brought an end to 13 years of socialist rule in Spain. The victorious conservatives of the Popular Party were associated with policies of centralisation and national unity, but their leader, Jose Maria Aznar, found his party to be 20 seats short of an overall majority in the new parliament. Consequently, he was obliged to set aside long-standing hostilities and court the favour of the Basque and Catalonian nationalists. Rather than reducing the influence of the regions, the Aznar administration has been obliged to devolve still more powers to them, while also allowing greater regional control of finances. These new concessions were presented as representing a positive move towards the final solution of the problem of minority nationalism in Spain, though in reality they were forced by electoral realities rather than principled conversion to the ideal of devolution.

Quoting Hartshorne, Paddison (1983, p. 97) describes how: 'federalism offers an institutional mode that balances the centrifugal and the centripetal forces within the state' to bind together the separate and diverse areas into an effective whole. This reflects the fashionable view that a sufficient supply of liberal and democratic provisions will enable culturally diverse groups to coexist within a federal state. However, the 'New Tribalism' of recent years seems to argue a different case. Canada is widely regarded as operating the most just and responsive of systems of federal government. Children in Quebec are banned from learning English in state schools until they are aged nine; the street signs are all in French and public employees may refuse to speak English – but this has not assuaged demands for an independent Quebec. The Parti Quebecois was formed as a moderate separatist party in 1967, the year when the French president, General de Gaulle, visited Canada and enraged Anglo-Canadian opinion by declaring, '*Vive le Quebec libre*'. It won its first election in the late 1970s; in 1980 it lost a referendum by a margin of 60–40 when it invited Quebeckers to vote on 'sovereignty-association' with Canada; and in 1993 the Bloc Quebecois became the official opposition in the federal parliament. Under the liberal federal constitution Quebec had developed its French identity. Car licence plates carry the legend '*Je me souviens*': 'I remember what has made me what I am', while:

> The harsh fact is that Quebec already feels like a different country. The wide boulevards of Quebec city make the province look like a chunk of France transplanted across the Atlantic. Quebec has its own jokes, its own food, its own celebrities. And as the Parti Quebecois likes to point out, at 7 million, its population is bigger than Denmark, Norway or Finland. (Travena 1995).

Despite the freedom to assert French identities, the Quebecois sense that their culture is besieged and feel that the English-speakers regard them as inferior and deny them respect. In the referendum held in 1995 the separatist cause failed by just one per cent.

The examples of Spain and Quebec appear to argue quite different cases, the former promoting devolution as an antidote to separatism but the latter seeming to favour the slippery slope analogy. In searching for unifying principles, perhaps we may only discover the unique?

■ *Chapter 6* ■

The International Dimension

Geography counts. Warsaw is not Johannesburg; Santiago is not Cairo. Marginalization in Liverpool is not the same as marginalization in Manila. The problems faced by women in Tokyo, Moscow, or Delhi or in the villages of Mali and Mexico cannot all be reduced to any simple equation. It is difficult to characterize even the operation of the states system in a way that captures the preoccupations of those living in the Middle East as well as those in Australia or China.

R. B. J. Walker (1988)

The process of interaction between communities takes place across as well as within political boundaries. Despite the waning of their influence (as explored in Chapter 3), states still command the international stage, so that the study of interstate relations still dominates the discipline of International Relations. In the course of the twentieth century, this discipline has developed and refined perspectives for the investigation of political behaviour at the international level, and it would be both wasteful and presumptuous for geographers to duplicate these efforts. Rather, we should seek to explore the ways in which spatially variable factors like place, location, terrain, culture and cultural modes of perception and decision-making serve to influence International Relations, and how political factors, such as territoriality, power, fear and conflict, exert their effects upon the geographical environment.

Before entering the international arena we should be aware of some terminological difficulties. Taylor (1995, p. 1) reminds us that: 'It is commonplace to note that the word international does not refer to what it describes – relations between nations . . . International as interstate is a product of the success of state-centred politics legitimating itself as national politics.' It is certainly the case that 'international' is most commonly used to describe relations between states rather than between nations. However, the use/misuse of the word is now so entrenched that it seems unlikely that it will be replaced by 'interstate', either in common parlance or academic usage.

■ Approaches to International Relations

There are several different approaches to the subject matter of the discipline of International Relations, and these are all of interest to political geographers working at the international level. Though not necessarily mutually exclusive, they represent different perspectives and emphases current within the subject, while also reflecting the significant stages in its evolution. Different authorities tend to identify a slightly different range of approaches, although the similarities between the identifications is far greater than the differences.

International Relations emerged as a subject in its own right at the end of the 1914–18 War, when political thinkers questioned the nature of a system that had allowed such destruction to happen. They sought to create a better one, framed in the values of Anglo-American liberal internationalism and buttressed by laws and institutions which would prevent a return to the mindless carnage that had marked the breakdown of the pre-war order. As the hopes for a peaceful and rational world order faded with the rise of totalitarian regimes during the 1930s, students of International Relations became divided between 'realists', who emphasised the essentially selfish and amoral nature of state behaviour, and 'idealists', who clung to the more traditional belief that good laws, proper institutions and democratic government could restore stability and decency to the international system. This opposition became known as the first debate in International Relations (Dalby 1991). Following the publication of E. H. Carr's *The Twenty Years Crisis* in 1946 and Hans Morgenthau's *Politics Among Nations* in 1948 the realist interpretation of international politics gained an intellectual ascendancy and attention was focused on state power, its composition and its applications when states engaged in the confrontational practice of power politics. At the time in the 1950s and 1960s when geography was undergoing its quantitative revolution and the emphasis was being placed on positivism and the conversion of geography into spatial science, International Relations was undergoing a comparable revolution as 'behaviouralists', who sought to apply the methodologies of science to the study of politics, emerged. Now the main schism in International Relations had come to lie between the behaviouralists and those who still supported the traditional view that scholars should study the questions which mattered rather than those that lent themselves to quantification and that political phenomena were too intricate and too unique to be suitable targets for positivist analysis. No victor emerged from this confrontation, the 'second debate' in International Relations, though it did give rise to a post-behaviouralist approach which seeks to assimilate the best features of each (Hastedt and Knickrehm 1991, p. 17).

More recently, the conceptual divisions in International Relations have become less clearly defined, though in addition to the enduring realist approach most authorities recognise a pluralist, a globalist and a neo-Marxist structural dependency approach, though to confuse matters, sometimes the pluralists and globalists are bracketed together while at others scholars group together the globalist and dependency approaches – compare, for example, Viotti and Kauppi (1993) and Hastedt and Knickrehm (1991). The pluralists argue that realists describe a world as it existed in the nineteenth century and that membership of the international system is no longer confined to sovereign states: now international organisations, transnational corporations, organised pressure groups or criminal organisations and other non-governmental actors all have their parts to play on the international stage. Realists may reply by claiming that pluralists place too much reliance on 'voluntarism' or human volition and on a naively optimistic regard for human nature. They may also suggest that the pluralist view is ethnocentric and based upon the American political system, which differs greatly from systems current in other parts of the world (Viotti and Kauppi 1993, pp. 248–50). The pluralists devalue the importance of power in controlling international affairs and argue that cooperation between the different actors also plays a significant role in international society. And as the challenges facing the world become ever more global in their extent, so the levels of interdependence and the need for cooperation must grow.

The followers of the dependency, international political economy or structuralist approach also question the realists' emphasis upon the sovereign state. They point out that while sovereignty is theoretically indivisible, the states of the developing world existed in an inferior or dependent position in their relationships with the most privileged states of the industrial world. Ideas drawn from Marxist theory were developed to interpret the shaping and domination of the Third World states by interests in the financial heartlands of the world. Critics of the approach argue that, like other theories based on Marxism, it reduces all explanations to 'economism' or the operation of the economic system and disregards the importance of non-economic factors. They also suggest that dependency may be a result of poverty rather than a cause of it and argue that the causes of poverty might be found within a Third World country, rather than being simply a consequence of the relationship with the external world. Other perspectives current in International Relations today include world order tendencies, which oppose the supposedly 'scientific' outlooks of the realists with normative discussions about how international affairs should be conducted: 'Asking questions about future possible worlds and the kinds of changes currently happening in global politics moves the focus of attention to ask questions about democracy, justice, ecology, and survival which are pressing political concerns that conventional international relations scholarship often cannot comprehensively address' (Dalby 1991, p. 264). Other approaches based on feminism or critical theory have also emerged.

Geographers exploring the conceptual world of International Relations will discover many themes that are familiar. Plainly, there are strong links between the behaviourist–traditionalist confrontation and the opposition between spatial science and the humanistic approach in geography. Less obviously, the pessimism of the realist approach echoes the fatalistic associations of environmental determinism, just as the optimism of the globalist perspective is reflected in the faith in the fundamental decency of human nature implicit in much of the thinking in environmental possibilism. Each of the approaches mentioned offers the geographer a different way of looking at the ways in which states, organisations and groups interact at the international level – and an appreciation of the alternative perspectives will further an understanding of this behaviour.

The realist perspective has certain inherent weaknesses, but it does assist in the construction of simple models of the international system. The actors in this system are the sovereign states, but now international organisations of states, transnational corporations and those other groups, such as Greenpeace, which can exert a significant effect upon international behaviour must also be regarded as actors. The states are still the dominant actors and the main motive force producing interactions in the system result from the pursuit by each state of its national (self)interest. Since the states exist in a closed system with finite resources, pursuit of the national interest must be a competitive process, a zero sum game in which one player's gain is a loss to other players.

Such a mechanistic approach can produce only the crudest model of the international system; the behaviour of states is really the behaviour of political decision-makers, so that international relations result from the deliberations of that hugely complex and unpredictable entity, the human being. Human decision-makers of all kinds do not base their judgements on the real world or phenomenal environment, but upon the world as it is perceived by their senses and moulded by their experiences: the behavioural environment (Kirk 1963). Thus:

> for all practical purposes we are not concerned with the unrecognizable absolute national interest but with those characterizations of national interest which form in the minds of political actors. Were the national interest readily identifiable and not amenable to varying interpretations, there would be little need for the elaborate diplomatic machines which most states support, and arguably, for political parties either. The national interest which concerns us here is a subjective phenomenon and so we can say that the fundamental motivation which helps to determine political behaviour at the international level is the pursuit of a perception of the national interest. (Muir and Paddison 1981, p. 196)

A fundamental characteristic of the realist approach has been the central role that it awards to power. To Morgenthau, politics was power politics, with the most significant outcomes being determined by inequalities in the spatial distribution of power throughout the world. (The practitioners of power politics treat power as the only important factor to be considered in International Relations, so that the interests of other parties are considered only to the extent that they command resources of power.) He regarded power as covering a wide spectrum of social relationships from outright physical violence to the most subtle of psychological influences; it was anything 'that establishes and maintains the control of man over man' (Morgenthau 1948, p. 9). Morgenthau took a very broad view of the domain of power, and for some like-minded scholars power is regarded as almost filling the arena that is politics. Potter's (1975, p. 173) definition of politics as concerning 'relationships of control and compliance between individuals and groups of individuals or agencies in society' is very close to the definitions of power offered by some realists. Others have seen the role of politics as being concerned with the management of power: 'Politics may be seen as the attempt . . . to eliminate from public life all powers that do not have the sanction of a public acceptance of their authority' (Scruton 1983, p. 366).

Power has meaning only in a relative sense. The power of one party is only effective in terms of its ability to coerce, influence or deter another party, and as Paddison (1983, p. 3) notes: 'Though opinions differ as to its possible definition, a widely held view is that a power relationship exists where A is able to get B to do something that the latter would not otherwise do.' It is plain that certain quantifiable ingredients, many of them geographical, must contribute to the power profile of a state – territorial extent, location on the globe, population size, energy production, numbers of fighter aircraft in service and so on must all exert an effect. This has inspired a number of attempts to devise 'magic' formulae which will express the power status of any state. Some of these have assumed that calculations based on physical resources are sufficient for the purposes of quantifying power, as with Ray's (1987) formula which considered that there were three essential dimensions to power which were based on demography, industrial strength and military might. Other researchers thought that allowance should be made for psychological factors, like morale; the extremely complicated analysis offered by German (1960) and involving no less than 26 variables was of this kind. Scarcely less daunting was Cline's equation:

$$\text{power} = C + E + M \times (S + W)$$

where C represented 'critical mass', this being a value for territory and population; E was a value for economic strength; M, a value for military strength: S, a value for strategy and W, a value for national will (Cline 1975).

Attempts such as these reveal the positivist approach at its most optimistic. Power cannot be quantified with any precision because it is relative not only in respect of the protagonists concerned but also in respect of a range of other variables, like the place and circumstance in which it is being applied. For example, during the post-war period the transmission of the power of the USA has been accomplished with much more success in the context of Central and South America than in that of the Middle East. Also, it must be remembered that in peacetime it is the perceptions rather than the realities of power which influence decision-making: 'With respect to policy-making and the content of policy decisions, our position is that what matters is how the policy-maker imagines the milieu to be, not how it actually is. With respect to the operational results of decisions, what matters is how things are, not how the policy-maker imagines them to be' (Sprout and Sprout 1957, pp. 327–8). Perceptions can diverge considerably from reality, and the injustices and fatal consequences of the Munich agreement might have been avoided had the British decision-makers not overestimated the power and resolve of the Nazi military machine as they existed in 1938. Very few diplomats indeed can have perceived the extent to which the might of the Soviet Union was illusory prior to the implosion of the Soviet state in 1989–91. Supporters and opponents of the system abroad must have been amazed to see the disintegration of a polity which they had held in awe, while the escalating changes 'also represented a massive general retreat from, and finally a rout of the old officially long-held and brutally defended claim that some kind of utopia was being built in the Soviet Union and Eastern Europe. There are few cases in history of an established regime collapsing so utterly, so swiftly and with so little resistance' (Denitch 1993, p. 465). Finally, any assumption that factors as elusive or volatile as morale, resolve or patriotism, or as ephemeral and conditional as leadership quality can be reduced to some numerical value is untenable.

A quite different approach to the interpretation of power was offered by Maull (1990), who made a distinction between 'hard power' and 'soft power'. Hard power, depending mainly upon military strength, was measured by the ability to command others to obey. Soft power was measured by the capacity to persuade – and he thought that Germany and Japan, as operators of soft power, were increasing their influence relative to that of the US, because they understood the need to cooperate and appreciated the importance of economic rather than military methods to furthering their national goals.

A rather different approach to the geographical concentration of power is represented by the concept of 'hegemonic cycles'. This was developed by Wallerstein (1984) and applied more particularly to political geography by Taylor (1993a). The Italian neo-Marxist, Antonio Gramsci, had developed the concept of hegemony in a class context, with the hegemonic class obtaining an ascendancy in the economic, social and political realms by persuading other classes to perceive the world in a manner favourable to this ascendancy. Taylor (1993a, p. 36) explains that in the arena of political geography: 'Hegemonic cycles focus upon one state, the hegemon, that for a short period is pre-eminently powerful economically, politically and culturally. The cycle consists of the rise and fall from this position.' This cycle commences when the hegemon achieves an advantageous position in manufacturing and broadens its leadership to include a command of the commercial and financial spheres. Meanwhile, it achieves a political dominance by leading an alliance of states in a successful confrontation with its chief rival and then proceeds to manipulate international affairs to its advantage; like Gramsci's hegemonic class, the hegemon is able to exert a cultural leadership and persuade others of the value of its liberal ideology, though after a short phase of 'high hegemony' its leadership role steadily declines.

The hegemon – Britain in the mid-nineteenth century and the US in the mid-twentieth century – was not just pre-eminent in the military arena but also possessed the resources of economic and cultural domination necessary to set its chosen agenda and enforce its chosen code of international behaviour:

> American hegemony, therefore does not only signify a shift in the identity of the hegemonic power . . . but also the institutions and practices the United States brought to the world by virtue of its dominant position. These have included mass production/consumption, limited state welfare policies,

Box 6.1 *Power systems*

Not only does power vary spatially in its intensity and concentration, it also ebbs and flows in the temporal dimension, so that yesterday's hegemon may become a puppet tomorrow. Differences in the way that power is distributed within the system of states produces different power systems which seem to be governed by different sets of rules. From the Treaty of Westphalia in 1648 up until the outbreak of war in 1914 a balance of power system held sway in which power was distributed between a number of great powers to produce a multipolar power system. The currency of this system was associated with a period of relative peace and stability which was advantageous to the British with their growing involvement in global commerce. Whilst no single state had the power to dominate the system, each great power sought to increase its wealth and might. Each also had an interest in preserving stability, and so the formation of one potentially aggressive alliance would be counterbalanced by the formation of a defensive alliance amongst the remaining powers. Within this system Britain, with its great navy and maritime interests, performed the role of the balancing power, and would lend its weight to the weaker of any two alliances, and thus restore balance and stability to the system. The collapse of the balance of power system and the outbreak of the 1914–18 War marked a fundamental watershed in political development.

Various other power systems can be identified, some of them imaginary and others real but all concerned with ways in which power can be distributed geographically. Kaplan (1957) described a range of theoretical power systems and evaluated the rules according to which such systems would operate; there was, for example, his 'tight bipolar' system, in which all the actors in the international system are integrated into one or other of two rival power blocs. After the 1914–18 War there was a power system which was multipolar but which lacked a balance of power mechanism, while after the 1939–45 War most of the former great powers slumped in relative importance and a bipolar system dominated by the US and the Soviet Union emerged. For a good three decades it appeared that China might be on the verge of transforming the bipolar power system into a tripolar one, but when fundamental change did arrive it resulted from the disintegration of the Soviet Union. In 1989 Fukuyama felt able to proclaim the end of history, his hugely discussed thesis being that democracy had achieved a victory over Marxism–Leninism and that this triumph of liberal capitalism was a permanent one which would therefore bring history to an end (Fukuyama 1989; 1992). Yet the current system is still not far removed from a multipolar arrangement in which Japan, China and the EU join the US as powers of the top rank.

> electoral democracy based on weak mass political parties, and government economic policies directed towards stimulating private economic activities. (Knox and Agnew 1994, p. 117)

The rise and decline of hegemons has been related to Kondratieff cycles (see p. 243), with the waxing and waning of British hegemonic power spanning the first and second Kondratieff cycles and the American hegemonic cycle being associated with the third and fourth Kondratieff cycles.

Naturally, the policies of a state will be strongly influenced by the evolving patterns of power concentration and dispersal. O'Loughlin (1991) remarks that in the Gulf War the US and UK shared the greatest commitment to fighting, while Japan and Germany were reluctant partners. He thought that the Germans and Japanese:

> clearly benefit from contemporary world economic and political arrangements, especially in rolling up huge trade surpluses, and they have no wish to upset the applecart. The USA and UK, by contrast, are declining economic powers but with disproportionate military strength and they wish to reorder the world system to their benefit. (ibid., p. 323)

Later he adds:

> One of the remarkable features of the post-war period was the constancy of USA containment of the USSR. With the disappearance of the USSR as the arch-enemy, the new geostrategy for the USA is only now being developed. One possibility is to create future opponents by defining a policy that prohibits the prominence of regional powers inimical to USA interests. (ibid., p. 326)

Power will continue to be a focus for political study and debate and geographers will continue to be interested in the ways that power is unevenly distributed throughout the political system, and in the ways that geographical factors contribute to the power profile of the state. This geographical contribution is likely to be both considerable and subtle, so that statements redolent of environmental determinism or crude geopolitics should be avoided. In evaluating state power – or, as they termed it, 'capability analysis' – H. and M. Sprout (1957, pp. 325–6) warned that:

> It is utterly meaningless to speak of capabilities in the abstract. Capability is always capability to do something, to bring about or perpetuate some state of affairs. Policy assumptions may be left implicit. But, unless some set of ends and means is envisaged, no calculation is possible, no inventory of environmental factors has any significance . . . The data of physical geography have no intrinsic political significance whatever. Nor have demographic, technological, economic, or other environmental data. Such factors acquire political significance only when related to some frame of assumptions as to what is to be attempted, by what means, when and where, and vis-à-vis what adversaries, associates and bystanders.

Finally, in advocating a fresh theoretical approach to International Relations which will be in greater accord with the changes to the international system engendered by the end of the Cold War, Halliday notes that:

> The neglect of the normative in most International Relations literature of the post-1945 epoch, be it in its North American or British variants, is in part to be attributed to the fear of falling into the mistakes of the inter-war 'utopians', in part the rather too close identification of the discipline with the priorities, and temper, of states

but, he continues,

> the neglect of the normative is, as much as anything, highlighted by the uncertainty which has come to prevail in public discussion, academic and other, in the aftermath of the Cold War, with anxiety about the overall direction of political life intersecting with the vacuities of post-modernism and ethical relativism. (Halliday 1994, pp. 241–2)

He believes that social scientists have failed to display independence and intellectual enterprise and writes that:

> The danger has not been that social scientists have been too removed from the concerns of power, political or entrepreneurial, but that they have not had enough distance from them, have not exerted themselves forcefully enough to rise above the supposed common sense of their epoch, and have consoled themselves with the vacuous and the insignificant: hence, on the part of the natural sciences, the effort devoted to weapons of mass destruction and the failure, till very late in the day, to predict the impact of mankind on the environment, distortions amply reproduced by the social scientists, including those in International Relations. (ibid., p. 244)

■ Interfaces

Until at least the 1970s, the literature of political geography was dominated by studies of frontiers and boundaries. Now such accounts are much rarer, perhaps partly because morphological approaches (concerning the physical form and structure of states) are unfashionable, and partly because scholars may feel that everything worthwhile that might be said about frontiers and boundaries already has been said. Whether or not this is the case with regard to the historically oriented type of boundary studies that were common in political geography, boundaries still perform crucial roles in conditioning human life. Their influence extends far beyond the control of trade and movement, and as Camilleri and Falk (1992, p. 237) describe:

> Boundaries are central to the discourse on sovereignty. It is not merely a case of physical boundaries which separate one sovereign state from another, but of cultural boundaries which separate the 'same' from the 'other', and of conceptual boundaries which distinguish the domestic from the international, community from anarchy, and the universal from the particular.

They then point out that:

> Within the boundaries imposed by the sovereign state it is possible for rights and obligations, order, freedom and other universal values to be articulated and in varying degrees given practical expression. Outside these boundaries there exists no order, no community, no framework for conducting normative discourse. All that exists is the mechanistic interaction of particular, often discordant wills, engaged in varying degrees of self-interested competition, conflict and co-operation. (ibid., pp. 237–8)

Boundaries still partition the world into a patchwork of sovereign territories, but the nature of the interactions which take place, or which are prevented, is changing: 'On the one hand, we observe the virtually universal recognition of territorial sovereignty as the organizing principle of international politics. On the other hand, because of the growth of transnational relations and interdependencies, there is a tendency toward erosion of the exclusivity associated with the traditional notion of territoriality' (Kratochwil 1986, p. 27).

The physical character of frontiers and boundaries can be summarised as follows:

> Boundaries have been loosely described as being linear; in fact they occur where the vertical interfaces between state sovereignties intersect the surface of the earth. Frontiers, in contrast, are zonal and therefore contain various geographical features and, frequently, populations. As vertical interfaces, boundaries have no horizontal extent, though the factor of border location can characterise surrounding landscapes, while a past frontier may be marked in a landscape long after the frontier concerned has advanced, receded or contracted. (Muir 1981, p. 119)

Most of the land surface of the world has been partitioned or 'privatised' in this way, although Antarctica was considered as *Res communis humanitatis* or a common human heritage resource in the Antarctic Treaty of 1959 – but: 'Eventually Antarctica may be privatized, along with the rest of the earth's land surface, and neither treaty nor customary international law will then apply there' (Johnston 1992, p. 221).

The oceans formed part of the global commons, but now substantial areas have been privatised into state ownership as international law has been modified to take account of the growing ability of states to defend their claims to ownership of offshore waters. Most states now claim a 12-mile wide territorial sea. By 1992, 154 states had signed the United States Convention on the Law of the Sea adopted at the UNCLOS III conference in 1982. This established the seaward extension of sovereignty over a 12-mile territorial sea, beyond which a contiguous zone may extend for up to 24 miles from the coast of the state concerned. Within this zone the state is considered to lack full sovereign territorial rights but it may exercise customs, immigration, sanitary and fiscal controls. Each coastal state may also claim an exclusive economic zone (EEZ) within which it exercises a right to explore, exploit, conserve and manage living or mineral resources of the sea, sea-bed and subsoil. This zone is not supposed to extend more than 200 nautical miles seawards from the coastal baselines from which the state projects its maritime claims. When these EEZs are subtracted from the High Seas, the extent of the maritime commons is reduced by one-third. As Glassner (1993, pp. 485–6) describes:

> More than half the combined EEZ of the world goes to only ten countries, of which six of the first seven are already rich (in order of size of maritime territory gained: the United States, Australia, New Zealand, Canada, Russia and Japan). All the top five gainers of submarine petroleum are also rich (United States, Russia, Britain, Norway, and Australia). Thus the poor countries, which began the drive for an EEZ and finally won acceptance for it, stand to gain relatively little from it.

The first United Nations Conference on the Law of the Sea in 1958 granted coastal states the exclusive rights to exploit the resources of the adjacent continental shelf and its subsoil, and the 1982 Conference modified the terms of the convention so that the rights extend to the outer edge of the continental margin or to a distance of 200 nautical miles form the coastal baselines. The remaining areas of sea-bed which are beyond the limits of national jurisdiction are designated International Sea-bed Area and exist under a common heritage regime which prevents appropriation by any state and demands exclusively peaceful exploitation.

Despite the efforts devoted to negotiating and codifying boundary-making principles, much remains to be achieved. Important conventions remain unsigned, sometimes because the developed states are reluctant to enter into any agreements which will constrain their ability to exploit the global commons. Meanwhile, as Johnston (1992, p. 216) describes:

> Environmental systems are rarely constrained by international boundaries and environmental processes cross them unhindered. Thus, however stringent the environmental laws in one state, its air, land water and soil are still open to pollution, deterioration and even destruction from activities that operate entirely beyond its boundaries and which are thus outside its control. Good laws in one place can be nullified by bad ones elsewhere.

Man-made boundaries effect the geographical partitioning of the world, and it can be argued that these boundaries are most significant by virtue of their function as barriers to normal human interactions. The barrier function is seldom enforced totally – one of the closest approaches to totality would be the isolation imposed from within on Albania in the years from 1960 until 1990, when Albanians were once more allowed to travel abroad. Normally, barrier functions are applied selectively to discriminate against certain patterns of trade, political or cultural contact, as when the Chinese authorities banned a Rolling Stones concert on the grounds that it would cause 'cultural pollution', or when a government decides to protect a fledgling textile industry by imposing a 10 per cent tariff on imports of manufactured cotton goods. Political geography has a long tradition of exploring the barrier effects of boundaries, going back to Brigham (1919) and continuing through landmark studies, like Mackay's (1958) investigation of the role of the international boundary as a barrier to social communication between French-Canada, English-speaking Canada and the USA, to Soja's (1968) use of transaction flow analysis to reveal changes in the patterns of cultural interaction after the states of East Africa gained independence.

Barrier effects are pronounced in the modern world, and although regional trading organisations have eliminated or reduced barriers to trade between their members, they have erected new tariff barriers to trade with non-members. Perhaps the most significant offender against the principle of free trade is Japan, which has combined a high exporting profile with a policy of shielding its industries from competing imported goods by using tariffs and quotas and by undervaluing the yen. In 1991, Japan's imports were worth $236 billion while Japanese exports were valued at $314 billion; in this year Japan took only 6 per cent of its imports from the European Community, yet the community took 20 per cent of Japan's exports. Despite its enforcement of unequal and protectionist trading policies, Japan is expanding its influence as a

Box 6.2 *Frontiers*

The oldest known words for a border zone, like the English 'march' or the German *mark*, derive from the ancient Indo-European root *mar-* and can be found throughout Europe. The word 'frontier' is believed to derive from the Latin *frons*, meaning 'forehead', and was first used to denote the borders between countries in the fifteenth century. According to McDonald (1978, p. 174): 'When the word was exported to the New World, undivided by countries and kingdoms, it took on fresh meaning, being used to differentiate the settled and known from the unsettled and hostile . . . The frontier then came to be associated less with a boundary line, and more with a certain way of life. Thoreau writes thus in *Walden*, where he says that "It would be some advantage to live a primitive and frontier life, though in the midst of an outward civilization, if only to learn what are the gross necessities of life".' Prescott (1978, p. 33) reminds us that: 'Political geographers use the term "frontier" in two senses; it can either refer to the political division between two countries or the division between the settled and uninhabited parts of one country. In each sense the frontier is considered to be a zone. There is no excuse for geographers who use the terms "boundary" and "frontier" as synonyms although it is not difficult to find geographers making this elementary error.'

Much of the discussion about frontiers has concerned the controversial ideas of Frederick Jackson Turner. In 1893, as a 31-year-old instructor at the University of Wisconsin, he delivered an address to the American Historical Association on 'The Significance of the Frontier in American History'. He began by pointing out that in 1890 the Superintendent of the Census had announced that it was no longer possible to recognise a frontier line in the American West – and Turner thought that this marked the end of the first period in American history. He believed that the frontier environment had created American society – a view that was very much in accord with the doctrine of environmental determinism which found favour in the US at that time. Europeans, according to Turner, had become Americanised as part of the process of responding to the various challenges which the frontier environments placed in their paths. As a patriotic American, Turner was keen to show that while the US may have had its cultural roots in Europe, it had progressed to develop its own distinctive identity. As the frontier of settlement had advanced into the Midwest, the dependence on England ceased and a mixed American nation, English neither in nationality or characteristics had come into being. These characteristics included restlessness, resourcefulness, inventiveness, exuberance, and above all, individuality and independence. Turner's ideas enjoyed a raptuous reception in the US, his audiences being delighted to imagine that they had acquired or inherited all the heroic and romantic qualities of resourcefulness associated with the frontier. Subsequently, however, they encountered widespread criticism. Berkhofer (1964) wondered why, if the frontier really were a place of democratic innovations where old values were shed, the constitutions adopted by the new states of the West were all modelled upon those of the old states of the East? He described how Turner was an American patriot with a mission to show that American history was unique and distinct from that of Europe; he did this by emphasising the interaction between the 'American social organism' and

Box 6.2 *continued*

American space, while failing to appreciate the significance of the European cultural baggage that the settlers brought with them to the frontier. Although Turner's ideas are now unfashionable, it may be worth considering that until they crossed the Mississippi/Missouri and entered the Great Plains, settlers had been moving through landscapes which were not hugely different from those of Europe. Perhaps the shock of the encounter with the vast emptiness of the dry Plains, their extreme climates and violent weather, may have done something to forge an American frontier identity?

leading participant in international commerce and manufacturing; Emmott calculates that there are more than 15 000 Japanese firms established around the world. The results of his survey suggest:

> a figure of more than 300,000 Japanese managers working in these firms around the world. If they are, on average, accompanied by one family member, the total associated with Japan's global reach becomes at least 600,000 people. It also means that every year roughly 50,000 managers return home from an overseas assignment, while roughly 50,000 more depart their homeland to begin one. (Emmott 1992, p. 5)

According to the World Bank the increase in enthusiasm for protectionist policies in recent years has reflected the continuing rise in exports from Japan and the newly industrialised countries of Asia and recession and unemployment in the Western developed countries, leading to rising job insecurity and growing demands for import controls.

Evidence can be found to support claims both for the growth and decline of boundary barrier functions in the modern world. Having noted the opening up of the East European power bloc and the signs of economic cooperation in the EC (EU), EFTA, NAFTA and ASEAN countries, Nijkamp (1994, p. vii) remarks that:

> Reality however, seems to be fairly harsh, in that vanishing borders do not necessarily imply more openness. Mankind seems to be keen in inventing new bottlenecks precluding a free movement of people, goods or information. Self interest or group interest is apparently a strong driving force which is often at odds with the social (or global) benefits of a borderless society and may thus destroy the dream of a flying carpet.

The uncertainty concerning the future – or even the current – state of affairs is echoed by O'Dowd, Corrigan and Moore, who write that

> The globalization of economic life and the restructuring of the international economy since the 1970s have generated a new social scientific interest in spatial questions but rather less interest in territorial boundaries . . . Yet, few borders anywhere have resulted from plebiscites or democratic negotiation at international level – instead, secret manipulations and some degree or threat of force are usually present . . . all of the European countries created in the last 150 years have border region problems arising from the demands of minorities seeking to realise their 'national' values within the framework of an organised state. (O'Dowd, Corrigan and Moore 1995, p. 272)

After studying the interplay of British, Irish, unionist, nationalist and European attitudes and policies in the Irish border zone these authors came to the surprising conclusion that:

> On balance, the evidence from Ireland's border region suggests that EU integration is not incompatible with economic peripheralization, consolidation of national boundaries and conflict over national sovereignty. The existing order of nation-states seems much more potent at the moment than moves towards an EU of multiple regional identities, overlapping jurisdictions and shared sovereignty. (ibid., p. 284)

The introduction of new political boundaries into an area or the upgrading of existing political boundaries can plainly have disruptive economic and social consequences. So too can the anticipation that such changes may take place, as evidenced by events in Quebec in the run-up to the referendum of October 1995 which produced a decision to remain in Canada by the narrowest possible of margins. Numerous firms left Quebec for other Canadian locations or prepared to leave in the expectation of a separatist victory, while the Prime Minister of Canada, Jean Chrétien 'has warned the French-speakers that they will become a tiny statelet, bereft of the economic umbrella of Canada, if Quebec says goodbye. English-speakers will leave, pulling out their factories and jobs. The US will not trade with Quebec on the same terms. But the committed do not hear him' (Freedland and Travena 1995). The Quebec issue demonstrated that separatism is not simply a consequence of the oppression or exploitation of a national minority; before, and much more so after the referendum of 1980 when Quebeckers voted to remain in Canada by a 60–40 margin, the authorities had sought to develop an equal, multicultural society. According to Woollacott, the events highlighted the illusory nature of the claim that modernisation militates against nationalism, with people becoming more alike and integrated as distances are shrunk and economic organisation crosses political boundaries. In the case of Quebec he found that:

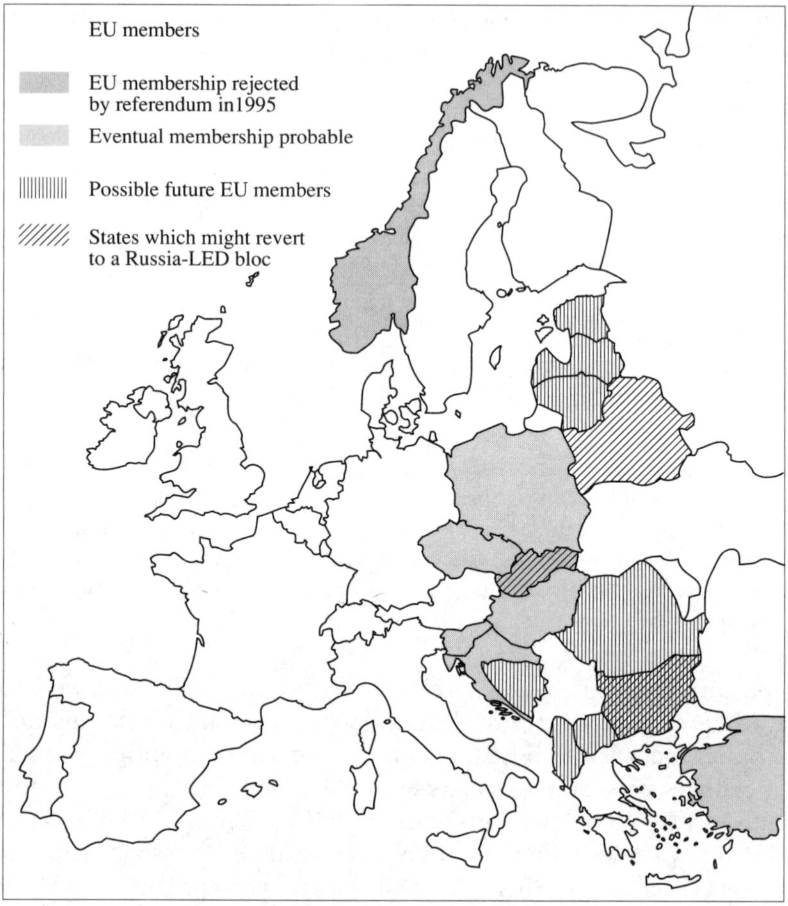

Map 9 Political and economic orientations within Europe

> Some would say that a mere vote cannot alter geography. Quebec remains where it is, as does English Canada . . . So what difference would a vote for independence make? The answer is that most people are not geographers or political scientists, and that it would make a huge, tearful and possibly rancorous difference. If the vote is in favour of 'sovereignty' then that will take the form of bargaining over economic and political relations between two peoples. If it is against, it will take the same form but more amicably, and with a less radical outcome. (Woollacott 1994)

In the former Soviet Union, former Yugoslavia and elsewhere the new nationalism has produced new or upgraded boundaries which have disrupted the established order. Kaldor (1993, p. 146) points out that:

> The new nationalism is different from earlier nationalism in a number of respects. First of all, it can be said that the new nationalism is anti-modern, whereas earlier nationalisms were part of the modern project . . . nationalism was an essential component of what we call modernity; it was linked to the rise of the modern state and to industrialization. Indeed the early nationalists were rather functionalist. Nationalism, for them, was part of the march towards progress. They viewed the nation-state as a viable political unit for democracy and industry . . . The new nationalism is anti-modern not only in the sense that it is a reaction to modernity but also in the sense that it is not a viable political project – it is out of tune with the times.

In comparison to the multitude of studies concerning the barrier effect of boundaries in disrupting 'natural' patterns of economic and social interaction, those which investigate the effects of the removal or diminution of boundary barrier effects are fewer. This is hardly surprising, for the rise of the international trading organisation is a relatively recent phenomenon. Reference has already been made to Kamann's (1994) exploration of national attitudes to management styles. The unification of Europe is associated with an increasing intensification of activities, with growing numbers of companies and organisations from different member states becoming engaged in contacts which are ever rising in their frequency and intensity. Managers and workforces from different cultural backgrounds are meeting and finding that they have different ways of doing things and different ways of looking at things. Different national workforces have different expectations of management and respond differently to management styles. Thus, 'The Dutch see work more as a way of making oneself useful to society than the Germans. The Germans focus to a much larger extent on the status and prestige derived from work' (ibid., p. 45).

Closer economic association can underline the inequalities between the rich and the poor. NAFTA is bringing the USA and Mexico closer together, the countries being separated by a boundary 2000 miles in length where one of the world's richest nations abuts the Third World. Hansen has studied the barrier effects of this boundary and describes how the establishment of US subsidiaries in Mexico has been associated with growing problems of chemical pollution. These are caused by the failure of the American concerns to abide by Mexican law and return their chemical waste to their parent companies. There is asymmetry in the international relationship, with different environmental standards and levels of enforcement on different sides of the boundary. Meanwhile:

> The prospect of a free trade agreement has generated unprecedented concern about environmental conditions in the border area. In particular, it is feared that U.S. manufacturing activities that have difficulty meeting U.S. pollution standards will move to Mexico in increasing numbers unless Mexican authorities enforce standards comparable to those in the United States. (Hansen 1994, p. 101)

The removal of political boundaries can have effects as traumatic as the imposition of barriers. Wild and Jones explored the spatial impacts of German unification following the fall of the Berlin Wall in 1989 and the full political union established in the following year, and found that it immediately exposed and accentuated the gulf that had developed following the division of German territory between the FRG and the GDR during the Cold War. The magnitude of the problem of reintegration had not been realised: 'The chronic weakness of the East German economy and the extent to which it lagged behind that of the West were vastly underestimated at the time of unification. But once its disastrous condition became properly known, euphoria was soon eclipsed by the sober realization of the immensity of the task ahead' (Wild and Jones 1994, p. 3). With the exposure to Western competition, the loss of markets in the collapsing economies of Eastern Europe and the consequences of operating obsolete machinery and plant, the east experienced a severe economic decline that did not bottom out until 1992, by which time productivity had fallen to about a quarter of the levels prevailing in the west of Germany. In the case of Berlin, Ellger (1992, p. 45) found that:

> In the long run, at least as far as employment is concerned, Berlin will lose workplaces in manufacturing, thus catching up with the de-industrialization processes elsewhere in Western cities. Producers of rather unspecialized electrical goods, paper-ware or food, for instance, will be leaving the city for suburban or rural locations in the Third World; with increasing land prices their space can be use much more profitably for office functions, i.e. by producer services.

Although the evidence relating to the barrier effect of modern boundaries is not clear-cut and can be contradictory, on the broad scale the globalisation of economic activities would appear to be unstoppable. This will increase the permeability of some economic barriers and lead to the disappearance of others. As the debates and disagreements current within the EU suggest, the diminution of the economic barrier effects associated with international boundaries may lead to a reactivation or an intensification of cultural separatism. But whether such cultural processes will be any more capable of resisting the pressures for integration associated with the revolution in information technology than the national economies were of opposing economic globalisation must remain to be seen.

■ Political geography and war

According to von Clausewitz (1908, p. 23), a Prussian veteran of the Napoleonic wars, war is the continuation of political intercourse 'with the intermixing of other means'. This implies that war is a natural part of the human condition, and leads us back to the issues of nature and nurture raised in Chapter 1. The military historian, John Keegan, reminds us of the intellectual discomfort which such questions provoke, for while disciplines like anthropology and archaeology reveal evidence of humanity's gory past, we prefer

> to recognise human nature as we find it displayed in the everyday behaviour of the civilised majority in modern life . . . Culture to us seems the great determinant of how human beings conduct themselves; in the relentless academic debate between 'nature and nurture', it is the 'nurture' school which commands greater support from the bystanders. (Keegan 1993, pp. 3–4)

However, he then proceeds to point out that: 'History lessons remind us that the states in which we live, their institutions, even their laws, have come to us through conflict, often of the most bloodthirsty sort' (ibid., p. 4).

Experts have tended to regard human aggression as a triumph of instinct or innate biological urges over cultural conditioning. Eibl-Eibesfeldt, when head of the Human Ethology Study Group at the Max Planck Institute of Behavioural Research, turned this argument around. In many species of animal, intraspecific aggression is heavily ritualised, so that it consists of displays of aggression and submission that do not lead to physical harm. Eibl-Eibesfeldt considered that this was basically true of human intragroup aggression too, where there are innate signals of submission which are sent by the defeated to the victor to prevent aggression between the members of a group from escalating into destructiveness: 'To some extent, a biological norm filter lays down the commandment: "Thou shalt not kill"' (Eibl-Eibesfeldt 1979, p. 240). Vayda described ritualised fighting among the clans of the Maring in New Guinea, where 'Nothing' fights occurred after slights and offences between groups had accumulated to a certain level. They were used both to test the military strength of the opposition and also to set the stage for negotiation:

> The men did not fight daily during the period of warfare. When it rained, both sides stayed in their houses, and, by mutual agreement, all combatants took a day off to repaint their shields, to attend to rituals in connection with casualties, or simply to rest. There could be intervals as long as three weeks during which active hostilities were suspended and the men worked at making new gardens. (Vayda 1976, p. 17)

Where aggression *between* groups rather than *within* groups is concerned, however, the situation is different, for it generally culminates in destruction: 'This is the result of cultural pseudospeciation, in the course of which human groups mark themselves off from others by speech and usages, and describe themselves as human and others as not fully human' (Eibl-Eibesfeldt 1979, p. 240). Eibl-Eibesfeldt believed that such reactions were underlain by the infant's fear and rejection of strangers and by primate territoriality, while war developed as a cultural mechanism in the competition between groups or pseudospecies for space and raw materials. Ritualised submission in the form of retreats by the vanquished should lead to the termination of hostilities, but such retreats became impossible because of the increasing shortage of empty spaces into which retreats could be made. 'In the course of pseudospeciation, man has superimposed a cultural norm filter that commands him to kill upon his biological norm filter, which forbids him to kill . . . The root of the universal desire for peace lies in this conflict between cultural and biological norms, which makes men want to bring their biological and cultural norm filters into accord' (ibid., p. 241)

While the political geographer cannot stay blind to the processes which produce war, his/her attention will focus upon territory, in terms of the way that territorial issues may be a cause or a justification for conflict and the way that warfare or the fear of warfare produces changes in the environment. In studying the language used to articulate territorial claims, Murphy has noted the steadily growing power of claims that territory historically belongs to a particular state and has been 'wrongfully' taken away. These concepts began with the Treaty of Westphalia and were rooted in Western concepts of property rights, so that during the formative period in the development of international law the state ideology commandeered concepts of individual property rights, including rights to restitution if property is stolen:

> The argument's ideological power lies both in its ubiquity and in its appeal to tradition. The contemporary discourse of territorial claim justification is so dominated by the historical argument that most other claims are either

> left unstated or are offered as support for the historical claim. Thus, when Somalia makes an ethnic claim about the Ogaden, or Ecuador raises geopolitical issues in connection with its claim to the area of northern Peru . . . or Togo advances the cause of the Ewes . . . each is tying ethnic claims to arguments for historical restitution. (Murphy 1990, pp. 544–5)

Changes in the ownership of territory can be the object or the consequence of war, and change seldom ends with a reversal of ownership. In the course of the wars in the former Yugoslavia, the conquest of territory was frequently followed by the imposition of policies of so-called ethnic cleansing, with the enforced removal or slaughter of any civilian members of the defeated nationality who still remained:

> Of the 202 mosques in the Banja Luka region of Bosnia-Herzegovina in 1992, only one has escaped not being dynamited, bulldozed or shelled out of existence. According to the vice president of the Banja Luka municipality, the systematic physical erasure of mosques from the landscape – some of which dated from the fifteenth and sixteenth centuries – is the only way to teach minorities to respect Serbian Law . . . This systematic erasure of history, organized sexual terrorism and relentless drive to create ethnically cleansed territory in the Banja Luka region of Bosnia is a microcosm of a world marked by crises of governance. (O Tuathail 1995, p. 260)

Civil Wars have their own political geographies, and McColl (1969) made a distinction between: *secessionist movements* struggling to detach a cultural territory from a larger entity; *rebellions*, which can concern local issues and which often have limited objectives; *revolutions* which involve struggles largely confined to members of the political elite; and *national revolutions*, which concern attempts by substantial portions of a state population to alter the entire state structure. His analysis of national revolution, as represented by Cuba of 1958 or Vietnam during the 1960s, had a powerful geographical dimension, and he considered that the basic tactic of the revolutionary was to establish an 'insurgent state' within the territory of the larger state. In some ways this anti-state is a microcosm of the surrounding state; it has its territory, population, core areas, administrative divisions, armed forces and 'state idea'. It provides the revolutionaries with a territorial stronghold, power base and launching pad for attacks, and in so doing it demonstrates the weakness of the state government, while providing the revolutionary leadership with a measure of legitimacy.

The creation of an insurgent state generally begins when a political opposition is declared illegal and is driven underground. On failing to secure an urban base, the revolutionaries then seek a safer rural foothold which is suitably located for both offensive and defensive guerilla warfare. Similar territorial bases are subsequently established throughout the state territory as the revolutionary movement gains strength and more guerillas are recruited. State and guerilla-controlled territories are then divided by transitional zones, which government forces may be able to control during daylight, but which become the domains of the guerilla at night; the main transport arteries often belong to this transitional category. The next stage in the guerilla advance from the various insurgent states involves the capture of towns and provincial capitals, until ultimately the state capital and the state itself may be taken over. A variation on this form of state capture can be found in places where different regional or ethnic insurgents compete for control. For example, in 1991, following the collapse of the regime of General Siad Barre and the slaughter of thousands of Somalis in fighting around the capital of Mogadishu, the state of Somalia had virtually ceased to exist and its territory was divided between six clans, each dominated by its own particular warlord.

Political geographical studies of the destructive consequences of warfare are not numerous; perhaps the most influential was Lacoste's study of the bombing of the dikes on the Red River in North Vietnam in 1972. This, he believed, was intended to cause catastrophic flooding in a river delta occupied by a highly concentrated civilian population of about 10 million people. He described how geography, as practised in its pre-academic guise, was intimately concerned with military tactics and strategy, and outlined too how a new 'ecological warfare' had been created which was associated with massive human assaults upon the environment: 'The Indo-Chinese war marks a new phase in the history of warfare, and also in the history of geography. For the first time in history, the modification and destruction of the geographical milieu (in both its physical and human aspects) is being used to obliterate those very geographical conditions which are indispensible for the lives of several million people' (Lacoste 1972, p. 246). However damaging the ecological warfare of the 1960s may have been, the future capability of environmental warfare – defined as 'the manipulation of the environment for hostile military purposes' (Westing 1984, p. 3) – is horrifying. Westing describes strategies like the destruction of the ozone layer above an enemy's territory, the use of chemicals and nuclear materials to poison water sources and the use of seismic sea waves to destroy coastal facilities.

Many of the geographical consequences of war are as obvious as they are gruesome. We know, for example, how modern warfare can virtually or temporarily annihilate a city in a matter of days or less –

as with the RAF and USAAF raids on Hamburg on 24–30 July 1943, which destroyed 80 per cent of the city's buildings and killed 30 000 of its inhabitants. According to UNICEF, a feature of modern warfare has been the increasing proportion of civilian mortalities. In the 1914–18 War civilian casualties were 14 per cent of the total; during the 1939–45 War 67 per cent of the people killed were non-combatants, while in recent wars – most of them occurring in the Third World – about 90 per cent of casualties have been civilians (1995). Most sickeningly, during wars fought during the last 10 years, 2 million children have been killed, 4–5 million disabled, 12 million made homeless and 10 million psychologically traumatised. During the Bosnian War, one child in four in Sarajevo was wounded and almost all experienced trauma from shelling; children under the age of 16 have recently been actively involved in fighting in 25 states.

We know how warfare can cripple the economy and society of a vast area of territory and Prendergast and Fieno have described how it has paralysed post-independence Africa and frustrated efforts at economic development. This is especially true for the Horn of Africa where it has intensified food shortages, killing untold numbers of non-combatants and disrupting every stage in the farming year. 'Wars also displace hundreds of thousands of people and obstruct relief programmes which could prevent most famine deaths. During wartime, food may be used as a weapon: one army may prevent the transport of food in order to starve the enemy. Under these circumstances, civilians always perish first' (Prendergast and Fieno 1993, pp. 344–5). The Gulf War was spatially confined and of very short duration, yet Barnaby notes that the total explosive yield of the weapons used by the coalition forces against Iraq was about 120 000 tons, the equivalent to ten Hiroshima atom bombs. Some 200 000 Iraqis were killed, representing about 1.2 per cent of the country's population (for purposes of comparison, about 4 per cent of the Vietnamese population was killed in the Vietnam War between 1965 and 1975). In addition, Iraqi troops set ablaze 580 oil wells and blew up 200 more; nearly 100 wells gushed uncontrollably into the sands to form black lakes. During the time when the oil wells were burning, between 3 and 6 million barrels of oil passed through the burning wells each day, with at least 430,000 tons of crude oil being combusted daily (Barnaby 1991, p. 168). As a result of the pollution from the oil fires, expanses of black, oily snow were encountered by skiers in the Himalayas and black rain fell in Iran, Afghanistan and Turkey. In the course of the war up to 3 million barrels of oil were spilled into the shallow waters of the Gulf and within months of the first spillages, 20 000 aquatic birds had been killed (ibid., p. 171).

A scarcely appreciated fact of warfare concerns the way that conflict (but not the consequences of conflict) is localised within the earth's land surface. Keegan points out that about 70 per cent of dry land is either too dry or too high or too cold to permit the conduct of sizeable military operations. Tundra, desert, rain forest and the great mountain ranges are inhospitable to armies, and though military manuals may discuss combat in such environments, in areas devoid of roads and water little more than skirmishing between specialist forces is possible. He notes that in the Second World War the desert armies of Rommel and Montgomery clung to the coast of North Africa and the Japanese conquest of Malaya in December 1941–January 1942 was achieved not through the jungle but along the well-engineered roads of the colony and by amphibious 'hooks' down its coastline, while: 'China's seizure of parts of India's mountain frontier in 1962, when attacks were mounted at heights above 16,000 feet, was staged by troops who had acclimatised for a year on the Tibetan plateau' (Keegan 1993, p. 68).

Whilst war obviously causes destruction, so too does the fear of war:

> Detrimental externalities arise as a nation responds to the arming of its adversary by increasing its defence spending so imposing costs on the whole community reflected in the 'sacrifice' of civil goods and services . . . also . . . defence spending, especially on defence R & D 'crowds out' valuable civil investment with adverse effects on a nation's growth rate and its international competitiveness. (Hartley 1995, p. 280)

The sums which states spend on armaments are fantastic. In 1993 a world total of $868.4 billion, amounting to 3.3 per cent of GNP was spent on armaments, with developed states spending $647.6 billion and developing states, all of which desperately needed to invest in food, health and development, spending $20.8 billion. Some 24.6 million people were serving in the armed forces of the world and the US exported armaments to the value of $10.3 billion (ACDA 1995). Hartley argues that defence activities can be treated as externalities; there are beneficial externalities, as when a nation safeguards its freedom, but there are also negative externalities. These occur, for example, in the form of opportunity costs, as when a country invests revenues which it can ill afford in armaments. In 1992 Malaysia ordered two warships from the UK at a cost that could have provided safe water for 5 million of its citizens for 25 years (Hartley 1995, p. 280). Noise pollution by military aircraft, environmental degradation in military training areas, the contribution to traffic congestion caused by military vehicles and the contamination of the environment by unexploded missiles, leaking fuel tanks, chemical spillages and nuclear materials all contribute to the burden of negative externalities. In the period 1984–1994 the US Department of Defense spent $11 billion on investigating and cleaning up contamination on American military bases and estimated that the completion of the task would cost up to $30 billion (CBO 1995).

> In recent years, the Pentagon generated between 400,000 and 500,000 tons of toxics annually, more than the top five U.S. chemicals companies combined. Its contractors produced tens if not hundreds of thousands of tons more. And these figures do not even include the large amounts of toxics spewing from the Department of Energy's nuclear weapons complex. (Renner 1991, p. 143)

The scale of the environmental damage attributable to military activities is awesome. According to Renner, US armed forces consume 3–4 per cent of the country's oil consumption and the global military consumes 25 per cent of all jet fuel; about 9 per cent of iron and steel production goes to military uses, while the global military consumes more aluminium, copper, nickel and platinum than does the Third World (ibid., pp. 137–8). He writes that the military requirements for land have risen greatly in the course of this century, so that today an area of territory equivalent in size to the state of Turkey or even Indonesia is reserved exclusively for military uses. 'During World War II, a US mechanised infantry battalion with about 600 soldiers needed fewer than 16 square kilometers to manoeuvre; a similar unit today has to have more than 20 times as much space' (ibid., p. 133). In the US the Department of Defense directly holds 100 000 square kilometres, an area roughly equivalent to the state of Virginia (ibid., p. 134). Recently, China has emerged as an important force in global arms dealing; its armed forces are believed to run more than 20 000 companies, including hotels, shops and airlines (Woollacott 1994)

In response to problems such as these, in recent years there has been a growing interest in the concept of 'environmental security', which appears to have emerged in the US in the 1970s in response to the first oil crisis. Finger (1991, p. 223) explains this as follows: 'In the past, the argument goes, states defined their security in military terms. Now, however, states must recognise that they are all dependent upon the biosphere: the term "national security" must be enlarged to include "environmental security".' However, he challenges the military model that seems to provide a background to the environmental security approach and which implies that states should collaborate in reaction to threats and fight them in the manner of a military campaign, and he points out that the security interests of the individual are not the same as the security interests of the state. He writes that: 'The idea of "environmental security" . . . blurs this difference of interests, deliberately ignores the different epistemological nature of individual and state security interests, and treats environmental degradation as a conceptual framework of military defence against environmental threats' (ibid., p. 224). He concludes that: 'The military must be addressed as a cause and not a cure of global environmental problems. In the long run, the industrial-military complex must be dismantled' (ibid., p. 225).

Working from the standpoint of critical geopolitics (see p. 235) Dalby has challenged the concept of security. He believes that: 'Security needs to encompass the interests of people, rather than just states, in gaining access to food, shelter, basic human rights, health care, and the environmental conditions that allow these things to be provided in the long term future' (Dalby 1992b). He describes how the military understanding is one of force and imposed solutions, one which involves secrecy, power and surveillance and he suggests that a similar dynamic works in ecological affairs: 'The metaphysics of domination is linked in environmentalist discourse to the theme of the domination of nature. Technology and industry exploit nature and remake it according to their demands' (ibid., p. 118). He believes that ways must be found of moving away from resource consumption models of development, just as the world is moving away from a realist model of an international society which is completely dominated by sovereign states. Meanwhile, a clearer and less ambiguous understanding of what is meant by 'security' must be attained, for: 'Security is both a term of Cold War discourse and a term that environmentalists and others would reformulate to shift political agendas. Security must now be constantly interrogated to reveal exactly who or what political order is being rendered secure' (ibid., p. 124).

■ Policy, decision and place

International policy-making is of great interest and significance to political geographers. Diplomats and other policy-makers who produce the decisions which then impact upon the setting do not form their decisions objectively or on the basis of a perfect knowledge of all relevant factors. The policies thus formed will be influenced by the geographical characteristics of the world – like relative location, resource distribution and so on – but these characteristics will be to greater or lesser extents distorted by the perceptual filters lodged in the psychological make-ups of the decision-makers involved. Also, it can be argued that cultural aspects, which vary from place to place, will affect the formation of policies, while different value systems acquired in the process of growing up within a particular society will influence the level of importance attached to different aspects of the environment. It is vital to remember that all political decisions are taken in respect of the perceived or behavioural environment rather than the real or phenomenal environment – even though it is the phenomenal environment which will bear their impact (Kirk 1963). This concept was encapsulated by the Sprouts (1957, p. 314), who wrote:

> Cognitive behaviourism per se postulates no particular theory of human motivation and no particular mode of utilizing environmental knowledge. It simply draws a sharp distinction between the *psychological environment* (with reference to which an individual defines choices and takes decisions) and the *operational environment* (which sets limits to what can happen when the decision is executed).

The mythical *homo economicus* or 'economic man', whose decisions were always founded on total information and formed to maximise economic advantage, was evicted from mainstream geography in the 1960s and early 1970s with the rise of behavioural geography, though he survived to infest political science for much longer. He was still surviving there when Franceisco and Gitelman (1984) studied political culture in the Soviet Union and found that while citizens were passive and deferential with regard to policy-makers they adopted confrontational attitudes towards those who were responsible for the implementation of policies. A study of culture and decision-making in China, Japan, Russia and the USA was undertaken by Gaenslen, who produced evidence to suggest: '(1) that Chinese, Japanese, and Russians tend to have somewhat different conceptions of "self" and "others" than do Americans, and that the former tend to be more collectivist than the latter; and (2) that these different conceptions have implications for collective decision making under conditions of complexity, uncertainty, and ambiguity' (Gaenslen 1986, p. 78). Policy-making can be affected by the psychological make-up of the leader (Singer and Hudson 1992) or by the nature of the structures created to furnish advice to the leader: it is suggested that the formal advisory system serving President Eisenhower worked well by persuading him not to intervene Vietnam in 1954, while President Johnson, who took the decision to intervene in 1965, was served less well by the informal arrangements that he had created (Burke and Greenstein 1989).

Since patterns of culture and socialisation vary considerably from place to place, it follows that the decision-maker's perceptions of the political milieu will also vary. This is reflected in General de Gaulle's statement of his own political geographical perspective in 1955: 'when all is said and done, Great Britain is an island; France, the cape of a continent; America, another world'. However, for several decades geographical influences have tended to be neglected in the social sciences. As Eagles has described, attention focused on the ways that polities and societies were being 'nationalised' by the processes of modernisation, while the development of higher levels of mobility were causing individuals to be atomised and social ties to be broken: 'Against this theoretical backdrop, political behaviour was primarily conceptualized as being shaped mainly by personal attributes such as gender, social class or status, education, attitudes, partisan identification, and so on' (Eagles 1995, p. 499). Despite this history of neglect for geographical influences, Eagles thinks that the importance of spatial and contextual influences on political behaviour is now being rediscovered. One reason for a revival of interest in the geographical factor may derive from changes in the nature of the political system, as suggested by Light (1994, p. 96): 'As a result of the recognition that the number of conventional conflicts in the international system had increased rather than diminished since the invention of nuclear weapons, the geopolitical fatalism of nuclear deterrence (the belief that nuclear weapons render geography irrelevant) has been replaced by a renewed interest in geopolitics in recent years.'

Since geographical influences affect human decisions in other areas, it is reasonable to suppose that those who are engaged in formulating international policies will also be affected by these influences. But demonstrating this in any specific and detailed manner is by no means easy. In 1955, 1956, 1959 and 1961 the Institute of European Studies carried out a remarkable survey of the opinions of key figures: 'In each of the three countries – Britain, France, and Germany – we had personal interviews with leading people in the major sectors of public life – government, politics, business, labor, military and intellectual life.' (Lerner 1967, p. 548). Earlier in the twentieth century, Europe had been at the power centre of the world, but as a result of the events of the 1939–45 War the Europeans became dependent on American policy and power, while during the 1950s the European leaders came to recognise that no European nation on its own could guarantee its own prosperity and security. Yet while the geostrategic thinking of members of the European elites had converged in some important respects, considerable differences existed. In answer to the question 'Do you consider collective defense more important than national sovereignty?', 95 per cent in Germany, 84 per cent in Britain but only 55 per cent in France gave the answer 'yes'. Plainly the community of interest was underlain by considerable differences from country to country in the perception of the homeland and its relationship with its political setting.

However, differences in perception of the political world exist within countries as well as between them:

> Decision-makers may agree that their state's existence is threatened but disagree about the source of the threat. This was true, for example, in the United States around the turn of the nineteenth century, when the Federalists believed France so much a menace that they favoured war with her. At the same time, the Republicans believed England an equal menace. (Jervis 1976)

At different times various political geographers have offered their geopolitical interpretations of the political partitioning of the world. More important for global society are the geopolitical world views which exist in the minds of political leaders. Here Boulding (1962) suggested a concept of 'critical boundaries', which are lines on the globe that are regarded as fundamental political and ideological watersheds which should always be defended and enforced. Subsequent events have shown how the criticality of some boundaries existed in the minds of influential policy-makers rather than in the world outside. Despite the eviction of American forces and influence from South Vietnam and the installation of a communist regime there in 1975, the non-communist regimes in the remainder of South East Asia did not fall in a domino fashion, while rather than crumbling, Western influence in the region has grown during the last two decades. The theme of the conditioning influence of geography on political perception emerged again in Sloan's (1988) study of the effects of geopolitics on US strategic policy since 1890.

Hastedt and Knickrehm (1991) have explored and contrasted the world views of the US, the Soviet Union and China. They show how questions of political perception governed American policy from the outset, initially in the rejection of a close British connection – and indeed of Europe and European political habits. Underlying George Washington's insistence on a destiny apart from that of the European powers 'was the belief that the United States and Europe were different (the United States was young, strong and liberal in outlook, while Europe was old, decadent and conservative in its ideology) and that involvement in European affairs could sap U.S. strength and dilute its uniqueness' (ibid., p. 77). Geographical factors strongly conditioned early American foreign policy, which was concerned with westward expansion and the annexation, conquest and purchase of territory; 'This westward expansion took place in the context of secure borders and hemispheric preeminence . . . not only did the oceans provide a large measure of security, but preoccupied with other concerns, the European powers showed little interest or ability to intrude into the Western Hemisphere' (ibid.). An important geographical factor has concerned the state's vulnerability to invasion and the terrible consequences of these invasions, which has produced a 'defensive expansionist impulse': 'Russian leaders have tried to substitute territory for secure borders. The more territory under Russian control, the further back becomes the starting point for the next attack, and the greater is the likelihood that the war will not have to be fought entirely on Russian soil' (Hastedt and Knickrehm 1991, p. 87). As a result of these experiences and perceptions, Russian foreign policy has a strong military aspect and has involved marshalling formidable resources of power while leaving neighbours uncertain of how these resources may be deployed.

Chinese political perceptions contrasted with the concept of state sovereignty developed in post-medieval Europe: 'China saw itself as the Middle Kingdom, the only power in a world of lesser states . . . The Chinese also rejected the European idea that peace was best ensured through a balance-of-power system. Confucian thought held that a natural order existed and that stability was obtained when this order was recognised' (ibid., p. 92). The Chinese did not regard their neighbours as equals and felt no compulsion to participate in international relations. Barbarian states related to the Chinese empire on an unequal basis, offering tribute to the emperor and sometimes receiving military protection in return. The question of perception is given a new twist when we apply our alien interpretation to the great creations of the Chinese Empire and interpret the Great Wall as a military frontier-work. In fact the Wall 'was more a product of the kind of state created within China than of the kind of pressure against China from the steppe. Naturally enough, it is the military aspect of the Great Wall that has commanded most attention, and this has distorted its historical significance' (Lattimore 1934, p. 434).

Recently, the appearance of critical geopolitics (see p. 235) has added a new dimension to approaches to foreign policy-making which are rooted in cognitive behaviourism. As Dodds (1993, p. 73) remarks, 'Representations of places and peoples as "foreign" are clearly crucial in the execution of foreign policy.' He describes experts, foreign policy professionals and media people as the state's privileged story-tellers who develop and rewrite scripts which simplify the world into more malleable forms (a script being a set of representations, descriptions, attributes and scenarios deemed necessary to define a place). The story-tellers serve to legitimate foreign policy; their perceptions of self and

Box 6.3 *Environmental Determinism*

This hypothesis, which has been presented with varying degrees of crudity, concerns the idea that free human choice is subordinated to the dictates of the geographical environment. It long predates the existence of academic geography and is evident in the thinking of classical writers, like Aristotle and Hippocrates, as well as in the work of later philosophers, like the Baron de Montesquieu, who believed that the differences between the peoples and societies of the world could be explained by reference to factors like the climates and soils of their homelands. In early political geography, environmental determinism was represented most influentially by Friedrich Ratzel and his notions about *Lebensraum* and by Halford Mackinder and his Heartland thesis. Subsequently, the emergence of a French school of geography, which was associated with environmental possibilism and incorporated characterisations of the milieu as the partner rather than the slave of human activity, provided a welcome counterbalance.

Geographers, on the whole, demonstrated maturity in rejecting the excesses of the environmentalist argument – though in both past and present others have been more prepared to accept simple cause and effect relationships between environmental forces and human actions. This is evident in the readiness of numerous high-ranking post-war American policy-makers to embrace crude geopolitical interpretations of the world as well as the earlier misrepresentations. Geography must accept ownership of such racially tainted crudities as Huntington's claim that the 'contrast between the energetic people of the most progressive parts of the temperate zone and inert inhabitants of the tropics and even of intermediate regions, such as Persia, is largely due to climate' (Huntington 1940, p. 471), but the following words, quoted by the Sprouts, express the views of a German diplomat: 'geographical position and historical development are so largely determining factors of foreign policy that, regardless of the kaleidoscopic change of contemporary events, and no matter what form of government has been instituted or what political party may be in power, the foreign policy of a country has a natural tendency to return again and again to the same general and fundamental alignment' (von Kuhlmann 1931, p. 179). But of course, 'To argue that the international environment determines a state's behaviour is to assert that all states react similarly to the same objective external situation' (Jervis 1993, p. 289).

Eventually, the Sprouts (1956) introduced a new reality and vitality into what had become a rather stale and tedious geographical debate with their explorations of the man–milieu hypotheses and their advocacy of what they termed cognitive behaviorism. Today professional geographers appreciate that the relationship between humanity and the setting operates through a complex network of channels associated with the economic, social, political, psychological and spiritual aspects of our existence, and that factors like culture, values, and personal predispositions can restrict or intensify the passage of information from the geographical environment to the brain.

otherness or foreignness will affect both policy and attitudes. Dodds concludes by explaining that:

> The contribution of critical geopolitics can be seen in two different ways. First, it puts the notion of space back into the centre of international politics. By refusing to treat space as simply a backdrop or stage for international affairs we can draw attention to how the construction of space is crucial to sustaining the drama of international life. Secondly, critical geopolitics can draw attention to how places and peoples are scripted by foreign policy discourse. Instead of seeking to legitimate or encourage these discourses, we can actually begin to challenge them. (ibid.)

■ *Chapter 7* ■

Geography, the State and the Third World

My map of Africa lies in Europe. Here lies Russia and here lies France, and we are in the middle. That is my map of Africa.

Bismarck, quoted in A. J.P. Taylor (1954), p. 294

But if the nation-state, as it has come down to us from the European examples, always ends in a mess – and so far it always has ended in a mess – what can be the future for the African examples?

B. Davidson (1990), p. 10

The term Third World was adopted by American writers from the original term of French origin, *le Tiers-monde*. Most of the general and theoretical writing in political geography relates to patterns and processes in the Western or developed world – although this bias is seldom announced. The Third World is different in so many respects that conditions and problems here merit special consideration. This is not to imply that the Third World exists as a coherent social, economic and political division of the Earth, for within the Third World there are enormous differences between the Newly Industrialised Countries (NICs) or the OPEC member countries and most African states, with much of Africa forming a Third World within the Third World. Kennedy (1994, p. 193) writes that: 'Nothing better illustrates the growing differences among developing countries than the fact that in the 1960s, South Korea had a per capita GNP exactly the same as Ghana's ($230) whereas today it is ten to twelve times more prosperous.' Africa, viewed by the World Bank as the most debt-distressed region of the world, contains three-quarters of the world's least developed countries and accounts for about half of the world's refugees (Ihonvbere, 1992).

The term Third World has been used to denote a grouping of economically underdeveloped states belonging neither to the First (advanced capitalist) or Second (state-socialist) worlds. Such a distinction was never satisfactory, and at the Bandung Conference of 1955 state-socialist China claimed membership of the Third World. Today, the United Nations has suggested that the 25 most economically backward states might be regarded as a Fourth World. At the same time, some might regard the NICs and OPEC countries as constituting a Fifth World, for just ten countries produce more than two-thirds of all manufacturing output in the Third World. Furthermore, if one were to take the sometimes stated view that the Third World is not defined upon economic bases but on political orientation (with the Third World standing somewhat apart from either the capitalist or state-socialist identity), then one could proceed to take the view that the collapse of the state-socialist systems has left us with only two worlds.

A different interpretation again is offered by Camilleri and Falk (1992, p. 72):

> The new international division of labour does not . . . treat the Third World as a homogeneous entity. We need to distinguish the East Asian NICs (recipients of export-orientated foreign investment) from the Latin American NICs (where foreign investment is directed largely to the home market), the oil-exporting countries, and the bulk of the less developed countries.

While political geographers have for long been interested to explore the division of the world into political macro regions, such divisions can be counter-productive and somewhat artificial (Crush and Riddell 1980). They may lead us to overlook the fundamental unity of the world and the interactions in the global system of states, with members of the system being linked by complex relationships of dependency, obligation and influence. However, in this chapter attention is focused on the Third World states of Africa, where the consequences of poverty and exploitation are seen at their starkest (Clapham, 1985).

Visions of dependency and the aftermath of empire

The nature of the Third World countries and of their exploitation by the advanced capitalist economies of the West are open to a variety of different interpretations, while completely opposed visions of the causes and cures for underdevelopment exist. One model holds that involvement in the world economy can save a Third World country from impoverishment; opposing it are the variants of the core–periphery model, which hold that economic destitution results from just such an involvement.

It was conventional to regard underdevelopment as a temporary condition which would be alleviated as the development process spread from the 'advanced' to the underdeveloped countries (Rostow 1971). However, it can be argued that underdevelopment is not endemic and innate in the Third World, but exists as a consequence of the relationship with capitalist societies and that it is virtually impossible for 'peripheral' countries to develop within a capitalist world economy. According to some dependency theorists, as a consequence of their traumatic first contacts and subsequent communications with the West, the societies of the Third World have become unable to survive without Western inputs of political and economic control and assistance. To quote Frank: 'Economic development and underdevelopment are the opposite faces of the same coin . . . One and the same historical process of the expansion of capitalism throughout the world has simultaneously generated – continues to generate – both economic development and structural underdevelopment' (Frank quoted in Brookfield 1975, p. 163). The capitalist countries, it is claimed, concentrated the profits created by Third World producers in the metropolitan centres of the West and created conditions of exploitation such that the only way in which a Third World country could aspire to development would require its prior isolation from the world economy. David Slater (1993, p. 432) regards the international dimension as fundamental:

> For the societies of Latin America, Africa and Asia the principles governing the constitution of their mode of social being were deeply moulded by external penetration. The phenomenon of colonialism, for example, represented the imposition and installation of principles of the political that violated the bond between national sovereignty and the constitution of social being. In this sense the geopolitical for these other societies has been grounded in the violation of their right to bear their own principles of social being . . . the end of colonialism has not signified the demise of such violations.

However, the association between the developed and the underdeveloped economies cannot simply be explained in crude terms of the exploitation of the latter by the former. Unequal as many or most such relationships may be, they involve interactions rather than one-way cause and effect relations; the underdeveloped countries can affect the developed ones for the worse as well as for the better. In 1994 the distinguished Amex prize was won by an essay by R. Brown and D. Julius which provided a post-industrial global analysis and emphasised the ability of developing countries to influence rather than just to respond to conditions in the metropolitan countries. The authors considered that developing countries are increasing their manufacturing exports to industrially advanced countries and at the same time reducing their imports from these countries. As a result, there is a deteriorating trade balance in manufactured goods for the advanced countries and the advanced countries are responding by financing the trade balance by selling services to the developing countries. Consequently, less manufacturing and more service employment are being found in the advanced countries as the export of services replaces the export of manufactures. (Opponents of this analysis might point out that, despite a temporary drop in the imports of manufactured goods by OPEC countries during the oil price slump of the early 1980s, between 1970 and 1991 the trade surplus in the export of manufactured goods from advanced to developing countries rose from $105 billion to $149 billion in real terms.)

A weakness of dependency theory concerns its difficulty in explaining the fact that a select number of Third World countries are undergoing a rapid process of industrialisation:

> a number of Third World countries – the NICs – emerged as significant industrial forces at the global scale during the 1960s and 1970s. The general claim that capitalism could not generate industrial development in the peripheral dependent economies was shown to be invalid. Not surprisingly, there have been many different interpretations of these 'anomalous' or 'deviant' cases. (Dicken 1992, pp. 443–4)

Another is a reluctance to acknowledge the importance of internal differences in resources, terrain and so on, as well as contrasts in history and culture in influencing the development prospects of a Third World country.

Dependency theories arose during the 1960s and 1970s from attempts to explain the failure of Latin American countries to develop by replicating the patterns of growth which had taken place in the US and Western Europe, as had been anticipated. According to the Truman Doctrine (presented to the US Congress in March 1947), the post-war world could be conceptualised as being politically and geographically partitioned between a free world (the West), a slave world (the Communist bloc) and a world composed of polities which had to choose between the two. Supporters of modernisation theory predicted a phase of transition, during which the underdeveloped countries would come increasingly to resemble the advanced countries of the West as they followed the path of progress charted by capitalism, industrialisation, technology, democracy and stability.

Later, it was argued by the dependency theorists that world capitalism cast the developing countries in a subordinate role of dependency; their economies were exploited by the dominant countries and their growth, stagnation or decline depended upon conditions within the dominant countries. They also argued that, as characterised by views and priorities current in the developed world, the Third World societies were devoid of history other than the history which began with their contacts with the West. In terms of this prevailing caricature these societies were provided with a destiny which was rooted in the assumption that they would modernise by mimicking the countries of the West, and it was also assumed that the relationships which existed between the West and non-West were beneficial for the developing world (Slater 1993, p. 429). As described by Slater (ibid.):

> In the encompassing context of North–South relations, the dependency writers constructed and deployed a geopolitical imagination which sought to prioritize the objectives of autonomy and difference and to break the subordinating effects of metropolis-satellite relations . . . The West might believe that it had a 'Manifest Destiny' to transmit and implant its way of life across the globe, but the ethnocentric presumption inscribed in its discourse of development was now challenged interrupted and destabilized.

Commenting on Slater's work, O Tuathail (1994a, p. 228) wrote that:

> the 'politics' of development for organizations such as the World Bank, the International Monetary Fund (IMF) and the Organization for Economic Cooperation and Development (OECD) is a politics circumscribed and disciplined by an unquestioned adherence to Western notions of modernity, progress and development. In other words, 'politics', for Western development organizations, is a management problem of the transition to modernity, a sticky stage that requires 'nation-building' interventions so societies can graduate to the status of mature, adult Western democracies.

Another characterisation of the global views of policy-makers was provided by O'Loughlin and van der Wusten (1986, p. 493): 'Traditionalists still dominate the foreign policy establishments in western nations. They view the globe in regional and ideological terms. By superimposing a vertical axis of technological advancement (north versus south) on a horizontal axis of ideology, socialist versus capitalist modes of production (east versus west), we obtain a quadripartite division of the globe.' They examined superpower interventions in the Third World and made a number of propositions: firstly, superpowers were more interested in their own geostrategic goals than in solving local problems; secondly, they showed few inhibitions in their political

Box 7.1 *Interpretations of empire*

It is one of the great ironies of political geography that the Age of Imperialism overlapped with the European Age of Nationalism, although the two movements espoused quite different values, for: 'the openended political and territorial expansion of the developed world across the globe and the absorbtion [sic] of foreign lands and peoples into the national–imperial state framework of the respective metropole . . . was from the outset irreconcilable, both logically as well as practically, with the territorially limited and socially homogeneous unit implied by the nation state' (Bassin 1987b, p. 115). How, then did this contradiction come about?

An influential early explanation of the causes of imperialism was provided by the English economist, John A. Hobson (1858–1940). He regarded imperialism as a search for captive markets and criticised the exploitation involved in the imperial relationship. Hobson considered that in the advanced countries problems were encountered when there were high rates of savings and the capacity to produce much more than could be consumed. These conditions would cause industrialists to search for opportunities to invest and sell their manufactures abroad (Hobson 1902). He agreed with Marx that capitalist competition would lead to rising levels of exploitation causing the impoverishment of the workers, who would then lack the money to purchase the products of capitalist industry. New outlets would be needed for the ever-rising production of capitalist industry, and the solution to this problem – as well as the problem of the shortage of attractive targets for investment in the developed world – could be found in the Third World. Imperialism would therefore benefit the capitalist, industrialist and financier and also the imperial bureaucracy and the military which buttressed empire. However, the competition between developed countries to establish overseas empires would lead them into contests which could culminate in conflict. He believed that the British colonisation of Africa after 1870 had benefited few but the army, arms manufacturers and shipping interests. (In Britain two decades earlier, Joseph Chamberlain had advocated a policy of imperialism as a means of increasing the influence of the UK in the face of the growing overseas influence of France and Germany; his supporters were known as imperialists, and their opponents, who favoured a concentration on domestic development, as Little Englanders.)

Lenin (1870–1924) was influenced by Hobson as he sought to explain the causes of war and exploitation and the failure to materialise of Marx's predictions concerning the falling rate of profit and its inevitable revolutionary consequences (Lenin, 1917). He argued that imperialism was the last stage of capitalism, arriving when smaller firms had been evicted from the system by huge corporations and monopolies which were overexploiting the domestic markets of the advanced capitalist countries. These concerns were therefore anxious to obtain profits by investment abroad and to expand foreign markets for their manufactures. The monopolies had developed their political influence, and they used these powers to urge governments to capture overseas colonies. And as their overseas interests grew, they were eager to further the export of imperialism so as to gain control of new sources of raw materials.

In developing his theory of imperialism, Lenin was seeking to explain why Marx's prediction of a proletarian revolution in the capitalist world had failed

Box 7.1 *continued*

to materialise – and why it could occur in his native Russia. This country lacked the characteristics of a capitalist economy ripe for revolution, but Lenin regarded it as the weakest link in the chain of imperialism. He argued that a few of the benefits deriving from the exploitation of colonial territories had filtered through to the working classes of the imperial countries, thus sapping their revolutionary fervour. But meanwhile, the struggle to control overseas markets drew the imperial powers into conflicts with each other which intensified as the territory available for annexation dwindled. He thought that imperialism was an inevitable component of progress, one which was bound to result from the establishment of monopoly capitalism. Though not without its merits, Lenin's economic theory of imperialism ignored a number of non-economic factors which were important in different imperial episodes. They include the urge to enhance the political and international status of the imperial country; racism, which casts the colonial subjects as inferiors and proper targets for domination; missionary motives; and historical accident.

More recent developments in the interpretation of imperialism are Wallerstein's world-system approach and its derivatives (Hopkins and Wallerstein 1982). The theories relate imperialism to cycles of economic growth and decline and to Great Power rivalries. Each Kondratieff cycle, lasting about 50 years (see Box 8.2) embraces a phase of growth and a phase of recession, while 'hegemonic cycles' last about 100 years and correspond to two Kondratieff cycles. During a phase of 'rising hegemony', technologies become concentrated in a favoured state, which develops a lead in productivity. Then, during the recession phase which follows, this 'rising hegemonic power' achieves a commercial superiority over its rivals. In the next phase of economic growth, the hegemonic state adds financial leadership to its industrial and commercial advantages, but in the following recession it encounters growing competition from rivals with productivity advantages, and it declines. During the next stage of economic growth, a new hegemonic power will emerge. According to Taylor (1989), during the final stage of the hegemonic cycle, periods of protectionism and formal imperialism are encountered as rival Great Powers struggle to preserve their shares of colonial territory in the 'periphery'. Hegemonic states have existed at three periods in history, with the Netherlands as the hegemonic state in 1620–75; Britain in 1815–73, and the US in 1945–67. In each case, hegemony was obtained by achieving productive efficiency, then commercial primacy and finally, financial dominance; hegemony was lost in the reverse order.

and military efforts to win influence in the Third World; thirdly, their interventions aggravated and prolonged local conflicts, particularly when they armed their allies; fourthly, they decry their rivals' efforts at destabilisation while seeking to conceal their own; fifthly, they claim to support normative principles of global order but their actions violate these principles; sixth their interventions in the most unstable parts of the world render the rest of the world unstable; seventh, their interventions hinder economic development in the Third World through military involvement and the linking of aid to alliances; and eighth, Third World investment in weapons diverts scarce funds from basic human services (ibid., p. 493).

Dependency theory provided a stepping stone on the way to the development of a world-system perspective, as described in Chapter 8. Now the problems of underdevelopment were presented in a truly global context as Wallerstein outlined the development of a capitalist world system consisting of a core, which was associated with the most advanced production and financial activites, a periphery, which supplied it with essential supplies of raw materials, and a semi-periphery, containing a mix of these operations and serving as a destiny for investment at times when wages in the core rose to unacceptable levels.

A variety of Marxist, neo-Marxist, non-Marxist and other perspectives offer different characterisations and interpretations of the Third World:

> To the pluralist, MNCs [multinational corporations] and international banks appear merely as other, potentially benign, actors. To the realist, they tend to be of secondary importance because of the emphasis on the state-as-actor. To the globalist, however, they are central players in establishing and maintaining dependency relations. To globalists of Marxist persuasion, MNCs and banks are agents par excellence of the international bourgeoisie. They represent two of the critical means by which Third World states are maintained in their subordinate position within the world capitalist economy. (Viotti and Kauppi 1993, pp. 457–8)

Dependency has its political as well as its economic dimensions, and during the Cold War era many Third World countries became entangled in the rivalry between the two superpowers. In the mid-1980s O'Loughlin (1986, p. 232) wrote that: 'By some accounts, the contemporary Third World is like the Balkans of the 1900–14 period as great-power tensions are expressed by alliances with local political forces and by pouring large amounts of military and economic aid to their allies.' He also thought that the blame for this instability did not attach solely to the superpowers, for: 'Leaders in Third World states, anxious to defeat external enemies or score internal political victories, blithely invite the superpowers to help achieve success and draw their state on to the front line of global competition. It would not be going too far to say that they make themselves pawns on the chessboard of hegemonic struggles' (ibid., p. 264). With the ending of the Cold War, however, several of the Third World states have found their superpower patrons to be less generous and less tolerant than before – in the way that the retreat of state governance in Zaire can be related, in part, to the decline in American concern for African geopolitics.

Imperialism and colonial boundaries – the African problem

In many parts of Africa the period of colonial rule lasted no more than a lifetime, yet it has utterly transformed the political geography and the nature of human existence on the continent. In the process of dividing the continent between imperial powers, spheres of influence concerning territories which were largely unknown were agreed in distant ministries or conference chambers, and lines were drawn upon maps in an almost total ignorance of the human and physical contents of the territories being partitioned.

Many of the divisions bore more relationship to the rivalries between Britain, France and Germany than they did to African realities. Before the 1880s, European influence was largely confined to the coasts of Africa, where forts, trading posts and refuelling stations were established. As the imperial process developed, the transformations affecting the colonial territories were heavily influenced by the histories and political geographies of the respective colonial powers (Packenham 1991). Being the leading naval power and enjoying a command of the global shipping lanes, Britain was able to penetrate the continent at will, and towards the end of the nineteenth century a British policy of colonising Africa from end to end had gelled; it produced a broad belt of British influence running continuously from Egypt to the Cape of Good Hope. As a Mediterranean rather than a global power, France directed her colonial control across this sea, establishing a zone of territories in North Africa and then seeking to expand her influence southward, beyond the Sahara. Initially, the German political leadership characterised colonialism as an adventure which would debilitate the imperial power, but later Chancellor Bismarck exploited opportunities to intensify Anglo-French rivalries in Africa, favouring first the French and then the British. As the great scramble for Africa gathered momentum a German presence in East Africa was established with the claiming of Tanganyika (Tanzania). German imperial expansion in Africa was undertaken with more regard for the European than the African situation: interests in Uganda and Kenya were relinquished to Britain in exchange for the tiny island of Heligoland, which controlled the approaches to the Kiel canal. Much German seizure of territory was accomplished to frustrate the ambitions of Great Power rivals, in the way that Togo was colonised to prevent a linking of the British Gold Coast and Nigerian dependencies, while the German efforts to expand northwards in Kamerun involved an attempt to break up the bloc of French sub-Saharan territory.

The ground rules for the European plundering of Africa were established at the Berlin Conferences of 1884–5, when the respective claims were outlined. As First (1983, p. 208) describes, 'The division of Africa was an extension of the struggle among the European powers of the nineteenth century, and Africa under colonialism was ruled as a promontory of European interests.' The political chicanery of the Great Power rivals had unfortunate consequences for the indigenous Africans. For example, Britain and Germany connived to award the Congo basin to Belgium in order to thwart French attempts to establish control of one million square miles of territory in the centre of the continent. The land was not then administered by the Belgian government but was severely exploited by the Congo Association, a private development company fronted by Leopold II of Belgium. So scandalous was the treatment of the Congo that when Leopold died in 1908 the Belgian government was shamed into taking over the administration of the territory. Similarly, the French expansion towards the Upper Nile in 1894–98 was unrelated to the interests of the Africans affected and was intended to put pressure on the British government in the hope that it would agree to the convening of an international conference on Egypt. At the Berlin Conferences the concept of spheres of influence generated from colonial toe-holds on the coast of the continent was widely applied (these spheres being described by Lord Curzon in 1907 as designated areas in which 'no exterior power but one may reassert itself'). As a result of the application of this concept the colonial powers 'thus acquired vast territories without having to perfect their title through effective occupation and administration of the vast hinterlands to their colonial enclaves. Since these areas were technically terra nullius (i.e., they belonged to nobody), considerable conflict could have developed from the inchoate titles in the absence of a multilateral agreement' (Kratochwil 1986, p. 39).

The motives which powered the process of imperialism were varied and occurred in complex combinations. The partition of Central Africa during the years 1875–85 was studied by Foeken (1995) who identified 13 different theories dealing with the causes of the partition of Africa; his identifications have considerable merit and can be summarised as follows. Firstly, according to **classical economic theory** states annex areas because their economies need a secure source of raw materials, an export market for their industrial products and an outlet for surplus

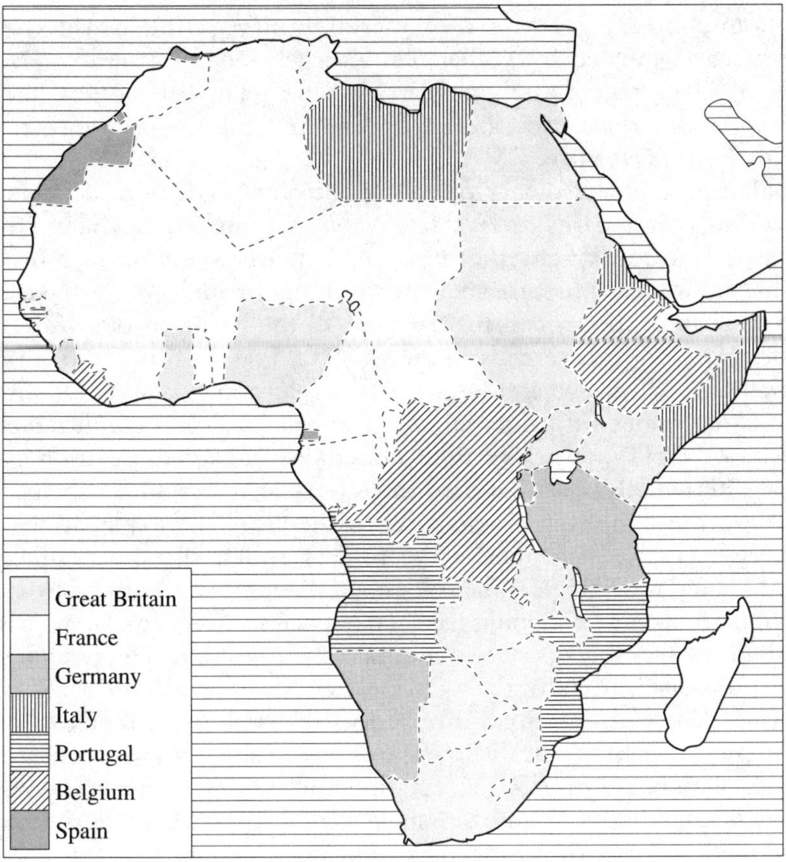

Map 10 The division of Africa into colonial territories, 1914

capital. Foeken identifies what he terms a **psychological variant of classical economic theory**, according to which statesmen in the European industrial states were convinced that imperialist policies were essential safeguards for their futures as industrial powers. He labels another general economic theory as **anarchistic theory**. It attributes the imperialism of the late nineteenth century to the anarchistic structure of the state system which lacked any mechanism for supra-national control, with states being obliged to pursue imperial policies because other states were distorting the patterns of commerce by erecting barriers to trade. The **closed door theory** interprets the German participation in the partition of Africa to Bismarck's fear that British and French protectionist policies in West Africa could leave the door to Africa and Asia closed to German trading interests. Another general economic theory relating to imperial policy is the **world-system approach** originated by Wallerstein and developed further by Taylor (1991a). This regards imperialism as being related to cyclical movements of economic growth and decline and the rivalry between the major powers (see Box 7.1).

Balance of power theory offers a political explanation of imperialism, which it regards as a safety valve for European Great Power struggles. According to the aims of Bismarck's diplomacy, Britain would be forced into agreement with Germany and France would be isolated, and the German involvement in the partition of Africa was undertaken with these ends in view. Next, Foeken lists the theory of **social imperialism**, whereby territorial expansion is cast as a political means of coping with internal social unrest and class conflict during phases of rapid industrialisation. Imperialism diverted attention away from internal stresses, alleviated the effects of recession and helped to preserve the established regime. Then there are the explanations for imperialism which emphasise the role of ruling elites; according to Schumpeter's **sociological theory**, imperialistic states are ruled by elites with nationalistic and militaristic tendencies. Accordingly, it is not capitalism and the quest for commerce that creates empire but the imperialist aspirations of the 'warrior class' (Schumpeter 1973). Related to this theory is the **mythical theory**, which has attributed French expansion in West Africa to the illusions of the politicians concerned, which were based on false expectations of the diplomatic reactions of other Great Powers (Kanya-Forstner 1972). Also related to the social elite theory is that of **prestige imperialism**, which involves an association between territorial expansion and national awareness and pride. In this way, imperialism, which nurtures the need for national self-aggrandisement and is fuelled by it, becomes an end in itself.

Then there are some theories that highlight the characteristics of the colonial territory. According to the **turbulent frontier** perspective, threats occuring along the frontiers of an empire can draw the imperial power further and further into territorial expansion as advances are made in the quest to achieve secure borders. British expansion in India, Malaysia and Africa have been offered as examples of this process at work, and it would also seem to apply to the Roman occupation of Britain. The **strategical theory** advanced by Robinson and Gallaher (1965) resulted from an analysis of British policy in Egypt and South Africa which concluded that nearly all the British interventions resulted from internal crises in the areas concerned which threatened worldwide British interests in influence and security. They also played down the importance of Great Power rivalries and considered that French colonial expansion in Africa was motivated by the search for compensation following the loss of French influence in the country to Britain in 1882. Finally, there was the **collaboration theory**, which claims that the occupation and governing of colonial territories was only made possible by the collaboration of indigenous elites (Robinson 1972). The friendly attitude of African leaders towards Europeans during the early stages of the partition of Africa concerned factors like the respect that they were shown by the European representatives and negotiators; hopes that the Europeans would offer them protection against hostile neighbours or subjects; the attraction of trading prospects, and also gifts, alcohol and deceipt.

Having evaluated all these theories, Foeken found that none of them was able to explain why a process of European territorial expansion started in Central Africa at the end of the 1870s. However, they were useful in explaining the results rather than the start of European expansion: 'The result is defined as the outcome of a series of political decision-making processes . . . Although these decision-making processes were influenced by a whole range of factors (on the international, national and individual levels), changes in the European power structure and ideological changes played an important role' (Foeken 1995, p. 97). He concluded by advocating the merits of using a behavioural approach in these areas of political geographical research:

> Finally, an analysis based on political decision making brings the stronger and the weaker aspects of the theories to the fore. Each theory contains elements which, for a certain actor and at a certain moment, may have been decisive in the process of decision making . . . Political decisions are seldom based on one single consideration, but it is always difficult to determine the relative weight of the various alternatives . . . What *is* clear, however, is that by carefully analysing how the European process of territorial expansion passed, statements about *why* it took place can be better supported. This is a political–geographical research area *par excellence*. (ibid., p. 98)

The most durable and troublesome aspect of the imperial legacy has been the network of colonial boundaries inherited by the successor states. Lines drawn on maps at the conference tables of Europe, according to the interplay of Great Power politics and in partial ignorance of the territories concerned and their human contents, have, for all their many faults, served to define the 'power containers' of the modern state system. As Griffiths (1986, p. 204) describes, 'The inherited political geography of Africa is as great an impediment to independent development as her colonially based economies and political structures . . . What were drawn as colonial boundaries have survived the transition from colonies to independent states and, more surprisingly, 25 years of African independence.' He adds that:

> The creation of long and narrow states such as The Gambia and Togo meant that development concentrated on the short sea coast remote from up-country regions. Many African states are too small to make viable economic markets and are below the threshold of any possible industrialization. Others are so large and diverse that effective government becomes difficult. There are 14 landlocked states in Africa, more than in the rest of the world put together. They all face chronic problems of access varying according to local circumstances. (ibid.)

Generally the colonial boundaries took no account of the societies which they combined or divided. The boundaries of Nigeria, which separated British, French and German colonial territory, split no less than 27 different tribal territories, including those of major groups such as the Yoruba, Hausa and Manga; on the other side of Africa, in the period 1875–85, the ancestral lands of the Muslim Somali people became divided between four non-Muslim imperial powers: Britain, Ethiopia, France and Italy. Frequently, boundaries were drawn through unmapped territory; often they would be tied to a loosely known river or range of hills and then divert arrow-straight along the lines of latitude or longitude which bestrode the unexplored areas. Prescott (1965, p. 65) has quoted the declaration concerning the agreed boundary between Portuguese Angola and German South West Africa as an example: 'The boundary follows the course of the river Kenene (Cunene) from its mouth to the waterfalls which are formed south of the Hunbe by the Kenene breaking through the Serra Canna. From this point the boundary runs along the parallel of latitude to the village of Andura.' He also quotes Sir Claude Macdonald's account of how colonial territory was allocated:

> In those days we just took a blue pencil; and a rule and we put it down at Old Calabar and drew that line up to Yola. The following year I was sent to Berlin to endeavour to get from the German authorities some rectification of the blue line . . . and . . . my instructions were to grab as much as I could. I was provided with the only map – a naval chart with all the surroundings of the sea carefully marked out, but the rest was white . . . [except] . . . for the river Akpayoff which started near the Calabar river and meandered for 300 miles on the map. That was to be the boundary . . . (however) . . . there was no such river and the only river there was 3 miles long. (Nugent 1914, p. 647)

While the inherited colonial boundaries disrupt the economic and social development of the continent and can exist as 'time-bombs waiting for a change of political circumstance to ignite the fuse' (Griffiths 1986, p. 209), the post-independence leaders have not engaged in a united movement to have them replaced or removed. In 1963 the member states of the Organisation for African Unity pledged to respect each other's sovereignty and territorial integrity. Plainly, the fear of territorial claims has exceeded the urge to achieve a rationalisation of boundaries.

■ Internal colonialism and political integration

The concept of internal colonialism, which implies the existence within a single polity of an unequal relationship involving a dominant and one or more subordinate cultural territories, was developed in the writings of Marxists, including Lenin and Gramsci. It can equally be explored and employed by non-Marxists, and it can be found to apply in various parts of the developed world as well as in the Third World: Hechter (1975) has argued that the persisting ethnic cleavages existing within Western states reflects the fact that these states were formed through the imperial conquest of one ethnic group by another. Political integration concerns the process by which the institutions of the state are made available to all members of its population, irrespective of their cultural or political backgrounds. It is associated with attempts to form a unified and harmonious national community which will buttress and enhance the power of the state concerned. The process of political integration can also be encouraged in multicultural Western societies, but in the Third World it is frequently regarded as an antidote to the divisive consequences of tribalism and as an essential component of nation building within ethnically diverse state populations which have very few shared traditions.

Particularly in the Third World, ethnic diversity has been viewed as a brake on development and a threat to the survival of the youthful and vulnerable state – as evident in 1964 in independence leader Kenneth Kaunda's repeated call for: 'One nation, one people, one Zambia.' For while some at least of the nation-states of Europe were privileged to develop in an organic manner, the states of the Third World have tended to have materialised out of the headlong retreat of colonialism and to have been propelled towards their places on the world stage untutored and unprepared. Their leaders, therefore, have exploited all movements and institutions which may secure and strengthen the state. Even Pan-Africanism, originally a vehicle for the reunification of

African peoples who were separated by the arbitrary partitioning of the continent, was pressed into service: 'But once the African nationalists obtained independence for their individual territories, Pan-Africanism was used by the new state elites to justify co-operation in preserving the existing political structures against common dangers of ethnic secession and irredentism which they claimed would lead to the Balkanization of Africa' (Hutchinson 1994, p. 153).

Before examining some of the problems of political integration in the Third World we should consider the nature of the state as it exists in Africa and perhaps a few other Third World countries. Often the state adopts a stance towards the rural society which is exploitative and aggressive. This has led several commentators to conclude that the African state acts as a ruling class (e.g. Callaghy 1984 and Stein 1985). Forrest rejects this analysis, claiming that if a class does not control the means of production (land, labour and tools) then it is not a ruling class and that the African state does not behave as a bourgeoisie in the manner described by Marx: the people who make up the state and hold power at the national level serve as political leaders and administrators but do not constitute a distinct ruling class.

> Thus the state in post-independent Africa is not a ruling class or a bourgeoisie, nor is it singularly beholden to the forces of international capitalism. It is, rather, an institutional composite of elites who hold national political power within a given territorial framework and who wield that power in order to advance their self-defined organisational, political and economic interests. (Forrest 1987, p. 70)

As Ihonvbere has described, it might have been hoped that the state would play a positive and leading role in the struggle to reverse underdevelopment, mobilise the masses and lay a viable foundation for self-reliance and self sustainment. However:

> The African experience has been radically different from that in both Europe and North America. The state has become a tool in the hands of a largely decadent, unproductive, corrupt and dependent dominant class. The state is used for accumulation as against legitimation purposes. Its structures, institutions and instruments are easily employed by the dominant forces to repress, exploit, suppress, and marginalize the masses. [Consequently,] the masses in Africa, relate to the state as an exploitative, coercive and alien structure. Its custodians lack credibility and legitimacy and are thus incapable of mobilizing or leading the people. Given the violent, coercive and exploitative nature of the state, the masses turn to ethnic, religious, and philanthropic organizations for hope, leadership, self expression and support. (Ihovbere 1994, p. 43)

At this point, Ihonvbere believes, the state becomes irrelevant in that it has lost its ability to provide leadership, and direction, mobilise human and material resources and effectively mediate class contradictions and conflicts. The difficulties associated with government become far worse when civil society is fragmented and the state adopts a role of actively encouraging division and doubt.

The African state will sometimes exist as a political vehicle which favours the interest of a particular ethnic grouping within a culturally diverse society. Quite frequently, political parties represent the interests of particular tribes or clans, in the way that the Inkatha Zulu party in South Africa represents Zulu interests or the Somali Patriotic Movement in Somalia represents the Ogaden clan. During the independence era of the 1960s, a number of failed attempts at defection took place as tribal leaderships sought to extract their territories from newly created states: the Ashanti from Ghana, the Buganda tribal kingdom from Uganda and the Ibo from Nigeria, last-named producing the destructive Biafra War of 1967–70. While ethnicity and ethnic-based conflicts were parts of pre-colonial life, sometimes the tensions of the post-colonial era may result from the privileged treatment accorded to particular groups during the colonial period. Whether or not divide-and-rule tactics were deliberately employed, unequal and discriminatory practices could ferment antagonisms between different groups. For example, under British rule the Ganda of Uganda were given preferential treatment in the education system and the Kamba were given a leading role in the Kenyan colonial forces.

In seeking to promote political integration the government should work to promote equality of opportunity across the ethnic spectrum and to produce a political party system which is not identified with sectional ethnic issues. Frequently, however, there are groups which cannot easily be assimilated or incorporated. The Tuareg are a people united by language and their traditional nomadic goat- and camel-herding culture who gained control of northern Mali and adjacent areas in the pre-colonial era. Their relations with Mali and with its negro population are difficult, not least because the Tuareg enslaved members of the black population in the eighteenth and nineteenth centuries. French rule was secured in 1898, and in 1960 the Mali Federation was granted independence, though within a few weeks Senegal withdrew. Drought and famine in 1984–5 produced a crisis which caused many Tuareg to become refugees, while those who remained in Mali were simultaneously excluded from positions of authority and exploited for taxes by the corrupt Moussa Traore regime. The Tuareg of northern Mali launched an armed uprising; some tribes and political organisations signed a settlement in 1992

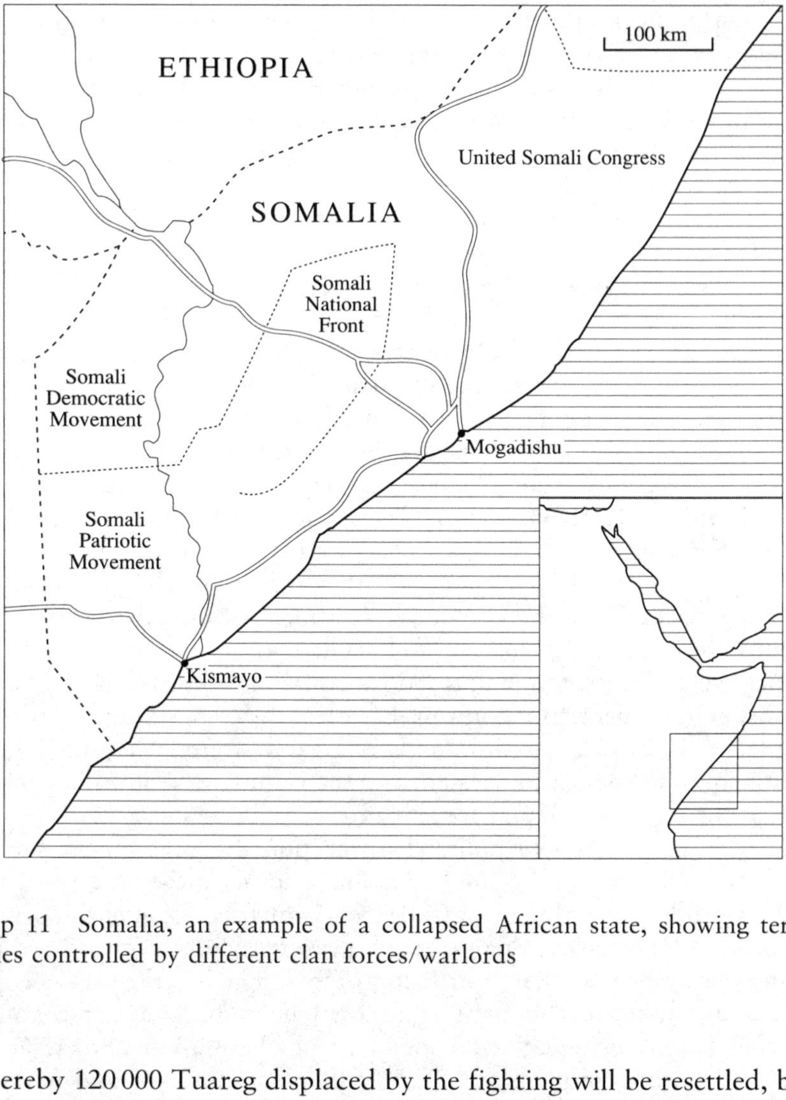

Map 11 Somalia, an example of a collapsed African state, showing territories controlled by different clan forces/warlords

whereby 120 000 Tuareg displaced by the fighting will be resettled, but some revolutionary factions are still pledged to the creation of an independent state covering the traditional Tuareg homeland of Azawad.

The droughts in sub-Saharan Africa during the modern era precipitated other conflicts of a political ecological nature. During the droughts of the early 1970s, large numbers of Fulani pastoralists migrated into Ivory Coast with their cattle (Bassett 1988). This migration was welcomed by the government, which was anxious to reduce its dependence on unreliable or expensive foreign suppliers of beef. However, the incursion of the Fulani and their herds caused mounting problems for the Senufo peasant farmers, who received no compensation for the damage caused to their crops. The problem was intensified as some politicians inflamed the situation by promising, if elected, to have the Fulani ejected, and during the spring of 1986 some eighty pastoralists were killed, causing a withdrawal of Fulani families from hundreds of camps. Because of intrigues and power struggles amongst politicians in the north of Ivory Coast, the official response to the killings was slow to arrive, and this was interpreted by both peasants and herders as denoting government approval for the atrocities.

In some cases, the exacerbation of ethnic rivalries was a consequence of political failure:

> Those who failed to gain power at national or local level tried to avoid permanent exclusion by exploiting communal divisions. Ruling parties and successful MPs did (and would) not attempt to recruit the support of all their constituents or every area of the country, and opposition groupings thus turned to the excluded or disfavoured candidates, families, ethnic groups, churches or Islamic organisations, areas etc. Long-standing local (and subsequently national) divisions became politicised, while party conflicts became redrawn and reconstructed as communal conflicts. (Allen 1995, p. 304)

Whether as a result of incompetence, corruption or evil intent, the handling of ethnic issues by Third World governments has frequently deepened the popular disillusionment with the state. It can be argued that ethnic divisions are not endemic and inevitable within African society, but that Africans will tend to seek solace in their tribal associations after the state has failed to deliver the promises of the pre-independence rhetoric and after the dominant elites have manipulated and exploited the ethnic factors to further their own interests. Having asserted that most Africans regard the state as a wicked, exploitative and coercive force, Ihonvbere (1994, p. 54) quotes Ake on the Nigerian case:

> Most Nigerians confront the state not as a public force but as an alien and hostile coercive power. This is all the more so because the Nigerian state, lacking autonomy, is immersed in the class struggle and is conspicuously a state for the few against the many, [and] because the Nigerian state tendentially appears as irrelevant or hostile, a critical condition for the transfer of loyalties to ecumenical levels is removed. Nigerians embraced ethnic identity all the more. The ethnic groups have been emotionally and materially supportive of their members, and do not rely on coercion. (Ake n.d., pp. 7–8)

Decolonisation, the 'soft' state and the collapsed state

Considerable attention has recently been given to the ideas of the journalist, Robert Kaplan (1994), concerning what he describes as 'the coming anarchy'. The collapse into anarchy of Sierra Leone has been represented as a microcosm for what is in store for West Africa and much of the underdeveloped world. According to Allen (1995, p. 318), however, 'The piece pulls together a familiar set of right-wing bogies: crime (as practised by non-whites, of course), AIDS, high birth rates (non-whites again), reversion to subnational loyalties, and the collapse of the state's capacity to police its citizens.' He shows that the states of Africa are following a variety of different political paths, and that as well as the negative aspects, recent history shows 'the desire and the capacity to experiment and innovate, and the presence of a persistent pressure for democratisation in African politics' (ibid.).

In the case of the collapse of Sierra Leone, which, with an average annual growth rate of 7 per cent between 1950 and 1972, had one of the fastest growing economies in West Africa, Zack-Williams (1990) believes that much of the blame must attach to internal corruption. He writes that:

> it is clear that successive governments in Sierra Leone have failed to seize the time and utilise even that small space for manoeuvre which imperialism had bestowed on them. We see that even the nucleus of democratic participation which was inherited from the departing colonialists was de-constructed and in its place kleptocracy reigned. (ibid., p. 33)

By 'kleptocracy' he refers to the emergence of an oligarchy with the specific project of creating a unity between the governing and ruling classes:

> Since the former has control over the formal state apparatus but lacks economic power, corruption is utilised as a vehicle through which economic hegemony can be attained. This process involves both the whipping up of xenophobic hysteria, as well as a de-politicisation of the population. This latter goal is usually achieved through the reification of the one-party state, as well as the strengthening of the oppressive state apparatus. (ibid., pp. 22–3)

While the economy of Sierra Leone declined,

> In order to finance its lust for imported luxuries, smuggling of the nation's precious minerals soon became common place, and the fine divide between

> state and private property disappeared. The kleptocracy forced out whatever semblance of democracy that had previously existed . . . Now, largely because the bourgeoisie was concerned with its regular forage into the national treasury without any inhibition or concern for those that produce the wealth of the nation, the latter in the main decided to opt out of the formal economy, by either smuggling cash crops across the border, or by abandoning cash crop production, and reverting to the production of subsistence crops. (ibid., p. 26)

The post-independence governments of Africa in general have proved to be vulnerable to internal forces, while their states have displayed a dangerous degree of 'softness'. The concept of hardness and softness in states has been developed by Forrest, who writes that:

> Since the attainment of independence, postcolonial states in Africa have attempted to augment state hardness by increasing their autonomy from social forces, carrying out the political penetration of society, extracting resources from the peasantry, and propagating ideological legitimation in order to defend and justify these activities. However, success in these goals has proved largely elusive, and so a significant degree of state hardness has not been achieved. (Forrest 1988, p. 437)

He considers that:

> While African states have managed to establish partial political autonomy, they remain to a large extent beholden to and dependent on social forces; despite an insistent drive to secure local level political control, local sociopolitical structures have in fact been able to elude the penetrative reach of central authorities; while states have managed to obtain a portion of rural wealth, peasant systems of production and trading networks remain mostly uncaptured by official cooperatives and marketing agencies; and government-promulgated ideological legitimation has been unable to convince the general populace of the worthiness of the state's hard-seeking activities. (ibid.)

Some have blamed the failure of the African state on the inability to break the ties with the previous colonial existence, so that there remains a continuity between the old dependence and the new. According to First (1983, p. 207):

> Many of the means and ends that made up colonial administration were inherited virtually intact by the independence governments. For the sediment of colonialism lies deep in African society. The armies are colonial products; the political system is largely a transplant, and a bad one at that; while the political rulers were trained or constrained by the colonial system.

In most African states, independence was not achieved as a result of mass struggle but arrived in a form offered by the colonial administration and accepted by the administration-in-waiting. Constitutions and forms of government developed over centuries of European political struggle and evolution were superimposed on societies with quite different histories and needs; as a result they failed again and again: 'From the end of 1960 to the beginning of 1962, 13 states revised their constitutions or produced altogether new ones' (ibid., p. 204). Meanwhile, children continued to be educated using subject matter borrowed from the national history of their former colonial masters and were examined according to standards set by the metropolitan examination boards, while students travelled overseas to study in the same universities that had graduated the administrators of the old empire. In the military field, the new officer corps was trained abroad in the traditions of Sandhurst, Cranwell or St Cyr.

> More than this, the armies of the new states were the identical armies that the colonial powers had built to keep their empires quiescent . . . Even when Africanized and run by commanders-in-chief who were nationals of their own countries, Africa's armies were an extension of the West. Where they had gone into battle in the pre-independence period, it had been for, not against the colonial power. (ibid., p. 218)

These armies have stood poised and ready to seize power whenever the civil regimes have faltered.

Davidson (1990) has compared the crisis of the nation-state in Africa with the fate which befell the states released from the Austro-Hungarian and Ottoman Empires. He thought that in both cases many of the states lapsed into military dictatorship, aggressive expansionism, forms of fascism and corruption and he considered that in Africa a new relationship must be established between the base and the centre. Rejecting both the capitalist and state socialist models, he notes that in the traditional indigenous political structures of Africa power began at the base of society. While it would not be practical to divide the continent into 500 units based on tradition rather than the 50 or so modern ones, the state should in the face of all its difficulties seek to develop a facilitating role: 'How to change around the government cadre from a "doer" and "dictator", to facilitating others to do, requires a fundamental change of attitude' (ibid., p. 15).

While Davidson draws analogies between Africa and the late nineteenth-century Balkans, Forrest (1994) sees parallels between post-colonial Africa and medieval Europe. He believes that in each case the state aspired to assert its power across the whole of its *de jure* national territory, but succeeded only partially and superficially, often being obliged to yield to local elites. In both cases, despite attempts by the central leaderships to establish formal political systems, politics remained focused on unbridled competition between factions of political elites and kin-, ethnic-, class-, regional- and clientele-based groupings. Political alliances and processes were unstable and unpredictable; 'Also, because of the organizational fragility of government agencies, powerful social forces – usually barons in Europe, ethnic and clientelistic groupings in Africa – were able to make their way into the heart of state power and assert their control over many official institutions and decision-making processes' (ibid., p. 261). Thus, three main features were shared by the weak states of independent Africa and medieval Europe: an administrative capacity too weak to achieve official goals; a low level of penetration by state authority due to the enduring power of local and intermediary authorities, and a dominance of informal politics. This dominance was associated with personal rule and ties, unlimited power struggles among factional groupings and the prevalence of force in general and *coups d'état* by military leaders in particular (ibid., p. 263).

In both cases too, powerful social groupings – barons in the case of medieval Europe and ethno-clientelist ones in that of post-independence Africa – were able to permeate the organisational boundaries of the state. Often they could affect or even dominate state policy-making, while when more than one faction of such groups penetrates the state then their rivalry and feuding intensify the levels of intrastate conflict (ibid., p. 291). However, despite these similarities, Forrest considered it unlikely that the African states will pursue paths similar to those followed by European states after the Middle Ages.

Allen investigated African states, seeking to discover whether they could be regarded as examples of the same political system. He concluded that a limited number of distinct historical paths could be discovered, beginning with two variants of the process of decolonisation. Then divergent paths resulted from differing responses to the political crises of the early post-independence era, and these produced contrasting forms of politics, termed **centralised bureaucratic politics** and **spoils politics**. In the period following independence, clientelism or patronage and bribery grew in importance, and:

> Within the new governments and ruling parties clientelism bred corruption . . . For those within the clientelist networks, loyalty to the party or its leaders was rewarded by access to valued resources. These could be passed on to more minor supporters and to voters to reinforce their loyalty – or

> they could be retained, for personal enrichment . . . Politics, politicians and their associates, and their entire political system became increasingly corrupt. (Allen 1995, pp. 304–5)

Opposition and popular reaction to corruption and the increasing factionalism within the ruling parties as groups tried to monopolise their control over state resources helped to produce a crisis of clientelism which often led to military intervention.

Centralised–bureaucratic politics results from attempts to resolve this crisis and produce stable, authoritarian systems. Clientelism, essential to party cohesion and mass consent, was retained; power was centralised in an executive presidency; the party was displaced as the main distributor and contestant for patronage by a bureaucracy that was answerable to the presidency, while representative institutions like parties, parliament, local government, elections and trade unions were downgraded or eliminated. These reforms provided a means of regulating clientelist competition. Previously, factional leaders competed to control resources and there was no way of controlling the process, but: 'With the creation of a powerful presidency, itself controlling directly considerable resources and able to exercise indirect control over still more resources through prefectral systems, competition could be regulated, and resource allocation overall less determined by the outcomes of clientelist competition' (ibid., p. 307).

Where the clientelist crisis was not resolved by adopting such centralising–bureaucratic structural reforms there was political breakdown and military intervention. Where an unresolved clientelist crisis persists to the point where the system breaks down completely, then spoils politics results. The dominant political faction denies access to resources to all other factions; there is wholesale corruption and looting of the economy, which affects its performance and produces economic crises; the government relies on bribes and force, while the absence of institutions for mediation means that discontent often leads to strikes or violence; the relationship between the state and the citizen is characterised by repression and violence; ethnic divisions may become increasingly important; instability becomes endemic, and there is an erosion of authority, popular alienation and a 'withdrawal from the state'. A further differentiation of political systems has resulted from popular responses to the breakdown of centralised bureaucratic politics and spoils politics. Economic decline and debt crisis could undermine the centralised–bureaucratic state leading to limited or cosmetic reforms of democratic renewal. Economic life in states dominated by spoils politics, with extreme levels of corruption and waste, tends to deteriorate more rapidly. The regimes of these states respond by intensifying 'spoils behaviour', which simply accelerates the disintegration of the state. It may then implode, and become, in Zartman's (1995, p. 7) words, 'a black hole of power'.

The collapsed state has become a characteristic part of the African political landscape. Allen points out that in the nine years since 1986 'we have witnessed the great majority of spoils systems moving towards state collapse accompanied by warfare, often highly destructive of society and the economy. Liberia, Somalia, Sierra Leone and Rwanda have already collapsed, while Burundi, Sudan and Zaire show clear and advanced symptoms' (Allen 1995, p. 314). In Liberia around 150 000 lives have been lost in recent internal struggles and in 1994 its territory had been divided between seven factions and Liberia had virtually ceased to function as a state; much of the population of Rwanda has been forced to live outside its boundaries, while Sierra Leone almost fails to exist as a sovereign entity.

> South Africans, Ethiopians and Malawians retain expectations for relatively new administrations. Uganda, Zimbabwe, Namibia and others run robust administrations. But in much of Africa – from Liberia to Somalia, Zaire to Nigeria – any belief that the state will look after the people, or at least not abuse them, has long since evaporated . . . The conflicts in Liberia, Sierra Leone or Somalia are a grasp at power with multiplying factions dividing the country between them. Rwanda may have appeared an ethnic confrontation but at its root it was a battle for power devoid of ideology. (McGreal 1994)

The collapse of some larger states, such as Nigeria or Zaire, could have consequences on a geopolitical scale for the rest of the continent. Zaire was propped up by the West during the period of the Cold War, but then left to crumble under the corrupt dictatorship of President Mobuto. By the mid-1990s it was plain that much of the apparatus of statehood had collapsed, with ever more territory sinking into anarchy as the state retreats. The regime maintains the power to preserve the President, but little more. In provincial towns civil servants were left unpaid and so abandoned their desks and began to work as subsistence farmers. All semblances of justice have been abandoned, with elements of the army operating without control in rural areas and, through their looting and murder, hastening the break between people and state.

Many of the problems of the weaker states of the Third World are rooted in history and the colonial experience. The present and the future contain problems of their own, and the information revolution and the expansion of communication systems may spawn a new set of challenges. In the words of a prominent UN official:

> Third world countries are one by one becoming 'ungovernable'. No matter what the complexion of the governments – right wing, left wing, military or democratic – they are all in situations of not being able to respond adequately to the expectations of their people: expectations aroused by the media, by communications, by education . . . it is my feeling that turmoil and tension in the Third World will eventually spill over national boundaries and threaten and endanger the very fabric of global peace and stability. (Corea 1990, p. 77)

European avarice created a world of sovereign states, each one cast in the European legal mould. The people of the newly emancipated African colonies could either accept the world of the national sovereign actor or else be denied a place on the diplomatic stage. Not surprisingly, the political codes and institutions which had evolved slowly according to the shifting nuances of European life often failed to flourish when superimposed on African society. How unjust that Europe so often expects the world to believe that this is all somehow the Africans' fault.

■ *Chapter 8* ■

Geopolitics, Globalisation and World Systems

When you're finally up at the moon looking back at earth, all those differences and nationalistic traits are pretty well going to blend and you're going to get a concept that maybe this is really one world and why the hell can't we learn to live together like decent people.

American astronaut Frank Borman, quoted in *Newsweek* (23 December 1968)

The only way to stop this evil is for all the red men to unite in claiming a common and equal right in the land, as it was at first, and should be now – for it never was divided, but belongs to all . . . Sell a country! Why not sell the air, the clouds and the great sea, as well as the earth? Did not the Great Spirit make them all for the use of his children?

Shawnee leader, Tecumseh (1810)

On 7 December 1972, an astronaut on the Apollo 17 space mission shot a series of photographs of the earth. One of these images, designated AS17–148–22727, was destined to become a symbol of the oneness of the earth. As described by Cosgrove (1994, p. 270): 'It captured, centerframe and with perfect resolution, the full terracqueous disk without a solar shadow or "terminator." The whole Earth, geography's principal object of study, had been photographed by a human eye-witness.' In the years which followed, this photographic image of the planet has supplanted the Mercator map and the cartographer's globe as an icon of the Earth.

The images obtained on the Apollo missions provided the global public with striking and timely reminders of the unitary nature of its fragile home. But some political geographers had for long been aware of the interconnected nature of the Earth, whereby significant changes in one part of the planet would in turn effect changes in all other parts. The study of geopolitics, often but not always undertaken at the global level, has been a component of geographical study throughout this century. At different times it has variously been lauded, derided and rehabilitated. Whatever its failings may have been, its great strength has been its ability to provide cogent reminders of the unity of the Earth. Formerly the factor of unity was invoked to demonstrate the transglobal potency of different forms of military power. In the geopolitics of the future, however, Earth unity concepts are most likely to express the ways in which ecological challenges span man-made boundaries and demand globally agreed solutions.

Geopolitics of the traditional kind was a risky affair involving speculation on the grandest possible of scales. It was never more than a component of political geography, but when it was discredited and rejected the whole subdiscipline was tarnished and entered into a decline that lasted for more than a quarter of a century. By the 1960s, geopolitics had come to represent everything that the prevailing opinion in geography disliked: it was based on subjective attitudes and an often crude environmental determinism, was unamenable to quantification and operated on the grandest of scales. When interest in political geography underwent a rapid revival during the 1980s, the rehabilitation process did not at first affect its geopolitical branch, but late in the decade a subdiscipline of critical geopolitics has emerged, which embodies much of the excitement but little if any of the tendentiousness which was often associated with the old geopolitics. Meanwhile, the globalisation of markets, manufacturing, finance and communications has given a new reality to ideas about the oneness of the Earth.

■ The geopolitical tradition

In practical terms, geopolitics must be as old as the quest for territory and security, as old as diplomacy, strategy, envy and fear. Alexander the Great must have indulged in geopolitical scheming, so too must Napoleon and many other commanders, emperors and conquerors. In the more scholarly sense, Admiral Alfred Thayer Mahan has been identified as the father of geopolitics, in which case the birth of the tradition must have taken place in Boston in 1890, with the publication of the Admiral's study of *The Influence of Sea Power upon History, 1660–1782*. It had to wait a further nine years before acquiring a name, for it was in 1899 that the Swedish political scientist, Rudolph Kjellen, used the term 'geopolitics' in an article on the Swedish boundaries. In 1905 Kjellen used the German *Geopolitik*, which was intended to denote 'the science of the state as a realm in space' – not that there was much that was spectacularly scientific about the work of Rudolph Kjellen, it being tinged by the extremes of nationalism and social Darwinism. Kjellen perceived the state as being comparable to a living organism, indeed, he implied that it had awareness, the power to reason and a will to live (Holdar 1992). Under the influence of Ratzel, who was currently refining his ideas in Berlin, Kjellen (1917) defined his *Geopolitik* as 'The science which conceives the state as a geographical organism or as a phenomenon in space.' This 'organism' was engaged in an unending contest for life-giving resources, of which territory was the most important.

As developed by its early practitioners in Europe, geopolitics was a crude creature of its times. It remained rooted in the old geographical materialism of the previous centuries. The weakness of such methods was recognised by the German communist geographer, Karl Wittfogel, in 1929 and O Tuathail (1994c, p. 314) has described how Wittfogel realised that geopolitics 'postulated that geographical factors, whatever their character (climate, soil, location, physical terrain, even race), directly influence political life', whereas in reality such geographical factors did not directly influence, but rather mediated the political aspects of life in human societies.

The first coherent description of the world as a functioning geopolitical entity was provided by the British geographer, Halford Mackinder, in 1904. When Mackinder revealed his ideas about his supposed 'geographical pivot of history' he did, if nothing else, issue a resounding reminder that the planet Earth was a closed system, where change in one part of the system would change the balance of relationships in all other parts.

During the 1920s, the focus of geopolitical effort shifted to Germany, and it was here that the subject acquired its severely tarnished image as a new school of geopolitics developed around Karl Haushofer (1869–1946). Parker (1994, p. 171) explains that:

> Following Germany's defeat in the First World War, Ratzel's ideas had been taken up by a group of German geographers who proceeded to use them as the basis for a systematic plan not only for the recovery of Germany but for the country's return to great power status. Their underlying contention was that while political geography was concerned with the spatial conditions of the state, geopolitics was concerned with its spatial requirements. The whole Nazi strategy for German domination in Europe was influenced by the ideas formulated by these geopoliticians.

Until relatively recently, it was commonplace for political geographers to make the clearest of distinctions between the corrupted geographers who placed geopolitics at the service of the Nazi state and the unblemished academic political geographers of the Anglo-American world. This was still the case as recently as 1986, when O'Loughlin and van der Wusten (1986, p. 484) wrote: 'Most political geographers have become so embarassed [sic] by the excesses of "Geopolitik" that they have shied away from research on international conflicts.' But it was also around this time that: 'interests long hidden in embarrasment [sic] began to re-surface. The term geopolitics, for example, abandoned in disrepute after World War II was revived in the late 1970s and 1980s' (Peet 1989, p. 258). Recent reappraisals by researchers such as Paterson (1987) and Bassin (1987a and 1987b) have tempered the earlier judgements on *Geopolitik* and have shown that the link between it and the Nazis was less direct than had been imagined. In 1924, Haushofer founded the remarkably popular journal, *Zeitschrift fur Geopolitik*. According to some modern commentators, this journal served to articulate and justify the loathsome territorial and ethnic policies of the Nazi state, and Cohen (1991, p. 556) writes that: 'The most direct, and infamous, geographical contributor to the concept of new world order was, of course, Karl von Haushofer, whose doctrine of Geopolitik became an intellectual underpinning for Nazi world conquest.' There are others, like Heske (1987), who stress the aristocratic viewpoint in Haushofer's writing, and O Tuathail (1994c, p. 319) writes that: 'Like other conservatives, Haushofer was actually quite hostile to "bourgeois" values and the "bourgeois" Weimar Republic. It was the coming together of a certain aristocratic *Weltanschauung* with the antimodernist counter-revolutionary zeal of the far right that made German geopolitics significant ideologically.' Yet whatever his private political stance may have been, there is no doubt that Haushofer along with his followers developed geopolitics as a potent tool for propaganda rather than enquiry. Even so, as Bassin (1987b) has revealed, the philosophies of *Geopolitik* and national socialism were not identical. The geopoliticians, heavily influenced by Ratzel's legacy, emphasised the importance of environmental determinism and 'natural laws' in shaping the destinies of societies, while in the view of the Nazis, race was the guiding factor. Thus two doctrines, one based on a mistaken understanding of geography and the other on a misrepresentation of genetics competed for attention (ibid.). Nevertheless, and though an admirer and associate of Hess rather than of Hitler, Haushofer actively supported the Nazis and not only published geographical propaganda helpful to their cause, but also broadcast such material monthly on nationwide radio.

The differences between academic political geography and the geopolitics being developed in Germany concerned the prescriptive

Box 8.1 *Mackinder and the Heartland*

Halford (later Sir Halford) Mackinder (1861–1947) was the first Lecturer in Geography to be appointed to a British university, taking a post at Oxford in 1887. He captured the imagination of a much wider audience in 1904 when he presented the first version of his geopolitical prophesy to the Royal Geographical Society in London. His ideas are of lasting value for two reasons: firstly, because they provided an early statement of the unified nature of the world, and secondly, because they continued to stimulate debate throughout the remainder of this century. And yet it would be difficult to regard Mackinder as a visionary. Some of his ideas were rooted in the organismic thinking of Ratzel (he believed a common blood coursed through the veins of generations who had occupied the same region). He combined his environmental determinism with notions that European civilisation was born of a struggle to resist invasions by Asiatic 'barbarians': these ideas were expressed in tones redolent of European supremacy which at best read like a 'ripping yarn', and at worst like colonial bigotry. His phrase 'world organism' has a modern ring, but this is juxtaposed with a simplistic environmental determinism which was beginning to seem jaded even in 1904, as the following quotation reveals: 'My aim will not be to discuss the influence of this or that feature, or yet to make a study of regional geography, but rather to exhibit human history as part of the life of the world organism. I recognize that I can only arrive at one aspect of the truth, and I have no wish to stray into excessive materialism. Man and not nature initiates, but nature in large measure controls. My concern is with the general physical control, rather than the *causes of universal history*' (Mackinder 1904, p. 422).

An important aspect of his interest in geographical controls concerned the attributes and relative potency of land power and sea power, a topic that he had already explored in his work, *Britain and the British Seas* (1902). He believed that past and future were explicable in terms of the juxtaposition of inner and outer crescent territory, which was accessible to sea power, and a vast pivot area, very roughly coincident with Russia, which, lacking the bays, inlets or navigable rivers which warships could penetrate, was immune to sea power. Throughout history, swarms of mobile nomads mounted on horses or camels had erupted from the secure citadel of the pivot area to beat on the walls of western civilisation. Now he believed that transcontinental railways were about to add a new dimension of potency to the land power of the pivot area: the train was heir to the horse and camel just as Russia was the heir of the Mongol empire. If Russian land power resources could be wedded to sea power – perhaps by an alliance with Germany or through a conquest of the Tsarist Empire by China – then world domination was within reach.

Mackinder modified his ideas in 1919 to take account of the events of the 1914–18 War, which had led him to believe that an invasion of his pivot area – now appearing as the Heartland – could be achieved via the East European steppes. And so he warned the diplomats engaged in shaping the post-war settlement that Germany and Russia should be separated by a tier of secure nation states, for any power that gained hegemony in Eastern Europe might conquer the Heartland and so gain dominion over the world (1919, p. 113):

Box 8.1 *continued*

> Who rules East Europe commands the Heartland:
> Who rules the Heartland commands the World Island
> Who rules the World Island commands the World

In his eighty-second year Sir Halford published another version (1943) of his geopolitical ideas, but this time he failed to command the attention of the Western world.

Mackinder was in the business of prediction, and so must be judged like any other tipster or seer by the accuracy of his forecasts. The web of transcontinental railways failed to materialise, and Russia's rise to superpower status took place under Stalin when the country's human, energy and mineral resources were mobilised in an authoritarian command economy behind the goal of industrialisation. And so it was the wealth rather than the desolation of the Heartland which proved decisive. His claim that: 'Nor is it likely that any possible social revolution will alter her essential relations to the great geographical limits of her existence' was inappropriate for a state soon to embark on an introspective policy of achieving Socialism in one country – and now it seems even less apt as the Russia of old implodes in the Yeltsin era (1904, p. 436). Mackinder gained supporters and apologists in every decade of this century, but this should not blind us to the fact that as a prophet he was a failure. It was the global breadth rather than the precision of his vision that should impress.

nature of the latter. This was evident to the geopolitician, Otto Maull, who wrote (1936, p. 31): 'Geopolitik is concerned with the spatial requirements of the state while political geography examines only its spatial conditions.' The most important intellectual components of Haushofer's geopolitics were the ideas of Ratzel, Kjellen and Mackinder, which were reworked to provide a geostrategic doctrine rooted in Ratzel's mystical notion of *Lebensraum* or the 'living space' of the state and in visions of a world composed of a heartland and pan-regions representing the German, Anglo-American and Japanese spheres. Thus, a tinkering with Mackinder's ideas produced a scenario in which the German-dominated Old World had been encircled and constricted by Anglo-American maritime power. Within these concocted realms, the (German) state was presented as a vital organism, ringed by hostile powers yet endowed with a natural right to expand at the expense of lesser, neighbouring organisms. According to the organismic theories derived from Ratzel, the vigorous [German] state had to devour more and more space in order to survive, and consequently boundaries were an artificial impediment to this natural process of growth. As with other kinds of mumbo-jumbo, these doctrines lacked logical consistency. For if earth and state really were

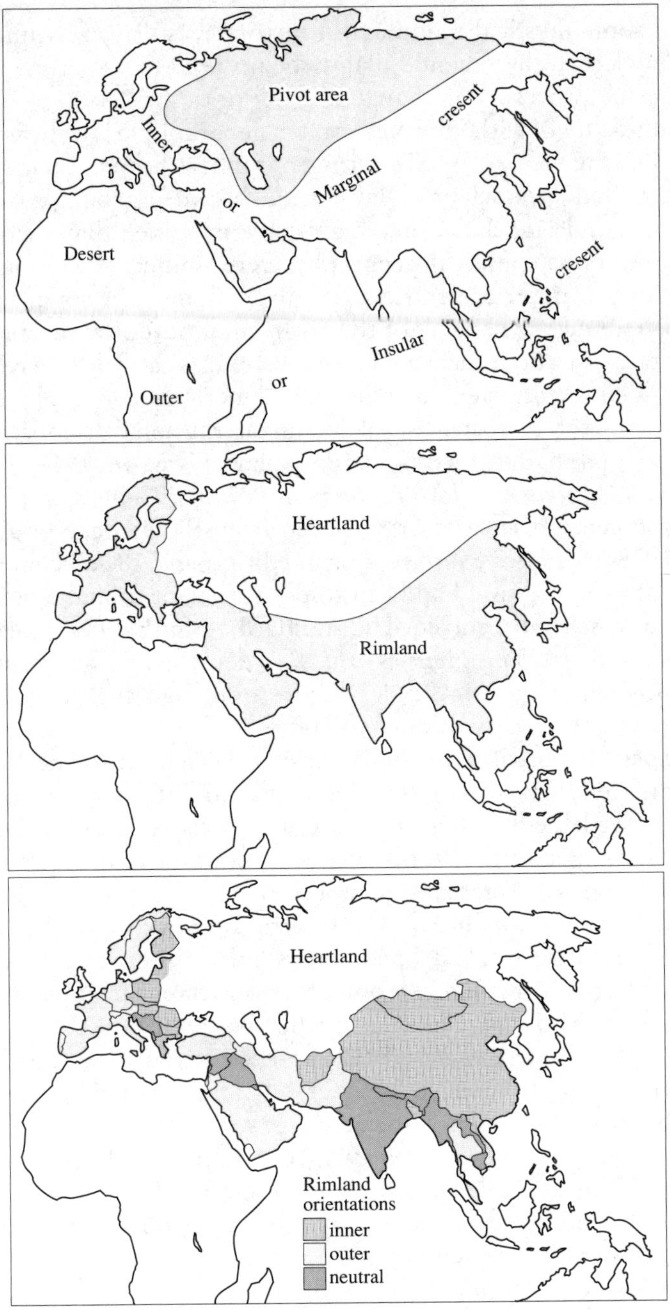

Map 12 Different versions of the geopolitical world
Sources: *above* – Mackinder (1904); *centre* – Spykman (1994); *below* – Meining (1956).

linked in some mystical union and if history was driven by immutable natural laws then there would plainly be no need to use propaganda to legitimise the processes of change.

Geopolitik died with the Nazi state; geography as well as history belonged to the victors. As Western geographers heaped their scorn on this discredited product of collaboration between geography and the state propaganda machine, one might have imagined that such experiments in 'applied' political geography were unique to Germany. Yet Mackinder had never pretended to be dispassionate: he sought to warn the British about the dangers of the Heartland, never the reverse. In the United States, at about the time that Haushofer's thoughts were turning towards *Zeitschrift*, the distinguished American geographer, Isaiah Bowman, sought to foster a Wilsonian internationalist consciousness in a state that had turned towards isolationism. In 1921, Bowman published *The New World: Problems in Political Geography*, a review of the emergent post-war world as seen from the vantage point of the US. By 1928 it had gone into its fourth edition and 18 000 copies of the English language edition had been sold – sufficient to make the book a popular best-seller by current UK standards (Smith 1986, p. 441). Yet for all its success, *The New World* was detached rather than sensational. Bowman, like Mackinder before him, had the geopolitician's ability to visualise the world as an entity.

As a specialist advisor to the American delegation to the Versailles peace conference, Bowman was one of the architects of the post-war territorial settlement. Thus it was not surprising that in Germany, where resentment at the Versailles terms smouldered, he came to be regarded as one of America's geopoliticians: ' "Geopolitics" became a convenient and fashionable word: all forms of work by geographers for the state could be dubbed "geopolitics". In public discourse, many began to refer to Bowman as "our" geopolitician, including anti-Nazi thinkers whom Bowman counted within his own ranks' (O Tuathail 1994c, p. 321). At the end of 1941 the US entered the Second World War, and ten months later, in October 1942, Bowman, who was plainly ruffled by remarks which associated his work with geopolitics, published a rebuttal, 'Geography Versus Geopolitics', in the journal of the American Geographical Society. Here there appeared the sentence that would be remembered as the epitaph for Geopolitik: 'Geopolitics is simple and sure, but, as demonstrated in German writings and policy, it is also illusion, mummery, an apology for theft' (Bowman 1942, p. 658). In reality, however, it was not geopolitics that had so outraged Bowman, but the nature of its development within a power that was hostile to his own country's interests and values. As O Tuathail (1994c) describes, in the self same year that Bowman unleashed his attack on 'geopolitics' he lavished high praise on a geopolitical work directed at assisting the policy-makers of the US: Nicholas J. Spykman published his *America's Strategy in World Politics* in 1942 and his more influential work on *The Geography of the Peace* two years later.

Long before Mackinder's death, the German geopoliticians had begun to rejig his ideas, while Spykman's work marked the beginning of a similar, ongoing, Anglo-American tradition. He took Mackinder's 'inner or marginal crescent' of lands which surrounded the 'pivot area or Heartland', renamed it as the 'Rimland', predicted that Britain and the USSR would be post-war rivals for the control of the Rimland and encouraged American statesmen to operate a form of containment policy to prevent the Rimland from subsiding under Soviet control. As an interesting postscript to the Spykman debate, in 1992 Nijman published the results of an elaborate quantitative investigation based on data concerning conflict and cooperation in US–Soviet relations during the four decades following 1948. The 20 countries in which the US and the Soviet Union had the most serious conflict were revealed, and they very largely formed a crescent around the Soviet frontiers, similar to Spykman's Rimland. These results certainly validate the Rimland hypothesis, although it could be argued that, Rimland or no Rimland, such results were easily predictable given, firstly, the global reach of US power compared to the regional reach of Soviet power, and secondly, the long-term operation of an American policy of containment, which ringed the Soviet Union in countries bound to the US in defensive treaty organisations.

Next in the geopolitical line and with a rather different vision stood the airman, de Seversky. His work is of lasting interest in terms of the political perception of space rather than because of any continuing geopolitical importance. Geographers and strategists had become accustomed to perceiving the world in terms of a Mercator map projection rather than a globe. To further his case for dramatic increases in American air power, de Seversky presented the world as it appeared in an azimuthal equidistant projection centred on the North Pole. At once it became obvious that the territories of two superpowers clasped the northern latitudes, with the US being within combat range of Soviet bombers approaching via the polar wastes rather than the Atlantic or Pacific. He plotted the ranges of contemporary aircraft to produce a geopolitical 'Area of Decision', with each superpower being entirely within reach of the bomber forces of the other, and he proceeded to advocate a policy of American air supremacy, considering that the only valid role for land forces involved defending the Arctic territories against a Soviet invasion of the American continent via the Bering Straits.

De Seversky was not the first to recognise the geopolitical significance of the map; the German geopoliticians had often exploited the nuances of trick cartography as a propaganda weapon, while the Pole, Jan Kowalewski (1892–1965), who served in British Intelligence and who greatly feared Soviet expansion, described how different forms of perception and cartographic presentation could greatly affect the interpretation of a situation:

> He was very aware that the same distribution or relationship on a global scale could be shown differently on different projections. The spheres of influence of the USSR and the USA could be seen as two halves of a tennis ball . . . On conventional maps the Soviet bloc could be seen to be encircled by the USA, with its many bases and allies, but from another angle the USA could be seen as encircled by the USSR and its allies, especially with the establishment of a Soviet military presence in Cuba after 1959. (Cole 1990, pp. 67–8)

The 'map-as-log' has been described by Anderson (1991, p. 175):

> In London's imperial maps, British colonies were usually pink-red, French purple-blue, Dutch yellow-brown, and so on. Dyed this way, each colony appeared like a detachable piece of a jigsaw puzzle. As this 'jigsaw' effect became normal, each 'piece' could be wholly detached from its geographic context . . . In this shape, the map entered an infinitely reproducible series, available for transfer to posters, official seals, letterheads, magazine and textbook covers, tablecloths, and hotel walls.

Perhaps the most lucid statement of the political significance of the map was provided by Lacoste (1973, p. 1):

> It is important that we gain (or regain) an awareness of the fact that the map, perhaps the central referent of geography, is, and has been, fundamentally an instrument of power. A map is an abstraction from concrete reality which was designed and motivated by practical (political and military) concerns; it is a way of representing space which facilitates its domination and control. To map, then, means to formally define space along the lines set within a particular epistemological experience; it actually transposes a little-known piece of concrete reality into an abstraction which serves the practical interests of the State machine; it is a tedious and costly operation done for, and by the State.

In 1956, Meinig swung the geopolitical spotlight back to Mackinder's Heartland. Both Heartland and Rimland were retained in forms very similar to those presented by Spykman a dozen years earlier, but here the author was at pains to emphasise that the orientations of Rimland states could change from the outward or maritime to the inward or continental. Here was the most acceptable exposition of the Heartland concept because it recognised that human will rather than environmental controls could govern the political orientation of states. However, Meinig's ideas scarcely amounted to a geopolitical revelation: the diplomacies of both the US and the USSR had given efforts to manipulate the political orientations of strategically located states their highest priority throughout the Cold War. Meinig was really only describing what had been glaringly obvious for many years. Nevertheless, geopoliticians not only *described* the strategic realities of the Cold War, they also helped to *shape* them: Cohen (1991) and Brown (1989) note how Acheson, Brzezinski, Dulles, Eisenhower, Haig, Kennan, Kissinger, Nixon, Nitze, Rostow and Taylor amongst the policy-makers were influenced by geopolitical theories. Cohen (1991, p. 552) adds: 'Outdated versions of the Heartland–Rimland theory remained a tool for containment strategy long after that strategy had proved wanting.'

Grandiose visions tended to flash brightly but briefly across the geopolitical firmament, yet Cohen built a personal tradition of geopolitical analysis which has spanned most of the post-war era. In 1964 he offered his blueprint of a world divided into 'geostrategic regions' which were gaining reality as nation states surrendered some of their identity in the face of pressure from supranational forces. These were subdivided into 'geopolitical regions', which exerted tactical rather than strategic influences upon global affairs. Two large regions of the world containing numerous states remained unintegrated: the Middle East and South East Asia. These strategically located regions were caught between the conflicting spheres of influence of the superpowers and were designated as 'shatterbelts'. Like Meinig, Cohen recognised that the superpowers competed for the loyalty of lesser powers and he considered that some sort of isostatic balance of power existed, so that as one competitor suffered a setback in one location it would compensate by intensifying its efforts to exert influence in another part of the world.

As Cohen's work developed, the emphasis that he placed upon complex interactions between states and on evolutionary change in the world rather than the crude environmentalism favoured by the old geopoliticians became increasingly evident. In 1990 he rejected the crude and outmoded concepts and suggested that geopolitical developments of a more subtle nature should be anticipated, with second-order powers and what he termed 'gateway states' playing increasingly important roles in global affairs. When he next published his ideas, in 1991, Cohen argued that at the highest geostrategic level there were two realms: the trade dependent Maritime realm (roughly Western

Europe, Africa and the Americas) and the inner-oriented Continental realm (embracing the Soviet Union and China). Most of the second-level regions were contained within these realms, but three lay outside either realm: the independent region of South Asia, the Middle East Shatterbelt, defined as a zone of contention caught between the two realms, and the emerging Gateway region of Central and Eastern Europe, which was a transitional zone that could facilitate contact and interchange between the two realms. In an upbeat postscript written to take account of the recent dramatic events in the doomed USSR and Yugoslavia, he observed that:

> Political systems that unravel so quickly are indeed cause for concern. The basis for this unraveling, the popular urge and will for democratic and human rights, also offers the hope that novel, more responsive systems are in process of being forged that will speedily contribute to a new, more stable, and peaceful map of the world. (ibid., p. 579)

With its relative complexity and its emphasis on the continuous processes of 'dynamic equilibrium', Cohen's recent work may seem to be far removed from that of Mackinder and his followers. On the other hand, the Heartland (the Soviet Union and China) is still there, and Cohen writes in the old prescriptive manner: he addresses himself to the US and says what it should do, and when he uses the word 'we' it is normally 'we Americans' that he means, as in: 'We should retain air and sea bases only where we are broadly welcomed as strategic partners' (ibid., p. 577).

Most of geopolitics was supposed to be about predicting the future; sometimes it got things wrong, while often the predictions amounted to little more than statements about the obvious. In retrospect, one might argue that it was really about announcing the preoccupations, anxieties and fantasies of the present, whether these took the form of Tsarist bogeymen arriving by train or Soviet bombers whirring unseen across the Arctic.

Some at least of the inconsistency associated with geopolitics concerned uncertainties surrounding the fundamental question of the relative importance of geography. Sometimes practitioners plumbed the depths of environmental determinism, with their excesses perhaps discouraging others from allowing geographical factors their real influence. This uncertainty about the proper weighting of evidence was recognised by writers as diverse as Lacoste and Cohen. The former wrote: 'In international relations, what we call "Geography" is subjected to two contradictory appraisals. The influence of factors considered to be geographic is either greatly exaggerated or nearly overlooked, in spite of obvious territorial imperatives' (Lacoste 1984, p. 213), while the latter wrote that: 'The American geopoliticians [like Dulles, Kissinger and Brzezinski] grasped spatially obsolete views because of their limited understanding of geography. For theirs was and is a definition of the discipline that is static, deterministic, and naive' (Cohen 1991 p. 552).

Geopolitics was always essentially a creature of its time, as the final example will show. In 1967, B. M. Russett published a study which involved an extremely technical factorial analysis of 54 variables for 82 countries. It was considered that if vast amounts of social, economic and cultural data were subjected to computer analysis then (and to cut a long story short) a new regionalisation of the world could be accomplished. These regions would not be the subjective creations of the old-school geopoliticians and geographers, but would be regions with a demonstrably objective existence. Different sets of regions were produced, some based on sociocultural homogeneity, some on voting groupings in the United Nations, and some on membership of international organisations. It all seemed most impressive. But this was 1967; quantification was all the thing – the more mind-numbingly complicated the better. This was the time when insecure social sciences were seeking to justify their existence by proclaiming themselves to be 'proper' sciences and backing up the claim by affecting scientific methods. Looking back, I am not sure whether this factor analysis and Q analysis taught us much about the regions of the world that we had not known or needed to know – but it certainly said plenty about the current state of the social sciences.

After being in decline for around a quarter of a century, geopolitics began to experience a revival. According to Hepple (1986, p. 521): 'in the last decade geopolitics has crept back into use, and geopolitical analysis of both global and regional problems has become more common'. He thought that this return to favour was due to diverse reasons, including the need for better forms of analysis to interpret the increasingly complex and multipolar world and the fact that policy-makers like Kissinger and Nixon chose to dabble in geopolitics, and raised its popularity and fashionability. Geographers, he thought, had a valuable role to play, but they should be more historically and politically sensitive than some of their predecessors. His concluding words anticipated the rise of critical geopolitics:

> An . . . important task is the historical and critical critique of geopolitics. Geopolitics must come to terms with its past, and examine the nature of its discourse. It is somewhat remarkable that geopolitics has not so far attracted more attention from those interested in social theory in human

> geography, for geopolitics is probably the outstanding example of a set of concepts originating in geographical analysis that has been absorbed into social and political practice. (ibid., p. 534)

Critical geopolitics

In the early 1970s one might have predicted with some confidence that, while political geography perhaps had brightening prospects, there would be very little future for geopolitics, which seemed destined to become no more than a colourful, risqué and rather wayward chapter in the history of geographical thinking. In the event, geopolitics has undergone a revival following the emergence of a new approach known as 'critical geopolitics' (though geopolitical research not rooted in social theory has also prospered). Students encountering the approach for the first time may be somewhat confused as to who or what is being criticised – and why, while the various biographers of the movement appear to disagree as to what was the seminal work. Their sense of confusion may not be eased on reading:

> A critical geopolitics is one that refuses the spatial topography of First World and Third World, North and South, state and state, its emphasis is on the precariousness of these perspectival identities and the increasing rarefaction of geopolitical identities. To frames it juxtaposes flows, to imaginations it juxtaposes vertigos. It withdraws organizing perspectival frames . . . and undermines the subject that it is supposed to know. (O Tuathail 1994a, pp. 231–2)

Those not completely bemused by such intellectual pyrotechnics may have grasped that critical geopolitics is concerned with upsetting established ideological apple carts. Elsewhere, O Tuathail (1994c) provides a more extended explanation. Presented as an approach rather than as a theoretical system, critical geopolitics is rooted in the poststructural movement which arose in France in the 1960s and involved thinkers such as J. Derrida (b.1930) and M. Foucault (1926–84), who followed different routes when applying 'deconstruction' to unsettle truth claims. O Tuathail allocates three dimensions to the approach or project of critical geopolitics. The first dimension is associated with the deconstruction of traditions of geopolitical thinking, in other words, revising and re-evaluating the ways in which the history of the discipline has been presented. The second dimension concerns an attempt to engage with the actual practice of statecraft, which has involved attempts to discover how those involved in statecraft have spatialised international politics. The third dimension challenges and displaces conventional understandings of geographical factors in global politics and questions the very meaning of 'place' and 'politics'. The definition of 'critical' remains open to question, for as O Tuathail (1994c, p. 314) observes: 'Within the history of geopolitics, some intellectuals could be simultaneously described as critical of geopolitics yet also geopoliticians; figures who defined their intellectual politics in opposition to geopolitics yet nevertheless worked within the conceptual infrastructure of geopolitics.'

A measure of vagueness persists. Critical theory, according to Cox (1981), is a theory which stands apart from the existing order and challenges it, though different writers take different views of the closeness of the associations between critical theory and postmodernism and postmodernism and post-structuralism, while some but not all work closely within the conceptual guidelines of the Frankfurt School and Jurgen Habermas (b.1929). While critical geopolitics brings some exciting and challenging new perspectives to bear upon the world and its ways, the terminology employed is often difficult and esoteric. It is certainly true that while the average butcher or baker could understand exactly what Mackinder was getting at, today the student really needs an understanding of post-structuralism to understand just what some critical geopoliticians are saying, and quite why they are saying it in that way.

Perhaps the first works to appear within the outlines of modern critical geopolitics were published by Agnew and Corbridge in 1989 and by Dalby in 1991, though O Tuathail wrote on the nature and language of the 'new geopolitics' in 1986. But the approach was anticipated in the writings of others, notably the French scholar, Yves Lacoste. A communist whose thinking soared above the ungainly Marxist analyses current in geography at the time, Lacoste was producing work in the 1970s which still seems remarkable fresh. He saw quite clearly that:

> Geography, as one mode of representing the world, is inevitably involved with ideological issues . . . Long before it was addressed to students, geography was addressed to kings, princes, diplomats, and military leaders. As a concise method of describing space, in both its human and physical characteristics (as we conventionally classify them), geography became transposed into terms amenable to management by the State, in the form of social organization and control, and also warfare. (Lacoste 1973, p. 1)

Lacoste considered that conventional geopolitics was tarnished by the manipulation of geographical evidence to suit the purposes of imperialism and conquest. It could develop out of lazy, misguided thinking, and, when adopted by the mass media, it could involve fraudulent, jingoistic hyperbole. Yet he also believed that it could be possible to produce a scientifically detached geopolitics, an alternative geopolitics that was capable of taking an elevated view of global affairs and engaging in objective enquiry which was untainted by association with state or empire. In exposing the motives and inconsistencies in established geopolitics, Lacoste anticipated the critical geopolitics of the 1990s, though whether all the new geopoliticians would accept the possibility of a clear-seeing, far-sighted geopolitics that was uncontaminated by human interests seems unlikely.

One of the objectives of critical geopolitics concerns the analysis of statecraft or foreign policy, which is a very relevant topic for geopolitical enquiry because its practitioners are involved in forming and appraising interpretations about spaces and places. Dodds has explained how foreign policy practices involve the development of 'script' and story-telling, the former being representations or collections of attributes, scenarios and descriptions which define places within the context of foreign policy and which may be identified by examining the utterances of policy-makers. He writes: 'Critical geopolitical writers attempt to investigate carefully how descriptions of places and people are stitched together to narrate and "explain" events. Foreign policy professionals are understood as the "master" story-tellers; their interpretations and utterances are crucial to the legitimation and justification of the practices of foreign policy' (Dodds 1994, p. 276).

Critical geopolitics diverges from geopolitics of the traditional kind, and in several respects its perspectives are fundamentally different, for instead of concentrating on identifying the influence of geographical factors on the formation of foreign policy, workers in this field will tend to explore how policy-makers construct their representations of the world and how these perceptions affect their interpretations of places. (Put in this fashion it becomes plain that there must be a strong, if not spoken, link between critical geopolitics and aspects of behavioural geography, which commanded great attention during the 1970s.) Critical geopolitics is a part of a much wider movement which includes International Relations and, indeed, all the social sciences: 'The aim of Critical Theory is the "restructuring of social and political theory" which involves both challenging positivist approaches to social science and proposing alternatives' (Brown 1994, p. 58).

Another quotation which, perhaps unintentionally, highlights the link between critical geopolitics and behavioural geography is provided by Slater in his exploration of the way that conceptualisations of development in the post-war period contain and express geopolitical imagination: 'new imaginations will need to include more self-reflexivity for the writer who imagines since, across the interface between development studies and political geography, the decolonization of the imagination is as critical as is the need for critique' (Slater 1993, p. 433). As Slater remarks, in its early years critical geopolitics has been concerned largely with the international or global level (though it could equally operate at the level internal to the state), and also concerned largely with the spatial representation of international politics by a whole state community of policy-makers (though it could consider the representations of individuals) (ibid.).

Critical geopolitics is an important offshoot of the introduction of critical social theory to the study of International Relations. Critical sociology set itself the task of unmasking the discrepancies between society's formal values and goals and the reality of the ways in which institutions actually behave. In this way society is obliged to confront these inadequacies, thus developing a critical awareness that can become a significant force for change. It does not constitute the only approach on offer in the area of political geography, and in the late 1980s and early 1990s in journals like *The Professional Geographer* and *Progress in Human Geography*, O Tuathail's advocacy of critical geopolitics has been contrasted with the positivist, problem-solving approaches of O'Loughlin and van der Wusten (O'Tuathail 1987). Meanwhile, Taylor's championing of a quite different world-systems approach (see p. 239) produced a triangular theoretical contest. In these respects the situation today does not seem to be greatly different from the picture in 1991, when Dalby (1991, p. 278) wrote:

> It would be very premature to make an argument that postmodern perspectives are the wave of the future, or the 'next stage' for political geography. In terms of substantive work it seems likely that world systems theory perspectives will continue to flourish . . . Quantitative and peace-science approaches are likely to continue too . . . in terms of global politics at least three schools are working on it!.

World-systems theory

In a sense world-system theory is the most global of all approaches because it places overriding emphasis on the existence of the world as a single system. World-system theory represented a reaction to theories about development which were current in the 1950s and 1960s, and it offers a penetrating questioning of many of the traditional assumptions of International Relations. The body of theory arose from the writings of André Gunder Frank, Samir Amin and, particularly,

Immanuel Wallerstein. Wallerstein (1983) expressed a belief that geography did not exist – and so the chances that world-system concepts would exert much influence upon geographers must have seemed remote in the earlier part of the 1980s. Nevertheless, these ideas were introduced to geographers by Taylor in 1986 and subsequently developed to provide the organisational framework for his work in political geography. Meanwhile, the same ideas were being applied by Knox and Agnew (1989) to produce an influential introduction to the theory and practice of economic geography.

Two types of 'dualism' in development studies were opposed by the world-system theorists. Firstly, they opposed the idea that 'under-developed' countries could achieve modernisation if resources could be shifted from the traditional sector of their economies into the modern sector. Secondly, they opposed the tactics of the communist parties which favoured alliances with the national bourgeoisies of the developing countries against feudal landowners and foreign multinational corporations. They countered such dualist interpretations with a 'monist' analysis, claiming that there were not two different economic sectors, however defined, but a single whole, the capitalist world economy.

This emphasis on the oneness of the world ran counter to the thinking that was current in the 1950s and 1960s. Then it was assumed that the escape from 'underdevelopment' involved each 'backward' country in following the path to progress which the developed countries had already charted. Frank and his supporters in the 'dependency' school argued that the reasons for underdevelopment were not to be found by looking at Third World societies individually and in isolation: their problems were a direct result of their relationship with the developed countries. The theme of global interaction was being advanced meanwhile in the realm of International Relations, where the world had traditionally been regarded as being fragmented amongst a multiplicity of free-standing sovereign entities. The world-systems approach is one which minimises the importance of individual states, arguing that their subordination to the world system is so great that it is unrealistic to regard them in isolation.

Like Marxism, from which it derives much of its inspiration, world-system theory is a holistic doctrine which offers all-embracing analyses of economics, history and politics. Although Wallerstein highlights the existence of the world as a single system, he regards it as being divided into three components; the core, the periphery and the semi-periphery. Capitalism provides the system with its logic, with capitalism being exported by European imperialism and imposed upon the world, so that from the sixteenth century a single world system had come into being. Every state, according to the theory, must be located in one or other of the positions in the capitalist world economy, though this location is not fixed for all time. The core has a membership of those countries which have industrialised, engaged in commerce and established advanced systems of farming. As the core countries competed for markets in the periphery, the global division of labour came into being, with the core countries providing first manufactured goods and then machine tools and infrastructure, like railways or telephone systems. The division of labour was founded on exploitative relationships between the core and the periphery, with the countries of the core having capital-intensive production and those of the periphery having narrowly based economies dependent upon labour-intensive industry and the employment of coerced labour in the production of cash crops.

Within this system, which takes its motive power from competition between the different nation-states, the semi-periphery has a crucial role to play. It occupies a middle position between the periphery and the core, and states can rise or fall, depending upon their economic fortunes, from one position to another. The members of the semi-periphery have characteristics shared with states in both of the other positions, being both the victims of exploitation and the exploiters of others, so that while the core exploits both the periphery and the semi-periphery, the semi-periphery is also exploiting the periphery. The presence of a semi-periphery is necessary to bring stability to the highly exploitative system because it prevents the formation of an anti-core alliance embracing all non-core countries. As Taylor (1993b, p. 11) explains: 'in any situation of inequality three tiers of interaction are better than two tiers of confrontation. Those at the top will always manoeuvre for the "creation" of a three tier structure whereas those at the bottom will emphasize the two tiers of "them and us"'. The semi-periphery has a particularly important role because it is the most dynamic position and serves as the incubator for change. During recessions, economic restructuring takes place and zones rise or sink through the semi-periphery. It is at such times that the class struggle is most intense, and supporters of world-systems analysis interpret unrest in Latin America and Eastern Europe during the 1980s in terms of stresses in the periphery during a phase of restructuring.

The three-tiered structure is one of the basic elements of the world economy, and Wallerstein identified two more. Firstly, there is the existence of a single world market which operates according to capitalist principles, causing competition and price cutting between different producers and fostering uneven economic development. He believes that the capitalist world system is driven by the goal of ceaseless accumulation, the process by which capital is reproduced at an ever growing scale through the reinvestment of profits. This results in phases of growth and the periods of stagnation when the restructuring of the world economy takes place.

Secondly, there is a multiple state system, for while the market became global as a result of European colonialism, political power remained fragmented. This 'inter-state system' is essential for the survival of the world economy, for if one power were able to extend total global domination the system would be transformed into a 'world-empire'. Although this has not happened, at certain times different states have been able to exert a commanding influence over the economic, political and military arenas and thus to act as hegemonic powers. From the mid-eighteenth century to the late nineteenth century England, having eclipsed the Netherlands and then France in mercantilist contests, became the hegemonic power, while after the Second World War the US commanded a position of enormous influence and was able to impose a relative order on the world system, until the onset of a decline resulting from increasing competition from Europe and Japan and the costs resulting from the Cold War.

Wallerstein's world-system theory borrows heavily from Marxism, leaning towards Trotskyism in some respects and diverging from Marxism in others. Like Marxism, it predicts that events will culminate in crisis, although Wallerstein does not share the sure conviction that socialism will arise victorious from the ashes of the capitalist order. Instead, he suggests that either socialism will triumph or else some new mode of production will be created to perpetuate the inequalities of capitalism.

World-systems theory has had an enormous influence upon modern thought, but it has also encountered a number of criticisms. Its emphasis on the interrelated nature of the world has been widely welcomed, but critics like Cooper (1981) have suggested that the insistence upon the global perspective is over-extreme. To this Taylor (1986, p. 286) replies that: 'Just because we are dealing with a world economy does not mean that local forces are any less important . . . What it does mean is that they must be seen in a new light, as part of a larger unfolding system.'

Dale (1984) has questioned the assumptions of the theory in terms of the ways it emphasises the essential similarity of nation-states. Firstly, he questions the assumption that the pre-capitalist history of states is irrelevant. If this were the case, neither the Norman conquest nor

Magna Carta would be significant to an understanding of contemporary England, or, as Dale (ibid., pp. 200–1) puts it:

> What this assumption means is that capitalism carries all before it. It sweeps away, neutralizes or ignores all existing institutions, ideologies, groupings etc . . . Taking the assumption at face value would mean, for instance, that there were no relevant pre-capitalist differences between, say, Japan and Britain, and that such differences as we can see between them in, say, production relations, result only from the impact of capitalism.

Secondly, he attacks the assumption that the capitalist world economy has the same effect on all the territories that it penetrates, and he asks whether we would expect a (lastingly) different impact on nation states whose first experience of the capitalist world economy came through the medium of British, as opposed to French, Portuguese or Dutch colonialism? He goes on to add that this is plainly a complicated and difficult question to answer – and this is his point. Thirdly, he questions what he calls 'the assumption of the normative superiority of the indigenous' or the unjustified and unprovable claim that were it not for the cruel intervention of the capitalist world economy the world would be a better place, full of independent nations.

The philosophies of both Marx and Wallerstein are odd mixtures of supposedly scientific principles and judgements about what ought to be. Both are associated with structuralist thinking (that is to say they are both associated with the idea that expert intellectual enquiry can reveal enduring structures underlying human designs yet invisible to the uninitiated, and with the anti-humanist belief that man is what structures beyond his conscious will or control compel him to be). This structuralism has been attacked by Corbridge (1991, p. 205) in terms of what it excludes: 'The main structures of the world economy, we are told . . . are the world class system, the core/periphery hierarchy, the inter-state system, and the world market. (This is fair enough, but there is not a lot of room here for ecology, territory or demography, let alone agency or culture).' In the same fiercely hostile review, Corbridge describes the 'bleak world-view . . . throughout which the ghost of an agent-less structuralism is resurrected in its worst form . . . A monolithic and deeply unattractive capitalism is continually opposed to a prospective and attractive socialism with no thought for the failings of the latter or the possibility of reform within the former' (ibid., p. 206).

A more restrained though highly influential critique of world-system theory was provided by Worsley in 1983. He questions whether the 'capitalist world-system' is in reality a system, capitalist and global.

Box 8.2 *Kondratieff cycles*

In 1926, the Russian economist, N.D. Kondratieff, identified long waves composed of a phase of rising prices followed by a phase of deflation. He studied English trade and believed that periods of expansion could be recognised occurring on a cycle of about 50 years. The existence and character of these long waves have been debated, but those who believe in them attribute them to technological advances and believe that important innovations have tended to be bunched together. Thus a cycle which is said to have peaked around 1980 was supposedly associated with innovations in microelectronics, information systems, biotechnology and robotics. Even so, the recognition of these cycles is by no means cut and dried: the 1989 and 1994 editions of Knox and Agnew's *Geography of the World Economy* reveal some quite glaring discrepancies. The 1989 edition has the fourth cycle peaking in 1966 rather than 1980, with 1980 actually being located quite close to the *bottom* of a trough. Equally, innovations involving motor vehicles and petrochemicals were firstly associated with the 1966 peak, whereas in the 1994 edition they are linked to the 1920 peak.

Supporters argue that the clusters of innovation cause the economy to expand, with the high costs of introducing the new technologies causing a 20-year-long phase of high inflation. The phases of economic expansion are separated by periods when gains are consolidated, and when the new technologies have been established and have become routine there is a deflationary phase as the economy dips towards recession.

World-systems theory has incorporated the concept of Kondratieff cycles, attributing the cycles of expansion and stagnation to the operation of the capitalist system where decisions are made by a multitude of independent entrepreneurs. During the phases of growth, all the entrepreneurs see an advantage in investing in the installation of the new technology, but the result of all this investment is overproduction, which brings the growth phase to an end. During the phases of stagnation, the opportunities to prosper are considered to be poor and so the entrepreneurs underinvest in the production process. Meanwhile, the economy is being restructured to prepare for the assimilation of the next cluster of innovations which will initiate the next phase of economic expansion. During the stagnation phases, zones, states and areas are moving up and down through the semi-periphery, which has no fixed geographical form and is in a state of flux. And it is at times such as this, when economic restructuring of the semi-periphery takes place against a background of economic recession, that the class struggle occurs in its most intense form. In this way the semi-periphery becomes the focus for political change.

Writing at the time when the Cold War was still very much a going concern, Worsley pointed out that instead of wholeness one found a world that was fundamentally divided between two competing socio-economic systems, capitalism and communism: 'Hence for most of us, the distinction between "capitalism" and "Communism" is the first pluralist distinction with which we commonly operate' (Worsley 1983, pp. 513–14). True to the Trotskyist tradition, Wallerstein refused to countenance the notion that socialism could exist in a single country or group of countries rather than on a global basis (for Trotskyites have devoted amazing energies to their internal disputes about whether the USSR was state capitalist or some sort of a deformed workers' state). But Worsley points out that whatever the Marxist nuances of the debate may be 'the fact of the matter is that these countries are organized on quite different lines from capitalist societies in every institutional sphere and it is these internal arrangements that constitute their distinctive character' (ibid., p. 521). With their command economies, collectivistic production and the distribution of essential goods based more on need than demand, the Warsaw Pact countries formed a very distinctive group. One might argue that the fall of the Berlin Wall and the fragmentation of the USSR now renders such objections irrelevant. But world-systems theory is an all-embracing and all-pervading analysis, so that if the theory was wrong in 1983 it must also be wrong today.

The difficulty with holistic theories is that one is expected to accept them in their entirety rather than pick and choose those ideas and outlooks which seem most attractive or relevant to the understanding of a particular problem. When a holistic theory is demonstrably unworkable it should, according to its own terms, be jettisoned in toto, though there have been inumerable attempts to patch up the widening holes in Marxism. In the section which follows, apparent failures of the world-systems approach to explain the vital contemporary process of globalisation are described, and this question presents the theory with a major – some say terminal – challenge.

There is no doubt that world-systems theory can be applied to produce valuable work in political geography. Taylor used it to provide the organisational framework for a highly successful textbook: 'A crucial advantage of this decision was that the "scale problem", so debilitating of other texts, became part of the theoretical structure itself' (Taylor 1993b, p. xii). His work played a major part in the revitalisation of the subject in the late 1980s. More recently, a conference held in Washington DC in 1993 has resulted in the publication of an important book (Knox and Taylor 1995) which explores the relationship between research into world cities and world-systems analysis. There can be no doubt that world-system theory will continue to be adopted as a theoretical framework for work in political geography for some years to come. In this respect it has succeeded where other systems-based approaches, which seemed to harbour so much useful potential for application in political geography during the 1970s, have failed.

Globalisation and world unity

Globalisation has been making its stealthy advance for some time, but society has only quite recently become aware of the crucial transformations which it is imposing upon the world. It provides us with the most insistent reminders of the oneness of this world, while confronting us with uncertainties and fear as we struggle to appraise its consequences for the coming generations. There is, however, a long and respectable tradition which has the political unification of the globe as its ultimate goal, although the contribution of geographers to the debate on global unity has been modest. This may seem surprising when the potential contribution that geographical expertise could make is taken into account.

Some globalising tendencies have existed for many years, but the roots of the globalisation process can be traced to the new economic conditions associated with the post-1945 peace and the American partial hegemony. People experiencing the post-war political and economic environment in the West were developing new habits of thinking. They began to think less in terms of the performance of their particular national economies and to attach more significance to the trading conditions governing the expansion of the world economy. Trade expanded rapidly and fairly continuously, and as it did so, the economies of the Western world became interlinked, while transnational corporations began to emerge as significant actors upon the economic scene: 'In 1960 the top 200 global industrial corporations accounted for some 17.7 per cent of GNP in the non-planned economies. By 1980 their share had increased to 28.6 per cent. Transnational firms based in the United States accounted for 80 per cent of its exports and over half its imports' (Camilleri and Falk 1992, p. 70). As the trend towards globalisation continued, labour, production and credit became more mobile as the huge corporations explored ways of cutting production costs and maximising output. It was realised that modern manufacturing had few demands for skilled and experienced factory labour forces and could be shifted around the globe in the pursuit of cost advantages.

In the early 1970s the oil crisis resulted in a severe recession in the West, leading to a restructuring of the world economy. Firms collapsed, merged, were taken over and recombined, and in the course of this activity the merging of enterprises based in different states set the trend for a more transnational industrial complexion, as described by Camilleri and Falk: 'Between 1973 and 1978 European firms were involved in 4,612 mergers, and in the same period 623 US firms were taken over by Canadian, European and Japanese firms. In 1979 alone and again in 1980, more than 600 US firms were taken over by foreign transnationals' (ibid., p. 73). Already the tendency towards global money markets had become apparent, with the leading US banks increasing their influence in Latin America and establishing footholds in Europe and the Far East during the 1960s, and during the 1970s and 1980s the dramatic expansion of the Eurocurrency market undermined the ability of national governments to control the flow of money. Meanwhile, the revolution in information technology provided the necessary equipment for a vast and almost instantaneous global traffic in investment and speculation. In 1987 an average of about $420 billion crossed the floor of the world's foreign exchanges each day and by 1995 this figure had risen to about $1000 billion dollars a day. As national governments found control of the financial markets slipping away, it was ironic that many of the innovations which provided globalisation with its technical base were the products of national governmental initiatives. Satellite communications and the associated rocketry were the offspring of the 'Space Race' between the two superpowers; the Internet was created by the Pentagon in the late 1970s and divested in 1986, while the International Monetary Fund and the World Bank which have moulded the form of global finance and trading were formed for intergovernmental relations.

We have already encountered globalisation in its role as one of the forces which combine to undermine the authority of the state; now we encounter it as a force imposing a form of unity upon the world. It involves 24-hour global money markets, revolutions in information and communications technology and gigantic business corporations whose comings and goings are hard to trace. It has been involved in the creation of new power units in the global landscape, with the largest US company, General Electric, having assets of $251 billion, a sum greater than the national assets of all but the world's ten largest states.

Not all the transnational corporations are gigantic, nor do the TNCs always perform as discrete entities. Knox (1995, p. 4) has described how they are bound in associations by elaborate networks of joint ventures, cross-licensing research, shared ownership, and so on: 'Through such arrangements, for example, Chrysler is linked to Mitsubishi, Samsung, Fiat, and Volkswagen; GM to Toyota, Isuzu, and Suzuki; Ford to Mazda, Jaguar, and BMW; Nissan to Volkswagen and Daewoo; Mitsubishi to Hyundai; Renault to Volvo.' Emmott (1993, p. 41) has described how the development of a stable, global business has been thwarted by fierce competition between the new entrants to the global markets, which also compete with the older American multinationals and with local firms, while even more importantly: 'the past decade has enabled small firms to become global, both as a way to grow rapidly and as a way simply to spread more widely. Most notably in the computer business, firms like Compaq and Dell became global almost before they had become big players in the domestic market.'

Though globalisation has been linked to the formation of great transnational corporations, there are those who argue that it can encourage smallness, and small- and medium-sized firms have increased rapidly in recent years both in the manufacturing and service sectors, often combining to pool services, share research costs and spread risks. The futurologist, John Naisbitt (1994), has coined what he calls 'the global paradox': the bigger the world economy, the more powerful its smallest player. He argues that: 'Big companies are breaking up and becoming confederations of small, entrepreneurial companies in order to survive . . . At once the global economy is growing while the size of the parts is shrinking . . . In the years ahead all big companies will find it increasingly difficult to compete with smaller, speedier, more innovative companies' (ibid., p. 50). The removal of barriers to international trade has made it easier for smaller companies to gain access to markets, while the deregulation and globalisation of financial markets give the smaller companies better access to capital than ever before. At the same time, in a situation where consumers demand the most up-to-date personalised or designer products rather than the old cheap, and standardised mass-produced factory goods, the small firm enjoys much more flexibility to switch production than does its large competitor.

An important feature of the TNCs, which are as yet far from being endangered species, concerns their footloose nature and readiness to switch production around the world to exploit quite small and transient cost advantages. As Reynolds has shown, this feature constitutes a powerful problem for the world-systems approach:

> While historically it may be true that semi-peripheral states have been the more innovative politically and economically, the rise of flexible production and global Fordism over the past two decades have seriously undermined the ability of core states to regulate the capital–wage labour relationship within their boundaries and, as a result have also begun to undermine the core/periphery relationship itself. (Reynolds 1992, pp. 396–7)

He adds that the apparent demise of Fordism in the core, coupled with the rise of state corporatism involving aggressive state intervention in the national economy (which world-systems theory associates with the semi-periphery) in parts of the periphery like South Korea and Taiwan, may spell the swan song for the world-systems approach itself (ibid., p. 397). As an indication of the significance of the trend, in the

Box 8.3 *The Pacific rim and Asian values*

The effects of globalisation are not confined to the commercial and financial arenas, but may spill over into cultural areas, as evidenced by the currently fashionable idea that to survive in conditions of intense globalised competition, Western societies should adopt what are referred to as 'Asian values'. The four East Asian 'tiger' or 'dragon' economies, Hong Kong, Singapore, South Korea and Taiwan, have all experienced recent export-led growth, while Thailand, Malaysia and Indonesia have become significant forces in manufacturing. Kennedy (1994, p. 197) writes that: 'Because of this staggering level of development, economists in East Asia invoke the image of the "flying geese," with Japan the lead bird, followed by the East Asian NIEs [Newly Industrialised Economies], the larger South-East Asian states, and so on.' He believes that these economically successful societies contain certain basic characteristics which, taken together, help to explain their growth. Firstly, he mentions an emphasis on learning and educational competitiveness deriving from Confucian educational traditions (12 of the 14 members of the 1989 cabinet of Taiwan had obtained PhDs abroad). Secondly, the countries concerned had high levels of national savings, with fiscal measures, low levels of personal taxation and import controls being employed to nurture a savings culture, thus making funds available for investment in domestic manufacturing and commerce. Thirdly, there were stable, authoritarian governments, and fourthly a commitment to production for export. Stubbs (1994, p. 366) emphasised factors more of a geopolitical nature in explaining the coherence of the region when he wrote that: 'the arc of countries at the eastern edge of the Asian land mass fronting the Pacific Ocean has been moulded into a region by the interplay of American and Japanese geo-political and geo-economic interests . . . The combination of America's commitment to containing Asian communism and Japanese companies' use of the region as an export platform to maintain their world-wide competitiveness has resulted in the emergence of an increasingly interdependent set of economies that may be set alongside the European Community and North American Free Trade Area as a key region in the rapidly changing global economy.' He believes that the main factors bringing the parts of the region together have been investment and trade involving Japanese firms and Japanese government aid building on a platform created by American aid donated during the Cold War campaign against Communism in Asia. Pacific rim state policies have tended to be interventionist in the economic and financial arenas and sometimes repressive in political terms, but to assume low profiles with regard to welfare. Schwartz (1994, p. 272) writes that: 'Industrialisation in Taiwan and South Korea has many institutional pieces found in Latin America and Eastern Europe. As in Latin America, the state played a major role in the industrialization process. The state started many basic industries, and state or state-controlled banks channeled investment funds to the private manufacturing sector. The state also controlled access to the domestic market, using tariffs and quotas to exclude imports and capital controls to limit TNC access. And the state systematically repressed labor.'

In the West it has been argued that to compete with the South-East Asians, Western workers will have to become more like them. These arguments appeal strongly to right-wing interests, particularly those linked to the UK

Box 8.3 *continued*

government, who desire a reduction in wages, workers' protection and the welfare state. Such interests would not only welcome a state redesigned according to a generalised South-East Asian model to become more authoritarian, more hostile to immigration, yet far less inclined to extract taxes to support a state welfare system, but they also argue for the adoption of 'Asian values' which they associate, above all, with an emphasis upon the supposed obligations of the family as opposed to the duties of the state. They believe that by transferring the responsibilities of the Western welfare state to the individual families, great savings in state expenditure could be made, which would allow a sharp fall in levels of taxation, releasing funds for investment. However, one cannot realistically compare the populations of the East and West; Europe has an ageing population which is set to decline in numbers, and, for example, almost one-fifth of France's population is aged over 60. In contrast to the pronounced 'greying' of Europe, the South East Asian countries have young, vigorous populations: the needs for state health, caring services and pensions are far less in these places. Equally, Asiatic societies are not alike, and there is no single set of Asian cultural values. The South-East Asian countries accommodate multicultural societies, each culture having its own distinct characteristics. The Buddhists of Thailand are noted for their tolerance, the overseas Chinese for their remarkable business acumen, which often gives them incomes several times those of their neighbours, and for their obsessive fascination with luck and gambling: 'For centuries the Thais and immigrant Chinese have coexisted with remarkably little strain [in Thailand], with neither religion (Buddhism), social customs (drinking and gambling) nor culinary habits (pork-eating) creating distinctions. In Muslim Malaysia or Indonesia and Brunei, these divergent habits count a lot against Chinese; in Buddhist Thailand or Roman Catholic Philippines they fit much better into the dominant social ethos' (Clad 1991, p. 150).

period 1963–81 the export of manufactured goods from the Third World rose at the rate of 46.87 per cent per annum (Dicken 1986, p. 38). New technologies had led to a deskilling of work, so that the low-cost and overabundant labour forces of the newly industrialising countries of the periphery could be employed to perform tasks which were or would have been previously located in the industrialised countries of the core.

As yet, there is still scope for debate about the true nature and implications of globalisation. Some commentators believe that what should properly be regarded as accelerating internationalisation is being mistaken for globalisation, and Hutton (1995) remarks that: 'Ford may produce a global car, but 80 per cent of its fixed assets are in the US; even the "global" Pepsi Cola and McDonald's have more than half of their fixed assets in the US' (Hutton 1995). He also remarks that the 'globalisation myth' has become a source of delight to the right and one of despair for the left:

> The globalisation thesis is no more than an argument deployed by the right to cow the left – but it is in danger of rebounding on the right. Because while it may serve the political purpose of persuading workers in the industrialised West that they have to accept ever-worsening pay and conditions, and social democrats that welfare systems are costly burdens that must be privatised, it also denudes the few international institutions that exist of the political and financial support necessary to upgrade their capacity to shape and manage current trends'. (ibid.)

So globalisation could become a self-fulfilling prophecy, for if governments become convinced that they are powerless to act in the face of the power of global capitalism, then they may fail to impose the essential policing and regulation of global financial markets.

Other researchers regard globalisation as a very real and powerful tendency. The political scientist, David Held (1991), has identified what he believes to be the three main socio-political consequences of the process. Firstly, it concerns the way that the economic, political, legal and military interconnectedness will impose change upon the sovereign state from above. Secondly, it concerns the manner in which 'local and regional nationalisms' are eroding the nation-state from below. Thirdly, it concerns the ways that the interconnection of the parts of the world produces chains of interlocking political decisions which in turn have their impacts upon national political systems. The first and third points are self-explanatory, but the second requires more amplification since there might seem to be a contradiction between the concepts of globalisation on the one hand and localised nationalism on the other. This, in fact, lies in the territory of Naisbitt's global paradox and he expresses it in the form: 'The more universal we become, the more tribal we act', and he explains: 'Minority languages all over the world are achieving a new status as people hold more tightly to their heritage as ballast to the creation of a larger, more economically homogeneous world' (Naisbitt 1994, p. 51).

Held has explored the political consequences of globalisation, while Anthony Giddens has outlined the sociological implications. He explains that it would be wrong to understand globalisation only in terms of global economic integration: 'Globalisation really refers to a new agenda for our lives – an agenda in which distant happenings directly affect local life, and in which what we do as individuals can have global consequences' (Giddens 1995). In many quarters including that of the 'New New Right' in the US this has encouraged the notion that the only kind of government that can exist in an era of globalisation is a minimalist government, shorn of some roles, like welfare, with others slimmed down and with many former governmental decisions being taken by market forces. Giddens believes that an antidote to these right-wing forces should be found by exploring new ties between the regional and the global. This would require governments to filter democracy downwards as well as upwards: 'A global society moving towards greater sexual equality cannot be one in which traditional family systems remain intact. Yet it might become a society which finds ways of reconciling equality and solidarity in family life; and governments can help to promote such an aim' (ibid.).

However, it would be rash to assume that reason will prevail amid the stresses imposed on state-bound societies by globalisation. According to Camilleri and Falk (1992, p. 254):

> the state will function as the principal arena of conflict, giving expression to and institutionalizing the tensions between competing values, interests and organizational principles. It will continue to provide a highly visible stage on which will be played out class and power antagonisms related to the restructuring of global economic processes and the ensuing patterns of stratification, inclusion and exclusion.

Within the state there may be a tug o' war between those who seek to explore and develop more localised patterns of community, locality and autonomy and those who cling to the established traditions of nation, state and sovereignty. While emphasising these tensions, they also downgrade the significance of conflicts between state sovereignty and international interdependence, though recent experience in post Maastricht Europe might argue otherwise. Within the British Tory party such stresses approached terminal proportions in the mid-1990s, though the arguments could be fraught with contradictions: 'To the Tory Eurosceptics, anything more than a common market Europe is a threat to national government. Yet national sovereignty is eroded more than anything else by the uncontrolled spread of market forces' (Giddens 1995).

Globalisation should not be about the obliteration of individuality, locality or regionalism by monolithic forces, but rather about relationships between the world and its components. By definition it is only possible because all the world's parts are engaged in an interactive dialogue. So while it may terminate some established avenues of opportunity, it will bring others into being. Globalisation is not a policy but rather a phenomenon which has resulted from the clustering of a host of technological innovations, economic tendencies and entrepreneurial acts. Globalisation of a different kind is an aspiration proclaimed by members of a minority who believe that the best or the only way of achieving peace, justice and the rational management of global affairs, challenges and resources is by the adoption of some new form of world order, frequently a world government. The fact that such a dramatic and drastic development has never appeared to be a forseeable probability is insufficient justification for geographers' disregard of the topic. No specialists are better placed to advise on the potential and pitfalls of world government in terms of resource management and distribution, or better able to take an overview of issues like environmental pollution, demography, urbanisation, transport, inequality and their interactions. The tradition is honourable and quite long. Amongst the earlier philosophers, none has had a greater influence on geographical thinking than Immanuel Kant (1724–1804). His ideas have conditioned the understanding of the place of geography within the sciences, the relationship between geography and history, the French possibilist school of geography, the Chicago school of sociology, critical theory and even postmodernism (May 1970). Kant (1795) was also an advocate of a 'universal international state' which would impose peace upon the territorial struggles of warlike humanity (Kant 1795).

It is arguable that political geography's most fruitful associations are those with International Relations, and within this subject a powerful world order movement has emerged (see pp. 163 *et seq.*). The globalists reject the other two main perspectives. They believe that the realist views are increasingly anachronistic and more appropriate to an understanding of European diplomatic history in the nineteenth century. They maintain that military power is less potent as a means of obtaining success in international affairs and that cooperation can play a role as important as that of power politics. They perceive a world in which there is a growing interdependence between the actors, which include international organisations, TNCs and guerilla groupings as well as states, and an increasingly global aspect to the nature of the problems that confront them. They believe, too, that such problems may only be solved by cooperation and the adoption of global management systems and they tend to be optimistic about the prospects for reform. An early articulation of the globalist case for global interdependence in the environmental, economic and human rights realms was provided by Pirages in 1978.

Deriving from the changing perspectives in International Relations have been themes concerned with the problems of world order (Dalby 1991, p. 263). Researchers who were deeply concerned about problems of ecological destruction, peace and human rights combined in the World Order Models Project (WOMP), the Committee for a Just

Box 8.4 *Large-scale historical change*

As defined by Little (1994, p. 9), 'Large-scale historical change refers to transformational movements in world history: for example, the demise of antiquity, the rise of feudalism and the emergence of modern capitalism.' Interest in the topic has grown fairly recently in relation to the fall of the Berlin Wall and the Soviet bloc and the identification of a new world order. O'Loughlin (1990, p. 322) noted that: '1989 will occupy a leading position as one of the most important years of the century. Global divisions and expectations about relations between states, established in 1945, were shaken to their foundations by events in central and eastern Europe.' He predicted that in political geography as in other disciplines, this would lead to a questioning of basic principles. It was at this time that an employee in the US State Department, Francis Fukuyama (1989), published a paper on 'the end of history' which stimulated an enormous discussion of his claim that the US had emerged victorious from the confrontation between the two superpowers, the liberal democratic values of the West had triumphed and the world would now experience accelerating economic interaction while war would recede. A little later, O'Loughlin warned about the need to distinguish between presumed defining moments in history and fadism: 'In 1987, Paul Kennedy's thesis of "American decline" was the rage, followed in 1988 by the "revivalist" argument that the evidence to support Kennedy's position did not exist. In 1989, Francis Fukuyama's thesis on the "End of history" got most of the attention, especially with its declarations that the USA was the only superpower left after the cold wars and that major global war was unthinkable. After August 2, 1990, the day Iraq invaded Kuwait, the "end of history" was converted into its corollary, that the USA could and should reconstitute a "new world order"' (O'Loughlin 1991, p. 322). Various systems of thought, including concepts of hegemonic cycles or world-systems analysis, can be applied to explore world order issues, but what all the great changes have revealed is a shortage of intellectual tools suitable for the analysis of change.

World Peace and the Global Civilisation Project and published their work in the journal *Alternatives*. To those who would deny the validity of normative views, Dalby replies:

> Asking questions about future possible worlds and the kinds of changes currently happening in global politics moves the focus of attention to ask questions about democracy, justice, ecology, and survival which are pressing political concerns that conventional international relations scholarship cannot comprehensively address. WOMP's overall significance may be to challenge the conventional categories of international relations by exploring beyond these limitations and investigating attempts to imagine politics in other ways. (ibid., p. 264)

Groom and Powell agree that the issue of world government is important and suggest that the period around 1960 marks an evolution in world politics wherein the concept has become increasingly relevant, but they believe that the interpretations are as yet only loosely formed: 'The growth of issues of global governance is a characteristic of our times. But global governance has an amorphous quality so that there is, as yet, no conception of a whole. In short, global governance is a theme in need of a focus' (Groom and Powell 1994, p. 81).

Probably the most convincing argument in favour of regarding any exploration of the case for world government as an exercise in futility has concerned questions of culture and political perception. For, since the mature and somewhat similar nations of Western Europe are currently experiencing great difficulty in accepting the quasi-federal institutional changes necessary for the formation of a more coherent regional grouping, how might one suppose that the diverse cultures of the world could countenance a global integration? Nevertheless, within the geographical literature a serious exploration of issues of global culture has recently emerged.

In the course of this century, perceptions of the world have changed immensely, and as Sturmer Smith and Hannam (1994, p. 74) explain: 'To talk of the world as a place is to imply that there is a commonality. The whole idea of a global economy and global politics makes an assumption that there is, to some extent, a global culture – that certain meanings can be understood worldwide.' They point out that the globalisation of culture could be interpreted in terms of dependency theory or world-systems theory. According to such a perspective, the wealthy nations could be seen as importing the produce and commodities of the world, while the flow of information proceeds in the reverse direction, with the major capitalist centres distributing news, data, literature, films, TV programmes, religion or academic texts to the remainder of the world. They show, too, that the powerful newsbrokers determine which news 'counts'; in 1986, for example, CNN's 'Headline News' drew 77 per cent of its items from the US, 6 per cent from Britain and Western Europe, only 2 per cent from Japan and a mere 0.5 per cent from the USSR (ibid., pp. 86–7).

If the advance of a hegemonic culture could be interpreted in terms of dependency theory, it could also be invoked in support of the rival modernisation theory. Featherstone (1993, p. 170) explains this as follows:

> One perspective on the process of globalization which was accorded a good deal of credibility until recently was that of Americanization. Here a global culture was seen as being formed through the economic and political

> domination of the United States which thrust its hegemonic culture into all parts of the world . . .That people in a wide range of countries around the world were watching *Dallas* or *Sesame Street* and that Coca-Cola cans and ring-pulls were to be found all around the world, was taken as evidence of this process.

However, he invokes postmodern developments, including the realisation that the non-Western world had histories of its own, to counteract the modernist assumption that history has a destiny and that Americanisation represents the destiny of global culture. He then turns to the assumption that, as defined by Little (1994, p. 9), 'Large-scale historical change refers to transformational moments in world history: for example, the demise of antiquity, the rise of feudalism and the emergence of modern capitalism'. Interest in the topic has grown fairly recently in relation to the fall of the Berlin Wall and the Soviet bloc and the identification of a new world order. O'Loughlin (1990, p. 420) noted that the density of contacts between nations will itself lead to a global culture and he emphasises the importance of distinguishing between the notion of a global culture and that of the nation-state. National cultures evolved in the face of strong pressures to create a coherent, homogenised common cultural identity and a global culture should in no manner be conceived as the culture of the nation-state writ large. It should not be assumed that increasing levels of contact with different cultures will produce more tolerant or cosmopolitan attitudes – it might in many cases lead 'to a retreat from the threat of cultural disorder into the security of ethnicity, traditionalism or fundamentalism, or the active assertion of the integrity of the national culture in global cultural prestige contests (for example the Olympic Games)' (ibid., p. 174). However, he thinks that it is also true that a global public opinion is beginning to emerge, as was evident in a worldwide convergence of attitudes towards events like the Lithuanian struggle for independence or the Gulf Crisis, which serve to demonstrate the existence of a world stage and the increasing tendency for the world to be regarded as one place.

The development of global culture and attitudes involve extremely complex and testing processes. At their best they can advance the progress of civilisation significantly. For as the world comes to be perceived as a locality – as a single place which is exposed and vulnerable to abuse – so it becomes more likely that the global ecological issues might at last receive the attention and action that they merit. Equally, the more that we incline to think in terms of a common humanity and less in terms of an 'us' and many 'thems', then the more we may be disposed to respect the humanity and rights of the vulnerable minority and the individual. Even so, such civilising attitudes will not be acquired in any simple and single process of conversion. Each stage in the advance towards a global culture will generate feelings of confusion and insecurity and be marked by processes of reaction and compensation, just as every encounter with the new and the different may require us to reappraise ourselves and our setting. As the middle classes in England have, during the last generation or so, experienced a new mobility associated with changes in the nature of employment, the transition has been marked by crises of identity, feelings of rootlessness and desires to manufacture home-places out of country-style pine, designer-built cottage gardens, Laura Ashley curtains, a clutter of lavender-scented knick-knacks from the National Trust shop and bookshelves stocked with whimsical and ill-informed volumes about old country customs, characters and places to visit. If changes from the regional to the national scales of living can create such crises of identity in a territory as small as England, the psychological turmoil associated with adopting a global culture would be immense.

Despite such difficulties, a progress in the direction of global values is undeniable, even if the precise destination remains debatable. Richard Falk, one of the most influential commentators on this globalism writes that: 'In effect, an emergent global ethos suggests the reality of a shared destiny for the human species and a fundamental unity across space and through time, built around the bioethical impulse of all human groups to *survive* and *flourish*' (Falk 1992, p. 198). However, 'For most people and leaders, this sense of shared destiny does not displace a persisting primary attachment to the state as a vehicle for aspiration and as an absolute, unconditional bastion of security' (ibid.), the attachment to the sovereign state being so deep-seated that the leaders of nuclear powers seem prepared to risk a 'nuclear winter' and the extinction of humanity in order to preserve state sovereignty. In the years to come, Earth and state will compete ever more strongly for our loyalty. The ecological need for a properly managed planet seems to be running ahead of the human ability to reform our political order in ways which may ensure a sustainable future for our species.

This increasingly repeated and insistent theme has been echoed once again in the report of the Commission on Global Governance (1995, p. 11):

> Mounting evidence indicates that human activities have adverse – and sometimes irreversible – environmental impacts, and that the world needs to manage its activities to keep the adverse outcomes within prudent bounds and to redress current imbalances. The links among poverty, population,

> consumption, and environment and the systemic nature of their interactions have become clearer. So has the need for integrated global approaches to their management and world-wide embrace of the discipline of sustainable development.

Specialists from the social sciences have contributed to the global debate, but geographers with invaluable expertise in the human or the physical aspects of their subject could and should consider issues of global management and planning. Our common plight compels us to think what was unthinkable.

■ *Chapter 9* ■

Politics of the Environment

The country was made without lines of demarcation, and it was no man's business to divide it. The Earth and myself are at one mind. The measure of the land and the measure of our bodies are the same . . . I never said the land was mine to do with as I chose. The one who has the right to dispose of it is the one who created it.

Thunder-Travelling-To-Loftier-Mountain-Heights (Chief Joseph) of the Nez-Perce tribe (19th century)

Our Earth is one, our world is not.

'Brundtland Report', World Commission (1987)

In June 1995, Shell capitulated in the face of a European campaign of boycotts organised by Greenpeace to oppose the deep water disposal of the obsolete Brent Spar oil rig. Shell was Europe's largest company with an income in the previous year of about £4 billion. The corporation had conducted a vigorous campaign of lobbying and had gained the support of the UK government for its strategy of deep sea dumping. However, when challenged by protests orchestrated by Greenpeace and built around the resurgent German Green party, Shell was obliged not only to abandon its plans for the Brent Spar rig, but also to jeopardise its relationship with its erstwhile ally, the UK government – a government then left isolated and appearing ridiculous after the corporate volte face. The campaign of opposition had gained the support of European governments, notably that of Germany, European politicians of several hues, consumer organisations and religious and educational groups. It was heralded as a triumph for grass-roots protest and consumer power and was the first great victory for a Europe-wide mobilisation of public opinion. A Danish government spokesperson declared that: 'People have been speaking with their hearts and not their brain on this. Ecology is now the ultimate political correctness. Today's consumers have been brought up to think very differently to their parents. The reaction we have been seeing has been due to education and culture and upbringing' (Vidal and Traynor 1995).

All the significant commentators agreed that the Brent Spar case represents a major landmark in the evolution and advance of green politics; it remains to be seen if it was also a watershed. If the well-being of the world depends upon humanity responding effectively to the environmental problems that it has created then salvation must seem to lie with non-governmental organisations (NGOs) or global governance, for the record of the sovereign actors in the realm of environmental policy-making is profoundly inadequate.

Numerous different disciplines with very different perspectives and resources of expertise are deeply interested in aspects of the politics of the environment. They include most of the physical sciences and most of the social sciences. Since the field of study involves such intense cross-disciplinary activity, the contribution of particular disciplines should, wherever possible, be quite sharply focused. Political geographers will be aware of problems like global warming or ozone depletion but not of the complex chemical and physical reactions and processes taking place. Rather, the involvement of political geography focuses firstly upon questions of 'institutional fit', concerning whether the geographical characteristics of the political agencies responsible for handling environmental issues are appropriate to this task. Secondly, it is concerned with exploring the processes of human agency, involving studies of how political opinions and decisions about the environment are formed and how they then impact upon the environment. This involves explorations in the realms of behavioural geography, with its emphases upon perception and decision-making and in the pluralistic approaches to politics, with their concern for the way in which different groups in society interact.

■ Sovereignty and the biosphere

Human history has been marked by a steady, but recently sharply accelerating rise in the scale at which episodes of environmental disruption operate. In some respects the human impact upon the environment may have become substantial at a relatively early stage in human development – it has been argued but not proved that the mass extinction of the larger palaeolithic fauna in northern Europe and North America was caused by human predation. In other respects, the human capacity to foul its nest remained modest until more recent times. Even in the medieval period, humanity lacked the capability for disruption on a grand scale. Restricted localities might be poisoned by the operation of lead smelters, the immediate settings of the (mostly tiny) towns could be polluted by smoke and sewage, while deforestation, hunting and increasing levels of disturbance would, in England for example, result in the successive extinction of the bear, the beaver, the wild boar and the wolf. Yet until the modern era, all the environmental problems attributable to human action could have been tackled effectively at one of the existing levels of government, whether that were the manor court or the state.

In modern times, however, humanity has been confronted by the internationalisation and globalisation of environmental problems, so that there is a glaring lack of spatial correspondence between the extent and reach of the state and the geographical scale of the challenges which it is required to meet. The nature of most environmental problems is such that we know *how* these problems should be tackled – by catching fewer fish, introducing population control policies, burning less fuel, and so on – but we lack the governmental structures that are needed to *implement* such solutions. This inadequacy has led Prins (1990, p. 722) to identify the 'incapable state':

> Underpinning any version of the social contract was the assumption that, by one means or another, the state could deliver satisfaction and protect its citizens . . . In 1990, for the first time since the rise of modern nationalism, the threat of major war has lifted; but at the same time the inability of states to protect their citizens to their own satisfaction from risk through poisoned water, air and food, from violent storm or rising sea level is revealed.

The theme of a citizens' interest in security which extends far beyond the boundaries of their state is echoed by other commentators. Dalby (1992a, p. 515) writes that:

> The economic security of the forest dwellers is determined by the survival of the forest, not the division of it into individual, precisely demarcated plots. Security for the rest of us likewise depends increasingly on the survival of an intact global ecosystem more than the inviolability of state borders. To maintain the global ecosphere as a functioning entity may well require that the political structures of the state be further called into question and the assumptions of absolute territorial sovereignty be further challenged in favour of ecologically based strategies.

Ironically, however, the need for some kind of supra-national body empowered to enforce global environmental policies has arisen in a period when fragmentation and a lack of confidence in the effectiveness of big government are rife: 'the need for stronger institutions comes at a time when the credibility of interventionist strategies has crumbled, capitalist market systems are seen to have triumphed over the command economy, and when more and more ethnic groups are demanding freedom to decide their own future' (Rees 1991, p. 293). In this section we explore the ways in which the state gained responsibility for the management of the environment and the problems which have subsequently derived from this.

The story of the relationship between humanity and its environment has significant philosophical and psychological overtones. Fundamental to the emergence of Western commercial and industrial society was a reorientation of thinking concerned with the place of humanity in the great scheme of things. As explained in Chapter 2, so-called primitive societies tended to subordinate the individual to the tribe or community and to regard human beings as existing in harmony with the natural order of which they were an integral part. Such ecofriendly perspectives were not universal in the ancient world, and certain cultures, like the Hebrews and the Greeks, which were accustomed to the struggle to survive in harsh or hostile environments thought that progress and prosperity could only result from the vanquishing of Nature by human determination and ingenuity (Passmore 1974). In Europe, early medieval society still subscribed in large measure to the widely held vision of humanity as part of Nature, the particular version of this doctrine provided by Christianity reasoning that the universe was governed by God's principles, the perfection of which contrasted to the flawed character of all human endeavours. Another aspect of the Christian attitude towards the environment concerned the model of the Great Chain of Being, which was conceived as an all-embracing hierarchy converging on God and descending via the angels to humans and then the lesser forms of life (Knill 1991, p. 239).

At the end of the Middle Ages, however, a very different interpretation emerged in the nascent capitalist societies of the West, with humanity regarding itself as having total dominion over Nature (Pepper 1984). Interestingly, the dichotomy between what O'Riordan terms the 'nature-as-usufruct' view and the 'nature-as-nurture' perspective still persist:

> Greens tend to see an interventionist perspective as the enemy, on the grounds that arrogance built on ignorance breeds disaster not only for humans but also for life on Earth in general. The intervenors genuinely believe themselves to be environmentalists. Their purpose is to improve the world by conscious planning and management, so that nature can be better off as much as the human race is upgraded. (O'Riordan 1989, p. 78)

At roughly the same time that humanity in the West was claiming some form of dominion over Nature, environmentalism also emerged: it was reasoned that while human beings operated a stewardship over Nature, they were also responsible for the consequences of their actions. Glacken studied the relationship between humanity and Nature and traced an evolutionary descent with continuity of substance but adaptations of form. He thought that Darwinistic ideas had challenged, though not completely vanquished, earlier notions of a divinely designed Earth, and he thought that throughout the history of Western thought, humans have regularly asked three questions about their relationship with the Earth:

> Is the earth, which is obviously a fit environment for man and other organic life, a purposefully made creation? Have its climates, its relief, the configuration of its continents influenced the moral and social nature of individuals, and have they had an influence in moulding the character and nature of human culture? In his long tenure of the earth, in what manner has man changed it from its hypothetical pristine condition? (Glacken 1967, p. 7)

It was at quite an early stage in the history of environmentalism that states began to assume a responsibility for handling environmental problems. In England, a Londoner was executed early in the fourteenth century for creating excessive smoke through burning coal, suggesting that the state already took its environmental responsibilities quite seriously; the first laws on water quality were enacted in 1388, while an Act to conserve wildfowl was introduced in 1534 (Johnson 1973). As the European mercantile powers expanded their control, commentators in the West began to relate the new lands which they encountered to the Eden myths and to stereotype indigenous people as 'noble savages' who were untouched by civilisation (Camilleri and Falk 1992, pp. 173–4). The fascination with the new, natural worlds led to the export of conservational practices, with the Assembly of Bermuda adopting legislation to control the taking of turtles in the early seventeenth century and trials of forest conservation, pollution control and fisheries protection being attempted on Mauritius in the late eighteenth century (Kennet 1974).

State involvement in conservation was carried a step further in 1878 with the creation of Yellowstone Park, the Earth's first national park. Here, the state sided with conservationists, naturalists and middle-class pressure groups seeking to protect this unspoilt expanse of Colorado against miners, loggers and industrialists. The park opened just one year after the crushing of its indigenous groups of native Americans by the forces of Generals Howard and Miles. The Yosemite National Park was founded in 1892, and in 1908 President Theodore Roosevelt convened a conference at the White House to consider a range of conservational proposals. (Although this Roosevelt is widely regarded as an important conservational pioneer he was remembered in Africa for the amount of big game which he shot while on safari, the slaughter being considered profligate even by the standards of those times.) The first of the African game parks to be established was the Kruger in South Africa, which was founded in 1898 after white hunters had virtually exterminated the elephant and rhino in the colony. Increasingly, the influential members of Western society were accepting that environmental issues were significant and should be entrusted to the state. When the British state first enforced game conservation policies in East Africa in the present century there was scant consideration for the fact that indigenous Africans had coexisted quite happily with game for millennia, and that current crises were very largely due to the hunting and farming activities of the whites: it was the Africans who faced eviction and exclusion when the national parks were instituted.

With the rise of corporate welfare considerations the state gained responsibility for framing and enforcing environmental health legislation, and with the growth of industry and the associated rapid and uncontrolled urbanisation, more effective public health policies were needed. In 1848 clean water legislation was adopted in response to an outbreak of cholera in London, other controls followed, but in the winter of 1952 smogs claimed the lives of more than 4000 Londoners. The Clean Air Act which followed in 1956 seemed, by its success, to demonstrate that forceful governmental action could eradicate environmental problems. Throughout the Western world there were urban industrial populations which appeared to have every reason to be grateful for the environmental health policies and regulations which their states had implemented.

The world of science had shown concern for environmental issues, though on the whole scientists perceived their mission as being distinct from that of the state. In 1827, J. B. Fourier had warned that industrial development could threaten the world climate (Ramanathan 1988, p. 299) and in 1896, S. Arrhenius provided what is still regarded as an effective account of the process of global warming. In the course of the twentieth century the role of scientists in environmental affairs changed as science assumed a position of dependency upon government. During the wars of this century, members of the scientific community were recruited into government service in escalating numbers as parts of the national attempts to advance the technology of warfare, while during the Kennedy era in the US, the young President attempted vigorously to apply science and technology to global problems of medium-term planning. Numerous government think tanks were established and the state came ever closer to exercising a monopoly over the scientific expertise needed to confront environmental problems. In the post-Kennedy era, science often seemed to be serving as the handmaiden of the state and the opponent of environmental interests: 'Indeed, too often over this period, the role of scientists and official scientific institutions was to patronise so-called "emotional" and "irrational" expressions of public environmental concern – on issues much later acknowledged by official scientific bodies and institutions to be indeed genuine and serious problems' (Grove-White 1993, p. 21).

In all these ways the state came to be regarded as the proper vehicle for environmental policy, but it also became apparent that the state was frequently ill-suited for this role. In some very important respects, this inadequacy was due to a change in the scale of the environmental problems which were being encountered. As Camilleri and Falk (1992, pp. 176–7) explain: 'So long as the physical impact of human intervention remained largely contained within national boundaries, it was possible to believe that existing social structures could be successfully adapted to meet the challenges posed by the impact of human activity on one biosphere'; however, human intervention was creating problems of international and global dimensions so that: 'Some eighty years after the first national environmental conference had been convened in the White House, it was already becoming clear that the political organization of a world based upon sovereign states would have to undergo substantial modification in order to grapple more effectively with global problems arising from human intervention in the biosphere.'

Camilleri and Falk (1992) have provided the most effective critique of the role of the sovereign state in the formation and implementation of environmental policy. They show that: 'The vision of linear progress to a high-technology future is deeply embedded in the discourse of the modern state' (ibid., p. 182). By this they mean that the nation-state is engaged in a constant process of demolition and reconstruction which is necessary to keep it competitive within the global economic system, and in the pursuit of this high rate of 'progress' alternative technologies and social options tend to be marginalised. By pursuing modernism the state sacrifices important ecological concerns and creates a climate of uncertainty which may actually encourage civil society to concede greater powers to the state as people respond to crisis by seeking stronger leadership.

The compression of time scales has several important aspects. The dynamic of the market compresses attention spans; some large corporations have average time horizons for planning of around three years. Such corporations value profits in the near future much more than they value more distant profits or fear future losses. Consequently, economic development pursues short-term gain and is far less concerned about its longer term consequences for the environment. The state might be expected to regulate such environmentally unacceptable behaviour, but in reality it contrives to intensify the adverse effects of the compression of time scales. Even the most superficial studies of government policy in Western democracies such as the US or UK will reveal that the prime objective of government appears to be that of securing re-election. Consequently, governments tend to neglect long-term concerns relating to the public good and to favour those policies which will buy short-term support. Essential programmes, like those needed to reduce energy consumption or cut emissions into the atmosphere, which would impose costs upon the electorate, will be set aside in favour of more 'popular' policies – like manufacturing bursts of economic expansion to enhance the 'feel-good factor' as an election approaches, irrespective of the environmental damage or inflationary consequences associated with such measures. Thus:

> The short time scales of corporations, which ascribe far higher value to profits now than to future profits or losses, combine with the electoral time scales of political parties and governments to produce a process of development which is insufficiently sensitive to long-term ecological damage . . . In the short term the close planning horizon of any single government is likely to distract it from initiating those difficult changes which will produce little result by the next election, but may be essential for the amelioration of long-term environmental degradation. (ibid., p. 184)

In the UK, where the 'first-past-the-post' electoral system has tended to produce majority governments and adversary politics rather than coalition and consensus, the effects of short-termism can be seen at their worst. During the post-war period the alternation of governments has been associated with a traumatic alternation of policies as socially oriented and market oriented policies have succeeded each other in step with the succession of Labour and Tory governments. Wherever an environmental problem is subjected to state policy-making then the approaches to its solution are likely to be severely contaminated by extraneous political considerations. In many cases the ruling party will prefer to ignore a problem whose solution demands the diversion of resources or the sacrifice of party political doctrines. 'Goal conflicts or trade-offs (e.g. with consumption and economic growth) may come to dominate the decision-making process. Spending on pollution control is still widely perceived as a threat to economic growth and hence political stability' (Boehmer-Christiansen 1994, p. 70).

While jealously cherishing its sovereignty, the state finds its supremacy repeatedly compromised in its dealings with economic corporations. Particularly following the rise of the TNCs, governments are anxious to create the commercial environments which will attract rather than repel the establishment of new enterprises and industries. For the working population of the state this may mean the dismantling of legislation created to safeguard standards of safety at work, to establish minimum wage levels and to provide security of employment. For the environment this can imply the dilution or non-enforcement of essential legislation and the toleration of activities and discharges which degrade it but which make a positive contribution to the balance of payment statistics. Through their reluctance to challenge or regulate companies which could suffer a loss of business or might relocate abroad, governments reveal their obsessive fascination with economic competitiveness and the balance of trade and the emptiness of many of their environmental claims and pledges. In such ways, environmental concerns are continually subordinated to the promotion of growth – with this growth promotion being the very cause of much of the environmental degradation.

Not only does the state fail to regulate polluting enterprises and corporations and itself indulge in similarly irresponsible short term policy-making, it is also the initiator and sponsor of projects which may damage the environment. Most states are associated with developments which are national in scale, including the development of transport networks, military capabilities and systems for the generation of energy. Some state-sponsored developments which are considered by government to be of central importance to the preservation of national sovereignty can constitute a distinct threat to members of that national community. This is particularly true in the case of nuclear power generation, which may be adopted to buttress sovereignty by obtaining materials for the manufacture of nuclear weapons, by reducing dependence on external sources of oil, coal or gas, by obtaining energy at (supposedly) more competitive prices or by reducing the power of trade unions in existing energy production industries. But such a nuclear strategy might then rebound on the sovereignty principle by assisting in the emergence of an international anti-nuclear movement. 'National states lost control of events as citizens, often acting across state boundaries, confronted the plans of industry and governments alike. Increasingly citizens saw themselves as battling not for national but international objectives in a global arena in which their state was only one protagonist among many' (Camilleri and Falk 1992, p. 192).

Though infatuated with international economic competition and slavish in the pursuit of modernity, the state as a principal actor in the environmental arena also suffers from defects which do not result from muddled thinking or mistaken priorities. Here we encounter the problem of 'institutional fit' and the fact that the individual sovereign state is far too small to cope with issues which are international or global in their reach. Porter and Brown (1991) have considered issues that have prompted the formation of global political concern – like whaling, ozone depletion and the trade in toxic waste – and argue for radical transformations which require the development on the part of humanity of a new geopolitical consciousness and the establishment of global governance to preclude the selfish exploitation of resources by individual nation-states. Stone (1993) also explored the question of institutional fit and suggested that a global trust fund should be instituted to protect global common property resources, the fund to be financed by taxes on environmentally damaging activities. He also advocated the establishment of global 'guardians' to speak out for the habitats and species whose interests go unrepresented in environmental affairs.

Also in the early 1990s, Byers explored the incongruities between the natural boundaries of ecosystems and the boundaries of states, and discovered many anomalies (Byers 1991). He described a world divided into about 168 sovereign entities, of which the ten largest then controlled some 52 per cent of the Earth's land surface. Many illogicalities were noted, including that of the Pacific island state of Kiribati, consisting of 33 islands with a total land area of 819 square kilometres. Though having a population of only 60 000, Kiribati, by virtue of the exclusive economic zone it derives from the Law of the Sea Convention of 1982, dominates an oceanic expanse of 4 980 863 square kilometres – an area larger than India! Byers noted the frequent incongruities between the boundaries of states and of bioregions, but claimed to detect a frequent correspondence between the borders of 'cultural nations' and bioregions. He quoted as an example the arid ecoregion of the Horn of Africa, inhabited by Somali nomadic pastoralists but (then) divided between four states.

The geographical foundations of Byers's case frequently appear to be rather shaky and one must doubt whether a redefinition of sovereign territory along biogeographical lines could provide an answer to problems which often seem to have sovereignty itself at their core. He advocated a modification rather than an abandonment of state sovereignty in order to recognise the 'ecogeographical' realities or biogeographical realms and, secondly, he argued that each bioregion should develop a basic resource self-sufficiency. As already described, Byers also thought that sovereignty bargains, whereby a state surrendered some measure of control over its constituent nations and bioregions, might increase the overall effectiveness of state sovereignty and he suggested Ethiopia, which was weakened by the fact that rebel fronts controlled parts of its territory, as an example. He concluded that: 'Sovereignty bargains will have to be made at all levels of the "ecopolitical heirarchy" – local, subnational, national, multilateral, and global – in order to build institutions that can resolve ecologically rooted conflicts and create ecologically sustainable development' (Byers 1991, p. 73).

In 1974 Hardin had argued that the answer to the environmental 'tragedy of the commons' problem was viable world government. Eighteen years later, Johnston (1992) realised with some reluctance that such a solution might not be avoidable. Having noted the global scale of most serious environmental problems he pointed out that:

> Tackling large-scale problems at large scales is very substantially hampered by another 'spatial reality'. The world is divided into a large number of independent territorial containers, which we call states. Each is sovereign over its own territory, and tackling the world's environmental problems involves some (probably very considerable) yielding of that sovereignty in order to ensure practices which will protect the environment and sustain its productivity. (ibid., p. 227)

He concluded that:

> The problems posed in this paper are large, and the apparent solution – an international state, or 'Leviathan-writ-large' – contains within it many dangers of an overweening power . . . The implicit conclusion here is that, unless real progress can be achieved through international treaties soon, such an overweening state may be the only salvation for the environment and for humanity. (ibid.)

While the possible alternatives are numerous and varied, authorities are moving ever closer to a consensus that the state is an impediment rather than a useful instrument in the proper regulation of the human relationship with the environment. As Falk (1992, p. 199) describes: 'The consequences of nuclear winter or global warming and ozone depletion, of rainforest destruction, of air and ocean pollution are quite literally shattering to human prospects. This mismatch between capabilities and challenges is bound to cause severe tensions between state and society in the years to come.'

■ Pressure groups, parties and decision-making

If environmental politics was not about places, their condition, use and the way that opposed groups would like them to be and be used, or if political choices and decisions did not impact upon places and change

Box 9.1 *Hardin and the tragedy of the commons*

Garrett Hardin's article (1968) on the tragedy of the commons was but six pages in length yet its themes have been recounted on countless occasions. It was based on an obscure pamphlet on population control issued in 1833 by William Forster Lloyd, an amateur mathematician. The notion of the commons can provide a metaphor of the anarchical nature of international society and the consequences which flow from this. Visualise an old English village which has a common pasture on which all the villagers are entitled to graze their livestock. The villagers continue to add to their herds so long as each additional animal yields some degree of profit. Eventually, however, overgrazing will completely ruin the common for all the graziers. Each villager has a personal interest in continuing to add beasts to the common, yet all also have a common interest in adjusting grazing to the carrying capacity of the resource. Each villager also knows that if he or she adds just one more animal to the common it will not instantaneously cause the ruin of the pasture. In addition there is a 'free-rider' problem: if some villagers act in an ecologically responsible manner and withdraw livestock from the common then they will bear the entire costs of conservation, while their selfish neighbours will reap the benefits and continue to overgraze the resource to the point of its extinction.

The metaphor demonstrates the lack of coincidence between individual and collective interests. Individuals have an interest in continuing to pillage a dwindling resource unless co-operative action or intervention by some external agency can impose a system of sustainable use which will benefit the whole community. Hardin invoked the Commons to support population control and wrote: 'The only way we can preserve and nurture other and more precious freedoms is by relinquishing the freedom to breed, and that very soon' (Hardin 1968, p. 1248). The tragedy of the commons has also been applied to many situations of resource exploitation and it can be used to demonstrate the problems associated with a global society dominated by sovereign states. Because the states are sovereign there is no overriding authority and each state will pursue its selfish interests to the point where scarce global resources are contaminated or exhausted. So as with the villagers, the state's short-term interests in maximising its share of resources may conflict with the long-term communal or global interest in maintaining the bases of life. Laver (1986, pp. 359–73) identified three possible solutions to the dilemma: privatisation of the common; the conclusion of collective agreements between the users, and regulation by an external body. The privatisation solution would not be appropriate to an international or global problem. A collective international agreement might be useful in regulating access to the resource providing that all the parties to the agreement honoured their undertakings – but if any should not then there is no supreme power to enforce the settlement. An external body empowered to regulate the behaviour of subordinate states does not exist – though increasing numbers of experts are beginning to regard global governance as a serious response to the tragedy of the world's commons.

them, then there might be no geographical case for studying environmental politics. The fact that places and people are engaged in a continuous interaction, which often takes on a political character as issues of use and amenity arise, locates environmental politics at the core of political geography. Much as a geomorphologist might seek to understand the evolution of a physical landscape by studying the processes of uplift and degradation which had formed it, so the political geographer must study the human processes of perception and decision-making in order to understand how the pattern of development of a place has been determined. Here, the topic of politics and the environment is approached by exploring how individuals and groups become politicised with regard to environmental concerns; how the public perceives such issues; how pressure groups and political parties serve to articulate popular demands concerning the environment; and how government responds to environmental issues.

□ *The environment as an issue*

In many respects environmental protest is a recent phenomenon, although concern and an awareness of the environmental consequences of human actions must be as old as history. Around 500 BC, Plato warned that Greek farmers were courting disaster by allowing their stock to overgraze the hills and destroy the forests. In the 1660s the diarist, John Evelyn, tried to mobilise support against atmospheric pollution in London by publishing a pamphlet, 'Fumifugium', in which he complained about 'that hellish and dismal cloud of seacoal perpetually overhead' (Evelyn 1661). Protests with environmental overtones took place in post-medieval England, although they were associated with questions of rights of ownership than with environmental degradation. In 1649 a group of radicals known as 'The Diggers' or 'True Levellers' began to dig up common land at Walton-on-Thames, with the intention of establishing a commune which would recreate the golden age of equality and justice wrongly imagined to have existed before the Norman Conquest, when the earth was 'the common treasury of mankind'. During the eighteenth and nineteenth centuries, Parliamentary Enclosure resulted in scores of local protests against the privatisation of traditional commons.

It was in the course of the nineteenth century, when issues of environmental concern apparently multiplied apace with industrialisation, that the distinction between environmental protests based on principle and those based on NIMBYism ('not in my backyard') became apparent. In the latter category, there were numerous protests by rural landowners who were horrified by their encounters with the air pollution, woodland destruction, trespass, poaching and road, rail and canal construction which were associated with the rapid expansion of the industrial cities. Other protests were based on moral or aesthetic principles, usually in connection with some disturbing aspect of the advance towards modernism. In the English Lake District the poet, William Wordsworth, campaigned vigorously against the projected Kendal and Windermere Railway during the 1840s, even if the cause did not bring forth the best from his pen (1844):

> Is there no nook of English ground secure
> From rash assault? Schemes of retirement sown
> In youth, and 'mid the busy world kept pure
> As when their earliest flowers of hope were blown,
> Must perish; – how can they this blight endure?

In the Yorkshire Dales in the 1870s the historian, T. D. Whitaker, complained about the aesthetics of Parliamentary Enclosure and the effects on the landscape of building new field walls: 'the fine swelling outlines of the pastures, formerly as extensive as large parks, and wanting little but the accompaniment of deer to render them beautiful, are now strapped over with large bandages of stone, and present nothing to the eye but right lined and angular deformity' (Whitaker 1878, p. 4). In addition to the expression of aesthetic concerns, the nineteenth century also witnessed the first systematic attempts to chart the human impact on the environment. In 1864 the American scholar and diplomat, George Perkins Marsh, published *Man and Nature*, a landmark study in which he attempted to assess the character and extent of the transformations which had been wrought upon the natural world.

In the West the modern environmental movement was a child of the 1960s, though some of the foundations were created in the 1950s. It was in the 1950s that television introduced the wonders of an as then less spoilt natural world into countless homes; in the UK viewers accompanied David Attenborough and Armand and Michaela Dennis on their safaris; soon German viewers would be warming to the conservational messages of Bernhard Grzimek, while the French followed Jacques Cousteau on his voyages on threatened oceans. An important benchmark in the popularisation of environmental concern was reached in 1962 when Rachel Carson published the results of her investigations into the contamination of the natural world by agricultural pesticides, and although the chemical industry sought to buy up the entire print run, *Silent Spring* enjoyed a remarkable success. Americans were shaken by the realisation that their national emblem, the bald eagle, faced extinction as a result of the presence of DDT in the food chain (von Weisacker 1994, p. 13). In West Germany, in 1969, Willy Brandt campaigned successfully for election on issues which included an assault on atmospheric pollution and the creation of 'blue skies over the Ruhr' – and as Federal Chancellor he gave a high priority to environmental issues. By the end of the decade, public opinion in the US had forced the adoption of a National Environmental Policy Act and a Clean Air Act, while water pollution and toxic chemicals had gained popular recognition as major problems in most West European countries and would become important political issues in Japan during the early 1970s.

The designation of 22 April 1970 as Earth Day symbolised the growing importance of the environmental movement. The demonstrations against the war in Vietnam and the student unrest of 1968 stimulated a public awareness of the possibilities of protest throughout the West, while the recent emergence of environmental principle groups, like Greenpeace, with mass memberships assisted in the organisation of protest. The first modern environmental protest in the UK took place in May 1971 when supporters of the new Friends of the Earth organisation dumped 950 bottles outside the headquarters of Cadbury Schweppes in London in protest at their introduction of non-returnable bottles. In the following year, the Club of Rome (an independent group formed around the Italian industrialist, Aurelio Peccei and the diplomat, Alexander King) published its environmental report *The Limits to Growth*, which sold more than 20 million copies worldwide (Meadows *et al.* 1972). Despite the impact which the grim forecasts made on global opinion, the appearance of *The Limits to Growth* marked the beginning of a division between the developed countries and the Third World on environmental matters. At the United Nations Conference on the Human Environment held at Stockholm in 1972 opinion in the Third World had plainly been offended by the apparent hypocrisy in the attitude that: 'First the North gets rich through unfettered growth at the South's expense, then, having gained all the wealth, the North tells us the limits to growth have been reached' (von Weisacker 1994, p. 38).

The repressive regimes in the communist world delayed but could not prevent the emergence of environmental movements. The first organisation to emerge was the Polish Ecology Club, which appeared after the Gdansk strikes of September 1980 and soon secured a membership of more than 1000. It disseminated information about pollution and campaigned for the closure of a polluting aluminium plant near Krakow. With the imposition of martial law in 1981 the PEC went underground, but resurfaced after the Chernobyl disaster of 1985. The first Hungarian environmental organisation was founded in 1983 to oppose the construction of a giant hydro-electric dam on the Danube. It was refused an official permit but continued as an unofficial organisation, the Danube Circle or 'the Blues'. In 1989 more than 100 000 Hungarians demonstrated in Budapest against the Gabcikovo-Nagymaros dam in a protest which signified the fall of the Communist Party. After Chernobyl, the floodgates to environmental protest were opened in Eastern Europe and each Warsaw Pact country developed its own Green movements. With the collapse of communist power in the USSR and the break-up of the federation, Green organisations developed in most of the new republics. Green protest was often a metaphor for demands for general political reform while many groups were concerned with opposition to particular local polluting activities, and it is estimated that by 1992 Leningrad alone contained more than 300 environmental groups (Jancar 1992, pp. 162–3). Meanwhile in the West, by the late 1980s the membership of environmental groups in Britain had grown to exceed that of the trade unions (McCormick 1989).

□ *Popular perception of environmental issues*

In seeking to conceptualise the ways in which environmental issues come to command public attention and inspire demands for change reference can be made to the work of Solesbury (1976). He describes a 'public agenda', a notional list of the most important matters which are the subject of political debate and on which popular opinion is calling for action: 'Over time the agenda changes as matters get dealt with or no further action is required and new issues arise to take their place on the agenda for consideration' (ibid., p. 380). Thinking in terms of this agenda, we can see that environmental matters scarcely featured on the public agenda before the 1960s, but have seldom been removed from it since 1970. In order to feature upon the agenda an environmental 'situation' must be converted into an 'issue', that is to say, it must gain a sufficient measure of public consent that the situation is bad and must be improved. Once an issue has gained public recognition it invites a response from government in the form of a policy designed to correct the situation giving rise to the issue. In this way the situation of atmospheric emissions becomes an issue of pollution when debate and complaints reach a critical level. Government may then respond by producing clean air legislation to eliminate the situation. However, not all issues are able to command the attention of government, for many issues simultaneously compete for government time, resources and recognition.

In order to proceed through the policy process an issue must be able to command government attention, claim legitimacy as a proper subject for such attention and invoke action. Each issue – like water pollution or juvenile crime – has its own particular qualities which may help or hinder its progress towards invoking a response. Solesbury suggested that the main attributes could be summarised under the headings of 'particularity' and 'generalisation'. Particularity concerns the ability to be exemplified by particular events, which will assist public identification with the issue. In this respect ozone depletion, which is invisible to the public at large, is more poorly endowed than river pollution, which can produce sensational media images of shoals of dead fish and swirls of scum. Generalisation relates to the extent to which an issue can be related to a more general system of values and political concerns, in the way that an authoritarian party may relate issues of vandalism on public housing estates to its general perspectives on class and law and order. Similarly, a socialist party is likely to view issues of industrial pollution within its doctrine of capitalist exploitation.

Some important environmental issues may fail to get the initial public attention that they merit because they are invisible or intangible and their appreciation requires acts of abstract reasoning. Prins (1990, p. 729) described the dilemma as follows:

> by the time they are unambiguously overt, things may be too far gone to retrieve the situation. This is the modern catch-22: When you don't see it, you can still act to prevent it but it is denied status by 'realist' politics, so you can't; when you do see it and it is granted status and you could act, you probably can't because natural processes have passed a point of no return.

However, he thought that public opinion had a vital role to play in the salvation of the world. Every aspect of communications and information technology should be used to force an act of collective public imagination about environmental matters, for only this could shortcircuit the 'official' selective, linear thinking which insulates issues from one another, ignores effects on interests located outside a narrow circle and which can only be fired to take action by a crisis. One way of achieving this, he thought, might be by making people more altruistic for selfish reasons. Here he quoted the example of the argument (at the Montreal Protocol conference in 1990) that giving China and India CFC substitutes to reduce the destruction of the ozone layer was the best way to protect European skins in the northern and southern hemispheres.

Solesbury's recognition of the 'public agenda' had been preceded by an attempt by Downs (1972) to characterise the 'issue-attention cycle' which was followed by American public opinion. In the first phase, the problem exists but is not recognised; in the second, the discovery of the problem was followed by public enthusiasm for the issue, both often being prompted by dramatic events; in the third phase, an appreciation of the complexity and costs of the problem develops; in the fourth phase, public interest gradually declines, and in the fifth, post-problem, phase there are periodic resurgences of interest in 'solutions' or their failure. A more refined exploration of the issue–attention cycle was developed by Sandbach (1989), who noted a fluctuation in interest in environmental issues in the years around 1970, when the environment became a focus for popular attention, only to be displaced by seemingly more pressing concerns about the economy and employment. Subsequently, environmental issues became a more reliably stable focus for concern, although in the years around 1990 the tendency for environmental issues to be supplanted by economic concerns in times of recession was again confirmed.

While some environmental issues may fail to capture the attention of the public, some have the capacity to ignite popular concern. Often, difficult problems of interpretation will be involved, for most environmental problems involve complex interactions and experts may offer conflicting explanations. This is certainly the case with global warming, and as de Freitas (1991, p. 11) explains: 'Calls for action have put enormous pressure on governments to formulate policies in response to the perceived threat. Despite the political momentum generated, there has been little progress in national and international policy formulation. One reason for this is that there are so many areas of uncertainty and confusion.' He concludes that:

> the basis of political and policy response to the greenhouse crisis is, in part, popular perception of the problem. Clearly the level of informed public discussion has experienced a dramatic upswing. It is equally clear that the discussion is tainted with half truths and oversimplifications. This, together with inaccurate and poor quality forecasts and environmental false alarms, could produce bad policy decisions.

□ *Policies, pressure groups and parties*

Individual activists generally come to realise that their attempts to intervene more effectively in the political arena will be enhanced by membership of a group or party. The choice of which organisation to join will be heavily influenced by the question of ideology. It will soon be found that fragmentation is a characteristic of the environmental movement and that there is not one Green doctrine on offer, but many. O'Riordan (1989) has described how all societies are divided between those who regard Nature as inherently exploitable and resilient and those who recognise that the human capacity to destroy its setting is greater than the ability to restore the damage. He writes that:

> Greens tend to see an interventionist perspective as the enemy, on the grounds that arrogance built on ignorance breeds disaster not only for humans but also for life on Earth in general. The intervenors genuinely believe themselves to be environmentalists. Their purpose is to improve the world by conscious planning and management, so that nature can be better off as much as the human race is upgraded. (ibid., p. 78)

Countless people would class themself as being Greens according to this simple division, but beneath the Green umbrella we find enormous divisions in terms of class, attitudes and goals.

During the 1980s there was a revitalisation of popular interest in environmental issues. In the US this is said to have been largely due to a reaction to the anti-environmental policies of the Reagan administration, while in Europe it involved the successful emergence of Green parties and the forging of Green support for anti-nuclear activism which was accompanied by a succession of issues – like global warming, the ozone hole, tropical forest destruction and oil spills – which obtained mass-media coverage (Cutter 1994, p. 218). In the UK the rise of the new environmentalism during the 1990s has been closely linked to opposition to new road building programmes.

The new environmentalism is built upon radical ideologies, including deep ecology, ecoanarchism and ecofeminism:

> Their goal is to achieve a social system based on the principle that every part of nature and all natural systems have intrinsic value and rights that humans must except [sic]; humans do not dominate nature, rather they are a part of it. The restructuring of society to eliminate domination, where all elements (human and nonhuman) are treated fairly, and sustainable societies are nurtured, is the ultimate objective of the new environmentalism. (Cutter 1994, pp. 217–18)

However, these principles do not provide a political programme around which all shades of the new environmentalism can unite. For example, Pepper (1993) has described how, while both support revolutionary change, the 'green greens' lean towards anarchist principles, reject political organisations and favour direct action, while the 'red greens' depend upon Marxist analysis and strategies. Yet though the Green movement may be as Balkanised in the UK as elsewhere, during the early 1990s one witnessed the amazing scenes of ultra-leftist New Age Travellers campaigning (almost) shoulder to shoulder with the rural stalwarts of the Tory parties against government road building plans. Any government which can forge alliances between its best friends and most implacable foes has surely achieved a degree of political incompetence of epic proportions. Later in the year, the French government managed to antagonise virtually every other government and every nation in the world – including its own – by testing nuclear weapons at Mururoa atoll in the Pacific.

One of the clearest explanations of the formless character of Green ideology was provided by Knill (1991, p. 241), who wrote:

> ecologism is very different to environmentalism, sustainability is the key, feminism is an integral component of the Green perception, and even light Green and dark Green are distinguished, but as with Green politics itself, the core is not readily apparent. Instead it appears to be a political movement built up around a number of principles which are instinctively accepted as being correct by the followers, with no-one seeming terrible sure why.

While exposing the nebulous nature of Green politics, Knill believes that it is possible to recognise a Green paradigm which provides a challenge and an alternative to the dominant Western environmental paradigm. He writes that: 'Nature is a complex system in which humans have a role to play, but Green thinking points out that the system is not there for the sole benefit of *homo sapiens*. It makes no sense for one part of the whole to exploit another to the ultimate detriment of the greater whole' (ibid., p. 239). The Green paradigm regards human society as an ecosystem which forms part of a larger system and rejects the notion that the Earth is a collection of resources available for people to dispose of as they wish. Actions are regarded as being good when they tend towards the stability and integrity of the system, while concepts of 'rights' and 'value' have little place within the paradigm. Essentially it assumes that any ideology which assumes that people have a central position in the universe will prove to be faulty. Yet despite the viability of the Green paradigm, the formation of successful Green parties is hampered by factionalism and disputed values. This factionalism is made more intense by the fact that at least the other parties with anthropocentric perspectives have, in the human good, a system of priority and a yardstick against which policy can be judged.

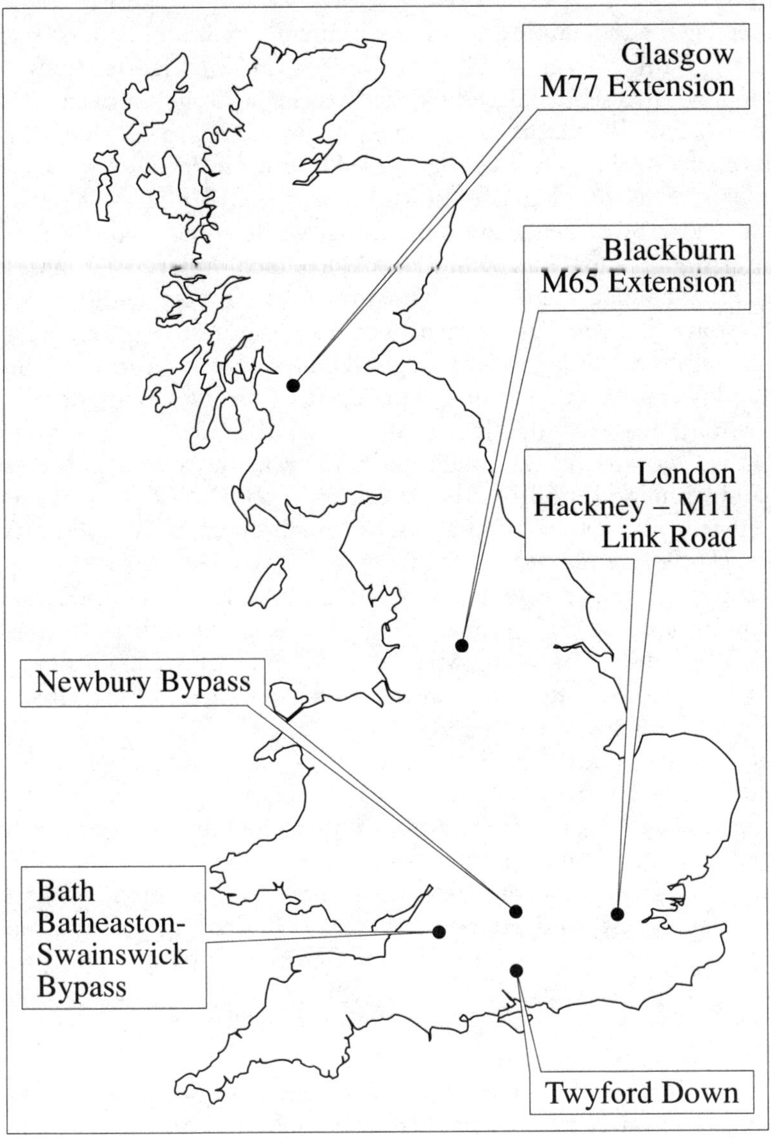

Map 13 Hotspots in recent campaigns against roadbuilding in the UK

The modern rise of the environmental movement has been paralleled in the social sciences by the growth of interest in pluralism, and in both, pressure groups have an important part to play. These can be regarded as being political groups which differ from political parties in that they campaign according to a narrower spectrum of policies and do not seek to exercise the formal powers of government (Muir and Paddison 1981, p. 119). While Green parties suffer to varying degrees from the ideological problems already described, the Green movement has spawned a multitude of environmental pressure groups operating at all levels from the global to the local. Here we immediately encounter problems of terminology, for some writers regard interest groups and pressure groups as being the same thing, while some favour a division of pressure groups into what may be called 'interest groups' and 'principle groups'. Here, the distinction is made between groups, like professional associations, which exist to promote the self-interests of their members and those groups which exist to promote moral principles and social values, like opposition to fox hunting. On the whole this sort of classification, as offered by Allison (1975, pp. 110–12), is useful, although one must remember that in the realm of environmental politics the rise of the 'NIMBY' results in the emergence of individuals and groups which claim to be campaigning on issues of principle – and to some extent may be doing so – but which are largely motivated by matters of self-interest. However, the NIMBYs have no monopoly on hypocrisy: 'In an increasing number of cases, the "selfish" middle class accusation seems to be thrown in simply to bolster anti-conservation arguments which are themselves selfish and sectional' (Perman 1973, p. 238).

McCormick studied environmental pressure groups in the UK and found the same variety in their types and aims as we have seen in Green ideology: 'There are sectional groups with demands which can often be conceded with minimal public controversy. There are economic and ideological groups. There are functional groups (mainly pursuing economic interest) and preference groups ("united by common tastes, attitudes or pastimes"). There are emphasis groups . . . and promotional groups' (McCormick 1991, p. 10).

Environmental pressure groups have the influencing of the policy-making process as their *raisons d'être*. In seeking to achieve this goal they mobilise their resources, with each particular group having its own distinctive resource profile. The size of its membership and membership quality in terms of expertise, influence, wealth and commitment; access to the governmental power centres; experience acquired in previous campaigns, and the prestige of the group, can all be significant. In another sense, resources can be classified as sanctional resources, which concern the ability to impose sanctions and discomfort upon an adversary (as when campaigners involve the mass media in their opposition to a hostile development), and non-sanctional resources. The latter are generally less effective but would exist, for example, when an environmental group is a repository for expert information needed by the government.

In one of the earliest geographical excursions into pluralism, Kasperson (1969) studied how a natural resource management system competed for investment needed to reduce 'stress'. This stress might originate in the physical or the man-made environment and concerned noxious or potentially noxious forces which could be brought to bear upon the individual. It could result from a traumatic event or the gradual worsening of a situation and might be caused by flooding, pollution, a riot, and so on. The concept of 'strain' was related to that of stress and it referred to the individual's perception and reaction to the stress and involved the notion of there being a threat to the manager or to the system within which he/she worked. The environmental manager concerned would evaluate the stress imposed by a particular issue or incident within the context of all the other stresses which were acting upon the political system, would attempt to assign a relative priority to it and, within the context of his/her managerial goals and values, would assess the various alternative strategies for coping with the stress-inducing situation. In many respects and cases, environmental pressure group activity involves imposing stress upon institutions and enterprises. The groups lack the resources of power or the legitimacy that would be needed to reverse a decision which in some ways threatens the environment by institutional means. Their greatest successes tend to result from their ability to expose government or developers to intolerable levels of stress resulting from public contempt or ridicule, these being produced by high profile campaigns in which the mass media have been heavily involved.

□ *Environmental policy-making*

Pressure groups help to focus and articulate public concerns about the environment but they are unable directly to formulate and implement appropriate policies; rather, they exist to influence government at its various levels. A simple model of the political system was provided by Easton (1957). Here, the government will recognise process and convert into policies only those *demands* which have obtained sufficient levels of *support*. Such a model can provide a starting point for analysis providing that policy-making is not conceived in too mechanistic a fashion. It is useful to remember that demands for government action may be disregarded if they lack influential support from some sections of the public, and one should also remember that political systems and

Box 9.2 *Pluralism*

In essence, pluralism is a theory that political power is dispersed widely amongst different groups in society rather than being the exclusive prerogative of a particular ruling elite or class. The theory derives from the work of R. A. Dahl (1961), who studied political affairs in New Haven and concluded that the broad parameters of power included groups and individuals who contributed to the decision-making process in ways which might have been overlooked by the supporters of a more elitist theory. In many respects, pluralism is an extension of the liberal theory of the state developed by Hobbes and Locke, who believed that the state arose from a social contract entered into by individuals who sought protection from the brutality and uncertainties of life in the state of nature. According to their formulations, the state served as a neutral referee which arbitrated upon conflicts within society and was guided by the public interest. Pluralism is an optimistic characterisation of the political system which considers that all groups enjoy access to government, that democracy essentially works and that elected politicians and government employees are accountable to the electorate.

Various different political philosophies take issue with pluralism and believe that political power is effectively monopolised by members of an elite, like the capitalist class or the military–industrial elite. Marxists do not accept the characterisation of the state as an impartial referee; they believe that it is a product of the class system and that it exists to perpetuate exploitation in the interest of the ruling class. Marxists would point out that whatever pressure group activity may exist, gross inequality remains: 'Today polluting industries, traffic hazards and other environmental disturbances are unevenly distributed so that the better off have prime access to higher quality environments. The rich and dominant class have been able to manipulate political institutions so that planning reinforces their narrow needs' (Sandbach 1984, p. 195). Anarchists also regard the state as an instrument of the ruling class, but while Marxist-Leninists seek to gain control of the state on behalf of the proletariat, anarchists seek to destroy it. At the opposite political extreme to the anarchists, the so-called New Right also regard the state as a monstrosity which insinuates itself into every aspect of life. Sometimes the New Right criticism of big government spills over into attacks on democracy itself, which is said to encourage politicians to 'buy' votes with promises of new state benefits, policies and agencies.

The Canadian economist, J.K. Galbraith (1962) has developed a neo-pluralistic theory of the state which emphasises the complexity of society and removes the naive optimism associated with earlier pluralistic analyses. It recognises the fact that some of the interests which seek to influence government – like big business with its partial command of the mass media – are much more powerful than others. Today, any neo-pluralist theory must take account of the rise of the transnational corporation with its enormous influence over governments and their policies. In one somewhat unsympathetic review of approaches to environmental problems, the pluralistic interpretation is characterised as follows: 'In a typical liberal and pluralistic account, environmental problems arise at various stages during the process of industrialization. Consequent strains lead to the development of social movements. The state, pressure groups, and the public react to these problems

Box 9.2 *continued*

and, depending upon the nature of the political system, there are varying degrees of consensus and conflict before acceptable solutions are found' (Sandbach 1989, p. 198). In a more upbeat account, Smith (1983, p. 125) concluded that: 'The increasing role played by pressure groups and the importance of public participation . . . have been shown to be significant factors in the decision-making process. For example, the satisfaction of needs in urban areas, based on conservation principles, means looking at and coming to terms with the area as a whole, especially with the aspirations and energies of the residents who are the most important of all the resources available to that area.'

politicians tend to favour some members of society over others. At a relatively early stage in the growth of environmental groups in the UK, Lowe (1977, pp. 54–5) found that:

> With growing emphasis on public participation in statutory planning, serious problems of equity arise because certain areas and sections of society are not effectively organised to protect their interests in the environment: certain sections of the community lack the available resources to sustain effective pressure group activity, and some local political cultures are unreceptive to group activity.

At the same time, very powerful vested interests may apply pressure on government to resist any calls for environmental reforms, and 'To a large extent those who currently benefit from the existing modes of development and political order are those least likely to take environmental arguments seriously or to wish to initiate dramatic changes' (Dalby 1992a, p. 511).

Government is not just a mechanism for processing the supported demands arising from its environment, it will originate its own policies and will have its own ideological perspectives. Sandbach (1980) described the scientific and ideological views relating to the limits to growth debate and identified three main perspectives which could be related to political stances. The conservative or neo-Malthusian position took a pessimistic view of the future and considered that tight controls would be necessary. The liberal or economic technological fix position was optimistic and considered that future shortages would be avoided by new discoveries or improved technologies, while the radical or Marxist position argued that under a state planned economy and workers' control resources of food, shelter and energy would be regarded as precious and wastage would be greatly reduced.

While different ideological perspectives may be brought to bear upon environmental problems, the problems themselves tend to occur – or rather to be recognised – in an unpredictable manner, with some threats existing for some time before they are recognised, whilst unforeseen accidents and disasters may suddenly propel an issue on to the public agenda, as occurred with marine oil pollution after the Torrey Canyon disaster of 1967 or radiation contamination after the Chernobyl disaster of 1986. As Rees (1991, p. 293) explains:

> This 'react and regulate' approach is known to be costly: it inevitably follows, rather than prevents, pollution damage, and policy makers, regulators and the regulated constantly find themselves chasing last year's hare. In the meantime new hares are busily entering the race as scientific knowledge improves, a different potential threat is identified and an awakening public awareness creates demand for further action.

Environmental problems tend to be associated with complex physical interactions, so that governments are obliged to call upon expert advice. However, Boehmer-Christiansen (1994, p. 76) warns us not to imagine that the making of environmental policy can be represented by a rational, linear, technocratic model such as may be found in text-books and where: 'Expert knowledge is seen as the foundation of policy because it reveals both unacceptable damage and the options for rational choice by which undesired damage can be avoided or repaired. From these options, government is assumed to select by optimizing not its own, but society's benefits.' In reality a host of factors complicate the policy-making process and Boehmer-Christiansen contrasts the rational model with one based on the real world:

> In this interactive and non-linear world, knowledge itself is also filtered by culture, self interest (economic, ideological and political), channelled and expressed through institutions (which may be open or closed to other members of society). These filters also test any options for consistency/compatibility with their own survival, pre-existing priorities and policy goals. This then leads to selection of environmental targets which are considered achievable in the given context. (ibid., p. 78)

Experts of different kinds have their own vested interests which they are likely to promote as part of the advice which they proffer: lawyers will argue for new laws, engineers for investment in research for new technologies, and so on. Governments, meanwhile, may seek to put their own gloss on particular problems, while: 'Political elites without capacity for corrective, effective control are most likely to deny significance to an environmental threat. They may promise action and engage in symbolic gestures without providing any practical instruments and resources for achieving proclaimed goals' (Boehmer-Christiansen 1994, p. 71).

Government approaches to environmental problems tend to be rooted in self-interest which often favours short-term sectional interests within the national community rather than the global environment. Prins (1990, p. 711) has criticised such 'linear' thinking based on narrowly conceptualised calculations of self-interest:

> 'Linear' thinking . . . insulates issues from one another, and it ignores the effects of outcomes on actors and interests outside a fairly narrow circle. It takes for granted that a political issue has a beginning (response to a demand or pressure), a middle (the working out of tensions for and against action), and a finite end. The politics of the environment, however, just aren't like that.

Whilst the rational models of policy-making embody assumptions that government seeks to maximise the public good, a more realistic interpretation of policy towards the environment will focus upon the desires of government to secure its own re-election in the short to medium term and to promote the success of its national manufacturers in a competitive global environment: 'Most governments have no difficulty in endorsing the view that global policies are needed to control the pace of environmental change: indeed most refuse to take unilateral actions which would affect the relative competitiveness of their business on world markets' (Rees 1991, p. 293).

The pre-eminence of narrowly and slantedly perceived national interest in forming policies in relation to global environmental issues has recently been explored by Rowlands (1995). He showed that the German government was sympathetic to policies for the limitation of greenhouse gas emissions, because Germany had already achieved considerable gains in energy efficiency and had developed a major stake in the market for environmental protection products. The government of the Netherlands was particularly forceful in pushing for carbon reductions because the Netherlands might be severely inundated in the event of rising sea levels resulting from global warming, but in contrast, the oil exporting countries of the Middle East were opposed to controls on fuel consumption.

National governments are still the most powerful actors upon the international stage and they remain unready to accept the need for global solutions to global problems. In performing their roles on the global stage, the national politicians still play to sectional domestic audiences and still seem to imagine, even in an age of an awesome assemblage of challenges to human survival, that the fudging of issues is a goal rather than a recipe for disaster. In addition to pursuing narrow state-centred policies, the states also combine in antagonistic blocs. The 1972 Stockholm conference became divided on North–South lines as the Third World delegates regarded environmentalism as a means of protecting the privileges of the First World while leaving the Third World countries mired in technical dependence and poverty. The 1992 Rio Earth Summit was supposed to produce a series of legally binding international accords on issues such as climatic change, toxic wastes, biodiversity and forests, but produced a 'framework convention' which was sufficiently diluted and amorphous as to cause little offence to any sovereign interest. In the US President Bush had become convinced that the control of greenhouse gas emissions and other environmentally desirable policies would damage the national economy and so he adopted a hostile attitude:

> The legally binding documents were so eviscerated as to have no practical impact. President Bush coyly resisted committing himself to a Rio appearance until after the CO2 accords had been cleansed of any binding language about levels of emissions and timetables for their reduction . . . The U.S. government announced its resistance to the biodiversity treaty on the grounds that the U.S would not pay for preservation outside its borders, nor hamper its biotechnology industries. (Hecht and Cockburn 1993, p. 96)

Having reviewed the current state of environmental politics it would be difficult to disagree with Dalby (1992a, p. 513) that

> given the disproportionate use of resources by the developed world and the poverty of much of the rest of the planet, conservation is clearly something that needs to start in societies that are the most profligate users (and wasters) of resources. But international arrangements to ensure that resource flows are maintained, and their price kept low, may well reinforce the current economic discrepancies allowing continued destruction of the environments of resource producing areas and continued pollution where the products of these resources are eventually disposed.

A recent and authoritative analysis of the crisis of global environmental change and the nation state has been provided by Hurrell (1994, p. 146), who found that: 'The increased seriousness of many environmental problems provides one of the most intuitively plausible reasons for believing that the nation state and the system of states may be either in crisis or heading towards a crisis.' He found, as we have, that running through the writing on the subject is the sense 'that the state and the fragmented system of sovereign states are less and less able to guarantee the effective and equitable management of an interdependent world in general, and of the global environment in particular' (ibid.). He thought that there were three main arguments that the nation-state was in, or heading for crisis in relation to the environment, and he identified them as follows. Firstly, the system of nation-states can no longer provide a viable political framework for the collective management of the global environment. Secondly, an increasing number of individual nation-states are found to be unable to provide localised order and are incapable of enforcing an adequate degree of environmental management within their own borders. Thirdly, environmental problems are themselves helping to erode the image of the state as the exclusive or primary focus for human loyalties and the new environmentalism is helping to stimulate the creation of a new sense of planetary consciousness which is leading to new, non-territorially based forms of political identity. However, Hurrell (ibid., p. 165) does not believe that the state system can simply be swept away:

> The state system may be part of the problem but it is also an essential part of the solution. The lack of global solidarity about resources and environmental issues is not primarily rooted in the state system but in the inability of human beings to agree on the nature and seriousness of the environmental threats, on the meaning of sustainability, and on the principles of global environmental management.

It seems likely that global environmental crisis will be encountered before any radically different political system can be put in place. As yet, global governance may be no more than a mirage of a flicker of light glimpsed through a mist. Really, our problem is not a problem of the environment but a problem of humanity. The remarkable success of the human animal was due not so much to an enlarged brain or an opposable thumb as to adaptability. It was this that allowed us to colonise the planet from the equators to the polar latitudes, displacing other life-forms as we advanced and multiplied. Yet now our responses to challenge and opportunity may seem to have become ossified. We see problems that are big enough to fill the sky. We know how they are caused, and we know how to begin to put them right. Yet our political systems seem to have lost the capacity to respond effectively. Political life has fallen so deeply under the tyranny of party politics that the whole rhythm of life runs according to a four or five year electoral cycle. No leaders dare to care about what may happen beyond the next election nor to recognise any threat greater than that which is posed by the rival party. If we have lost the political adaptability which will be essential to the rehabilitation of the Earth then our future as the dominant species must be in doubt. The people, meanwhile, have surrendered to a different tyranny, one which underpinned the long-outmoded world of mercantilism and was reborn in the gimcrack arena of Thatcherism and Reaganomics. Balance of trade figures are king and all must pay fealty to this mad monarch by working and worrying about work until all thoughts of the meaning and value of life are forgotten in the fog of fear. And all the while the time runs out.

Conclusion: The Shape of Things to Come?

The millennium approaches: the rusty Iron Curtain has fallen and there is much talk of the 'New World Order'. Political geography has grown up in a world composed of sovereign states. It matured on a planet contested between two superpowers – a world in which the rules were stark and simple. But that world has gone, leaving far more scope for hypothesis and uncertainty. In the old world of the 1950s and 1960s there did not seem to be a great deal that was wrong that could not have been fixed at a summit conference between the leaders of the two superpowers. Any modern summit would have to accommodate a coachload of leaders, and looming over them would be challenges of a global nature, many of which they might not fix even if they wanted to. In the last years of this century, old certainties are undermined and new rules are needed to make sense of what is happening.

Once, election results seemed to be determined by the size of rises in domestic incomes, the level of inflation and the unemployment rate. Today, *uncertainty* seems to be becoming a major consideration influencing voters' choices, especially in countries whose governments' enthusiasm for deregulation and flexibility, policies which are regarded in mainstream thinking as being essential in order to compete in a globalised economy, have led to widespread fears of job insecurity.

It seems that uncertainty flourishes in a globalised world – and this is clearly true in the realms of political prediction:

> some analysts see political authority fragmenting into even smaller parcels. Others see authority consolidating into large, competitive military or trade blocs as the number of rival centers of power expand. Some perceive science and technology propelling the world into abundance and affluence; others see it breeding chaos and environmental destruction. And some project the spread of democracy worldwide, whereas others forsee a resurgence of hypernationalism and cultural clashes between civilizations . . . and a rekindling of support for strong (and, potentially, war-waging) autocratic rulers. (Kegley and Wittkopf 1995, p. 7)

Whatever the detail of their analyses, all experts seem to recognise the paramount nature of change:

> The old state system is resolving itself into a complex of political–economic entities: micro-regions, traditional states, and macro-regions with institutions of greater or lesser functional scope and formal authority. World cities are the keyboards of the global economy. Rival transnational processes of ideological formation aim respectively at hegemony and counterhegemony. Institutions of concertation and co-ordination bridge the major states and macro-regions . . . The whole picture resembles the multilevel order of medieval Europe more than the Westphalian model of a system of sovereign independent states that has heretofore been the paradigm of international relations. (Cox 1994, p. 53)

As Graham Smith has noted:

> With the demise of state socialism and the end of the Cold War, a common consensus has emerged in both popular and scholarly discourses that we have come to the end of an historical epoch . . . For the New Right, the end of the Cold War represents nothing less than the 'end of history', and the victory, reflected in the revolutionary years of 1989 and 1991 in Eastern Europe and the Soviet Union, for economic and political liberalism, a triumph for the west that presages the global universality of capitalism and the end of Communism. (Smith 1993, p. 76)

He then reviewed the leading approaches to the World Order that was associated with the Cold War era and found them all wanting. Traditional geopolitics embodied a Western-centric assumption that what gave the Cold War its underlying momentum was Soviet expansionism: in claiming to guard against such encroachment the United States could seek to legitimise its own military encroachments. The balance of power models failed to take account of non-state global actors and social changes within states, while: 'in viewing world politics solely through the prism of an inter-state system fluctuating around a geopolitical equilibrium, such accounts failed to predict the Cold War's eclipse' (ibid., p. 79). Meanwhile, world-systems theory failed to recognise the complexity of bilateral and multilateral political, military and other relationships, and, in particular, it largely ignored the fundamental division of the world between the competing social systems of capitalism and Communism.

As an alternative, Smith offered a thesis of 'post-Stalinism' and 'Atlanticism'. The unique character of the Cold War was provided by its existence as a conflict between the rival social systems of capitalism and socialism, with their different perspectives on ownership, different ideologies and their tendency continually to generate competing geopolitical interests. Each system was not homogeneous, and though each had a superpower at its core, variation within the systems also existed – as in the manner that Labour governments in the UK differed quite considerably from Republican administrations in the USA. In a sense, each system needed the other, for both were founded on an ongoing external threat and on the high levels of military spending associated with facing the threat.

By the early 1980s, however, both economic systems and their respective superpower core states were showing signs of decline. For the US, the costs of maintaining a worldwide military role were beginning to hurt, while the trend towards the globalisation of capital was leaving the Soviet world financially sidelined at a time when the post-Stalinist economy was constricted by bureaucratic central planning; was shaped to meet the demands of war rather than to satisfy domestic needs, and yet was barred from economic reform for fear of what the social and political consequences of reform might be. As the Soviet Union became unable to resource economic development or permit reform in Eastern Europe, so the Warsaw Pact countries sought to modernise by turning to Western sources of investment. At the same time, in the Soviet Union the privileged caste of party members was being eclipsed by a new, more cosmopolitan, educated elite, as meanwhile the differentials in living standards widened. Post-Stalinism was unable to prevent economic stagnation and living standards fell at a stage when it was also unable to exclude Western media images which revealed the gulf in living standards between the socialist and capitalist worlds. Thus, while the USA may have been in decline, the rate of decline was far faster in the Soviet Union – and the collapse of this superpower resulted in the creation and existence for a while of an essentially mono-polar power system.

In 1989 Fukuyama wrote his celebrated article on 'The End of History?' for the journal *The National Interest*. He argued that a remarkable consensus concerning the legitimacy of liberal democracy had emerged throughout the world over the past few years, 'as it conquered rival ideologies like hereditary monarchy, fascism, and most recently communism' (Fukuyama 1992, p. xi). He went further, and claimed that the establishment of liberal democracy may constitute the end of human ideological evolution and the ultimate form of government – thus ushering in the end of history. He believed that the tyrannies of the Left and the Right were ultimately compelled to surrender when confronted with modern technology, which bestows such advantages on those states which possess it, and which was combined with the struggle of people to be recognised as human beings with worth and dignity. Thus:

> The most remarkable development of the last quarter of the twentieth century has been the revelation of enormous weaknesses at the core of the world's seemingly strong dictatorships, whether they be of the military–authoritarian Right, or the communist–totalitarian Left. From Latin America to Eastern Europe, from the Soviet Union to the Middle East and Asia, strong governments have been failing over the last two decades . . . A liberal revolution in economic thinking has sometimes preceded, sometimes followed, the move towards political freedom around the globe. (pp. xiii–xiv)

News of the death of history has been greatly exaggerated, and even some form of resurrection of the Soviet bloc cannot yet be ruled out. It is still possible to imagine a Russia that reverts to a form of Stalinism and which succeeds in reclaiming some of its former Republics – like Belorus – and possibly even one or two former satellites – perhaps Bulgaria or Slovakia. With a fervent and aggressive nationalism probably linked to some Brezhnev-style form of Stalinism, such a state would indeed be a most unpleasant and dangerous creature. Before too long it would perish, the victim of the same economic inadequacies which brought down its predecessor. But in the meantime it could accomplish a great deal of damage at home and abroad. Nationalism can be a welcoming refuge for embittered failures; writing of the rise of the nationalist Vatra Romaneasca movement in Romania, Gallagher (1992) describes how it can appeal to those 'searching for alternative legitimizing symbols with which to make sense of their lives. . . Nationalism is well placed to fill the ideological vacuum left by the collapse of communism.'

This speculation lies in the realms of the possible, but the existence of globalisation as a major cause of change in the years to come is absolutely certain. During the last century the core of advanced manufacturing has drifted westwards, from Victorian England across the eastern seaboard states and Midwest of the US to California, and it will soon settle on Asia's Pacific rim. This does not imply that an Asian power is poised to exert a global hegemony, but it does seem likely that three great power clusters or geostrategic regions – South-East Asia, North America, and Europe – will dominate the political and economic life of the world in the first decades of the twenty-first century. Such changes can not be regarded with complacency by the communities of the West, for globalisation is associated with ever-intensifying competition in an ever-expanding range of activities. Thus far, globalisation seems to have had only a minimal effect on employment levels in the West, though its effects in reducing wage levels may already have been significant. However, were globalisation to lead to a marked levelling down in Western standards of living, it is conceivable that the great economic blocs, the EU and the NAFTA might resort to forms of protectionism.

It would be wrong to characterise the world of today and tomorrow as being crudely split into some sort of threefold core, NIC and periphery division. Far more realistic is the image of a continuum from rich to poor in which the position of the economic contestants is forever shifting as the affluence deriving from advantage becomes in turn a source of weakness, and so helps to promote another shuffling of the economic pack. Thus in Taiwan, the first Asian NIC to become established, labour is now ten times as expensive as it is in mainland China: within the Pacific rim the world exists in an economic microcosm, with the more developed countries shedding low-tech industries to those that are in earlier stages of industrialisation.

The rise of Asia will have profound repercussions for the whole of the world; already the rates of growth are stunning, with the Chinese economy doubling in size every decade and that of India at last being poised for spectacular growth. This rise will not be confined to the economic arena, and the cultural consequences must be considerable. In some respects the omens here are not auspicious, and China and India rank fourth and fifth in the world in respect of their emissions of greenhouse gases (*World Resources* 1990–1, p. 345). Still, they are respectively associated with beliefs which emphasise the need for environmental harmony and the respect for all forms of life, so it can only be hoped that these deeply ingrained values will triumph over the pragmatism and arrogance which, in China particularly, is causing enormous damage to overworked environments. Globalisation is normally associated with a politics which holds the state in low regard. There is no doubt that politicians have lost their freedom to manipulate national economies, but it is also the case that there has been very considerable state involvement in controlling the development of Asia's most rapidly growing economies. In Malaysia, Taiwan and several other cases, government has been associated with heavy and sustained investment in growth industries, while government enthusiasm for low levels of taxation has allowed high levels of private investment in the domestic economies. State welfare spending is very low in the Asian economies, partly reflecting youthful population structures as well as the traditional cultural attitudes towards family obligations – but in terms of the policing and regulation of society the state is much more prominent and interventionist, with lower premiums being placed on human rights and individual freedom.

The rise of Asian influence should not be taken necessarily to presage a further reduction in the importance of the state. Within the societies of South-East Asia – with the exceptions of rogue and oppressive regimes like those of Burma and China – government tends to be held in quite high regard. The widespread contempt for government, such as one finds in the US, is not encountered; instead, the state is respected in the manner of a wise patriarch by societies more conditioned by habit to the acceptance of authoritarian rule.

The geopolitical outlines of the New World Order are still in the process of forming, and though power may be concentrated in the three geostrategic regions of power concentration already mentioned – North America, Europe and the Pacific rim – other aspects remain blurred. Here it might prove useful to review Cohen's (1964) concept of 'shatterzones', which he identified as being large, strategically located regions occupied by a number of states caught between the conflicting spheres of influence of greater powers. The shatterzones of today and tomorrow do not match this description, for there are no longer two great superpowers competing for the allegiance of the unaligned states. But there certainly are zones of instability running between, beside, or even through the geostrategic regions. Their significance is augmented as the former bipolar tensions give way to the *regional* contests and rivalries which will be characteristic of the twenty-first century. The old shatterzone of the Middle East remains a zone of instability, with the appetite for reprisals and war amongst the disadvantaged Arab and Lebanese populations being replenished on every occasion that Israel vengefully devastates refugee camps and civilian settlements in the territory of its neighbours. A new zone of instability runs along the southern margin of Russia, through the youthful republics derived from the disintegration of the old Soviet Union. Here, Muslims, Russians and Christians exist in varying numerical proportions and in varying states of tension, with the spectre of Muslim fundamentalism poised to throw the region into a turmoil of incompatible identifications. Next, there is the prospect of rivalry between China and Japan when these traditional enemies vie for leadership of the Asian geostrategic region. For decades Japan has been able to shelter under the American nuclear umbrella and has capped defence spending at 1 per cent of GDP, but such arrangements may not persist as China grows rapidly in economic strength and reacts aggressively to Taiwan, a lesser rival. Other notable regional tensions will include those between North and South Korea and India and Pakistan.

In the world that awaits, migration is sure to be a cause of very considerable tension too. It will take place as advancing economies outstrip domestic labour supplies, and already one worker in every seven in Malaysia is a migrant from countries like Indonesia or Bangladesh. Other migrants will be refugees from overpopulation, environmental deterioration, famine or war and hosts of economic

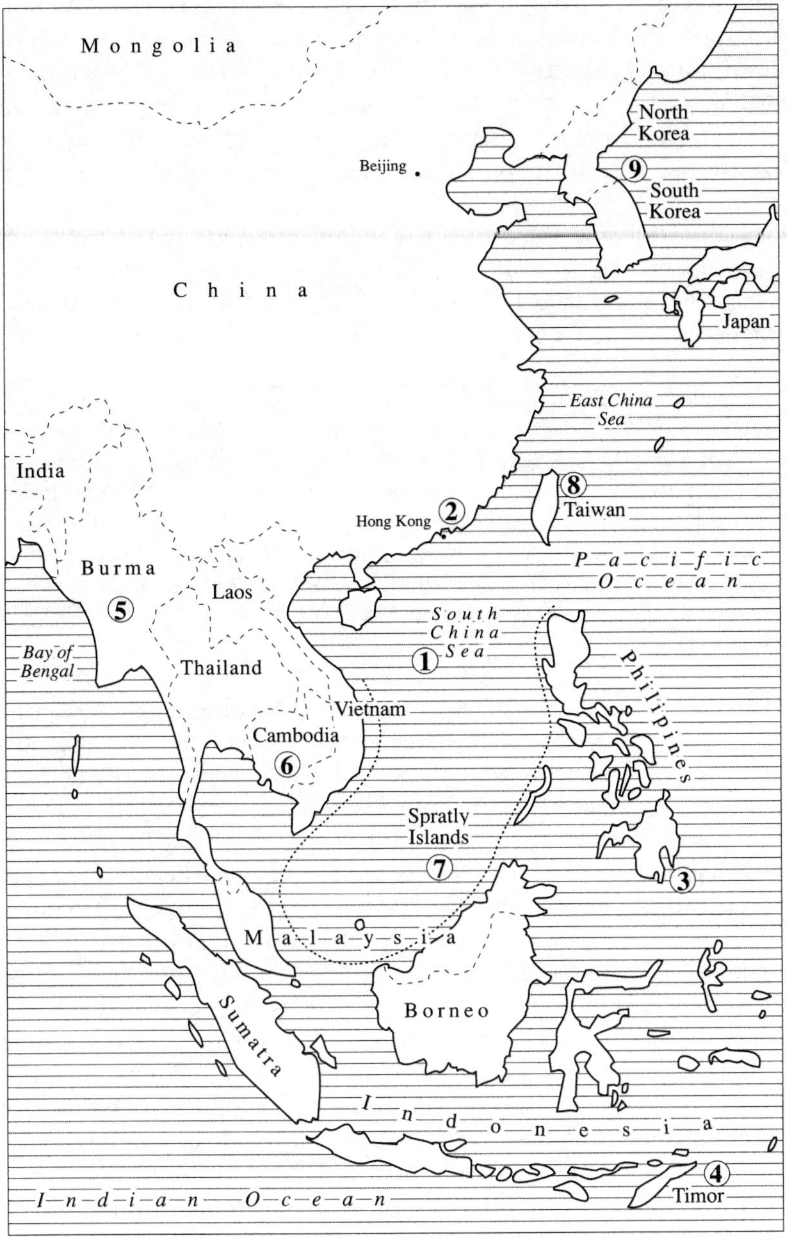

Map 14 Pressure points in South-East Asia: the dotted line denotes the extent of the Chinese claim to sovereignty over the South China Sea, Spratly Islands and beyond

migrants will struggle to gain access to the more prosperous parts of the world. According to Castles and Miller (1993, p. 124): 'The North–South gap – the differentials in life expectancy, demography, economic structure, social conditions and political stability between the industrial democracies and most of the rest of the world – looms as a major barrier to the creation of a peaceful and prosperous global society. International migration is a major consequence of the North-South gap.'

In addition to the intercontinental and international movements of people, throughout the developing world there are surges of people moving from rural to urban settings. Never before have questions and problems of identity been so prominent:

> New social movements converging around specific sets of issues – environmentalism, feminism and peace – have grown to a different extent in different parts of the world. More amorphous and vaguer movements – 'people power' and democratization – are present wherever political structures are seen to be both repressive and fragile. These movements evoke particular identities – ethnic, nationalist, religious, gender. They exist within states but are transnational in essence. The indigenous peoples' movement affirms rights prior to the existing state system. (Cox 1994, pp. 54–5)

The shift from the village to the city or urban ghetto can never be less than traumatic, while in the European homelands of nationalism, individuals and societies which have not yet accomplished the mental adjustment in identification from the nation-state to the European Union are now confronted with the psychological challenges posed by globalisation. Meanwhile, streets and neighbourhoods are shared between those who can enjoy and develop the rights, privileges and identification associated with citizenship, and others to who these are denied.

There has been speculation about the consequences of globalisation for nationalism and for human identifications with locality and place, but most remains uncertain. Globalisation and regional integration must surely be weakening more traditional loyalties. If nation-states endure – as they probably will for quite some time to come – it will be because people are not yet ready to make the transition from a nation-state-based form of mental bonding to some other form of psycho-political association. But:

> the age of migration could be marked by the erosion of nationalism and the weakening of divisions between people. Admittedly there are countervailing tendencies, such as racism, the 'fortress Europe' mentality, or the resurgence

> of nationalism in certain areas. The decline of national divisions is likely to be uneven, and setbacks are possible, especially in the event of economic or political crises . . . [yet the] globalisation of migration provides grounds for optimism, because it does give some hope of increased unity in dealing with the pressing problems which beset our small planet. (Castles and Miller 1993, p. 275)

Ultimately, however, human survival will depend upon the creation of the transnational and global political structures which are needed if we are to meet the environmental challenges of the twenty-first century.

References

Aase, T. H. (1994) 'Symbolic Space: Representations of Space in Geography and Anthropology', *Geografiska Annaler* (76 B) 111–31.

Abdel-Malek, A. (1977) 'Geopolitics and National Movements: An Essay on the Dialectics of Imperialism', *Antipode* (9) 28–36.

ACDA: (1995) *World Military Expenditure and Arms Transfers, 1993–4* (Washington DC: US Arms Control and Disarmament Agency).

Agnew, J. (1987) *Place and Politics: The Geographical Mediation of State and Society* (Boston: Allen & Unwin).

Agnew, J. (1995) 'The Rhetoric of Regionalism: The Northern League in Italian Politics, 1983–94', *Transactions of the Institute of British Geographers*, n.s. (20) 156–72.

Agnew, J. and Corbridge, S. (1989) 'The New Geopolitics: The Dynamics of Geopolitical Order', in R. J. Johnston and P. J. Taylor (eds), *A World in Crisis* (Oxford: Basil Blackwell).

Ake, C. (n.d.) 'Theoretical Notes on the National Question in Nigeria', Department of Political Science, University of Port Harcourt, Port Harcourt, Nigeria.

Allen, C. (1995) 'Understanding African Politics', *Review of African Political Economy* (65) 301–20.

Allison, L. (1975) *Environmental Planning, A Political and Philosophical Analysis* (London: Allen and Unwin).

Anderson, B. (1991) *Imagined Communities*, 2nd edn (London: Verso).

Anderson, J. (1989) 'Nationalisms in a Disunited Kingdom', in J. Mohan (ed.), *The Political Geography of Contemporary Britain* (London: Macmillan), pp. 35–50.

Anderson, P. (1983) 'The Absolutist States of Western Europe', in D. Held (ed.), *States and Societies* (Oxford: Martin Robertson).

Ardrey, R. (1967) *The Territorial Imperative: A Personal Inquiry into the Animal Origins of Property and Nations* (London: Collins).

Armitage, P. (1992) 'Indigenous Homelands and the Security Requirements of Western Nation-States: Innu Opposition to Military Flight Training in Eastern Quebec and Labrador', in A. Kirby (ed.), *The Pentagon and the Cities* (Newbury Park, Call.: Sage) pp. 126–53.

Armstrong, J. (1982) *Nations Before Nationalism* (Chapel Hill: University of North Carolina Press).

Barnaby, F. (1991) 'The Environmental Impact of the Gulf War', *The Ecologist* (21) 166–72.

Bassett, T. J. (1988) 'The Political Ecology of Peasant-herder Conflict in the Northern Ivory Coast', *Annals of the Association of American Geographers* (78) 453–72.

Bassin, M. (1987a) 'Imperialism and the Nation State in Friedrich Ratzel's Political Geography', *Progress in Human Geography* (11) 473–95.

Bassin, M. (1987b) 'Race Contra Space: The Conflict Between German Geopolitik and National Socialism', *Political Geography Quarterly* (6) 115–34.

Beetham, D. (1984) 'The Future of the Nation State', in G. McLennan, D. Held and S. Hall (eds), *The Idea of the Modern State* (Buckingham: The Open University).

Bell, E. (1995) *The Guardian*, 26 February.

Berkhofer Jr, R. F. (1964) 'Space, Time, Culture, and the New Frontier', *Agricultural History* (38) 21–30.

Berner, E. and Korff, R. (1995) 'Globalization and Local Resistance: The Creation of Localities in Manila and Bangkok', *International Journal of Urban and Regional Research* (19) 208–22.

Black, R. (1991) 'Refugees and Displaced Persons: Geographical Perspectives and Research Directions', *Progress in Human Geography* (15) 281–98.

Blaut, J. (1986) 'A Theory of Nationalism', *Antipode* (18) 5–10.

Blij, H. J. de (1967) *Systematic Political Geography* (New York: John Wiley).

Boehmer-Christiansen, S. (1994) 'Politics and Environmental Management', *Journal of Economic Planning and Management* (37) 69–85.

Boulding, K. E. (1962) *Conflict and Defense: A General Theory* (New York: Harper & Row).

Bowman, I. (1921) *The New World: Problems in Political Geography* (New York: World Books).

Bowman, I. (1942) 'Geography Versus Geopolitics', *Geographical Review* (32) 646–58.

Brigham, A. P. (1919) 'Principles in the Delimitation of Boundaries', *Geographical Review* (7) 201–19.

Brown, C. (1994) 'Critical Theory and Postmodernism', in A. J. R. Groom and M. Light (eds), *Contemporary International Relations Theory* (London: Pinter) pp. 56–68.

Brown, S. (1989) 'Inherited Geopolitics and Emergent Global Realities', in E. K. Hamilton (ed.), *America's Global Interests* (New York: W. W. Norton) pp. 166–77.

Brubaker, W. R. (1992) *Citizenship and Nationhood in France and Germany* (London: Harvard University Press).

Brubaker, W. R. (ed.) (1989) *Immigration and the Politics of Citizenship in Europe and North America* (London: University Press of America).

Brunn, S. D. and Yanarella, E. (1987) 'Towards a Humanistic Political Geography', *Studies in Comparative International Development* (22) 3–49.

Buck, N. (1990) review of J. A. Agnew and J. S. Duncan, *The Power of Place: Bringing together Geographical and Sociological Imaginations* (Boston and London: Unwin Hyman, 1989), Sociology (24) 555–6.

Burke, J. P. and Greenstein, F. (1989) *How Presidents Test Reality: Decisions on Vietnam 1954 and 1965* (New York: Russell Sage Foundation).

Buttimer, A. (1990) 'Geography, Humanism and Global Concern', *Annals of the Association of American Geographers* (80) 1–33.

Byers, B. (1991) 'Ecoregions, State Sovereignty and Conflict', *Bulletin of Peace Proposals* (22) 65–76.

Callaghy, T. M. (1984) *The State–Society Struggle: Zaire in Comparative Perspective* (New York: Columbia University Press).
Camilleri, J. A. and Falk, J. (1992) *The End of Sovereignty* (London: Edward Elgar).
Carr, E. H. (1945) *Nationalism and After* (London: Macmillan).
Carr, E. H. (1946) *The Twenty Years Crisis: 1919–1939* (London: Macmillan).
Carson, R. (1962) *Silent Spring* (Boston: Houghton Mifflin).
Castles, S. and Miller, M. J. (1993) *The Age of Migration* (London: Macmillan).
Cathcart King, D. J. (1988) *The Castle in England and Wales* (London: Croom Helm).
CBO (1995) 'Cleaning-up Defense Installations: Issues and Options' (Washington, DC: Congressional Budget Office).
Clad, J. (1991) *Behind the Myth: Business, Money and Power in Southeast Asia* (London: Grafton Books).
Claessen, H. J. M. and Skalnik P. (eds) (1978) *The Early State* (The Hague: Mouton).
Clapham, C. (1985) *Third World Politics: An Introduction* (London: Croom Helm).
Clausewitz, C. von (1908) *On War*, vol. 1, tr J. J. Graham (London).
Cleland, C. E. (1973) *Art of the Great Lakes Indians* (Michigan: Flint Institute of Arts).
Cline, R. (1975) *World Power Assessment* (Washington, DC: Georgetown University Centre for Strategic and International Studies).
Cohen, S. B. (1964) *Geography and Politics in a World Divided* (New York: Oxford University Press).
Cohen, S. B. (1990) 'The World Geopolitical System in Retrospect and Prospect', *Journal of Geography* (89) 2–14.
Cohen, S. B. (1991) 'Global and Geopolitical Change in the Post-Cold War Era', *Annals of the Association of American Geographers* (81) 551–80.
Cole, J. P. (1990) 'The World of Jan Kowalewski: Pawns in Other People's Games', *Scottish Geographical Magazine* (106) 66–74.
Commission on Global Governance, (1995) *Our Global Neighbourhood* (Oxford: Oxford University Press).
Connor, W. (1978) 'A Nation Is a Nation, Is a State, Is an Ethnic Group, Is a . . .', *Ethnic and Racial Studies* (1) 377–400.
Connor, W. (1990) 'When Is a Nation', *Ethnic and Racial Studies* (13).
Connor, W. (1993) 'Beyond Reason: The Nature of the Ethnonational Bond', *Ethnic and Racial Studies* (16) 373–89.
Cooper, F. (1981) 'Africa and the World Economy', *African Studies Review* (14) 1–86.
Corbridge, S. (1991) 'Cheap Bananas and Global Capitalism', a review of C. Chase-Dunn (1989), *Global Formation: Structures of the World Economy*, in *Journal of Historical Geography* (17) 204–7.
Corea, G. (1990) 'Global Stakes Require a New Consensus', ifda dossier, 78, July/September, quoted in Camilleri and Falk (1992) p. 57.

Cornell, J. (1988) 'The Transformations of Tribe: Organization and Self-concept in North American Ethnicities', *Ethnic and Racial Studies* (11) 27–47.

Cosgrove D. and Daniels, S. (1988) *The Iconography of Landscape* (Cambridge: Cambridge University Press).

Cosgrove, D. (1994) 'Contested Global Visions: One World, Whole Earth and the Apollo Space Photographs', *Annals of the Association of American Geographers* (84).

Coughlin, C. (1995) 'Trojan Horse at the Heart of Europe', *Sunday Telegraph*, 19 February.

Council of Europe, (1992) 'Les Incidences de l'Achèvement du Marche Unique sur les Regions Frontalières', draft by C. Mestre based on trend report by R. Kovar and D. Simon cited in L. O'Dowd, J. Corrigan and T. Moore, 'Borders, National Sovereignty and European Integration: The British Case', *International Journal of Urban and Regional Research* (19) 272–85.

Cox, R. (1981) 'Social Forces, States and World Order', *Millennium: Journal of International Studies* (10) 126–55.

Cox, R.W. (1994) 'Global Restructuring: Making Sense of the Changing International Political Economy', in R. Stubbs and G.R.D. Underhill (eds), *Political Economy and the Changing Global Order* (London: Macmillan) pp. 45–59.

Crush, J.S. and Riddell, J.B. (1980) 'Third World Misunderstanding', *Area* (12) 204–6.

Cuba L. and Hummon, D. (1993) 'A Place to Call Home: Identification with Dwelling, Community and Region', *Sociological Quarterly* (34) 111–31.

Curzon of Keddleston, Lord (1907) 'Frontiers', the Romanes lecture, Oxford.

Cutter, S.L. (1994) 'Environmental Issues: Green Rage, Social Change and the New Environmentalism', *Progress in Human Geography* (18) 217–26.

Dahl, R.A. (1961) *Who Governs?* (New Haven: Yale University Press).

Dalby, S. (1991) 'Critical Geopolitics: Discourse, Deterrence and Dissent', *Environment and Planning D: Society and Space* (9) 261–83.

Dalby, S. (1992a) 'Ecopolitical Discourse: "Environmental Security" and Political Geography' *Progress in Human Geography* (16) pp. 503–22.

Dalby, S. (1992b) 'Security, Modernity, Ecology: The Dilemmas of the Post-Cold War Security Discourse', *Alternatives* (17) 95–134.

Dale, R. (1984) 'Nation State and International System: The World-System Perspective', in G. McLennan *et al.* (eds), *The Idea of the Modern State* (Oxford: Oxford University Press) pp. 183–206.

Daley, S. (1995) 'A Small Corner of Africa that is Forever Germany', *The Guardian* 8 September.

Davidson, B. (1990) 'The Crisis of the Nation-states of Africa', *Review of African Political Economy* (49) 9–21.

Dawkins, R. (1976) *The Selfish Gene* (Oxford: Oxford University Press).

de Freitas, C.R. (1991) 'The Greenhouse Crisis: Myths and Misconceptions', *Area* (23) 11–18.

De Seversky, A. P. (1950) *Air Power: Key to Survival* (New York: Simon & Schuster).
Denitch, B. (1993) 'Eastern Europe: Prospects after Communism', in P. Bennis and M. Moushabeck (eds), *Altered States* (New York: Olive Branch) pp. 465–73.
Deutsch, K. W. (1953) 'The Growth of Nations', *World Politics* (5).
Deutsch, K. W. (1961) 'Social Mobilization and Political Development', *American Political Science Review* (55) 493–514.
Deutsch, K. W. (1966) *Nationalism and Social Communication*, 2nd edn (New York: MIT Press).
Deutsch, K. W. (1981) 'The Crisis of the State', *Government and Opposition* (16) 331–43.
Dicken, P. (1986) *Global Shift, Industrial Change in a Turbulent World* (London: Harper Row).
Dicken, P. (1992) *Global Shift, The Internationalization of Economic Activity*, 2nd edn (London: Paul Chapman).
Dickens, P. (1990) *Urban Sociology: Society, Locality and Human Nature* (New York: Harvester Wheatsheaf).
Dodds, K.- J. (1993) 'Geopolitics, Experts and the Making of Foreign Policy', Area (25) 70–4.
Dodds, K.- J. (1994) 'Geopolitics in the Foreign Office: British Representations of Argentina, 1945–1961', *Transactions of the Institute of British Geographers* n.s. (19) 273–90.
Downs, A. (1972) 'Up and Down with Ecology: The Issue Attention Cycle', *The Public Interest* 38–50.
Driver, F. (1991) 'Political Geography and State Formation: Disputed Territory', *Progress in Human Geography* (15) 268–280.
Duncan, J. and Duncan, N. (1988) '(Re)reading the Landscape', *Environment and Planning D: Society and Space* (6) 117–26.
Eagles, M. (1995) 'Spatial and Contextual Models of Political Behavior: An Introduction', *Political Geography* (14) 499–502.
Earle, T. (ed.) (1991) *Chiefdoms: Power, Economy, and Ideology* (Cambridge: Cambridge University Press).
Easton, D. (1957) 'An Approach to the Analysis of Political Systems', *World Politics* (April) 383–400.
Eibl-Eibesfeld, I. (1979) *The Biology of Peace and War: Men, Animals and Aggression* (London: Thames & Hudson).
Ellger, C. (1992) 'Berlin: Legacies of Division and Problems of Unification', *The Geographical Journal* (158) 40–46.
Emerson, R. (1960) *From Empire to Nation* (Cambridge, Mass.: Harvard University Press).
Emmott, W. (1993) *Japan's Global Reach* (London: Arrow).
Engels, F. (1972) *The Origin of the Family, Private Property and the State* (New York: International Publishers).
Entrikin, J. N. (1994) 'Place and Region', *Progress in Human Geography* (18) 227–33.

Esping-Andersen, G. (1990) *The Three Worlds of Welfare Capitalism* (Cambridge: Polity Press).
Evelyn, J. (1661) 'Fumifugium Or the Inconvenience of the Aer and Smoake of London Dissipated' (reprinted 1961, 1972, Brighton: National Society for Clean Air, 39pp.).
Eyles, J. (1990) 'Group Identity and Urban Space: the North American Experience', in M. Chisholm and D. M. Smith (eds), *Shared Space, Divided Space, Essays on Conflict and Territorial Organization* (London: Unwin Hyman) pp. 46–66.
Falk, R. (1992) *Explorations at the Edge of Time* (Philadelphia: Temple Press).
Fawcett, C. B. (1919) *The Provinces of England* (London).
Featherstone, M. (1993) 'Global and Local Cultures', in J. Bird, B. Curtis, T. Putnam, G. Robertson and L. Tickner (eds), *Mapping the Futures, Local Culture and Global Change* (London: Routledge) pp. 169–87.
Ferguson, Y. (1991) 'Chiefdoms to City-state: The Greek Experience' in T. Earle (ed.), *Chiefdoms: Power, Economy, and Ideology* (Cambridge: Cambridge University Press) pp. 169–92.
Finger, M. (1991) 'The Military, the Nation State and the Environment', *The Ecologist* (21) 220–5.
First, R. (1983) 'Colonialism and the Formation of African States', in D. Held (ed.), *States and Societies* (Oxford: Martin Robertson).
Foeken, D. (1995) 'On the Causes of the Partition of Central Africa, 1875–85', *Political Geography* (14) 80–100.
Forrest, J. B. (1987) 'The Contemporary African State: A Ruling Class?', *Review of African Political Economy* (38) 66–70.
Forrest, J. B. (1988) 'The Quest for State Hardness in Africa', *Comparative Politics* (20) 423–41.
Forrest, J. B. (1994) 'Asynchronic Comparisons: Weak States in Post-colonial Africa and Mediaeval Europe', in M. Dogan and A. Kazancigil (eds), *Comparing Nations* (Oxford: Basil Blackwell) pp. 260–96.
Franceisco, W. D. and Gitelman, Z. (1984) 'Soviet Political Culture and Covert Participation in Policy Implementation', *American Political Science Review* (78) 603–21.
Frank, A. G. (1975) quoted in H. Brookfield, *Independent Development* (London: Methuen).
Frankel, J. (1964) *International Relations* (London: Oxford University Press).
Freedland, J. and Travena, C. (1995) 'A Bright New Dawn of Storm Clouds Ahead?', *The Guardian*, 26 October.
Frelick, W. (1993) 'Closing Ranks: The North Locks Arms Against New Refugees', in P. Bennis and M. Moushabeck (eds), *Altered States* (New York: Olive Branch) pp. 162–75.
Friedmann, J. (1986) 'The World City Hypothesis', *Development and Change* (17) 69–84.
Fukuyama, F. (1989) 'The End of History', *National Interest* (16) 3–18.
Fukuyama, F. (1992) *The End of History and the Last Man* (New York: Free Press).

Gaenslen, F. (1986) 'Culture and Decision Making in China, Japan, Russia and the United States', *World Politics* (39) 78–103.
Galbraith, J. K. (1962) *The Affluent Society* (Harmondsworth: Penguin).
Gallagher, T. (1992) 'Vatra Romaneasca and Resurgent Nationalism in Romania', *Ethnic and Racial Studies* (15) 570–97.
Garau, P. (1989) 'Third World Cities in a Global Society Viewed from a Developing Nation', in R. V. Knight, and G. Gappert (eds), *Cities in a Global Society* (London and Newbury Park, Cal.: Sage).
Gellner, E. (1964) *Thought and Change* (London: Weidenfeld & Nicolson).
Gellner, E. (1983) *Nations and Nationalism* (Oxford: Blackwell).
German, F. C. (1960) 'A Tentative Evaluation of World Power', *Journal of Conflict Resolution* (4) 138–44.
Germani, C. (1995) 'An Ancient Mythical Warrior Gives the Kyrgyz Hope in a New World', *Baltimore Sun*, reprinted in *The Guardian*, 19 September.
Ghazi, P. (1994) 'Too Many Kids', *The Observer* 4 September.
Giddens, A. (1984) *The Construction of Society: Outline of a Theory of Structuration* (Cambridge: Polity Press).
Giddens, A. (1985) *The Nation State and Violence*, (Cambridge: Polity Press).
Giddens, A. (1990) *The Consequences of Modernity* (Cambridge: Polity Press).
Giddens, A. (1991) *Modernity and Self-Identity: Self and Society in the Late Modern Age* (Stanford, Cal: Stanford University Press).
Giddens, A. (1995) 'Government's Last Gasp', *The Observer*, 9 July.
Glacken, C. (1967) *Traces on the Rhodian Shore* (Berkeley: University of California Press).
Glassner, M. I. (1993) *Political Geography* (New York: John Wiley).
Gottmann, J. (1951) 'Geography and International Relations', *World Politics* (3) 153–73.
Gottmann, J. (1952) 'The Political Partitioning of Our World: An Attempt at Analysis', *World Politics* (4) 512–19.
Gottmann, J. (1973) *The Significance of Territory* (Charlottesville: University Press of Virginia).
Gramsci, A. (1971) *Selections from the Prison Notebooks* (London: Lawrence & Wishart).
Gray, J. (1994) 'Kill the Leviathan', *The Guardian*, 3 October.
Griffiths, I. (1986) 'The Scramble for Africa: Inherited Political Boundaries', *Geographical Journal* (152) 204–16.
Groom, A. J. R. and Powell, D. (1994) 'From World Politics to Global Governance – a Theme in Need of a Focus', in A. J. R. Groom and M. Light (eds), *Contemporary International Relations: A Guide to Theory* (London: Pinter).
Grove-White, R. (1993) 'Environmentalism: A New Moral Discourse for Technological Society?', in K. Milton (ed.), *Environmentalism, The View From Anthropology* (London and New York: Routledge).
Gurr, E. R. and Harff, B. (1994) *Ethnic Conflicts in World Politics* (Boulder, Col.: Westview Press).
Halliday, F. (1994) *Rethinking International Relations* (London: Macmillan).

Hammar, T. (1990) *Democracy and the Nation State* (Aldershot: Gower).
Hansen, N. (1994) 'Barrier Effects in the US-Mexico Border Area', in P. Nijkamp (ed.), *New Boundaries and Old Barriers in Spatial Development* (Aldershot: Avebury) pp. 87–104.
Hardin, G. (1968) 'The Tragedy of the Commons: The Population Problem has no Technical Solution; It Requires a Fundamental Extension of Morality', *Science* (162) 1243–8.
Hardin, G. (1974) 'Living on a Lifeboat', *Bioscene* (24) 561–68.
Hartley, K. (1995) 'Defence and the Environment: an Economic Approach', *GeoJournal* (37) 277–82.
Hartshorne, R. (1950) 'The Functional Approach in Political Geography', *Annals of the Assocation of American Geographers* (40) 95–130.
Harvey, D. (1973) *Social Justice and the City* (London: Edward Arnold).
Harvey, D. (1975) 'The Geography of Capital Accumulation: a Reconstruction of the Marxian Theory', *Antipode* (7) 9–21.
Harvey, D. (1989) *The Condition of Postmodernity: An Enquiry into the Origins of Cultural Change* (Oxford: Basil Blackwell).
Harvey, D. (1993) 'From Space to Place and Back Again: Reflections on the Condition of Postmodernity', in J. Bird, B. Curtis, T. Putnam, G. Robertson and L. Tickner (eds), *Mapping the Futures, Local Cultures, Global Change* (London: Routledge), pp. 3–29.
Hastedt, G. P. and Knickrehm, K. M. (1991) *Dimensions of World Politics* (New York: HarperCollins).
Healey, D. (1995) 'Not a Very Solid State', *Sunday Times*, 5 March.
Hecht, S. and Cockburn, A. (1993) 'Eco-Tiers: Rio and Environmentalism After the Cold War' in P. Bennis and M. Moushabeck (eds), *Altered States* (New York: Olive Branch) pp. 95–104.
Hechter, M. (1975) *Internal Colonialism* (London: Routledge).
Hechter, M. and Levi, M. (1979) 'The Comparative Analysis of Ethno-regional Movements', *Ethnic and Racial Studies* (2) 260–74.
Heidegger, M. (1971) *Poetry, Language, Thought* (New York: Harper & Row).
Held, D. (1991) 'Democracy, the Nation-state and the Global System', in D. Held (ed.), *Political Theory Today* (Cambridge: Polity Press) pp. 197–235.
Henley, J. (1995) *The Guardian*, 24 January.
Hepple, L. W. (1986) 'The Revival of Geopolitics', *Political Geography Quarterly* (5) 521–36.
Hernandez, J. (1985) 'Improving the Data: A Research Study of New Immigrants', in L. Maldonado and J. Moor (eds), *Urban Ethnicity in the US* (Beverly Hills: Sage).
Herz, J. E. (1957) 'The Rise and Demise of the Territorial State', *World Politics* (9) 473–95.
Heske, H. (1987) 'Karl Haushofer: His Role in German Geopolitics and Nazi Politics', *Political Geography Quarterly* (5) 267–82.
Hitler, A. (1940) *Mein Kampf* (New York: Reynal & Hitchcock).
Hobbes, T. (1968) *Leviathan*, C. B. Macpherson (ed.) (Harmondsworth: Penguin).
Hobsbawm, E. J. (1968) *Industry and Empire* (Harmondsworth: Penguin).

Hobsbawm, E. J. (1984) 'Mass Producing Traditions', in E. J. Hobsbawm and T. Ranger (eds), *The Invention of Tradition* (Oxford: Clarendon Press).
Hobson, J. A. (1902) Imperialism, (London: George Allen & Unwin).
Holdar, S. (1992) 'The Ideal State and the Power of Geography: the Lifework of Rudolf Kjellen', *Political Geography* (11) 307–23.
Hooper, J. (1995) *The New Spain* (Harmondsworth: Penguin).
Hooson, D. (ed.) (1994) *Geography and National Identity* (Oxford: Blackwell).
Hopkins, T. K. and Wallerstein, I. (1982) *World System Analysis: Theory and Methodology* (Beverly Hills: Sage Publications).
Horsman, M. and Marshall, A. (1994) *After the Nation State* (London: HarperCollins).
Huntington, E. (1940) *Principles of Human Geography* (New York: Wiley).
Hurrell, A. (1994) 'A Crisis of Ecological Viability? Global Environmental Change and the Nation State', *Political Studies* (42) 146–65.
Hutchinson, J. (1994) *Modern Nationalism* (London: Fontana Press).
Hutton, W. (1995) 'Myth that Sets the World to Right', *The Guardian* 12 June.
Hutton, W. and Linton, M. (1994) 'Four Nation Poll', *The Guardian*, 2 April.
Ihonvbere, J. O. (1992) 'Surviving at the Margins: Africa and the New Global Order', *Current World Leaders* (35) 1053–72.
Ihonvbere, J. O. (1994) 'The Irrelevant State: Ethnicity and the Quest for Nationhood in Africa', *Ethnic and Racial Studies* (17) 42–60.
James, P. E. (1959) *Latin America*, 3rd edn (New York: Cassell).
Jancar, B. (1992) 'Chaos as an Explanation of the Role of Environmental Groups in East European Politics', in J. W. Rudig (ed.), *Green Politics Two* (Edinburgh: Edinburgh University Press).
Jervis, R. (1976) *Perception and Misperception* (Princeton: Princeton University Press), chapter 1, reproduced in Viotti and Kauppi (1993) pp. 286–304.
Johnson, S. P. (1973) *The Politics of the Environment* (London: Stacey).
Johnston, R. J. (1982) *Geography and the State* (London: Macmillan).
Johnston, R. J. (1986) *On Human Geography* (Oxford: Basil Blackwell).
Johnston, R. J. (1990) review of J. A. Agnew and J. S. Duncan (eds), *The Power of Place* (Boston and London: Unwin Hyman, 1989) in *Progress in Human Geography* (14) 447–8.
Johnston, R. J. (1991) *A Question of Place: Explaining the Practice of Geography* (Oxford: Basil Blackwell).
Johnston, R. J. (1992) 'Laws, States and Super-states: International Law and the Environment', *Applied Geography* (12) 211–88.
Johnston, R. J. (1993) 'The Rise and Decline of the State', in P. J. Taylor (ed.), *Political Geography of the Twentieth Century* (London: Belhaven).
Johnston, R. J. Gregory, D. and Smith, D. M. (eds), (1994) *The Dictionary of Human Geography*, 3rd edn (Oxford: Blackwell).
Johnston, R. W. (1985) *The Politics of Recession* (London: Macmillan).
Jones, S. B. (1954) 'A Unified Field Theory of Political Geography', *Annals of the Association of American Geographers* (44) 111–23, reprinted in de Blij (1967)

Kaldor, M. (1993) 'The New Nationalism in Europe' in P. Bennis and M. Moushabeck (eds), *Altered States*, (New York: Olive Branch) 141–52.

Kamann, D.- J. (1994) 'Spatial Barriers and Differentiation of Cultures in Europe', in P. Nijkamp, (ed.), *New Boundaries and Old Barriers in Spatial Development* (Aldershot: Avebury) 35–63.

Kant, I. (1795; 1957) *Perpetual Peace*, trans. L. Beck (New York: Liberal Arts Press).

Kanya-Forstner, J. S. (1972) 'French Expansion in Africa: The Mythical Theory', in R. Owen and B. Sutcliffe (eds), *Studies in the Theory of Imperialism* (London: Longman) pp. 277–94.

Kaplan, M. A. (1957) *System and Process in International Politics* (New York: Wiley).

Kaplan, R. (1994) 'The Coming Anarchy', Atlantic Monthly (February) 44–76.

Kasperson, R. E. (1969) 'Environmental Stress and the Municipal Political System', in R. E. Kasperson and J. V. Minghi (eds), *The Structure of Political Geography* (London: University of London Press).

Keegan, J. (1993) *A History of Warfare* (London: Hutchinson).

Kegley Jr., C. W. and Wittkopf, E. R. (1995) *World Politics, Trend and Transformation*, 5th edn (New York: St Martin's Press).

Kennedy, P. (1991) *Preparing for the Twenty-First Century* (London: Harper-Collins).

Kennedy, P. (1993) *Preparing for the Twenty-First Century* (London: Fontana).

Kennet, W. (1974) 'The Politics of Conservation', in A. Warren and F. B. Goldsmith (eds), *Conservation in Practice* (London: Wiley).

Kesselman, M. and Rossenthal, D. (1974) 'Local Power and Comparative Politics', *Sage Professional Papers in Comparative Politics*, vol. 5, no. 49 (Beverly Hills, Cal.: Sage).

Kidron, M. and Segal, R. (1991) *The New State of the World Atlas*, 4th edn (New York: Simon & Schuster).

Kirk, W. (1963) 'Problems of Geography', *Geography* (48), pp. 357–71.

Kjellen, R. (1917) *Der Staat als Lebenform* (Leipzig: Hirzel).

Knight, R. V. and Gappert, G. (eds) (1989) Preface in *Cities in a Global Society* (London and Newbury Park, Cal.: Sage) quoted in Berner and Korff (1995) p. 208.

Knill, W. G. (1991) 'Green Thinking: Politics or Paradigm?', *Area* (23) 238–44.

Knox, P. L. and Agnew, J. (1989) *The Geography of the World Economy* (London: Edward Arnold).

Knox, P. and Agnew, J. (1994) *The Geography of the World Economy*, 2nd edn (London: Edward Arnold).

Knox, P. L. (1995) 'World Cities in a World System' in P. L. Knox and P. J. Taylor (eds), *World Cities in a World System* (Cambridge: Cambridge University Press) pp. 3–20.

Knox, P. L. and Taylor, P. J. (eds) (1995) *World Cities in a World System* (Cambridge: Cambridge University Press).

Kohl-Larsen, L. (1958) *Wildbeuter in Ostafrika* (Berlin).

Kratochwil, F. (1986) 'Of Systems, Boundaries and Territoriality: An Inquiry into the Formation of the State System', *World Politics* (39) 27–53.

Kuhlmann, R. von (1931) 'The Permanent Basis of German Foreign Policy', *Foreign Affairs* (9).

Kummer, H. (1971) 'Spacing Mechanisms in Social Behavior', in D. F. Eisenberg and W. S. Dillon (eds), *Man and Beast: Comparative Social Behavior*, Smithsonian Annual 3: Washington, DC.

Lacoste, Y. (1972) 'Bombing the Dikes: A Geographer's on-the-site Analysis', *The Nation*, 9 October, 298–301, republished in *Antipode* (5) (1973) 1–13 and reprinted in R. Peet (ed.) (1977), *Radical Geography* (London: Methuen) pp. 244–61.

Lacoste, Y. (1973) 'An Illustration of Geographical Warfare: Bombing of the Dikes on the Red River, North Vietnam', *Antipode* (5) 1–3.

Lacoste, Y. (1984) 'Geography and Foreign Policy', *SAIS Review* (4) 213–27.

Lapham, L. H. (1988) 'Notebook: Leviathan in Trouble', *Harper's Magazine*, September.

Lattimore, O. (1934) *The Monguls of Manchuria* (New York: John Day).

Laver, M. (1986) 'Public, Private and Common in Outer Space', *Political Studies* (34) 359–73.

Leakey, R. and Lewin, R. (1992) *Origins Reconsidered. In Search of What Makes Us Human* (New York: Doubleday).

Leitner, H. (1995) 'Internal Migration and the Politics of Admission and Exclusion in Postwar Europe', *Political Geography* (14) 259–78.

Lenin, V. I. (1917) *Imperialism: The Highest Stage of Capitalism.*

Lerner, D. (1963) 'Will European Union Bring About Merged National Goals?', *Annals of the American Association of Politics and Social Sciences*, 34–45, reproduced in H. J. de Blij (1967) *Systematic Political Geography* (New York: John Wiley) pp. 545–56.

Ley, D. and Samuels, M. S. (1978) 'Introduction: Contexts of Modern Humanism in Geography', in D. Ley and M. S. Samuels (eds), *Humanistic Geography* (London: Croom Helm).

Leyton-Brown, D. (1994) 'The Political Economy of North American Free Trade', in R. Stubbs and R. D. Underhill (eds), *Political Economy and the Changing Global Order* (London: Macmillan) pp. 352–65.

Licht, S. (1993) 'After Yugoslavia', in P. Bennis and M. Moushabeck (eds) *Altered States* (New York: Olive Branch).

Light, M. (1994) 'Foreign Policy Analysis', in A. J. R. Groom and M. Light (eds), *Contemporary International Relations: A Guide to Theory* (London: Pinter) pp. 93–108.

Little, R. (1994) 'International Relations and Large-Scale Historical Change', in A. J. R. Groom, and M. Little, (eds), *Contemporary International Relations: A Guide to Theory* (London: Pinter) pp. 9–26.

Lloyd, W. F. (1833) *Two Lectures on the Checks to Population* (Oxford: Oxford University Press).

Locke, J. (1965) *Two Treatises of Government* (New York: New American Library).

Lorenz, K. (1966) *On Aggression*, transl. by M. Latzke (London and New York: Methuen).

Lowe, P.D. (1977) 'Amenity and Equity: A Review of Local Environmental Pressure Groups in Britain', *Environment and Planning* (9).
Mackay, J.R. (1958) 'Interactance Hypothesis and Boundaries in Canada: A Preliminary Study', *Canadian Geographer* (2) 1–8.
Mackinder, H.J. (1902) *Britain and the British Seas* (London: Heinemann).
Mackinder, H.J. (1904) 'The Geographical Pivot of History', *Geographical Journal* (23) 421–44.
Mackinder, H.J. (1919) *Democratic Ideals and Reality: A Study in the Politics of Reconstruction* (London: Constable).
Mackinder, H.J. (1943) 'The Round World and the Winning of the Peace', *Foreign Affairs* (21) 595–605.
Mann, M. (1984) 'The Autonomous Power of the State: Its Origins Mechanisms and Results', *Archives Européennes de Sociologie* (25) 185–213.
Marquand, D. (1988) *The Unprincipled Society* (London: Fontana).
Marsh, G.P. (1864) *Man and Nature; Or Physical Geography as Modified by Human Action* (New York: Scribners).
Marshall, T.H. (1950) *Citizenship and Social Class* (Cambridge: Cambridge University Press).
Marston, S.A. (1989) 'Adopted Citizens: Discourse and the Production of Meaning Among Nineteenth Century American Urban Immigrants', *Transactions of the Institute of British Geographers*, n.s. (14) 435–45.
Marx, K. (1968) *Preface to a Contribution to the Critique of Political Economy, Karl Marx: Selected Works* (London: Lawrence & Wishart).
Marx, K. and Engels, E. (1976) *The Communist Manifesto* (Harmondsworth: Penguin).
Massey, D. (1993) 'Power-Geometry and a Progressive Sense of Place', in J. Bird, B. Curtis, T. Putnam, G. Robertson and L. Tickner (eds), *Mapping the Futures, Local Cultures, Global Change* (London: Routledge).
Maull, H. (1990) Germany and Japan: The New Civilian Powers', *Foreign Affairs* (69) 91–106.
Maull, O. (1936) *Das Wesen der Geopolitik* (Leipzig).
May, J.A. (1970) 'Kant's Conception of Geography and its Relation to Recent Geographical Thought', University of Toronto Department of Geography Research Publications 4, Toronto.
McCarty, H.H. (1960) quoted in E.N. Thomas, 'Maps of Residuals from Regression: the Characteristics and Uses of Geographical Research', Report no. 2, Department of Geography, State University of Iowa.
McColl, R.W. (1969) 'The Insurgent State: Territorial Bases of Revolution', *Annals of the Association of American Geographers* (59) 613–31.
McCormick, J. (1989) *The Global Environment* (London: Belhaven).
McCormick, J. (1991) *British Politics and the Environment* (London: Earthscan), quoted in M. Newsom (ed.), *Managing the Human Impact on the Natural Environment* (London and New York: Belhaven, 1992).
McDonald, P. (1978) 'Frontiers', *Area* (10).
McGreal, C. (1994) 'Inside Africa', *The Guardian*, 3 October.
McGreal, C. (1995) 'Liberia Follows the Tortured African Path to Disintegrating Nation States', *The Guardian*, 10 February.

Meadows, *et al.*, D. (1972) *The Limits to Growth, Report of the Club of Rome* (New York: Universal Books).
Meinig, D. W. (1956) 'Heartland and Rimland in Eurasian History', *Western Political Quarterly* (9) 553–69.
Mellor, R. E. H. (1975) *Eastern Europe* (London: Macmillan).
Mellor, R. E. H. (1989) *Nation State and Territory* (London: Routledge).
Merrifield, A. (1993) 'The Struggle over Place: Redeveloping American Can in Southeast Baltimore', *Transactions of the Institute of British Geographers*, n.s. (18) 102–21.
Mintel (1995) *Regional Trends*, 18–19 Long Lane, London.
Mojtahed-Zadeh, P. (1994) 'Mapping the New World Order; Appreciation: Jean Gottman', *The Guardian*, 6 May.
Mooney, J. (1973) *The Ghost Dance Religion and Wounded Knee* (New York: Dover), quoted in P. Slowe, *Geography and Political Power* (London: Routledge, 1990).
Moran, T. H. (1990) 'The Globalization of America's Defense Industries: Managing the Threat of Foreign Dependence', *International Security* (15) 57–100.
Morgenthau, H. (1948) *Politics Amongst Nations: The Struggle for Power and Peace* (New York: Alfred Knopf).
Muir, R. (1976) 'Political Geography: Dead Duck or Phoenix?' *Area* (8) 195–200.
Muir, R. (1981) *Modern Political Geography*, (London: Macmillan) 2nd edn.
Muir, R. and Paddison, R. (1981) *Politics, Geography and Behaviour* (London and New York: Methuen).
Murdoch, J. and Marsden, T. (1995) 'The Spatialization of Politics: Local and National Actor-spaces in Environmental Conflict', *Transactions of the Institute of British Geographers*, n.s. (20) 368–80.
Murphy, A. G. (1990) 'Territorial Claims', *Annals of the Association of American Geographers* (80) 531–48.
Murray, R. and Boal, F. W. (1979) 'The Social Ecology of Urban Violence', in D. T. Herbert and D. M. Smith (eds) *Social Problems and the City* (Oxford: Oxford University Press) pp. 139–57.
Nairn, T. (1977) *The Break-Up of Britain: Crisis and Neo-Nationalism* (London: New Left Books).
Nairn, T. (1988) *The Enchanted Glass: Britain and its Monarchy* (London: Chandos).
Naisbitt, N. J. (1994) *Global Paradox* (London: Nicholas Brearley).
Nientied, P. (1985) 'A "New" Political Geography: On What Basis?' *Progress in Geography* (9) 597–600.
Nijkamp, P. (1994) Preface in P. Nijkamp (ed.), *New Boundaries and Old Barriers in Spatial Development* (Aldershot: Avebury).
Nijman, J. (1992) 'Limits of Superpower: The United States and Soviet Union Since World War II', *Annals of the Association of American Geographers* (83) 681–95.
Nugent, W. V. (1914) 'The Geographical Results of the Nigeria–Kamerun Boundary Demarcation Commission', *Geographical Journal* (44) 630–51.

O Tuathail, G. (1986) 'The Language and Nature of the New Geopolitics – the Case of US–El Salvador Relations', *Political Geography Quarterly* (7) 73–85.

O Tuathail, G. (1987) 'Beyond Empiricist Political Geography: A Comment on van der Wusten and O'Loughlin', *Professional Geographer* (39) 196–7.

O Tuathail, G. (1994a) 'Critical Geopolitics and Development Theory: Intensifying the Dialogue', *Transactions of the Institute of British Geographers*, n.s. (19) 228–38.

O Tuathail, G. (1994b) 'Political Geography I: Theorizing History, Gender and World Order Amidst Crises of Global Governance', *Progress in Human Geography* (19) 260–72.

O Tuathail, G. (1994c) 'The Critical Reading/Writing of Geopolitics: Re-reading/Writing Wittfogel, Bowman and Lacoste', *Progress in Human Geography* (18) 313–332.

O Tuathail, G. (1995) 'Political Geography 1: Theorizing History, Gender and World Order Amidst Crises of Global Governance', *Progress in Human Geography* (19) 260–72.

O'Dowd, L., Corrigan, J. and Moore, T. (1995) 'Borders, National Security and European Integration: The British Irish Case', *International Journal of Urban and Regional Research* (19) 272–85.

O'Loughlin, J. (1984) 'World-power Competition and Local Conflicts in the Third World' in R. J. Johnston and P. J. Taylor (eds), *A World in Crisis* (Oxford: Basil Blackwell) pp. 231–68.

O'Loughlin, J. (1988) 'Political Geography – Bringing the Context Back', *Progress in Human Geography* (12) 121–38.

O'Loughlin, J. (1990) 'Political Geography: Attempting to Understand a Changing World Order', *Progress in Human Geography* (14) 420–37.

O'Loughlin, J. (1991) 'Political Geography: Returning to Basic Conceptions', *Progress in Human Geography* (15) 322–39.

O'Loughlin, J. and Wusten, H. van der (1986) 'Geography, War and Peace: Notes for a Contribution to a revived political geography', *Progress in Human Geography*, (10) 484–510.

O'Riordan, T. (1989) 'The Challenge of Environmentalism', in R. Peet and N. Thrift (eds), *New Models in Geography* (London: Unwin Hyman).

Oppenheim, L. (1952) *International Law*, vol. 1, 7th edn (London).

Packenham, T. (1991) *The Scramble for Africa: The White Man's Conquest of the Dark Continent from 1876–1912* (New York: Random House).

Paddison, R. (1983) *The Fragmented State: The Political Geography of Power* (Oxford: Blackwell).

Pahl, R. E. (1975) *Whose City? and Further Essays on Urban Society* (Harmondsworth: Penguin).

Pahl, R. E. (1979) 'Socio-political Factors in Resource Allocation', in D. T. Herbert and D. M. Smith (eds), *Social Problems and the City* (Oxford: Oxford University Press).

Painter, J. (1995) *Geography, Politics and Political Geography* (London: Edward Arnold).

Painter, J. and Philo, C. (1995) 'Spaces of Citizenship: An Introduction', *Political Geography* (14).
Parker, G. (1994) 'Political Geography and Geopolitics', in A. J. R. Groom and M. Light (eds), *Contemporary International Relations: A Guide to Theory* (London: Pinter) pp. 170–81.
Parker, G. and Brown, J. W. (1991) *Global Environmental Politics* (Boulder, Col.: Westview).
Passmore, J. (1974) *Man's Responsibility for Nature* (London: Duckworth).
Paterson, J. H. (1987) 'German Geopolitics Reassessed', *Political Geography Quarterly* (5) 75–85.
Peet, R. (1989) 'Introduction: New Models of the Nation, State and Politics', in R. Peet and N. Thrift (eds), *New Models in Geography*, vol. 1 (London: Unwin Hyman), pp. 257–65.
Pepper, D. (1984) *The Roots of Modern Environmentalism* (London: Croom Helm).
Pepper, D. (1993) *Eco-socialism from Deep Ecology to Social Justice* (New York: Routledge).
Perman, D. (1973) *Cublington: A Blueprint for Resistance* (London: The Bodley Head).
Piaget, J. and Inhelder, B. (1956) *The Child's Conception of Space* (London: Routledge & Kegan Paul).
Pirages, D. (1978) *The New Context for International Relations: Global Ecopolitics* (North Scituate: Duxbury Press).
Porter, G. and Brown, J. W. (1991) *Global Environment Politics* (London: Westview).
Potter, D. (1975) 'Communication, Nation and Politics', in *Making Sense of Society*, Block 3 (Milton Keynes: Open University Press).
Poulantzas, N. (1968) *Political Power and Social Classes* (London: New Left Books).
Pounds, N. J. G. and Ball, S. S. (1964) 'Core Areas and the Development of the European State System', *Annals of the Association of American Geographers* (54) 24–40.
Prendergast, J. and Fieno, J. (1993) 'Crises in the Horn of Africa', in P. Bennis and M. Moushabeck (eds), *Altered States* (New York: Olive Branch) pp. 343–9.
Prentice, R. (1990) 'The Manxness of Man: Renewed Immigration to the Isle of Man and the Nationalist Response', *Scottish Geographical Magazine* (106) 75–88.
Prescott, J. R. V. (1965) *The Geography of Frontiers and Boundaries* (London: Hutchinson).
Prescott, J. R. V. (1978) *Boundaries and Frontiers* (London: Croom Helm).
Prins, G. (1990) 'Politics and the Environment', *International Affairs* (66) 711–30.
Ramanathan, V. (1988) 'The Greenhouse Theory of Climate Change: A Test by an Inadvertent Global Experiment', *Science* (240) 15 April.
Ratzel, F. (1897) *Politische Geographie* (Munich and Berlin: R. Oldenbourg).

Ratzel, F. (1901) 'Der Lebensraum, Eine Biogeographische Studie', in K. Bucher *et al.* (eds), *Festgaben für Albert Shaffle zur Siebenzigsten Wiederkehr Laupp'schen Buchhandlung*, pp. 101–89.

Ray, J. (1987) *Global Politics*, 3rd edn (Boston: Houghton Mifflin).

Rees, J. (1991) 'Equity and Environmental Policy', *Geography* (76) 292–303.

Renfrew, C. (1972) *The Emergence of Civilisations: The Cyclades and the Aegian in the Third Millennium BC* (London: Methuen).

Renner, M. (1991) 'Assessing the Military's War on the Environment', in L. R. Brown (ed.), *State of the World 1991* (New York and London: W. W. Norton) pp. 132–52.

Rex, J. (1968) 'The Sociology of a Zone in Transition', in R. E. Pahl (ed.), *Readings in Urban Sociology* (Oxford: Pergamon Press) pp. 211–31.

Reynolds, D. R. (1992) 'Political Geography: Thinking Globally and Locally', *Progress in Human Geography* (16) 393–405.

Robinson, R. (1972) 'Non-European Foundations of European Imperialism: Sketch for a Theory of Collaboration', in R. Owens and B. Sutcliffe (eds), *Studies in the Theory of Imperialism* (London: Longman) pp. 117–42.

Robinson, R. E. and Gallagher, J. (with A. Denny), (1965) *Africa and the Victorians: The Official Mind of Imperialism* (London: Macmillan).

Rokkan, S. and Urwin, D. W. (1983) *Economy Territory Identity, Politics of West European Peripheries* (London: Sage).

Rokkan, S. and Urwin, D. W. (eds) (1982) *The Politics of Territorial Identity: Studies in European Regionalism* (London: Sage).

Rostow, W. W. (1971) *Stages in Economic Growth: a Non-Communist Manifesto*, 2nd edn (Cambridge: Cambridge University Press).

Rousseau, J.-J. (1913) *The Social Contract and Discourses*, trans. G. D. H. Cole (London: Dent).

Rowlands, I. (1995) *The Politics of Global Atmospheric Change* (Manchester: Manchester University Press).

Rowntree Foundation (1995), *Inquiry into Income and Wealth* (York: Rowntree).

Russett, B. M. (1967) *International Regions and the International System: A Study in Political Ecology* (Chicago) repr. Greenwood Press, Conn. 1975.

Sack, R. D. (1980) *Conceptions of Space in Social Thought: A Geographic Perspective* (London: Macmillan).

Sack, R. D. (1983) 'Human Territoriality: A Theory', *Annals of the Association of American Geographers* (73) 55–74.

Sack, R. D. (1986) *Human Territoriality* (Cambridge: Cambridge University Press).

Sandbach, F. (1980) *Environment, Ideology and Policy* (Oxford: Blackwell).

Sandbach, F. (1984) 'Environmental Futures', in D. Massey and J. Allen (eds), *Geography Matters* (Cambridge: Cambridge University Press).

Sandbach, F. (1989) Environment, Ideology and Policy (Oxford: Basil Blackwell).

Sauer, C. O. (1952) 'Agricultural Origins and Dispersal', Bowman Memorial Lecture Series 2 (New York: American Geographical Society).

Schebesta, P. (1941) *Die Bambuti-Pygmaen von Itruri* (Brussels).
Schumpeter, J. (1973) 'The Sociology of Imperialisms', in R. J. Art and R. Jevis (eds), *International Politics, Anarchy, Force, Imperialism* (Boston: Little, Brown) pp. 304–82.
Schwartz, H. M. (1994) *States Versus Markets* (New York: St Martin's Press).
Scruton, R. (1983) *A Dictionary of Political Thought* (London: Pan Books).
Shack, W. A. (1978) 'Open Systems and Closed Boundaries: The Ritual Process of Stranger Relationships in New African States', in W. A. Shack and E. P. Skinner (eds), *Strangers in African Society* (Berkeley: University of California Press).
Sheridan, J. E. (1966) *Chinese Warlord: The Career of Feng Yu-hsiang* (Stanford, Cal.: Stanford University Press).
Short, J. R. (1993) *An Introduction to Political Geography*, 2nd edn (London: Routledge).
Sidaway, J. D. (1992) 'Mozambique: Destabilisation, State, Society and Space', *Political Geography* (11) 239–58.
Siegfried, A. (1913) *Tableau Politique de la France de l'Ouest* (Paris: A. Colin).
Simon, D. (1995) 'The World City Hypothesis: Reflections from the Periphery', in P. L. Knox and P. J. Taylor (eds), *World Cities in a World System* (Cambridge: Cambridge University Press) pp. 132–56.
Singer, E. and Hudson, V. (eds), (1992) *Political Psychology and Foreign Policy* (Boulder and Oxford: Westview Press)
Slater, D. (1993) 'The Geographical Imagination and the Enframing of Development Theory', *Transactions of the Institute of British Geographers* n.s. (18) 419–37.
Sloan, G. R. (1988) *Geopolitics in United States Strategic Policy, 1890–1987* (Hemel Hempstead: Harvester Wheatsheaf).
Slowe, P. (1990) *Geography and Political Power* (London: Routledge)
Smith, A. D. (1981) 'War and Ethnicity: The Role of Warfare in the Formation, Self-image and Cohesion of Ethnic Communities', *Ethnic and Racial Studies* (4) 375–397.
Smith, A. D. (1986) *The Ethnic Origins of Nations* (Oxford: Basil Blackwell).
Smith, A. D. (1988) 'The Myth of the Modern Nation and the Myths of Nations', *Ethnic and Racial Studies* (ll) 1–26.
Smith, A. D. (1989) 'The Origin of Nations', *Ethnic and Racial Studies* (12) 340–67.
Smith, D. M. (1990) 'Introduction: The Sharing and Dividing of Geographical Space', in M. Chisholm and D. M. Smith (eds), *Shared Space, Divided Space: Essays in Conflict and Territorial Organization* (London: Unwin Hyman) pp. 1–21.
Smith, D. M. (1994) 'Social Justice', in R. J. Johnston, D. Gregory and D. M. Smith (eds), *The Dictionary of Human Geography* (Oxford: Basil Blackwell) pp. 563–6.
Smith, G. (1990) 'The Soviet Federation from Corporatist to Crisis Politics', in M. Chisholm and D. M. Smith (eds), *Shared Space, Divided Space* (London: Unwin Hyman) pp. 84–105.

Smith, G. (1993) 'Ends, Geopolitics and Transitions', in R. J. Johnston (ed.), *The Challenge for Geography* (Oxford: Basil Blackwell) pp. 76–99.
Smith, G. (1994a) in D. Gregory, R. Martin and G. Smith (eds), *Human Geography, Society, Space and Social Science* (London: Macmillan).
Smith, G. (1994b) *The Baltic States: The National Self-determination of Estonia, Latvia and Lithuania* (London: Macmillan).
Smith, G. (1996) pers. comm.
Smith, N. (1986) 'Bowman's New World and the Council on Foreign Relations', *Geographical Review* (76).
Smith, P. M. (1983) 'Political Conflict over the Physical Environment: Three Case Studies in Conservation', in M. A. Busteed (ed.), *Developments in Political Geography* (London: Academic Press) pp. 69–128.
Smith, S. J. (1989) 'Society, Space and Citizenship: Human Geography for the New Times?' *Transactions of the British Institute of Geographers* n.s. (14) 144–56.
Soja, E. J. (1968) 'Communication and Territorial Integration in East Africa: An Introduction to Transaction Flow Analysis', *East Lakes Geographer* (4) 39–57.
Solesbury, W. (1976) 'The Environmental Agenda', *Public Administration* (54) 379–97.
Sowell, T. (1981) *Ethnic America: A History* (New York: Basic Books).
Sprout, H. and M. (1956) *Man–Milieu Relationship Hypotheses in the Context of International Politics* (Princeton: Centre for International Studies).
Sprout, H. and M. (1957) 'Environmental Factors in the Study of International Politics', *Journal of Conflict Resolution* (1) 309–28.
Spykman, N. J. (1942) *America's Strategy in World Politics* (New York: Harcourt Brace Jovanovich).
Spykman, N. J. (1944) *The Geography of the Peace* (New York: Harcourt Brace Jovanovich).
Steed, M. (1986) 'The Core-Periphery Dimension of British Politics', *Political Geography Quarterly* supplement to vol. 5, S91–S103.
Stein, H. (1985) 'Theories of the State in Tanzania: A Critical Assessment', *Journal of Modern African Studies* (23) 44–62.
Stone, C. D. (1993) *The Gnat is Older than Man: Global Environment and Human Agenda* (Princeton, NJ: Princeton University Press).
Stubbs, R. (1994) 'The Political Economy of the Asia-Pacific Region' in R. Stubbs and G. R. D. Underhill (eds), *Political Economy and the Changing Global Order* (London: Macmillan) pp. 366–377.
Sturmer Smith, P. and Hannam, K. (1994) *Worlds of Desire, Realms of Power: A Cultural Geography* (London: Edward Arnold).
Sudjic, D. (1995) 'Megalopolis Now', *The Guardian*, 24 June.
Supple, B. (1983) States and Industrialization: Britain and Germany in the Nineteenth Century', in D. Held (ed.), *States and Societies* (Oxford: Martin Robertson).
Sutton, I. (1975) *Indian Land Tenure, Bibliographical Essay and Guide to the Literature* (New York: Clearwater).

Swift, R. (1994) *New Internationalist*, (257) July.

Tate, N. (1995) 'Friends, Subjects, Citizens . . .', *The Guardian*, 5 September.

Taylor C. and Muir, R. (1983) *Visions of the Past* (London: J. M. Dent).

Taylor, A. J. P. (1954) *The Struggle for Mastery in Europe, 1848–1918* (Oxford: Clarendon Press).

Taylor, P. J. (1986) 'The World-Systems Project', in R. J. Johnston and P. J. Taylor (eds), *A World in Crisis* (Oxford: Basil Blackwell).

Taylor, P. J. (1989) *Political Geography: World Economy, Nation-state and Locality* (London: Longman).

Taylor, P. J. (1991a) 'Political Geography Within World-systems Analysis', *Review* (14) 387–402.

Taylor, P. J. (1991b) 'The English and their Englishness: "A Curiously Mysterious, Elusive and Little Understood People"', *Scottish Geographical Magazine* (107) 146–161.

Taylor, P. J. (1993a) 'Geopolitical World Order' in P. J. Taylor (ed.), *Political Geography of the Twentieth Century: A Global Analysis* (London: Belhaven Press) 31–61.

Taylor, P. J. (1993b) *Political Geography: World Economy, Nation-State and Locality*, 3rd edn (Harlow: Longman).

Taylor, P. J. (1994) 'The State as Container: Territoriality in the Modern World-System', *Progress in Human Geography* (18) 151–62.

Taylor, P. J. (1995) 'Beyond Containers: Internationality, Interstateness, Interterritoriality', *Progress in Human Geography* (19) 1–15.

Teitz, M. B. (1968) 'Towards a Theory of Urban Public Facility Location', *Papers and Proceedings, Regional Science Association* (2).

Telles, E. E. (1995) 'Race, Class and Space in Brazilian Cities', *International Journal of Urban and Regional Research* (19) 395–406.

Thompson, M. W. (1987) *The Decline of the Castle* (Cambridge: Cambridge University Press).

Thranhardt, D. (1995) 'Germany: An Undeclared Immigration Country', *New Community* (21) 19–36.

Tilly, C. (1975) 'Reflections on the History of European State-making', in C. Tilly (ed.), *The Formation of Nations and States in Western Europe* (Princeton, NJ: Princeton University Press) pp. 601–38.

Travena, C. (1995) 'A Bright New Dawn or Storm Clouds Ahead?', *The Guardian*, 28 October.

Turner, F. J. (1893) 'The Significance of the Frontier in American History', *Report of the American Historical Association*, 199–227.

Unicef (1995) *State of the World's Children.*

United Nations High Commission for Refugees (UNHCR) (1993) *The State of the World's Refugees* (Harmondsworth: Penguin).

US Department of State (1989) *World Refugee Survey* (Washington: Government Printing Office).

Vayda, A. (1976) *War in Ecological Perspective* (New York).

Vidal, J. and Traynor, I. (1995) 'Green Victory Brings on Shell Shock', *The Guardian*, 21 June.

Viotti, P.R. and Kauppi, M.V. (1993) *International Relations Theory, Realism, Pluralism, Globalism*, 2nd edn (New York: Macmillan).

Vulliamy, E. (1995) 'Nothin is Sacred in the Apache Nuclear Feud', *The Observer*, 21 May.

Vyner, B.E. (1993) 'The Territory of Ritual: Cross-ridge Boundaries and the Prehistoric Landscape of the Cleveland Hills, Northeast England', *Antiquity* (68) 27–38.

Walker, R.B.J. (1988) *One World Many Worlds: Struggles for a Just World Peace* (Boulder: Lynne Rienner).

Walker, R.B.J. (1990) 'Security, Sovereignty and the Challenge of World Politics', *Alternatives* (15) 3–27.

Wallerstein, I. (1974) *The Modern World System* (London: Academic Press).

Wallerstein, I. (1983) 'An Agenda for World-Systems Analysis', in W.R. Thompson (ed.), *Contemporary Approaches to World-system Analysis* (Beverly Hills: Sage) pp. 299–308.

Wallerstein, I. (1984) 'Long Waves as Capitalist Process', *Review* (7) 559–75.

Weisacker, E.U. von (1994) *Earth Politics* (London and New Jersey: Zed Books).

Wellhofer, E.S. (1995) ' "Things Fall Apart; The Centre Cannot Hold": Cores, Peripheries and Peripheral Nationalism at the Core and Periphery of the World Economy', *Political Geography* (14) 503–20.

Westing, A. (ed.) (1984) *Environmental Warfare: A Technical, Legal and Policy Appraisal* (London: Taylor & Francis).

Whitaker, T.D. (1878) *History of Craven*, 3rd edn (Parish of Carlton).

Whittlesey, D.S. (1935) 'The Impress of Effective Central Authority upon the Landscape', *Annals of the Association of American Geographers* (25).

Whittlesey, D.S. (1939) *The Earth and the State* (New York: Holt).

Widgren, J. (1990) 'International Migration and Regional Stability', *International Affairs* (66) 749–66.

Wilbur, C.M. (1968) 'Military Separatism and the Process of Reunification under the Nationalist Regime', in P.T. Ho and Tang Tsou (eds), *China in Crisis*, vol. I, book I (Chicago: University of Chicago Press).

Wild, T. and Jones, P.N. (1994) 'Spatial Impacts of German Unification', *Geographical Journal* (160) 1–16.

Williams, C. (ed.) (1982) *National Separatism* (Cardiff: University of Wales Press).

Williams, C.H. (1988) 'Conceived in Bondage – Called unto Liberty: Reflections on Nationalism', *Progress in Human Geography*

Williamson, T. and Bellamy, L. (1987) *Property and Landscape* (London: George Philip)

Woollacott, M. (1994) 'A Mad World of Rambos', *The Guardian*, 14 November.

Woollacott, M. (1995) 'Side by Side but Separate', *The Guardian*, 28 October.

World Resources 1990–1

Worsley, P. (1983) 'One World or Three? A Critique of the World-system Theory of Immanuel Wallerstein', in D. Held (ed.), *States and Societies* (Oxford: Martin Robertson) pp. 504–25.

Zack-Williams, A. B. (1990) 'Sierra Leone: Crisis and Despair', *Review of African Political Economy* (49) 22–33.

Zaidi, I. H. (1966) 'Towards a Measure of the Functional Effectiveness of a State: The Case of West Pakistan', *Annals of the Association of American Geographers* (56) 24–40.

Zartman, I. W. (ed.), (1995) *Collapsed States: The Disintegration and Restoration of Legitimate Authority* (Boulder, Col.: Lynne Rienner).

Index